THE ROUTLEDGE COMPANION TO PERFORMANCE PRACTITIONERS

The Routledge Companion to Performance Practitioners collects the outstanding biographical and production overviews of key theatre practitioners first featured in the popular *Routledge Performance Practitioners* series of guidebooks.

Each of the chapters is written by an expert on a particular figure, from Stanislavsky and Brecht to Laban and Decroux, and places their work in its social and historical context. Summaries and analyses of their key productions indicate how each practitioner's theoretical approaches to performance and the performer were manifested in practice.

All 22 practitioners from the original series are represented, with this volume covering those born before the end of the First World War. This is the definitive first step for students, scholars and practitioners hoping to acquaint themselves with the leading names in performance, or deepen their knowledge of these seminal figures.

Franc Chamberlain is Professor of Drama, Theatre and Performance at the University of Huddersfield, UK and the series editor for *Routledge Performance Practitioners*.

Bernadette Sweeney is Professor of Theatre and Performance Studies at the School of Theatre & Dance at the University of Montana, USA and co-editor with Franc Chamberlain of the expanded *Routledge Performance Practitioners* series.

ROUTLEDGE THEATRE AND PERFORMANCE COMPANIONS

The Routledge Companion to Scenography
Edited by Arnold Aronson

The Routledge Companion to Adaptation
Edited by Dennis Cutchins, Katja Krebs and Eckart Voigts

The Routledge Companion to Butoh Performance
Edited by Bruce Baird and Rosemary Candelario

The Routledge Companion to Theatre, Performance and Cognitive Science
Edited by Rick Kemp and Bruce McConachie

The Routledge Companion to African American Theatre and Performance
Edited by Kathy A. Perkins, Sandra L. Richards, Renée Alexander Craft, and Thomas F. DeFrantz

The Routledge Companion to Theatre of the Oppressed
Edited by Kelly Howe, Julian Boal, and José Soeiro

The Routledge Companion to Theatre and Politics
Edited by Peter Eckersall and Helena Grehan

The Routledge Companion to Dance Studies
Edited by Helen Thomas and Stacey Prickett

The Routledge Companion to Performance Practitioners
Edited by Franc Chamberlain and Bernadette Sweeney

The Routledge Companion to Performance Philosophy
Edited by Laura Cull Ó Maoilearca and Alice Lagaay

The Routledge Companion to Theatre and Performance Historiography
Edited by Tracy Davis and Peter Marx

For more information about this series, please visit: www.routledge.com/handbooks/products/SCAR30

THE ROUTLEDGE COMPANION TO PERFORMANCE PRACTITIONERS

Volume One

*Edited by Franc Chamberlain
and Bernadette Sweeney*

LONDON AND NEW YORK

First published 2021
by Routledge
2 Park Square, Milton Park, Abingdon, Oxon OX14 4RN

and by Routledge
605 Third Avenue, New York, NY 10017

First issued in paperback 2022

Routledge is an imprint of the Taylor & Francis Group, an informa business

© 2021 selection and editorial matter, Franc Chamberlain and Bernadette Sweeney; individual chapters, the contributors

The right of Franc Chamberlain and Bernadette Sweeney to be identified as the authors of the editorial material, and of the authors for their individual chapters, has been asserted in accordance with sections 77 and 78 of the Copyright, Designs and Patents Act 1988.

All rights reserved. No part of this book may be reprinted or reproduced or utilised in any form or by any electronic, mechanical, or other means, now known or hereafter invented, including photocopying and recording, or in any information storage or retrieval system, without permission in writing from the publishers.

Trademark notice: Product or corporate names may be trademarks or registered trademarks, and are used only for identification and explanation without intent to infringe.

Publisher's Note
The publisher has gone to great lengths to ensure the quality of this reprint but points out that some imperfections in the original copies may be apparent.

British Library Cataloguing-in-Publication Data
A catalogue record for this book is available from the British Library

Library of Congress Cataloging-in-Publication Data
Names: Chamberlain, Franc, editor. | Sweeney, Bernadette, 1969– editor.
Title: The Routledge companion to performance practitioners/edited by Franc Chamberlain and Bernadette Sweeney.
Description: Abingdon, Oxon; New York, NY: Routledge, 2020. | Series: Routledge theatre and performance companions | Includes bibliographical references and index.
Identifiers: LCCN 2019053698
Subjects: LCSH: Theatrical producers and directors – Biography. | Choreographers – Biography. | Theater – History. | Acting – History. | Dance – History. | Performance art – History.
Classification: LCC PN2205 .R59 2020 | DDC 792.02/320922 [B] – dc23
LC record available at https://lccn.loc.gov/2019053698

Volume One:
ISBN: 978-1-03-239992-8 (pbk)
ISBN: 978-0-367-41732-1 (hbk)
ISBN: 978-0-367-81599-8 (ebk)

Volume Two:
ISBN: 978-1-138-95375-8 (hbk)
ISBN: 978-1-315-66720-1 (ebk)

Set:
ISBN: 978-0-367-90348-0 (hbk)
ISBN: 978-1-003-02798-0 (ebk)

DOI: 10.4324/9780367815998

Typeset in Bembo
by Apex CoVantage, LLC

*For our families, those close by, those far away,
and in memory of those who are no longer with us.*

CONTENTS

Acknowledgements   ix
List of contributors   x
Introduction   xii

1   Stanislavsky (1863–1938)   1
    Bella Merlin

    1.1   Biography in social and artistic context   1
    1.2   Description and analysis of *The Seagull*   23

2   Meyerhold (1874–1940)   43
    Jonathan Pitches

    2.1   A life of contradictions   43
    2.2   Meyerhold's key production: *The Government Inspector*   64

3   Copeau (1879–1949)   86
    Mark Evans

    3.1   The life of Jacques Copeau   86
    3.2   Copeau's ideas in production: *Les Fourberies de Scapin*   109

4   Laban (1879–1958)   132
    Karen K. Bradley

    4.1   Laban's core: biography   132
    4.2   The Tanztheater and analysis of a work: *Die Grünen Clowns*   156

5	Wigman (1886–1973) *Mary Anne Santos Newhall*	173
	5.1 Mary Wigman: a life in dance	173
	5.2 Mary Wigman as choreographer: choosing the focus	208
6	Chekhov (1891–1955) *Franc Chamberlain*	230
	6.1 Biography and context	230
	6.2 Chekhov as director	251
7	Brecht (1898–1956) *Meg Mumford*	273
	7.1 A life in flux	273
	7.2 *The Caucasian Chalk Circle*: a production model	299
8	Decroux (1898–1991) *Thomas Leabhart*	322
	8.1 A Promethean life	322
	8.2 Decroux as director/creator: how did Decroux make a performance?	348
9	Ohno (1906–2010) and Hijikata (1928–1986) *Sondra Fraleigh and Tamah Nakamura*	371
	9.1 Butoh shapeshifters	371
	9.2 Dances of death, sacrifice, and spirit	390
10	Littlewood (1914–2002) *Nadine Holdsworth*	409
	10.1 Biography in political, social and artistic context	409
	10.2 Description and analysis of *Oh What a Lovely War*	431
Index		*453*

ACKNOWLEDGEMENTS

Bernadette Sweeney: I would like to thank Franc Chamberlain for sharing this editing task with such grace and rigour. I would like to recognize the support of my colleagues at the University of Montana School of Theatre & Dance, most especially John DeBoer, Pamyla Stiehl, Mike Monsos and Erin McDaniel. I would like to thank my family Bryan, Ruby and Saoirse Sweeney Ferriter for their love and laughter, my siblings and my parents Mary and Ted Sweeney – their unfailing love, support and belief in education are gifts that I will always treasure.

Franc and Bernadette would like to thank Ben Piggott, Kate Edwards and Laura Soppelsa at Routledge for their patience and support with this project.

CONTRIBUTORS

Karen K. Bradley is Associate Professor Emerita in Dance at the University of Maryland, College Park. She is a certified movement analyst in Laban Movement Analysis.

Franc Chamberlain is Professor of Drama, Theatre and Performance at the University of Huddersfield UK and the Series Editor for Routledge Performance Practitioners.

Mark Evans is Professor of Theatre Training and Education at Coventry University.

Sondra Fraleigh is Professor Emeritus of dance and somatic studies at the State University of New York at Brockport. She chaired the Department of Dance at SUNY Brockport and has been a faculty exchange scholar for the State University of New York. Her innovative choreography has been seen in theatres in New York, Germany and Japan, and she is often a guest lecturer in Europe, America and Asia. Fraleigh is the Founding Director of Eastwest Somatics Institute for the study of dance and movement therapy, a member school of ISMETA, International Somatic Movement Education and Therapy Association

Nadine Holdsworth is Professor of Theatre and Performance Studies at the University of Warwick.

Thomas Leabhart is Professor of Theatre and Resident Artist at Pomona College, California. He edits *Mime Journal*, performs and teaches internationally and was for a decade a member of the artistic staff of Eugenio Barba's ISTA (International School of Theatre Anthropology).

Bella Merlin is Professor of Acting and Directing in the Department of Theatre, Film and Digital Production, University of California, Riverside.

Meg Mumford is Senior Lecturer in Theatre and Performance Studies at the University of New South Wales, Australia.

Tamah Nakamura is a professor at Chikushi Jogakuen University, Fukuoka, Japan. Her areas of expertise are contemporary Japan, popular culture and gender. Research interests include artistic inquiry and butoh. She has published articles and presented on butoh in Japan and internationally.

Jonathan Pitches is Professor of Theatre and Performance at the University of Leeds in the School of Performance and Cultural Industries. He is Founding Co-editor of the journal *Theatre, Dance and Performance Training*.

Mary Anne Santos Newhall is Professor Emerita of Dance at the University of New Mexico, where she also served as Associate Dean for Research in the College of Fine Arts. She is also a research director for the American Dance Legacy Initiative at Brown University.

Bernadette Sweeney is Professor of Theatre and Performance Studies at the School of Theatre & Dance at the University of Montana, USA and Co-editor with Franc Chamberlain of the expanded *Routledge Performance Practitioners Series*.

INTRODUCTION

Franc Chamberlain and Bernadette Sweeney

The *Routledge Performance Practitioners* series was conceived, at the end of the last century, as a series of handbooks on key figures in twentieth-century performance practice some of whom would, of course, be still practicing into the new century. Each volume aimed to provide a basic theoretical and practical grasp of the practitioner's work and was structured around four major sections: (i) biography in social and artistic context, (ii) a summary and analysis of key writings (iii) description and analysis of a key production or productions and (iv) practical exercises. Each of these sections was framed by some guiding questions that were designed to keep the focus on the contemporary relevance of the practitioner's work. The aim was for the books to be useful in the studio and able to inform creative practice and for each volume to be written by a practitioner-academic, someone who was able to conduct the necessary scholarly research as well as having an understanding of how this material worked in practice. The working assumption was that someone who had an embodied understanding of a practitioner's working practices would have a better grasp of how the more theoretical aspects of the work could be understood *through* practice – but that brings with it another set of problems (see below).

Odd as it might seem, there wasn't a series of short, introductory texts on key performance practitioners in English at the turn of the twenty-first century. There was the excellent *Directors in Perspective* series from Cambridge University Press, but their emphasis was more of an historical rather than a practical one and so didn't address the aim of being useful in the studio processes of making performances. The books in the Cambridge series may have been written *about* exercises and devising or compositional techniques, but they didn't provide readers with material that they could try out in their own processes of performance making.

The first four volumes of the *Routledge Performance Practitioners* series appeared during 2003: Stanislavsky, Meyerhold, Chekhov, and Lecoq. The volume on Michael Chekhov appeared in the autumn of 2003 but, as per the publisher's normal convention, 2004 is the date on the copyright page. The publication of Mary Richards' volume on Marina Abramović, the twenty-first to appear, brought the first iteration of the series to a close in 2010. In 2018 the twenty-one original books began to be reissued in bright new covers, some texts fully revised, and by mid-2019 the complete set was available. In 2018 a decision was made to re-open the series and start commissioning new volumes and adjusting the focus to include the work of ensembles. The initial series proposal had conceptually embraced the inclusion of ensembles but Routledge's decision at the time was to stay with individual figures. There has been a growing interest in the

Introduction

work of ensembles in recent years, and the collection of essays and snapshots in the collection edited by Britton (2013) offers a good grounding in the field.

The exclusion of ensembles from the first twenty-one volumes of *Performance Practitioners* raises the question as to how the various practitioners were selected for inclusion. Given the explicit focus on performance practice and, perhaps more implicit emphases on processes of training and devising, it is not surprising that dramatists were ruled out.

As the series was focused on key practitioners (indeed, the first proposal referred to 'Key Performance Practitioners' as the series title) there was the notion that anyone who was proposed for inclusion would have a sufficiently high profile within the curriculum of Higher Education Institutions in the UK and the US. Stanislavsky was an obvious person to include, perhaps too obvious, and there was no shortage of books on his work. Bella Merlin, who authored the volume on Stanislavsky in the series, had already published a very useful handbook before beginning work on her book for the series. Meyerhold, on the other hand, was a practitioner with high name recognition in the field, but there was very little available that would provide an effective introduction to his practice in the studio.

In addition to Stanislavsky and Meyerhold, the big names were easy to call to mind: Grotowski, Lecoq, Artaud, Brecht, Graham, Laban, Copeau, Abramović, Wilson, Boal, Bausch, Brook. Making a case for inclusion on the basis of their prominence in the field, and consequently their marketability, was simple enough. From the very beginning of the commissioning process, it was clear that monographs would be sought on these luminaries. It is, of course, easy to argue that some of these figures are more important than others or to suggest that some should be replaced. Is Wilson more important than Kantor? Or Mnouchkine? What about Lee Strasberg or Stella Adler? Or Rachel Rosenthal and Liz LeCompte? Don't they belong in this company? Or Michael Chekhov? Shouldn't he be included at the top table? And they are mostly male and, with the exception of Ohno and Hijikata, of European heritage. Where are the practitioners with disabilities? Aren't they just as important?

Deciding who the most important practitioners are depends on the position from which the evaluation is made. Is it possible to imagine the history of mime over the past century without paying attention to the work of Decroux? No, Decroux must figure in any consideration of modern mime – but shouldn't Suzanne Bing also be there? What about a history of American dance without Martha Graham? Or Katherine Dunham? Why not Tadashi Suzuki?

The construction of a series such as *Routledge Performance Practitioners* provides material for these debates, but the debates themselves generate claims for the inclusion of other practitioners. The operational openness of the series (it was never intended to be a 'Top 21' but to continue growing) allows for the possibility of adaptation, of becoming more diverse as the field changes. But, as a series published by a major company, attention always has to be paid to the relative marketability of a book. That doesn't mean that only those already recognized as major figures can be published, but that a volume on a minor figure might need to be balanced by one on a major figure.

Sometimes the editors went in search of authors, and sometimes authors came with their own proposals; some proposals were so obscure or radical that it wasn't possible to enact them at that particular point in time. Perhaps some of these figures will be included in the new iteration of the series.

Some of the major figures mentioned above did not appear in the original series list: Lee Strasberg, Katherine Dunham, Peter Brook, Martha Graham, Suzanne Bing, Stella Adler, Rachel Rosenthal, Liz LeCompte, and Antonin Artaud. At some point these were all under consideration for inclusion, some were contracted but never completed, for others it proved difficult to find someone either suitable or interested to take on the task. Hopefully, in the future, these omissions and absences will be addressed and new figures will come to the fore and be included. Some are already under contract.

One problem that occurred on more than one occasion was where the subject of a proposed volume was still alive and did not want to co-operate with the project. This could be where the author's first-hand knowledge of the practitioner's work could pose a problem. If the author were to go ahead and write the book anyway, and they would be perfectly entitled to do so, they might jeopardize their relationship with the practitioner and, in at least one instance, this led to the dropping of the project.

The series was never designed to be 'complete' or to represent a fixed canon but, by bringing together this collection of practitioners into a single volume it can appear that it is *these* twenty-two practitioners and no others who represent *the* key performance practitioners. That is not the intention at all. Each author makes a case for the importance and relevance of the individual practitioner and the significance of their work for contemporary practice without excluding the contributions of others.

It would not be practicable to bring together all twenty-one monographs into a single book, and the two volumes of *The Routledge Companion to Performance Practitioners* include roughly half of each title in the series comprising sections (i) biography in social and artistic context and (iii) description and analysis of a key production or productions.

Themes

The task of compiling the material in this volume has provided fresh opportunities for considering the relationships between the different practitioners. The architecture of the series, with each book following a similar pattern, facilitated comparisons and the recognition of some shared themes. True, there are many ways in which the work of these practitioners can be considered in isolation and an emphasis on what makes their work unique, but they inevitably reference the influences and legacies of other practitioners in the series. This is true even when Stanislavsky, Meyerhold, and Copeau are being considered; there is no original source, but practitioners who are constantly in dialogue with the work of each other. When these interactions are considered, a number of parallels in the experiences of theatre making, conceptualization and experimentation become apparent.

The chapters in this volume are listed in order of the practitioners' birth dates which can give a sense of who came first and offer some intimations of the lines of influence and transmission. This is a claim to treat with some suspicion, however, particularly when periods of activity cross, but it does seem possible to trace out meaningful lines of influence. The following chapters evidence how, for example, Halprin looks to Grotowski; Lepage looks to Halprin; Mnouchkine looks to Lecoq; Boal to Brecht, Barba to Grotowski, Kantor looked to Meyerhold and Wigman looked to and away from Laban. But this implied linearity can be deceiving – in many cases, over the course of their artistic careers, these practitioners have been influenced by those who followed, are younger and earlier in their career, or by political, social or artistic movements and moments that resonated or continue to resonate across artistic, geographical, and other boundaries.

The gathering of the material for this volume has brought into sharper focus a number of shared ambitions, themes, and ways of looking, with practitioners striving in different ways to solve the same problem, or innovate in similar ways. These shared concerns range from the broader political ones to more focused artistic issues and are evidenced in their biographies and in their productions.

Introduction

It is interesting to note how many of these practitioners were revolutionary in some way – whether they were involved in fomenting explicit social revolution or were engaged in an artistic revolution that might shift the way in which the world is perceived. For some of these practitioners this seems more apparent, or familiar, than with others: Boal was looking to use theatre to rehearse for revolution; Brecht and Littlewood were looking to give agency to the audience so the audience could change what they considered to be possible or desirable and consequently enact social change; Abramović seems to have sought to incite change through risk, often to herself. But other names that have become synonymous with mainstream practice were revolutionary too – Stanislavsky would be the most obvious example here. Stanislavsky was looking to reinvigorate acting as an art and his series of approaches is well documented here and elsewhere. He is an example of a practitioner whose work became set and distributed in a certain phase (reliance on the emotion memory) because of its dissemination, and although he is one of the practitioners who learned from his students, these discoveries (more centred on the physical) were made later and didn't circulate as freely for a long time. Merlin (2018), in the second chapter of her book on Stanislavsky in the series, discusses the problems with the dissemination of Stanislavsky's work outside of Russia and the difficulties that have plagued English translations of his writings.

Many of the practitioners featured here lived through tumultuous times of one kind or another. Some were directly affected by this unrest, with a number going into exile such as Brecht, Boal, Laban, and Chekhov, while others like Wigman remained at risk under oppressive regimes, experiencing censorship, incarceration, torture or even, as was sadly the case with Meyerhold, execution, for their artistry, innovation, and resistance. Much of this work thus evolved in the shadow of tyranny and at great personal cost to the practitioners themselves. It is also interesting to note through this exercise how theatre functions as a global community: practitioners are not only influenced by each other, but look out for one another, as evidenced by the petition by international practitioners for Boal's release from prison when he was incarcerated and tortured by the Brazilian dictatorship in 1971. Another example of international solidarity was the theatre artist-led petition against the US State Department's refusal to permit Grotowski's *Teatr Laboritorium* to enter the country in 1968, which resulted in the company being allowed in in 1969. The playwright Arthur Miller was a signatory in both cases.

Freedom of movement can be viewed, historically, as a key generator of exchange and education for the artist and, when this is threatened, as some would argue it is right now in our current political moment, it endangers the generation of art, ideas, the philosophies of theatre making, and the dissemination of artistic knowledge.

Some of the practitioners featured here were more obviously affected by the politics of their day than others. Some brought their responses to bear in the content of their work, in its form, in how they developed their companies, ensembles, the hierarchies of organization, in their engagement with the audience or their arrangement and configuration of space. Some companies had more open and dialogical structures because of the authoritarian politics of their respective regimes. What the practitioners featured here share, however, is a focus on process and the work of the ensemble (however it may be formed), with the possible of exceptions of Hijikata and Ohno, and Abramović.

While Barba cultivated an ensemble with unknown, untrained actors, others like Kantor sought to work with established professionals; some like Halprin moved outside the mainstream and sought alternative collaborators. By contrast, Mnouchkine has maintained a company but renewed the membership over a long period of work. Someone like Lecoq was more focused on pedagogy while Grotowski's work moved outside of theatre altogether, and then returned.

Meyerhold was influential in his early efforts to reject psychological realism, and many of the others experimented with form as we see in Wigman's, Decroux's and Copeau's focus on the body. Other experimentations with form include Laban's and Bausch's work with Tanztheater, Wilson's work with an objective rather than subjective actor, Wilson's and Abramović's experimentation with duration, Boal's use of agency, and Lepage's work with split subjectivity and media. In a bid to reinvigorate their practices, a number of these practitioners looked back into the pasts of their own cultures to seek out abandoned or diminished forms. The interest of Meyerhold, Copeau, and Lecoq in *commedia dell'arte* is one example of this.

They simultaneously looked outwards to other cultures sharing a fascination with the performance forms of the various Asian cultures in particular (*inter alia*, Brecht, Wigman, Mnouchkine, Lepage, Grotowski, Barba). This courts the danger of an accusation of cultural appropriation. Other rituals and traditions, such as those of various cultures of Africa or Bali, can be found throughout in a reaching out beyond the borders of the 'West' to reinvigorate western practices. Looking to other cultures is a long held tradition across forms of performance, where it becomes problematic is in the cases of appropriation rather than exchange – a fetishization of otherness for profit, ridicule or crude entertainment. Nonetheless the influences of non-western actors, practices, rituals and design recur across the twentieth and into the twenty-first century. This interest in the 'other' poses questions: what were these practitioners looking for in these engagements and did they find it? Not just the artists featured here, but others, such as Brook, Gregory, Yeats and Craig were consistent in their search for a quality they felt lacking in European theatre – was it a deliberation, spirituality, stillness, simplicity, discipline? Obviously, it is reductive to search for a single answer, as the sources are as various as their impacts, but in much of the work that follows we see this fascination manifest, not just in the work as staged, but in the studio practices and rehearsal techniques. This was often used as a foundation for building the ensemble, alongside a sharing of personal stories, skills and music. Those non-western practitioners featured here such as Boal, or Hijikata and Ohno, have created specific relationships with western traditions, through opposition or absorption.

Practitioners were sometimes looking to bring some kind of spiritual experience to their practice and/or by extension, to their audience. A return or retreat to nature, was sometimes a pathway to an alternative spirituality, or a way of being in the world. Both Stanislavsky and Copeau took their actors out of the city and into the countryside, while Chekhov established his studio in the idyllic surroundings of Dartington Hall, and then of Ridgefield in Connecticut. Grotowski and Halprin engaged with the natural world in both their training and in the production of the work, in a way that resulted in the audience being participants rather than 'merely' spectators or observers. This move to the natural world could perhaps be equated with the search for non-western influences in a rejection of commercialism, capitalism, and the treatment of art and performance as commodities. This immersive experience in the natural world was perhaps a progression of efforts to rethink the audience experience within the formal theatre space – to reconfigure the space, treat the work as a ritual, and to reject the formal traditions of dramaturgy, psychological realism, and form.

Practitioners featured were actively looking to reinvigorate the imaginations of the actors and thus of the audience. Visual art, architecture, and design drives the work of Kantor, Wilson, and Lepage, for example, while rhythm and musicality were key to the work of the dance theatre practitioners like Wigman and Bausch. Song was significant in the work of Littlewood and Brecht, in slightly different ways. Some of these practitioners chose very controversial forms or subjects such as nudity, high risk, profanity, or unflinching challenges of accepted norms or histories: Halprin, Kantor, Abramović, Grotowski. While some looked to embrace life, the environment or spirituality, others like Hijikata and Ohno, Kantor or Abramović went further to investigate the performance of darkness, death, and the subjugation of the self.

Many of these studies in the following chapters also cite Artaud as an influence, and given the lack of a specific method or practice left by Artaud to facilitate and deliver his extreme demands, it is intriguing to see the variety of practices that claim his influence. Lecoq cites Artaud and Copeau as key influences, Mnouchkine cites Artaud too, while Abramović's work could be a considered as an embodied engagement with his philosophies.

The *Routledge Performance Practitioners* series was formed to focus on practice, and these books evidence the sharing and perhaps demystification of these studio practices, and provide a look at how these practices can serve in the building of any performance ensemble. Living lineage informs creativity, but texts, video, and other documentation can solidify and extend this legacy. Of course the act of generating written texts on practice can be limiting and lead to misunderstanding and misinterpretation – but can also lead to new departures and ways of working. One of the things that can evade documentation is the way performers learn through practice and pass on this living legacy through embodiment. Thus, many of us will have encountered these practices before without necessarily knowing their source.

Here we also encounter the gap between theory and practice – the ethics of work espoused can sometimes idealize our sense of the practitioner, or conversely construct a somber authoritarian figure far removed from the warm individual who might have been encountered live in the rehearsal room. None of these figures was living or working without the real human weaknesses, flaws, or follies of the rest of us, and much of their work was actually developed in a bid to counter the dangers of the ego. In his book *To the Actor*, Chekhov highlights this when he asks the reader for help – here he breaks down the fourth wall in a way, but in an appeal to the reader rather than the spectator. This gives agency to the reader, as he and others did for the audience member, but it also points to the openness in the work and a lack of completion that only the reader or audience member can resolve.

Perhaps this is our cue to reiterate Chekhov's appeal to the reader, you, to help us through your own practice to continue the relevance of the work and artistry of the theatre practitioners featured in this companion.

Reference

Britton, John (ed.) (2013) *Encountering Ensemble*, London: Bloomsbury.

1
STANISLAVSKY (1863–1938)

Bella Merlin

1.1 Biography in social and artistic context

Introduction

→Actor↗Director→Husband←Director↖Father→Actor↙Director↗Teacher↑

The challenge for anyone tracing Stanislavsky's biography is that the path isn't linear. Sometimes he ditched an idea only to pick it up again years later; at other times, the preoccupations of his mature life can be traced right back to his childhood. He was full of contradictions and experimentations, and he was often an artistic maverick. One thing's for sure: this is a man who was passionate about theatrical 'truth'. His evolution as a theatre practitioner can be divided into four broad sections: the amateur years, the director dictator, round-the-table analysis and the final legacies. There are times when the work of the *director* dominated, then for a while the *writer* became central, and at other times *actor training* was foregrounded. Added to all this, there were political events in Russia which influenced and censored his choice of vocabulary, and various artistic 'isms' (including Naturalism and Symbolism) also played their part in defining Stanislavsky's 'system'.

The amateur years: 1863–98

Kostya Alekseyev

Born in 1863 into one of Russia's wealthiest families, Konstantin Sergeyevich Alekseyev was the second of nine siblings. Along with four brothers and four sisters, his childhood was spent at the theatre, opera, circus and ballet: arts and entertainment formed the family's staple diet. It was no surprise when, in 1877, his father converted a room at their country house into a theatre, where the children produced plays for the guests' entertainment. Here, at the age of fourteen, Kostya began writing up these forays into drama; his youthful eagerness to analyse his own work would, later in his adulthood, inform his acting 'system'. By 1885 – aged twenty-two – his Notebooks were filled with increasingly sophisticated questions: 'What is the physiological aspect of the role? The psychic aspect of the role?' (Stanislavsky cited in Benedetti 1999: 23). Already he had made the vital connection between body and mind.

Kostya's young professional life was spent in the family textile business, although his passion for theatre soon hurled him into a series of ventures, not the least of which was the Alekseyev Circle, his family's highly acclaimed acting troupe. When the Circle folded in 1888, Kostya fuelled his love of performing by secretly appearing in a host of risqué amateur theatricals. To protect the family's reputation, he adopted the stage name, 'Stanislavsky', after a ballerina whom, as a young boy, he had lovingly adored from afar. Before long, the 'Stanislavsky' cover was blown, when his father discovered him cavorting in a lewd French farce and immediately prompted him to legitimise his acting. Thereupon, Stanislavsky undertook his next entrepreneurial project, the formation of the Moscow Amateur Music-Dramatic Circle. Within months, this had given way to the far more ambitious Society of Art and Literature, involving fellow collaborators, Fyodor Komissarzhevsky (an opera singer) (1832–1905) and Aleksandr Fedotov (a director) (1841–95). Working with theatre professionals provoked in Stanislavsky a serious need to question his own acting.

An early glimpse of a 'system'

His first major engagement with the Society was in 1888 taking the lead role in Pushkin's *The Miserly Knight*. The experience threw up three concerns: What were the differences between 'character' acting and 'personality' acting? How could actors stimulate their imaginations and therefore their 'creative will'? And how did actors 'get inside' the director's ideas?

The first concern arose because Stanislavsky envisaged himself as a dashing 'personality' actor, and the Miserly Knight as a romantic lead; Fedotov, however, saw the role as a decrepit old man. Given that Stanislavsky was only twenty-five, this was clearly a case of casting against 'type'. Not quite knowing what to do with the part, he adopted an externalised style of 'character' acting that he knew was really lacking 'something'. This gave rise to his second concern: how to stimulate the imagination? In an attempt to find the 'something' lacking, he spent a night locked in the cellar of a castle. This experiment was his first intuitive understanding of what he was later to call affective memory, whereby actors find an analogous situation from their own experience that mirrors the character's fictional life. In typical fervour, Stanislavsky went to an extreme. By setting up a real situation, he hoped that, once he returned to the rehearsal room, his memory of the gloomy experience would provide the elusive 'something' that was currently missing in his 'Knight'. He was wrong: all he got was a cold (and his imagination seemed none the sharper). The third difficulty in his rehearsal of *The Miserly Knight* was that Fedotov had very specific results that he wanted him to achieve. Yet Stanislavsky had no method for personalising those results, and all he could do was mimic them. Although it was frustrating, the seeds of his 'system' had been planted: how was he to move from external result to internal process?

A production of Krilov's *The Spoiled Darling* distracted him for a while that year. His leading lady was a charming actress, Maria Perevoshchikova (1866–1943), who also hid behind a stage name, that of 'Lilina'. They fell in love, were married in 1889, and spent the rest of their lives as partners and workmates.

The distraction of love didn't last forever. The internal/external acting dilemma arose again in 1896 when Stanislavsky played Othello. One of the biggest influences on his performance style was the great nineteenth-century actor, Mikhail Shchepkin (1788–1863). Shchepkin believed that the key to 'truthful' acting was to 'take your examples from real life'. Following Shchepkin's advice, Stanislavsky found a real-life 'image' upon which to base his interpretation of Othello – it was an Arab whom he met and befriended in Paris. He then set about crafting a 'mask' for himself based on the flesh-and-blood Arab acquaintance. The 'mask' was precise in its external detail, but inside there was nothing living, it was just an imitation. *Othello* threw up more concerns for the ever-questioning Stanislavsky: When does an actor 'become' the character? And how does the actor observe life and then turn those observations into 'creative will', or 'inspiration'? Stanislavsky had tried to incarnate a 'truthful', psychological portrait, and yet nothing emerged but a skilful sculpture.

But why was Stanislavsky so preoccupied with the psychology of acting? Turning to the state of Russian theatre at the time soon explains his heartfelt frustration.

The state of the arts

Theatrical repertoire in Russia towards the end of the nineteenth century was in a quagmire of stagnation. The Imperial theatres (those subsidised by the State) dominated Moscow and St Petersburg and, along with a smattering of privately owned venues, they operated under the beady eyes of Tsar Nicholas II's censors. Their hawkish gaze kept a tight rein on any play whose subject matter might be deemed politically or personally subversive. 'Safe' theatrical fare consisted of melodramas and vaudevilles, hastily translated from the French and German originals, though occasionally an innovative piece of new writing surfaced. Describing his play, *The Last Will*, Vladimir Nemirovich-Danchenko (1858–1943) wrote that:

> This play greatly pleased the actors. It was written as was said in those days, in soft tones; it did not offend anyone and revolutionised nothing; the chief thing about it was its excellent roles: big scenes with temperament and effective exits.
>
> *(Nemirovich-Danchenko 1937: 12)*

Not only does Nemirovich admit here that the more timid the play, the more likely its success, but also he reveals the importance of the actors.

Russian theatre of the nineteenth century was actor-driven: the idea of a director shaping a production was unheard of. In fact, 'The role of stage director was a very modest one; it had neither a creative nor a pedagogic content. Actors listened to him merely out of politeness' (ibid.: 29). But there's no need for a director when you already know what's required of your acting. In a repertoire where melodrama predominated, actors were cast to a formulaic type known as an *emploi*. This meant that each performer specialised in a particular role, such as the romantic lover, the comic flunkey or the bumbling father, according to his or her personality and stature. This *emploi* then became the blueprint for any role that the actor played. The audience grew familiar with both the actor and the *emploi*, and began to expect it at every performance, regardless of the play. The result of the audience's expectation was the development of a 'star system', as 'actors lost their independence and went into the service of the crowd' (Stanislavsky 1984: 105). The 'big scenes with temperament and effective exits' referred to by Nemirovich involved the star actors being 'called out' by the audience in the middle of a scene to come centre stage and receive wild applause. The remaining onstage cast froze, doll-like, until the adored actor had finished bowing, at which point the action of the play could resume. It was the playwright's job to incorporate these moments into a script, and the more famous the actor the more effective exits would be required. Here, then, was no ensemble acting: here was a theatre dominated by a 'star system'.

The situation was exacerbated by the frighteningly short rehearsal periods, which often resulted in actors simply not knowing their lines. And yet it was hardly their fault. At a time when leisure pursuits were limited, a rapid turnover of repertoire was a prerequisite of any business-minded theatre. Consequently, rehearsal time for a new production was a rarity, not a necessity. Quantity ruled over quality, leading to a situation where most performers had greater need of a prompter than a director. To save them from embarrassment, the prompt box was situated

Down-Stage-Centre and sunk into the floor. It was not uncommon for much of a play's action to be performed 'DSC', so that the actors could be prompted through their entire performance.

The 'star system' also impacted on the design of a show. Designers were still unusual in most theatres, and the rapidity of the repertoire's turnaround prohibited anything more ambitious than the recycling of old productions. Sets were dragged from the store, with stock canvas backdrops depicting dining rooms, gardens, or parlours, reappearing regardless of the genre or form of the play in question. As for costume design, this was determined by the leading actresses, each of whom was expected to supply her own wardrobe. Should the leading lady choose to wear crimson in the third act, then woe betide the female juvenile if she decided to wear red! An actress's acclaim lay in direct proportion to the voluptuousness of her wardrobe; therefore, money was vital and that often meant relying on a wealthy patron. As one actress of the time declared: 'How could you have a career without a wardrobe. What is an actress without costumes? She is a beggar; her route to the stage is cut off' (Velizarii cited in Schuler 1996: 31). Wealth and wardrobe swung an actress's fate: acting processes were the last consideration.

For all their influence, the professional acumen of the 'stars' was questionable. Before the monopoly of the Imperial theatres was abolished in 1882, actor-coaching was rare. Even when training programmes did become established, 'many actresses and actors firmly rejected the idea that acting was a learned skill' (ibid.: 39). So how did young actors acquire their craft? By imitating the great performers, of course! Even Stanislavsky confessed that his usual practice as an amateur was to copy blindly his favourite artist of the Imperial Maly Theatre. He memorised every bit of business in the great actor's interpretation of a role, learning the full range of his gestures and intonations, and leaving Stanislavsky's own directors with nothing to do. After all, he had already 'acquired' his performance, albeit second-hand. But how else could young actors learn when there was no written 'manual' that might help them? Thus, a type of performance evolved in which shouting, exaggerated gestures and simple characterisations were all 'larded with animal temperament' – and that was considered 'full-toned acting' (Stanislavsky 1984: 40). The artistic climate into which Stanislavsky emerged as a theatre practitioner was fairly bleak: a chaos devoid of coherent stage pictures, design concepts, directorial decisions, trained professionals and ensemble companies. Under these conditions, and without an acting 'A–Z', Stanislavsky began his process of 'revolution'.

The theatrical revolution

Stanislavsky's theatrical revolution began in earnest with his famously long conversation with Vladimir Nemirovich-Danchenko on 22 June 1897. Nemirovich was an award-winning playwright and teacher at the Philharmonic School and, on his instigation, the two men met at the stylish Moscow haunt, the Slavyansky Bazaar. Having been struck by Stanislavsky's acting, and knowing of the family's wealth, Nemirovich invited him to discuss the prospects of founding a new theatre. His intention was to harness the talent of his own pupils with Stanislavsky's amateur colleagues; at the same time, he couldn't disguise the fact that he had an eye on those Alekseyev roubles. . . . The meeting lasted from 2 p.m. until 8 a.m. the following morning, during which time the two men heatedly debated artistic ideals, staging techniques, discipline and ethics, organisational strategies, future repertoire and their respective responsibilities. The only major hiccup was Stanislavsky's refusal to jeopardise his family's fortune. Nonetheless, the pioneering discussion forged an alliance and, by the summer of the following year, the first season of the fledgling Moscow Art Theatre was deep in rehearsal, with Stanislavsky serving as an actor and director.

His main artistic concern was that the new company should explode the emptiness of traditional theatre practice; instead, plays should be infused with psychological content. The troublesome question was whose task was it to create that psychological content: the actors or the directors? Knowing no better, Stanislavsky began with the Director.

The director dictator: 1891–1906

Where the ideas came from

Stanislavsky's directing strategy involved a 'production plan', which he created by filling a play-text with a myriad of details that he thought out before rehearsals began. The details concerned every aspect of the play: how to move, how to act, where and when to change positions (a little like working out the 'blocking'), even the kind of voices that he thought the actors should use. Once the production plan was prepared, the actors then had to carry out his directions with total and unquestioning precision.

The summer of 1898 wasn't the first time Stanislavsky had used a production plan. He had in fact developed this practice out of two formative encounters with professional directors in his early career. The first of these was Fedotov of the Society of Art and Literature, whose directing style had revealed to Stanislavsky the value of preparing a careful and artistic plan. It wasn't always easy, however, to convert the plan – or *mise-en-scène* – into actual stage pictures. Fedotov often resorted to demonstrating for his actors the style or the physicality that he wanted them to use. The trouble was that their performances often consisted of nothing more than poor imitations of his exciting demonstrations. (Stanislavsky himself had fallen victim to this with his Miserly Knight in 1888.) A second major influence on Stanislavsky's directing style emerged in 1890, when the German Saxe-Meiningen players performed in Russia. Their director, Ludwig Chronegk (1837–91), choreographed the company with a discipline so military that vast and dynamic crowd scenes could be incorporated into his productions. Stanislavsky was extremely impressed with the ensemble effects, as well as the details of lighting, scenery, costume and sound. It was the first time that he had seen authentic-looking sets and heard made-to-order soundscapes, and he was so bowled over that he attended all the performances, devoting an entire album to careful notes and drawings of each play.

With a combination of Chronegk's autocratic discipline and Fedotov's understanding of the 'blocking', or *mise-en-scène*, Stanislavsky began his first directing job for the Society of Art and Literature in 1891 with *The Fruits of Enlightenment* by Lev Tolstoy (1828–1910). By 1898, when the infant Moscow Art Theatre staged *The Seagull* in its opening season, Stanislavsky had had seven years to establish his particular directing style, which toppled dangerously towards dictatorship.

Putting it into practice

Although the history of *The Seagull* by Anton Chekhov (1860–1904) is discussed in greater detail in section 1.2, there are a number of important points to be raised here. *The Seagull* was unlike anything seen on the stage before. There were no traditional character 'types', nor any recognisable structural devices, such as exposition (the unravelling of the plot) and dénouement (the revelatory climax). Instead, Chekhov introduced 'inner activity' to the dramatic form, full of nuances and suggestions. These innovations were exceptionally challenging to actors and audience alike. In fact, the play's 1896 premiere at the Aleksandrinsky Theatre in St Petersburg was a legendary 'failure'. Without the familiar conventions and formulae, the acting company floundered. Chekhov himself could hardly help: he was neither an actor nor a director and had no means of alerting them to the delicate style of playing. Robbed of their usual *emplois* (types), the actors had nothing to sustain them.

Enter Stanislavsky, two years later, to rise to the challenge with the Moscow Art Theatre. He immediately put his directing method into practice. Hiding in a study in the Ukraine, he beavered away diligently from 12 August until 20 September 1898 to construct the production plans. They included extensive character notes and detailed staging, from the barking of dogs to the croaking of frogs to create a realistic atmosphere. Although Stanislavsky didn't understand the play, the imaginative details of his *mises-en-scène* somehow unlocked the difficulties of Chekhov's psychological writing in a way that the Aleksandrinsky company had previously failed to do. As the plan of each act was completed, Stanislavsky sent the notes to Pushkino near Moscow, where Nemirovich-Danchenko rehearsed them with the newly formed acting company. The relay between Stanislavsky and Nemirovich was by no means satisfactory: it meant that Chekhov's intentions were filtered through two directors before the actors' interpretation was even considered. Not that it would have made much difference: Stanislavsky had yet to appreciate the personal contribution that actors themselves could make. Nonetheless, his choices as a director were so evocative that Chekhov honoured the production plans as 'amazing, the like of which have never been seen in Russia' (cited in Benedetti 1990: 79).

The pitfalls of the mise-en-scène

Stanislavsky's success in creating the *mises-en-scène* lay in his ability to turn the nuances of Chekhov's script into very specific directions for the actors. Unfortunately, the details that worked on paper in the Ukraine didn't always translate smoothly to the rehearsal room in Pushkino. Part of the problem was that, whether he knew it or not, Stanislavsky was setting in motion two revolutions at the same time. The first revolution concerned *theatre production* and the actual attention to detail on stage, and the second revolution focused on *acting styles* and the 'truthful' portrayal of what he called the life of the human spirit (Stanislavsky 1984: 171). In the summer of 1898, he possessed the tools with which to tackle only the first (the external form) and not the second (the inner content). Without addressing form and content together, he was in danger of exchanging one convention – demonstrational acting – for another convention – Naturalism.

Naturalism was introduced to the international literary scene in 1868 by the French writer, Émile Zola (1840–1902). The preoccupation of the Naturalists was to investigate 'man' as a product of his heredity (his genes) and his environment (his upbringing): are we simply born the way we are or can we do something about it? To examine this essentially scientific theory, Zola recreated in his novels a 'slice of life' – an imitation of the real world; a fictional 'crucible' in which human behaviour could be analysed and dissected.

Stanislavsky was clearly intrigued by the imitation of real life as his *Seagull* production plan illustrates (see section 1.2). However, he was so insistent on naturalistic detail that Chekhov's initial thrill with the production plan was completely wiped out. He grew incensed at the pedantic 'truth' that Stanislavsky demanded of the actors – 'But the theatre is art! . . . You forget, you don't have a fourth wall!' (Chekhov cited in Melchinger 1972: 4).

In Stanislavsky's defence, he struggled hard to penetrate the complex writing of Chekhov, whose new dramatic form was steeped in contradictions. The idiosyncrasies of the characters couldn't always be formulated intellectually on the pages of a production plan: they required the breath of the live actors. Yet they were caught in a 'catch-22': the script needed the actors' psychological-physical selves, but they had no psychological-physical acting vocabulary. At this stage in his career, Stanislavsky was really none the wiser, and all he could do was resort to the same level of whip-cracking that he had used with the Society of Art and Literature. He later confessed that:

> I was helped by the despotism I had learned from Chronegk. I demanded obedience and I got it ... I cared little for the inner emotions of the actor. I sincerely thought it was possible to order others to live and feel according to another's will. I gave orders to all and for all places of the performance and these orders were binding for all.
> (Stanislavsky 1984: 41, 43)

The subjugation of the actors

Of course it was impossible to 'order others to live and feel according to another's will', and the Art Theatre actors were adrift in the whole process. They needed guidance as to how they might flood the externally imposed actions with their own inner life, but their director couldn't give it. They were utterly frustrated. After all, the Moscow Art Theatre had been founded to revolutionise all aspects of the theatre, and yet here was Stanislavsky, blatantly denying one of its crucial components – the acting ensemble – its own creative freedom. As Vsevolod Meyerhold (1874–1940), one of its dynamic young actors, complained:

> Are we the cast really supposed to do *nothing but* act? We also want to *think* while we're acting. We want to know *why* we are acting, *what* we are acting and who we are teaching or criticizing by our acting.
> (cited in Benedetti 1991: 45)

Despite the cast's complaints, Stanislavsky persisted with his autocratic directing for all of Chekhov's successive works: *Uncle Vanya* (1899), *Three Sisters* (1901) and *The Cherry Orchard* (1903). His insistence that they accept his production plans continued to cause grief among his actors, who felt robbed of their potential input. Working on *Uncle Vanya*, Olga Knipper (1868–1959), one of the Art Theatre's founder members and Chekhov's wife, was obliged to abandon her own characterisation of Elena before she had had the chance to develop it properly. Stanislavsky found her interpretation 'boring', and insisted that she adopt *his* concept instead, saying it was 'essential for the play'. Knipper wrote to Chekhov, declaring that it was 'awful to think of the future, of the work ahead, if I have to resist the director's yoke again' (cited in Benedetti 1991: 65). New rehearsal methods were becoming a matter of artistic urgency.

A taste of his own medicine

By 1902 – scarcely four years into its existence – the Moscow Art Theatre faced a potential crisis. It was widely accused of being too naturalistic, and disagreements between Stanislavsky and Nemirovich-Danchenko over creative style had grown acute. Added to this, the ensemble was disrupted when the valued actor, Meyerhold, was deliberately omitted from the list of Art Theatre shareholders. He quit the company, taking with him a number of angry allies. There was a general state of artistic and internal turmoil. Stanislavsky's faith in his own acting was cracking, and a series of collisions with Nemirovich-Danchenko fuelled his crisis of confidence. Referring to his interpretation of Satin in *The Lower Depths* (1902) by Maksim Gorky (1868–1936),

Nemirovich declared that Stanislavsky needed a new method of acting. He had worn out his old method, and it was time to show himself 'to be a different performer from the one that the Art Theatre had come to know' (Nemirovich-Danchenko cited in Benedetti 1991: 140).

Stanislavsky's personal dissatisfaction was exacerbated in 1903. He was working with Nemirovich on the role of Brutus in Shakespeare's *Julius Caesar*, during which time, Nemirovich was evolving his own theory of the 'creative producer'. As the director of *Julius Caesar*, Nemirovich adopted a stance that was startlingly reminiscent of Stanislavsky's own dictatorial intransigence:

> My production plan is a complete treatise. . . . I have prepared everything . . . with great care and intend to dragoon the cast into what I have written with conviction. . . . I see the tone and tempo of the second act, especially for Brutus, *absolutely* differently from you. . . . And I intend to follow my line without restraint.
> *(Nemirovich-Danchenko cited in Benedetti 1991: 155)*

Stanislavsky felt straitjacketed by Nemirovich's direction, and suddenly he realised the fundamental problem with the production-plan technique. Because the ideas in the *mise-en-scène* were not the actors' own, but were forced upon them by the director, they struggled to find their own *inner justification* for their onstage actions. Without a real sense of inner justification, the *mise-en-scène* – however imaginative – was no more 'truthful' than the clichéd, representational acting from which Stanislavsky wanted to break. Once he understood this, he realised that supreme power had to be taken from the director. His unsettling experience on *Julius Caesar* convinced him that the production-plan technique was 'despotic'. Now he sought new strategies, in which directors studied their actors beforehand and depended on their contribution in rehearsal. That didn't mean that detailed research into the playscript wasn't essential. It was simply a question of how and by whom this work should be done. In his search to create the 'life of the human spirit', Stanislavsky turned his attention away from the *director's* interpretation of a play to the *company's* creative contributions.

Round-the-table analysis: 1906–early 1930s

What was it and why do it?

It was time to give the actors some power. Stanislavsky threw away the notion that he should devise the *mise-en-scène* on his own; instead, he gathered the acting company around the table, where together they unravelled a playtext and its characters. Their detective work took a variety of forms: they retold the content of the play, and made lists of all the facts, events, and given circumstances proposed by the playwright. They thought up questions and provided the answers. They studied the words and pauses between them. They invented past and future lives for the characters. They analysed the play's structure, breaking it into sections – or bits – and finding names for the characters' objectives – or tasks. There were discussions and debates, which sometimes focused on spatial relationships, sometimes on psychological motivations. All these differing practical methods were 'part of the single process of analysis, or coming to know the play and your parts' (Stanislavsky 2000b: 155).

The aim of Stanislavsky's round-the-table analysis was very specific: through discussing the play, the company could feel that they 'owned' the production, that they all had responsibility for the creation of their characters and atmospheres. So discussions weren't head-bound and intellectual, but imaginative and even emotional. Harnessing emotions was a key concern for Stanislavsky during this stage of his professional evolution. Thus, he developed the concept of 'affective memory', a term adopted from the French psychologist, Théodule Ribot (1839–1916). At its most simplistic, the sequence behind affective memory (or 'emotion memory') was easy: actors began by remembering from their own life an experience that was analogous to an event in the play. They then conjured up memories of all the physical and sensory details that were originally connected with that personal experience. Once these memories were sufficiently powerful, the actors related them to the given circumstances of their *characters'* situations, so that the fictional roles could be flooded with real emotional content. (Stanislavsky had hoped that this would happen with the night in the cellar and the Miserly Knight!)

The combination of imagination, emotional recollection and textual analysis certainly fuelled Stanislavsky's rehearsal practices in the early 1900s. With his growing need to identify the tangible means of bringing to the stage 'the life of the human spirit', his round-the-table discussions extended from several hours to several months, as the actors became more and more involved.

Assailing actor training through the theatrical studio

If his actors were to become increasingly involved in the creative process, the very foundations of *actor training* would have to be reconsidered. It was all well and good experimenting in the rehearsal room, but what if the actors' basic tools were rusty, or even dormant? Stanislavsky knew that he had to go right in at ground level – via the classroom. The attachment of a drama school to the Moscow Art Theatre had always been a significant part of Stanislavsky and Nemirovich's plans and, from the moment the Theatre was founded, ongoing classes were an accepted part of the timetable. However, the acting disciplines at the Theatre's school as it existed in 1902 were fairly traditional, with classes in diction, declamation, singing, recitation, dance and juggling. What was needed was an entirely new technique, in which the actors' inner life was also considered.

Stanislavsky's fascination with 'inner life' may well have been sparked by various stimuli – from his own practical research and from his reading all things scientific and philosophical. One such stimulus was a critical article entitled 'Unnecessary Truth', written in 1902 by Valery Bryusov (1873–1924), a leading exponent of the Russian Symbolist movement. For Bryusov, theatre production and the *art of the actor* were the same thing: one couldn't exist without the other. This clearly sparked something in Stanislavsky's thoughts about the nature of *actor training* on the one hand, and the nature of *theatrical performance* on the other. He was becoming increasingly disenchanted with the dominating style of psychological realism in the MAT, and so it was to Symbolism that he turned. During the 1904–5 season, he decided to stage three plays by the Belgian playwright, Maurice Maeterlinck (1862–1949). The content of these Symbolist dramas soon highlighted – even more than the naturalistic texts – that the live contribution of the performers was vital for exploring their ethereal, 'spiritual' quality. Unfortunately, his actors just weren't equipped to balance the technical demands of performance with the esoteric content of the plays.

Symbolism thrived in the first two decades of the twentieth century. At its heart lay the desire to transcend the crude realities of everyday life that the Naturalist movement strove to imitate. Instead, the Symbolists explored the way in which supernatural and mystical reverberations impacted on 'man's' existence. Bryusov's article attacked naturalistic detail, arguing that the only 'real' thing on the stage was the actor's physical body.

How then was Stanislavsky to train them? He understood through his work on the Symbolist plays that acting was a 'two-way street': inner life couldn't exist without the human 'casing' of a physical body, yet the outmoded representational school of acting had proved that physicality alone was shallow and boring without the actors' 'inner' connection. Stanislavsky recognised Bryusov's declaration that theatre was a *physical* medium; at the same time, he saw that his actors' bodies were fairly limited compared with ballet dancers or gymnasts. He was in another 'catch-22': he yearned for physically versatile performers, yet he had no means of training them. To help him in his dilemma, he turned to the 'new ways' that were being explored by former company member, Vsevelod Meyerhold. Meyerhold hungered for a performance medium that was physical, political and unashamedly theatrical. In response to the potential of Meyerhold's dynamic techniques, Stanislavsky set up an offshoot of the Moscow Art Theatre in 1905, and they called it the Theatrical Studio.

The Theatrical Studio proved to be Stanislavsky's first concrete step towards developing a psychophysical training ground in which the actors' psychology and physicality were equally important. It was 'neither a ready-made theatre nor a school for beginners, but a laboratory for more or less mature actors' (Stanislavsky 1982: 430). Stanislavsky was to fund it, while Meyerhold, whom he invited back into the fold after three years' absence, was given artistic and pedagogical freedom. The techniques proposed by Meyerhold in the Theatrical Studio were truly progressive. He abandoned discussion and focused on improvisation. (In many ways, his practices were precursors of those adopted by Stanislavsky almost thirty years later with his Method of Physical Actions and Active Analysis.) Yet it quickly transpired with Meyerhold's production of Maeterlinck's *The Death of Tintagiles* that the Theatrical Studio was trying to run before it could walk. There was still no specific vocabulary with which to tackle an acting revolution. Neither Meyerhold's Biomechanics (a precise form of acrobatic-based training) nor Stanislavsky's 'system' had yet been formulated. Added to which there was an inherent contradiction between Stanislavsky's artistic ambitions and those held by Meyerhold. Meyerhold pursued the path of *physical* theatre, in which there was little room for psychology or emotion. Stanislavsky, on the other hand, was striving for a *psycho*physical theatre, where gesture was invested with *emotional* content, as well as theatrical expression. And so, in spite of – or perhaps because of – Meyerhold's innovative ideas, the Theatrical Studio closed after only five months. The political upheaval caused by the first Russian Revolution in 1905 might have been partially responsible for the Studio's demise. Unfortunately, it doesn't dispel the unavoidable dichotomy that existed between the two directors' idealistic visions and the reality of their pursuits. Nonetheless, the role of the Theatrical Studio as a pioneering forum for testing some kind of psychophysicality is profound.

The holiday in Finland

The following year – 1906 – proved to be a critical one in terms of the development of Stanislavsky's 'system'. The closure of the Theatrical Studio, along with Chekhov's death, the failure of the Symbolist plays, a dissatisfaction with the artistic ethos of the Moscow Art Theatre, political and social unrest throughout Russia, financial disaster and a growing despair with the inadequacies of his own craft forced Stanislavsky to reassess the basic mechanics of acting. His relationship with Nemirovich-Danchenko had been deteriorating for several years, and at various times both parties had threatened to quit the company. The cause of the disputes was complex, but at the heart of it lay the fact that Nemirovich was a *writer* and a *director*: the text and the final production were for him the critical elements. Stanislavsky, on the other hand, was an investigator, an experimenter, as well as a director. He now believed that the *actor* was at the heart of the performance and, at this stage in his artistic credo, he didn't revere the writer. (He had even suggested during their 1904 production of *Ghosts* by the realist dramatist, Henrik Ibsen (1828–1906), that he rewrite the opening lines, as the text didn't fit his physical actions.) It was, therefore, extremely depressing when, in 1906, while touring with the Art Theatre in Europe, Stanislavsky found that his own acting had become mechanical and empty. In a state of personal unrest, he took his family on a much-needed holiday to Finland. Once there, he hid away in a darkened room, smoked endlessly and surrounded himself with twenty years of notebooks, each filled with his scribblings on acting, rehearsing and directing. He began a complicated and soul-searching attempt to organise formally a practical acting 'system'.

Stanislavsky believed that his evolving 'system' was essentially a means of applying natural and biological laws to the conventions of the theatre. He took as his starting point moments in his own stage experiences and his observations of famous actors, when spontaneity seemed to take over and 'the life of the human spirit' appeared on the stage. He then tried to isolate those moments, analyse them and put them back together in a formalised way *via* his 'system', so that all actors at any time could tap into their own spontaneous inspiration. Although he took many years to develop it thoroughly, his 'system' had two distinct but parallel branches: (1) practical exercises to develop the actor's physical, vocal and emotional instrument (Actor Training or *the work on the self*); and (2) methods of round-the-table analysis to explore forensically the hidden mysteries of a script (Rehearsal Techniques or *the work on the role*).

The *work on the self* also had two (interdependent) prongs – inner and outer. (You could say that inner work trains actors to be imaginatively playful and outer work trains them to be technically adept.) In the course of time, Stanislavsky developed exercises to help inner preparation through meditation, relaxation, concentration and imagination (all of which were tools that he probably acquired through his reading of yoga books, as we'll see later). This inner work was paralleled with the outer preparation of the actor's raw materials. Those raw materials included a strong voice, perfect diction, plasticity of movement, a characterful face and expressive hands, a vivid imagination and 'an infectious stage charm' (Stanislavsky cited in Gorchakov 1985: 194). Because these tools were in a continual state of development, Stanislavsky believed that every actor should complement his or her professional stage work with lifelong training to accommodate those changes.

Work on the role consisted of round-the-table analysis, as well as entering into the character's psychology through historical research, imagination and affective memory. Stanislavsky's intention was that the 'bi-focal' preparation of *the self* and *the role* would help actors to dive into a 'creative state'. The 'creative state' was one in which they felt so physically, mentally and emotionally open that they could stimulate their 'creative will'. The 'creative will' was the dynamo for acting in a spontaneous, exciting and unexpected way.

Having begun the process of creating a 'system' in Finland, Stanislavsky then used the various studios that emerged alongside the Moscow Art Theatre's main house in the years between 1905 and 1927 as 'laboratories'. In these 'laboratories', he explored different genres of play, trying out numerous experiments to combine the two aspects of his 'system': Actor Training and Rehearsal Techniques. The most significant 'laboratory' was arguably the First Studio, formed in 1912 and devoted to theatrical adventures involving the genius actor, Mikhail Chekhov (1891–1955), and the pioneering director, Evgeny Vakhtangov (1883–1923). The Studio was headed by Leopold Sulerzhitsky (1872–1916), a striking individual who became a huge influence on Stanislavsky....

THE IMPACT OF SULERZHITSKY

With an eclectic past as a singer, artist, fisherman, scholar, shepherd, sailor and political prisoner, 'Suler' was introduced to Stanislavsky in 1900 and he quickly became a respected friend. Suler was deeply spiritual and, when Stanislavsky became fascinated by the Symbolist plays with their exploration of the human soul or spirit, Suler's background and temperament were perfectly suited to assisting him. In fact, he was first officially employed by Stanislavsky as his personal assistant in 1906 – around the time he was beginning to formulate his 'system'. Suler remained his collaborator for many years despite the fact that Nemirovich was suspicious of his influence and refused to acknowledge him officially as a member of the MAT staff. Suler's most profound contribution to Stanislavsky's development was his introduction of Hatha yoga into the actor-training programme.

> **Hatha yoga** dates back more than 5,000 years, the word 'yoga' meaning 'union, to join or yoke together'. The basic principle of Hatha yoga is that exercise (asana) combines with breathing (pranayama) to relax the body and integrate the mind and emotions. It's unlikely Stanislavsky knew the (now) familiar postures of yoga, but he certainly employed the connection between breath, relaxation and the creative state.

Two key productions in the Moscow Art Theatre's main house were used to experiment and test out these new acting tools. They were the allegorical *The Drama of Life* (1907) by Nobel prize-winning Norwegian author, Knut Hamsun (1859–1952), and the more naturalistic drama, *A Month in the Country* (1909) by Ivan Turgenev (1818–83). In both productions, Stanislavsky served as director, as well as taking the role of Kareno in the first and Ratikin in the second.

The Drama of Life was the first production in which Stanislavsky consciously examined 'the *inner character* of the play and its roles' (Stanislavsky 1982: 474). The 'system' was still in its embryonic state, and he lacked the strategies to execute this work succinctly and effectively. Nonetheless, the particular experiment that he undertook in rehearsals focused on intangible levels of communication, that he called 'irradiation' or communion. Indeed, communion was a concept stemming from Suler's Eastern meditational practices.

One experiment with communion in rehearsals for *The Drama of Life* involved complete immobility. During this particular exercise, Stanislavsky forbade his actors to use any external means of presenting a character – neither gesture nor movement. Instead he wanted:

> bodiless passion in its pure, naked form, both naturally and emanating directly from the soul of the actor. For the transmission of this . . . the artist needed only eyes, face and mime. So let him, in immobility, live through the emotion he has to transmit with the help of feeling and temperament.
>
> *(cited in Worrall 1996: 173)*

Through the 'immobility' exercise, Stanislavsky wanted his actors to realise how powerful stillness and silence could be. He also wanted them to feel the resonances of their own emotional repertoires and the wealth of information that they could glean from each other just by allowing the space between them to be 'alive' [...].

Two years later – in 1909 – Stanislavsky's rehearsals for *A Month in the Country* involved an even stranger new practice. Up until now, he had adopted a predominantly cerebral approach as a director, either through production plans (such as *The Seagull*) or round-the-table discussions. However, the more he experimented with psychophysical exercises involving the actors' bodies and imaginations, the more he questioned intellectual activities. Not quite daring to let go completely of the brain-based preparatory work, Stanislavsky came up with a curious blend of analysis and spirituality for *A Month in the Country*. As usual, the first rehearsals took place round the table. Rather than embarking on discussions of context or dramatic structure, Stanislavsky began to dictate, and the actors carefully noted down, 'the symbolic designations of the various emotions and inner states' suggested by the text (Koonen cited in Worrall 1996: 186). These 'symbolic designations' ranged from a question mark indicating 'surprise', or a question mark in brackets indicating 'hidden surprise', to a large dash denoting 'stage apathy', a cross denoting 'the creative state' and an upward-pointing arrow denoting 'the transition from apathy to the creative state'. The hieroglyphics littered the text to signpost the characters' emotional journeys, which the actors were then expected to experience. This was all very strange: to ask the actors to embody big emotional transitions at the points the director indicated was far more complex than Stanislavsky's former insistence on detailed, naturalistic *mises-en-scène*. As actress Alisa Koonen (1889–1974) declared: 'The exercises associated with the "system" turned out to be difficult all round. What was demanded was not simply the mechanical execution of the task, but also our inner participation' (cited in Worrall 1996: 186).

To some extent, Stanislavsky's bizarre exercises in immobility and hieroglyphics go to show that he knew that he was on to something exciting with the idea of 'inner life' and 'creative state'; he simply didn't know how to access them formally. There was a danger that the hieroglyphics were just another form of artistic straitjacketing, no better than a production plan. By 1910, however, Stanislavsky's rehearsal methods had been simplified: the actors were now asked to identify the rather more attainable 'bits' of a text (often translated as 'units') and 'tasks' of a character (often translated as 'objectives') [...]. This process combined and activated what Stanislavsky called the three inner motive forces (often translated as 'inner psychological drives') of thought, will and emotion. Through intellectual analysis (via the thought-centre), the actors determined what they were *doing* (in the action- or will-centre) and why they *wanted* to do it (through the emotion- or feeling-centre).

By 1910, the major components of bits, tasks, affective memory, inner motive forces and communion had been identified. Stanislavsky's 'system' was coming into focus [...].

The importance of yoga

For more than ten years, Stanislavsky continued to refine his 'system', supplementing his practical experiments by delving into books on psychology, philosophy and yoga. Indeed, he openly noted how he combined science, thought and metaphysics in the shaping of his actor training. And yet the real impact of this interdisciplinary research is only recently coming to light. Stanislavsky scholars and practitioners have acknowledged for some years the importance of Suler's collaboration with Stanislavsky. However, it's really only now that we're beginning to understand the profound impact of Eastern philosophy and yoga on the entirety of his evolving 'system'.

A key player was Nikolai Demidov (1884–1953). As a 25-year-old medical student and friend of Sulerzhitsky, Demidov was initially hired as the physical and moral educator of Stanislavsky's son, Igor. Over the next thirty years, Demidov became Stanislavsky's 'right-hand man', offering up insights into human behaviour, editing his writings and running the Fourth Studio at MAT between 1921 and 1925. As Stanislavsky was grappling with concrete terminology for his acting 'system', Demidov drew his attention to two books by Yogi Ramacharaka which had recently been translated into Russian: *Hatha Yoga, or the Yogi Tradition of Philosophical Well-Being* (1909) and

Raja Yoga, or Mental Development (1914). These books seem to have provided Stanislavsky with all manner of tools for his 'system'.

First of all, we have the *structure*. In brief: one book, *Hatha Yoga*, provides exercises in physical postures, relaxation, breathing and inner rhythm. The other, *Raja Yoga,* aspires to inner-outer coordination and stillness of the mind. Inherent in yoga is the idea of centres (or *chakras*) of energy through the body. In other words, the physical and the psychological are both delineated *and* interwoven (like Stanislavsky's *An Actor Prepares* and *Building a Character*).

Then we have some *terminology*. Ramacharaka used words including tasks, bits of information, relaxation, concentration and wants, as well as highlighting the power of the breath. In fact, Demidov asked Stanislavsky why he was trying to invent exercises and names for things that had long ago been discovered in yogic practices – at which point he indeed turned his attention to Ramacharaka's words. It's exciting to understand that Stanislavsky combined his understanding of psychology (drawn largely from Ribot, with affective memory and his concept of radiating and emanating energy) with yogic thoughts. He wanted to find a 'system' that created a body-mind-spirit continuum for the actor both in the process of creating a role and working in an ensemble. It was the combination of science and ancient spiritual practices that helped him in that task.

> **Ramacharaka** was one of the various names adopted by American lawyer and philosopher William Walker Atkinson (1862–1932). His two books *Hatha Yoga* (Russian publication 1909) and *Raja Yoga* (Russian publication 1914) focused on a modern Americanized version of self-improvement, with an emphasis on the power of the solar plexus and *prana* energy as the essence of authentic communication. *Prana* is mentioned many times by Stanislavsky in *An Actor Prepares* […], though edited out of Benedetti's 2008 translation, *An Actor's Work*.

The state of 'I am'

During this period of intense practical research, the double-pronged training of 'work on the self' and 'work on the role' led Stanislavsky to adjust his definition of what he had previously called 'personality' acting. He had come to believe that, if actors really wanted to stir their creative wills, they could only work from their own raw materials. Rather than donning a character like a cloak, they had to put themselves into the characters' circumstances and ask themselves: 'What would *I* do in this situation? What do I *want*? Where am I *going*?' By stimulating these questions, the actors' vibrant, living, breathing temperaments were directly linked to the circumstances of the play.

There was a significant difference between this new kind of 'personality acting' and the kind for which Stanislavsky had yearned in his vainglorious, swashbuckling youth as the Miserly Knight. Although actors might now *begin* with their own personality, they didn't stop there: they stepped *beyond* their individual *emplois* into the character as written by the playwright. This transition provoked many questions for Stanislavsky about the relationship between actor and role and, in 1914, he altered his notion of the 'creative state' to the state of I am: 'I am in this situation (albeit imaginary), so I will respond as truthfully as I can for the character'. (This is sometimes translated as 'I am being'.)

What caused Stanislavsky to shift his understanding of acting in this way? Quite possibly it was his exploration of metaphysics: for Ramacharaka, full consciousness of being oneself – being

'I' – was the truth of human existence. Quite possibly it was Stanislavsky's ongoing grappling with stage nerves: after all, in the state of 'I am', the actor is ideally so united with the role that any sense of physical awkwardness evaporates. Quite possibly it was the result of drastic international events as much as personal artistic probings that caused him to change his terminology. In 1914, the year in which the First World War broke out, Stanislavsky found himself caught in the Swiss frontier town of Immerstadt while travelling with some of his family and colleagues. Having been dragged from a train, accused of being a Russian spy and threatened with death at gunpoint, it's hardly surprising that his mind had turned to questions of existence and ideas of who 'I am'.

Some years later, in 1923–4, the Moscow Art Theatre embarked on two tours of America to ease the Theatre's ailing finances. The Americans had gone wild for the Russian 'psychological' acting, and were hungry for lectures and lessons to help them achieve equally detailed performances themselves. By 1924, Stanislavsky provided an actual step-by-step guide into the state of 'I am', beginning with factual knowledge of the play and ending with heartfelt emotion of the role. At the heart of this guide lay the actor's need to search for the 'right bait' (i.e. the right 'actions') to arouse their feelings. Then – having 'caught the feeling' – they had to learn how to control it: after all, inspirational acting depended on the fine balance between conscious control and subconscious spontaneity. (The fact that Stanislavsky placed 'actions' at the heart of the fourth stage signals that he was already moving towards the Method of Physical Actions and Active Analysis.)

Ultimately, the state of 'I am' is when the actor is as relaxed on stage as they are in real life so that everything they do operates according to the laws of human nature – despite the abnormal conditions of creating in public. 'I am' is really our natural state.

Dead Souls – *a turning point*

Stanislavsky's ideas never remained static for very long, which was why he considered that his 'system' was simply a toolkit to assist actors when they had trouble with a role, and certainly not a gospel. So when Nemirovich-Danchenko unexpectedly announced in 1911 that the 'system' was to be adopted by all the Moscow Art Theatre practitioners, Stanislavsky was far from pleased.

Even less pleasing was Stalin's own formalisation of the 'system' in 1934: this completely contradicted Stanislavsky's own belief that 'Nothing can be more harmful to art than the use of a method for its own sake' (1990: 142). Added to which, Stanislavsky was always experimenting, always moving on. So how on earth could his 'theories' be set in stone? In fact, after years of variations on round-the-table research, he came to the conclusion in 1932 that analysis could be limiting. And the production that brought Stanislavsky to this conclusion was Nikolai Gogol's (1809–52) *Dead Souls* (1846).

Four years before *Dead Souls*, in 1928, Stanislavsky had suffered a heart attack following a gala performance to celebrate the Art Theatre's thirtieth anniversary. During the gala, he'd given a speech praising the wealthy capitalist, Savva Morozov, who had invested in the theatre in its early years. His speech provoked a vicious onslaught in the communist press, and a heart attack ensued. Thereon in, terror of the Soviet regime took its toll on Stanislavsky's delicate health. He retired from acting and devoted his time to teaching and directing, including his production of *Dead Souls*.

To prepare for *Dead Souls*, his cast embarked on extensive research into Gogol's letters, biography, works and portraiture. One of the leading actors, Vasily Toporkov (1889–1970), grumbled that, while they all found the visits to museums and galleries fascinating and the discussions stimulating, they couldn't translate their intellectual investigations into anything useful on stage. Toporkov wasn't the only one to question the rehearsal methods. Another very experienced actress had serious problems. She was Stanislavsky's wife, Lilina, who had been with the Moscow Art Theatre since its foundation. For some reason during the rehearsals of *Dead Souls*, she seemed to abandon all her intuitive responses to the part and embarked instead on 'a painstaking, corroding analysis, with unnecessary reflection and excessive self-control'. Stanislavsky's advice to her was wonderfully reassuring, declaring that: 'It is not necessary for you to understand everything in the scene. Meticulousness can be a plague for the actor; he starts to split hairs, [and] place a mass of unnecessary details between himself and his partner' (cited in Toporkov 1998: 133).

Obviously, Stanislavsky had become as wary of extensive round-the-table analysis as he was of his former directorial autocracy. He now rejected the practice of telling actors to:

> 'Go on stage, perform your roles and apply what you have learned during the past few months of work around the table.' With a swollen head and empty heart, the actors go on stage and are unable to play anything at all. They need many more months in order to discard the superfluous, to select and assimilate the necessary, in order to find themselves – even at moments – in the new role.
>
> *(Stanislavsky cited in Moore 1973: 31)*

The experience of *Dead Souls* had taught Stanislavsky that actors have to 'let go of their homework'. That doesn't mean they shouldn't do the preparation in the first place, but – just as a pianist stops thinking about digital dexterity when he's playing a concerto – so too should actors 'forget' their preparation at the point when it has served its purpose. Accurate research was no longer as interesting to Stanislavsky as unexpected interpretations and the possibility of inspiration.

How then might actors experience artistic inspiration? By now Stanislavsky knew that the answer lay in *action*: finding the right action was the challenge to which he turned his attention in his final voyage of discovery.

The final legacies: 1930s–1938 and beyond

The opera-dramatic studio

At the age of seventy-three, Stanislavsky knew that the only way he could conduct his final experimentations was away from the main house of the Moscow Art Theatre. By the 1930s, the Art Theatre had long ago ceased to be a hotbed of theatrical innovation. Since it had been declared a paradigm of cultural heritage in 1917, it had become little more than a museum shackled to Socialist rule. Therefore, in 1935, Stanislavsky and his sister, Zinaïda, drew together a circle of young and talented protégés to open his last 'satellite laboratory' – the Opera-Dramatic Studio. It was situated in his own apartment on 6, Leontievski Lane in Moscow, and here he remained locked away for the rest of his life.

Joseph Stalin was elected general secretary of the Communist Party in 1922, from which position he defeated all major opponents, so that, five years after the death of Soviet leader, Lenin, in 1924, Stalin was in the position to become dictator of the USSR. His absolute – autocratic and cruel – Socialist power went unchallenged until his death from a stroke in 1953.

Stanislavsky (1863–1938)

Politically, Stanislavsky was well informed, but naïve. Although he read the written words of the newspaper, he had a peculiar ignorance – or blindness – to their subtext and undercurrents. As he grew older and sicker, and immersed himself more deeply in his practical research, he was oblivious to the fact that he was essentially under house arrest. He was, in the words of Joseph Stalin (1879–1953), 'isolated, but preserved'. All Stanislavsky's meetings were surreptitiously controlled by his doctors (and maybe his assistants, too) who themselves were under the strictest orders 'from above'. In secluded ignorance, Stanislavsky focused the Opera-Dramatic Studio on the process of training and rehearsal, without worrying about the results of a full-scale production.

The Method of Physical Actions

HOW IT CAME ABOUT

Stanislavsky's lifelong search was for a rehearsal technique that would engage body, mind and emotions simultaneously. His youthful experiments had led him to predetermine a *mise-en-scène* and then analytically research a text. But, by 1935, he seriously questioned whether either of those rehearsal methods was any good in terms of its psychophysical possibilities. His work in the early 1900s had convinced Stanislavsky that real human feelings were a vital part of good acting, and that every gifted performer possessed the appropriate raw materials. It was just a matter of finding the 'right bait' to arouse them. Over the years, he had tried to find the 'right bait' through analysis, observation, affective memory and imagination. The tricky part was that, once actors' emotions were aroused, they had to be able to stop them in an instant, and to change them as appropriate. Yet Stanislavsky recognised that the emotion-centre was highly capricious and, as such, almost impossible to manipulate consciously. The fascinating contradiction in the acting process, therefore, was how to arouse and then control something as teasingly uncontrollable as emotion.

Stanislavsky's career had been devoted to unravelling this troublesome contradiction, and by the end of his life, he believed that he had discovered a possible solution to the emotion/experience dichotomy. Instead of true emotion being the *end*-product of an acting technique, he wanted to devise a rehearsal process of which emotion was a *by*-product. In other words, he sought a process in which emotions arose inevitably from the actions, rather than actors consciously trying to squeeze emotions out of themselves. After all, the emotion-centre was only one piece in the jigsaw: an actor's intricate acting instrument also included the other two 'inner motive forces' of will and thought. Could it be that, if actors actively *did* something (will) and fully *believed* in what they were doing (thought), appropriate emotions might arise accordingly?

Action! Action! Action! became the focal point of Stanislavsky's new technique and, in 1935, he addressed his Opera students, proclaiming that: 'now we shall proceed differently. We shall create the line of physical action' (cited in Magarshack 1950: 389). That was the crux of it: *the line of physical action*, and the shift of emphasis from inner emotion to onstage action was described by his young actor Toporkov as 'one of Stanislavsky's greatest discoveries' (1998: 58).

'Physical actions' were small, achievable tasks that were directed towards the other actors on stage; the motives behind those actions were both practical and psychological. To illustrate what he meant, Stanislavsky took the example of the highly dramatic situation of the jealous composer, Salieri, plotting the murder of his archrival, Mozart. Salieri manages to poison Mozart by means of a series of simple physical actions: 'first by choosing a wine glass, next by pouring the wine, next by dropping in the poison, and only then by handing the glass to his rival' (Stanislavsky cited by Carnicke in Hodge 2010: 16). Through this kind of logical progression, actors found that small, achievable tasks could encapsulate great psychological complexities. So these actions weren't an end in themselves, but rather they propelled the actor into 'complex psychological emotional experiences' (Chushkin in Foreword to Toporkov 1998: 17). At the same time, they were so simple and direct that actors could accomplish them without any emotional strain whatsoever.

REHEARSAL TECHNIQUE: FINDING THE 'SCORE OF PHYSICAL ACTIONS'

The main purpose of the Method of Physical Actions was for actors to find the precise and logical sequence of actions that would enable their characters to achieve their 'tasks'. The technique for doing this was in fact very simple, and Stanislavsky's challenge to his company was provocative: 'Without any reading, without any conferences on the play, the actors are asked to come to a rehearsal of it' (2000b: 213). How on earth could they do that? Well, the only way to rehearse a play with so little preparation had to be through improvisation. This wasn't a new idea: Meyerhold had used improvisations extensively in the 1905 Theatrical Studio, and Nemirovich-Danchenko had also been an advocate of improvisation in rehearsal. Now, in 1935, however, the improvisations had a very specific goal: if the actors were going to identify precise and truthful physical actions, they needed to pay as much attention to detail in their improvisations as they had done previously with their round-the-table analysis. The main difference was that they were no longer sitting at the table with their heads in their books and their pencils in their hands. They now did their research *on the stage*, looking into their own human lives for whatever information they needed to achieve their characters' 'tasks'.

To help actors find that information, Stanislavsky proposed four easy steps. Step 1 was as simple as possible: the actors read a scene. Step 2 involved a small amount of discussion to clarify what the scene was about, how it divided into 'bits' and what was its main 'action'. In Step 3, the actors got up and tried out the scene using improvisation. They often began with a '*silent étude*', in which they worked attentively – but silently – through 'the line of physical action', testing whether the actions they had chosen during the preliminary discussions were appropriate or not [...]. After the étude, further discussions (Step 4) identified which moments had worked in the improvisation and which ones had fractured the logical line of physical action. Then the actors went back to Step 1 and read the scene again. Little by little, words were introduced into the études starting with their own improvised text, each time drawing closer and closer to the playwright's actual script. Throughout the whole process, they returned to the simple, ongoing sequence of reading, discussing and improvising. Through these developing improvisations, the actors were able to fine-tune their actions and fix them to form the scene's 'skeleton', known as the 'score of physical actions'. This precise score could then be repeated until habit became easy and ease became beautiful [...].

THE 'CREATION OF THE LIVING WORD'

In many ways, the 'score of physical actions' wasn't very different from the early, predetermined plan of a *mise-en-scène*, except that the process of discovery was the complete opposite. Stanislavsky no longer provided a shopping list of actions as he had with *The Seagull*. Instead, the actors themselves unearthed the moments of 'truth' – in the characters and in the action – through their psychophysical experience of *doing* the scene. Another reason for improvising was to personalise the learning of a text. Stanislavsky believed that:

> between our own words and those of another, the distance is of most immeasurable size. Our own words are the direct expression of our feelings, whereas the words of another are alien until we have made them our own, are nothing more than signs of future emotions which have not yet come to life inside us. Our own words are needed

in the first phase of physical embodiment of a part because they are best able to extract from within us live feelings, which have not yet found their outward expression.

(2000b: 100–101)

He even went as far as to forbid the deliberate memorising of the playwright's text in the early stages. If actors depended too heavily on a learned script, he believed it revealed their reluctance – or inability – to embody the character's life. 'It was considered the highest achievement if an actor could reveal the scheme of a scene by means of purely physical actions or with the minimum number of words' (Toporkov 1998: 160).

Of course, the time would come when the actors needed the actual text, at which point in rehearsals Stanislavsky fed them with the writer's words from the sidelines, like a football coach. They grabbed these words hungrily as – by this stage – the author's text expressed a thought or carried out a piece of action much better than their own made-up speeches. The result of this process was a seemingly effortless passage from (1) the actors' improvised text, through (2) the director's prompting from the sidelines, to (3) the actors finally knowing the lines because they wanted those very words, rather than because they had formally memorised them. If the actors followed this sequence, their spoken text became what Stanislavsky called the 'creation of the living word' (2000b: 262). Its roots ran deep into their psyches, emerging as the only way to express what was going on inside them. The truly exciting moment for an actor was when the playwright's text became *action* in its own right, the vital tool for really articulating the character's burning desires.

THE EMERGENCE OF CHARACTER

Because the emphasis of the early improvisations was on the actors' own words and real feelings, character was obviously not a major concern. In fact, 'character' was nothing more than the 'line of physical actions'. This in itself was joyously liberating. Because physical actions can come in an infinite variety of sequences and combinations, every actor had the potential to play a huge number of characters. Perhaps this was the greatest advantage of the Method of Physical Actions: it provided an easy means of expanding the actors' repertoires. No longer reliant on memories of previously experienced emotions, they could use physical actions to 'create experience where there [was] none to be remembered' (Mitter 1993: 20). In other words, murderous imaginings or analogous memories were no longer necessary for playing Macbeth. All the actor had to do was to establish a series of small achievable physical actions which by their very sequence revealed leadership, ambition, gullibility and the myriad of other qualities required for the part.

The Method of Physical Actions seemed to be a psychophysical 'cure-all'. Stanislavsky summarised it as the simultaneous creativity of all the intellectual, emotional, spiritual and physical forces of human nature: 'this is not theoretical, but *practical research* for the sake of a genuine objective, which we attain through physical actions' (2000b: 239; my emphasis). Yet there was still another step to be taken. His understanding of 'practical research' would in fact fuel his ultimate experiment in acting practice, now known as Active Analysis.

Active analysis

KEDROV AND KNEBEL

In the early twenty-first century, there was some debate among international scholars as to whether a difference actually existed between the Method of Physical Actions and Active Analysis. And there's no doubt the overlaps are considerable. The confusion was due in part to the fact that Stanislavsky was very old and sick when these experiments were in full throttle. He himself wrote down few of his findings, leaving his young actors, directors and teachers to hand down his 'lore' in his stead. Two individuals in particular were largely responsible for shaping his legacy: Mikhail Kedrov (1893–1972) and Maria Knebel (1898–1985). Kedrov and Knebel were both involved in Stanislavsky's last projects, and in 1948 they became directors of the Stanislavsky Drama Theatre, the venture born out of the Opera-Dramatic Studio.

Following Stanislavsky's death in 1938, Kedrov (who served as his assistant on *Tartuffe*, as well as playing the title role) pursued the idea of physical actions to extraordinary extremes. One of his students, the celebrated Russian actor, Albert Filozov (1937–2016), found that Kedrov's desire for the logic of 'Action! Action! Action!' was so dogmatic, that the Method of Physical Actions had 'in effect killed Russian theatre' (Filozov cited in Merlin 2001: 158). Kedrov's call for 'Action!' was undoubtedly influenced by Socialist Realism. In fact, it's thought that Kedrov might have been a government watchdog. He was certainly tasked with heading the Soviet commission to vet Stanislavsky's acting manuals (Carnicke in White 2014: 259). The Socialist Realists declared that there was nothing about 'man' that couldn't be changed by social reform. Reason ruled: emotion was out! With this in mind, it's clear to see how the logical sequence of the Method of Physical Actions, particularly as promoted by Kedrov, fell in line with the scientific, 'provable' aspect of Socialist Realism.

Maria Knebel, on the other hand, was far more interested in Stanislavsky's idea of 'analysis through action', or Active Analysis. Active Analysis was exactly what it said: the actors analysed their roles actively by using their bodies, imaginations, intuition and emotions on the rehearsal-room floor. So – just like the Method of Physical Actions – the detective work on a play was carried out by the actors using their entire beings and not just their intellects. Unlike the Method of Physical Actions, the 'logic' of physical actions, the 'scoring' of a role, was no longer such a big deal. Anything could provide the actors with valuable clues – the structure of a scene, the 'anatomy' of the play, the very *medium* of drama itself. So the logic of the sequence was less important than the experiential discoveries made through active research.

> **Socialist Realism** was a literary movement that came to prominence in 1934. Mirroring some of the elements of nineteenth-century Naturalism, it studied the behavioural patterns of human conduct. Unlike the Naturalists, however, the emphasis was now on environment, to the exclusion of heredity: in other words, we are not victims of our parentage, we can be whatever society wants us to be.

THE REHEARSAL PROCESS

In spite of its apparently holistic appeal, the rehearsal technique still had to have a very clear process. In many ways, it echoes the stages of the Method of Physical Actions, and can be broken down into a fairly straightforward sequence (as Carnicke has so skilfully done in Hodge 2010: 19).

First of all, the actors read the scene. Second, they assess the facts of the scene. This involves asking questions such as: What is the event? What are the protagonist's inciting actions and the antagonist's resisting counteractions? What is the style of the piece? What language do the characters use in terms of images and rhythms? 'Assessing the facts' constitutes a serious piece of textual analysis, also involving the discussion of 'bits' of action. This is important to remember, as otherwise it might seem as if Active Analysis is merely about getting up and sloshing about in generalised impro. The psychophysical information that actors glean from experiencing the scene through improvisation is undoubtedly vital. Yet it is only truly beneficial when the decisions that they make on the rehearsal-room floor are grounded in their detailed investigation of the script.

The third stage consists of the actors improvising the scene using their own words, incorporating any of the facts that they can remember. As with the Method of Physical Actions, they may start the improvisations with silent études to really bed their understanding of action, counter-action and event in their bodies and experiences.

Following the improvisation, the actors reread the scene and compare it with what they just experienced. They note which facts were retained and which were forgotten, and whether the inciting event took place. Rehearsing a play with Active Analysis consists of repeating this four-stage process of reading, discussing, improvising and discussing the improvisation. With each new improvisation, the actors strive to add more details of events, language and images.

The important shifting between table discussions and on-the-feet explorations ensures that the line of thought (what the character wants) and the line of action (how the character tries to get it) are first unlocked, and then interwoven. The analogy I always use is that the play is the trellis and the actors are the ivy. The director's task is to watch what unfurls in the improvisations and weave the ivy-actors round the trellis-play without disturbing the organic nature of the human process.

The fifth and final stage involves memorising the scene. It's important to realise that it isn't necessary to repeat improvisations *ad nauseam*. Once the heart of an encounter has been unpacked, the actors can then go away and learn the lines. In fact, if the improvisational work has been successful, they find that the scene virtually 'learns itself'.

'HERE, TODAY, NOW'

The power of Active Analysis lies in its immediacy. It acknowledges the reality of the situation ('Okay, we're on stage, so what shall we do?') and combines it with a sense of playfulness ('But what would we do *if* . . . ?'). Stanislavsky called it 'Here, Today, Now'. The actors are starting from *themselves*, so they have as much information as they need to kick-start the creative process into action. Because it's so effortless, the very pleasure of acting and the excitement of live performance become valid emotions in themselves. Whatever the actors have – here, today, now – are the physical and emotional tools with which they work. This state of being has profound effects both in rehearsal and in performance. *In rehearsal*, the knowledge that the work is simply Active Analysis – in other words, trying out ideas in three dimensions, and not just intellectually – serves as a huge liberation for the actors, daring them to be brave in their research. After all: 'A mistake in an *étude* isn't so terrible. The *étude* is a test, a quest, a verification, it is a step towards the creation of a role. It is a rough draft' (Knebel 1981: 17). Actors are therefore free to try out ideas and to reject readily what they have just found out, because all the time their imaginations are working keenly and adaptively.

In performance, the sense of improvisation carries all the way through from first preview to last night. Because the research is always 'Here, Today, Now', the actors take stock of their personal frames of mind each night, noting how they feel – even if it's tired, preoccupied, ill, or just not in the mood. This state then serves as the first piece of information, from which the necessary adaptations can easily be made.

Just like the Method of Physical Actions, Active Analysis is based upon simple actions; therefore, it requires no creative 'force' or impossible demands. All the actors have to do is to carry out those simple actions carefully and, as Knebel described it, that action will become their own. Once one simple action (e.g. 'I enter the room') has been accomplished, the second ('I throw down my backpack') follows, then the third ('I nuzzle my dog'), then the fourth and so on. With each action, the actors find that a familiar emotion flares up, and genuine feeling is awakened. It's an easy and effective osmosis from outer action to inner sensation, and back again.

THE REAL 'EXPERIENCING'

The emphasis on 'here, today, now' liberates us from the mythical belief as actors that we're supposed to feel what the character feels. But the character doesn't feel anything: it's just lines on a page. It's us – as living, breathing human beings – who feel. Not that that's always clear from Stanislavsky's own writing. One of the contradictions innate in his work – as he tried to evolve from a somewhat externalised actor in his youth to a more thin-skinned sensory performer – is his shift in defining what it means to 'experience' a role [...].

In Jean Benedetti's 2008 translation of *An Actor's Work*, Year One of the training programme is actually called 'Experiencing' (with Year Two focused on 'embodying'). In fact, Carnicke refers to *perezhivanie* ('living through' or 'experiencing') as Stanislavsky's 'lost term' (2009: 129–147). And it can really all be boiled down to the inescapable, beautiful *artificiality* of performing. The reality of being on stage or in front of a camera is that we commit to the given circumstances of the performance at the same time as wholly knowing that we *are* performing. To forget the latter would be a bold step *towards* madness and *away* from professionalism.

When Stanislavsky incites actors to 'experience' a role, he's ultimately inciting them towards the genuine act of *creating*. Create anew every night. Experience the actuality of what's going on every performance or every take. It's what he also calls being in a 'constant state of inner improvisation'. And the actor's organic sense of alternating between reality and fiction was, for Stanislavsky, necessary and healthy. In fact, we're at our most 'true' – our most 'real' – when our body, mind, spirit and whole natural organism exist within the actual framework of simultaneously pretending to be the character *and* acknowledging we're acting. That's the *real* experience. That's the experience in which we can know a genuine 'faith and a sense of truth' – because it actually exists, there's nothing fake about it. It is totally here-today-now.

And this is where Stanislavsky's 'system' and principles cross time and cultures and styles and intentions. A sense of vibrant presence can be as applicable to a toothpaste commercial, an episode of *The Handmaid's Tale*, a post-dramatic performance or *Pericles*. As Carnicke points out:

> If genuine experiencing is indeed the experience of performance itself and if this creative state allows for the alternation of contradictory states of mind, then by recovering Stanislavsky's lost term we can easily revisit his System [*sic*] from a postmodern angle and bring renewed vigor and relevance to his techniques . . . Stanislavsky's redefinition of truth as whatever happens during performance can take the contemporary actor into any dramatic style, including those yet to be invented.
>
> *(Carnicke 2009: 147)*

THE REAL STANISLAVSKY

For all the scholarship on Stanislavsky, the claims and counter-claims on what his 'system' really meant and how we should interpret it, it's actually through his letters that we truly come to know him.

It always seems a little prurient reading other people's letters, especially as so often they weren't intended for public consumption. Yet what emerges through those selected, translated and edited by Senelick (2014) is a fascinating insight into a man troubled with ill health, wracked by performance anxieties, tormented by personal fall-outs, fretting over rubles and budgets, wooing writers, massaging egos, diplomatically navigating government officials. And beyond the professional actor and theatre executive, we find a deeply loving husband and father. 'My dear precious boy,' he writes to his sick son, Igor. 'My dear and priceless clever-dick Kiryulya,' he writes to his daughter, Kira. 'Greetings, my bright, dove-grey-winged, tender, kind, clever, wonderful little angel!' he writes to his wife, Lilina. And we see the romantic artist, showing his passionate but platonic feelings for Isadora Duncan: 'I love you, I am in raptures over you and I respect you (forgive me!) – a great and admirable performer. Write me at least one little word, just so I know about your plans' (cited in Senelick 2014: 237).

In 2012, I revisited the Stanislavsky House Museum in Moscow, having not been there for nearly twenty years. I was struck by the quality of playfulness that hung in the air. 'Strange furniture from motley productions. Set models and stained glass. Photographs of Stanislavsky in various costumes and productions, including some in which he looked decidedly ham! One of the little curator ladies told me an amusing tale: one day, some visitors called upon Stanislavsky to find him (tall, aristocratic, shock of grey hair) crouching beneath the piano. "What are you doing?" they asked. "Finding out what it's like to be a mouse," he replied (no doubt those bright eyes twinkling from beneath his heavy brows)' (Merlin 2014: xvi–vii).

After all the complexities of his theories and systems, it was actually while exploring the simple elegance of playfulness that Stanislavsky died in this house, Number 6, Leontievsky Lane, in 1938. Years of smoking and endless working finally took their toll, and on 2 August he suffered a heart attack amid the paraphernalia of the Opera-Dramatic Studio. Along with a devoted wife and an extended theatre family, Konstantin Stanislavsky left behind him a teasing quantity of probings into acting and directing, and a number of publications full of tantalising discoveries, more of which will reveal themselves no doubt in years to come.

1.2   Description and analysis of *The Seagull*

Introduction

The Seagull has long been considered to have launched the success of the Moscow Art Theatre – if not revolutionised the art of acting as we know it today. And yet revolutionary endeavours are often the result of chance rather than intention and, in many respects, this was the case with the 1898 production of *The Seagull*. When all the components are considered together, it's almost remarkable that it became such a high point of modern theatre history, especially since the only person with any faith in the project was Nemirovich-Danchenko. So, what was it about the production that now renders it such a critical example of Stanislavsky's theories in practice?

In the course of the following [pages], we shall see where the seeds of many principles explored in *An Actor Prepares* (and later in the Method of Physical Actions and Active Analysis) first took root. What also emerges is that, curiously, Stanislavsky often felt he had no idea what he was doing. Yet a detailed study of his 'production plan' reveals why *The Seagull* became so significant, as Stanislavsky smashed existing rehearsal practices and pioneered modern methods of theatre-making.

The Seagull's *flight path*

Nemirovich-Danchenko's influence

Although the 'plan' of *The Seagull* was undeniably insightful, it's quite possible that Stanislavsky would never have chosen the play, had it not been for the literary taste and understanding of Vladimir Nemirovich-Danchenko. To appreciate his influence, let's return to the night of 22 June 1897 and the haunts of the Slavyansky Bazaar. . . .

It was Nemirovich who initiated the eighteen-hour meeting, driven by his thoughts on actor training as he taught it at the Philharmonic School. Besides encouraging his student-performers to be daring, fascinating and confident, he wanted them to be aware of relevant social issues, as well as the psychological development of dramatic characters and how to merge the actor's craft with the playwright's voice. These were issues about which he felt so passionate that he had to share them with Stanislavsky on that night in June. However, actor training wasn't their only preoccupation. In the course of the Slavyansky encounter, the two men discussed their desire for theatre to be collaborative, believing that all the roles in a play, however small, must be treated with the appropriate 'creative attitude'. So, late into the night, their discussion threw up ideas of an ensemble-driven theatre, the kind that would later prove vital for getting inside Chekhov's unconventional writing.

Possibly the greatest influence exerted by Nemirovich at the Slavyansky meeting was on the repertoire. While Stanislavsky was an ardent admirer of comedies and classics, Nemirovich argued vehemently that new writing should form the kernel of their pioneering enterprise. He was attracted by all things daring, and he recognised in *The Seagull* a play that abolished the normal rules of dramatic form. However, he didn't just have to convince the rather inexperienced Stanislavsky to appreciate the play's merits, he also had to persuade the writer to surrender it up to the infant company in the first place. He knew that Chekhov would be reticent and that a compelling sales pitch was needed, so Nemirovich wrote to the playwright, declaring:

> Only a literary man with taste would know how to present your plays, a man who knows how to appreciate the beauties of your works and who is, at the same time, an expert producer himself. Such a man I can truthfully claim to be.
> *(Nemirovich cited in Balukhaty 1952: 50–51)*

Nemirovich's 'pitch' continued, exclaiming that this was the only modern play and Chekhov the only living writer 'to be of any interest to a theatre with a model repertoire' (ibid.: 52). Perhaps the deal-clincher for Chekhov was Nemirovich's astute awareness that there was something special in the author's writing, something that demanded 'bridges' over which the producer must lead the audience to help them understand the images conjured up. Without these 'bridges', the play would simply fall into the 'crude conventions' so popular with the late nineteenth-century theatre-goer. In other words, Nemirovich knew the play was a challenge to the spectator – it was no easy watch, and that was what made it exciting and attractive to him as a producer. It may well have been his awareness of this that twisted Chekhov's arm.

Once he had convinced Chekhov to hand over *The Seagull* to the Moscow Art Theatre, Nemirovich then had to elucidate its many qualities to Stanislavsky, who in the meantime was struggling hard to comprehend the play. The first stage in mounting the 1898 production involved Nemirovich patiently unlocking for Stanislavsky the reverberations and complexities of the writing. It would then be Stanislavsky's task to convert those essentially literary ideas into appropriate stage pictures. The early discussions weren't easy and, over the course of many evenings, Nemirovich 'hammered all the beauties of Chekhov's work' into Stanislavsky's head (Stanislavsky 1982: 321). Thereafter, Stanislavsky travelled to the Ukraine to come up with his detailed production plan. Thus, the staging of *The Seagull* was a complete team effort: without Nemirovich, Stanislavsky probably would have avoided the play. Without Stanislavsky's vivid imagination and understanding of stage pictures, the Moscow Art Theatre might never have found its 'house style' (a style which was to define its international identity – even to the extent of adopting a seagull as a logo). And without the Moscow Art Theatre, Chekhov might have disappeared into theatrical obscurity. This serendipitous meeting of minds might explain why

The Seagull hadn't successfully taken flight before. After all, 1898 was not the first year in which the play was staged.

The Aleksandrinsky 'duck'

The year 1897 had seen the premiere of *The Seagull* at the Aleksandrinsky Theatre in St Petersburg. The first night proved to be disastrous, although following performances gained in success. Under the direction of Yevtikhy Karpov, the rehearsal schedule included one read-through, five half-day rehearsals and two dress rehearsals: unbelievable under any circumstances, let alone the production of a daunting new play like *The Seagull*. Karpov's production copy shows a scattering of stage directions, such as 'Trigorin walks to the back of the stage, then comes out to the front from left' (cited in Balukhaty 1952: 25), and mentions several props, including cigarettes, matches and a few wood shavings. A handful of sketches indicate certain positionings for the actors. But that's about it! Chekhov was due to turn up to the first rehearsal, but failed to show, leaving the initial reading of the script to the poor stage manager, with the result that the actors had no means of penetrating the play's haunting 'half-tones'. They couldn't understand how their personal *emplois* fitted into the style, as proven by the fact that the leading actress, Maria Savina, changed from Nina to Arkadina to Masha, before pulling out of the production entirely – all within eight rehearsals!

The first-night audience arrived expecting their favourite comedienne, Elizaveta Levkeyeva, to be presenting them with a rip-roaring comedy. Instead, they were left baffled and confused by the opening act with the character Konstantin Trepliov's 'symbolist' play, leading to cat-calls and whoops of disappointment. An account of the second night gives some indication of what the first night must have been like:

> what made all the difference and what distinguished the second performance from the first was that the actors had learnt their parts. They did not mouth their speeches any more, and that was why everybody got quite a different impression of the play.
>
> *(Tychinsky cited in Balukhaty 1952: 30)*

In a letter to Chekhov, Nemirovich recalls the words of a friend, who had seen the fourth performance, saying that 'the play could not possibly have succeeded in view of such an incredibly bad performance by the cast and such an utter lack of understanding of the characters and their moods' (Nemirovich cited in ibid.: 31). The reviews endorsed the comments of the audience, declaring that 'The play is impossibly bad' and that 'From all points of view, whether of idea, literature or stage, Chekhov's play cannot even be called bad, but absolutely absurd' (Nemirovich-Danchenko 1937: 65). All this goes to prove just how great was the challenge that lay before Stanislavsky in preparing his production plan and, in retrospect, how extraordinary was the collective achievement of Chekhov, Nemirovich and Stanislavsky in producing the final result.

The Seagull *flies*

Stanislavsky's method

Stanislavsky's first reaction to the play was one of complete incomprehension. He himself admitted that, as soon as he was left alone with the script, he felt bored! Yet little by little as he sat in his brother's study in Kharkov, he fell under the play's spell. His reaction was entirely instinctive, as – intellectually – he could hardly grasp what the play was about. Maybe the very fact that he didn't have an intellectual grasp enabled him to operate on a deeper, more intuitive level, and he began to experience the life of *The Seagull* with his 'inner eye and ear' (Stanislavsky cited in Balukhaty 1952: 54). The resulting production plan left Nemirovich amazed at Stanislavsky's fiery and highly gifted imagination. As Stanislavsky completed the plan of each scene, he sent it to Nemirovich, who began the initial rehearsal with a four-hour discussion of the first two acts. He then passed on to the actors the gestures, movements, rhythmic choices and interpretations made by Stanislavsky (and tweaked by himself). Of the twenty-six rehearsals, Nemirovich led fifteen and Stanislavsky nine; including three dress rehearsals, a total of eighty hours was spent rehearsing *The Seagull* with all its nuances and textures. Although the cast was so nervous on the first night, most of them were sedated and 'Stanislavsky's leg developed a nervous twitch during the play-within-the-play scene' (Senelick 2014: 116), the production was a colossal success – and theatre history was made!

Act 1

THE FIRST IMPRESSIONS

Stanislavsky's production plan looks very much like a traditional prompt copy, in the sense that the script appears on the left, with numerically ordered notes on the right-hand page indicating where and how the characters move and talk. Accompanying the notes are a myriad of sketches. Perhaps one of the most striking features of the first page is the highly detailed ground plan of the set for Act 1. Hot-houses, a lake, a stream, a bridge, bushes and sunflowers mark out the landscape, along with various paths and trees. A rocking bench is placed directly at the front of the stage, signalling that, at some point, the actors will break a major theatrical convention and sit with their backs to the audience, as indeed they do during Konstantin's play. Although the detail of the ground plan is startling enough in itself, its sense of perspective is fascinating: as spectators, we are invited to feel that what we see on the stage is only a 'slice' of the life that actually exists in the play. We are encouraged to imagine that, when the actors exit the scene, they don't return to their dressing rooms to sip coffee and smoke cigarettes, but, rather, they continue the lives of their characters beyond the boundaries of the stage. In other words, a highly elaborate invitation to 'realism' is presented to the audience simply from the first visual image of the set.

Then once we start reading the production plan, we discover that, even before the curtain is raised, a whole atmospheric (almost cinematic) lighting and soundscape has been designed to conjure up the play's inner life:

> The dim light of a lantern on top of a lamp-post, distant sounds of a drunkard's song, distant howling of a dog, the croaking of frogs, the crake of a landrail, the slow tolling of a distant church-bell – help the audience to get the feel of the sad monotonous life of the characters. Flashes of lightning, faint rumbling of *thunder* in the distance. After the raising of the curtain a pause of ten seconds.
>
> *(Stanislavsky cited in Balukhaty 1952: 139)*

[...] Stanislavsky has often been (wrongly) accused of inviting actors to ignore their audiences, and to focus all their attention behind the imaginary fourth wall. Yet straight away in the production plan, we see that he wants to weave a spell over the audience, through their senses as well as their intellects. The fact that he requires a ten-second pause once the curtain has been raised indicates his desire to create a sense of suspense, as if we should count the seconds between the flash of lightning and the crash of thunder to see how close the storm is coming. The use of 'pathetic fallacy' (whereby the weather reflects the inner life of characters) is prevalent throughout the production plan, adding to the subtle levels upon which the play operates. The ten-second pause as the curtain rises would also have given the original spectators a chance to absorb the details of a set that Stanislavsky knew would challenge their usual expectations of painted stock canvases.

MASHA AND MEDVEDENKO

Stanislavsky's understanding of psychophysical behaviour is immediately revealed with the arrival of the first two characters – Masha and the schoolteacher, Medvedenko. Throughout the play, Masha is seen to be earthy and noisy: she does solid physical things. She slurps her tea loudly, she sniffs snuff and, here, she cracks nuts. As we shall see, her noisy behaviour is often placed at exactly the point where she can gain attention, or 'pull focus'. She is a needy character, in an environment where there are far more interesting and beautiful females whose needs will be served more swiftly. Medvedenko smokes heavily during the whole play. In other words, he surrounds himself in a cloud of impenetrable dinge, preventing himself from seeing what is really going on in front of his very nose with Masha and her affections. By giving actors simple physical activities, Stanislavsky is able to touch upon deeper psychological implications. Although the audience may not consciously pick up on the reverberations, he has provided his actors with wonderful nuances with which to inform their characterisations.

Perpetuating the illusion that the life of the characters goes beyond the confines of the stage, Stanislavsky ignores Chekhov's stage direction that Masha and Medvedenko sit down (Chekhov 1990: 1). Instead, he uses their two-page dialogue to zigzag on and off the stage, as if they are taking an after-dinner walk. These aren't two characters who have come here to present a piece of dialogue to an eagerly attentive audience: instead, we as spectators are encouraged to feel as if we are eavesdropping on a conversation that is taking place almost casually. (Just as we might if this were film.) Stanislavsky breaks their dialogue into sections as they exit the stage and return, rather like a pendulum. This gives us the sense of life passing in its usual way, but also that this life is fateful – its course is unalterable; what happens between Masha and Medvedenko is inevitable. In the brief pause in their dialogue (specified by Chekhov, ibid.: 2), during which they momentarily exit, the hammering of the workmen grows louder. Once more, the soundscape is used to create a sense of tension, of imminent foreboding.

ENTER SORIN AND KONSTANTIN

Realism leaps to the fore with the arrival of Konstantin (Kostya) and Sorin. Where Chekhov has '*Enter right*, SORIN *and* KONSTANTIN' (ibid.), Stanislavsky describes how they 'walk through some bushes on to the path, pushing the branches out of their way, bending down, climbing over garden seats' (Stanislavsky cited in Balukhaty 1952: 141).

Instantly we have a sense that we are in a part of the garden not used very often. There is a feeling of awkwardness, and even of subterfuge when, some lines later, Masha and Medvedenko 'emerge from behind a bush' (ibid.). Maybe all will not be what it seems....

The combination of Masha, Medvedenko, Sorin and Konstantin sets up a fascinating cobweb of tempo-rhythms. When Konstantin requests that they leave: 'Medvedenko begins to walk away obediently. Masha remains standing, deep in thought. Sorin sits down on the rocking bench, swaying up and down' (ibid.: 143). This juxtaposition of images illustrates Stanislavsky's musicality – in terms of rhythm and stage pictures. At the same time, it reveals his intuitive understanding of what he would later call in *An Actor Prepares* the 'inner motive forces': thought, feeling and action [...]. Medvedenko has a linear path: he is action-orientated. He does what he is told: his sense of etiquette and manners is acute. Masha has no path at all: she is static. Her thought-centre governs her at this moment. Sorin strikes up a miniature pendulum motion, not dissimilar to the bigger pendulum created by Masha and Medvedenko walking from one side of the stage to the other. Sorin's path has movement, but goes nowhere, just like his whole life. We discover during the course of the play that he has big dreams and desires, but no longer the physical stamina to activate them. In the middle of these three constrained tempo-rhythms, we see Konstantin, utterly driven by his over-stimulated emotion-centre. Masha is torn between two lovers – the methodical, action-based schoolteacher and the imaginative, emotion-based writer. But she knows with whom her destiny lies: as if 'awakening from a reverie' (Stanislavsky cited in Balukhaty 1952: 143) she follows Medvedenko out.

A COMPLEX DIALOGUE!

The dialogue between Sorin and Kostya is very complex, as it involves working with a prop, inner actions versus outer activities, inner/outer tempo-rhythms, central and peripheral actions, and tiny details versus the bigger picture. Let's unpack all these.

Props were an important part of Stanislavsky's growing awareness of psychophysicality, so it is not by chance that Konstantin arrives carrying a bundle containing Nina's outfit for his play. The relationship between an actor and a prop can access deep psychological information and add unconscious layers to the spectators' perception of events. There is an intimacy evoked by Konstantin handling Nina's costume, as well as establishing him as the director of his play. He is forming and shaping not only her performance but also the experience that he wants his audience (particularly his mother and her writer-lover) to undergo. The image becomes startlingly clear when, some time later in Act 1, Nina arrives and Konstantin 'starts unfolding Nina's costume. . . . During this scene, Nina undoes her hair and drapes herself in a sheet. Konstantin is assisting her, pinning her stage costume for her here and there' (ibid.: 153). There is a naive eroticism attached to them mutually preparing her to be exhibited before the man (Trigorin) who ends up becoming her lover. Certainly, when Stanislavsky eventually sets up the scene for Konstantin's play, there is a significant sense of sexual awareness, as the prop evolves from inanimate bundle to revealing adornment: '[Nina] is draped in a white sheet, her hair hangs loosely down her back, the sheet, as it falls down her arms, forms something that resembles a pair of wings, through which Nina's bust and arms are faintly outlined' (ibid.: 159). Here, with Sorin, however, the prop is used to reveal the underlying tension. Konstantin tries to balance the bundle against the side of the table and, on failing, throws it down on the ground. His action is performed without comment as an accompaniment to the dialogue, and yet, through the bundle's 'lack of cooperation', we see Konstantin's frustration that he can't control Nina. And she's late! The physical activity reverberates with psychological metaphor. There is a similar effect with the rocking bench: Sorin constantly tries to stabilise it, while Konstantin unsettles it every time he leaps up and down.

The contradiction between inner action and outer activity is cleverly encapsulated in Stanislavsky's stage directions for Konstantin's long speeches that rail against his mother and art. Stanislavsky specifies that Konstantin remains lying on the bench for the duration of the dialogue. He then juxtaposes the stillness of the posture with sudden outbursts of excitability – Kostya puffs a cigarette, shakes off the ash, tears up flowers and grass-stalks, abruptly sits up and then lies down again. This sequence reveals the conflict within Kostya's inner motive forces: by lying still, his body (action-centre) is trying to contain the explosiveness of his emotion-and thought-centres, which every so often get the better of him through these abrupt physical actions. It is all very clever, as a dynamic tension is created between Kostya's inner and outer tempo-rhythms. Added to this, Kostya's actions become more *central*, as he becomes more agitated. In other words, the tearing of the flower or the shaking of ash are actions at the *periphery* of his body, whereas 'slapping his leg nervously' and 'beating his breast in agitation' (ibid.: 147) reveal how his intensifying frustration becomes directed towards himself rather than the physical objects around him.

With regard to visual pictures, Stanislavsky develops the tension between inner feeling and outer expression in the changing spatial relationships between Sorin and Kostya. At the start of the dialogue, Kostya lies on the bench with his head in his hand: it's casual and devil-may-care. As the tension rises, he changes to sit looking out front, before the final – more confessional or confrontational – posture in which he straddles the bench face to face with Sorin. Throughout these changing images, Sorin remains grounded and still: he yawns, hums and whistles – his tempo-rhythm is legato. Konstantin paces, smokes and tears things – his tempo-rhythm is staccato. There is a musicality in the stage pictures as a whole and in the individual gestures of the two characters. A moment of comedy is reached at the end of the dialogue, when Nina arrives, Kostya leaps up from the bench and Sorin almost falls off, having clung on for dear life throughout the exchange. As Kostya loses his emotional balance, Sorin almost loses his physical balance.

DANCING AND MUSIC

The arrival of Nina is illustrated in Stanislavsky's production plan with a flurry of small drawings, as Nina, Sorin and Kostya almost dance around each other – age and ill health encounter youth and hopeful love. Following Sorin's departure, the text between Kostya and Nina is quite sparse – leading, of course, to the kiss lasting 'five seconds' (ibid.: 153). Littered around this dialogue are numerous stage directions with specific details for almost every line and pause: this is clearly an early kind of a Method of Physical Actions. Twice Kostya seizes Nina's hand, twice she pulls it away, the second time 'running off rapidly' (ibid.) to sit elsewhere. Taken as a whole, the stage picture consists of Konstantin trying to tie Nina down with kisses, while she constantly flies away – like a seagull? Their objectives vividly contradict each other, creating – as a result – exciting, detailed action.

By contrast, the exchange between Dorn and Polina, which follows Kostya and Nina's encounter, has very few directions. It is the same in Act 2, when Trigorin has his long speeches to Nina about playwriting. This may be because Stanislavsky was going to play Dorn at one point and then he took the part of Trigorin. Perhaps he considered it unnecessary to give himself stage directions. The ensemble interactions surrounding Konstantin's play, however, are extremely detailed, revealing Stanislavsky's great understanding of how the musicality of the collective voices could be drawn out. Nowhere is this more clearly seen than with the estate manager, Shamrayev, who is evidently the 'bass' instrument. Inspired by Shamrayev's tale of the famous singer, Silva, Stanislavsky creates a repeating motif, a kind of psychological gesture for the actor to integrate into his characterisation. Shamrayev becomes a bassoon-like buffoon, who, at inappropriate moments, honks the bass notes. One example follows the collapse of Kostya's play, when ethereal singing is heard across the lake. In the pause during which the other characters listen, somewhat haunted, Shamrayev leaps on a tree stump and starts conducting. Cleverly, Stanislavsky allows a moment of melancholy stillness – obviously intended by Chekhov, who inserted a pause (Chekhov 1990: 14) – but he instantly undercuts the latent sentimentality with the brusque humour of the estate manager.

SOUNDSCAPES

The moment of the singing also introduces another vital component into the production plan, again prefiguring filmic devices: that of underscoring the action with soundscapes. This effect not only creates atmosphere but also takes the spectator on a particular emotional journey. In the middle of Kostya's play, the distant tolling of a church bell sounds. At this stage, it provokes a sense of foreboding, as well as reminding us of a world beyond the garden of Arkadina's estate (as does the singing across the lake). When the same bell is sounded during Nina's return visit in Act 4, we are flung back to this moment in Act 1 and reminded of the inevitability of Nina's sorry plight.

Sound effects are even more imaginatively created through the counterpoint of characters' voices and preoccupations. Shamrayev's crassness in telling the story of Silva, accompanied by his coarse laughter, clashes with the delicacy of emotions exchanged between Nina, Trigorin and Arkadina. The 'musical score' suggested by Stanislavsky is highly expressive:

> No one laughs, Shamrayev, on the other hand, bursts out laughing even louder, then stops abruptly, repeats once more, 'Bravo, Silva!' and falls silent as suddenly as he began. A pause of fifteen seconds. No one stirs. The only sounds are the distant singing of the peasants, the croaking of the frogs and the cry of the corncrake.... Another pause of ten seconds.
>
> *(Stanislavsky cited in Balukhaty 1952: 169)*

This soundscape delicately takes the spectators on a subconscious exploration of circles of attention: from the bass voice of Shamrayev, to the vocal silence of each character's individual preoccupations, to the world beyond the estate and, in the final silence, back to their own preoccupations. The audience is being catapulted between the inner world (or microcosm) of the characters, and the outer world (or macrocosm) of Russia.

The closing image of the first act, which at the Art Theatre's premiere left the audience suspended in silence before bursting into tumultuous applause, is heavily cinematic in its use of soundscape. Masha's sobs at realising the futility of her love and life are cross-faded to the sound of Konstantin playing a 'frenzied waltz' (ibid.: 175) on the piano. To an almost melodramatic cacophony of sound, including the tolling of a church bell, a peasant's song, frogs, corncrakes, the knocking of the nightwatchman, 'and all sorts of other nocturnal sound effects' (ibid.: 175), the curtain falls! Whether a director today would want to try out all of Stanislavsky's idea is debatable. Nonetheless, implicit in this stage direction is the creation of atmosphere: that atmosphere is as vital for the audience's emotional journey as it is for the actors' sense of realism. Although he was greatly misunderstood at the time – not least by Chekhov – Stanislavsky's exploration of sound was essentially aimed at gelling the actors and the audience into one theatrical experience in which they could all develop a sense of faith and truth.

Act 2

MASHA'S TEMPO-RHYTHMS

The opening stage directions for the second act are once again highly cinematic in detail, with the continuing idea of a 'pathetic fallacy' (where the weather reflects the characters' states of mind). The curtain of Kostya's makeshift stage is now 'waving in the wind and flapping against the sides of the platform' (ibid.: 179), mirroring his own tattered art and heart. Within this opening exchange, Stanislavsky has incorporated a number of physical activities for characters, which reveal their underlying tensions. Masha noisily drinks her tea throughout this scene (just as, in Act 1, she cracked nuts and, in Act 3, 'she eats noisily' (ibid.: 211)). Her noisiness serves as both a kind of attention-seeking to upstage Arkadina's reading of the Maupassant novella, and a 'naturalistic' indication of her social upbringing; after all, she is the daughter of the brusque estate manager, Shamrayev. Stanislavsky's detailed consideration of Masha's character in this scene reveals his concern for every part in the ensemble. In her short exchange with Nina about Konstantin's writing, Stanislavsky specifies precisely the changing tempo-rhythms that Masha is to use with each sentiment. She begins by speaking 'her words very rapidly and a little sharply', followed by a pause, after which she continues 'in quite a different, dreamy voice' (ibid.: 183): this betrays her deepening emotion memory as she vividly recalls Konstantin's own reading, at the same time as providing a moment of comedy when Sorin finally erupts with a snore. Although the counterpoint of Masha's musing and Sorin's snoring is provided by Chekhov in the text, Stanislavsky carefully directs the actress playing Masha through a series of adapting tempo-rhythms to gain the maximum comic potential.

SONGSCAPES

At several points throughout the production plan, Stanislavsky indicates that characters sing. The singing provides another texture to the soundscape, while also operating on an emotional/psychological level. This is exactly the case during the discussion of Sorin's health near the beginning of Act 2, when Dorn begins to hum a melody (as indeed he often does throughout the play) and Arkadina provides a harmony. This musical accompaniment to the discussion of Sorin's life suggests that the characters are avoiding their concern about his health. In other words, Stanislavsky adds layers to a scene beyond and beneath the actual words, so that the text ceases to be a conversation about Sorin's life and instead becomes a scene about other people's *attitudes* to his life: their singing effortlessly expresses the subtext.

PHYSICAL ACTIVITY VERSUS PSYCHOLOGICAL ACTION

Dorn and Arkadina's singing is in itself a physical activity. Again, in Act 2, Stanislavsky uses physical activities to highlight characters' social status. (Don't forget that the influence of environment and heredity on psychology and social status was an important aspect of the Naturalist movement.) So, after the sipping of tea by the assembled company, Shamrayev arrives and continues his dialogue, 'stuffing bread into his mouth and washing it down with tea' (Stanislavsky cited in Balukhaty 1952: 187). Their etiquette (notwithstanding Masha's noisy slurping) is offset by Shamrayev's brusque practicality. In fact, cups of tea are used with comic regularity to express a character's inner life. When Polina and Dorn are left alone after Arkadina's row with Shamrayev, Polina 'drinks up her cup of tea at one gulp' (ibid.: 191), as if the downing of hot liquid reflects her desire to devour Dr Dorn.

The exchange between Dorn and Polina is larded with comic frustration, endorsed by the bizarre picture of Dorn doing his gymnastic exercises. He walks up and down a plank throughout Polina's entreaties, as if balancing on a tightrope. By distracting himself from the conversation like this, he seems to behave like an annoying child, refusing to engage with the adult conversation that Polina is anxious to pursue. In other words, Stanislavsky presents their conflicting objectives (Polina's to engage Dorn, Dorn's to deflect Polina) in broad, physical pictures, where psychology and physicality are inextricably linked. (He may also be weighing up his love-options between Polina and Arkadina, walking the plank of passion, so to speak?)

It is the constant juxtaposition of physical activity with psychological action and spoken text that marks out Stanislavsky's production plan of *The Seagull* as revolutionary and extraordinary. Even when Chekhov gives characters monologues, Stanislavsky justifies the text with a physical activity. So he takes Chekhov's stage direction that Nina gives Dorn some flowers (inciting Polina to 'tear them up and throw them on the ground' (Chekhov 1990: 26)) and creates a further 'dialogue' between the flowers and Nina. During her speech about famous actresses, 'she sorts out the flowers and makes a little bunch of them' (Stanislavsky cited in Balukhaty 1952: 193).

Her action transports the monologue from a theatrical device to a conversation with herself, as, through the prop (the flowers), she 'arranges' or 'makes sense' of the situation.

AN INTIMATE STYLE OF ACTING

In many ways, moments such as Nina with the flowers are like cinematic close-ups. The precision of the physical activity guides the audience's eye towards very specific details. Although cinema was in its infancy at the time that Stanislavsky composed his production plan, many of his ideas illustrate the way in which he explored the same kind of intimate contact that on-screen close-ups can allow. This is absolutely clear in both exchanges that Nina has in Act 2, the first with Konstantin and the second with Trigorin. Throughout these two encounters, Stanislavsky makes references to eye contact. Having presented Nina with the dead seagull, Konstantin 'looks intently and reproachfully' at her, while she 'is unable to look him straight in the face' and, thus, 'lowers her eyes' (ibid.: 193). Eventually, she turns her back on him, thereby avoiding eye contact altogether. In sharp contrast to this encounter, Nina's relationship to Trigorin is unashamedly intimate: during the conversation, she 'gazes entranced into Trigorin's pensive eyes' (ibid.: 197). Stanislavsky even stresses that, in the course of Trigorin's long speech about his writing: 'it would be advisable for Nina not to change her position, but go on looking into Trigorin's eyes all the time with rapt expression' (ibid.). The insistence on eye contact suggests a specific kind of acting. As we have already touched upon in section 1.1, it was quite common for actors to present most of their performance Down-Stage-Centre and directly out to the audience. This was partly because stage lighting was still fairly primitive and 'DSC' was a prime spot, and partly because the actors were then close enough to the prompter to be guided through an ill-rehearsed performance. However, Stanislavsky's directions invite an intimate style of acting, involving a real level of 'communion', which also requires 'limitless attention to your partner' (Stanislavsky cited in Gorchakov 1985: 318). Facial expressions change, and eye contact varies in intensity: Stanislavsky draws the audience in, so that they can watch human interaction under a microscope. Although we have now become used to such detailed acting through the media of film and television, we have to remind ourselves of how revolutionary it would have been for an audience who were accustomed to the grand gesturing and loud oratory of nineteenth-century melodrama.

Comparing the two encounters between Kostya and Nina, and Nina and Trigorin also highlights the way in which Stanislavsky explored spatial dynamics. Although the majority of illustrations in his production copy are ground plans of the stage, from time to time he embellishes his stage directions with sketches of the characters. In the first dialogue, Stanislavsky shows Konstantin with his foot on a tree stump, and between him and Nina is a shotgun, upon whose barrel he leans. So, an implement of death (the gun) is placed between them along with a dead seagull; at the same time, a status game is being played, with Kostya above Nina in terms of height. Taken as a whole, the picture is threatening, rather than tender: it certainly doesn't look like a love scene. However, according to Stanislavsky's sketches, the dynamics between Nina and Trigorin are entirely different. At first, she sits herself in a hammock, against whose side Trigorin leans casually. Then a little later, he crosses to a seat Down-Stage-Right, and Nina sits herself on a cushion at his feet. On both occasions, he is above her in terms of height, yet each time the picture is one of fascination, interest and flirtation, not intimidation as it is with Konstantin. The fact that Stanislavsky chooses to provide sketches of these two exchanges demonstrates that he wanted these spatial and pictorial comparisons to be made by the audience, either consciously or subconsciously. The final sketch that he provides of Nina and Trigorin shows them sitting together on the bench. Now they are on equal footing: they have both understood that they are in love with each other, although between them still lies the macabre body of the dead seagull, like a fateful totem. Chekhov's intention that the seagull should be a metaphor throughout the play is embellished by Stanislavsky through positioning the characters in various spatial relations to the bird.

The penultimate stage direction of Act 2 explores the different intentions behind the various characters' eye contact. As Arkadina 'throws a quick glance at [Nina] through her lorgnette', she leads away Trigorin, who is 'still staring at Nina' (Stanislavsky cited in Balukhaty 1952: 207). Images of eyes and seeing permeate the production plan. Who really sees what's going on? In the world of actors and writers, who can really tell truth from artifice? Undoubtedly, Stanislavsky is bravely following Chekhov's lead of combining realism with symbolism, the physical with the metaphysical. And yet he was constantly haunted by a sense of self-doubt. His final direction of Act 2 is bold in terms of its theatricality, and yet Stanislavsky's notes to Nemirovich indicate his insecurity:

> During the final pause of ten seconds it might not be a bad idea for the curtain on the platform to start swaying violently and flapping against the platform (as a hint of what is to be mentioned in Act IV). The danger is that it might produce a rather ridiculous effect. Should we try it?
>
> *(ibid.)*

On the one hand, Stanislavsky seems to know that he is challenging convention; on the other hand, he is aware of the fine line between dramatic experimentation and melodramatic device. These doubts simply reinforce the fact that *The Seagull* was successful almost in spite of itself.

Act 3

NATURALISTIC DETAILS

The floor plan for Act 3 instantly reveals the innovative quality of the stage design. The interior of a room is shown, complete with parrot in cage, and yet it is all presented on an angle, enhancing the feeling that we are watching a slice of life rather than a neatly prepared box set for a play. The angle of the design suggests that the house – and the characters' lives – stretch far beyond the boundaries established by the stage. In contrast to the vivid soundscapes of the first two acts, Act 3 begins with a simple clock ticking. During his lifetime, Stanislavsky was often ridiculed by fellow practitioners (not least of whom was Chekhov himself) for his enthusiastic love of sound effects. His argument was that, paradoxically, we notice silence much more acutely through the use of sound: the simplicity of the clock ticking suggests the chilling calm before a storm.

These details of set and sound remind us of the Naturalist movement. As stressed already, a crucial component of Naturalism was the role that heredity and environment played in the development of an individual. At the beginning of Act 3, Stanislavsky gives Masha a simple physical gesture, which links her back to Dr Dorn in Act 1. She pensively traces lines on the table-cloth with her fork, just as Dorn pensively traces with his stick on the ground throughout the fracas following Kostya's play. There is an implication in *The Seagull* that Dorn might be Masha's biological father (her heredity), and yet Shamrayev is her familial father (her environment). Therefore, juxtaposed with her quiet thoughtfulness is her brusque coarseness. During this encounter with Trigorin at the top of Act 3, Stanislavsky is thorough in the details concerning Masha's character:

> It can be seen from the way in which she fills the glasses that she is an expert at that kind of thing.... Does it all with assumed gaiety, with the devil-may-care air of a

student. . . . One arm akimbo, like a man, clinks glasses energetically, also like a man. . . . Masha empties her glass at one gulp and has a bite of something (she eats noisily), then slaps Trigorin on the back. . . . Leaning with her elbows on the table, bends over towards Trigorin.

(Stanislavsky cited in Balukhaty 1952: 211, 213)

This collection of stage directions illustrates two aspects of Stanislavsky's intentions for his production plan. Just as we saw at the top of Act 2, he was eager to give as much attention to the minor characters as to the principal roles in order to encourage a style of ensemble acting. The second intention is the way in which he sets up a very clear relationship between the actress playing Masha and the props with which she works. The aplomb with which she fills the glass and drinks the liquid, and her physical contact with the table, give us a clear insight into her psychology and her backstory. These naturalistic details also serve to undercut any sentimentality that might lie in the text. So, for example, when Masha asks Trigorin to sign a book for her, she speaks 'while struggling into rubber goloshes and buttoning her coat' (ibid.: 213). In other words, Stanislavsky cunningly provides the actress with a vigorous, practical, physical activity while her text is poetic and imaginative. This contrast reveals the contradictions within Masha's personality: she wants to be a Nina but she has to be a Polina.

SUBTEXTS AND PAUSES

As Masha exits, Nina enters. Following the plan established in Act 2, the close-ups of eye contact are once again put under the microscope in her exchange with Trigorin. More interesting at this point is the use of the pause. It is believed that the term 'subtext' (*padtekst* – 'beneath the text') was introduced into theatrical vocabulary by Nemirovich-Danchenko and Stanislavsky, when they were first tackling *The Seagull*. We often articulate our subtext through pauses. And indeed at the point in this dialogue where Trigorin reminds Nina of the dead seagull, Chekhov has inserted a pause. Then, to illustrate that dramatic pauses are never just empty silences, Stanislavsky provides an extensive stage direction. After a moment's awkwardness, Nina jumps to her feet to leave the room, but Trigorin catches her hand to stop her. She stands with her back to him in silence, as Trigorin raises her caught hand to kiss it. Gently she withdraws her hand from his lips and moves to the stove, where (just like Dorn and Masha lost in thought) she traces something with her finger. This is a moment of decision for her. That tracing finger marks a resolution: she turns quickly to Trigorin to finish her speech and immediately exits. The details piled into that one 'pause' indicate a whole sequence of conflicts *between* the two characters as well as *within* each of the two characters. Their emotions battle with their thoughts, their desires battle with their sense of duty. The vividness of Stanislavsky's imagination has jam-packed that one moment with a complexity of realistic human responses, full of varying tempo-rhythms and life-changing decisions.

EATING LUNCH: A PHYSICAL DISTRACTION TO HEIGHTEN TENSION

Stanislavsky's intuitive sense of musicality collides the delicacy of Trigorin and Nina with the brassier notes of Arkadina in her conversation with Sorin. Once again, Stanislavsky changes a solemn dialogue about Sorin's health into a piece of light naturalistic conversation by having Arkadina eat her lunch as a backdrop to the text. The noisy clatter of her knife and fork conflict with Sorin's tentative attempts to find the appropriate moment to ask her about money. Their contradictory objectives create a sense of comic tension: Sorin doesn't want to spoil her lunch, which is exactly what he knows will happen as soon as he mentions money.

Stanislavsky's musical understanding of the conversation continues after the moment at which Sorin dares to broach the subject. The changes of tempo-rhythm between the characters, as well as the actual aural accompaniment of Arkadina's eating are delightfully observed. Arkadina stops eating, she frowns, she thinks, she plays with her knife. She stops eating again. She shakes her head slowly. She quickly fills her glass. She starts eating vigorously. At the point at which she 'cannot stand it any longer, she throws down her knife (a clatter of dishes on the table) and, like the thoroughly spoilt woman she is, bursts into tears' (Stanislavsky cited in Balukhaty 1952: 219). She then buries her face in a napkin and remains sitting motionless. The comedy arises from the incongruity of her lack of interest in Sorin's health versus the emotional response that the issue of money arouses in her. However, when Sorin's fainting fit reveals his dreadful physical state, Stanislavsky insists that the audience be plummeted into the seriousness of the situation to the same degree that Arkadina is:

> This scene should be played as realistically as possible, so as to deceive the audience. It should be played in a way to convince the audience that Sorin is dying. That would greatly heighten the suspense of the audience and its interest in what is taking place on the stage.
>
> *(ibid.: 221)*

Here we see Stanislavsky playing a dramatic game with the spectators, seducing them into a suspension of disbelief. He uses Arkadina's seeming lack of interest in Sorin to create a false sense of security for the audience, before plunging them into an uneasy anxiety. His stage direction also implies that the actor playing Sorin mustn't indulge in any melodramatic clichés: the acting is to be as realistic as possible.

AN EARLY METHOD OF PHYSICAL ACTIONS

The constant interplay between big emotions and physical activities continues through Act 3 into the dialogue between mother and son surrounding the head-bandaging. Initially Arkadina's task of reapplying Konstantin's dressing is extremely practical and realistic, as Stanislavsky provides details of filling a glass of water, pouring it into a soup plate, mixing it with disinfectant, tearing rags, folding rags and soaking rags: the paraphernalia of naturalism offsets the emotive dialogue. As their passions rise, however, Stanislavsky writes various psychological gestures into the characters' demeanour, revealing how those big emotions are displaced into physical tics. Thus, we have Arkadina drumming nervously on the table and tapping her foot on the floor. These peripheral movements of her body show that, although she remains sitting, she is boiling like a kettle, until the moment at which 'beside herself, she flings the end of the rolled up bandage ... in Konstantin's face' (ibid.: 227). What Stanislavsky achieves by listing the medical details of preparing the bandage is the creation of a tragicomic resonance when he reaches Chekhov's own stage direction: *Tears the bandage off his head* (Chekhov 1990: 41). After all of the attention mother pays son, Kostya rips off the dressing and hurls it at her.

In many ways, this is another early form of the Method of Physical Actions, in that Stanislavsky takes the actors from simple practical tasks through to psychophysical gestures combining seething inner emotions with rapid physical actions. Therefore, Arkadina goes from drumming the table, to tearing the bandage, to crashing her chair to the floor. The sequence, or score, of physical actions builds to a crescendo in proportion to her inner emotions. The actors' relationships with props, as well as with each other, serve as a realistic texturing of the spoken word. There is a wonderfully ironic moment at the end of the dialogue, when Trigorin arrives and Kostya runs out. To distract from her obvious distress, Arkadina starts carefully putting Trigorin's papers into his case: her physical action stands in stark contrast to Konstantin's own destruction of his manuscripts in the final act of the play.

PLAYING WITH GENRE

From time to time in his production plan, Stanislavsky reveals his awareness that he was playing with dramatic forms as much as exploring new avenues of staging. Halfway through the argument between mother and son, Stanislavsky incites his actors with the words: 'To make the play more dynamic and more comprehensible to the audience, I would very much advise the actors not to be afraid of the *most glaring* realism in this scene' (cited in Balukhaty 1952: 229). Then again, during the lovers' tiff between Arkadina and Trigorin, Stanislavsky inserts the note that she 'embraces him, kneels before him, acts a real tragedy, or rather melodrama' (ibid.: 233). He converts Arkadina's play-acting, implicit in the text, into overt vocabulary concerning theatrical forms, as she 'speaks in the tone and with the sort of pathos usually employed in melodrama' (ibid.: 235). Stanislavsky acknowledges that Arkadina has an objective to achieve – 'to seduce Trigorin' – and he encourages the actress playing the role to exploit recognisable theatrical conventions to fulfil that objective. This is a sophisticated metatheatrical device, in which the actress playing Arkadina is exploiting various dramatic forms in order that the character of Arkadina can reach her psychological objective.

THE MUSICAL PLAYOUT

The dialogue between Trigorin and Arkadina is the last in a series of 'duets' that comprise this highly musical act. We weave from the poignant comedy of Masha and Trigorin to the lyricism of Trigorin and Nina, followed by the high comedy of Arkadina and Sorin, which ends in an abrupt moment of potential tragedy with his fainting fit. The contrasting dialogues between Konstantin and Arkadina (tragicomedy) and Trigorin and Arkadina (comedy) bookend each other, before the orchestral finale of the act in which the entourage take leave of their estate. It is particularly worth noting in this section the way in which Stanislavsky personalises the ensemble. The character of the maid (until this point unmentioned) is shown to be wonderfully spunky, being the only one not to bow low to Arkadina, but, rather, being pictured looking displeased. Another maidservant in the crowd has a baby who starts to cry, thereby adding to the cacophony of farewell frenzy. Any sentimentality at the grand departure is entirely undercut by Polina and her plums, one small line of Chekhov's text which is turned by Stanislavsky into a whole farcical routine! It begins with Polina squeezing her way through the crowd of domestics into the front hall to give Arkadina a basket of plums. Half a page later, Arkadina goes out to the carriage, at which point Polina runs back into the dining room to fetch the plums that her mistress has (intentionally?) forgotten. Arkadina's giving of a ruble to be shared between three servants causes another crush, through which Polina once more pushes with her basket of plums, accompanied by the old retainer, Yakov, who shuffles through the crowd to retrieve a forgotten suitcase. Although Chekhov himself inserted some of the business with the plums, Stanislavsky has taken the idea to a further comical degree, from which the final moment of intimate solitude between Trigorin and Nina emerges with heightened poignancy.

From a distance of over 100 years, the way in which Stanislavsky specifies the lengths of various kisses is rather droll. Ten seconds is the duration of Nina and Trigorin's final kiss, compared with the mere five seconds granted Nina and Konstantin in Act 1. Of course we can guess the degrees of intimacy in their respective kisses, but ultimately it's the sustained moment of hiatus in the middle of the frantic departure that seems to be most important here. It's fairly unlikely that Stanislavsky stood with a stopwatch in rehearsals making sure that the kisses lasted their specified time. But the point really is that Stanislavsky's attention to detail once more illustrates his understanding of musicality, realistic acting and contradictory tempo-rhythms and atmospheres.

Act 4

TYING UP LOOSE ENDS

After the vigorous departure and the sound of carriage bells at the end of the previous scene, Act 4 begins with a specified pause 'of between ten and fifteen seconds' (Stanislavsky cited in Balukhaty 1952: 247). Then Stanislavsky begins to paint with both colour and sound. The reddish glow of the stove fills the room, while the atmospheric soundscape reveals the change in season and psychological climate. Wind and rain beat against the windows causing the panes to rattle. Medvedenko enters, chilled to the marrow and stamping his feet – a stage direction which is underlined with red pencil in the prompt copy, illustrating Stanislavsky's fervour to create the feeling of an outside world, a world beyond the confines of the stage.

In this final act, Stanislavsky completes images and ideas that he has set up in the previous three acts, not least of which is the musicality of the production plan. Konstantin's piano playing becomes a literal score accompanying Polina and Masha as they make up Sorin's bed. Masha's physical actions complement the soundscape: as she 'sighs' then 'shuts the lid of the snuff box fiercely' (ibid.: 253), the contrast between the sustained sigh and the staccato snapping of the lid conjures up the contradictory emotions within Masha herself. The piano music is also used very consciously as a source of affective memory for Polina: Stanislavsky explicitly explains how Polina's thoughts in listening to the music drift back to memories of her own love affair with Dr Dorn.

Throughout the play, we have seen how Dr Dorn's inner life is manifested by his continual humming – an idea provided by Chekhov in the script and amplified by Stanislavsky in the production plan. It usually indicates that Dorn is preoccupied with something other than the present moment. This device reaches a climax in his curious exchange with Sorin, during which Stanislavsky has the able-bodied doctor almost dancing round the wheelchair-bound invalid. Over a page of dialogue between the two characters, Sorin is stuck with his dreams and his newspaper, while Dorn 'perambulates' around the room, humming. At the end of the exchange, Chekhov specifies a pause (Chekhov 1990: 53). This pause is made extremely full in Stanislavsky's production plan: Dorn is lost in his tune, Sorin is lost in his newspaper and Konstantin 'stares motionlessly in front of him. Masha looks wistfully at Konstantin, and Paulina [sic] at Dorn' (Stanislavsky cited in Balukhaty 1952: 257). Stanislavsky again uses a kind of stage close-up to take us right into the characters' very thoughts. Even when Dorn eventually sits down, it's in a rocking chair, as if he of all the characters can settle least easily.

The rocking chair is used as a very specific device during Konstantin's account of Nina's life: as the story grows sadder, Dorn's rocking becomes slower and slower, 'until at last, at the pause, he stops rocking himself altogether' (ibid.: 259). The rocking chair is seen to be an outer manifestation of Dorn's inner state. With the Method of Physical Actions, and certainly with Active Analysis, actors can strike up a relationship with anything that provides them with appropriate psychophysical information. It may be a prop, a sound, a lighting effect, or, of course, another actor! Here – for the actor playing Dorn – it's a piece of furniture.

Bella Merlin

BUILDING TENSION AND DISSOLVING ATMOSPHERES

Throughout Konstantin's story of Nina, the recollections of unfortunate events in her professional or private life are given an eerie underscoring. So, when Kostya describes how Nina made 'a complete mess' of her private life, there's a pause and what Stanislavsky simply calls 'sound effects'. These are repeated when Kostya declares that her stage career 'was an even worse failure'. A pause and the same sound effects are again elicited by the debate surrounding whether she had any talent or not. (It's curious that, given all his specificity in the rest of the production plan, Stanislavsky doesn't specify what the particular sound effects are here.) The fourth moment occurs in response to Kostya's confession that Nina never admitted him to her hotel, and the final combination of 'pause and sound effect' reverberates after his revelation that 'She kept saying in the letters that she was a seagull' (Chekhov 1990: 54). The pay-off for the fivefold 'pause and sound effect' moments occurs when, towards the end of Konstantin's story, the pause is followed by the sound of carriage bells signalling the arrival of Arkadina. The sobering recollections of Nina are superseded by the girlish sleigh-bells of the woman who got the man.

Arkadina's arrival collides with the established atmosphere, shattering the solemnity with her kisses and chocolates and throwing off of gloves. Curiously, the older woman's behaviour is seen as more girlish than the 'real' life into which Nina threw herself. The texturing of atmospheres is taken a step further by Stanislavsky's stage directions, in a way that prefigures Act 1 of *Three Sisters*, when one upstage conversation between the soldiers unwittingly comments on a downstage conversation between the three sisters. Here, in *The Seagull*, Stanislavsky stresses that Masha's sullen acknowledgement that she is married and unhappy provokes an awkward pause 'during which the conversation of the group up-stage can be heard (it is here that I would make them burst out laughing suddenly at some of Dorn's witticisms)' (Stanislavsky cited in Balukhaty 1952: 265). So, was it in fact Stanislavsky who first gave to Chekhov the idea of counterpointing stage dialogue, a technique that seemed so revolutionary and unexpected in *Three Sisters*?

REAL OR RIDICULOUS? PLAYING WITH CIRCLES OF ATTENTION

Stanislavsky is certainly not afraid of adding to the text on occasion. One of these moments occurs in this act when Masha sees off Medvedenko, 'giving him instructions concerning their child' (Stanislavsky cited in Balukhaty 1952: 267). Similarly, when the lotto game begins, Stanislavsky suggests that Masha call out numbers in addition to those specified by Chekhov in the script. Far from being maverick with the text, both of these suggestions enhance the realism of everyday life that Stanislavsky was keen to perpetuate. Once or twice, however, his embellishments seem a little overzealous. Chekhov writes that Konstantin starts to play a melancholy waltz off-stage, after which Arkadina steals attention by showing the company the brooch that she was recently given. Stanislavsky extends this instance to almost ridiculous ends:

> A pause. Shamrayev takes brooch and examines it in the light of the candle. The game halts for a little while. Shamrayev turns the brooch round and round before the light of the candle, while the rest look on.... *The Pause* [underlined in ink]: wind, rain, rattling of windows, from the distance the sound of the piano (played by Konstantin). The pause lasts ten seconds.
>
> *(ibid.: 269)*

Despite the excess of this stage direction, Stanislavsky is clearly trying to establish the musicality and atmosphere by means of as many different layers and textures as possible. He goes on to specify that Masha calls out the lotto numbers in a 'mournful monotonous voice' (reflecting the tone of Konstantin's piano playing), while Arkadina chats in a 'very cheerful voice' (contradicting the tone of her son's music). From time to time, Shamrayev drops his bass '*à la Silva*' impression in to make her laugh. Into this soundscape of voices and music, Stanislavsky adds Dorn's habitual humming and Sorin's timely snoring! The multiplicity of emotional reactions is heightened, not only by the words that the characters speak, but the manner in which they speak them and the accompanying noises that they make.

What Stanislavsky is doing here is creating four very distinct circles of attention. The first is within the characters' own heads, be it Masha's monotony or Dorn's humming. The second is within the room, mainly through the gregarious outbursts of Arkadina and Shamrayev during the lotto game. The third circle encompasses the rest of the house as we hear Konstantin's melancholy waltz. Every so often, Stanislavsky reminds us of the outside world: for example, '*A very long pause*' as the characters exit out to dinner is followed by 'wind and rain' and interspersed with 'Animated conversation in the dining room' (ibid.: 273). The constant dynamic tension between outer world (in which Nina lives) and inner world (in which Trigorin temporarily resides) is tightened, with Konstantin psychologically trapped in a nebulous hinterland between the two.

NINA AND KONSTANTIN'S FINAL ENCOUNTER

The aural textures develop when Nina arrives and, falling upon Konstantin's chest, begins to sob. We then hear 'The sound of a church-bell in the distance; in the dining room Madame Arkadina's and Shamrayev's laughter' (Stanislavsky cited in Balukhaty 1952: 275). In Act 1, Stanislavsky set up the connection between the church bell and Nina's character: now the solitude of the church bell tolling versus the sound of the dinner guests laughing serves as a painful commentary on Nina's current situation. Curiously, Stanislavsky himself is rather coy about this device. When the laughter is heard a second time in the dining room – just at the point when Nina bursts into sobs on her line, 'And Lord help all homeless wanderers' (Chekhov 1990: 62) – he adds: 'This is a very clumsy stage effect, but it never misses with an audience. I do not, of course, insist on it' (Stanislavsky cited in Balukhaty 1952: 277). He is aware that he may be ladling on the sentiment in a potentially 'melodramatic' manner; and yet, there's a cruelty in the device which undercuts the sentiment. And – like any good producer – he doesn't want to miss a trick with the audience if it will achieve a succulent theatrical experience.

As the play draws towards its emotional climax, Stanislavsky is acutely aware of the journey on which he wants to take the audience. Whereas Chekhov writes in a pause after Kostya asks Nina why she must leave, Stanislavsky insists: 'No pause here under any circumstances' (ibid.: 279). He senses where the impetus of the scene is vital, and a pause here would only break the characters' emotional intensity. Two lines later, however, when Nina asks for a glass of water, he allows enough silence for the sound of the glass knocking against the jug to be heard, followed by a snatch of the conservation in the dining room. In other words, the tiny detail of the intimacy between Nina and Konstantin is juxtaposed with the bigger social gathering, which includes – of course – the dangerous Trigorin.

The directions provided for the last few moments of Kostya and Nina's *affaire* pile image upon image, with the howling wind and the beating rain increasing in volume as Nina recalls some of Konstantin's play. Bells toll, windows break, doors close and footsteps disappear to the sound of laughter and the knocking of the nightwatchman. The sequence concludes when 'Konstantin stands without moving, then he lets fall the glass from his hand', accompanied in the production plan by Stanislavsky's own self-deprecating comment that 'this, too, is rather a cheap stage effect!' (ibid.: 283). It's almost as if Stanislavsky can't help himself: he wants to create the maximum dramatic and emotional scene, while teetering on a knife-edge between realism and melodrama.

DRAWING TO A CLOSE

Chekhov knew that he was breaking all the accepted theatrical conventions with the ending of *The Seagull* and, in turn, Stanislavsky endeavoured to create a dramatic climax for a deliberately anticlimactic play. The plot is: Konstantin destroys all his manuscripts (attended to in great detail by Stanislavsky, and expressed very simply by Chekhov as '*Over the next two minutes he silently tears up all his manuscripts and throws them under the desk*' (Chekhov 1990: 65)). Then the 'mob' returns. Stanislavsky creates a vast whirlwind of lively activity, with laughter and lotto, followed by a gunshot and a pause of five seconds. From the dance of action, the characters freeze in a *tableau vivant*, 'afraid to breathe' (Stanislavsky cited in Balukhaty 1952: 285), as they await the return of Dorn, who goes to discover the cause of the gunshot. Stanislavsky guides both the actors and the audience into one extreme close-up on Dorn's face: the doctor begins disconcertedly, then he 'changes the expression of his face before the eyes of the audience' (ibid.). He deflects attention from himself with his usual humming, and then 'When nobody can see him, his face again expresses concern and shock' (ibid.). Stanislavsky provides the actor with very technical facial details, which must then be justified and filled with the appropriate inner content. By these means, he keeps the spectators' attention finely focused on the doctor's face.

Right up to the final moment, Stanislavsky is keen 'to keep the audience in suspense' (ibid.: 287). The very last stage direction in the production plan continues the musical texturing of vocal timbres (Masha's monotonous voice calls out the lotto numbers against Arkadina's soft, gay humming). At the same time, he takes the audience right to the brink of resolution, but then denies them: 'Trigorin, shaken and pale, walks over to the back of Madame Arkadina's chair where, however, he stops dead, for he cannot summon enough courage to break the terrible news to her' (ibid.). Unable to let the final line of Chekhov's text stand alone – '[Konstantin] has shot himself' (Chekhov 1990: 167) – Stanislavsky adds these details of Trigorin's failed attempt to tell Arkadina. And yet he still manages to leave us hung in a moment of indecision, honouring Chekhov's desire that the audience be denied its usual theatrical expectations.

A hive of scribbled sketches fills the final page of Stanislavsky's plan, reflecting the highly choreographed sense of the entire production score. The detail of sound, lighting, spatial relationships, physical activities, psychological gestures, intonations and pauses clearly marks *The Seagull* out as a milestone in the development of Stanislavsky's ideas. It also prefigures many of the components of his 'system'. Characters play definite actions on each other as they strive towards their own significant objectives. Naturalism, realism and symbolism brush with tragedy, comedy, melodrama and absurdism in a truly inspirational production plan.

Further reading

Allen, D. (1999) *Stanislavski for Beginners*, London: Writers & Readers.
Balukhaty, S. D. (ed.) (1952) *The Seagull Produced by Stanislavsky*, trans. D. Magarshack, London: Dobson.
Benedetti, J. (1990) *Stanislavski: A Biography*, London: Methuen.
Benedetti, J. (1991) *The Moscow Art Theatre Letters*, London: Methuen.
Benedetti, J. (1994) *Stanislavski: An Introduction*, London: Methuen.
Benedetti, J. (1999) *Stanislavski: His Life and Art*, London: Methuen.
Berne, E. (1964) *Games People Play: The Psychology of Human Relationships*, London: Penguin.
Boleslavsky, R. (1933) *Acting: The First Six Lessons*, New York: Theater Arts Books.
Carnicke, S. M. (2009) *Stanislavsky in Focus: 2nd Edition: An Acting Master for the Twenty-First Century*, Abingdon: Routledge.
Chekhov, A. (1990) *The Seagull*, trans. M. Frayn, London: Methuen.
Cole, T. (ed.) (1983) *Acting: A Handbook of the Stanislavski Method*, New York: Crown.
Cousin, G. (1982) 'Stanislavsky and Brecht: The Relationship between the Actor and Stage Objects', unpublished thesis, Exeter: University of Exeter.

Damasio, A. (1994) *Descartes' Error: Emotions, Reason and the Human Brain*, New York: Penguin.
Donnellan, D. (2005) *The Actor and the Target*, London: Nick Hern Books.
Edwards, C. (1966) *The Stanislavski Heritage: Its Contribution to the Russian and American Theatre*, London: Peter Owen.
Evans, M. (ed.) (2015) *The Actor Training Reader*, Abingdon: Routledge.
Gauss, R. B. (1999) *Lear's Daughters: The Studios of the Moscow Art Theatre 1905–1927*, New York: Peter Lang.
Gillett, J. (2014) *Acting Stanislavski: A Practical Guide to Stanislavski's Approach and Legacy*, London: Bloomsbury.
Gorchakov, N. M. (1985) *Stanislavsky Directs*, trans. M. Goldina, New York: Limelight Editions.
Gordon, M. (1987) *The Stanislavski Technique: Russia: A Workbook for Actors*, New York: Applause.
Gordon, M. (2010) *Stanislavsky in America: An Actor's Workbook*, Abingdon: Routledge.
Gutekunst, C. & Gillett, J. (2014) *Voice into Acting: Integrating Voice and the Stanislavski Approach*, London: Bloomsbury.
Hodge, A. (ed.) (2010) *Actor Training*, Second Edition, Abingdon: Routledge.
Hulton, D. & Kapsali, M. (2016) *Yoga and Actor Training*, Abingdon: Routledge.
Ignatieva, M. (2008) *Stanislavsky and Female Actors: Women in Stanislavsky's Life and Art*, Maryland: University Press of America.
Knebel, M. (1981) 'On Analysis through Action of a Play and a Role', trans. A. Law, unpublished paper.
Leach, R. (2003) *Stanislavsky and Meyerhold*, Bern: Peter Lang AG.
Leach, R. & Borovsky, V. (eds.) (1999) *A History of Russian Theatre*, Cambridge: Cambridge University Press.
Leiter, S. (1991) *From Stanislavsky to Barrault: Representative Directors of the European Stage*, New York: Greenwood Press.
Levin, I. & Levin, I. (2002) *The Stanislavsky Secret: Not a System, Not a Method But a Way of Thinking*, Colorado Springs: Meriwether.
Lewis, R. (1986) *Method or Madness?*, London: Methuen.
Magarshack, D. (1950) *Stanislavsky: A Life*, London: Faber & Faber.
Malaev-Babel, A. & Laskina, M. (eds.) (2016) *Nikolai Demidov: Becoming an Actor-Creator*, trans. A. Malaev-Babel, A. Rojavin & S. Lillibridge, Abingdon: Routledge.
Melchinger, S. (1972) *Anton Chekhov*, New York: Ungar.
Merlin, B. (2001) *Beyond Stanislavsky: The Psycho-Physical Approach to Actor Training*, London: Nick Hern Books.
Merlin, B. (2008) '*An Actor's Work* Is Finally Done: A Response to the New Jean Benedetti Translation of Stanislavski's *An Actor's Work*', cw.routledge.com/textbooks/Stanislavski/downloads/bella-article.pdf.
Merlin, B. (2012) 'Where's the Spirit Gone? The Complexities of Translation and the Nuances of Terminology in *An Actor's Work* and an Actor's Work', in *Stanislavski Studies*, Iss. 1, February, London, stanislavski.studies.org/wp-content/uploads/Bella_Merlin_Stanislavski_Studies_1.pdf.
Merlin, B. (2014) *The Complete Stanislavsky Toolkit*, Revised Edition, London: Nick Hern Books.
Merlin, B. (2016) *Facing the Fear: An Actor's Guide to Overcoming Stage Fright*, London: Nick Hern Books.
Mitter, S. (1993) *Systems of Rehearsal: Stanislavsky, Brecht, Grotowski and Brook*, London: Routledge.
Moore, S. (ed.) (1973) *Stanislavski Today: Commentaries on K. S. Stanislavski*, New York: American Center for Stanislavski Theater Art.
Moore, S. (1979) *Stanislavski Revealed: The Actor's Guide to Spontaneity on Stage*, New York: Applause.
Moore, S. (1984) *The Stanislavski System: The Professional Training of an Actor*, New York: Penguin.
Nemirovich-Danchenko, V. (1937) *My Life in the Russian Theatre*, trans. J. Cournos, Boston: Little, Brown & Co.
Pitches, J. (2006) *Science and the Stanislavsky Tradition of Acting*, Abingdon: Routledge.
Pitches, J. (ed.) (2012) *Russians in Britain: British Theatre and the Russian Tradition of Actor Training*, Abingdon: Routledge.
Redgrave, M. (1958) *Mask or Face: Reflections in an Actor's Mirror*, London: Heinemann.
Richards, T. (1995) *At Work with Grotowski on Physical Actions*, London: Routledge.
Schuler, C. (1996) *Women in the Russian Theatre*, London: Routledge.
Senelick, L. (trans. & ed.) (2014) *Stanislavsky: A Life in Letters*, Abingdon: Routledge.
Stafford-Clark, M. (1990) *Letters to George*, London: Nick Hern Books.
Stanislavsky, K. (1938) *Chayka: V Postanovke, Regissers Kaya Partitura Stanislavskovo*, Leningrad: Isskustvo.
Stanislavsky, K. (1948) *Stanislavsky Produces Othello*, trans. Dr H. Nowak, London: Geoffrey Bles.
Stanislavsky, K. (1958) *Stanislavsky's Legacy: Comments on Some Aspects of an Actor's Art and Life*, trans. E. R. Hapgood, London: Max Reinhardt.
Stanislavsky, K. (1973) *On the Art of the Stage*, trans. D. Magarshack, London: Faber & Faber.
Stanislavsky, K. (1980) *An Actor Prepares*, trans. E. R. Hapgood, London: Methuen (first published in Britain 1937).

Stanislavsky, K. (1982) *My Life in Art*, trans. J. J. Robbins, London: Methuen (first published 1924).
Stanislavsky, K. (1984) *Selected Works*, trans. V. Yankilevsky, Moscow: Raduga.
Stanislavsky, K. (1990) *An Actor's Handbook*, trans. E. R. Hapgood, London: Methuen.
Stanislavsky, K. (2000a) *Building a Character*, trans. E. R. Hapgood, London: Methuen.
Stanislavsky, K. (2000b) *Creating a Role*, trans. E. R. Hapgood, London: Methuen.
Stanislavsky, K. (2008a) *An Actor's Work*, trans. J. Benedetti, Abingdon: Routledge.
Stanislavsky, K. (2008b) *My Life in Art*, trans. J. Benedetti, Abingdon: Routledge (first published 1924).
Stanislavsky, K. (2009) *An Actor's Work on a Role*, trans. J. Benedetti, Abingdon: Routledge.
Stanislavsky, K. & Rumyantsev, P. (1998) *Stanislavski on Opera*, trans. E. R. Hapgood, New York: Routledge.
Styan, J. L. (1984) *Realism and Naturalism: Modern Drama in Theory and Practice Volume 1*, Cambridge: Cambridge University Press.
Tcherkasski, S. (2016) *Stanislavsky and Yoga*, trans. V. Farber, Abingdon: Routledge & Wroclaw: Icarus Publishing.
Thomas, J. (2016) *A Director's Guide to Stanislavsky's Active Analysis, Including the Formative Essay on Active Analysis by Maria Knebel*, London: Bloomsbury.
Toporkov, V. O. (1998) *Stanislavski in Rehearsal: The Final Years*, London: Routledge.
White, R. A. (ed.) (2014) *The Routledge Companion to Stanislavsky*, Abingdon: Routledge.
Whyman, R. (2008) *The Stanislavsky System of Acting: Legacy and Influence in Modern Performance*, Cambridge: Cambridge University Press.
Whyman, R. (2013) *Stanislavski: The Basics*, Abingdon: Routledge.
Worrall, N. (1996) *The Moscow Art Theatre*, London: Routledge.
Zarrilli, P. B. (2009) *Psychophysical Acting: An Intercultural Approach after Stanislavski*, Abingdon: Routledge.

2
MEYERHOLD (1874–1940)

Jonathan Pitches

2.1 A life of contradictions

Meyerhold's life was abruptly brought to an end in the basement of a prison in Moscow over sixty years ago. He was an old man, nearing his seventies, and had dedicated over two-thirds of his life to the Russian theatre, much it to the cause of Communism after the Russian Revolution in 1917. After a life-long career of innovation and experiment his presence as a theatrical figurehead was deemed too dangerous by the Soviet authorities. He was tortured, 'persuaded' to confess to charges of spying and finally shot, a little less than a week after his sixty-sixth birthday.

It was the last of many contradictions in Meyerhold's life. From his theatrical theories to his relationships with others, Meyerhold courted controversy, even to the extent of promoting dissent among his audiences:

> If everyone praises your production, almost certainly it is rubbish. If everyone abuses it, then perhaps there is something in it. But if some praise and others abuse, if you can split the audience in half, then for sure it is a good production.
>
> *(Gladkov 1997: 165)*

His was a theatre based expressly *on* contradiction, a theatre which strove not to smooth out problems or to resolve paradoxes but to let them resonate within the minds of his performers and his audiences. A divided audience, Meyerhold argued, was more likely to engage at a deeper level with the content of the production, to turn in on itself, discuss and debate. We have all travelled back from the theatre with friends and talked about the spectacle we have just enjoyed. But how much more lively is the discussion if, for some reason, we don't agree on everything we have seen? This was Meyerhold's logic and it informed much of his practice.

There were contradictions in Meyerhold's life as well. Often labelled an opponent of Stanislavsky's, he ended his career holding the reins of his teacher's last directorial project, described by the dying Stanislavsky as his 'sole heir in the theatre' (Benedetti 1990: 345). Although he was reputed to be a dictator and a control freak, Meyerhold's workshop nevertheless produced a startling range of theatrical freethinkers, each one capable of enriching the

Russian tradition in their own right. Notorious for being difficult to work with, his record of collaboration with musicians, artists, playwrights and co-directors belies this image, and instead defines a man with an irrepressible desire to move with the times and to learn from the people who defined those times.

Meyerhold undoubtedly manufactured some of this controversy, but the one contradiction over which he had no control was his relationship with the political powers of Soviet Russia. He was overtly supportive of the new powers from the earliest opportunity and much of his work in the early 1920s was geared to furthering the cause of the new Soviet regime. It is difficult to believe, then, that those who embraced Meyerhold's vitality in the early years of the Revolution were also responsible for extinguishing it. But this was precisely what happened. It may have taken over twenty years for the turnaround to be completed but its conclusion was undeniably decisive. What is more, Meyerhold's fate was anything but unique. He was joining a long roll-call of artists whose love of experimentation finally became an unendurable threat to the leader of the Soviet Union, Joseph Stalin.

But why begin here, at the end of Meyerhold's story, rather than at the beginning? First, because Meyerhold's death offers us a measure of how seriously the authorities in the Soviet Union (and before the Revolution, under the Tsar) viewed the art of the theatre. British politicians no longer see the theatre as posing a threat to their authority, and the fact that people might be killed in order to silence its voice is almost incomprehensible to us today. But in the post-revolutionary climate of the new Soviet Union, live theatre was viewed as one of the most effective tools of communication – not least because most of its audiences were unable to read. To be in control of this weapon of communication gave the director great power, but it was power that came at a cost and for many Soviet artists the weapon proved double-edged.

Second, by reversing the chronology of his story, we are recognising that any version of Meyerhold's life is somehow uncontrollably coloured by his death. The bitter irony of his demise hangs over his work, constantly reminding us of the volatile context within which he was practising his art. In a way, this foreknowledge captures the kind of attitude Meyerhold himself wanted to inculcate in his audiences. He, like Bertolt Brecht, did not want his spectators to focus their 'eyes on the finish' (Brecht 1978: 37), but instead to engage in the material of the production in a consciously enquiring manner. For this reason, Meyerhold delighted in revealing the mechanics of the theatre. He filled his productions with self-conscious theatricalities, arranging the order of the scenes in such a way that they might collide against one another rather than seamlessly fuse together. We might conclude from this that, in Meyerhold's thinking, people's lives are similarly unpredictable. They do not unfold in a smooth, organised way (as the naturalistic repertoire often suggested), but are multifaceted, problematic and surprising. In Meyerhold's own case this could not have been more true.

So, with our eyes diverted from the finish and focused now on the course, let us examine the episodes of Meyerhold's life, from his early years before he met Stanislavsky to the final period of his career before his arrest by the NKVD (the no-less-brutal predecessors of the KGB). We will cover the following ground:

- Apprenticeship (1874–1905)
- St Petersburg (1906–17)
- Meyerhold and the Revolution (1917–22)
- The Meyerhold Theatre (1922–31)
- The death of Meyerhold and his theatre (1932–40)
- Meyerhold today.

Meyerhold (1874–1940)

Apprenticeship (1874–1905)

Life before the Moscow Art Theatre

As the eighth child of the family, Vsevolod Meyerhold had to work hard to make an impression. He was born into the affluent family of the German vodka distiller, Emil Meyerhold, on 28 January 1874, and, recognising that he would never inherit the family business, he developed a much closer relationship with his mother, Alvina, than with his businessman father. At such a distance from the head of the family, the young Meyerhold did not find himself obliged to espouse all of his father's values. Instead, he mixed with the workers from the distillery and attended music concerts and the theatre. The artistic influence was so great that at the age of nineteen he was already able to define his career path, claiming an even earlier calling in his diary:

> I have talent, I know that I am a good actor.... This is my most cherished dream, one I have thought about almost since I was five.
>
> *(Gladkov 1997: 4)*

But the decision to enter the theatre wasn't as clear cut as it might have seemed. Two alternative careers presented themselves to Meyerhold – one as a lawyer, the other as a violinist. In fact, it was the former occupation which first beckoned him and which provided his escape route from the provincial town of Penza to the bustling city of Moscow. Meyerhold began reading for a degree in law at Moscow University in 1895, after graduating with some effort from his school in Penza. Once in Moscow he faced what he called 'a crossroads' in his life (Gladkov 1997: 91), torn by the equally appealing possibilities of a theatre training or a career as a second violinist in the University orchestra. Failing the orchestra's audition made the decision not to play 'second fiddle' unnecessary and instead, in 1896, he went into two years of actor training with the playwright and director Vladimir Nemirovich-Danchenko at the Moscow Philharmonic school. Music continued to play a significant part in Meyerhold's career, however, and although he gave up the violin and later looked back at his failure with some relief, he never turned his back on the discipline of music itself. Indeed, the *musicality* of many of his productions is a notable characteristic of his directorial approach.

Vladimir Nemirovich-Danchenko and Konstantin Stanislavsky

Nemirovich-Danchenko is best known for his stormy relationship with the director Konstantin Stanislavsky and for co-founding the Moscow Art Theatre (MAT) with him, arguably the most famous theatre in all of Russia. But before he began this collaboration with Stanislavsky in 1898, Nemirovich had already established a well-earned reputation as a creative artist and, if anything, it was he who was the most experienced theatre professional in the early days of the MAT. For his part, Stanislavsky had begun cutting his teeth as an actor and a director ten years earlier at the semi-professional dramatic society known as the Alexeiev Circle. There, he developed an impressive range of character roles, many of which were revived under the auspices of the MAT.

Nemirovich was not an actor. Essentially he was a literary man with an intuitive eye for great writing. It was he, for example, who first recognised the dramatic talent of Anton Chekhov, calling for *The Seagull* (1896) to be awarded the Griboedov literary prize in place of his own play: *The Worth of Life* (1896). But although his talents lay first and foremost with the dramatic text, he also had experience as a director and, judging by the range of activities he lists in his autobiography, was clearly interested in teaching too. Meyerhold's tuition, he tells us, 'went far beyond the bounds of first experiments in stage technique'. It also involved:

> Psychological movements, everyday features, moral questions, emotional mergings with the author, aspirations towards frankness and simplicity, the quest of vivid expression and diction, mimicry, plastics, self-assurance.
>
> (Nemirovich-Danchenko 1968: 46)

It may not immediately be clear what he means by 'everyday features', but Nemirovich's commitment to *simplicity* on stage and his call for a vivid *expressivity* in the performer are characteristics clearly reflected in the later practice of Meyerhold. Even more important, perhaps, is the implicit relationship indicated here between the inner and outer work of the performer – *psychological movements* as Nemirovich calls them – for this all-important relationship, often referred to as *psycho-physicality*, is a dominant theme in the Russian tradition of acting and we will encounter it in many guises in this book.

Meyerhold, Stanislavsky and The Seagull

Meyerhold graduated from the Moscow Philharmonic in March 1898, sharing the top prize for acting with Olga Knipper – Chekhov's future wife and soon-to-be star of the MAT. Nemirovich had already seen the potential of the young artist, describing him in his memoirs as having 'excellent directing quality and not a little technical skill' (Nemirovich-Danchenko 1968: 123).

Both graduates joined the newly founded Art Theatre that year, as the talent drawn from both Stanislavsky's Circle and Nemirovich's school was merged to form the revolutionary new theatre. But although he had begun as an advocate of Meyerhold's, Nemirovich's support of him did not last and he offered no resistance when the company was reorganised in 1902, leaving the young actor without a job.

In the intervening four years (1898–1902), Meyerhold played an impressive range of parts (eighteen roles, from blind prophets to princes), developed a passion for Chekhov's writing and, most significantly, observed a highly innovative and self-critical actor-director at work. Of all Meyerhold's creative relationships, his time with Stanislavsky was the most influential, not because Meyerhold followed in his teacher's footsteps – he didn't – but because the two men shared a fundamental belief in the complete training of an actor and in the need to experiment continually. Stanislavsky's famous System did not begin to be formulated until 1906, after Meyerhold had left the MAT, but his first experiments in realising a text with the emphasis on psychological truth were already being made as early as 1898 – with the revival of Chekhov's text, *The Seagull*.

After taking the role of Vassily Shouisky in the inaugural production of the Art Theatre, *Tsar Fyodor Ivanovitch* in October 1898, Meyerhold was given the pivotal role of Konstantin Treplev in Stanislavsky's production of *The Seagull*. Kostia (Treplev's diminutive name) is a young experimental playwright, still living in the shadow of his successful actress mother, Arkadina, and fighting to assert his independence as a writer. He is deeply in love with Nina, another aspiring young artist, and casts her in his own highly stylised and symbolic play-within-a-play. Sitting in the audience at Treplev's play is the already established writer, Trigorin, Arkadina's lover. Trigorin, though, soon develops an amorous interest in Nina, becoming Kostia's rival in both professional and personal terms. Thus, the fortunes of the young moderniser, Kostia, are contrasted with the older Trigorin (representing a kind of established orthodoxy), with Nina as focal point.

Meyerhold (1874–1940)

This typically Chekhovian love triangle was given a further twist by the casting of Stanislavsky as Trigorin. Critics have been quick to point out the uncanny similarities between the power dynamic at work in the MAT and that reflected in Chekhov's play, especially when you imagine these words being spoken by the young innovator, Meyerhold/Treplev:

> What we need are new artistic forms. And if we don't get new forms it would be better if we had nothing at all.
>
> *(Chekhov 1991: 63)*

It wasn't long before Meyerhold himself was saying as much, criticising the Naturalism of the MAT and forging the same theatrical path as Treplev: towards Symbolism and a theatre of stasis. As Nina remarks of Treplev's play: 'It doesn't have much action, your play – it's just a kind of recitation' (Chekhov 1991: 66).

A baptism of fire: The Fellowship of the New Drama

Between being sacked by the MAT Board in 1902 and his return to Moscow in 1905, Meyerhold was busy. He seems to have put contingency plans in place for his inevitable ousting from the MAT, booking a theatre south of Moscow in the Ukraine for the next season, 1902–3. Here, in Kherson, Meyerhold joined up with another forced exile – Aleksandr Kosheverov – and, with a troupe of disaffected actors from the MAT, founded what was eventually called The Fellowship of the New Drama. Meyerhold's industry during this season and the next (1903–4) is captured explicitly in the appendix of Meyerhold premières in Robert Leach's book, *Vsevolod Meyerhold* (1989: 194–196): three pages of productions, 140 in all, with Meyerhold taking forty-four roles himself, as well as finding time to translate Georg Hauptmann's text, *Before Sunrise,* from the original German.

What greater baptism of fire can one imagine? Before The Fellowship, Meyerhold had had precious little directing experience. Relatively speaking, he had lots of time to work on his roles and to reflect on the nature of his task as an actor at the MAT. With his days in Kherson often involving the launch of two new productions in a single day, Meyerhold had little time to innovate – or to engage in the pre-rehearsal discussions he argued had been lacking in Stanislavsky's approach. But he did necessarily grapple with the practical difficulties of staging Russian classics (Gogol, Ostrovsky), European Naturalism (Ibsen, Hauptmann, Zola), his beloved Chekhov *(The Seagull, The Wedding, The Cherry Orchard)* and Shakespeare *(A Midsummer Night's Dream, The Merchant of Venice)*. He also began his relationship with Maeterlinck, unconsciously laying the foundations for a return to Moscow in decidedly different circumstances from those in which he left.

By 1905 the MAT was seven years old and its founders, Nemirovich and Stanislavsky, were recognising the need to introduce new blood and to reflect more clearly the contemporary movements in Western drama. Stanislavsky's own words, penned in his autobiography, *My Life in Art* (1924), are interestingly more redolent of Treplev's than Trigorin's:

> Like me, [Meyerhold] sought for something new in art, for something more contemporary and modern in spirit. The difference between us lay in the fact that I only strained toward the new, without knowing any of the ways for reaching and realizing it, while Meierhold thought that he had already found new ways and methods which he could not realize partly because of material conditions, and partly due to the weak personnel of the troupe . . . I decided to help Meierhold in his new labors, which as it seemed to me then, agreed with many of my dreams at the time.
>
> *(Stanislavsky 1980: 429–430)*

Stanislavsky's assessment, written some nineteen years after the events he is describing, was accurate on a number of counts: Meyerhold *did* represent a modernist challenge to the orthodox repertoire of the MAT and he was, in all aspects of his life, responsive to the 'contemporary . . . spirit' or Zeitgeist. It was for this reason that he later embraced the scientific theories of the reflexologist, Pavlov, and why he brought in the constructivist artists Popova and Stepanova to work with him just after the Revolution.

The Theatre Studio and The Death of Tintagiles

Meyerhold's love of innovation may also explain why he accepted Stanislavsky's invitation to return to his Alma Mater as co-director of the Theatre Studio. For this project, entirely funded by Stanislavsky's own money and therefore independent of the main theatre, offered Meyerhold an opportunity to develop an alternative directorial approach – what he called *stylisation*. He had recognised the challenges posed by symbolist texts during his time with the Fellowship and had offered a sensitive reading of Chekhov's symbolic last play *The Cherry Orchard*. But with three productions a week to put on in Kherson, he plainly did not have enough time to devote to any kind of training for his actors, least of all a training in the kind of stylised, highly gestural acting he was looking for in his vision of Maeterlinck's plays.

The Theatre Studio offered him that space. It was, in Stanislavsky's words, 'a *laboratory* for more or less mature actors' (1980: 430, my italics). As such, it embodied the principles of innovation, stylistic experimentation and secluded interrogation which Meyerhold sought to reproduce in many different contexts later in life.

In cultural terms, the move from Naturalism (the attempt to *recreate* life on stage in all its detail) to Symbolism (the attempt to *evoke* and *suggest* a life beyond the material world) was not entirely surprising. Over a decade earlier, the French theatre had fought the same battle – with André Antoine's tiny Théâtre Libre, the bastion of fourth-wall Naturalism, giving way to the symbolist stages of the Théâtre d'Art and Lugné Poe's Théâtre de l'Œuvre. In a sense, the Russian theatre was simply staging the same theatrical revolution as France had done ten years earlier.

But in acknowledging that they needed a counter-repertoire of non-naturalistic plays, Stanislavsky and Nemirovich were echoing a tension felt by the naturalists themselves. Many of the key movers in Naturalism – Ibsen, Strindberg, Hauptmann and (in a different way) Chekhov – all seem to have found the restrictions of Naturalism too great and, as a consequence, allowed their ideas to move into other fields of drama. Strindberg's *Miss Julie* may have had a preface hailing the birth of Naturalism, but his emphasis on the symbolism of the props (the beheaded greenfinch as a symbol of Julie's impending fate, for example) and the atmospheric lighting in the play already signed a progression away from the material conditions of the kitchen sink towards a more implicit realm of communication.

It was this implicit realm, a suggestive, obscure and imaginative world, which Meyerhold tried to create in his Theatre Studio and, specifically, in his production of Maeterlinck's *The Death of Tintagiles*. Here, Meyerhold looked back to his own fascination with music and with theatrical simplicity to define an approach which exploited both characteristics. Movement was kept to a minimum, with Meyerhold defining what gestures the actors could make in a prescriptive 'score' or prompt copy. All the energy of the actor was concentrated into the eyes and lips, creating what Meyerhold called an 'exterior calm which covers volcanic emotions' (Braun 2016: 63). Maeterlinck's words were not spoken naturalistically but 'coldly coined . . . free from the familiar break in the voice' (ibid.) and the effect must have been rather like a sleepwalker concealing a terrible story. All of this was performed in front of a single backdrop – at first just plain – and underscored by a musical accompaniment which was designed to complement exactly the stylised action.

Resisting the usual three-dimensional models, the designers for this production (Nikolai Sapunov and Sergei Sudeikin) painted impressionistic pictures to capture the atmosphere of the plays. The intention was to keep the stage as dark as possible, so as to let the audience complete the story in their own minds and thus, as Meyerhold put it, be transformed into a 'vigilant observer' (Braun 2016: 65). The essence of Meyerhold's symbolist approach is therefore made clear: to enhance the imaginative input of the spectator by *making strange* the actor's body and voice and placing them in a darkened, non-specific theatrical environment. *Plasticity* (the movements of the actor) works alongside *musicality* (in the voices of the actors and in the composer's score) to create a sometimes harmonious, sometimes dissonant theatrical effect.

For Stanislavsky, viewing the dress rehearsal of *The Death of Tintagiles* in October 1905, this strangeness added nothing to its credibility. He had seen an earlier rehearsal in a small workshop space during the summer of that year and had been impressed. But now in the larger proposed home of the Theatre Studio, with no fewer than 700 seats (Braun 1995: 41), the intended suggestive style was lost. This was exacerbated by Stanislavsky's insistence that the lights should be turned up, killing the symbolist aura of other-worldliness and revealing the holes in Meyerhold's production.

By the end of that year Meyerhold had left the MAT for a second time and was bound for St Petersburg. But he did not leave Moscow empty-handed; he had experienced a model of discipline, of innovation and of expressive acting in his time with Stanislavsky which was to have a lasting impression on his work, a debt he was happy to acknowledge:

> You who knew Stanislavsky only in his old age can't possibly imagine what a powerful actor he was. If I have become somebody, it is only because of the years I spent alongside him. Mark this well.
>
> *(Gladkov 1997: 149)*

In St Petersburg, Meyerhold rekindled his interest in Maeterlinck and by the next year was directing one of the most celebrated names of the Russian theatre, Vera Komissarzhevskaya, at her own Dramatichesky Theatre in another of his plays, *Sister Beatrice*. Thus began an extended period (from 1906 to 1917) living and working in what was then the capital of Russia.

St Petersburg (1906–17)

Vera Komissarzhevskaya

From a distance it is hard to see why Meyerhold and Komissarzhevskaya (1864–1910) formed a working relationship: he, a relatively inexperienced graduate of an art theatre, dedicated to the pursuit of new forms and she, a widely known actress of the State theatre, famed for her naturalistic roles playing Ibsen's Nora and Nina in the first ever production of Chekhov's play in 1896.

The daughter of one of Stanislavsky's early collaborators, Fedor Komissarzhevsky, Vera Fedorovna Komissarzhevskaya began working in the theatre in 1892 and from 1896 to 1902 rose to stardom as the principal actress at the State-supported Imperial Theatre – the Aleksandrinsky – in St Petersburg. She was, in many ways, one of the first method actors. She had a reputation for accepting roles close to her own nature and for engaging emotionally with the character at a very deep level. 'My nature requires me to feel with my characters,' she argued: 'I don't know how to act any other way. I have to wash each role in the blood of my own heart' (Schuler 1996: 166). Such emotionalism would not have recommended her to Meyerhold. His own acting style was reserved and he harboured a deep-seated distrust of unrestrained passions in performance. This was, in part, due to a disturbing experience in his early life in which he empathised so closely with the title role of a play called *The Madman* that he began to consider himself deranged: 'I lived every line,' his biographer, Nikolai Volkov, records him saying, 'I thought I was insane' (Hoover 1974: 5).

Much of Meyerhold's later work reflects the fear he had of this kind of hypnotic acting and his repudiation of Naturalism is often seen in the same light, as a rejection of psychologically driven drama. Why, then, did he collaborate with Komissarzhevskaya, an actress who excelled on both counts?

One answer is that they shared the same desire to refresh the repertoire of the Russian theatre. Another, more cynical suggestion, comes from Catherine Schuler:

> Meyerhold came to St. Petersburg not because he believed in Komissarzhevskaia's vision or mission but because a contract with the Dramaticheskii Theatre was a ticket out of the provinces.
>
> *(Schuler 1996: 174)*

Certainly, Meyerhold had learnt from his days in Kherson (and from a revived attempt to stage a modern repertoire in Tiflis, after the failure of the Theatre Studio) that producing the 'New Drama' in such provincial circumstances was never going to be easy. St Petersburg, he must have thought, offered him a far more discerning audience as well as a flourishing avant-garde movement.

But although the latter was true (Meyerhold did mix with range of artistic modernisers including many symbolists in St Petersburg), this did not save him from accusations of betrayal and of pretentiousness, specifically for his treatment of Ibsen in his première production. His new directorial approach was first seen with *Hedda Gabler,* a naturalistic text, written by Ibsen in 1890 and dealing with some of the Norwegian's favourite themes: inheritance, power, social influence. Meyerhold's production, though, was anything but naturalistic. With Komissarzhevskaya in the title role, Meyerhold wanted to challenge directly the style for which she was renowned and which had come to characterise his old hunting ground, the MAT:

> Is life really like this? Is this what Ibsen wrote? Life is not like this, and it is not what Ibsen wrote. *Hedda Gabler* on the stage of the dramatic theatre is *stylised*. Its aim is to reveal Ibsen's play to the spectator by employing new unfamiliar means of scenic presentation.
>
> *(Braun 2016: 81)*

These new means of expression included a timeless costume design which aimed to capture the *essence* of the character. Oversized furniture was used to break up the natural perspective for the audience and the stage space itself was distorted, flattened, to provide a playing area just twelve feet deep. Spectators were not simply peeping in on a room full of people living their lives, as the Naturalism of the play demands, but viewing a scene in which the space itself suggested the thematic concerns of the play – a 'cold majesty', as Meyerhold puts it (Braun 2016: 81).

Meyerhold's work on *Sister Beatrice* continued this stylised approach, although here the text lent itself more readily to such treatment. Once again, Komissarzhevskaya took the title role and once again the depth of the stage was limited. In this instance Meyerhold had his cast working on a platform just seven feet deep – no deeper than the average bathroom – although the width of the stage was far greater. The result was a kind of theatre sculpture – or bas-relief – in which Komissarzhevskaya and company were grouped into starkly expressive tableaux, reminiscent of religious paintings. Following the work he had done at the Studio on *The Death of Tintagiles*, the gestural language of the actors was carefully prescribed and choreographed so that together the ensemble created a predominantly pictorial impression. Meyerhold actually brought paintings into the rehearsal room as a stimulus, merging the different shapes to create a new but nevertheless highly orchestrated look to the production.

With all these anti-illusionary devices in place, Komissarzhevskaya's specifically empathetic style of acting had to adapt in some way, although, interestingly, she did not reject all of her previous techniques. She still personalised the role and still drew on her inner resources to lend an energetic charge to it. At the same time, her voice captured the stylised musicality Meyerhold had been looking for in his first Maeterlinck production at the Theatre Studio. Frantisek Deák has documented the production in some detail:

> Komissarzhevskaya used two different voices. The voice for the Virgin Mary was like 'pure sound of an unknown musical instrument', a depersonalized sound. The voice for Beatrice, even when keeping with the rhythm imposed by Meyerhold, had certain emotional undertones and personal quality ... It is quite possible that Komissarzhevskaya's identification with the part, which was against the Symbolist esthetic of a detached representation, was one of the reasons for the great success of the production.
>
> *(Deák 1982: 50)*

Unfortunately, *Sister Beatrice* was alone in being both critically and commercially acclaimed. Other productions failed, due either to the cast's unease with Meyerhold's experimentation or to the inappropriateness of the lead role for an ageing principal actress. Meyerhold's relationship with Komissarzhevskaya began to show its weaknesses and his time at her theatre was running out. But there was one more major event to grace the stage of the Dramatichesky Theatre, an event which fitted perfectly Meyerhold's ideal of a divided audience: his production of the symbolist farce, *The Fairground Booth* (1906).

Meyerhold, Blok and the Balagan

By the time Meyerhold produced his play in December 1906, Aleksandr Blok (1880–1921) had already made his name as a poet and was an established figure in St Petersburg literary circles. His early work was charged with a darkly romantic spirit and was often inspired by his relationships – actual or virtual – with women. As an adolescent he had fallen for a married woman twice his age and captured this youthful spark of love in his writing:

> I did not know, unhappy one, that embraces were so hot.... She, inflamed with the fire of passion, wanted to melt my heart.... She boiled with love's desire! But I held my mind captive with a cold thought, and only at moments, ardently, I believed and thirsted.
>
> *(Forsyth 1977: 20–21)*

Even in the flush of adolescent hormones one can detect a sense of detachment in this extract, an ability of Blok's to sit back from the experience and apply a 'cold thought' to the proceedings. Such critical detachment is evident in far greater measure in his first play, *The Fairground Booth*, or, in Russian, *Balaganchik*.

In addition to a booth at fairs, *Balagan* also has associated meanings – farce, clown, playacting, showman – all of which mark a distinct shift in tone from the sombre statuesque atmosphere of

Sister Beatrice. In fact, Blok's drama openly ridicules the portentous seriousness of the symbolist movement, revelling instead in the characteristics of the popular theatre: audience involvement, riotous action, unashamed theatricality.

In part, this shift in allegiance – for Blok was considered to be 'the greatest Symbolist' (Banham 1992: 103) – was stimulated by a growing sense of pessimism and a desire by Blok to satirise his own troublesome relationships in dramatic form. The narrative thread to the play thus bears a marked similarity to the complicated love triangle he himself was immersed in at the time. His wife, Lyubov Mendelyeva (Columbine in the play) had fallen in love with another famous symbolist writer, Andrei Bely (Harlequin), with Blok (Pierrot) the lamenting victim:

> PIERROT: Where are you faithless one? ...
> Beneath your window, plaintively,
> My guitar will twang as you whirl with friends.
> I'll rouge my face that glimmers moonily,
> Pencil eyebrows, stick a moustache on.
> My poor heart – can you hear it, Columbine
> Sobbing out its melancholy song?
> *(Green 1986: 48)*

Perhaps we should note here that, in real life, Blok was far from an innocent victim and engaged in the same infidelities as his wife. In his drama, though, the love triangle drives the simple plot, with Harlequin/Bely leading Columbine/Mendelyeva away to enjoy a wintry sleigh ride and Pierrot/Blok following dejectedly after.

It is here, at the moment in the play most steeped in romantic imagery – soft snow falling, sleigh bells chiming – that Blok's sense of detachment (his 'cold thought') surfaces, not to dampen the atmosphere but to inject a mischievous vein of humour:

> PIERROT: O in his toils he'd entangled her,
> With laughter and jingling bells.
> Then he drew her wrap about her
> And flat on her face she fell!
> *(Green 1986: 52)*

In fact, Columbine has turned into a cardboard cut-out and Pierrot and Harlequin spend the rest of the evening walking the streets together, gazing not into the eyes of their mutual love but nestling cheek to cheek with each other!

Blok never takes himself too seriously in this play. Nor does he allow his characters to get caught up in predictable theatrical situations. Instead, they exhibit a refreshing sense of self-irony and are capable of making huge emotional shifts: from jealous desperation to glee, from ardent passion to whimsical disinterest. For all these reasons Blok's *Fairground Booth* was a model of the kind of drama Meyerhold wanted to produce.

From the Symbolism of Maeterlinck Meyerhold had found a distinct *physical* approach to performance, an expressive mode of non-naturalistic acting which characterised much of his later work. But the symbolists were often accused of being removed from reality in their mystical pursuit of the immaterial, an accusation which Meyerhold could not bear. Blok satirises this characteristic in his play, opening the drama with a chorus of Mystics who exude all the signs of Symbolism to a deliberately laughable degree. At the same time Blok is drawing on a number of conventions associated with a much older tradition of theatre, a tradition to which Meyerhold became inextricably connected and which he wrote about at length later in his career: the popular theatre.

It will already be evident in the extracts from *The Fairground Booth* that the dramatis personae (Blok's list of characters) bears no resemblance either to Naturalism or to Symbolism. Blok is not trying to represent real people with real names. Nor is he attempting to revive the dark atmosphere of castles and knights. Instead, he is looking to the popular tradition of *commedia dell'arte* for his characters, a theatrical form which first grew up in Europe in the sixteenth and seventeenth centuries and which in part informs the English pantomime. Let us spend a minute detailing the key characteristics of this all-important form of theatre.

Commedia dell'arte

Commedia dell'arte was founded on stock characters including Harlequin (or Arlecchino), Pierrot and Columbine, Blok's three chosen types, as well as a host of others such as Pantalone and Il Dottore (the doctor). It was an improvised form, based loosely around scenarios and punctuated with moments of comic business or *lazzi*. Before it became drawn into the establishment (it was eventually scripted and lost its spark), *commedia* was performed in a wide range of public places, adapting to every space with its flexible, booth-like staging. It was predominantly concerned with matters of sex and status, pitting servants against masters in endless comic mishaps. Primarily an external form of theatre, the *commedia* actors were not burdened with creating psychologically coherent characters, but were free to improvise using a conventional physical language instantly recognisable to the audience. Most of the characters wore a half-mask, revealing the mouth and chin but concealing the more expressive part of the face. These masks were often distorted with large noses and prominent features, giving rise to an exaggerated sense of character. *Commedia* was 'popular' because it did not rely heavily on the written word. It was a visual form, brought *to* the people by a travelling troupe of professionals and pitched at a local level. As a mask-based performance it was played outwards, making a direct connection with its spectators and engaging them in a two-way relationship.

For Meyerhold, who himself played Pierrot in Blok's play, the spirit of *commedia* was significant in many ways. First, because it placed more emphasis on the *physical* craft of the actor. *Commedia* performance was a highly skilled job and called on many aspects of an actor's training, aspects which Meyerhold believed had been undervalued in the Russian theatre of the early 1900s: physical dexterity, precision, balance, heightened expressiveness. Second, it established a different relationship between the actor and the text, empowering the performer to grab the audience's attention through their own improvisatory skill. Third, the *commedia* characters were types – masks – and were not therefore bound by the psychological laws Stanislavsky was attempting to uncover in his System. People were not asked to *believe* in them in the same way as they were to believe in Treplev or Nora. Instead, the masks could be seen for what they were, fictional dramatic creations fulfilling a function within the overall piece. Finally, *commedia* captured the spirit of surprise which we have already seen Blok exploiting in *The Fairground Booth*. Rather than the slow build-up of tension – the incrementally structured rhythms of Naturalism – *commedia*, and by extension Meyerhold's theatre, could undergo sharp changes in atmosphere and collisions of ideas and of styles, all of which were designed to keep the audience alert and responsive.

Writing six years after the production of Blok's play, Meyerhold was drawn back to the *commedia* characters of *The Fairground Booth* to illustrate this particular characteristic (what we will later come to understand as the *grotesque*):

> Depth and extract, brevity and contrast! No sooner has the pale, lanky Pierrot crept across the stage, no sooner has the spectator sensed in his movements the eternal

tragedy of mutely suffering mankind, than the apparition is succeeded by the merry Harlequinade. The tragic gives way to the comic, harsh satire replaces the sentimental ballad.

(Braun 2016: 163)

Meyerhold's Fairground Booth

In Meyerhold's production of *Balaganchik* these surprising shifts of tone, already endemic to Blok's style, were intensified by his directorial choices. The chorus of Mystics, who in Blok's original disappear into their own costumes like burst effigies, in Meyerhold's production transform into cardboard statues, mirroring the demise of Columbine and setting up the absurd entrance of the Author perfectly:

> Ladies and Gentlemen! I apologize to you most humbly, but I must disclaim all responsibility! They are making a laughing stock of me! I wrote a perfectly realistic play.
>
> (Green 1986: 51)

Accentuating the already obvious theatricality of the piece, Meyerhold placed the whole of the action in a booth of its own:

> This booth has its own stage, curtain, prompter's box and proscenium opening. Instead of being masked by the conventional border, the flies, together with all the ropes and wires, are visible to the audience; when the entire set is hauled aloft in the booth, the audience in the actual theatre sees the whole process.
>
> (Braun 2016: 85)

The best way to gauge whether such starkly self-conscious theatricality (what we now call *meta-theatricality*) was effective is to examine the audience's reaction. Meyerhold intended his spectators to be anything but passive and, on the first night on 30 December 1906, they reacted in just the way he wanted. It was proof of what he called 'true theatricality':

> The auditorium was in uproar as though it were a real battle. Solid, respectable citizens were ready to come to blows; whistles and roars of anger alternated with piercing howls conveying a mixture of fervour, defiance, anger and despair: 'Blok – Sapunov [the designer] – Kuzmin [the composer] – M-e-y-e-r-h-o-l-d, B-r-a-v-o-o-o.'
>
> (Braun 1995: 65–66)

What better response could the director dedicated to splitting his audience's allegiances and to fomenting controversy have wished for? It was testament to Meyerhold's directorial vision and to the modernism of Blok's text that there was such an emphatic reaction to the production – a production which we can now say was one the most significant of all of Meyerhold's experiments.

Meyerhold remained in post as artistic director at Komissarzhevskaya's theatre for almost another year, but, after repeated differences of opinion with the rest of the management, parted company with the theatre in November 1907.

For Komissarzhevskaya, the collaboration had been little short of a disaster. She had received very few good notices and had placed the theatre's finances in a precarious position. For Meyerhold, the results of his time with Vera Fedorovna could be measured in very different terms. Via Blok, he had begun a lifelong association with *commedia* and with the popular theatre in general. He had concluded a brief but highly influential period of experimentation with symbolist theatre, devising an aesthetic of stylisation and of musicality which informed much of his later work. And, perhaps most significantly, he had started to dismantle the conventions of the theatre at their very base, producing a style of heightened theatricality and of shocking unpredictability which shaped both his training methods and his work as a director.

Servant of the state or underground subversive? The Imperial Theatres and the development of the studios

The years at Komissarzhevskaya's theatre had cast Meyerhold in the role of a radical reformer – a reputation which carried far and wide. The path, seemingly, was set out for him: to develop the laboratory work he had begun in Moscow with Stanislavsky and continued in St Petersburg and to consolidate his search for 'new forms' as a director. The best place to do such work must surely have been in the studios and intimate theatres in which he had begun this quest. But Meyerhold did not continue in this direction, at least not visibly. Instead, he took his chance in the theatres which seemed most in opposition to his project of reform – the Imperial Theatres. It was a typically unpredictable move, taking Meyerhold into the world of large-scale, State-funded performance. The Imperial Theatres, numbering five in all, were based in St Petersburg and Moscow and in many ways were the antithesis of the art theatre movement in which Meyerhold had flourished: there was a deeply ingrained hierarchy among the actors and no tradition of the director being a creative artist, as Meyerhold saw the role.

Meyerhold was appointed director to the St Petersburg Imperial Theatres in April 1908 by the chief administrator Vladimir Telyakovsky, a man who clearly shared the young director's contrary attitude to life:

> I became interested in him when I heard unflattering opinions of him on all sides.
> When everyone attacks a man, he must be of some importance.
>
> *(Hoover 1974: 51)*

Thus began almost a decade of work for Meyerhold, taking him from the aftermath of one failed revolution (in 1905) to the very day in which the Tsarist regime began finally to crumble for good, in February 1917.

The pace of production slowed considerably in his new job. No longer was Meyerhold overseeing the kind of hectic schedule he had experienced in the provinces. Here, he could enjoy a lengthy period of research similar to that which Stanislavsky and Nemirovich had called for back in 1898, although in a very different environment to the MAT. He read avidly, wrote articles and collaborated closely with artists and choreographers, including the designer Aleksandr Golovin.

But with only two productions a season to direct, Meyerhold did not simply spend his time preparing for the operas and classics he was to direct at the Imperial Theatres. Instead, he 'moonlighted' as director and teacher on a range of small-scale, innovative ventures, in conditions which could not be more different from the Aleksandrinsky or Marinsky Theatres: cabaret venues, tiny stages, rooms in his own flat and in others' houses. Meyerhold, in effect, began to live two very different lives – the one public and high profile, the other low key and exclusive. It was a theatrical twist to his own existence which Meyerhold must have relished.

Dr Dapertutto

Meyerhold's double life was given further dramatic symbolism when he adopted the pseudonym, Dr Dapertutto, a character created by one of his favourite authors, E.T.A. Hoffmann, and who symbolised many of the contradictory qualities Meyerhold saw in himself. Taking on the role of Dapertutto allowed Meyerhold to continue his experimental work without breaking his contract with the Imperial Theatres. It was a compromise from the management which had far-reaching implications, for without the 'other side' to his work Meyerhold would not have begun his programme of teaching or have developed his interest in the popular theatre. Both of these strands, as we shall see, had much to do with his theatrical direction after the Revolution.

In an article entitled 'The Fairground Booth', written in the middle of his Dapertutto period, in 1912, Meyerhold defined his aspirations for the future by recalling the past:

> The cult of the cabotinage, which I am sure will reappear with the restoration of the theatre of the past, will help the modern actor to rediscover the basic laws of theatricality.
>
> *(Braun 2016: 152)*

The cabotin was a strolling player, able, as Meyerhold puts it, 'to work miracles with his technical mastery' and capable of keeping 'alive the tradition of the true art of acting' (Braun 2016: 148). He was a model of the kind of self-aware, physically dynamic style of performance we have already seen in Blok's play of the same name. But Meyerhold was not just celebrating old alliances in this article. He was defining his own way of working for decades to come: a fusion of traditional and modern theatrical techniques. Tradition was assured by Meyerhold's continued interest in popular forms, including *commedia dell'arte*. The 'new' was to be found in his collaborations with contemporary playwrights, designers and composers as well as in the terminology which began to emerge later from the experimental work. Meyerhold's message was simple: in order to innovate you have to renovate – and he meant the popular theatres of old.

His production of *Columbine's Scarf*, freely adapted from a pantomime by Arthur Schnitzler and staged as part of a varied programme of events in a tiny theatre in October 1910, illustrates this idea. Returning to the story of Pierrot, Harlequin and Columbine, Meyerhold worked closely with the designer Nikolai Sapunov to create what Konstantin Rudnitsky calls 'chaotic and dynamic stage designs' (Rudnitsky 1988: 15). The physicality and magical trickery with props in this production owed a significant debt to the *commedia* style but the *grotesque* imagery and atmosphere achieved by Meyerhold and Sapunov spoke directly to the contemporary concerns of the country. As Meyerhold's biographer, Volkov states: they 'saw clearly into the ugliness of everyday life in Russia' (Braun 1995: 101). Such a mixture of old and new pre-empts the approach Meyerhold took in 1926 with his masterpiece production of Gogol's *The Government Inspector* and we will be looking in detail at this work in section 2.2. But it also characterises a general tendency of Meyerhold's work to synthesise the ancient and modern, an approach begun at the Dramatichesky Theatre with Komissarzhevskaya and developed in the guise of Dapertutto.

Meyerhold's studios

Meyerhold's teaching programme, designed to create this 'modern actor', was also formulated under the name of Dapertutto and looked again to *commedia* for inspiration. Having taught acting technique in a music, drama and opera school in 1909, Meyerhold formed a specialised group two years later, along with the young director, Vladimir Solovyov, to continue his research into *commedia* techniques. Principal among their repertoire was the one-act play *Harlequin the Marriage Broker*, penned by Solovyov himself in the manner of a *commedia* scenario. Meyerhold's own description of the harlequinade captures the knockabout style very effectively:

> Striking one's rival across the face ... one character carrying off another pick-a-back; fights, blows with clubs, cutting off of noses with wooden swords.
>
> *(Braun 2016: 173)*

Here, in this improvised theatre piece, are the seeds of what was later to be called biomechanics – Meyerhold's acting system, devised as a counterpoint to Stanislavsky's System (with a capital 'S'). After the Revolution, these loosely defined *lazzi* became tightly controlled études such as 'The Slap', 'The Stab with the Dagger' and 'Throwing the Stone', names which betray their history in Italian popular theatre and which [...] are still taught by Russian masters today.

At this stage, though, the work had not been fully formalised. Instead, it was music which provided the controlling influence among the playfulness:

> The actor ... is free to act *ex improvisio*. However the actor's freedom is only relative because he is subject to the discipline of the musical score.
>
> *(Braun 2016: 172)*

We may recall that Meyerhold's early work with Maeterlinck placed great stress on the musical score. Indeed, almost all of the significant production work of Meyerhold relied heavily on the musical accompaniment devised by the composer as well as on the essential *musicality* of the performers. Here, Meyerhold is making clear that the discipline of music (in tension with the freedom of improvisation) is as fundamental to an actor's training programme as it is to the production work – two sides of the theatrical equation which Meyerhold was to bring together after the Revolution.

By 1914 Meyerhold was including Shakespeare and Spanish theatre in his teaching, as well as examples of the modern drama in Russia. A year earlier (in September 1913) he had secured a specified venue for an actor's Studio and now he was beginning to clarify its aims. These included a detailed study of *commedia* techniques, run by Solovyov, exercises in rhythm, and movement classes devised by Meyerhold himself. In the same year (1914) his Studio published the first of nine editions of a journal entitled *The Love of Three Oranges,* in which the practical activities of the Studio were documented and dramatic scenarios, poems and critical articles were published. Aleksandr Blok remained a collaborator on this project, heading up the poetry section, but Meyerhold took overall editorial control.

A 1916 edition of the periodical illustrates just how far the aims of the training had extended. Among thirteen subjects highlighted for discussion, the following areas of expertise are listed:

- the comic, tragic and tragicomic (or grotesque) masks;
- the nineteenth-century Russian classics including Gogol;
- the popular theatre, the circus, and the Hindu and Oriental theatres;
- contemporary theories of the theatre, including Meyerhold's own;
- the role of the director and designer.

(Braun 2016: 186–187)

It was a daunting and highly ambitious list, illustrating just how highly Meyerhold valued the past theatrical contributions of both East and West and pointing clearly to the kind of actor he wanted to create: rounded, informed and flexible.

Masquerade

Whilst Meyerhold developed this laboratory of actor training, he was continuing in his role as Imperial Theatre director, overseeing highly elaborate, some might say extravagant, theatrical (and operatic) spectacles. The ultimate in this alternative strand of work, the jewel in his double life, was his production of Lermontov's *Masquerade* in 1917. In all aspects *Masquerade* was a grand production. It had taken seven years to come to fruition, delayed by the onset of war in 1914 and, according to Marjorie Hoover, by the extensive archival research Meyerhold conducted in preparation (Hoover 1974: 67). It involved a cast of 200, two-thirds of whom were choreographed by Meyerhold in one group in the opulent ball scenes which punctuate the action of the play. Its designs (again by Golovin, Meyerhold's close collaborator in this period) were highly elaborate and technically demanding – nothing was recycled from old stock. And its impact, irrespective of the richness of the settings at this sensitive time in Russian history, was huge – it remained in the repertoire of the Aleksandrinsky theatre until the Second World War.

But for all its grandiose indulgence, Meyerhold's production bore the hallmarks of his earlier work in the experimental theatre. Music underpinned all aspects the performance, the text was rearranged into episodes à la Blok's *Fairground Booth* and the manipulation of props on stage owed a significant debt to his Studio's experiments with *commedia* – indeed, some of the younger actors from the Imperial Theatre attended Meyerhold's laboratory.

At the same time, *Masquerade* anticipated some of the techniques Meyerhold was to perfect in his post-revolutionary period, chiefly in terms of its staging. Realizing that the dynamic force of the play would be compromised by lengthy set changes, Meyerhold devised a *mise-en-scène* (setting) which leapt from forestage, to mainstage, to a series of intimate 'substages', sectioned off by screens and borders. The director could thus ensure a swift transition between scenes – the early manifestation of what was later called *kinetic staging* for his production of *The Government Inspector* – while assuring that the proscenium arch did not act as a barrier between audience and performer.

Meyerhold had come a long way from his days on tour in the provinces. He was now, at the age of forty-three, a significant figure in the mainstream theatre world of tsarist Russia, famed for his highly skilled direction of large casts as well as for the development of an innovative system of actor training. As the shots began to ring out at the beginning of the second Revolution, corresponding exactly with the opening of Meyerhold's *Masquerade,* the question remained: would he be as important a figure in the new world order?

Meyerhold and the Revolution (1917–22)

Of course, looking back, the answer to that question is easy. Meyerhold's career as a director is best known for his *post*-revolutionary productions, among which must be listed: *Mystery Bouffe* (1918 and 1921), *The Magnanimous Cuckold* (1922), *The Death of Tarelkin* (1922), *The Government Inspector* (1926), *Woe to Wit* (1928) and *The Bedbug* (1929). But at the time it was hardly a foregone conclusion that the Imperial Theatre director would succeed in the transformed political landscape which emerged after February and October 1917.

There are two dates because there were two significant stages to the overthrowing of the Tsar's ruling class. The first February uprising led to what was called the Provisional Government – a compromise in which the Tsar stood down and control of the country was given over to an unelected group of academics, industrialists and lawyers. The Bolsheviks (or Reds) did not recognise the new government and began to return to Russia from exile, sensing that the time had come for a full-scale overturning of the country's power base. Very quickly they began to swell their ranks, mainly with workers, soldiers and sailors, and the party membership rose from a handful of people in February to a third of a million by October (Fitzpatrick 1982: 46). With such growing support, and with the Provisional Government struggling with decisions over the war campaign (there was still one year left of the First World War, remember), the possibilities of a coup – a violent insurrection to overthrow the government – grew. And on 24 October this was what happened: the sitting government, headed by Aleksandr Kerensky, was 'stormed' and subsequently thrown out.

You may be familiar with the famous images created by one of Meyerhold's students, Sergei Eisenstein, which recount this momentous occasion: hordes of soldiers stream into the Winter Palace in St Petersburg (then Petrograd), firing on the resistant enemy and heroically taking the territory of the Palace and with it the power of the country. But these images in Eisenstein's film, *October* (1928), are fictional and romanticised. In reality, there was little or no bloodshed, the battleship Aurora did not fire a shot and Kerensky was let out of a side door and allowed to flee. Even so, there had been a successful overthrowing of the vestiges of the old order and in its stead was Bolshevism.

Meyerhold, who was always responsive to the spirit of the time, reacted quickly to the new powers and within three weeks of the October Revolution had already attended a meeting called by the minister for education and the arts, Anatoly Lunacharsky. He found himself with only four other enthusiasts at this gathering (out of a possible 120) and must have thought that his chosen profession was anything but committed to the new regime. Of the other four who did turn up, he knew Blok and had already met Mayakovsky, the playwright and poet, who was to become one of the most important figures in Meyerhold's career. Very soon Meyerhold was brought on to the board of the new theatre department within Lunacharsky's ministry, The Theatre Department of the Commissariat of Enlightenment (TEO), and by September of the next year (1918) was heading up the Petrograd branch of this organisation. He had also joined the Bolshevik party and was consciously manoeuvring within the party's bureaucratic structures.

Meyerhold produced Mayakovsky's play *Mystery Bouffe* (the first Soviet play, as it was known) in the same year, for the first anniversary of the Revolution and he went on to direct two others: *The Bedbug* and *The Bathhouse* (1930). *Mystery Bouffe*, in Mayakovsky's own words, is: 'A Heroic, Epic, Satiric Representation of our Era' and this description amply captures the scope and immediacy of his text. It is a modern day parable play, telling the story of the Revolution through a series of biblical episodes which have clear associations with the events of October 1917. Mayakovsky was so keen to see the play reflect the times in which it was being produced that he wrote a small explanatory note to the second version of the play (1921):

> In the future, all persons performing, presenting, reading or publishing *Mystery Bouffe* should change the content, making it contemporary, immediate, up to the minute.
> *(Mayakovsky 1995: 39)*

Meyerhold too wanted to use his immediate cultural and political environment in his work as a director and this may be one reason why he and Mayakovsky collaborated so effectively together. For Meyerhold, the 'change' in response to the Revolution could be seen in the language he began to adopt to express his theatrical thinking. Where before it was the popular theatre which underpinned much of the training system he was devising, now, in the new post-revolutionary climate, it was science and industry, specifically objective psychology and Taylorism. For it was these two areas which the new ruling order wanted to see developed.

Biomechanics, Pavlov and Taylor

[...] Here we can note a distinct change in expression concerning his emergent acting system. After 1917, and specifically after the civil war between the White Army and the Reds had been won, the influences of *commedia,* oriental theatre and the circus were subsumed under the banner of biomechanics, a banner which was waved by Meyerhold and his students in a range of public locations in the early 1920s. This did not mean that he rejected these traditional forms as a basis for his system, but rather that the training system he taught from 1921 in Moscow had a distinctly different method of *articulation* – one which drew on two major figures in the thinking of the time: Ivan Pavlov (the objective psychologist) and Frederick Winslow Taylor (an American industrialist).

Often this scientific basis to Meyerhold's work is criticised for being superficial or badly thought out. Edward Braun calls it 'specious' (Braun 2016: 225), for example – that is a deceptively attractive theory but ultimately a false one. But while Meyerhold served to gain a lot from connecting his work with some of the favoured ideas at the time, he did also find something of practical help in these supposedly unconnected disciplines.

From Pavlov, the man best known for his experiments on dogs, Meyerhold borrowed the idea that behaviour is best understood as a chain of reflex responses to the external world. Pavlov's theory was resolutely objective: we don't act but *react,* in response to the different stimuli of our environment. This pattern of behaviour, Pavlov maintained, was as true for humans as it was for the animals in his laboratory. 'Chain reflexes' (our reactions connected together in a long 'domino line' of responses) are what he calls 'the foundation of the nervous activities of both men and of animals' (Pavlov 1927: 11). Meyerhold tested this idea in his own laboratory, not on dogs but with actors.

From Taylor, Meyerhold took the idea of smoothly executed, rhythmically economical actions. As a man driven to obsession over the question of efficiency, fluent movement was something Taylor himself had been preaching to raise the levels of productivity in factories in America. He broke up the work of his labourers into simple and connected 'tasks' and then gave each task a maximum time in which it could be completed. The aim was high productivity – a watchword of the new Soviet powers too – and Meyerhold pursued it with characteristic vigour. He even called for the 'Taylorization of the theatre' to reduce a four-hour theatre piece to just sixty minutes (Braun 2016: 245).

In theoretical terms, biomechanics is a fusion of these two ideas. It is an objective system, focusing on the external apparatus of the actor and designed to create a responsive, efficient and *productive* actor. Although the work of the performer was far removed from that which was done in the factories, Meyerhold wanted to claim an allegiance with industry. An effective theatre piece (the 'product' of the theatre) is one which 'hits the mark' and succeeds in communicating its message, just as an efficient factory may produce goods without waste and to specification.

Constructivism in The Magnanimous Cuckold *and* The Death of Tarelkin

Meyerhold was not alone in the pursuit of factory-like efficiency. Concurrent with the developments in industry and science, the fine arts were responding to the shift in emphasis brought about by the Revolution. In no other art movement was this more explicitly captured than in

Constructivism. Aleksei Gan, one of the more radical of their number and a kind of Treplev for the modern age, explains:

> The socio-political system conditioned by the new economic structure gives rise to new forms and means of expression. The emergent culture of labor and intellect will be expressed by *intellectual material production*.
>
> *(Bann 1974: 37, my italics)*

Although Gan's extremism led him to attack all art, including Meyerhold's, his statement has some affinity with the core of Meyerhold's practice at the time: to focus on conscious, creative *work*. For the constructivists this meant a move away from the art of the easel to sculpture and poster production. For Meyerhold it meant centring attention on the principal material resource of the theatre – the actor's body. For both, the emphasis on *products* led to a celebration of the possibilities of the machine – that which produces things – and this is clearly expressed in the designs Lyubov Popova created for Fernand Crommelynck's *The Magnanimous Cuckold*.

In keeping with the philosophy of the constructivists, Popova transformed the Meyerholdian stage into a machine, casting the actors as workers within the theatre factory. Any attempt at representation was banished beyond the highly stylised wheel which dominated the backdrop (the central character, Bruno, is a miller). Instead of rooms, chairs and realistic properties there were ramps and walkways, and the usual flats, borders and curtains were disposed of to reveal the stark brick wall of the theatre. But while the stage may have resembled the skeletal structure of a huge machine, the actors were not reduced to automatons. They retained all the vigour, playfulness and dexterity of Meyerhold's earlier experiments in *commedia*. As the critic Boris Alpers explains:

> The strong, agile, physically robust actor filled the stage with his self-possessed movements. It was as though he impersonated the new man freed from the power of things.
>
> *(Symons 1971: 84)*

Thus, Meyerhold effected yet another fusion of old and new, bringing on to his stage what James M. Symons tellingly calls 'twentieth century, machine-age versions of that cabotin of whom Meyerhold had spoken so fondly in 1912' (ibid.: 83). Alma Law has documented the whole production in some detail and the mixture of slapstick, *commedia*-style acting with the modernist environment of Popova's constructivist set comes through very clearly in her descriptions:

> The construction aided the actors in much the same way that a properly designed machine enables a worker to perform more efficiently. . . . The action demanded acrobatic virtuosity and split second timing as a whirlwind of blows, leaps, falls and somersaults all but swallowed up Crommelynck's text.
>
> *(1982: 71–72)*

In the same year (1922) Meyerhold collaborated with another Constructivist, Varvara Stepanova. For the production of *The Death of Tarelkin*, by Aleksandr Sukhovo-Kobylin, Stepanova produced a similar machine-like set, this time with a huge meat mincer-cum-cage as the centrepiece. She also created stylised costumes, akin to the uniforms worn by convicts, and so retained the anti-illusionary approach of her colleague, Popova. Once again, the moving parts of the set were complemented by the dynamism of the actors and the pictures which survive of the production indicate a style of acting which was close to that seen in American film comedies featuring the Keystone Cops and Charlie Chaplin.

There were other experiments, but these two productions capture the essence of the union of biomechanics and Constructivism and mark an extreme in Meyerhold's experimentation. After this, Meyerhold began to return to more representational settings, although the self-conscious theatricality of these landmark productions remained in his later repertoire.

The Meyerhold Theatre (1922–31)

While he worked to achieve a coherent aesthetic on stage, things behind the scenes were anything but stable for Meyerhold. In May 1919, he had been forced out of his job at the Petrograd TEO by a bout of tuberculosis and retired south (to Yalta) to recuperate. The civil war was still in full flight and he was arrested by the Whites, imprisoned and almost executed, three months after leaving Petrograd. A year later he was summoned to return to public life by Lunacharsky and arrived in Moscow in September 1920. Here, for just over five months, he took overall charge of the theatre department of Lunacharsky's ministry, now covering the whole of the Soviet Union, and launched repeated attacks on the establishment theatres, including the MAT, for their outmoded repertoires and dated style. In late February 1921 he resigned from his position and concentrated his energies on his alternative to the Academic (or state subsidised) theatres – the Russian Soviet Federal Socialist Republic (RSFSR) Theatre No. 1, where he produced the second version of Mayakovsky's *Mystery Bouffe* and a radical adaptation of Emile Verhaeren's *The Dawn*. Ten months after this, on 6 September 1921, the RSFSR theatre was closed and Meyerhold was once again looking for work.

There followed a complex period in which Meyerhold taught his emergent system of biomechanics and began to make public his findings: first, under the auspices of the State Director's Workshop (GVYRM) and then, in January 1922 under the name of GVYTM, the State Theatre Workshop. Later, this second workshop was merged with others under the umbrella of GITIS, the State Institute of Theatrical Art, and it was here where Meyerhold worked most closely with the filmmaker Eisenstein. GITIS still exists today, although it is now called the Russian University of Theatre Arts, and still has classes in biomechanics, taught by Gennadi Bogdanov, among others. Finally, after breaking away from GITIS, Meyerhold's own workshop was given the name GEKTEMAS (State Experimental Workshop) in 1924.

The theatrical outlets for all this 'laboratory' work were the performances created by Meyerhold's students at the Sohn Theatre – the dilapidated space Meyerhold appropriated in 1922 and which served as his main performance space for almost a decade. During this period, at what became known as the Meyerhold Theatre, the revolutionary director put on some of his most celebrated work, often drawing on the workshop for his casts and achieving a mixture of school, theatre and experimental laboratory that remains an ideal for many directors today. The work in biomechanics did not emerge on the stage directly; the études were never 'quoted' as such, apart from one moment in the *Magnanimous Cuckold*. But the symbiotic relationship of workshop and theatre established by Meyerhold meant that his dramatic productions were always *informed* by the training in biomechanics. This is perhaps most clear in his ground-breaking production of *The Government Inspector* – the most remarkable of his productions from this period.

That story will be told in section 2.2 and the context surrounding his 1926 production is best described in that section of the book. For now it remains for me to conclude the history of Meyerhold's career by returning to the events with which we began this section: the decline of his theatre and his ultimate extermination.

Meyerhold (1874–1940)

The death of Meyerhold and his theatre (1932–40)

If the 1920s for Meyerhold were characterised by glittering innovation and an immediate responsiveness to things current, then the 1930s would best be described as a period of stagnation. It was a time when Meyerhold retreated further into the classical repertoire and during which he found it increasingly difficult to practise his craft without intervention or criticism. His range of chosen plays had never been entirely contemporary – the nineteenth-century writers, Gogol, Ostrovsky and Sukhovo-Kobylin, figure prominently in the 'golden age' of his theatre in the previous decade. But these classic playwrights had always been set among the works of new playwrights – Mayakovsky and Erdman, for example – or had themselves been subject to some radical interpretation and/or adaptation. By 1932, the pace of the premières emerging from the Meyerhold Theatre had slowed considerably and the choice of plays was beginning to look dangerously removed from the context of Soviet Russia. Robert Leach lists just eight 'new' productions between 1932 and 1938 (the date when Meyerhold's theatre was finally 'liquidated') and these include revivals of his pre-revolutionary masterpiece *Masquerade* and a return to Griboedov's play *Woe from Wit*, which he had originally staged in 1928 (Leach 1989: 202).

I say 'dangerously' because, increasingly, the presence of Soviet 'censors' was being felt by theatre directors, restricting what new work there was and ensuring that each production toed a party line. The man at the end of that line was Joseph Stalin who, after a bitter internal battle, had taken over from Lenin after his death and from 1928 had taken responsibility for the industrialisation of the country with his first Five Year Plan. By the early 1930s, his control over the party was talked about in terms redolent of Constructivism: he was running a party 'machine', with a well-oiled bureaucracy and a determined aim of productivity. But to keep such productivity going, it was necessary for all the separate parts of the machine to work together – to agree – even if that meant compromising the democratic ideals with which the Bolshevik Revolution had begun. This was as true for the arts as it was for agriculture or engineering and in practice it meant a party style: Socialist Realism. All other approaches were denounced as 'formalist', originally a term without prejudice but which became the ultimate condemnation for work which (supposedly) loved itself at the expense of any social message.

Socialist Realism, described by one Russian critic as 'Naturalism without the nature', was defined in 1934 by its key theorist, Andrei Zhdanov, as 'revolutionary romanticism' (Gorky et al. 1977: 21). It was a style of art which was unflinchingly positive in its presentation of the Revolution and pointedly organised, as Zhdanov puts it, towards 'remould[ing] the mentality of the people in the spirit of socialism' (ibid.: 24).

As such, Socialist Realism sought a response from its audience in direct contrast to that which Meyerhold had been trying to achieve. Meyerhold's ideal was a divided, debating audience. Zhdanov wanted *everybody* to celebrate the successes of the Revolution. The two were bound to come into conflict, all the more so if you consider the absence of any contemporary plays in the repertoire of the Meyerhold Theatre during this period. Meyerhold began to be vilified in the press and accused of formalism. Questions were asked about his current work and about the experiments of the past and he was forced to defend himself from the accusation that his was an 'alien theatre', working against the national cause. One such defence came from Meyerhold in 1936. Using imagery which was tragically prescient, he spoke on the subject of criticism:

> Both as an actor and as a director, my body is so covered in wounds from the critics' shafts that there doesn't seem to be a part left unscathed.
>
> *(Braun 2016: 263)*

Two years later Meyerhold's theatre was closed, after a final matinée of *The Government Inspector*. For a short time he was adopted by his old mentor, Stanislavsky, and given the job of finishing his opera production *Rigoletto* – Stanislavsky was in the last months of his life. It was a final statement from the teacher that, irrespective of the differences they had experienced over the years, he valued his student's contribution above all.

But this new horizon proved a false one and Meyerhold was arrested on charges of espionage, of plotting to assassinate Stalin and of being part of a counter-revolutionary Trotskyist organisation. For fifteen years following his execution in 1940 Meyerhold's name was erased from Russian theatre history and his face removed from theatre portraits. His close collaborators were terrified into silence and his acting system, biomechanics, was never mentioned. Only after Stalin was dead did the slow process of rehabilitation begin.

After Meyerhold

Fortunately for us, there were people, even in such extreme circumstances, who did not forget Meyerhold and his work. One of these was a young actor called Nikolai Kustov.

Kustov was a collaborator with Meyerhold in the 1930s and taught biomechanics in the same period. Kustov's figure is immortalised in a series of pictures from this time, taken as he performed the actions of the étude 'Shooting the Bow' on a beach (Zarrilli 1995: 94–95), and his work with Meyerhold's biomechanics has similarly defied the passing of time. For Kustov came out of retirement in the 1970s and taught eight actors, working at the Theatre of Satire in Moscow, the art of Meyerhold's biomechanics. By then, he was physically weak and unable to perform the études himself but he nevertheless passed on five of the original études to his actors, two of whom (Gennadi Bogdanov and Aleksei Levinski) are still teaching today.

In doing so, Kustov was defying Stalin's death sentence, keeping alive the spirit of Meyerhold's work, which, for all of the documentary evidence available, nevertheless only truly persists in the body of the actor. What follows is an invitation to continue this process.

2.2 Meyerhold's key production: *The Government Inspector*

Gogol's challenge

Think of yourself as a director for a moment. You have Nikolai Gogol's nineteenth-century comedy, *The Government Inspector* (1836), in your hands and you are looking at the final page. Here's Gogol's extended stage direction, the moment with which he concludes his play:

> *The* MAYOR *stands in the centre, like a pillar, with his arms outstretched and his head flung back. To the right are his* WIFE *and* DAUGHTER, *their entire bodies straining towards him; behind them stands the* POSTMASTER, *transformed into a sort of question mark, facing the audience; behind him stands the* SCHOOLS SUPERINTENDENT, *with a look of helpless innocence; behind him and at the far side of the stage, three visiting ladies, leaning against one another with the most satirical expression on their faces, are looking straight at the* MAYOR'S *family. To the left of the* MAYOR *stands the charities warden, his head cocked to one side as if straining to listen; behind him the* JUDGE, *with his arms stuck out, is practically squatting on the floor, and moving his lips, as if trying to whistle. . . . Behind him,* KOROBKIN, *facing the audience with his eyes screwed up, directs a look of contempt at the* MAYOR; *and behind him again, at the other side of the stage, stand* BOBCHINSKY *and* dobchinsky, *their arms outflung towards each other, open-mouthed*

and goggle-eyed. The other guests stand around like pillars. The petrified company maintain their position for almost a minute and a half. Then the curtain is lowered.

(Gogol 1997: 100)

You may well be asking yourself: 'How on earth am I going to do that?' How am I going to capture the audience's attention for a full ninety seconds, as they watch a frozen dumb show of 'petrified' characters?

Now ask your next question as a director: what does this conclusion tell me about Gogol's theatrical vision? Why does he ask so much of an audience at this critical moment in the play? As a skilled dramatist, Gogol would be well aware of the dangers of this finale: losing the audience's attention, leaving them on a low point, or worse still inviting them to point out any flaws in the quality of the actors' freeze. But he knew, too, the impact that such a moment could make if it were successfully realised on stage, how electrifying such unabashed theatricality could be in the hands of a master director.

In effect, Gogol is challenging the director to ask themselves the question: Do I have sufficient creative, imaginative and performative resources within my company to stage this piece?

Meyerhold's response

By the time Meyerhold attempted to direct Gogol's play in 1926, he had built himself a considerable reputation for meeting such theatrical challenges. From his early days on tour with the Fellowship, through the double life he led in St Petersburg, to the founding of his own theatre in Moscow, he had staged well over 100 productions, and proved himself to be an exceptionally versatile director.

But of all his productions, Meyerhold's response to the challenge of *The Government Inspector (Revisor* in Russian) was particularly remarkable. There are many reasons for this, most of which I hope will be highlighted in this section. But one central reason needs stressing from the outset: Gogol's play was tailor-made for Meyerhold's theatre. If you look back to the stage direction above, you can see why. This incredible *coup-de-théâtre* incorporates many of the devices we have already encountered in Meyerhold's work:

- The deliberate choreography of the characters within the stage space.
- The sense of the stage as a picture or composition.
- The use of an exaggerated and expressive physical style.
- The use of the face as a mask.
- The mixing of opposites.
- The direct connection with an audience.
- The elongation of an action to make it strange.

With such a stylistic meeting of minds it was only a matter of time before Meyerhold took on Gogol's classic text, for *The Government Inspector* was the ultimate test of how his theories combined with his practice.

It is for this reason that his production is so worthy of another look. It is a measure of how well Meyerhold managed to synthesise his ideas into one performance. What's more, it is relatively easy to find material to make this judgement. In addition to the original source (Gogol's play), a whole host of people have documented their responses to Meyerhold's 1926 production – actors, theatre critics, academics, politicians – so there are several resources we can turn to in fleshing out our understanding of the work.

One key objective for this section must be to place Nikolai Gogol in context, to draw out his intentions as a playwright, and to summarise the contents of the play itself. But my overriding aim is to use Meyerhold's production to exemplify this meeting point between theory and practice. A production is one of the most powerful indicators of how a practitioner's thinking and training come together. It is where creativity meets with hard graft, where technique confronts the imagination, and where abstract thought informs concrete actions. For this reason I have punctuated the material of this section with some practical suggestions of how to draw on Gogol's text in the spirit of Meyerhold. This section may be treated as a precursor to the next, or it might be returned to after reading up on what Meyerhold asked of his actors in the studio. Either way, Meyerhold's theory and practice are best thought of as two halves of a complex and creative equation called 'performance', not as separate activities.

So how did Meyerhold managed to stage this amazing ending? Konstantin Rudnitsky, one of the most important commentators on Meyerhold, offers this description:

> The curtain rose, and the spectators saw the characters of the show frozen in the poses indicated by Gogol. The sculptural group was immobile. Only after a long pause did the spectators guess that before them were not actors but dolls – that the 'mute scene' was truly mute and dead.
>
> *(Rudnitsky 1981: 417–418)*

Meyerhold's response to the challenge set by Gogol exactly ninety years earlier was characteristically imaginative: substitute mannequins for the actors in the blink of an eye and Gogol's metaphor of petrification is transformed into a concrete image on stage. What's more, if you can perform it with such a theatrical sleight of hand that the assembled audience are fooled, then they too will be drawn into the silent moment, made mute by the miraculous appearance of puppets. This was Meyerhold's answer to Gogol. He gulled his audience into believing that the cast were still on stage and then pulled the rug from beneath them. Surprise, surprise!

But who are these people who turn to stone in front of your eyes? Why are they moved to such hysteria? And what has the Mayor done which makes him the focus of everything? More fundamentally, who created these characters? Who is Nikolai Gogol? And where does he fit into Russian theatre history? Once we have established these facts, we can return to Meyerhold's production of Gogol's play and to the task in hand – a practical exposition of what has frequently been called Meyerhold's 'masterpiece', one of the landmark productions of the twentieth century.

Nikolai Gogol: the comet

Gogol's artistry, concentrated as it was into a period of just eight years (1829–36), has been likened to the lifespan of a comet:

> Bursting suddenly upon the landscape, burning itself out quickly, but transforming the configuration of Russian literary culture.
>
> *(Ehre, in Gogol 1980: ix)*

With only three plays to his name – *The Marriage, The Gamblers* and *The Government Inspector* – Gogol's explosive impact is surprising, particularly as almost all of his reputation as a dramatist rests on the last play in this list. But by the time Meyerhold produced *The Government Inspector,* Gogol was firmly established as a comic genius and his play was inextricably connected to some of the biggest names in Russian theatre history: Mikhail Shchepkin, Konstantin Stanislavsky and Michael

Chekhov. After Meyerhold, came other significant productions of the play – including Georgy Tovstonogov's staging in 1972 and, in 1985, Richard Eyre's production for the National Theatre in London. Perhaps the image of Gogol as a comet points not only to his fiery presence at the time but also to his play's enduring ability to 'come round again' and enlighten new audiences.

Gogol was born in the Ukraine in 1809, at a pivotal time in Russian history. Developing later than most European countries, Russia was slowly moving away from its feudal past and waking up to the influence of capitalism. Russia's professional theatre was only fifty years old and the influence of Europe was just beginning to impact on the native culture. In short, it was a time of transition and transition creates tensions, between the customs of the past and the needs of the future. Gogol was at the heart of many of these tensions. His work was acclaimed by left- and right-wing critics alike. He was a figure of radicalism as well as of conservatism. He founded the new movement of Realism but used well-established conventional caricatures to do so. He wrote caustic social satire, but escaped the wrath of the censor.

Indeed, the period in which he was writing was simultaneously a 'golden age' of Russian literature and a period of frightening Tsarist repression. Even though Nicholas I 'turned his country into a barracks staffed by spies and informers' (Worrall 1982: 19), stifling all manner of creative expression, Gogol was part of a burgeoning of home-grown literary talent, including the novelist Dostoevsky and Gogol's friend Pushkin. (A similar tension between State and artist was to be found in the latter part of Meyerhold's career, although in his case the Tsar's oppressive force had been replaced by the equally totalitarian General Secretary of the Communist Party, Joseph Stalin.)

At first, Gogol wanted to be part of the bureaucratic world of nineteenth-century Russia, moving to its capital, St Petersburg, in 1828 and finding work in the Ministry of the Interior. But he quickly tired of the ministry and moved from what he called such 'stupid and senseless work' (Magarshack 1957: 69) to a teaching career, first in an Institute of Young Ladies and then as a history lecturer at the University. After a promising start, his performance as an academic went the same way as his career in the ministry, a result no doubt of his sheer hopelessness as a lecturer! Turgenev, an equally gifted dramatist and friend to Gogol, recognised immediately that his talents lay elsewhere.

> We were all convinced . . . that he had no idea of history, and that . . . professor [Gogol] had nothing in common with Gogol the writer.
>
> *(Magarshack 1957: 102)*

By the end of 1835 Gogol had accepted Turgenev's argument. He left teaching and dedicated his time exclusively to writing, completing in that year alone an impressive range of work, including his dramatic masterpiece, *The Government Inspector*.

For this play, Gogol's creative energy was at its peak. It took him under two months to write and just four more to get passed by the censor, rehearsed and staged at the Aleksandrinsky Imperial Theatre in St Petersburg. By one of those strange coincidences so often thrown up by history, it was the very same theatre Meyerhold was to work in, over seventy years later during his Dapertutto period.

Gogol's Government Inspector

What happens in the play

Gogol's play hinges on the trademark convention of comedy – mistaken identity. The dignitaries of an unnamed provincial town, hundreds of miles from anywhere, have become accustomed to their particular way of life. Led by the Mayor, they are vain, self-interested, corrupt and divisive, values which are rewarded in this unfortunate town. But something has arisen to undermine the status quo. The Mayor has received a letter from his friend warning of an impending visit from a Government Inspector – an official charged with rooting out the very practices which have become second nature to the town's ruling class.

Act 1

Flushed with panic, the Mayor invites his governing council to his house to tell them the news. They are: the Judge, Lyapkin-Tyapkin; the Charities Warden, Zemlyanika; the Schools Superintendent, Khlopov; the Physician, Doctor Gibner; and the Postmaster, Shpyokin. Later they are joined by two landowners, Dobchinsky and Bobchinsky, and by the Chief of Police – all of the town's officials crammed into the Mayor's room.

In any other town the Mayor's news would be highly confidential. But in this provincial backwater the people thrive on whispers, forgotten confidences and shared intelligence. Despite the Mayor's grandiose attempts to capitalise on the moment, the Postmaster has already heard the news and the two landowners, also operating on third-hand information, burst into the meeting with news of a discovery: the Inspector, they claim, has already arrived and is staying at the local inn.

Thus, the seed of delusion is planted in the minds of the officials. Khlestakov, a lowly clerk from St Petersburg, on his way home from the capital, is elevated in the eyes of the town to a senior government official. He may not look the part but that's because he's travelling 'incognito', the people reason. They automatically assume, of course, that the St Petersburg government operates in the same underhand manner as they do.

Act 2

Thinking fast, the Mayor suggests that he visits Khlestakov in his hotel room to begin a process of covert persuasion or 'buttering up'. First, Khlestakov's bill must be paid, then he must come and stay with the Mayor and after that he must be wined and dined, with an all-expenses-paid tour of the town thrown in. For Khlestakov and his servant Osip, the Mayor's visit to their room comes just in time, saving them from certain eviction at the hands of the landlord for not paying their bills.

Act 3

We rejoin the town's 'best' after Khlestakov has been taken for the tour. The officials once again crowd into a room in the Mayor's house and Khlestakov is introduced to the family: Anna, the Mayor's wife, and Marya, his daughter. Now decidedly drunk, Khlestakov's natural arrogance and imagination lead him to concoct an elaborate and ever more magnified version of his life in St Petersburg. In an attempt to impress both Anna and Marya, Khlestakov concludes his outburst with the ludicrous claim that he is to be created a field marshal as early as tomorrow. He then makes a hasty exit to sleep it all off! With wanton ambition and deep-seated pretensions to be 'better than they are', the townspeople, including the wily Mayor, swallow all of Khlestakov's lies.

Act 4

Next day, the Judge and his fellow councillors plan to 'buy the ear' of Khlestakov. One by one they approach the hungover clerk to persuade him to accept a bribe. Always needy and open to offers, Khlestakov accepts each one, raising the stakes as the officials flock through his room.

Meyerhold (1874–1940)

Next in line are the workers, led by a chorus of indignant shopkeepers, eager to inform on the corrupt practices of the Mayor. True to form, Khlestakov soon loses interest and, like a tired child, rejects the remaining petitions. Instead, he composes a letter to his friend, basking in his new-found status and satirising the townspeople. Osip, the thinking half of the duo, has made him aware that their luck is bound to run out soon, so Khlestakov – at this point behaving like a hormonal teenager – attempts to woo the Mayor's wife *and* his daughter. He concludes the act with a perfunctory offer of marriage – to Marya – and then departs swiftly, his pockets stuffed with the Mayor's money.

Act 5

With a field marshal for a son-in-law, the Mayor revels in his family's fortune, accepting the applause of a host of guests all scrabbling for a piece of their new-found prosperity. That is, until the Postmaster arrives, who, in an echo of the first act, brings in a letter of monumental significance. As a habitual reader of everyone's mail, the Postmaster has opened Khlestakov's letter to his friend. In doing so he is forced to see himself and the rest of his corrupt colleagues through someone else's eyes, a vision he particularly enjoys sharing with the Mayor. The panic that ensues is only heightened by the final revelation: the real Government Inspector has arrived and is awaiting the Mayor's presence at the inn. Each character turns slowly to stone as the cataclysmic response to the news literally petrifies the company. We have arrived back at the grotesque dumb show with which we began this section.

I have summarised the story of the play in some detail for two reasons: (1) so that, before you have actually read the play, you have a sound grasp of the events and the order in which they occur – you should then be able to put the theatrical choices made by Meyerhold into some kind of context; and (2) so that you have enough material to go on for the following practical exercise:

Now you have recorded your findings, you will have begun the process of making practical notes on three key areas of theatrical analysis: plot, characterisation, and themes and symbols.

Box 2.1

- Recalling Marinetti's speed-version of *Othello* from the last section, get into a group of four (although any size, including solos will do).
- As a group read the plot summary above.
- Tear up some paper into a number of small pieces, about the size of an envelope.
- Start the stopwatch.
- Spend three minutes deciding upon the main events of the play.
- Perform a three-minute version of your edited play, using the pieces of paper as props in as many ways as you can.

Now, reflect on the choices made in the following manner:

- List the events you chose to include in your three-minute version.
- List the characters you included in your three-minute version and note briefly how you distinguished between them.
- List the number of different things you used the paper for.

Plot (the organisation of events)

When Gogol sat down to compose *The Government Inspector* he had a story in his head – given to him by Pushkin as a matter of fact. In the process of writing the play, he then had to decide how to *tell* that story. In other words, he translated a chronological narrative into a *plot*. (You have done something similar in creating your three-minute version of Gogol's play, devising a plot from a plot!)

There are some things worth noting about Gogol's plot before we see what Meyerhold chose to do with it:

1. It is divided up into five acts, the traditional subdivision of a full-length play at the time.
2. All of the action takes place within the isolated town.
3. The action is squeezed into a period of less than two days.
4. Act 2 is set in the hotel room. All the other acts are set in the same room in the Mayor's house.
5. Khlestakov is only present in the middle of the play – Acts 2–4.
6. The Mayor appears in every act.
7. The play has a carefully constructed cyclical form: it begins with the announcement of an Inspector (the false one) and ends with the announcement of an Inspector (the real one); it begins with a letter which *conceals* the truth and ends with a letter which *reveals* the truth; it begins in panic, with the Mayor surrounded by his citizens and ends in panic in the same way.

Effectively, Gogol sticks closely to the dramatic unities in *The Government Inspector*, setting the whole piece in the one location (with a switch within the town to the hotel), over a period of little more than twenty-four hours. He concentrates the appearances of his anti-hero (Khlestakov) into the middle of the play, while the Mayor has an overarching and controlling function throughout. The pivotal action of the play is the gradual exposure of Khlestakov to the townspeople, one after another: first, in Act 2, to the Mayor, Dobchinsky and Bobchinsky; next to the Mayor's family, and then, in Act 4, to a whole parade of people, from the Judge to the Sergeant's Widow. Khlestakov is thus revealed as a kind of 'serial responder' to the town's community.

Characterisation

First, look back to the list of characters gathered around the Mayor in Act 1 – their names give us a clue as to the kind of characters they are. Some of these clues are obvious – Dobchinsky and Bobchinsky are clearly a duet, for example. But some of them are hidden in Gogol's language – Zemlyanika means 'strawberry', for instance, and Khlestakov, 'whippersnapper'. To help us out, Gogol provided detailed notes to some of the characters, in an article entitled 'Advice to Those Who Would Play *The Government Inspector* as it Ought to be Played', published after his death in 1846:

> KHLESTAKOV: Everything about him is surprising, unexpected. For a considerable length of time he cannot even surmise why people are showing him such attention. . . . The actor playing this role must have an extremely multifaceted talent, capable of expressing the diverse characteristics of a person.
> MAYOR: He senses that he is a sinner, attends church . . . but the temptation of easy gain is great. From beginning to end he finds himself in a more heightened emotional state than he has ever experienced. . . . Shifting from terror to hope and joy excites his senses.

> ZEMLYANIKA: Physically gross, but a subtle crook.... Despite his clumsiness and obesity, he is always quick on his toes.
> DOB/BOBCHINSKY: Both are short, squat, have little pot-bellies, and resemble one another in the extreme ... the actor must ache with curiosity and be afflicted with a wagging tongue if he wants to play these roles well.
> KHLOPOV: He quivers like a leaf at the news of the government inspector: all [the actor] has to do is convey perpetual terror.
>
> *(Gogol 1980: 170–174)*

There are several characteristics here which prefigure Meyerhold's style of acting: the clear delineation of the *external* features of the role, the sharp changes in characters' emotional states, the sense of Khlestakov as a 'montage of different masks', and the consistent feeling of surprise and contradiction in many of the parts.

But, in spite of these features, Gogol also informs us in this essay that the characters must *not* be caricatured, 'exaggerated or hackneyed' (ibid.: 169). Instead, the parts must be played modestly and sincerely with the actor looking to 'common mankind' (ibid.) for a model. With such heightened expressivity highlighted in his notes for the actors, this realistic note appears contradictory.

In fact, Gogol's direction is pointing to the serious intention behind his play. He didn't want it to be written off as a superficial vaudeville, composed simply as a diversion for the upper classes. He saw *The Government Inspector* as a didactic piece, designed with an intelligent and 'detached' (ibid.) audience in mind. The play's purpose, he argued, was to pinpoint the failings of society and then hold them up for scrutiny, aims which could scarcely be met if the actors resorted to empty caricature.

Ninety years on, this underlying 'realism', or social message, appealed in equal measure to Meyerhold, whose own pursuit of a detached and critical audience was never far away from Gogol's. Indeed he went as far as to reject some of his trademark influences in the pursuit of the Gogolian style:

> We must avoid in particular, anything which smacks of buffoonery. We mustn't take anything from the *commedia dell'arte*.... The course to be held is one which leads towards tragedy.
>
> *(Worrall 1972: 76)*

Themes and symbols

Take a look back at the list of things you symbolised with the paper. They will probably include the Mayor's and Khlestakov's letters – two pivotal props in the play which open and close the piece. Your list may also have included the petitions from the workers, perhaps juxtaposed with the bribes of the Judge and his colleagues. You may have transformed the paper into a love note or a poem to symbolise Khlestakov's wooing of the Mayor's wife and daughter. And, at some point, you almost certainly will have used them as roubles to stuff Khlestakov's pockets.

Using such a simple and transformable material as paper to make different props focuses attention indirectly on some of the underlying images and themes in the play. Think of the associations which come with these props and we get a direct indication of Gogol's thematic content. Such a list could include: officialdom, bureaucracy, corruption, secrecy, oppression, the power of the pen, the power of the rouble, power itself (and its abuses), coercion, manipulation and role play.

Now, if we connect these ideas with some of the other themes in Gogol's play we can begin to get an indication of its complexity. I'll keep the list down to those themes which engaged Meyerhold in his production: the dream, greed versus hunger, the power of the lie, dislocation, masking and disguise, transformations, the grotesque, sexuality, rich versus poor, bribery, Tsarism, formality and crudity, and madness.

It is a diverse and inspiring list of thematic concerns, some of which we have encountered before (masking, the grotesque) and others which are new – the question of 'unreality' or the dream, for example. It is testament to the richness of Meyerhold's vision that his production – four hours long in total – dealt with all of these themes, weaving them together in a performance of such significance that one commentator called it 'The key to all the secrets of his work' (Symons 1971: 149).

Let's turn, then, to unlocking this much lauded production to see for ourselves how Meyerhold realised these ideas on stage.

Meyerhold's Government Inspector

Director as author

It has become customary to call the outstanding 1926 production of Gogol's play, 'Meyerhold's *Government Inspector*', but before we sweep over this shift of emphasis let's recognise the significance of substituting director for playwright. After all, naming Meyerhold as the 'author' of the production constitutes a massive challenge to the hegemony of the playwright. It is a categorical statement in favour of the 'theatre theatrical' as opposed to the literary theatre and it marks in general terms the ascendancy of the director in the twentieth century.

In the case of Meyerhold, the designation was not just making a philosophical point. It was a practical indication of the extent to which Meyerhold was prepared to adapt Gogol's text to his own ends. During the process of rehearsal and performance Meyerhold changed:

- The structure of the text (from acts to episodes).
- The genre of the text (from comedy to tragicomedy).
- The setting for the play as a whole (from an undefined provincial backwater to the capital).
- Individual locations within the play (from just the hotel and the room in the Mayor's house to multiple locations inside and outside the house).
- The number of characters (specifically introducing three new characters).

In making these changes, he worked not from one canonical text but from all six versions created by Gogol in the drafting and redrafting process. Meyerhold also looked further afield for inspiration, using ideas from Gogol's final play *The Gamblers,* as well as material from his novels and short stories. Although this radical approach to Gogol had its critics (those who thought it was extending the remit of the director too far), Meyerhold's creativity offers us a model of directing/devising today. The underlying principles he espoused in his production are as pertinent now as they ever were:

- Be bold with your vision of the production.
- Research around the text, using as many different and related sources as possible.
- Make connections between the context of the play and conditions today.
- Be prepared to adapt the text to meet the needs or desires of your company.
- Integrate your training into your performance work.

The production

In order to illustrate how Meyerhold synthesised his ideas into one theatrical vision for his *Government Inspector*, I am going to revisit some of the key theoretical terms encountered in the previous section with specific reference to the production. I am also going to highlight the kind of training underlying the performances in the play. We'll look at the following interconnected areas: montage in practice; musicality and rhythm; the design; acting style; the training beneath; and the grotesque.

Montage in practice

Central to Meyerhold's adaptation of Gogol was the reorganising of the text. He rejected the five-act structure detailed above and structured the play in terms of episodes, numbering fifteen in all:

Gogol's Government Inspector	*Meyerhold's Government Inspector*
Act 1	Episode 1: Chmykhov's Letter
	Episode 2: An Unforeseen Occurrence
Act 2	Episode 3: After Penza
Not in Gogol	Episode 4: Unicorn
	Episode 5: Filled with the Tend'rest Love
Act 3	Episode 6: The Procession
	Episode 7: Behind a Bottle of 'Tolstobriucha'
Not in Gogol	Episode 8: An Elephant Brought to its Knees
Act 4	Episode 9: Bribes
	Episode 10: Mr High Finance
	Episode 11: Embrace Me Do
	Episode 12: The Blessing
Act 5	Episode 13: Dreams of St Petersburg
	Episode 14: A Fine Old Celebration
	Episode 15: Unprecedented Confusion

(Adapted from Worrall 1972)

This wholesale re-plotting of Gogol's play, and the addition of new scenes, were two clear reasons why Meyerhold declared himself the author of the production. So why make these changes?

First, the shift from acts to episodes changes the *rhythm* of the text. Gogol's five-act structure obeys closely the so-called three Aristotelian unities: time, place and action (although Aristotle actually only mentioned two). Over a period of less than two days, with the vast majority of the time spent in the Mayor's chambers, the action builds gradually to a crescendo (the dumb show). Meyerhold's episodes fragmented this gradual rhythmic development, creating instead a series of shorter 'hits' or shocks. Coupled with his use of multiple locations, the result of this kind of editing was to develop a more fluid and *associative* feel. Norris Houghton contrasts Meyerhold's approach with the seamless arrangement of scenes in Stanislavsky's theatre:

> At the MXAT [Moscow Art Theatre] these *kuski* [bits] are segments of text which are rehearsed separately but when performed flow without a break, so that one is aware only of the *continuity* of the act. Meyerhold divided the act into small episodes so that each ... example of the *jeu de théâtre*, may have *individual* expression. ... Thus the whole production becomes like an 'improvization' or 'variations on a theme'.
>
> *(Houghton 1938: 122, my emphases)*

It is no surprise, then, that when Stanislavsky staged the play he chose to accentuate the feeling of 'continuity' by telescoping the action of Gogol's drama into one day. (He played the last act in ever-dwindling light as the sun set on the Mayor and his community.) Meyerhold's episodic structuring retained Stanislavsky's principle of segmenting the play into named 'bits', but rejected the idea of overall continuity. Instead, each episode could be viewed *individually*, as a self-supporting 'play in itself', or a *'jeu de théâtre'*, as Meyerhold put it – the author's 'thought in theatrical form' (ibid.: 117).

This brings me to the second reason for the episodic treatment: *montage*. Meyerhold's production of *The Government Inspector* conformed to Eisenstein's theory of montage. It was structured to maximise the theatrical impact of the play on the audience using short sharp shocks or 'attractions' and it played with the spectators' capacity to link ideas, juxtaposing different images to create another (arguably higher) level of meaning. In short, the episodic structure led Meyerhold to think like a film director, serving up the action in what he called a series of 'close-ups' (Rudnitsky 1981: 390), contrasted with wide-shots. I will return to this point when we talk about the production's design, but here the point concerns the audience: how did they assimilate what was fed to them in these close-ups?

The best way to answer this question is to look at an example: episodes 7–12. At this point in Gogol's play (the end of Act 3), Khlestakov has collapsed from drink and departs for the night. The officials allow him a night to sleep it off and visit him the next day (in Act 4). But Meyerhold saw an opportunity to create some vivid associations in the audience's mind:

Episode	Content of scene	Thematic associations
7	Khlestakov's boasting	Drunkenness/The power of the lie
8	Khlestakov's nightmare vision	Drunkenness/Desire/Corruption
9	The bribe machine	Drunkenness/Bribery/Corruption
10	The merchants' petitions	Injustice/Indifference/Bribery
11	Khlestakov's wooing	Lust/Desire/Bourgeois formality
12	The betrothal	Unreality/Indifference/Corruption

Filling in material not originally included in Gogol's text, Meyerhold moved from the end of the boasting scene (Episode 7) with Khlestakov asleep on the sofa, to Episode 8, 'An Elephant Brought to its Knees'. This latter *jeu de théâtre* saw Khlestakov visited by a nightmarish gallery of townspeople, filing past him as he 'slept' on the sofa. Episode 9, 'Bribes', then merged all the separate inducements offered by the officials into one terrifying theatrical moment, a 'bribe machine'. Simultaneously all the officials' hands appeared from doors at the back, mechanically waving packets of money and chanting. Episode 10 moved to the merchants' petitions. With a huge table slanted across the stage to separate the two parties, the shopkeepers assailed Khlestakov en masse, urging him to support their cause. Episode 11 had Khlestakov dancing a formal quadrille with Marya and Anna, and declaring his undying love for each of them respectively. Finally, Episode 12 staged a trance-like blessing for Khlestakov and Marya before the former abruptly departed leaving the family in a continued state of somnambulism.

Following the thread of associations from episode to episode allows us to see the impact of Meyerhold's montage. What, for Gogol, was simply a change of acts, marking the end of one day and the dawning of another, becomes in Meyerhold's version a richly suggestive juxtaposition of ideas. The drunkenness of the previous episode (7) is carried over into the scenes of bribery. The next episode (8) becomes strangely distorted, therefore, by Khlestakov's inebriated perspective. This justifies the nightmarish expressions on the townspeople's faces and their dreamlike status, drawn as they are from Khlestakov's lustful imaginings. As Lunacharsky, the government minister for Arts and Education at the time, describes:

> He dreams of lines of flirting women, of trembling hands with offerings stretched out to him, of piles of envelopes with money falling down on him like rain.
>
> (Lunacharsky 1978: 67)

This image, once implanted in the audience's mind, is then juxtaposed with the bribe machine episode (9), when the officials shower him with money for real. Associations between the images of money, bribery, self-indulgence and drunkenness thus build as we enter into the next three episodes 10–12. The final idea, of course, which is implicit in Gogol but exploded out of Meyerhold's montage, is that Khlestakov's wooing of the women and his ultimate betrothal to Marya is also a corrupt and distorted commercial exchange, albeit of a higher order.

By far the best way to get a feeling for what Meyerhold was doing with his montage is to create an 'episode' of your own. That way you can begin to see how Meyerhold's mind was working when he approached Gogol's text, a definite bonus if you are to take this kind of practice any further. Box 2.2 gives a suggestion as to how you might begin this process, using Meyerhold's idea of 'filling in' material absent from the text.

Musicality and rhythm

At this point we need to step back and revisit the idea that Meyerhold's episodic structure celebrates the *individuality* of each scene. Clearly, this can only partly be true if what we have said about his use of montage is correct. A montage only begins to have an effect when it is viewed as a whole, when the collision of theatrical images is processed by the brain and an overall response is activated. Stand-alone scenes, then, need an overall structure and for Meyerhold this came from music; he even coined a new term for the integration of music and action in his production of *The Government Inspector:* 'musical realism'.

Box 2.2

- Take Gogol's text (Steven Mulrine's 1997 translation is a relatively new and accessible version) and read Act 1 (pp. 3–18).
- Discuss the major events, focusing mainly on the Mayor's reading of his letter.
- Working individually, recreate, in your imagination, the journey the letter might have taken to get to the Mayor's front door. Remember, the town is in the middle of nowhere and Russia is an immense country. The letter could have passed through many different environments – from snowscapes to sunny beaches.
- Share your thoughts and collate a picture of the most elaborate journey imaginable.
- Split into smaller groups and divide the journey up between you.
- Working primarily in a physical way, restricting the use of voice to ambient noises only, recreate the journey of the letter. The only prop you can use is a piece of paper to symbolise the letter.
- Link the work by insisting that one of the group passes the letter on to the next group. Again, ensure this transition is imaginative and well executed.
- Perform the episode, defining the space by locating a symbolic letterbox somewhere on stage (a chair will do). The episode can then conclude with the delivery of the letter.
- Reflect on the work created and discuss the effect of juxtaposing this episode with the opening of Act 1.

This much-debated term encapsulates a number of ideas, both large and small. In particular, it has implications for how we understand three key aspects of Meyerhold's theatrical thinking:

1. His overall vision of the actor.
2. His orchestration of action within scenes.
3. His overall approach to the play.

For the most fundamental of these questions, his overall vision of the actor, Paul Schmidt, a translator of writings on Meyerhold, offers a helpful analogy:

> When you watch [the Japanese musician] Yo-Yo Ma play the cello, you watch the physicality of the performance. That is, his physical relationship with the instrument and the way his body moves – that's all you can see, you can't see his mind, his training. You can watch his body move, his features, his face move and you listen to the music as he makes it. Impossible to slip even a knife point between the physicality of what you see and the music itself. You are watching a physical embodiment of the music.
>
> *(1998: 83)*

As a strings player himself, this explanation would have appealed to Meyerhold. The actor must emulate the integration of music and movement achieved naturally by a great musician. What Yo-Yo Ma is exhibiting is precisely this: an unconscious and seamless synthesis of movement and music, underpinned by years of training. He has achieved the state of 'physical musicality'.

But the actor has more work to do than this. Yo-Yo Ma's movements may be deeply informed by his understanding of the music he is making, but they are nevertheless arbitrary. He's in a constant state of improvisation as far as his external features are concerned. Meyerhold's actors had to *consciously* embody a very precisely prescribed physical score and had little room for any deviations from that score. In a sense the biomechanical actor has to think the other way round – to 'make movement' and imbue it with a sense of musicality. In Meyerhold's own words: 'The actor must know how to act "with the music" and not "to the music"' (Gladkov 1997: 115).

One such actor who understood perfectly this distinction was Erast Garin, Meyerhold's choice for the pivotal role of Khlestakov. Garin's interpretation of the clerk from St Petersburg clearly embodied this concept of musicality. Indeed, the contemporary descriptions of his performance point consistently to his *dance-like* quality, the result, perhaps, of his creative fusion of music and movement.

This was no more evident than in Episode 7, when Khlestakov/Garin danced a drunken reel, staggering from sofa to chair and from wife to daughter, as he told his ever more fanciful autobiography. The entire scene was dictated by the rhythmic shifts of Garin. First, as he began his speech, those gathered were entranced by the slow rhythms of his hypnotic tale, then he leapt up at the sound of Marya shrieking, jerking convulsively and causing the officials to tremble. He then boldly disarmed one of the soldiers and swung his sabre perilously around his head, before collapsing into the Mayor's arms (see Bogdanov 1997, for a fragment of this moment on film). The action was underscored by a waltz entitled 'The Fire of Desire Burns in My Blood', stressing in musical terms one of the overpowering themes of the scene and anticipating Khlestakov's efforts at seduction in Episode 11.

Rudnitsky makes explicit the musicality of Meyerhold's approach in this scene:

> The director's score for the episode was built on the sudden, practically unfounded alteration of Khlestakov's rhythms. Khlestakovianism was revealed by the lack of

motivation for the rhythmic shifts and was brought to a concentration of essential tragic absurdity when the officials, trembling with terror, shook and stood helplessly before the snoring monster from St Petersburg.

(Rudnitsky 1981: 402)

Thus, the absurdity of the officials' plight was communicated through the rhythmic structure of the scene. The erratic movements of Garin's Khlestakov somehow symbolised the ludicrous and illogical fawning of the town's dignitaries. Meyerhold's directorial score, his rhythmic orchestration of the activities of his cast, worked to reveal the themes of the episode and to determine its tragicomic genre. It was an essentially *operatic* approach with movement, sound and speech all playing their part in the creation of meaning.

This snapshot from the production gives an idea of Meyerhold's overall intentions. He viewed the actor and the composer in the same terms: both were charged with the task of expressive communication within a tightly controlled time structure. Meyerhold's job was to oversee the process so that the 'variations on a theme', as Houghton called the episodes, came together in a coherent manner.

In a very real way, Meyerhold was a kind of *conductor* of the production, defining a precise structure within which his actors could find their own expression. Ultimately the use of 'real' music, live or recorded, was subordinate in his mind to the actors internalising the *concept* of musicality, as Garin managed to do in the scene above. In fact, Meyerhold wanted finally to drop the use of any musical soundtrack, defining a vision of the performer which is reminiscent of Schmidt's cello player:

Music is [the actor's] best helper. It doesn't even need to be heard, but it must be felt. I dream of a production rehearsed to music but performed without music. Without it and yet with it, because the rhythm of the production will be organized according to music's laws and each performer will carry it within himself.

(Gladkov 1997: 115)

Design

The keystone in realising this musical vision of the play was the production's design. Meyerhold believed this so firmly that he took responsibility for it himself, recognising that his complex orchestration of events could only successfully be achieved if the design was fully in harmony with the rest of the production. There *was* a credited designer for the show, Victor Kiselyov, but he simply delivered Meyerhold's overall concept.

The design is a crucial aspect of any production, primarily because it organises the key dimension of an actor's world: *space*. As such, a design dictates:

- the movements of individual performers;
- the physical relationship *between* characters;
- the composition of any groupings or sub-groupings;
- the atmosphere of a particular scene.

A design also encompasses the look and feel of the props and furniture: those objects most closely related to the work of the actor. It can create a visual context for the action of the play and may suggest important details such as period, place and social position.

Rejecting Gogol's provincial location, Meyerhold set his *Government Inspector* in a city just like the capital, St Petersburg. He retained the Tsarist context of the play and used the production to satirise pre-revolutionary bourgeois values. Many critics, though, saw the parallels with post-revolutionary officialdom, and these cannot have been entirely unwarranted. To emphasise the extravagance of the ruling class, Meyerhold portrayed the Mayor's house as vast, setting each episode in a different room and giving the women, in particular, added costume changes. He also exaggerated the size of the Mayor's furniture, creating a distorted and unsettling vision of a moneyed class.

But perhaps most important of all the design choices made by Meyerhold was the way in which he chose to 'serve up' his production to his spectators. He understood that it was not so much *what* they viewed but *how* they viewed the production that was important. The 'rhythm' of the episodic structure had in some way to be translated into the design so that the audience could appreciate the play in its new format. Meyerhold's answer was bold and ingenious, he called it 'kinetic staging'.

The word 'kinetic' comes from the ancient Greek verb *kinein*, 'to move', and Meyerhold's design was founded on this principle. It was a 'moving' stage. He realised that unless the scenery could be turned around between scenes very quickly the whole production would come to a standstill. So, in characteristic fashion, Meyerhold looked back into the past to find a solution for the present. He created a modern-day classical stage, fusing the *theatron* of the ancient Greeks with the up-to-date cinema techniques of the day.

The backdrop was dominated by a series of eleven doors, fashioned out of hardwood and arching across the whole of the back of the stage. Two more pairs of doors were situated on each side, towards the forestage, totalling fifteen – the number of episodes in the play. This was the 'wide-shot' or open stage, used for five of the episodes. The rest of the scenes (with one exception) were staged on a tiny platform, just 4.25 by 3.5 metres (Braun 1995: 231), which was wheeled out silently through the middle doors at the back. Here was the similarity with the Greek stage, for Meyerhold's truck closely resembled the *ekkyklema* of classical tragedy, designed to roll out precisely composed tableaux of death in plays such as Aeschylus's *Oresteia*. Meyerhold also used his *ekkyklema* to reveal frozen figures, but with his 'close-ups' the ensemble sprung into life as the episode began. The only other scene – Episode 3 – was flown in as an entirely separate set.

The detailed pattern of wide-shots (on the open stage) and close-ups (on the platform) was as follows:

Episode	Title	Staging
1	Chmykhov's Letter	Platform
2	An Unforeseen Occurrence	Platform
3	After Penza	Flown-in 'room'
4	Unicorn	Platform
5	Filled with the Tend'rest Love	Platform
6	The Procession	Open stage (+ balustrade)
7	Behind a Bottle of 'Tolstobriucha'	Platform (+ split balustrade)
8	An Elephant Brought to its Knees	Open stage
9	Bribes	Open stage
10	Mr High Finance	Open stage (+ long table)
11	Embrace Me Do	Platform
12	The Blessing	Platform
13	Dreams of St Petersburg	Platform
14	A Fine Old Celebration	Platform
15	Unprecedented Confusion	Open stage

This table of Meyerhold's staging reveals some interesting facts about his directorial thinking for *The Government Inspector:*

1 The uniqueness of the scene in the hotel room – After Penza.
2 The concentration of attention on the small platform, even for large scenes.
3 The range of different locations suggested by the platform.
4 The extent to which he felt it necessary to delineate the space of the open stage with other pieces of furniture or scenery.
5 The constant need to keep the production *moving*.

In terms of the staging of After Penza, Meyerhold was honouring Gogol's original text. The hotel *is* unique in the play. It contains the only scene to take place outside of the Mayor's house, the only moment where we see *real* poverty and grime as opposed to the metaphorical dirt of corruption. Flying the whole episode in from above stressed that the hotel was 'another world', populated not by masters, as with the rest of the play, but by servants.

The second point relates to one of the boldest design choices of all. With a large stage and a huge cast at his disposal, Meyerhold chose to restrict the majority of the action to a platform a little less than fifteen metres square. This did not mean, however, that he neglected to use the full ensemble for the platform scenes. On the contrary, Meyerhold meticulously composed huge canvases made up of fifty or more actors, all beautifully crammed on to the platform. He likened it to 'construct[ing] a palace on the tip of a needle' and it was a central part of his philosophy of acting. 'Having constructed such a platform, it became possible for me to comprehend the beauty of . . . *self-limitation,*' he argued, adding that *restrictions* encourage 'true craftsmanship' (Rudnitsky 1981: 391). It was a message which spoke volumes, not just about the production but about the acting system which informed the work: biomechanics.

The last three points may be dealt with as one. The use of the platform allowed the multiple locations of the production to be changed almost instantaneously, for there was not just one platform but two. While one scene was playing in front of the doors the next scene could be set behind them, and at the end of the episode the two could be swapped. Thus, the production was always 'on the move', fluidly transforming from location to location and punctuated by the open-stage scenes. These Meyerhold used carefully, either to allow for an unusually expansive vista (as in the Bribes scene), to suggest the outdoors (as in The Procession) or to accentuate the divide between Khlestakov and the townspeople (as in Mr High Finance). Meyerhold also reserved the open stage for the final episode, stripping back all the properties and furniture used before to present his gallery of mannequins: the emptiness of Tsarist Russia underlined in a deft theatrical coup.

Acting style: Chaplin meets Hoffmann

If Meyerhold likened his design to the cinema, he also appealed to the movies in describing the style of acting he was looking for in his cast:

> Remember Chaplin . . . what complicated scenes he does, or Keaton – and he acts in a space of a couple of yards, sometimes half that, sometimes simply sitting on a chair.
> *(Hoover 1974: 160)*

Chaplin and Keaton, as silent-movie stars, encapsulated the physical clarity and economy of craft Meyerhold was seeking in his production. Both could express a virtuosic range of skills and yet still hit their mark for the camera. They understood the power of 'composition' on the big screen, using all of their physical resources to tell the story. And they caught the essence of the genre Meyerhold wanted – the mix of tragedy and comedy, melodrama and farce. Meyerhold also recreated the frantic rhythms and knockabout action of the Keystone Cops in the final episode (15), choreographing a comical and panic-stricken exit by the police, following the announcement of the real Inspector's arrival. He enjoyed the satirical mix of authority and buffoonery just as much as the early American filmmakers.

The other frequently cited influence is that of E.T.A. Hoffmann, especially in relation to Garin's playing of Khlestakov. This is how his first entrance, in After Penza, was described by one critic:

> He appears onstage, a character from some tale by Hoffmann, slender, clad in black with a stiff mannered gait, strange spectacles, a sinister old fashioned tall hat, a rug and a cane, apparently tormented by some private vision.
>
> *(Braun 2016: 266)*

Hoffmann's influence explained Meyerhold's sinister reading of Khlestakov, also partly inspired by Michael Chekhov's dark portrayal of the character in 1921. The entrance seems consciously to reverse that of Coppelius in Hoffmann's *The Sandman* (1816), who, rather than descending the staircase like Garin, climbs the stairs, putting the fear of God into the child, Nathaniel:

> The image of the cruel sandman now assumed hideous detail within me, and when I heard the sound of clumping coming up the stairs in the evening I trembled with fear and terror.
>
> *(Hoffmann 1982: 87)*

Meyerhold wanted to induce echoes of this response in his audience, justifying the panicked reactions of the dignitaries in the previous episode by showing Khlestakov as an altogether more calculating and mysterious individual than was customary.

Many critics have highlighted this departure from the tradition of playing Khlestakov, using it as evidence of yet more radical reinterpreting by the director. But Meyerhold's choices were surprisingly in tune with Gogol's view of the character. Although he clearly believed the servant, Osip, to be Khlestakov's mental superior, Gogol does describe the St Petersburg official as 'phantasmagorical', adding, as we noted in the section on characterisation: 'everything about him is surprising, unexpected' (Gogol 1980: 173).

It was this idea of 'unpredictability' that became the leitmotif for the characterisation of Khlestakov: physically, vocally and rhythmically. Like a storyteller, he transformed from one character to another, changing his 'mask', as the critic Boris Alpers noted, to fit the moment. One minute he was an invalid with the Mayor, broken by poverty and clutching a stick, the next he was a puffed-up and accusatory officer, transforming himself with a simple waft of his cloak. Such instability of character served only to increase his air of mystery.

So what was the result of this mixture of Hollywood and Hoffmann? Nick Worrall picks up the account where we left off. Dressed in the black garb described above, Garin paused on the landing of the flown-in scene. Next:

> He came down the stairs. Then, instead of turning into the room, [he] advanced straight forwards, as if threatening to enter the auditorium. Then he stopped, turned suddenly to the left, presenting his profile to the audience and, with a swift movement, cracked

his cane sharply across the table. He then detached a [bread] roll [from his button hole] and held it out to Osip – 'Here, it's for you'.

(Worrall 1972: 82)

The fusion of the sinister and the farcical is beautifully caught in this extract. First, like a grim reaper, Khlestakov glides into the space, wielding his cane like a scythe. Next, he plucks an incongruous bread roll from his costume and with great seriousness proffers it to his hungry servant. The moment is both comic and tragic, a collision of ideas perhaps best symbolised in the emblem of the cane: is it Chaplin's or Coppelius's? Take your pick!

The training beneath: biomechanics in The Government Inspector

If you were to compare *The Government Inspector* (1926) with a production from earlier in the decade – *The Magnanimous Cuckold* (1922), for example – you might well conclude that there was *no* evidence of any biomechanics in Meyerhold's masterpiece. Whereas the constructivist stage for Crommelynck's play reflected the new machine age, with the actors recreating the étude of 'The Slap' within the performance, the nineteenth-century setting for *The Government Inspector* seemed far removed from its contemporary context and the performers offered no obvious indications of any biomechanical training.

But this did not mean, of course, that there *was* no training. In fact, Meyerhold's approach to Gogol's play confirmed a new maturity in the way he integrated his teaching in the studio with his directing in the theatre. Rather like his ultimate dream of a musical production without the music, biomechanics was also 'silent' or unseen in *The Government Inspector*. But it was no less influential for that.

Indeed, Meyerhold's seamless assimilation of training and text offers us a model of how to relate 'process' to 'product'. The shapes and rhythms of the études cannot simply be lifted, unchanged, on to a stage and imposed on a character. They must be absorbed, embodied, made part of you in some way. Only then is it possible to exploit creatively the underlying theatrical skills developed by the training. As Meyerhold himself said, 'technique arms the imagination' (Schmidt 1996: 41), and he drew on both to realise his vision of Gogol's drama.

With a trained eye, the 'unseen' elements of biomechanics come into focus. They are evident in the:

- rhythms of the actors;
- discipline of the ensemble;
- constant surprises;
- gestural patterns of the performers;
- dance-like quality of the action;
- extensive 'play with props';
- conscious attention to external form;
- responsiveness of the actors.

Some of these things may not be clear [yet], but a good number of these ideas should now be familiar to you. You may indeed be able to add to this list. With these aspects in mind, then, read the following description from one of the most celebrated ensemble moments in the production (Episode 14). See if you can identify the latent influence of biomechanics:

> The small platform was framed by the splendid restless drawing of a gold triple mirror, filled to the limit by figures of officials and their wives, and soldiers. Uniforms shone, women's bare shoulders gleamed. Guests continued to arrive with a happy roar. There

was nowhere to sit, chairs were being brought in, floated over heads, rocked, were put down. The Jewish orchestra behind the scenes played a march.... The mass of humanity ... wavered, shifted, babbled and pressed toward the Mayor and Anna Andreevna, who were in the right corner of the platform. Then the postmaster appeared and made his way through the crowd, jumping on chairs, falling down and disappearing from view. When he stopped, finally, clutching the fateful opened letter in his hand, the entire crowd immediately changed its orientation and pressed to the left corner, where the reading began.

(Rudnitsky 1981: 417)

Thus, the moment where the Postmaster reads Khlestakov's incriminating letter is set up. It was a scene which simply could not have been either conceived or achieved without an understanding of biomechanics.

The overall structure of the moment mirrors that of an étude: the *otkaz,* or preparation, is extensive and drawn out as the Postmaster fights to get a seat; the *posil',* or action, is marked by the ensemble's rapid change of orientation; and the *tochka,* or 'end point', is the instant held by the Postmaster as he prepares to read the letter. (This is the moment which is documented in the famous photograph.)

The rigid discipline of the ensemble testifies to the collective training of biomechanics, slowly building up an unspoken understanding between actors which is underpinned by a strong sense of rhythm. Here, there are two rhythms at work – the individual bumbling of the Postmaster, set against the collective rhythm of the mass as they respond to the new focus and pan round to take in the letter.

The game with the chairs (reminiscent of companies such as Complicite) is a development from the work with sticks. Props became beautiful in the hands of Meyerhold's actors – a result of arduous work balancing, throwing and catching various objects in the studio. The music of the orchestra lends the whole passage with the chairs a feeling of a formal dance, even though chaos reigns on the platform.

But of course, the final measure of the discipline of this scene is that chaos *doesn't* actually reign. We only see the external and carefully composed *form* of chaos. No one falls off from the huge pyramid, no one breaks the rhythmic cohesion of the ensemble, everyone works together to build their palace on a needle point. This must have been the ultimate test of Meyerhold's adage that limitations breed artistry and it can only have come from the training which preaches the same message: biomechanics.

The grotesque – the synthesis of Meyerhold's ideas

By now, is should be clear why Meyerhold's *Government Inspector* is so important. It constitutes the grand synthesis of his ideas. It is empirical evidence of the mature director-author displaying his undisputed talent for directing. I am by no means the first to argue this, but I hope that this section has illustrated something new: the way in which this seminal production acted as a locus for so many of Meyerhold's activities and theories.

One of the clearest indicators of this is the extent to which the production achieved Meyerhold's defining style: the grotesque. For the grotesque by nature is synthetic, it borrows from a range of sources and combines them in unusual and thought-provoking ways. It does this with the aim of shifting an audience's perspective, surprising them into new discoveries. For Meyerhold the grotesque was an intrinsic aspect of Gogol's dramaturgy:

> Gogol was fond of saying that funny things often become sad if you look enough at them. This transformation of mirth into sadness is the conjuring trick of Gogol's dramatic style.

(Braun 2016: 263)

Having seen too many frothy, vaudeville-inspired versions of Gogol's text, Meyerhold wanted to shift its genre into the darker, more challenging arena of tragicomedy. He looked to Hoffmann, as we have seen, for one model of the grotesque and to Chaplin for another. He combined slapstick clowning with the stark images of death in the dumb show. He designed his stage so that it could constantly mutate and transform. He peppered the production with theatrical surprises and unexpected delights. He drew out the hitherto understated satirical bite of Gogol's play. He included elements of the mysterious and of 'other worldliness', particularly in the drunken episodes. And, in his creative montage, he 'stretched' the play, reconfiguring it in order to shift the audience's perspective. In a way, this was a theatrical response to what Gogol is saying above about perception: look long enough at this play (just over four hours, in fact) and you will begin to see it differently.

All of these techniques are part of Meyerhold's overarching pursuit of the grotesque. But the ultimate question remains: how did they impact on the audience? The eyewitness testimonies are sharply divided on this question. *The Government Inspector* led to huge debates and disputes in the press and had stimulated three book-long critiques within a year of its opening. This was, of course, the ideal response for Meyerhold, who revelled in controversy and worried if too many people praised his productions.

Such disagreement is in itself evidence of the grotesque at work, challenging its audiences, unsettling them and forcing them to see things differently. Harold Clurman, the American writer and director, who saw the production in the 1920s, puts his finger on this effect beautifully:

> A strange feeling comes from this production: it is very funny and it's very tomblike. It has a definite macabre quality – cold, beautiful, grimacing, distorted and graceful. . . . The production ends with the actors running off stage laughing while on stage we see the prototypes who are puppets. Meyerhold's *Revisor* [*The Government Inspector*] is a masterpiece, but somehow not a warming one, it leaves one slightly uncomfortable.
>
> *(Clurman 1998: 80)*

There could be no better measure of the power of the grotesque, no clearer indication of how seriously Meyerhold had taken Gogol's challenge and how effectively he had risen to it.

There were fewer landmark productions after *The Government Inspector* at the Meyerhold Theatre. Soon the pressure of censorship was to increase to a level which clearly stifled the creativity of the Master. But this time the limitations imposed on Meyerhold were not the kind which led to greater artistry. They led instead to public criticism, to interrogation, to prison and finally to execution. After symbolising such a creative fusion of Meyerholdian techniques, *The Government Inspector* became one of the productions cited as evidence of Meyerhold's anti-governmental stance. It was simply (and chillingly) labelled a 'mistake'.

Vsevolod Meyerhold paid the ultimate price for making things uncomfortable.

Further reading

Books and articles

Banham, Martin (ed.) (1992) *The Cambridge Guide to Theatre,* Cambridge: Cambridge University Press.
Bann, Stephen (ed.) (1974) *The Tradition of Constructivism,* New York: Da Capo.
Barba, Eugenio and Savarese, Nicola (1991) *A Dictionary of Theatre Anthropology: The Secret Art of the Performer,* trans. Richard Fowler, London: Routledge.
Benedetti, Jean (1990) *Stanislavski: A Biography,* London: Methuen.
Braun, Edward (1995) *A Revolution in Theatre*, London: Methuen.

——— (ed.) (2016) *Meyerhold on Theatre*, Fourth Edition with an Introduction by Jonathan Pitches, London: Bloomsbury Methuen Drama.
Brecht, Bertolt (1978) *Brecht on Theatre,* trans. John Willett, London: Methuen.
Carter, Angela (ed.) (1990) *The Virago Book of Fairy Tales,* London: Virago Press.
Chekhov, Anton (1991) *Plays,* trans. Michael Frayn, London: Methuen.
Clurman, Harold (1998) 'An Excerpt from Harold Clurman's Unpublished Diary', *Theater* 28(2): 79–80.
Deák, Frantisek (1982) 'Meyerhold's Staging of Sister Beatrice', *The Drama Review* 26(1): 41–50.
Eisenstein, Sergei (1988) *Writings: Vol 1, 1922–1934,* trans. and ed. Richard Taylor, London: British Film Institute.
Fitzpatrick, Sheila (1982) *The Russian Revolution 1917–1932,* Oxford: Oxford University Press.
Forsyth, James (1977) *Listening to the Wind: An Introduction to Alexander Blok,* Oxford: William A. Meeuws.
Frost, Anthony and Yarrow, Ralph (1990) *Improvisation in Drama,* London: Macmillan.
Gladkov, Aleksandr (1997) *Meyerhold Speaks, Meyerhold Rehearses,* trans. Alma Law, London: Harwood Academic Publishers.
Gogol, Nikolai (1980) *The Theater of Nikolay Gogol,* trans. and intro. Milton Ehre, Chicago, IL: University Press of Chicago.
——— (1997) *The Government Inspector,* trans. Steven Mulrine, London: Nick Hern Books.
Gordon, Mel (1995) 'Meyerhold's Biomechanics', in Philip Zarrilli (ed.) *Acting (Re)Considered,* London: Routledge.
Gorky, Maxim, Radek, Karl, Bukharin, Nikolai and Zhdanov, Andrei (1977) *Soviet Writers Congress 1934: The Debate on Socialist Realism and Modernism,* London: Lawrence & Wishart.
Green, Michael (ed.) (1986) *Russian Symbolist Theatre,* Ann Arbor, MI: Ardis.
Hawkins-Dady, Mark (1987) 'Gogol's "The Government Inspector" at the National Theatre, 1985', *New Theatre Quarterly* 3(12): 358–376.
Hodge, Alison (ed.) (2010) *Actor Training,* Second Edition, London: Routledge.
Hoffmann, E. T. A. (1982) *Tales of Hoffmann,* trans. R. J. Hollingdale, London: Penguin Classics.
Hoover, Marjorie L. (1974) *Meyerhold: The Art of Conscious Theater,* Amherst, MA: University of Massachusetts Press.
Houghton, Norris (1938) *Moscow Rehearsals,* London: George Allen & Unwin.
Ibsen, Henrik (1980) *Plays: Two,* trans. Michael Meyer, London: Methuen.
Law, Alma (1982) 'The Magnanimous Cuckold', *The Drama Review* 26(1), Spring: 61–86.
——— and Gordon, Mel (1996) *Meyerhold, Eisenstein and Biomechanics,* London: McFarland.
Leach, Robert (1989) *Vsevolod Meyerhold,* Cambridge: Cambridge University Press.
——— (1994) *Revolutionary Theatre,* London: Routledge.
——— (2010) 'Meyerhold and Biomechanics', in Alison Hodge (ed.) *Actor Training,* London: Routledge.
Lunacharsky, A. V. (1978) 'Gogol-Meyerhold's "The Inspector General"', *October* 7, Winter: 57–70.
Magarshack, David (1957) *Gogol: A Life,* London: Faber & Faber.
——— (1986) *Stanislavsky: A Life,* London: Faber.
Mayakovsky, Vladimir (1995) *Mayakovsky: Plays,* trans. Guy Daniels, Evanston, IL: Northwestern University Press.
Nemirovich-Danchenko, Vladimir (1968) *My Life in the Russian Theatre,* trans. John Cournos, New York: Theatre Arts Books.
Pavlov, Ivan (1927) *Conditioned Reflexes: An Investigation of the Physiological Activity of the Cerebral Cortex,* trans. G. V. Anrep, New York: Dover Publications.
Pérez Sánchez, Alfonso E. and Gállego, Julián (1995) *Goya: The Complete Etchings and Lithographs,* Munich: Prestel-Verlag.
Pitches, Jonathan (2007) 'Tracing/Training Rebellion: Object Work in Meyerhold's Biomechanics', *Performance Research* 12(4): 97–103.
——— (2009) *Science and the Stanislavsky Tradition of Acting,* London and New York: Routledge.
——— and Shrubsall, Anthony (1997) 'Two Perspectives on the Phenomenon of Biomechanics in Contemporary Performance: An Account of Gogol's "Government Inspector" in Production', *Studies in Theatre Production* 16: 93–128.
Rudlin, John (1994) *Commedia dell'Arte: An Actor's Handbook,* London: Routledge.
Rudnitsky, Konstantin (1981) *Meyerhold the Director,* trans. George Petrov, Ann Arbor, MI: Ardis.
——— (1988) *Russian and Soviet Theatre,* trans. Roxane Permar, London: Thames & Hudson.
Schmidt, Paul (ed.) (1996) *Meyerhold at Work,* New York: Applause.

—— (1998) 'Acting Music, Scoring Text', *Theater* 28(2): 81–85.
Schuler, Catherine (1996) *Women in Russian Theatre: The Actress in the Silver Age*, London: Routledge.
Stanislavsky, Constantin (1980) *My Life in Art,* trans. J. J. Robbins, London: Methuen.
Symons, James M. (1971) *Meyerhold's Theatre of the Grotesque: Post Revolutionary Productions, 1920–1932*, Coral Gables, FL: University of Miami Press.
Taylor, Frederick Winslow (1947) *Scientific Management,* New York: Harper & Row.
Worrall, Nick (1972) 'Meyerhold Directs Gogol's "Government Inspector"', *Theatre Quarterly* 2: 75–95.
—— (1982) Nikolai Gogol and Ivan Turgenev, London: Macmillan.
Zarrilli, Phillip (ed.) (1995) *Acting (Re)Considered,* London: Routledge.

Films and videos

Bogdanov, Gennadi (1997) *Meyerhold's Theater and Biomechanics,* Berlin: Mime Centrum (video).
—— (1998) *Meyerhold's Biomechanics and Rhythm*, 6 Volumes, Exeter: Arts Documentation Unit (video).
—— and Raüke, Ralf (1995) *Meyerhold's* Throwing the Stone, Exeter: Arts Documentation Unit (video).
Chaplin, Charlie (dir.) (1936) *Modern Times*, 87 minutes (film).
Eisenstein, Sergei (dir.) (1928) *October*, 90 minutes (film).
Levinski, Aleksei (1995) *Meyerhold's Biomechanics: A Workshop,* Exeter: Arts Documentation Unit (video).

3
COPEAU (1879–1949)

Mark Evans

3.1 The life of Jacques Copeau

In the history of the French theatre there are two periods: before and after Copeau.
(Albert Camus in Saint-Denis 1982: 32)

Jacques Copeau's international success in the fields of journalism, playwriting, directing, acting and teaching represent a level of achievement unmatched in the history of modern French, and perhaps even modern European, theatre. At a time when French theatre was desperately in need of direction and purpose, Copeau, through his writing, his teaching and his practice, offered inspiration and a ceaseless pursuit of quality. His influence on French cultural policy has been profound and his work has also left its mark on the practice and policy of major British and American theatrical institutions. Copeau brought to the theatre of his time a new vitality, purposefulness and energy; an energy based on the actor's physical skills, on a vision of the role of theatre, and on an instinctive feel for the rhythmic and structural demands of a play. In his search for a revitalised theatre – for a theatre which, as in Ancient Greece or Medieval Europe, was able to play a social and moral role with the community – he drew together the influences of other innovators such as Edward Gordon Craig, Adolphe Appia, Emile Jaques-Dalcroze and Konstantin Stanislavsky into a unique and successful synthesis. His innovative work on the use of masks, improvisation, mime and physical expression, as training tools for the actor and as elements within the creation and presentation of performance, have led to his current recognition as a key figure in the history of what is now referred to as 'physical theatre'.

Copeau's influence on the development of twentieth-century theatre practice has been diverse and extensive. His commitment to a true ensemble company where actors would play leading roles in one production and minor parts in the next, where the repertoire would include classical revivals and contemporary writing, was a profound influence on the founding principles of the Royal Shakespeare Company in the early 1960s. His belief in the value of a complete and rounded education for the student actor – preparing not just for the theatre of yesterday, but also for the theatre of today and tomorrow – can be seen underpinning the philosophies of many of the leading European and American drama schools. Copeau wrote many articles and pamphlets, but, unlike Konstantin Stanislavsky or Michael Chekhov, he left no handbook outlining his techniques. Though he promoted a broad cultural education for his students, he was equally clear that study through reading was not the way to educate the actor. His legacy has been a practical one; a way of crafting drama handed down by teachers and practitioners, learned through experience and participation. The purity and simplicity of his purpose and his work, his belief in the moral and social power of theatre, and his passionate commitment to the training of the actor's body and mind as well as their voice, have shaped and inspired the work of so many of those who followed after him, both in France and further afield. Much that is now commonplace in contemporary theatre practice can be traced directly back to the work of Copeau and his small group of collaborators during the few decades between the two World Wars. If his influence is not so clearly evident at the start of the twenty-first century, then that is in part because it is so firmly embedded in the cultural framework of the British, European and American theatre industries that it has become taken for granted.

My own introduction to Copeau's work came during my three years as a mime student in London and Paris during the early 1980s. While I grappled with the rigorous and exacting demands of corporeal mime and physical theatre techniques, I found myself curious to discover more about the history and background of the skills that I was acquiring. Copeau's influence has in this sense been a constant presence throughout my career – through my training with Jacques Lecoq, my work in community theatre, and my own teaching. Though Copeau began as a journalist and wrote many pamphlets, articles and lectures, my own experience confirms for me that his theatre methods have been kept alive not only through publication, but also through their dissemination down a line of teachers and students, directors and actors – a living and changing heritage against which his writings need to be seen not as the main text, but as the footnotes, anecdotes and appendices. This book aims to draw attention to Copeau's achievements, practices and ideas so that they may continue to enrich and encourage the practice of new generations of theatre makers.

The formative years

Jacques Copeau was born on 4 February 1879, at 76 rue du Faubourg Saint-Denis in the 10th Arrondissement of Paris. The France in which he grew up was a country of political uncertainty, a country still dealing with the aftermath of the Franco-Prussian War (1870–1871). The war had been a bitter conflict, leading eventually to the end of the Second Empire and the beginning of the Third Republic in France, and the founding of the German Empire. When peace returned to France, it brought with it relative economic prosperity and a growth in cultural activity. Over the following decades France continued to struggle with some profound political and social problems, most notable of which was the notorious Dreyfus affair in which a Jewish soldier was wrongly accused of treason; at the same time, Paris became one of the great cultural capitals of the continent, drawing to it modern artists and writers from all corners of Europe. This social and economic climate enabled middle-class families, such as that of Victor and Hélène Copeau, to prosper and survive, and perhaps encouraged their son's cultural dreams and aspirations. They were a reasonably well off middle class family who owned a small iron factory in Raucourt in the Ardennes, and although they themselves had no notable literary or theatrical connections or background, their son found inspiration in the occasional family trips to performances, the family's small library of melodramas, and from the games and flights of imagination that filled his childhood days. The young Copeau used to imagine the rooftop and courtyard views from his family's house as a stage for his childhood fantasies. His mind, even at that early stage, noting the dramatic potential of the bare architectural spaces – 'like a desert sunrise or a stage after the performance' (Copeau 1990: 5) – and the rich details of everyday activity around him. His childhood passion for games was intense. In his later work, Copeau was often to return to his childhood games and imaginings with a deeply felt sense of their value:

> The mind of a child wanders amid such semblances. He links his own fairyland to the bits of reality that he observes with a relentless eye and absorbs with a bold heart. This is the way we compose our first dramas, which we try out in our games and mull over in silence.
>
> *(Copeau 1990: 6)*

Copeau was a pupil at the Lycée Condorcet (in the nearby 9th Arrondissement) from 1889 to 1897, during which time he attended various theatre performances at the Théâtre-Libre, the Comédie-Française and the Châtelet: 'I used to sneak out of the house to go and spend the few sous I had carefully saved from my pocket money to attend the theatre' (Copeau 1990: 211). The director André Antoine was an important and significant early influence, as he was for many young theatre enthusiasts at the end of the nineteenth century. Copeau was riveted by Antoine's performance in Jules Lemaitre's *L'Age Difficile*, 'Everything he did fascinated me' (ibid.), and, despite the differences in their ideas, Antoine was to prove a friend and supporter of Copeau's work in the years to come.

In his final year at the Lycée, Copeau's first play, *Brouillard du Matin* (*Morning Fog*), was performed by his fellow pupils. The young Copeau was enthused by the success of his first experience of making theatre; the fact that it was his own play, put on by himself, must have been important in nurturing his inner belief in the value and power of theatre.

André Antoine (1858–1943) was a key theatrical reformer and a leading figure in the development of theatrical naturalism. In 1887, with the support of Émile Zola, the novelist and critic who had founded the Naturalist movement in literature, Antoine established the Théâtre Libre. Through his work he stressed the close and scientific observation of everyday life over conventional play construction and hackneyed acting techniques. He later managed both the Théâtre Antoine and the Odéon, retiring after the First World War to concentrate on dramatic criticism. His influence both in France and further abroad was profound, and his support for the next generation of dramatists and theatre-makers was generous and influential.

In September 1897 he visited London with his father, seeing the famous English actor-manager Sir Johnston Forbes-Robertson (1853–1937) and the leading actress Mrs Patrick Campbell (1865–1940) in *Hamlet*. On his return he enrolled at the Sorbonne for a degree in literature and philosophy, however he was far more enthusiastic about attending the latest theatre shows than he was about attending his lectures. What money he had he continued to spend on going to performances at the Théâtre Antoine and at the Théâtre de l'Oeuvre, two of the leading avant-garde theatres of the time. He was present at the opening night of Alfred Jarry's *Ubu Roi* in 1896, a seminal moment in European theatre history (Donahue, 2008: 5). Despite failing his written exams at the Sorbonne, Copeau continued with his own writing, completing a one-act play, *La Sève* (*The Essence*), and drafting the first outline of his autobiographical play, *La Maison Natale* (*The Birthplace*). In June 1901 Copeau's father died; now in his early twenties, he decided to abandon his studies, preferring instead to see the world. He undertook a trip to Scandinavia, including a stay in Denmark where in June 1902 he married a young Danish woman, Agnes

Thomsen, whom he had first met in Paris six years earlier. Within the year, Agnes gave birth to their first child, a daughter, Marie-Hélène. Money was inevitably tight, but Copeau managed to support his family by giving private French lessons. At the same time, he continued with his writing, sending several articles to Parisian periodicals. One of these articles caught the eye of its subject, the author André Gide, who wrote to Copeau in Copenhagen, encouraging the young writer to continue with his efforts. This correspondence marked the start of a long and warm friendship between the two.

Gide persuaded Copeau to return to Paris with his young family. Copeau's original intention was to continue with his writing, however now that his father had died he was obliged once more to leave Paris – this time to manage the family's iron factory, which he did from 1903 until the business went bankrupt in 1905. His familial loyalty at this important point in his life is an early indicator of his strong sense of moral responsibility and of his personal resolve in the face of fate. As Copeau was ruefully to remark some twenty or so years later: 'From our twentieth or twenty-fifth year on . . . We cease to control our life; it controls us!' (Copeau 1990: 6).

> **André Gide** (1869–1951) was a French novelist and playwright, whose works explore the tensions between individual hedonism and moral responsibility. His dramatic work included plays as well as translations and adaptations of Shakespeare and Kafka. He received the Nobel Prize for Literature in 1947.

Copeau was now twenty-seven, but according to his friend Gide he looked ten years older; the cares and uncertainties of his twenties had clearly taken their toll. Once again he sought to establish himself in the theatre career he so earnestly desired. Despite his friends' continuing support and encouragement, he complained that he was getting nowhere, 'I do not have the right milieu' (Copeau in Kurtz 1999: 5). Copeau's sense of isolation has to be understood in its context; despite the activities of a few innovators, drama in Paris at this time was dominated by the commercial theatres of the boulevards, and by the artistic and cultural tastes associated with the *belle époque*. He found it difficult to consider how he could work in an art form seemingly so concerned with surface, success, and notoriety at any cost.

> The **belle époque** was marked by a taste for all things beautiful and ornate. This period was most particularly associated with the city of Paris between the years 1871 and 1914. Across Europe, scientific and political progress had made for a life that was, on the face of things, comfortable and satisfying – at least for the well-to-do. At its best, this period produced work which was graceful, luxurious to the eye, and enchanting, such as the decorative flourishes of *Art Nouveau*. At its worst, it could produce frivolous and sensational novelty and superficial effect. In the Parisian boulevard theatre of the turn of the century this lead to a system dominated by the egos of star actors and fascinated by the spectacular, the sentimental, the melodramatic and the trivial.

In order to support his family, he turned instead to the world of modern art and, with a recommendation from his friend the painter Albert Besnard, gained work as an exhibition director and salesman at the Georges Petit Gallery. Copeau continued working at the gallery for four years, juggling his work with his writing – doing what he could to champion theatrical reform, and to demand moral integrity and artistic rigour from the critics. In 1907, he was offered the opportunity to take over from Léon Blum as drama critic for the *Grande Revue* – a post which finally gave him access to a wider public. This proved to be an important turning point in Copeau's fortunes, as two years later, Copeau, together with Gide, Jean Schlumberger, André Ruyters and Henri Ghéon, founded the *Nouvelle Revue Française*, which was to become one of the leading French journals of the early twentieth century. Finally Copeau had the financial security he needed to support his family, and more significantly to pursue his own interests in theatre.

Copeau could now start to devote more time to his writing and to his own creative interests. He cut his teeth as a critic by writing for a wide range of journals and newspapers between 1905 and 1913. He was recognised as an important and successful critic – widely read, culturally knowledgeable, perceptive and incisive (Paul 1977: 221). Compared to the polite, anecdotal and descriptive style of most of his contemporaries, Copeau's reviews lambasted the mediocrity and complacency of the Paris boulevard theatres, and repeatedly called to question the extensive commercialisation of the theatre of the time. Underlying his critical writing was a belief in theatre's potential to reveal the true inner dimensions of human life. What Copeau could not bear was the empty theatricality of the commercial theatres, where tricks, traditional stage 'business', hackneyed dialogue and over-simplified ideas of character and motivation brought popular success but revealed little of consequence about the nature of human existence (ibid.: 226).

His first opportunity to put his own head over the parapet came with an invitation from Jacques Rouché to write a play for the 1910–1911 season of the Théâtre des Arts. Copeau chose to adapt and stage Fyodor Dostoyevsky's novel *Les Frères Karamazov* (*The Brothers Karamazov*). The production opened on 6 April 1911, and was hailed as a resounding success by the Parisian critics. It was to be revived three times by Copeau during the decade or so that followed. On the heels of this success he was able to visit London and discuss an English revival of *Karamazov* with the actor-manager Herbert Beerbohm Tree, and also to meet the dancer Isadora Duncan. Over the next year, he saw the Ballet Russes perform in Paris, and visited London where he attended a performance of Harley Granville Barker's production of *Twelfth Night* and met with the playwright George Bernard Shaw. Without a doubt the success of *Les Frères Karamazov*, and his subsequent contact with some of the key figures of European theatre, was a major factor in Copeau's decision in 1913 to follow his own vision and form a new theatre company.

Harley Granville-Barker (1877–1946) was an English actor, director, critic and playwright. After initial success as an actor, Granville-Barker took out a lease on the Royal Court Theatre in London in 1904, where he produced plays by some of the leading European playwrights of the period: George Bernard Shaw (1856–1950), Henrik Ibsen (1828–1906) and Maurice Maeterlinck (1862–1949). He also produced several of his own plays, as well as ground-breaking productions of Shakespeare's *Twelfth Night* and *The Winter's Tale*. His productions were notable for their lack of declamatory diction, the continuous flow of scenes, the use of open staging, and an emphasis on ensemble performance. In 1923 he moved to Paris, where he began a highly influential series of *Prefaces to Shakespeare* (1927–1948), in which he offered the first comprehensive analysis of the plays from the perspective of the modern actor and director. After working in America during the Second World War, he returned to Paris in 1946, where he died later that year.

The Théâtre du Vieux-Colombier (1913–1917)

In starting up his own company, Copeau's ambition was no less than to rebuild the art of theatre from the base up. He proposed a theatre that was 'simple but inventive' (Bradby and Williams 1988: 15), a theatre that would integrate play and performance, with a repertoire based on the classics (principally Shakespeare and Molière) as well as new writing. He intended the emphasis to be on faithful productions, honest and imaginative acting, and minimal stage effects – allowing the poetry and truth of the playwright's work to come through unsullied and pure. In order to achieve this the first and most obvious requirement was a space, and Copeau found what he was looking for in the Théâtre de l'Athénée Saint-Germain, at 21, rue du Vieux-Colombier (the road after which it was to be renamed). The location was far enough away from the boulevards to avoid unwanted competition and comparison, and also sufficiently convenient for his supporters within the intellectual communities of the Left Bank. He saw immediately that the stage and auditorium of the old theatre building would need to be redesigned – eschewing the conventional ornate decoration for a simple, functional stage which would allow direct contact between the actor and the audience. The process of redesigning the new space and of organising and planning his new company led Copeau into a period of research. He threw himself into correspondence with many of the key figures of European theatre, including Edward Gordon Craig, Konstantin Stanislavsky, Harley Granville-Barker and Adolphe Appia.

He hired a young company of ten actors to form the core of his company. Some were actors he had already worked with, others he interviewed and hired specifically for this new project. In auditioning for the company he looked for indications of the natural and unforced talent and openness that he wanted to bring back to the stage. One young actress, Suzanne Bing, only accepted the salary he offered on condition that she did not have to buy her own costumes – a traditional responsibility of the hired actor, sometimes at considerable expense to themselves. Copeau accepted her conditions and in an instant he did away with a convention which had financially burdened actors for centuries, and which forced onto the stage a visible reminder of the financial status separating the star and the humble player (Kurtz 1999: 12). Why did these young actors follow a relatively unknown director on such a risky and unconventional venture? Copeau's secret was his ability to inspire others – his vision of what theatre could be and what it could do was passionately felt and eloquently communicated. It was also timely; he appealed to and grasped the imagination and idealism of the young actors of the time, giving their aspirations focus and direction, challenging their creativity in ways that they had probably never experienced before. He intended his new company to work as a disciplined ensemble – a truly innovative theatrical ambition, as, for many years, the pattern of employment had been based around clearly delineated hierarchies in which 'stars' were hired to perform their 'set pieces' alongside companies of jobbing actors. In order to achieve this radical change he realised that he would have to re-educate the young actors who would form the core of his new company. Copeau's primary aim was to free his actors from the dangers of *cabotinage*.

Though a formal training programme was not an option at this early stage, Copeau decided that he nonetheless needed to take his young actors 'outside the theatre into contact with nature and with life!' (Copeau 1967: 452). The location he chose was Le Limon, a small village in Seine-et-Marne a little over sixty kilometres east of Paris, where he owned a family property. This period of training, rehearsal, discussion and preparation was a nourishing experience for all concerned – bonding the group of actors into an ensemble and helping to establish a company ethos, shared aims and ambitions. The strict training regime included: swimming, fencing, rhythmical exercises, play-reading, and improvisation; actors were fined for lateness and non-attendance. Copeau also employed open air rehearsals, the simple setting intended to encourage the actors to get used to a lack of technical effects. On a less pragmatic level, he may also have felt that working in the open air in a more rural environment encouraged a different kind of truthfulness and naturalness; in making nature the measure against which his endeavours were compared he was seeking a more profound set of criteria for good acting than those established through nothing more than repetition and tradition. The results were promising, but inevitably limited, prompting Copeau to reflect that it would take 'at least two or three years to get a decent company together' (Copeau in Rudlin 1986: 12). Nonetheless, we can see that from the earliest days of the Vieux-Colombier, training and education were an integral part of Copeau's project, and informed the structure of the company's typical day.

> **Cabotinage** – Copeau speaks of *cabotinage* as a disease, 'the malady of insincerity, or rather of falseness. He who suffers from it ceases to be authentic, to be human' (Copeau 1990: 253). He used the term to identify the qualities which he most vehemently despised in the commercial actor: the cult of the star performer, the falseness of the 'ham' actor, the use of superficial technique and empty histrionics. It is interesting to note the different emphasis the Russian theatre director Vsevelod Meyerhold (1874–1940) gives to the same qualities: 'the cabotin can work miracles with his technical mastery; the cabotin keeps alive the tradition of the true art of acting' (Meyerhold 1981: 122). Though both directors employed a vibrant sense of rhythm, play, comedy and imagination within their work, their differing use of this term indicates key differences between their conceptions of the role of the theatre (see Rudlin 1986: 36–37).

One of Copeau's shortcomings during this period, both as an actor and as a director, was his lack of experience; his ideas outran his practice. He tended to rely on the simple delivery of the text at the expense of discovering its living theatrical expression. At this stage in his career as a director his passion for perfection and precision sometimes left little room during rehearsal for the actors' own creative exploration of their roles. His company fondly nicknamed him *le patron*, and indeed, throughout his theatrical life, he tended to find himself drawn to the role of the father-figure, the 'host', the friendly manager, and the 'skipper of the ship'. It needed the polite criticism of one of his young associates, the actor Charles Dullin, who had worked with him on *Les Frères Karamazov*, to point out to him that: 'in *listening to actors*, [you] are allowing yourself to be seduced *by the text*, and in your mind [you] are making up for the shortcomings of their interpretation – and therefore not drawing out a full performance' (Dullin in Rudlin 1986: 13). At this stage in the work of the young company it was Dullin and Louis Jouvet who were encouraging a less intellectual and more direct, spontaneous and physical approach; Copeau's confidence in his ideas and in his abilities as a teacher and director was still developing.

> **Charles Dullin** (1885–1949) and Louis Jouvet (1887–1951) both joined the Vieux-Colombier in its early years. Dullin eventually left to form his own company in 1919. He later established himself as a key figure in French theatre through his work at the Théâtre de l'Atelier as an actor, director and teacher. Jouvet, who had performed in *Les Frères Karamazov* (*The Brothers Karamazov*), joined the Vieux-Colombier as stage manager (regisseur). He left Copeau in 1922 in order to form his own company, and, like Dullin, he enjoyed considerable success in his own right. They were both members of the Cartel des Quatres ('Group of Four'), which dominated Parisian theatre after the First World War, and shared in the directorship of the Comédie-Française for a short period.

Copeau (1879–1949)

The Théâtre du Vieux-Colombier announced its opening to the people of Paris with a bold and simple poster proclaiming its aims and ambitions and calling on the young and cultured of the city for support. It opened its doors to the public on October 22, 1913, with *Une Femme Tuée Par La Douceur* (*A Woman Killed with Kindness*) by Thomas Heywood and *L'Amour Médecin* by Molière. The new company's subsequent repertoire combined classical plays and new writing in equal measure and was met with interest and enthusiasm by the serious theatregoers of Paris. Though Copeau sometimes struggled to achieve the fluidity of expression to which he aspired as a director, nonetheless the freshness and vitality of his productions shone through. The young company was obliged to forge its identity within the crucible of its public performances; but the benefit was a collective inner strength and a subtle understanding of each other's acting that was to produce, at the very end of the season, a success which justified all his efforts and made Copeau confident of the route he now wished to take.

The company's first major success, *La Nuit des Rois* (*Twelfth Night*) by William Shakespeare, opened on 19 May 1914 to almost immediate critical acclaim. By the opening night the company were exhausted – Copeau and Jouvet had been up all night organising the lighting, and the costume designs were finished as the actors prepared to go on stage and perform. Copeau's single-minded dedication to simplicity, sincerity and detail, coupled with the bonding experience of the limited training spell in the country and a season's experience of collaboration, produced fine ensemble playing and high performance standards. The risk had finally paid off. So successful was Copeau's lyrical, comical and inventive interpretation of Shakespeare's play, that the company received numerous invitations to tour. In late summer 1914 preparations for touring and for the next season were well underway when war was declared; suddenly fate had swung against Copeau – he and his actors were dispatched to the Front and his theatre was requisitioned as 'a shelter for refugees and soldiers on leave' (Kurtz 1999: 32).

Copeau and Craig

> There has not been a single artist of the theatre during the last twenty-five years who is not indebted to a greater or lesser extent to Gordon Craig.
>
> *(Copeau 1990: 14)*

Copeau had heard of Craig's work and was a subscriber to Craig's influential journal, *The Mask*. He had asked Craig for permission to publish some of his writings and designs in the *Nouvelle Revue Française* (Bablet 1981: 183), and subsequent correspondence between the two men confirmed their shared views on theatre and the Arts. When he was invalided out of the French auxiliary forces in April 1915, Copeau decided to make use of his time by visiting those people whose work he saw as complementary to his own ideas and aspirations. His first visit was to Edward Gordon Craig's school in Florence during the autumn of 1915.

Edward Gordon Craig (1872–1966) was a major influence on the development of European and American theatre practice and design. He started his career as an actor (he was the son of the famous actress Ellen Terry) but quickly turned to work behind the scenes. His innovative ideas on the use of space, lighting and staging levels had a profound effect on the development of stage design. Despite some notable collaborations (he designed Stanislavsky's 1911 production of *Hamlet* at the Moscow Arts Theatre), Craig struggled to see his ideas realised in practice. He settled in Florence in 1908, where he ran a school of theatre and from where he edited his journal, *The Mask*. He wrote profusely about theatre – its practice, its history and its theories – and his writings can be seen as a manifesto for much contemporary theatre and performance practice (e.g. the works of Tadeusz Kantor, Robert Wilson, Robert Lepage).

It was this meeting which helped to convince Copeau of the importance of training new actors, of 'welcoming the young', for a rejuvenated theatre. Craig's aim was to provide within his school an environment that enabled and encouraged creative experimentation. Both Craig and Copeau agreed on the importance of developing a high level of technical skill:

> It is neither talent nor ideas that are lacking, nor heart, nor need. It is the discipline of craft which once reigned over even the most humble endeavor. It is the rule that to think well leads to the ability to do well, competency with perfection in mind. Art and craft are not two separate entities.
>
> *(Copeau in Felner 1985: 37)*

Furthermore, both believed in the value of study programmes that encouraged the student to acquire a full and rich understanding of the wider cultural environment.

Copeau shared Craig's recognition of the important role of the director and designer in the creation of a new artistic vision for the theatre; where he differed with Craig was over the role of the actor within this vision. While Craig's disenchantment with conventional acting led him towards reconfigurations of the actor as a kind of marionette to the will of the director, Copeau was convinced that the actor must remain a central part of the theatre event and its creation. On the other hand, Craig's vision of a stage stripped of the fussy decorative naturalism of the nineteenth century and his ideas for creating atmospheric spaces within which theatre could generate a new synthesis of scenic movement and *mise-en-scène*, provided Copeau with affirmation for his own idea of a *tréteau nu* on which the actor could (re)create a poetics of theatrical expression. Having looked at Craig's designs and discussed with him the use of screens and the principle of the single scene, Copeau was enthused enough to write to Jouvet: 'it is exactly what we need for our stage … One might be able to improve a few details in the course of working with this material, but as it stands, it satisfies *all our needs*' (Copeau in Bablet 1981: 184). Craig also showed Copeau an idea for a stage lighting scheme that avoided the contemporary fashion for footlights and battens. All these ideas came together in Copeau's imagination, building a realisable image of a theatre which, incorporating permanent stage architecture, use of levels and steps, could finally achieve 'an unbroken transition from auditorium to stage' (Bablet 1981: 185).

By the time Copeau had to leave Craig and return to France, he had arrived at his own assessment of Craig's ideas. While he valued Craig's flashes of insight, vision and erudition, which could be both illuminating and inspiring, he also recognised the lack of clear direction which could make Craig's work sometimes seem to be 'so useless and almost puerile' (Copeau 1990: 17). Copeau's comments betray a frustration with Craig's idealism; he believed that Craig was wrong to avoid the necessity to *realise* a new theatre, not merely to dream of it. How could any 'movement for the renewal of dramatic art which is not accompanied or necessitated by the production of new work' possibly be 'realistic, living, necessary' (ibid.: 18)? Furthermore, whereas Craig saw the theatrical event in terms of staging, design and lighting, Copeau sought to achieve his effects through the actor's 'gracefulness, his airs, his acting and delivery' (ibid.: 19). As Craig himself admitted to Copeau, 'You believe in the actor. *I do not*' (ibid.: 22). Copeau was to continue his journey of study and reflection deeply inspired, greatly excited, certain of his own route, and also convinced that: 'there is infinitely more soul and a more fertile seed-bed in my little theatre, which exists and lives with all of its poverty and imperfections' (ibid.: 19–20).

Copeau, Jaques-Dalcroze and Appia

In 1915 Copeau had acquired a short pamphlet on the work of Emile Jaques-Dalcroze (Jaques-Dalcroze 1913). Inspired by Jaques-Dalcroze's work, Copeau willingly accepted a government invitation to spend a short period in Geneva as a cultural ambassador for France during the summer of 1916, as this meant that he was able to visit Jaques-Dalcroze's school regularly and to watch Eurhythmic classes (Copeau 1990: 59–62). He took with him his daughter, Marie-Hélène, and a member of his company, Suzanne Bing, both of whom were to become invaluable and committed associates in his future work.

> **Emile Jaques-Dalcroze** (1865–1950) was an unlikely figurehead for the development of early twentieth-century movement and dance. A portly and dapper composer and music teacher, he had begun his work on movement in order to find a method to release his music students' natural understanding of rhythm. In adding rhythm to gymnastic education, Jaques-Dalcroze emphasised the dynamic qualities of the body over the static, regimented practices of the previous century. For him, rhythm was a universal and essential component to all expression. After being dismissed from his post as Professor of Harmony at the Geneva Conservatoire he continued to teach, founding his own school. His movement work was quickly recognised as a pleasurable and liberating alternative to the functional, mechanical exercise of traditional drill and the rigidly formal vocabulary of the ballet, offering instead a unified and expressive approach which could be adapted to several potential uses.

Copeau shared with Jaques-Dalcroze a passionate interest in exploring how the mental and physical facilities of the performer could be developed to the point where 'the muscles would do the will of the mind easily and quickly' (Spector 1990: 56–57). He had a deep respect for Jaques-Dalcroze's empirical approach, the way that he worked from experience, through improvisation and experiment, encouraging his students to reflect constantly on the emotional effect of their practice (Copeau 1990: 60). The entire body and person of the performer might in this way be unified in theatrical expression, precisely the effect that Copeau wanted his young actors to achieve.

He was impressed enough with Jaques-Dalcroze's work to try a few experiments of his own in Paris, and later to invite a young student of Jaques-Dalcroze, Jessmin Howarth, to work as movement teacher with his company. Miss Howarth was to travel with the company to New York in 1917 and reportedly 'not only drilled the troupe regularly each day in rhythmic gymnastics but also observed each rehearsal' (Rogers 1966: 178–179). The experiment did not work; Miss Howarth, and a later replacement, Jane Erb, were both dismissed by Copeau. Despite such problems, Copeau and Jaques-Dalcroze shared a life-long admiration for each other's work, each recognising in the other a fascination with the interaction of rhythm and movement in the work of the actor and performer.

Whilst in Switzerland, Copeau also took the opportunity to visit the designer Adolphe Appia, who had collaborated with Jaques-Dalcroze in setting up the innovative training establishment for Eurhythmics at Hellerau, in Germany.

> **Adolphe Appia** (1862–1925) had been inspired in his youth by the work of the composer Richard Wagner, in whose compositions he saw a vision of a theatre of the future. His innovation was to set aside the traditional conventions of staging and work solely from the inner qualities of the music or text itself. He rejected pictorial staging and focussed instead on the three dimensional dynamics of people moving in space. To this end he proposed a simple space, using movement, lights and stage levels to create his effects. In 1906, Appia attended a demonstration of 'Eurhythmics' by Jaques-Dalcroze and his students. Jaques-Dalcroze's work offered a way in which the actor's body could take its central place as a carrier of the action without breaking the rhythmic spell of the music. Appia began a collaboration with Jaques-Dalcroze which was to last through various projects and productions, including the influential school of Eurhythmics at Hellerau in Germany, until Appia's death in 1928.

Copeau called Appia his 'master' (Hayman 1977: 86), and shared with him a belief in the primacy of the actor within the theatrical event. Copeau remained in contact with Craig, Appia and Jaques-Dalcroze throughout his life, and his debt to their pioneering work is clear. His conversations with all three confirmed his conviction that the conventional hierarchy of the nineteenth-century stage – spectacle, music and effect over the spoken word, the rhythms of the text and the scenic interplay of the actor and space – should be challenged and changed. Copeau had the insight, the theatrical experience and the working environment in which to resolve the problems such innovations posed. In an important sense, Copeau was the conduit through which the idealistic visions of Craig and Appia could find theatrical realisation. As Copeau himself was to write to Appia:

> What shocks me, and worries me, is that you and Craig, you are building the theatre of the future without knowing who will live there, what kind of artist you will put on the stage, or house in the very theatre you wish to welcome them. It seems to me, Appia, that I alone have begun at the beginning in taking on the job of forming a troupe of actors.
>
> *(Copeau in Felner 1985: 39)*

The Vieux-Colombier in New York (1917–1919)

In January 1917, Copeau was again dispatched as a cultural ambassador by the French Ministry of Fine Arts. This time he was sent to the United States as part of a drive by the French Government to encourage American involvement in the First World War and to counter the influence of the German theatre in New York at this time – a task made all the more urgent by the terrible events on the battlefields of France, where several of his first company had already fallen. His lectures were an unusual success, given that they presented a profound critique of the dominant commercial theatre in America. The lecture tour resulted in a lively interest in the work of the Vieux-Colombier Theatre. An invitation was made to bring his troupe to New York, with financial support from the wealthy banker and philanthropist Otto Khan, who was eager to help introduce the new European stagecraft to American audiences. There were difficulties to overcome, it would mean bringing together a troupe of performers that had been disbanded for several years; identifying a suitable venue; and, less attractive to Copeau, the manipulation of the troupe's repertoire to suit American tastes and interests. The tour was an inherently risky venture. Several months of planning and organisation had to take place, including the search for and redesign of a suitable New York theatre. However Copeau succeeded in gathering together almost all of his pre-War company, and his previous theatrical success also allowing him to recruit several talented new actors. The season opened at the Garrick Theatre in New York on 27 November 1917 with a performance of Molière's late farce, *Les Fourberies de Scapin*. The success of this and other productions speaks volumes for the young company's ability to overcome the problems of language and culture. This was in no small part a result of the emphasis Copeau placed on simple staging and expressive physical movement. As a director he was learning to pay careful attention to the rhythm of the text, its dramatic choreography and poetry. His New York revival of *Les Frères Karamazov* (*The Brothers Karamazov*) also demonstrated an increasingly confident grasp of psychological characterisation. Copeau's knowledge of Stanislavsky's techniques for psychological realism was, of course, limited, and it was to be another six years before the visit of Stanislavsky and the Moscow Art Theatre to New York, however his intuitive understanding of the need for sincerity and truth on stage enabled him and his company to achieve some success in this respect. It is a mark of the achievement of Copeau's young company that the programme for the New York season could proudly announce that:

> The Théâtre du Vieux-Colombier is the youngest of French theatres, and the only one which can be compared to those numerous artistic stages that have been created abroad during these last twenty-five years.
> *(from 'French Théâtre du Vieux-Colombier', programme for New York season, 1917–1918, Fonds Copeau, Bibliothèque nationale de France, p. 3)*

Both the lecture series and the New York tour served their purpose in generating interest in French culture, but they also had a significant influence on the development of the American Little Theaters.

The Little Theater movement found inspiration in Copeau's commitment to effective dramatic expression, the work of native playwrights, a rejection of the commercial theatre system, and to creating and building an audience sympathetic to the work (Kurtz 1999: 48). The Vieux-Colombier's visit to New York thus played a vital role in re-establishing the international importance of French theatre. Nonetheless, despite this recognition, Copeau's intentions were more straightforwardly to nurture and protect the integrity of the Vieux-Colombier Theatre's mission. The New York season was actually important to Copeau because it gave him an opportunity to explore in more depth and detail the ideas gleaned from his visits to Craig, Jaques-Dalcroze and Appia, and through his correspondence with Stanislavsky.

The **Little Theater movement** began in America around the second decade of the twentieth century. The movement arose as a response by the cultured middle classes to the popular success of the early cinema and to the perceived irrelevance of the commercial theatre to contemporary issues. Its members sought to promote 'serious' theatre, putting on their plays in community venues and small, intimate performance spaces, rejecting detailed naturalistic staging, experimenting with form, and encouraging new writing. The movement was also closely associated with the development of drama studies in American universities and colleges.

His success in America, while significant, was only partial. The audiences were selective in their taste and he was forced to compromise with his programming in order to ensure an adequate degree of box office success. The conditions of his tour and the nature of his financial backing meant that he was reliant on a society audience who were not naturally in tune with his ideas and ideals. A proportion of the audience and critics seemed to have expected something richer, more elaborate and ornate, something more star-studded and flamboyant, than the typically simple and uncluttered productions which Copeau had delivered. But over the duration of the tour, as a result of sticking to some of his plans and compromising on others, Copeau's work had begun to find regular followers and friends. Nonetheless, Copeau's workload during the tour followers and friends. Nonetheless, Copeau's workload during the tour was gruelling – between November 1917 and March 1919 he produced 44 different plays (Harrop 1971: 115–116). Eventually, the stress of such an extensive and demanding schedule took its toll on the actors' energies, and Copeau became aware that not all his actors were able or willing to explore the new challenges he wished to confront. Company cohesion started to suffer. Despite the overall sense of success, and despite the strong friendships and associations he had made, it must have been a sweet relief for Copeau eventually to return to Paris and to resume his own creative mission once more.

The company returns and the school re-opens (1919–1924)

By 1919, Copeau's international success as a director of both classical revivals and modern plays meant that he had become established as a leading figure in French and world theatre. However, this success and recognition was not enough to lift the Vieux-Colombier out of financial danger. In part this was because the theatre could only hold 363 people – minute in comparison to the cavernous capacity of the major boulevard theatres – but Copeau was resolutely against any form of financial support (government or private) which might, as he saw it, bind him to another's agenda: 'I don't want state funds, they would choke me' (Copeau in Kurtz 1999: 69). It is fascinating for us today that such a distinctive and rigorous theatre experiment could occur on such a scale, with virtually no state support, relying almost entirely on private finance, box office income and patronage. For Copeau, meaningful experiment could not happen without freedom from outside interference, nor away from the support of a loyal public:

> The Vieux-Colombier is not a fantasy of amateurs or intellectuals concocted to tickle the curiosity of snobs and to win for itself the ephemeral favor (*sic*) of great philanthropists. It is a work of slow construction, open to all workers of the theatre, and destined for the general public which must give it life.
>
> *(ibid.: 70)*

Copeau chose to open the company's new Paris season in February 1920 with a production of *Le Conte d'Hiver* (*The Winter's Tale*), adapted from Shakespeare by Copeau himself and Suzanne Bing – a story of rebirth and forgiveness, appropriate for a country recovering from the ravages of a long war. However, the surprise hit of the season was to be his production of Charles Vidrac's play *Le Paquebot Tenacity*. This play was full of naïve charm, staged with simplicity and sensitivity, preferring understatement and subtlety to the overblown acting of the boulevards. The uncluttered, poetical realism of these productions set out clearly the guiding principles of Copeau's directorial style.

Buoyed by the recent critical acclaim, and encouraged by the support of friends and enthusiasts through Les Amis du Vieux-Colombier (The Friends of the Vieux-Colombier), Copeau now entered into a period of well-earned professional success and intense theatrical activity. During the first season before the War, less than one-sixth of the Vieux-Colombier's performances had been of new work – now, during the 1920 season, nearly half of the plays Copeau produced were new works (Kurtz 1999: 68). This change in emphasis marked a real turning point for Copeau's original mission – the rejuvenation of French theatre could not take place solely through a return to the classics, the lessons learnt from the past must be brought to the service of the theatre of today. The Vieux-Colombier, through its successes, had become the fashionable place to go, and new playwrights strove to get their plays put on there. Copeau's theatre offered an environment that welcomed playwrights as a key creative force within the theatre; he encouraged writers to explore the 'poetic' possibilities of drama as a medium, and crucially offered them the theatre resources to do so. Writers such as Georges Duhamel (1884–1966), Jules Romains (1885–1972) and Charles Vildrac (1882–1971) responded willingly to this opportunity and began the re-invigoration of theatre writing which was to place French drama at the heart of European theatre over the next four decades.

At last Copeau felt able to restart the Vieux-Colombier School. His initial attempts in 1913, and again in 1915, to provide a training regime for the actor had been stalled as a result of the outbreak of war. He had always intended that a school for actors would be the foundation stone of his project to rejuvenate the theatre. He knew that despite his own and his company's success, more work needed to be done in order to develop a genuinely spontaneous, sincere and vital theatre. While his dream of establishing a school that would run alongside the theatre company was not entirely innovative – other schools for actors had already opened their doors across Europe (e.g. Beerbohm Tree's Academy of Dramatic Art in London and Stanislavsky's Studio in Moscow) – nonetheless Copeau's school offered a new and serious challenge to the dominance of the Conservatoire Nationale de la Musique et d'Art Dramatique as the principal centre for actor training in France. The Conservatoire primarily drilled students, through the most pedantic and functional of training regimes, to become actors of set roles with the Comédie-Française – what Copeau offered was, in comparison, nothing short of revolutionary in its focus on creativity, spontaneity and physicality.

The Vieux-Colombier School (1920–1924)

The School opened its doors once more in February 1920, the first year intended as a pilot enterprise involving a limited number of students. The first classes were held in a barn in the Theatre's courtyard, but this space proved too cramped and the School soon moved a short distance away to better facilities at 9, rue du Cherche-Midi. Difficult experiences with some actors during the New York tour meant that Copeau had become convinced that the future lay with training children rather than re-educating actors who had already been formed by what he saw as a corrupting system: 'the only hope we can have in the future of the theatre is . . . the training of children' (Copeau in Kusler 1979: 20). The first classes therefore focussed on teaching the young group voice technique, simple characterisation and group performance. This work laid the foundation stones for the more ambitious plans for the school in the following year.

The inclusion of classes for children was important; Copeau did not want the school to be restricted to training actors for the company. Instead he aimed to provide within the School a space for exploration and experiment, as well as for the public dissemination of his ideas. Copeau had always aimed to open a school before starting a theatre company, but initially he felt that he had 'neither the authority nor the means to do so' (Copeau 1990: 28). He realised the impossibility of managing the School alongside all his other responsibilities, and asked the philosopher, novelist, playwright and poet Jules Romains (1885–1972) to be Director of the School. Romains was, by inclination and belief, as committed as Copeau to the idea of developing a community of actor-artists. For Copeau inclusion of the School brought his whole enterprise closer to the great models of the past, the theatrical 'families' of the *commedia dell'arte* troupes and the great Japanese Nōh companies, in which training, living and performing became part of an indistinguishable blend of activity.

The legacy of the visit to New York was evident through some important developments within the company, which now did much to shape this next phase in Copeau's work. The actress Suzanne Bing had become increasingly involved with the teaching of student actors. Whilst in New York, she had visited schools and observed children's games and play; this led to a fascination with improvisation, animal mimicry, games and the basic skills of what was later to become modern mime. Working closely with Copeau, she developed these elements as key features of the teaching and training at the Vieux-Colombier School. During this period, Bing was to become the key figure in the day-to-day work of the school. She had a close understanding of Copeau's aims and her commitment to the development and success of the School was such that she was prepared to give up acting with the company in order to make it happen: 'It was necessary that I chose between the theatre and the school' (Suzanne Bing in Mignon 1993: 204, author's translation).

> **Suzanne Bing** (1887–1967) was a leading actress and teacher at the Vieux-Colombier, with Les Copiaus and later with the Compagnie des Quinze. She married the composer Edgar Varèse (1883–1965) in 1906, moving with him to Berlin in 1907. In 1913 she and her husband divorced, she had trained at the Conservatoire d'Art dramatique and it was to the Paris theatre that she now returned, joining the Vieux-Colombier Theatre in its first season. She had an affair with Copeau, with whom she had a son, Bernard Bing, born in 1917. She became one of Copeau's closest associates; she was a key member of the teaching staff at the Vieux-Colombier School and later a leading member of Les Copiaus and the Compagnie des Quinze. Her teaching was highly influential in the development of modern mime and mask improvisation techniques, and of physical training for actors.

At the same time, Jessmin Howarth's attempts to train the actors in the basics of Eurhythmics had proved less than successful, perhaps her inexperience had been at fault but the result was that her classes had been poorly attended. Copeau had also become increasingly disillusioned with Eurhythmics, which he found prone to artificiality and self-consciousness: 'It cannot be directly applied to our training. It already bears within itself an affectation' (Copeau in Kusler 1979: 18). After Howarth's departure, her teaching input was split between dance classes, the 'natural gymnastics' of George Hébert, and movement improvisations led by Bing.

Suzanne Bing had taken notes on Howarth's movement classes, focusing on aspects of interest to her (silent pantomime, sensory experience, the essential rhythms of characters) which she was now able to integrate into her own teaching. In synthesising these influences, Bing was a crucial contributor to Copeau's efforts, helping to draw together his many ideas and principles into a coherent method of actor training. Copeau's frequent and prolonged lecture tours, and his work as a director and actor with the Vieux-Colombier company, meant that Bing's teaching was effectively the heart and core of the work at the School. Copeau's close personal relationship with Bing meant that he was always in touch with the developments at the School, and he liased frequently on the students' progress. Suzanne Bing has not generally been credited for the hugely significant contribution she made to the School (Jean Dorcy (1961) mentions her only twice in his account of Copeau's achievements); to her fell the task of testing many of Copeau's pedagogical ideas through practice, and through her teaching she was to develop much of the detail of corporeal mime technique and mask improvisation. For a detailed discussion of Bing's contribution, see Donahue (2008, 95–125) and Fleming (2013).

George Hébert (1875–1957) was a significant influence on the development of physical education in France. After a career as a naval officer, during which he noted with fascination the natural fitness, strength and flexibility of the 'button boys' who climbed the rigging of the tall ships, he travelled extensively, observing the physical prowess of indigenous peoples who had not had any form of formal gymnastic training. Later, as a teacher of physical education at the College of Rheims, he formulated his own theories and principles based on the 'natural' practices he had observed and on Ancient Greek physical ideals. His system rejected the mechanical repetition of the dominant Swedish method, and proposed that physical education should be linked to an observation of and interaction with Nature. Hébert sought physical development through 'organic resistance, muscularity and speed', basing all exercise around walking, running, jumping, crawling, climbing, balancing, throwing, lifting, swimming and self-defence. He was an early advocate of exercise for women. His influence can be seen in the development of obstacle course training, the physical theatre training of Jacques Lecoq (Murray 2003: 30), and even in the contemporary urban extreme-sport of 'free-running' or *parkour*.

For Copeau, the first and most important task of the school was to rediscover the rules of theatre. This was to be achieved through the complementary activities of experiment (using improvisation and physical technique), and of historical research (in particular into the theatrical traditions of Ancient Greece, the Middle Ages and the Renaissance). The resulting programme of study indicates Copeau's determination that his students should see their training as the preparation of an artist, not the drilling of a journeyman. They were to become, 'interpreters of dramatic forms whose realisation we have as yet not been able to imagine for lack of a proper instrument' (Copeau in Kusler 1979: 20). The next three years of the school represented the most complete expression of Copeau's work on the training of the actor. The newly expanded programme of training, which began when the School opened in its most complete form in 1921, included three strands which represented the main aims of the school: courses for the general public; courses for student actors and other theatre artists; and courses for young people and children without previous acting experience. Of these strands, by far the most important to Copeau was the last – it was in this group of apprentice actors, untainted by the bad habits which he saw as endemic in the profession, that he saw the possibility for a theatre art of the future. The apprentice group started in 1921 as a small class of six students, at the core of which were several pupils, including his own daughter Marie-Hélène, who were to stay with Copeau's project for the rest of the decade. It was with this young group that Copeau and Bing felt able to make their most profound experiments in actor-training; it was in their classes that Copeau first introduced the mask as a training device. And it was this apprentice group, directed by Suzanne Bing, that produced a revival of the classical Japanese Nōh play, *Kantan*, that, for those who saw it, marked the highpoint of the School's achievement. The mix of family, friends and newcomers, the atmosphere of experiment and playful innovation, helped to foster the spirit of a company and school linked by connections which went deeper than professional and commercial need.

The work of the school was so new and innovative, that there were few markers for Copeau, Bing and the other teachers to follow other than their own instincts and experience, and Copeau's knowledge of developments elsewhere in Europe. Inevitably, as one of his students noted, 'discovery became the common task of master and student' (Michel Saint-Denis in Kusler 1979: 30), with Copeau counting on his students to help him move the work forward. The enthusiasm of the students was high, the atmosphere a heady mix of invention, discovery, liberty and discipline. Enthused by the success of the School, Copeau re-organised the whole enterprise, moving his colleague Jules Romains to oversee the expanded public course provision (and eventually removing him altogether from the School), so that Copeau could take more active charge himself.

Copeau and Stanislavsky

Just as he had found inspiration in the staging concepts of Craig and Appia, Copeau now found another mentor who could provide an equally compelling vision of the art of the actor. He had written to the Russian actor, theatre director, and teacher Konstantin Stanislavsky as early as 1916, sure that there was much in common between his ideas for the Vieux-Colombier and Stanislavsky's work at the Moscow Art Theatre.

> **Konstantin Stanislavsky** (1863–1938) is probably one of the most influential teachers and directors in the history of Western theatre. In 1898 he co-founded, with Vladimir Nemirovich-Danchenko (1858–1943), the Moscow Art Theatre. He revolutionised the actor's craft, building a process through which the actor could repeatedly achieve a high level of psychological realism. He directed the first productions of most of Anton Chekhov's plays. Though stripped of his wealth after the Russian Revolution, he continued to teach, direct and act until his death. His influence owes much to the success of his books, available in English as *An Actor Prepares*, *Building a Character*, and *Creating a Character*. Recent studies (e.g. Merlin 2003) have highlighted the importance of his later work on Physical Actions and Active Analysis, ideas which share with Copeau's work an emphasis on improvisation and physical engagement with text and character.

Stanislavsky replied to Copeau, excited by the possibility of an international studio which might bring together leading artists from around the world. Copeau was equally enthused, but by the time he attempted to contact Stanislavsky again the February revolution had occurred and Stanislavsky's private fortune and his family's business had vanished. However the friendship which they had established was to endure the distance and difficulties of the next five years, and on the 29 November 1922 Stanislavsky and the Moscow Art Theatre travelled from Berlin to Paris as part of an extensive tour. Copeau was at the Gare du Nord railway station to welcome Stanislavsky, and two days later they met to discuss further the creation of an international centre of theatre art. Copeau and Stanislavsky kept in close contact during the Moscow Art Theatre's visit to Paris and on 21 December a midnight reception was held for Stanislavsky at the Vieux-Colombier. Copeau gave a dinner at a nearby restaurant, also attended by Harley Granville Barker, and then, a few days later, Stanislavsky and his company set sail for New York.

Copeau and his company had the opportunity to watch Stanislavsky's productions of *Fiodor*, *The Lower Depths*, *The Brothers Karamazov*, and *The Cherry Orchard*, and they were very much impressed by what they saw. The opening production of *Fiodor* was nearly a disaster when the sets and costumes did not arrive until the very last minute, however Copeau and his company may have appreciated the subsequent simplicity – all the most elaborate effects were abandoned and the performance took place with the theatre lighting at full throughout. Although they did not know the detail of Stanislavsky's System until much later, when the key texts were translated and published, the Vieux-Colombier company were, in the words of Michel Saint-Denis, 'converted' (Saint-Denis 1967: 111). What Copeau learnt from Stanislavsky was threefold: 'the importance of sincerity and truth, that action must be linked to a psychological state, [and] that movement should originate from need' (Felner 1985: 39). Copeau recognised Stanislavsky as 'the master of us all' (Copeau in Felner 1985: 39), and Stanislavsky's Moscow Studio provided an important model for the future development of the École du Vieux-Colombier.

The retreat to Burgundy – Les Copiaus (1924–1929)

Stanislavsky's visit to Paris seems to have renewed Copeau's determination to recommit to his original vision for a new kind of theatre. The Vieux-Colombier continued successfully for another year after Stanislavsky's visit, but in 1924 Copeau made the unexpected announcement that he intended to close both School and Theatre. This radical and impulsive decision, taken at a point when his own reputation and that of the Vieux-Colombier was at its height, seemed to many to be a retrograde and capricious step. But for Copeau, the subsequent retreat to the countryside with a small group of young followers represented his final chance to achieve the theatre of which he dreamed. He recognised the enormous risk that he was taking: 'I have left everything. I am playing the last chance of my life' (Copeau in Kusler 1979: 50), but his determination was unshakeable. Copeau 'bequeathed' his Paris company and repertoire to Jouvet before his departure. His influence, through Jouvet's work and the work of the other members of the Cartel des Quatres, would dominate the development of theatre in Paris between the Wars. But this was a world on which Copeau was once more turning his back, setting out to renew his search for a simple, pure and popular theatre – even if it meant starting again almost from scratch.

> The **Cartel des Quatres** was an informal alliance, begun in 1927, between four influential theatres and their directors: Louis Jouvet, Charles Dullin, Gaston Baty, and Georges and Ludmilla Pitoëff. They all committed to a policy of respect for the text, simple staging and a serious approach to the poetic function of drama. It did much both to foster the growth of serious drama production between the Wars, and to protect Copeau's legacy and influence.

In re-locating that autumn to the remote rural village of Mourteuil in Burgundy, Copeau was not only committing himself (and the thirty-four students, writers, artists and actors who chose to follow him) to the cause of regional theatre, but also in many respects turning his back on Parisian and European modernity in search of a more regenerative vision of theatre (Ward 1996: 173). Disillusioned and disheartened by the failure of his autobiographical play *La Maison natale* (1923) to find favour with the Paris critics, he must also have been facing a crisis of direction. To complicate matters, he was leaving the capital at a time of increasing financial difficulties across Europe, and a time of high taxation for the theatres in France – another possible motive for his decision to close the Vieux-Colombier (Carter 1925: 161). However his intention was not simply to relocate his existing work, but rather to explore a new kind of theatre: a theatre involved in and evolving from the working life of the community in which it was based, producing work relevant to the conditions of life within that community; a theatre which was pure, simple and rigorously focussed on the actor's skills.

Such a retreat attempted also to remove the company from the commercial pressures of the theatre world in Paris. Copeau had spent his early adulthood running a small family factory, and although this had given him a genuine appreciation of the value of craft and honest labour, he must have had no particular desire to find himself permanently tied to the tiller of a theatrical equivalent. At the Vieux-Colombier, the need for the continuous production of successful performances had increasingly tended to dominate over the activity of the School. Pressure had grown for a move to larger premises, for the acceptance of subsidy, but Copeau was reluctant to compromise his vision because of financial constraints. He must have hoped that the retreat to Burgundy would allow the balance to shift back in favour of experiment and exploration. His clear interest in the work with the apprentice group (based largely on the group of children who had started at the School in 1920) had, towards the end, created jealousies and divisions within the company and the School, and the decision to make the break must in part have meant that he could now draw a line under some of those fractures and schisms.

In November 1924 Copeau gathered together the small company (which included his own daughter Marie-Hélène, and the young Etienne Decroux) in order to announce his aims for his new project. The emphasis within this enterprise was to be on the moral responsibility of the actor, the importance of personal discipline, respect for fellow artists, the value of individuality, sincerity, intelligence and good humour. The organisation of the company in Burgundy was in many ways a continuation of the regime Copeau had established for the final year students of the school in Paris. They continued to help with cleaning, kept a log of their activities and held meetings to discuss their work (Kusler 1979: 36). The cohesion of the group was strengthened by the interlocking family units of which it was now composed.

Etienne Decroux (1898–1991) enrolled as a student at the Vieux-Colombier School in 1923. He followed Copeau to Burgundy, but left after five months as a result of the company's initial problems. He then worked with Baty and Jouvet, and later joined Dullin at the Théâtre de l'Atelier as an actor and mime teacher, where he worked for eight years. In 1931 he met with the young actor Jean-Louis Barrault, and together they began working on what was to become the basis of Decroux's concept of corporeal mime. Decroux performed in mime performances, plays, and films (including the famous film *Les Enfants du Paradis*), but perhaps his greatest legacy is as a teacher – alongside the international mime artist Marcel Marceau (whom he taught) and Jacques Lecoq, Decroux is one of the central figures in the history of modern mime.

For some of Copeau's literary friends, including the writer André Gide, the retreat to the countryside represented an act of misguided romanticism. For Gide, the sanctity and purity of which Copeau dreamed were a seductive illusion. Gide's criticisms were effectively countered by later commentators (e.g. Bentley 1950: 48–51), who recognised that the important quality of such an experiment was not the end result so much as the process itself. Nonetheless, the retreat to Burgundy was a venture balanced for its success on a knife's edge. Copeau was tired and unwell after years of managing the Vieux-Colombier – his commitment and dedication would not let him slacken, and as with so many of his ventures he found it hard to delegate responsibility. Furthermore, money was short – the Vieux-Colombier had drained a lot of Copeau's personal resources, and the company finances were complicated and confusing. Although Copeau had made thorough preparations for the setting up of the Vieux-Colombier, this new move had been relatively sudden and impulsive and consequently seemed more reckless to his concerned friends. Copeau felt a deep sense of responsibility for his young company, and this transposed itself into a rigorous insistence on self-discipline, re-inforced by various sets of rules and regulations. Copeau's Catholic beliefs led him to insist on an almost monastic devotion to communal self-sufficiency; in those early months living conditions were hard and money was scarce, illness was also rife. The company was forced to throw together two performance pieces, which they presented in Lille as part of an unsuccessful attempt to raise money. By late February, it was clear that the project, as initially conceived by Copeau, could not continue; he had no option but to disband the group.

What Copeau appears not to have expected was the internal momentum which had built up of its own accord amongst his young company. The basic conditions, the return to nature, and the strong sense of community that the retreat had provided, had fostered an instinctive interest in ritual and festivity and in the exploration of dramatic responses to the rhythms and celebrations of the countryside. The strict rules had helped to cultivate a disciplined work-ethic, but had also engendered a rich counter-seam of playfulness, irreverence and spontaneous celebration. A small number of the original group decided to stay on in Pernand-Vergelesses and continue the work, including: Suzanne Bing, Michel Saint-Denis and Leon Chancerel (1886–1965).

Michel Saint-Denis (1897–1971) was Copeau's nephew. He became a student at the Vieux-Colombier School and followed Copeau to Burgundy in 1924 to become a key member of Les Copiaus. When the troupe was disbanded Saint-Denis founded the Compagnie des Quinze with his former colleagues and the young company achieved consider able success. He settled in London in the early 1930s and alongside his achievements as a director he also co-founded the influential Old Vic Theatre School. He had a profound influence on the development of actor training in Europe and North America and was one of the original artistic directorate of the Royal Shakespeare Company.

Within a few months, Copeau, assisted by Saint-Denis, had drawn together a new smaller group from the few followers who had stayed on in Burgundy. The company's log-book notes that the local people, punning on Copeau's name, had started to call the group 'Les Copiaus' (or the Little Copeaus). The company now adopted this title, a name which reflected the strong connections with Copeau's vision and yet also suggested lightness, youth and humour. Copeau continued to participate as a writer and an actor, though large portions of his time were also taken up with raising funds through lecture tours and personal appearances. Certainly Copeau's continued presence (however distant at times) meant that he maintained a clear control over the general direction of the work. This arrangement was not without its difficulties and its tensions. For some of Les Copiaus, *le patron*'s control of the group sometimes felt oppressive. Just as Dullin and Jouvet had eventually needed to become independent of the Vieux-Colombier, so too the members of Les Copiaus, already straining at the leash, increasingly sought to explore their own creative instincts. Copeau had always been gifted at developing the talents and creativity of others, and Les Copiaus are a significant success in this respect. The price of his success, however, was that despite being on the verge of achieving his prophetic vision of a small troupe of actor/artists who would tour a repertoire of classic and devised performances to the people, Copeau seems to have struggled to find a new role for himself within this democratic and youthful project.

Les Copiaus' early performances were collages of rural life, which, although initially thrown together in haste, showed an increasing confidence in the new skills and artistic processes which they were acquiring and developing. The performances would typically contain a prologue, short scenes and one-act plays, and entertainments including songs and dances. Characters and scenarios were created and developed through observation, mask-work and improvisation, and then later worked into the performances. The working day for the company and the young students revolved around a programme of gymnastics and mime exercises, voice exercises and general theatre classes in the mornings, followed by improvisation, games, rehearsal, devising and group work in the afternoons. Sessions were also organised to work on mask-making, singing, music and design. The days were long, the work demanding, with each member also taking on general company tasks and responsibilities. All of these features contributed to the company's sense of identity, coherence and purpose, foreseeing the kind of communal practices that would later form the basis of the work of experimental practitioners such as the Polish director Jerzy Grotowski (1933–1999) and the director of the Odin Teatret, Eugenio Barba (1936–).

Protracted and increasingly frequent absences from Pernand-Verglesses meant that Copeau became progressively more distanced from Les Copiaus and their work. The absences were necessary; despite their relative self-sufficiency the young group still relied upon the income from Copeau's many lectures, readings and other professional activities for their financial survival. In the interim, the company continued to experiment and improvise around their own ideas; the training also continued, led by the older members of the company. As indicated above, such separations between the 'master' and his students eventually created tensions within the community. The younger students found themselves having to adapt to the increasing need to perform rather than train. Their loyalties must also have felt stretched between Copeau and the senior company members who wanted to develop the company's work along their own lines of interest. Suzanne Bing kept a faithful record of the group's work (Gontard 1974), but she clearly felt her position was somewhat compromised by her intimate relationship with Copeau and, possibly as a result, tended to put a generally positive gloss on his absences and the relationship between the group and its *patron*.

Things came to a head in March 1928, when the company premiered a new show, *La Danse de la Ville et des Champs* (*The Dance of the Town and the Fields*), which had been devised and rehearsed with very little input from Copeau himself. The first performance took place in front of a full house including old friends, former colleagues and Copeau. For many watching, the performance was a triumph of collaborative creation, an accomplished example of ensemble acting which demonstrated the power and effectiveness of choral movement, physical acting and mask-work (see Rudlin 1986: 109–110 for a full description). The next day the company assembled to hear Copeau's critique of the piece: it was devastating. Expecting notes for improvement, the troupe listened in a state of shock and dismay as Copeau derided their efforts and their work. He finished his critique with the word: 'Dust'. The actor Jean Villard-Gilles, several years later, still recalled the bitter disappoint of this moment: 'All our efforts, all our passions, all our joy – there was nothing left. Nothing found favour in his eyes' (Villard-Gilles in Rudlin 1986: 110).

There are several possible reasons for Copeau's destructive response to his students' work: possibly he had sought to bring the young troupe, elated by their success, back to earth; perhaps he found it difficult to accept the achievements of the Copiaus without his guiding presence; he might have found the relaxed and easy-going atmosphere that tended to permeate the group in his absence problematic for his natural asceticism; it is even possible that his increasingly strong religious sense found the work ultimately too secular. Whatever the reason, Copeau's crushing dismissal marked a watershed moment in his relationship with Les Copiaus. The company continued for one more year, adding new productions to their repertoire and even devising new collaborative performances (once again without Copeau's participation), but finally dispersed for good in 1929. The core of Les Copiaus was to continue, reforming as the Compagnie des Quinze, under the leadership of Michel Saint-Denis. Although the ways had parted, both Copeau and his former colleagues retained a very warm and real affection for each other – Copeau continued to support his former students' work, and they never forgot the legacies he had left them: of rigour, commitment, passion and creativity. The explorations the group had undertaken had proved that a new *commedia* was indeed possible; they had brought back to life traditions of masked improvisation and popular theatre which were timely and which offered an invigorating new energy to the theatre. Ironically it was perhaps the very rigour, passion and energy which had made the experiment possible which had in the end brought about its eventual demise. The Vieux-Colombier experiment, which had started at one end of the decade and transformed itself through various stages including the retreat to Burgundy and the work of the Copiaus, had, it seems, reached its natural conclusion. Copeau's project to rejuvenate the theatre had finally reached the fulfilment of its first phase; over the next three decades his former pupils continued the work they had begun together – establishing important regional and national theatre initiatives and passing on the skills and techniques they had acquired under Copeau.

Popular theatre, the Comédie-Française, and sacred drama (1929–1949)

Once again Copeau's personal theatrical mission was drifting into disarray. In a manner reminiscent of his departure from the Vieux-Colombier, the end of the Burgundy experiment came quite quickly and unexpectedly. At the same time his inner life was going through a period of profound change as he continued to come to terms with the personal and artistic implications of his conversion to Catholicism. For two years he now retreated from practical theatre work as he wrestled internally with his creative impulses and his beliefs, unsure in which direction he should travel next. Eric Bentley (1950: 50) suggests that the tensions between Copeau's Catholicism and his commitment to the rediscovery of dramatic expression were profound and antithetical, leading Copeau eventually to compromise the rigour of his dramatic explorations. Certainly, throughout his life in the theatre, Copeau struggled between public exhibition and celebration, and personal seclusion and self-denial. Inevitably his choice of direction at this point in his life was shaped by the reality that he now lacked a troupe of his own, though he toyed occasionally with the possibility of re-grouping the Vieux-Colombier company (Kurtz 1999: 132). He was by now an international theatrical figurehead, and continued to lecture and give readings both in France and abroad; but he relied upon invitations to direct. His first opportunity was an offer to mount a mystery play, *Santa Ulvina*, at Florence in 1933. The production enabled Copeau make use of a medieval site, the cloisters of Santa Croce, and to explore the potential the site offered for experiment with the position of the audience, the use of the *tréteau*, and the movement of actors across broad open spaces. However, as John Rudlin points out, Copeau's interest at this time was actually less to do with these aspects than with 'his new quest for theatre-as-communion' and 'the actual popularity of theatre' (Rudlin 1986: 116). The strength of Copeau's religious convictions meant that he now believed that any new popular theatre must also be a religious theatre, or at least, as John Rudlin suggests, a theatre that has a role in revealing and confirming social morality. For Copeau, the idea of a 'popular' theatre was strongly linked with his faith in the social value of the great theatres of the past – of Ancient Greek drama and the European medieval mystery plays – theatres which offered models for simple but profound dramatic expression. Through his talks and his writing, in particular his essay 'Le Théâtre Populaire' (Copeau 1941), he advocated for a decentralised structure for theatre in France, for a theatre that could function not only to rebuild a sense of French cultural pride and identity at a time of German Occupation but also to respect and respond to the diversity of French culture as represented in the regions outside Paris. This was to be one of his most important and lasting legacies.

Copeau's return to Catholicism was the result of several complex factors and much personal soul-searching. Certainly on a wider social and cultural scale we can understand his personal decision as a subconscious response to the increasing spiritual unease that was pervading Europe during the 1930s. There was a common perception in some quarters that society was entering a period of moral danger caused by the pressures of modern urban life, increasing secularisation and threats to national culture. Copeau's work in Florence on two grand-scale religious dramas was clearly part of a search for a new unifying role for theatre. Mass performances, pageants and rallies were popular throughout Europe at this time, though put to very different ends according to national political agendas (i.e. the Nazi mass movement choirs for the 1936 Olympics). The complex issues of nationalism and the expression of national and popular concerns through art were of course to be become pressing concerns with the outbreak of war in 1939.

In 1940, at a time of crisis for the French nation, Copeau was offered the directorship of the Comédie-Française. He had initially been approached about running the theatre in the mid-1930s, but having made his conditions clear he found that the Government fought shy of the kind of changes he proposed, and his appointment was shelved. By 1940 much had changed: France had surrendered to Germany, Paris was occupied, and French theatre needed strong leadership if it was to maintain a valuable cultural role in this difficult environment. This was not a post that he would naturally have sought, and the likelihood is that he thought he might be able to be an agent of long overdue change and renewal. He was only partially successful and resigned several months later, having fallen out with the German authorities and the Vichy Government, who demanded that he put pressure on his son Pascal to quit the Resistance (Kurtz 1999: 145). This cannot have been an easy decision for him, and he left Paris again for Pernand in order to escape the 'vanity and *cabotinage*' (Copeau in Rudlin 1986: 118), and to live a relatively quiet life based once more in his beloved Burgundy. News of Michel Saint-Denis' successes in London must have given him cause for great pride, and perhaps encouraged him to continue to direct. Copeau's final major production was a further re-working of the 'mystery play' form, *Le Miracle du Pain Doré* (*The Miracle of the Golden Bread*), in 1943. The performance took place in the cloisters of the Hospices de Beaune, and drew extensively on his experiences in Florence, on his previous work on the Greek chorus and the Japanese Nōh Theatre, and on his understanding of Appia's ideas of the relationship between theatre and music (Rudlin 1986: 120).

The **Vichy Government** was established after the Franco-German armistice in June 1940. The agreement allowed Germany control of north and western France, whilst the Vichy Government, lead by Marshall Pétain, retained control of the south (it was based in the city of Vichy) and the French colonial empire. Pétain assumed personal control of the government, effectively dismissing the Senate and the Assembly. To this extent his values of patriotism, family, religion and hard work became the dominant values which he sought to promote within the 'new' France. In 1942 his regime assisted in the deportation of French Jews to the concentration camps.

Despite the exercises in popular religious drama, Copeau seems by the 1940s to have lost the driving passion for his work which marked his earlier years. In part his declining health was to blame, he suffered from thickening of the arteries (atherosclerosis) for a large portion of his later life. He was, as a result, no longer able to take on the sheer volume of work that he had managed in his former days. There are suggestions (Added 1996) that Copeau's writings at this time can be seen as in some senses favourable towards Pétain's right-wing ideology. Such a view represents a misunderstanding of Copeau's passionate pride in his national culture and of his commitment to a theatre which speaks to the common people as well as to the theatrical *cognoscenti*. His writings on popular theatre, his period at the helm of the Comédie-Française, and his epic productions of religious plays are in this sense the activities of a man searching for that which could heal, unite and give purpose to a country riven and humiliated by defeat and occupation. Though his work as a director was minimal after the War, his desire for recognition as a writer did not leave him, and he continued to write plays and to publish articles about his experiences and ideas, up until his death on 20 October 1949 at the Hospice in Beaune – the very place where a few years earlier he had staged his last production.

Le patron

The psychological forces that contributed to Copeau's charisma and energy were also the source of some of his inner struggles and personal disappointments. His life was driven by contradictory impulses that must have created powerful tensions for him. Despite a strong moral and religious sensibility, he had several affairs outside his marriage – one of which resulted in a child; it is possible that the pressure of reconciling his sexual energies with the guilt he must have felt as a result of his strong Catholic beliefs may have intensified his zeal for purity, discipline and rigour in his theatre work. Copeau was a man of great energy and conviction, a charismatic figure able to draw others to him and to enthuse them with his own vision; but, although others held him in deep affection, it is difficult to tell how much at peace he was with himself. His intense passion for theatre sometimes meant that he trod a lonely path – he was not a man who found compromise easy, and he demanded the best from himself and from those he worked with. Copeau liked to take on everything himself – he knew every aspect of the making of theatre from personal experience, and he encouraged his students and fellow actors to do the same. If there is one criticism of his dedication and enthusiasm it might perhaps be that it left him too demanding of himself to become a great actor or a great playwright (an ambition he had cherished from childhood). Though he achieved success in both these areas, his real talent lay in directing and teaching, in encouraging, shaping and developing the creative abilities of others. In this he was supremely gifted, and it is here that his influence on the future development of theatre practice and cultural policy was most profound.

3.2   Copeau's ideas in production: *Les Fourberies de Scapin*

Jacques Copeau recognised that a renewed French theatre could not and should not blindly turn its back on the past. To do so would be to ignore the vital energies and the powerful sense of scenic poetry which he believed informed the work of the great dramatic authors. Throughout the most productive phases of his career, Copeau brought the same experimental rigour to his revivals of classic plays as he did to the work of new French playwrights. In fact, it would be fair to say that a large part of his reputation as a powerful force in French and European theatre was based on his revivals of works by classic playwrights such as Shakespeare and Molière. In some respects the motivation for Copeau in mounting revivals was clearer and more immediate. For over two hundred years, the Comédie-Française had regarded itself as the 'spiritual home' of Molière and the classic French dramatists, Copeau was to attempt nothing less than a full-scale assault on this cultural dominance.

> The **Comédie-Française** is the national theatre of France, and the oldest national theatre in the world. Founded after Molière's death in 1673, it has survived several historical crises which have seen it divide and re-unite. Its reputation is based largely on its productions of classic French playwrights such as Molière, Racine and Corneille, though it has also produced notable productions of modern writers. The director-ship of the Comédie-Française is a state appointment; the post was briefly held by Copeau in 1940.

This chapter will examine a key production from one of the most productive periods of Copeau's career. Between *Une Femme Tuée par la Douceur* (*A Woman Killed with Kindness*) in 1913 and his departure for Burgundy in 1924, the Vieux-Colombier Theatre, under Copeau's direction, produced something in the region of 147 productions (including revivals). Such a large and varied body of work makes the task of picking one production very difficult. Several of his productions (e.g. *La Nuit des Rois* (*Twelfth Night*), *Les Frères Karamazov* (*The Brothers Karamazov*), and *Le Pacquebot* (*Tenacity*) are already covered in some detail elsewhere (Kurtz 1999; Rudlin 1986). Equally not all of his productions with the Vieux-Colombier give us useful insights into his later work in Burgundy. Copeau was never closely associated with any one particular contemporary playwright, as Stanislavsky was with Anton Chekhov for instance; however, if there was one constant lodestar guiding Copeau's career it was Molière. Molière's life and work, as we have already seen, represented so much of what Copeau aspired to achieve within a living, artistic and socially purposeful theatre. Copeau produced most of Molière's plays at some point during his career, but one production in particular can be seen as central in the development of his ideas and practices, the late comedy *Les Fourberies de Scapin* (*The Tricks of Scapin*). The play was first performed by the Vieux-Colombier company in the Garrick Theatre in New York on 27 November 1917 and remained in the repertoire until 13 May 1922, when it was presented in the open air outside the Church of Saint-Sulpice in Paris; the production's four and a half year life-span thus encompasses probably the most productive and critically successful period for both Copeau and his company. It is during this period that Copeau is able to realise for the first time many of his most cherished ambitions: the secure commencement of the Vieux-Colombier School, the nurturing of new theatrical talent, the development of improvisation within rehearsal and training, the use of masks in training, and the exploration of the skills and traditions of the Italian *commedia dell'arte*. *Les Fourberies de Scapin* provides us with an insight into the significant links between Copeau's work in direction and performance and his ideas for the rejuvenation of the theatre. There is certainly much of interest in the later work of Les Copiaus; but the work after 1924, whilst it reflects Copeau's visionary influence, relies less on his own personal contribution. Adequate records, reviews, photographs and testimonies survive for Copeau's productions of *Les Fourberies de Scapin* to enable us to examine the production in sufficient detail – in particular Louis Jouvet's carefully annotated edition of the play (Molière 1951) provides details of some of Copeau's original stage directions and represents perhaps the closest we can get to a textual recreation of one of his productions.

Copeau (1879–1949)

Les Fourberies de Scapin *(The Tricks of Scapin) by Molière*

In 1920 Copeau gave a production of *Les Fourberies de Scapin* by Molière. Set on a bare platform, ruthlessly lit like a boxing ring, it recaptured the spirit of the Commedia dell'Arte without any laborious imitation of the past.

(Saint-Denis 1960: 22)

Les Fourberies de Scapin is one of Molière's late three-act farces; it was first performed in Paris at the Palais Royal (the home of Molière's company) in 1671, two years before his death. At first sight it seems a strange choice for Copeau to mount a revival of such a light piece at the start of such an important event as the Vieux-Colombier's first season in New York, but the play was chosen for two very specific purposes. On the one hand, the play represented a piece of cultural propaganda; it was intended to warm the American audience to the French people – the performance was introduced by Suzanne Bing, who greeted the audience, offering 'a smile from France in the midst of war' (Bing in Kurtz 1999: 53). Bing's greeting was followed by an introduction in which each member of the company announced their name and responsibility. Copeau was very aware of the need to explain what the company were about to present – its relationship to their work as a whole, and to the principles underpinning their performances. On the other hand, the production represented a return to the basics of theatre and acting; Copeau's own statement reveals his commitment to the search for what is direct, simple and self-renewing in theatre: 'I am simply a man who performs his job as best he can, learning it each day, and each day discovering something he did not know the day before' (Copeau in Kurtz 1999: 53). This statement is on one level offered as a simple gesture of modest humility in front of a new audience, but we can also read it as an indication of the 'attitude' with which Copeau intended that the play should be performed. Acting was a serious job – a task that the actor had to undertake 'as best he can' – and the work should be undertaken with as little fuss as possible. It was the duty of the actors therefore to apply themselves whole-heartedly to the task of embodying the characters' actions, without embellishment. Furthermore, the actors should pour their interest into what they were doing, absorb themselves in the task – the process of acting thus became a journey for the actor, and the art of acting was always coming into knowledge and never fully achieved.

In much the same way that Shakespeare had, by this time, become iconic within British theatre, Molière had also acquired a similar status within the French theatre. Copeau's production broke away from the reverential and tired traditions of the Comédie-Française to present the play with a vigour, physicality and playfulness which critics had not experienced before – 'Molière reborn!' exclaimed one reviewer (John Corbin, *The Times*, 2 December 1917). What Copeau possessed was an ability to draw out of his actors performances which *embodied* the words and made physically present the energies, rhythms and playfulness of the text. However despite the production's originality, Copeau was adamant that he was not so much revolutionising theatre as rediscovering its essential principles. To make this clear he declared that 'This production of *Les Fourberies* is in the traditional category, it is not revolutionary' (Copeau in Molière 1951: 21, author's translation).

The Vieux-Colombier's first production of the play met with a generally positive reception in New York. Audience numbers were smaller than expected, perhaps because the piece was considered too light and farce too insignificant a medium for an audience who had come expecting something more weighty and profound. Most critics were intrigued and amused by the play's staging, fascinated by the *tréteau nu*, and engaged by the cast's playfulness and directness. Copeau's atmospheric and emotionally intense adaptation of Dostoyevsky's novel, *Les Frères Karamazov* (*The Brothers Karamazov*), which was revived a few months later, did better box office – it was more in line with the popular tastes of the New York theatre-going public. Nonetheless, *Les Fourberies de Scapin* offers an important illustration of the kind of actor-based theatre which Copeau had advocated so strongly during his lecture tour the previous winter: 'Here was a play acted with the body far more than with the brain or the voice' (Kurtz 1999: 53). The production was woven through with a simplicity, freshness, imagination and vigour which must have been a pleasant surprise to any for whom Molière had become little more than an historical figure or a 'national treasure'.

Copeau's belief in the play and its importance in relation to the company's mission was not shaken by the reaction in New York. He decided to restage *Les Fourberies de Scapin* as part of the company's new season on their return to Paris. No doubt he wished to reassert his personal belief in the production, and also perhaps to fine tune it in more sympathetic surroundings. The Paris critics were more receptive to his innovations, though their comments still betrayed a lingering scepticism that the piece was significant enough to merit Copeau's attention. What the critics missed was the value of Copeau's work for the working-class theatre-goer. Maurice Kurtz relates how Georges Vitray, one of Copeau's actors, overheard a worker express to a friend his amazement, after seeing *Les Fourberies*, that, '*mon vieux*, you know what? They don't have stage sets. They sit right on the steps so you *see the words*' (cited in Kurtz 1999: 84). What better expression could there be of Copeau's special talent for making the text come alive with a physical presence. *Les Fourberies de Scapin* was also an important production for Copeau's own personal creative journey. It marked a key stage in his exploration of the skills and techniques of the *commedia dell'arte*, an exploration which was to culminate in the 'new Commedia' created by Les Copiaus. It introduced the *tréteau nu* (bare platform) which Copeau borrowed from the medieval theatre, as a central element in a simple and uncluttered staging system. Equally, the open-air performance of the play in May 1922, in the Place Saint-Sulpice in the Latin Quarter of Paris, can be seen in hindsight as a pre-cursor of the 'booth' theatre performances of Les Copiaus and of the public pageantry of Copeau's later sacred plays.

The play: a synopsis of the plot

Les Fourberies de Scapin is a three-act prose comedy, set in Naples. Below is an outline of the plot:

Act 1

The young Octavio panics when he hears the news from his valet Sylvestre that his father, Argante, is returning, eager to marry him off to Hyacinthe, the absent daughter of his old friend Géronte. In despair Octavio turns to Scapin for advice and help. He describes the situation to Scapin, explaining his friend Léandre's love for a young gypsy girl, Zerbinette, and his own affections for another poor young woman, whom he has only just married three days ago. The young woman, who unbeknown to Octavio is actually Géronte's daughter Hyacinthe, enters and they both proclaim their undying love for each other. Scapin agrees to help the lovers, he starts by teaching Octavio how to stand up to his father's questioning. Despite Scapin's tutoring, Octavio runs off as his father enters, leaving Scapin and Sylvestre to face the wrath of Argante, who has just heard of his son's marriage to an unknown girl. Scapin argues that Octavio was forced into marriage by the young woman's family, plotting that Argante will forgive his son if he thinks that he was simply unfortunate enough to be 'caught out'. Nonetheless Argante threatens that the marriage must be annulled, despite Scapin's appeals to the damage that might be done to his own and his son's reputation. Scapin has begun to lay his plot and now recruits Sylvestre as a player in his scheme.

Act 2

Argante and Géronte bicker with each other over the cause of the problems besetting their marriage plans for their off-spring, blaming each other's bad parenting. Argante leaves having hinted that Géronte should look to the behaviour of his own son, Léandre. Léandre enters and is confronted by his father who, before he leaves for his house, demands to know the truth about what has gone on. On meeting Octavio and Scapin, Léandre accuses his valet of betraying him. He threatens Scapin with a beating unless he owns up to what he has done – Scapin owns up to several misdemeanours, but not to telling Géronte about Léandre's romance. Carlo, a rascal, enters and tells Léandre that gypsies have his beloved Zerbinette and that unless he pays them at once he will lose her forever. Léandre now has to beg Scapin to help him out, and Scapin makes him take back all the names and insults he has just been called before he agrees to help both Octavio and Léandre raise the cash they need to solve their problems. Scapin then tells the two lovers to fetch Sylvestre while he engages with Argante, who is still determined to get his son's marriage annulled. Scapin lies that the family of Octavio's wife are willing to fix a quick annulment for a large sum of money. Scapin, wheedles and connives, trying everything to get Argante to agree to pay the sum Octavio requires, two hundred pounds. Sylvestre enters, disguised as a villainous member of the wife's family, and hearing from Scapin of Argante's reluctance to pay up threatens to kill him. Argante, terrified, hides behind Scapin and listens and watches as the disguised Sylvestre shows how Argante will die when he finds him. This convinces Argante, who, as soon as Sylvestre has left, gives Scapin the money. Scapin then turns his attention to Géronte, pretending to search desperately for him in order to let him know that his son has been kidnapped by sailors from a Turkish galley who are demanding five hundred guineas in ransom. Géronte too falls for Scapin's tricks and, reluctantly, hands over the money. Scapin gives the money to the two lovers and swears to get his revenge on Géronte for the way he has treated him.

Act 3

Hyacinthe and Zerbinette are brought together for safety, under the care of Sylvestre and Scapin. Zerbinette expresses her resolution that she shall not return Léandre's love until she is sure of his hand in marriage. Zerbinette tells Hyacinthe that she does not know who her parents are. Scapin suggests that it is the ups and downs of love and life that make both enjoyable. The others go off leaving Scapin to meet Géronte. Scapin tells Géronte that Octavio's wife's family now want to have him killed because they think it is his fault that Argante wants the marriage annulled. Scapin offers to help Géronte escape the wife's family by hiding him in a sack. Once Géronte is in the sack Scapin pretends to be a member of the villainous family and interrogates himself over his master's whereabouts. He then pretends to be hit while protecting his master's father, whilst beating the sack and giving Géronte a good hiding! Eventually Géronte can take no more and gets out of the sack, Scapin runs away. Géronte is furious with Scapin's trick, but is met straightaway by Zerbinette. She is laughing at what has happened to her, and tells him the story: about how a young man fell in love with her, how the gypsies she was with would not part with her without being paid a large sum of money, and how the young man's foolish father was tricked out of a large sum of money by a servant. Géronte reveals that he is the father and leaves to search for his son. Zerbinette confesses to

> Sylvestre that she has 'spilt the beans'. Argante and Géronte meet together, realising that Scapin has hoodwinked them both. Géronte also bewails the news he has just received that his daughter from his secret first marriage, whom he has not seen for many years, has been lost at sea. At that moment his child's old nurse enters. She has been trying to seek out Géronte, unable to find him because he had changed his name. She confirms that Géronte's daughter is near at hand, but she also announces that his daughter is married – without his consent because they had not been able to find him. Argante and Géronte, surprised but happy, go to see Hyacinthe. Sylvestre brings Scapin up to date with events and warns him that the old men are after him. Octavio tells his father he will remain married to his wife whatever his father thinks, only to find that his father is more than happy with the match as his son has in fact made the desired match himself. Zerbinette apologises to Géronte for laughing at his predicament, but he still refuses to let her be married to his son. Léandre enters to declare that the gypsies have just revealed that she came from Naples and from a well-to-do family. He shows a bracelet which the gypsies also took – Argante recognises the bracelet and realises that Zerbinette is his own long-lost daughter! Carlo brings in Scapin, dying, mortally injured by a falling mason's hammer, and seeking forgiveness for his sins. Argante and Géronte forgive him everything and everyone goes in for the wedding feast.

Notice the plot structure. The play uses stock characters – masters and servants, rich fathers, lovers, lost children, scoundrels – in conventional story lines – the lost child is rediscovered, the thwarted lovers find true happiness, the wily servant outwits his master. This kind of narrative structure, which may to some modern audiences seem a little contrived and cliché-ridden, nonetheless has a long and healthy pedigree. The plot is based on the *Phormio* of the Roman playwright Terence, which Molière knew well, and also draws on the tricks and traditions of the Italian *commedia dell'arte* (a successful Italian troupe shared the Palais Royal with Molière's company). Scapin is the son of Brighella, a well-established stock character within the *commedia* repertoire; he is a crafty character whose name comes from the Italian for 'escape' or 'run away'. Molière's intention in writing and presenting this play was thus two-fold: this play is an unashamed demonstration of his skill and wit as a playwright and an actor (Molière himself played Scapin); and, it is a clear acknowledgement of the importance and value of such traditional skills and knowledge, skills and knowledge that are part of the foundations on which he built his more ambitious and innovative plays. On another level there is some evidence that Molière produced *Scapin* for more strategic reasons – his company had struggled to compete with the commercial success of the Italian troupe in Paris, *Scapin* was an attempt to reclaim the popular ground on his own terms. No doubt Copeau too believed in the need to provide an introduction to his new and experimental staging ideas that was also popular and accessible.

Why did Copeau choose this play?

For Copeau, the decision to produce any play by Molière could never be accidental. Molière was a profound and lasting source of inspiration for him: an example of the role of playwright/director/actor/manager which he himself played within his company, a representative of the values which he was seeking to re-establish in French theatre. Copeau was later to pronounce that, 'It was under the invocation of Molière that the Vieux-Colombier was founded' (Copeau 1990: 142). Copeau's interest in Molière's short farces was motivated primarily by a wider interest in their roots in the lively and popular traditions of the *commedia dell'arte* rather than by any literary or academic interest.

Les Fourberies de Scapin is a playful piece of writing – it invites the actor to enjoy the act of performing, to use their skills with delight and to celebrate the theatricality of the stage. Copeau toyed with the idea that playwrights such as Molière and Shakespeare, who were not just writers but were actors as well, embedded into their writing indicators for the actor, subtle suggestions of movement, gesture, style, rhythm, character, and atmosphere: 'When a text is created for dramatic life, there is a necessary *mise en scène* within the work itself' (ibid.: 144). Though not completely wedded to the idea, he certainly found the notion of reading a text in this way an 'agreeable and fertile' (ibid.) approach for the actor. He thus understood the actor's job in relation to the task of discovering such indicators and translating them into action. It is in this sense that an actor can then be said to be 'obedient' to the text. Copeau suggests that such a reading of a theatrical text is not immediately evident to the literary critic, or to the academic, but that the ability to read a dramatic text as *theatre* is central to the staging of a text (and central to the skills of the actor). In order to read in this way, the actor requires an understanding of the playful possibilities of theatre – the actor must grasp how the internal logic of the *action* may be more important than any literal interpretation of what is spoken. Scapin's ruse to deceive Géronte into a painful beating, for instance, is pure theatre, illustrating how magical and fantastical the tricks of the performer can be. To the reader it seems little more than a clumsy piece of traditional stage business, hard to believe and lacking in psychological sophistication – but such a reading misses the point that Molière is trying to make. At one and the same time we see Scapin behave as a loyal servant protecting his master from a villain, and the old man getting kicked in the sack by the same servant – we see the actor playing a rogue playing a loyal servant. The logic of Scapin's actions and movements in this particular scene flow not from a simple psychological reading of the text, but from the logic of the body (what movement could follow from the position I am in now) and the logic of the imagination (how can I play with this situation or with this movement). Scapin's tricks are thus the tricks of the actor – we see both what is and what is not, we see the body transform and the imagination fly. The play is also a farce and relies upon pace, rhythm and timing to achieve its full comic effect, always balanced perilously on the edge of collapse and disaster. The actor playing Scapin must flirt with the possibility of failure, of being caught out by the master he is beating; the pretence must be played on a knife-edge of risk and believability. For Copeau, the particular features of farce, and of this play in particular, are not just comic devices but also represent the poetics of theatre *in action*, and indeed the fragility of our hold on life itself. The play provided a perfect arena in which Copeau could maximise the expressive effect of the rhythm and dynamics of the actor's movement. In fact, it is the play's very simplicity that makes it so attractive as a 'play-space' for the actor's imagination: 'There is in a work like *Les Fourberies de Scapin* a kind of playful elasticity which communicates, which allows the actor to be truly creative' (Copeau in Molière 1951: 28, author's translation).

Staging

The stage space

For Copeau's first production of *Les Fourberies* in 1917 at the Garrick Theatre, New York, the existing stage space was transformed. The stage surround was stripped of its conventional decoration and left simple, grey and empty, with a small platform (*le tréteau*) placed centre-stage. The proscenium arch was opened up, allowing the stage space to connect more directly with the auditorium. Four years earlier Copeau had written that his rejuvenated theatre would require a bare stage (Copeau in Cole and Chinoy 1970) and now, finally, here it was. The bare stage and the raised platform were intended to emphasise the presence of the actor, bringing the audience's attention to their movement and footwork. The platform consisted of four large, square pieces of wood, raised on trestles. It was accessed by five staircases each with four steps, two of the staircases being at the front and one on each of the other three sides. Between the front two sets of steps were several cubes which acted as a bench. For Copeau, this meant that: 'The stage is already action, it gives material form to the action' (Copeau in Knapp 1988: 208). The audience saw only the bare stage, the platform, and, at the back of the stage, an orange velvet curtain. This was a controversial and innovative staging experiment to take to the heart of New York theatre. With only the simplest props and staging, the actors were required to use all their skills to summon up not only the illusion of character, but also of place, time and atmosphere. The production of *Les Fourberies de Scapin*, in this respect, provided a particular impetus for the company's early experiments with mime techniques. It challenged their abilities to create character, place, time and mood with the simplest of resources; no doubt giving those in the company such as Suzanne Bing, who were later to teach in the school, much food for thought.

The staging drew directly on Copeau's knowledge of the booth theatres of sixteenth-century Europe. The raised platform, traditionally used to improve visibility for the audience, was the most direct reference to the earlier staging conventions. For the Vieux-Colombier company it created different levels for the stage action, a central focus for the audience's gaze, as well as a symbol of the simple authenticity they sought to bring to their playing. On a practical level, entrances and exits could no longer be as straightforward as opening or closing a door in a stage flat – the actor would need to enter several moments before their cue, in effect 'chasing' the action already on stage. The action would, in this manner, seem to 'wash' against the *tréteau* in waves, creating an ebb and flow of action and characters around the central focus point.

Lighting

Copeau had read about the ideas of Appia and Craig and had no doubt discussed ideas for lighting with both men during his meetings with them a few years earlier. In his early articles he had rejected the use of stage machinery:

> Being enthusiastic about the inventions of engineers or electricians always means giving usurped importance to canvas, painted cardboard, lighting arrangements – always means falling somehow or another into tricks. Old or new, we repudiate them all.
> *(Copeau in Guicharnaud 1967: 301–302)*

However, by the time he had completed his New York tour and returned to Paris, he had clearly recognised the value of a discreet, simple and unobtrusive use of lighting. His lighting plans for *Les Fourberies* drew on Craig's and Appia's innovations, and were also driven by his own determination to clear the stage space of unnecessary pretence. Michel Saint-Denis describes the stage of the 1920 revival as 'ruthlessly lit like a boxing ring' (Saint-Denis 1960: 22), implying that the lighting was bright, intense, and overhead – creating at once an image of openness and of focus, of risk and of excitement. The suggestion of a boxing ring, presumably enhanced by the presence of the raised platform of the *tréteau nu*, would have had some resonance for a cosmopolitan New York audience. The boxing ring had a special appeal within early twentieth-century culture; boxing was a popular form of male physical education, and an equally popular spectator sport (Ruffini 1995). Copeau would have been aware of the associations he was drawing on and no doubt he was not averse to aligning his performers with the lithe nimble athleticism of the modern boxer.

For the new Paris season in 1920, Copeau and Jouvet installed a new lighting system which did away with the conventional footlights and made innovative use of new lighting technology. Jouvet designed and installed a set of revolving lanterns mounted at corners above the space, and also an array of lights concealed within a triangular box structure and suspended directly over the playing space. These overhead lights had the effect of flooding the stage with light, vividly illuminating the movement and actions of the actors and emphasising this above all else. The removal of footlights meant that the melodramatic effect of under-lighting the actors was avoided. The overhead lighting also helped to establish the heat and brilliance of the play's Neapolitan setting. Several years prior to Brecht's earliest work as a director, Copeau was already employing some of the staging techniques which the German playwright/director was to make part of his own, more overtly politicised, theatrical language (simple staging, bright lighting, acknowledgement of the audience's presence). Copeau's agenda was not political, and his work is not as well known, but he was no less influential in revolutionising lighting design for the modern stage.

The actors

The part of Scapin was played by Copeau. By the time of the first performance in New York, Copeau was thirty-eight years old. He was taking on a major part in a classic farce, a part which required mobility, agility, comic timing and improvisatory skills which would challenge an actor half his age. Remarkably, given the other pressures on Copeau as leader of the company, he pulled it off with enormous success:

> Copeau brought out Scapin's turbulence, dynamism, and seemingly endlessly refreshing store of energy and imagination. He was movement incarnate, cascading motility, leaping here and there, with long and lithe strides, stopping but for seconds – just enough time to think up new tricks, new deceits, acrobatic stunts, and rogueries, thereby accomplishing his ends in the most theatrically perfect way possible.
>
> (Knapp 1988: 211)

Contemporary critics were struck by the plasticity of Copeau's performance, by 'its lightness of touch and mercurial swiftness of changing mood' (*Morning Sun*, 28 November 1917). The complete physicality of the performance contributed to the impression that every inch of the actor's body had become expressive: 'at once an athlete, a harlequin, a mimic and a comedian. He talks with his face, feet and hands as well as with his voice' (*Brooklyn Eagle*, 28 November 1917). At the same time, Copeau's understanding of rhythm and the dynamics of movement meant that his performance had 'smoothness' as well as 'dexterity and lithe vigour' (*The Literary Digest*, 15 December 1917). Acting the role of Scapin had a particular significance for Copeau, as he believed that Molière himself had played the part at the play's first performance. The connection between himself and his historical role model would not have been lost on him; like Molière, he was the creative and organisational linch-pin for his company. In this sense his performance can also be understood as a living homage to Molière, an interpretation further strengthened by his insertion of a company performance, after the New York opening, of a short devised spectacle 'The Crowning of Molière'.

The part of Géronte was played by Louis Jouvet, one of Copeau's closest colleagues in the early days of the company. Jouvet was a bold actor, capable of giving full rein to the complete range of Géronte's emotions. He combined a humorous portrayal of physical decrepitude with a convincing display of Géronte's rapidly changing emotions of greed, fear, anger and shame. Several New York critics picked out Jouvet's performance as equally accomplished and equally important to the success of the production as that of Copeau. Remarkably, Jouvet's acting success was achieved alongside his many other significant responsibilities within the company, including supervising the redesign of the Garrick Theatre for the New York opening.

Both of these actors performed the same parts when the production was revived in Paris. The actress Jane Lory also continued in the part of Zerbinette. But the long and stressful New York tour had marked an important watershed for the company, revealing to Copeau those actors whom he could trust and with whom he could work in the future. Suzanne Bing, Robert Allard, Romain Bouquet, André Bacque and Georges Vitray – all of whom had previously performed in *La Nuit des Rois* (*Twelfth Night*) – joined the cast in Paris, no doubt bringing with them the rich experience of classical comedy they had gained from the earlier Shakespeare production. Copeau continued to devise short improvised prologues for the play, all of which drew on the traditions of the *commedia dell'arte*. His own direct involvement in the play gradually diminished until by the time of the open air performance in 1922 the part of Scapin was played by Georges Vitray.

Rehearsing and acting: the actor's approach to Les Fourberies de Scapin

Though Copeau was probably aware of the kind of rigorous textual analysis which characterised Stanislavsky's System, this was not an approach which he felt was appropriate for the kind of theatre he was seeking to create. As Stanislavsky was eventually to realise himself, too much analysis can paralyse the actor's natural instincts for action and play:

> It isn't necessary to do analysis to get into a character or a play. It is an instinct or a talent which one either has or not, and this instinct alone gives the sense, the rhythm, the pulse of the character or of the play to the actor, just like a director.
> *(Copeau in Molière 1951: 19, author's translation)*

In rejecting heavy-handed text analysis Copeau was not promoting some form of anti-intellectualism, rather he was advocating a recognition of the importance of the actor's instinctual responses, without which no amount of analysis could make the part or the play live. For Copeau, a play is not simply a collection of characters, but rather a work of art which has its own particular physicality, emotionality, spatiality and dynamics. This meant that the actor needed to read the play thoroughly but sensitively in order to grasp its overall atmosphere, mood and emotional dynamics. He describes the process as similar to woodcarving – the latent shape and structure is revealed gradually and through the interplay of the actor's technique and artistic sensibility. As the rehearsal readings progress, it becomes clear what is working and what is not, what the actors are finding that is vital and living in the play. In this sense, Copeau's acting and rehearsal 'technique' is one of playful physical expression combined with introspection and intuitive understanding. The actor and director have to bring into play their 'sense of theatre' – a sense which is a combination of critical understanding and of enjoyment and playfulness. Because this kind of understanding is not something which is easy to put into words, the emphasis in Copeau's rehearsals was on getting up and enacting the scenes, improvising and playing with the staging until it matched the director's and actors' senses of how the scene required itself to be played. Copeau allowed the actors to improvise around the text, sometimes for long periods, before drawing together elements from their play to form his final concepts for the *mise-en-scène* (Felner 1985: 42). The element that then linked the text and the movement in Copeau's technique was breath: 'To read a text, you must have sensitivity to the breath ... one speaks and acts as one breathes' (Copeau in Molière 1951: 24, author's translation).

This approach to acting and rehearsal was clearly well matched to a play such as *Les Fourberies de Scapin*. The play does not require deep and detailed analysis; its characters and its plot are easily recognisable and demand no profound psychological insights from the actors. The character's psychology, in so far as it is evident, is worn on the sleeve and exists less through subtext than through action and gesture. What is demanded is a sensitivity to rhythm and play, to the characters' physical pulse. Copeau believed that Molière's plays contained an implicit requirement for the actor to engage physically with the characters and the situations: 'There is a physical necessity made on the actor to be a dancer, feelingly to manifest this physical quality' (Copeau 1990: 144). The revealing word here is 'feelingly' – Copeau implies that the emotionality of the play is communicated not through the text or through the words, but through the physicality of the actor – their movements, gestures, actions. In so far as these physical elements are then organised, made meaningful and given intention, they become something approaching choreography. *Les Fourberies de Scapin* enabled Copeau to explore and develop this kind of approach to performance in detail. He realised that such a play could be interpreted as a kind of score for the actor – demonstrating to the young company how a writer could provide the sensitive actor with indications of the ebb and flow of the part and of the play, if they were open to receive it: 'This dance is in the text. It is not imagined' (ibid.). This kind of sensitive and sophisticated understanding of the dynamics of a play-text can easily be underestimated; several New York observers perceived nothing more than apparent exuberance, boisterousness and carelessness in the performances, with only the more perceptive critics recognising that these qualities were achieved with and through 'the most careful thought' (*New York Evening Post*, 28 November 1917).

Playing with objects

This vision of the rehearsal and acting process was an inclusive one, built on an holistic understanding of the actor's art. Thus, for Copeau even the smallest part of a scene has its value and importance. One wrong gesture or inflection can ruin the overall effect. Rather than ignore such problems Copeau preferred to go back on the scene and to modify the actions, checking how effectively everything hangs together. Rehearsing was a patient and careful procedure in which the company 'decoded' the play from words into actions whilst maintaining its essential coherence and quality. In a play such as *Les Fourberies de Scapin* even props had their special part to play and Copeau was insistent that their introduction into a scene had to be carefully worked out – on a bare stage props have an extra eloquence. We can look at an example of this by examining the way in which an umbrella or parasol was used to develop the playing of the character of Géronte. The parasol was itself an innovation – it is not specified in the original text, but was developed by Jouvet and Copeau as a simple way to indicate the heat of Naples and to provide the actor with a means of expression of character, intention and mood. The actor could open or close it, tap the ground, trail it behind him, point with it, use it as a weapon, or even as an extension of his own arm.

In pairs, look at the scene below (Act 3 Scene 2, author's translation) in which Scapin is talking to Géronte about the dangers facing him as a result of upsetting Octavio's bride's family.

GÉRONTE: What am I to do, my dear Scapin?
SCAPIN: I don't know, master – here's a bad business. I'm so scared for you I'm shaking from my head to my toes, and . . . what was that!

> GÉRONTE: Eh?
> SCAPIN: No. No, no, it's nothing.
> GÉRONTE: Can't you think of some way to get me out of this mess?
> SCAPIN: I can think of one way; but I would run the risk of getting beaten myself.
> GÉRONTE: Eh! Scapin, be a good servant: don't desert me, I beg you.
> SCAPIN: I'll try my best. I have a soft spot for you which won't let me leave you defenceless.
> GÉRONTE: You will be rewarded for it, I assure you. I promise you can have these clothes, when I've worn them a little longer.
> SCAPIN: Wait. Here's an idea, and I think it just might save your skin. Get inside this sack.
>
> Now, without the text, explore how both Géronte and Scapin might use the parasol:
>
> - defending
> - emphasising
> - hiding
> - dragging
> - disguising
> - protecting
> - comforting
> - restraining
> - pushing away
> - pointing/indicating
> - offering
> - getting attention
> - avoiding/dodging
>
> Now build a sequence which works with the lines, trying to keep the playfulness which you had when improvising. Look carefully at how your sequence works and consider also its rhythmic shape and structure – when is it hectic, when nimble, when slow and when frenetic. To what extent does the parasol assist in this? How much does it become an extension of the actor's body? How does it help to clarify meaning and intention? Can it be transformed to serve any other purpose?

Playing stock characters

The playing of stock characters is fraught with dangers, especially for the inexperienced or lazy actor. It can be only too easy to slip into a characterisation which is clichéd, two dimensional and predictable. Copeau recognised the challenge that a play like *Les Fourberies de Scapin* represented for his young troupe, but believed that the solution lay in trusting in Molière:

> Molière never created a mundane character, a stock character, as we say, or a fill-in, because he was a man of the theatre and he wrote for actors.
>
> *(Copeau 1990: 144)*

The characters may initially seem simple and stereotypical, but this is a misapprehension born from the expectation of psychological and social realism, from the dead-weight of tradition, and from a misunderstanding of the nature of this kind of comedy. Copeau saw this play as 'pure' theatre, and by this he meant that the internal logic which bound the play together and gave it coherence was not psychological, political or even entirely narrative, but essentially theatrical. Its driving energy was not that of the gentle drawing room comedy, but the lively 'ferocious' all-consuming energy of the *commedia dell'arte*. To play such characters demands a complete physical, vocal and mental commitment, as well as enormous fitness, agility and control on the part of the actors. The characters need to be able to turn on a sixpence, constantly on their toes in order to survive the twists and turns that fate throws at them. To achieve this kind of playing, actors need to be performing 'in the moment' – alive to all that is going on around them, to the possibilities their role offers, and to the potential offered by the objects, spaces and actors around them.

Playing the rhythm

Copeau came to theatre via the written media of playwriting and journalism, yet very early on in his career as a theatre director he realised the importance of the physical aspects of performance. We have already examined his commitment to the physical training of the actor – for the kind of theatre that he wanted to make he needed actors who were fit, strong, flexible and agile. Such physical ability needed however to be shaped and directed through the operation of a guiding set of aesthetic principles in order that it might become truly integral to the actor's art. The answer for Copeau, as for several other early twentieth-century theatre practitioners, came from the analysis of rhythm. Copeau, like Stanislavsky, Appia and Meyerhold, knew of the work of Emile Jaques-Dalcroze, and would have had some knowledge of the movement theories of Etienne Marey, Georges Demeny and Paul Souriau. Although by 1920 Copeau had rejected Jaques-Dalcroze's work as too formulaic and reductive, and Eurhythmics had been replaced by Hébertisme in the School curriculum, yet this should not be taken to mean that Copeau's interest in rhythm and acting was in any sense diminished. Rhythmic movement was, for Copeau, a way of opening up the actor to the rhythm of a piece of spoken text. He saw a direct relationship between reading dramatic text and rhythmic movement training (Copeau 1990: 58), which led him to believe that this kind of training must form the basis for a holistic training regime for the new actor. Copeau was critical of Jaques-Dalcroze's work with movement and spoken text, he found it affected and even a little ridiculous; but he knew instinctively that rhythmic awareness was a skill which the actor could and should possess.

What Copeau sought was to incorporate and internalise the sense of rhythm, in much the same way as Stanislavsky encouraged his students to explore what he called 'the inner tempo-rhythm' of a part. When he came to work on a play such as *Les Fourberies de Scapin*, Copeau saw immediately the importance of rhythm to the acting and to his own *mise-en-scène*. Right from the start of the play, Copeau wanted the actors' movements to give dramatic expression to the rhythms and dynamics within the play. Let's look at the opening scene and at Copeau's notes:

Les Fourberies de Scapin Act 1 Scene 1 (author's translation).

OCTAVIO: Ah! This is the worst news for a lover! What dire hardships I see coming my way! Silvestre, you tell me you've heard at the harbour that my father's coming home.
SILVESTRE: Yes.
OCTAVIO: And that he's arriving this very morning?
SILVESTRE: This very morning.

> OCTAVIO: And that he's coming back determined to get me married off?
> SILVESTRE: Yes.
> OCTAVIO: To the daughter of Signor Géronte?
> SILVESTRE: Of Signor Géronte.
> OCTAVIO: And that this girl is being summoned over especially from Taranto.
> SILVESTRE: Yes.
> OCTAVIO: And you had this news from my uncle?
> SILVESTRE: From your uncle.
> OCTAVIO: Who was instructed to do so in a letter from my father?
> SILVESTRE: By a letter.
> OCTAVIO: And you say that this uncle knows everything we've been doing?
> SILVESTRE: Everything.

The dialogue above appears quite bald and functional; Molière is using the scene simply to establish the plot and the characters. The structure is that of a double act routine, a rapid question-and-answer exchange between the anxious lover/son and the shifty servant. Let's look at what Copeau does with this section of the scene. According to Copeau's notes and stage directions (Molière 1951: 33), Octavio should enter suddenly from the left, extremely agitated, arms gesturing wildly to the sky, and pacing from left to right at the front of the stage. As Octavio gets to centre-stage Silvestre appears, on the same path across the stage, moving very slowly in contrast to his young master. As he does so he eats sunflower seeds which he takes from the pocket of his jacket. Octavio rounds on Silvestre, who responds incoherently, still chewing. This interplay continues between them, varying and developing as Octavio becomes more and more urgent and exasperated – pulling on his hat, waving his hands and so on. The exchange ends with Octavio walking backwards in front of Silvestre who slowly gains ground, finally reaching the steps on the right where he sits.

Straight away we can see that Copeau wants the two characters to be clearly differentiated by the rhythm of their movement. Furthermore, he intends that the rhythm of the movement creates and embodies the dramatic impact of the scene. In this scene, the rhythmic interplay comes from the rapid, anxious pacing of Octavio and the slow matter-of-fact chewing of Silvestre. Despite Octavio's role as the master and despite his attempts to impose his urgent rhythm on his servant, we can tell that it is Silvestre who is setting the pace and controlling the game. He plays with his master's agitation, setting a dramatic counter-context for the driving love story. Elsewhere in the play, the staging itself actively draws attention to the actor's rhythm. Copeau realised that the sound of footsteps, leaps, falls and the tapping of sticks and umbrellas could all variously function to announce someone's arrival, draw the audience's or the actor's attention, build suspense, increase the noise of a scene, or punctuate speech. Michel Saint-Denis (1982: 29) describes how the platform stage 'intensified, in a pleasant manner, the sounds made on it, either by the stamping, jumping feet of the younger characters or by the slow stomping of their elders accompanied by the tapping of their walking sticks'. John Rudlin (1986: 81) picks up on Saint-Denis' memories of the 'by-play of sound' created as the actors leapt from 'the hard coldness of the cement floor up to the warm, resounding wooden platform' (Saint-Denis 1982: 29), pointing out the manner in which the sounds created by Scapin's feet and Géronte's movements help to bring the comedy of the 'sack scene' in Act 3 Scene 2 to a riotous and noisy climax. We can see a similar but different effect later in the same scene when Géronte dances with rage as he listens to Zerbinette's story of his own foolishness – providing a counterpoint to the rhythm of her bubbling laughter. Similarly at the beginning of Act 2 Scene 1, we see Argante, hat in hand and dripping with sweat, bustle along in what may have seemed something like an agitated dance, performing what Knapp describes as 'arabesques' (Knapp 1988: 211) around the platform. In contrast, Géronte walks with short steps, sheltering his head from the sun with his parasol. The contrast is physical; there is an auditory and a visual contrast between the two old men, producing a counterpoint of rhythms and postures.

> With a partner, walk around the room, establishing a shared rhythm to your walk. Your walk should be neither too fast nor too slow. Now, while one of you maintains that rhythm, the other tries to walk at half the rhythm, and then twice the rhythm. Finally try to walk at the counter-tempo, in between your partner's footfalls. Change over. To finish, improvise an argument with your partner as you walk, allowing the changes in rhythm to take place as you engage with the argument with your partner. Perhaps you slow down your rhythm to make a point, or speed up your rhythm to express your frustration. Try to play with the rhythm, rather than let it dominate.
>
> Now pick a scene from the play – an argument, a love scene, a disagreement, or a plotting scene – and explore how the rhythm of the two characters' walks (or gestures, or speech) could be used to express physically the nature of the interplay between them. This same exercise could be developed further by using sticks, parasols, sacks, bags of money, food or a number of other properties as the medium for the rhythmic interplay.

Playing the space

Copeau intended the *tréteau* to be central to the staging of the play. In order to achieve this, he had to explore how the platform could be used as an integral part of the drama. Copeau discovered that as well as providing a clear and open space on which to expose the rhythmic interplay of the characters' movements, the platform stage could also function to create a physical expression of the characters' age and status – revealing their particular physical abilities. Copeau described it as operating, in this play, as a 'trap for old men' – giving them a sense of peril and danger and of the unknown. The young characters could leap on and off the platform, sometimes even using it as a kind of spring-board. The older characters were forced to clamber on and off, teeter on the steps or even go around it like an obstacle. The platform represented the status of the characters – achieving the platform indicating that a character had managed to assume status and/or authority within a scene – and of course the platform was dominated for most of the scenes by the figure of Scapin! How different this kind of playing is from the naturalistic drama – space is used symbolically, acoustically, rhythmically and dynamically, it comes alive and is an expressive element within the theatre event. The actors' posture, movements and gestures, and the fluid images which Copeau's *mise-en-scène* generate, are all shown in vivid relief against the bare stage and the *tréteau*. The effect is both sculptural and musical, creating dynamic living images and rhythmic counterpoints between characters. Even simple movements and gestures function musically, accumulating energy and rhythm, building their effect on the audience's imagination.

With no complex set changes to perform, the scenes can flow smoothly, quickly and efficiently one into the next – sometimes to magical effect, sometimes providing deliciously poignant overlaps as one character exiting nearly meets another entering. Place is established by a word and a gesture – in fact the overlay of fictive space (Naples) and theatrical space (the Vieux-Colombier stage) is made explicit through the very simplicity of the setting. This calls for a style of acting which is equally direct, and which can also move smoothly between the fictive and the overtly theatrical. Copeau found this quality in the naïve play of children and it is this playful but absorbed energy which seems to permeate his production notes.

Copeau's staging ideas have influenced several of the major figures of contemporary theatre. Peter Brook used similarly simple devices in several of his productions and theatrical experiments over the last thirty years. For his journey across Africa in the early 1970s his company used a large carpet to delineate the playing space; for his production of *La Tempête* he used a circular pit of sand; and, for his production of *Ubu*, a large industrial cable drum. Just as Copeau had done before him, Brook consciously made use of the qualities and associations of the materials and shapes of the set structures for his productions. The simple designs helped to establish the rhythms and dynamics of the piece as a whole. Both Brook and Copeau clearly searched for the simplest form of staging that would still be able to create a world which the play/text/improvisations could meaningfully inhabit. It is also possible to see similarities with the work of Steven Berkoff, who is equally sensitive to the playful possibilities of movement and space, using direction, rhythm and movement dynamics within bare spaces to establish place, mood and a sense of theatrical poetry.

A different kind of realism

Copeau was aware of Stanislavsky's production of *Les Fourberies de Scapin* at the Moscow Art Theatre. He had already noted that, 'Stanislavsky's *mise en scène* is unnecessarily realistic. In order to explain Scapin's sack, Stanislavsky puts a boat loaded with grain sacks at the back of the set, from which Scapin borrows the prop in the sack scene' (Copeau 1990: 261). For Copeau the 'location' of the sack was not important, it was there because it was needed: 'The sack was a traditional accessory in the theatre of the sixteenth century. It was frequently used' (Copeau in Molière 1951: 28, author's translation). Likewise, when the sack was finished with Géronte can simply kick it into the wings. Stanislavsky's productions relied for their veracity and inner logic on carefully worked out naturalistic details; Copeau believed that this kind of realism ignored the theatricality at the heart of Molière's theatre. Whereas Stanislavsky's approach to acting might certainly be capable of being adapted to nonnaturalistic plays, he seems to have struggled to develop an approach to staging which was as flexible. Copeau wrote in his notes that to base classical productions on the principles of realism was tantamount to a betrayal – it went against everything those plays stood for (ibid.: 19). This is of course not to say that Copeau entirely rejected realism – he advocated the use of elements of realism in order to maintain an appropriate feeling of vitality and relevance within the production – but he did not feel bound by the aesthetic logic of realism, and would transpose anachronistic realistic elements into period situations because he felt it was justified within the inner dynamics of the play (e.g. Géronte's umbrella). He rejected whole-heartedly the declamatory vocal delivery of the Comédie-Française, preferring instead a delivery which was natural, fluid and sensitive to the events on stage. Copeau specialised in giving dramatic readings – something he continued to do for most of his working life – and the simple, direct style of the reading was a style which infused the vocal delivery of the whole company. If this occasionally led to a slightly austere and presentational vocal style, nonetheless in the right circumstances it allowed the words to 'work' on the listener rather than requiring the actor to 'emote'.

Copeau (1879–1949)

Symbolism and scapin

Instead of a laboured realism, Copeau chose a simple bare staging – a choice which was undoubtedly influenced by his memories of the work of Craig and Appia. A clear stage would make room for the flow of movement which would bring the rhythms and dynamics of the play alive. Perhaps Copeau wanted, like Craig, to move beyond the suggestion of time and place towards some timeless representation of mood, ideas and a deeper dramatic reality, but he preferred to work on a less monumental and abstract scale. His staging did not set out to dwarf the actors but to provide them with a space which let their actions live and breathe, and which allowed the audience to feel closer to the stage and less intimidated by it. Like Craig he had a fine eye for the flow of lines of movement and action, but whereas Craig seemed happier working with inanimate objects, Copeau preferred the living movement of his actors. For both the aim seems to have been to create a space that in effect generates movement rather than simply framing it.

> Two years ago, I put on *Les Fourberies de Scapin*. In order to revive the movement with which the play was presented, I thought it advisable to conceive a stage lay-out which forcibly produced movement. So I imagined the tréteau, surrounded on four sides by steps, built in the centre of the stage, in order to compel the actors constantly to change position.
>
> *(Copeau 1990: 145)*

Copeau did not think of his theatre as 'symbolist', however he was aware of the symbolist movement and was in some respects closer to symbolism in his staging than to realism. His approach to staging aimed to humanise symbolism, bringing the scale of the poet's inner vision down to a more personal size. The characters of his dramas were always more than ciphers for the poet's inner mind – though Copeau championed the playwright as the poet of the theatre, he would never conceive of a theatre in which the actor/character was a mere pawn to the playwright's vision.

A useful comparison can be made with the early work of the London-based physical theatre company Complicite, for example *A Minute Too Late* (1984) or *Anything for a Quiet Life* (1987). In these shows, a seemingly simple and essentially comic narrative is set up around a group of clearly delineated characters; at the same time, a minimal but flexible staging allows the actors to pursue wonderful flights of fantasy and imagination, executed with physical skill and acrobatic agility. The whirling plot narratives, and the dreamlike fantasies weaved around them, leave us touchingly aware of the fickleness of fate and the futility of our struggle to stay on top of events. The lightness, joy, freshness and technical expertise of these productions gives us some insight into the possible effect which a production such as *Les Fourberies de Scapin* might have achieved, as well as demonstrating the continuing influence of Copeau's innovations.

Framing the event

For the first performance Copeau decided that the production needed some kind of introduction. In fact the evening was advertised as being composed of three parts: *L'Impromptu du Vieux-Colombier* by Jacques Copeau, *Les Fourberies de Scapin* by Molière, and *Le Couronnement de Molière* (*The Crowning of Molière*). There were several reasons for this. On one level Copeau was simply copying a tradition used by many renaissance playwrights – the use of a prologue and epilogue served to introduce the company and the work to an audience. In the context of the New York tour, the framing pieces also served to provide an introduction to the style of the company and to create an ambience for the evening as a whole. *L'Impromptu* offered the audience a form of introduction to the actors, using a format which was both traditional and yet which also emphasised the theatricality of the event. After a welcome address by Suzanne Bing, Copeau called on the 'spirit' of the theatre, represented by the dancer Jessmin Howarth, to inspire the company. His words echo Oberon's instructions to Puck, invoking the mystery of theatre tradition and the ritual power and magic of the stage. *L'Impromptu* finishes with Copeau calling out to the company who respond in chorus that they are ready, the stage manager then gives the traditional signal for the start of the play by knocking three times and the play begins and is acted 'sans interruption dans un mouvement rapide' (Copeau 1984: 175). The lack of an interval and the rapid pace clearly signal Copeau's conviction that the artistic integrity of the production was more important than the need to accommodate the conventional breaks. He was certainly convinced enough of the benefits of a form of improvised prologue to invent several other semi-improvised scenarios to introduce *Les Fourberies de Scapin* when it was revived again in Paris.

At the end of the play, after the curtain calls, Copeau placed the other short piece, *Le Couronnement de Molière*. A bust of Molière was brought on to the middle of the *tréteau*, and placed on a pedestal. The bust then became the focal point of a solo dance-drama; a performance quite probably choreographed by Jessmin Howarth, and thus drawing on a mixture of Ancient Greek and Eurhythmic references. After this homage in movement, the dancer lifts a flute to his mouth and produces a sound which is echoed by the chorus of actors in the wings. The ritual and symbolic nature of the piece is reinforced by the appearance of several figures – Aristophanes, Terence, Plautus, Harlequin, Shakespeare, and others – representing the comic traditions of Europe – who also dance in homage to Molière. Eventually all the various symbolic figures dance a *farandole* around the stage. The music ends, and Jessmin Howarth enters as the spirit of the Vieux-Colombier. She dances, finishing by introducing on to the stage Copeau's two small children, Marie-Hélène and Edi, each holding a dove in a cage (a symbol of the Vieux-Colombier Theatre) which they offer to the bust of Molière. Copeau enters in the costume of Scapin, under the robe he wore for *L'Impromptu*. He holds the hand of his young son, Pascal, who carries a crown of laurels. They approach the bust; Copeau recites a homage to Molière, at the end of which he lifts up his son who crowns the bust with the laurels.

The ritual elements of *Le Couronnement de Molière* are clearly intentional. Copeau meant this final part of the evening as a serious and artistic act of homage. As with *Les Fourberies de Scapin* it is easy to see that in the wrong hands this piece could seem trite, quaint, and overly reverential. It is rescued by the qualities which mark out so much of Copeau's best work: its simplicity, its bravery, its sincerity, its purposeful integration of dance, voice and movement, and its ability to bring into play the 'heart' of the company – its beliefs, its family ethos and its theatrical reference points. There is an element of the self-conscious about the framing of the main performance in this way. Copeau spent a lifetime as an educator – teaching, lecturing and giving demonstrations – and an element of the educational and expository lingers around the manner in which the opening night was presented. But before being too quickly critical of Copeau, we must recognise that the impulse behind the whole event was not that the audience should forget themselves, but that they should be awakened to the extraordinary power and poetry of theatre and its particular relationship with its audience and with western cultural history. It is all too easy to view *L'Impromptu* and *Le Couronnement de Molière* as slightly embarrassing indulgences on the part of Copeau, but this is to miss their significance as important and carefully crafted framing devices for the main play, and to ignore the importance of these apparent dramatic 'trinkets' as foretastes of the more sophisticated and complex work, seven years later, of Les Copiaus.

Copeau (1879–1949)

Critical reaction

The reaction of the critics to *Les Fourberies de Scapin* also reveals something of the significance of this production. Some American critics found it difficult to accept a theatre production which was so radically different from the theatre traditions they were used to, but many could appreciate the innovatory value of the enterprise. The deceptive simplicity of Copeau's production meant that there was little to say about the décor and design. Some critics found it difficult to see why Copeau had chosen a light farce as his opening production – surely notable European theatre must be sombre and portentous, not playful and frivolous.

> The grand qualities of the play were lost on the American critics, surfeited as they were by the harsh and glittering obviousness of American theatre. The pure spirit of comedy, playing upon passions and foibles of simple human beings, could not hold them; it seemed not only superficial, but unsophisticated – surprising, coming from the French.
> *(Knapp 1988: 212)*

Despite some puzzlement over the opening 'Impromptu' and the final 'Crowning', there was general recognition of the quality of the performances: 'the performance of Molière's boisterous and primitive farce was accomplished in excellent style . . . there was always celerity, vigor, vivacity and veracity in the performance' (*Morning World*, 28 November 1917). It is evident that the company impressed the New York audiences with their skilful ensemble playing, perhaps more so because of the lack of décor and the simplicity of the play. Though the minimalist staging qualities of the production confused some critics, others recognised the possibilities the staging offered for the 'lively actor, childlike in his playful eagerness' (*Boston Transcript*, 28 November 1917). John Corbin, writing in the *New York Sunday Times* (December 1917) also recognised the innovatory success of the *tréteau nu*: 'an artistic perception as subtly intelligent as it is original'. The irreverent informality of the event clearly disturbed some, one letter to the *New York Times* (5 December 1917) complained that Copeau's 'conception of the character [of Scapin], his blending of the clown and of Mephistopheles makes a bizarre combination' and considered the whole production grotesque, annoying and bewildering. Others found the simple staging overstrained, 'to the point where it actually interposes a barrier to imagination instead of encouraging imagination' (George Nathan, *Chicago Herald*, 16 December 1917). But, in general, all relished the vitality of the performances:

> Their manner was so fresh and impulsive that the spectator could not escape the conviction that much of the business was actually improvised . . . beyond all else one noted the physical freedom and poise of the players, who had been trained not as actors alone, but as happy vigorous animals.
> *(Boston Transcript, 28 November 1917)*

Copeau himself had been a critic. He understood the importance of critical reviews – for the financial success of the company, and for the success of its artistic mission. The Copeau Archives in the Bibliothèque nationale de France contain an extensive set of reviews from both the New York and Paris productions. They confirm that many of Copeau's aims were successfully achieved. Furthermore, they help us to understand something of the significance of the production: the new standards it set for vigorous and spontaneous ensemble playing; the innovations it made in staging methods and lighting; and, the energy and rhythmic musicality of the physically trained performer.

Where next: a new commedia?

Copeau revived this production several times, culminating in the open-air performance in the Place Saint-Sulpice in 1922, and we can assume that he did so at least in part because it was good box office and popular with his audience and supporters. However, throughout his career Copeau refused to be driven solely by financial imperatives, and he would not have returned repeatedly to *Les Fourberies de Scapin* if it did not also embody the essential features of the theatre towards which he aspired. *Les Fourberies de Scapin* provided Copeau with the opportunity to develop his ideas about popular theatre, the physical actor, the ensemble and the *tréteau nu* by testing them in the public arena. The production needs to be seen as complementary to his work in the Vieux-Colombier School, and as part of the journey towards his later work with Les Copiaus. Key features of this production were to reappear in the work in Burgundy: the open and simple staging, the direct physical playing, the rapport between stage and audience, the use of simple texts and the emphasis on the theatrical event. In many senses then, we can see the seeds of Copeau's later work more clearly in *Les Fourberies de Scapin* than in many other productions.

Further reading

Added, Serge (1996) 'Jacques Copeau and "Popular Theatre" in Vichy France', in Günter Berghaus (ed.) *Fascism and Theatre: Comparative Studies on the Aesthetics and Politics of Performance in Europe, 1925–1945*, Oxford: Berghahn Books, 247–259.
Anders, France (1959) *Jacques Copeau et le Cartel des Quatre*, Paris: A. G. Nizet.
Auslander, Philip (1997) *From Acting to Performance: Essays in Modernism and Postmodernism*, London: Routledge.
Bablet, Denis (1981) *The Theatre of Edward Gordon Craig*, London: Eyre Methuen.
Balance, J. [Edward Gordon Craig] (1908) 'A Note on Masks', *The Mask*, 1: 11.
Barker, Clive (1977) *Theatre Games: A New Approach to Drama Training*, London: Eyre Methuen.
Barrault, Jean-Louis (1951) *Reflections on the Theatre*, trans. Barbara Wall, London: Rockliff.
——— (1961) *The Theatre of Jean-Louis Barrault*, trans. Joseph Chiari, New York: Hill & Wang.
Benedetti, Jean (1988) *Stanislavski: A Biography*, London: Methuen.
Bentley, Eric (1950) 'Copeau and the Chimera', *Theatre Arts*, January, 34: 1, 48–51.
Bradby, David (1984) *Modern French Drama: 1940–1980*, Cambridge: Cambridge University Press.
Bradby, David and Delgado, Maria (2002) *The Paris Jigsaw: Internationalism and the City's Stages*, Manchester: Manchester University Press.
Bradby, David and McCormick, John (1978) *People's Theatre*, London: Croom Helm.
Bradby, David and Williams, David (1988) *Directors' Theatre*, Basingstoke: Macmillan.
Callery, Dymphna (2001) *Through the Body: A Practical Guide to Physical Theatre*, London: Nick Hern Books.
Carter, Huntley (1925) *The New Spirit in the European Theatre 1914–1924: A Comparative Study of Changes Effected by the War and Revolution*, London: Ernest Benn.
Christout, Marie-Françoise, Guibert, Noëlle and Pauly, Danièle (1993) *Théâtre du Vieux-Colombier: 1913–1993*, Paris: NORMA.
Clurman, Harold (1945) *The Fervent Years*, New York: Alfred A. Knopf.
Cole, Toby and Chinoy, Helen Krich (eds.) (1970) *Actors on Acting: The Theories, Techniques, and Practices of the World's Greatest Actors, Told in Their Own Words*, New York: Three Rivers Press.
Copeau, Jacques (1931) *Souvenirs du Vieux-Colombier*, Paris: Nouvelles Editions.
——— (1941) *Le Théâtre Populaire*, Paris: Presses Universitaires de France.
——— (1963) 'Visites à Gordon Craig, Jaques-Dalcroze et Adolphe Appia', *Revue d'histoire du Théâtre*, 15ème année, December: 357–367.
——— (1967) 'An Essay of Dramatic Renovation: The Théâtre of the Vieux-Colombier', trans. Richard Hiatt, *Educational Theatre Journal*, Part 4: 447–454.
——— (1974) *Registres: Appels*, ed. Marie-Hélène Dasté and Suzanne Maistre Saint-Denis, Paris: Gallimard.
——— (1976) *Registres II: Molière*, ed. André Cabanis, Paris: Gallimard.

―――― (1979) *Registres III: Les Registres du Vieux-Colombier premiere partie*, ed. Marie-Hélène Dasté and Suzanne Maistre Saint-Denis, Paris: Gallimard.

―――― (1984) *Registres IV: Les Registres du Vieux-Colombier deuxième partie, America*, ed. Marie-Hélène Dasté and Suzanne Maistre Saint-Denis, Paris: Gallimard.

―――― (1990) *Copeau: Texts on Theatre*, trans. and ed. John Rudlin and Norman Paul, London: Routledge.

―――― (1993) *Registres V: Les Registres du Vieux-Colombier troisième partie, 1919–1924*, ed. Suzanne Maistre Saint-Denis, Marie-Hélène Dasté, Norman Paul, Clément Borgal and Maurice Jacquemont, Paris: Gallimard.

―――― (2000) *Registres VI: L'École du Vieux-Colombier*, ed. Claude Sicard, Paris: Gallimard.

Darwin, Charles (1872) *The Expression of the Emotions in Man and Animals*, London: John Murray.

Decroux, Etienne (1985) 'Words on Mime', trans. Mark Piper, *Mime Journal: Words on Mime*, Claremont, CA: Pomona College.

Doisy, Marcel (1954) *Jacques Copeau*, Paris: Le Cercle du Livre.

Donahue, Thomas (1991) 'Mnouchkine, Vilar and Copeau: Popular Theater and Paradox', *Modern Language Studies*, 21: 4, 31–42.

―――― (1998) 'Improvisation and the Mask at the École du Vieux-Colombier: The Case of Suzanne Bing', *Maske Und Korthurn*, 44: 1–2, 61–72.

―――― (2008) *Jacques Copeau's Friends and Disciples: The Théâtre du Vieux-Colombier in New York City, 1917–1919*, New York: Peter Lang.

Dorcy, Jean (1961) *The Mime*, trans. Robert Speller, Jr. and Pierre de Fontnouvelle, New York: Robert Speller.

Dukes, Ashley (1931) 'The English Scene', *Theatre Arts Monthly*, September, 15: 9, 715–719.

―――― (1935) 'The Scene in Europe: Theatre and School', *Theatre Arts Monthly*, April, 19: 4, 259–263.

Eldredge, Sears (1979) 'Jacques Copeau and the Mask in Actor Training', *Mime, Mask, and Marionette*, 2: 3–4, 1979–1980.

―――― (1996) *Mask Improvisation for Actor Training and Performance: The Compelling Image*, Evanston, IL: Northwestern University Press.

Eldredge, Sears and Huston, Hollis (1995) 'Actor Training in the Neutral Mask', in Philip Zarrilli (ed.) *Acting (Re)Considered: Theories and Practices*, London and New York: Routledge.

Evans, Mark (2009) *Movement Training for the Modern Actor*, London and New York: Routledge.

Feinsod, Arthur (1992) *The Simple Stage: Its Origins in the Modern American Theatre*, New York: Greenwood Press.

Felner, Mira (1985) *Apostles of Silence: The Modern French Mimes*, London: Associated University Press.

Fleming, Cass (2013) 'A Genealogy of the Embodied Theatre Practices of Suzanne Bing and Michael Chekhov: The Use of Play in Actor Training', unpublished PhD thesis, De Montfort University. Available from: www.dora.dmu.ac.uk/xmlui/bitstream/handle/2086/9608/Cassandra%20Fleming%20PhD%20 Thesis.pdf;sequence=1.

Frank, Waldo (1925) 'Copeau Begins Again', *Theatre Arts Monthly*, September, 9.

Frost, Anthony and Yarrow, Ralph (1990) *Improvisation in Drama*, Basingstoke: Macmillan.

Ghéon, Henri (1961) *The Art of the Theatre*, trans. Adele Fiske, New York: Hill & Wang.

Gignoux, Hubert (1984) *Histoire d'une Famille Théâtrale: Jacques Copeau – Léon Chancerel, Les Comédiens-Routiers, La Décentralisation dramatique*, Lausanne: Éditions de l'Aire.

Gontard, Denis (ed.) (1974) *Le Journal de Bord des Copiaus 1924–1929*, Paris: Seghers.

Guicharnaud, Jacques (1967) *Modern French Theatre: From Giraudoux to Genet*, New Haven, CT: Yale University Press.

Harrop, John. (1971) '"A Constructive Promise": Jacques Copeau in New York, 1917–1919', *Theatre Survey*, November, 12: 2, 104–118.

Hayman, Ronald (1977) *Artaud and After*, Oxford: Oxford University Press.

Hébert, Georges (1949) *L'Éducation physique par la méthode naturelle*, 10 vols, Paris: Librarie Vuibert.

Hobson, Harold (1978) *French Theatre since 1830*, London: John Calder.

Innes, Christopher (1993) *Avant Garde Theatre: 1892–1992*, London: Routledge.

Jaques-Dalcroze, Emile (1906) *Méthode Jaques-Dalcroze: Pour le dévèloppement de l'instinct rythmiques, du sens auditif et du sentiment tonal, en 5 parties*, Neuchâtel: Sandoz, Jobin & Cie.

―――― (1913) *The Eurhythmics of Jaques-Dalcroze*, introduced by Prof. M. E. Sadler, Boston, MA: Small Maynard.

Johnstone, Keith (1981) *Impro: Improvisation and the Theatre*, London: Eyre Methuen.

Kilby, John (2005) Personal email to author (8 April).

Knapp, Bettina (1988) *The Reign of the Theatrical Director: French Theatre: 1887–1924*, Albany, NY: Whitston.
Kurtz, Maurice (1999) *Jacques Copeau: The Biography of a Theatre*, Carbondale, IL: Southern Illinois University Press.
Kusler, Barbara Leigh (1974) 'Jacques Copeau's Theatre School: l'École du Vieux-Colombier, 1920–1929', unpublished PhD thesis, University of Wisconsin.
——— (1979) 'Jacques Copeau's School for Actors: Commemorating the Centennial of the Birth of Jacques Copeau', in *Mime Journal: Numbers Nine and Ten*, Claremont, CA: Pamona College.
Leabhart, Thomas (1989) *Modern and Postmodern Mime*, Basingstoke: Macmillan.
——— (1995) 'The Mask as Shamanic Tool in the Theatre Training of Jacques Copeau', in *Mime Journal: Incorporated Knowledge*, Claremont, CA: Pamona College, 82–113.
——— (2004) 'Jacques Copeau, Etienne Decroux, and the "Flower of Noh"', *New Theatre Quarterly*, November, 20: 4, 315–330.
Lecoq, Jacques (ed.) (1987) *Le Théâtre du Geste: Mimes et Acteurs*, Paris: Bordas.
Merlin, Bella (2003) *Konstantin Stanislavsky*, London: Routledge.
Meyerhold, Vsevolod (1981) *Meyerhold on Theatre*, trans. and ed. Edward Braun, London: Eyre Methuen.
Mignon, Paul-Louis (1993) *Jacques Copeau ou le mythe du Vieux-Colombier: Biographie*, Paris: Julliard.
Miller, Anna Irene (1931) *The Independent Theatre in Europe: 1887 to the Present*, New York: Benjamin Blom.
Milling, Jane and Ley, Graham (2001) *Modern Theories of Performance*, Basingstoke: Palgrave.
Mingalon, Jean-Louis (1999) 'An Interview with Marie-Hélène Dasté', *Mime Journal: Transmissions*, 11–27.
Molière (1951) *Les Fourberies de Scapin – mise en scène et commentaires de Jacques Copeau*, Paris: Éditions du Seuil.
——— (1962) *The Miser and Other Plays*, trans. John Wood, Harmondsworth: Penguin.
Murray, Simon (2003) *Jacques Lecoq*, London: Routledge.
Paul, Norman (1977) 'Jacques Copeau, Drama Critic', *Theatre Research International*, May, 2: 3, 221–229.
——— (1979) *Bibliographie Jacques Copeau*, Paris: Société les Belles Lettres.
——— (1987) 'Review of "Jacques Copeau" by John Rudlin', *Modern Drama*, December, 30: 4, 582–583.
Rogers, Clark (1966) 'The Influence of Dalcroze Eurhythmics in the Contemporary Theatre', unpublished PhD Thesis, University of Wisconsin.
——— (1969) 'Appia's Theory of Acting: Eurhythmics for the Stage', E. T. Kirby (ed.) *Total Theatre: A Critical Anthology*, New York: Dutton.
Rudlin, John (1986) *Jacques Copeau*, Cambridge: Cambridge University Press.
——— (1996) 'Play's the Thing', in *Mime Journal: Theatre and Sport*, Claremont, CA: Pamona College, 17–29.
——— (2000) 'Jacques Copeau: The Quest for Sincerity', Alison Hodge (ed.) *Twentieth Century Actor Training*, London: Routledge, 55–78.
Ruffini, Franco (1995) 'Mime, the Actor, Action: The Way of Boxing', in *Mime Journal: Incorporated Knowledge*, Claremont, CA: Pamona College, 54–69.
Saint-Denis, Michel (1960) *Theatre: The Rediscovery of Style*, London: Heinemann.
——— (1967) 'Stanislavski and Shakespeare', trans. Simone Sanzenbach, in Erika Munk (ed.) *Stanislavski and America: 'The Method' and Its Influence on the American Theatre*, Greenwich, CN: Fawcett Premier.
——— (1982) *Training for the Theatre: Premises and Promises*, London: Heinemann.
Sorell, Walter (1973) *The Other Face: The Mask in the Arts*, Indianapolis, IN: Bobbs-Merrill.
Spector, Irwin (1990) *Rhythm and Life: The Work of Emile Jaques-Dalcroze*, Stuyvesant, NY: Pendragon Press.
Taylor, Graham (1999) 'François Delsarte: A Codification of Nineteenth-Century Acting', *Theatre Research International*, 24: 1, 71–81.
Volbach, Walter (1965) 'Jacques Copeau, Appia's Finest Disciple', *Educational Theatre Journal*, December.
Waley, Arthur (ed. and trans.) (1976) *The NM Plays of Japan*, Rutland, VT: Charles E. Tuttle.
Ward, Nigel (1996) '"Théâtre Populaire": Ideology and Tradition in French Popular Theatre', in Ros Merkin (ed.) *Popular Theatres? Papers from the Popular Theatre Conference, Liverpool John Moores University, 1994*, Liverpool: Liverpool John Moores University, 172–182.
Williams, David (ed.) (1999) *Collaborative Theatre: The Théâtre du Soleil Sourcebook*, London: Routledge.

Archive material

'French Theatre du Vieux-Colombier', Programme for New York Season, 1917–1918. (Fonds Copeau – Bibliothèque nationale de France, Paris).

Copeau (1879–1949)

Other resources

For those interested in further study there is a substantial archive of material on Copeau's life and work available in the Copeau Archives (or *Fonds Copeau*) at the Bibliothèque nationale de France in Paris. An archive of material which previously belonged to John Ruldin is available at the Templeman Library of the University of Kent.

Websites

Bibliothèque nationale de France, Paris. Online, available: www.bnf.fr (20 September 2005).
Footsbarn, Maillet. Online, available: http://footsbarn.com (20 September 2005).
Jacques Copeau Archive, Templeman Library of the University of Kent, Canterbury. Online, available: http://library.kent.ac.uk/library/special/html/specoll/COPEAU3.HTM (20 September 2005).
Théâtre du Soleil, Paris. Online, available: www.theatre-dusoleil.fr (20 September 2005).
Théâtre du Vieux-Colombier, Paris. Online, available: http://vieux.colombier.free.fr (20 September 2005).

4
LABAN (1879–1958)

Karen K. Bradley

4.1 Laban's core: biography

Rudolf Laban never planned anything in his life. As a true visionary, he regarded life as one long improvisation. He described himself as salamander, and it is possible to see him that way – eyes darting to see everything, quick, constantly advancing. He has also been described as a genius, a manipulator and a womanizer – all of which turn out to be facets of this complex man; a man without a plan, but a man with a purpose. His purpose was to move ahead and to spread out. In photographs, he is leaning forward peering at us, challenging us to respond, to grab hold of the essence of life. His eyes have a twinkle in them. The twinkle is mischievous.

He never owned his own intellectual property; ideas flowed through him, coming from a vast number of sources, passing through his continually active mind and body, where he readily disbursed them to his followers. He did not see his work as a commodity. Despite the fact that money was always a problem for him, his work was not for sale.

Mary Wigman described him as a "great wanderer" (Wigman and Sorell, 1973, p. 32). Vera Maletic added that wherever he stayed, even if for a short while, he left his traces (1987, p. 13).

> **Mary Wigman** (1886–1973) was a choreographer and student of Laban's. She is considered one of the founders of modern dance in Germany.

To him, it was simple. In Laban's world, life was movement and movement was life. He was master of both the instant and the long-range horizon. Laban was also a recycler; he was pragmatic, opportunistic and conservative in the sense of making the best of a situation and the materials at hand, in the moment. At the same time, he saw the range of possibilities across a broad spectrum. Laban's view of the horizon did not lead to his forming intentions, however. The horizon merely provided a canvas for possibilities.

Some portray him as a trickster, and he loved play and playfulness. He was definitely a provocateur as well. But even though he could be quite naïve, he was no fool. He was a keen observer and saw human impulses and predilections that needed to come to fruition. He watched, and listened, and responded as a man fully in touch with the realities around him. Only in his political astuteness did he fail to attend soon enough; he admired power and so, as we shall see, became entangled with the Nazis for a time.

Laban was both naïve and wise. He was open to new possibilities and viewpoints and he could be dogmatic at times as well. Laban looked at phenomena from many perspectives. Some say he could see the trace forms of movement and the energies behind gestures. The desire to tap into and amplify the human movement story is what drew him to the theater (Kennedy Interview, July 8, 2004).

His student and colleague Kurt Jooss said that Laban's main interest was always a kind of educative and therapeutic approach. "He believed in the salvation of the science of dancing" (Partsch-Bergsohn and Jooss, 2002). In 1920, Laban even told Jooss that dancing would develop and would rescue a dissolute society.

> **Kurt Jooss** (1901–1979) was a dancer with Laban's Tanzbühne in the late 1910s and 1920s. He eventually established his own company, combining ballet with the Tanztheater work, and is best known for his antiwar ballet, *The Green Table* (1932).

Laban's life story is a tale of aspiration to deliverance and transcendence, but it is not the story of how he saved society. It is a story about the gifts of salvation and transcendence that he tried to give humanity, through movement. As we look at the last 150 or more years since Laban's birth, it is clear that humanity has, thus far, tended to ignore the gift.

Developing

Laban was born December 15, 1879, in Bratislava, the oldest of three children and the only boy. His father was an officer in the Austro-Hungarian army and his mother often traveled with her husband, leaving young Rudolf alone with his grandparents. From the hills above Bratislava, then called Poszny or Pressburg, he gained perspective. Looking down on the town: the church spires, the twisting streets and shops, the theater, and most vividly, the series of town squares, he could see humans in interaction, in expression, in community and in commerce. He could also see the heavens, majestic and massive, and sense his own small place within them. It was there in those hills that he first came upon the interweaving of nature and metropolis, the individual and the community, the quotidian and the performative that informed his later work.

His early teenage years were full of travel: to Sarajevo, Mostar, Istanbul and the like. Since his father was an officer, such deployments were not uncommon. As an inventive and self-possessed child, Laban roamed the countryside in these locales on his own. The natural formations of rocks, trees and terrain created a backdrop and set for his imaginative stories and plays. Local myths and folklore culture played an influential role in his creations of plays and puppet shows, and because of the travels, he picked up an international banquet of tales.

During his travels, Laban was exposed to both eastern and western sensibilities, studying under an Imam for a time.

> He drank in Middle Eastern philosophy and sacred practices ... Russian Orthodox Catholicism, Greek Orthodoxy, Turkish-style Muslim concepts and behaviour, extremist Sufi practices, as well as Catholic and Protestant Christian groups, all contributed to his awareness of religious possibilities and human behaviour.
>
> *(Preston-Dunlop, 1998, p. 3)*

While in Istanbul, according to Valerie Preston-Dunlop, he also encountered Sufism and Dervish dances. The exposure to mysticism, the crossing of boundaries between the waking and dreaming world, provided Laban with a holistic sensibility, launching him on a lifelong search for hidden meanings and allegorical symbology.

He was attracted to performance – theatrical, military, story-telling, puppetry – all forms of nonverbal, movement-based forms of human discourse. He wrote about his childhood Kasperl Theater (a Punch and Judy type of puppet stage). The character of Kasperl was based on his actor-uncle, Adolf Mylius (who had become a sort of black sheep of the family), and the devil character was called Napoleum, after Napoleon; these players conspired to find a blue flower that renders the finder immortal. The devil was banished and there was a joyful dance at the end. Laban, in *A Life for Dance* (written on the eve of the rise of Nazi Germany), concludes: "My childhood play has a happy ending. Time has taught me to think differently. It is the devil who more often than not gets to keep the blue flower" (1975, p. 9).

His relationship with his father was convoluted. As a military man, Papa Laban was not pleased that his only son chose the life of an artist over following in his footsteps. Nevertheless, Laban's father supported him financially through his turbulent years as a young artist in Paris.

His mother was more of a playmate. A painter, and a woman with liberal, if not socialist leanings, Marie von Laban encouraged the imaginative play and spectacles in which her son engaged.

During his later teenage years, the family lived in Budapest, where Rudolf was a bit of a man-about-town. Photos from this time show a dark-haired, slender, intensely focused man-boy, with an expressive eyebrow, and a sophisticated air. The family was upper-middle class and Laban was the oldest and a male. The city of Budapest had become a cosmopolitan and sophisticated Mecca for the Empire and the coffeehouses rivaled those of Vienna. In many ways, Laban could have easily wound up a shallow cad, for the café-society called him and he responded with enthusiasm.

But the muses also came calling early on and he was pulled in artistic directions and subsequently adopted a more focused and disciplined attitude than he might otherwise have had. Despite a privileged, but often lonely childhood, he had learned to observe human behavior. This visual perceptivity led him in the direction of the visual arts.

Laban was first drawn to painting as a vocation, primarily due to the tutelage of an artist whose values of "love of work, scrupulous fulfillment of duty and unaffected behaviour" (1975, p. 10) were a contrast with the indulged life he had been living as the only son of a high-ranking officer. As his visual training evolved, however, he began to see the movement within the static picture:

> It needed a special occasion to open my eyes to the fact that in the "moving picture" lies hidden a tremendously enhanced expression of human will and feeling ... Then came a memorable day when I discovered tableaux vivants.
>
> *(Laban, 1975, p. 11)*

He put together a series of these tableaux, with musical accompaniment, in such a way that each moment built on the last. When strung together, the theatricality and evolution of the static scenes took on movement and drama. He was still in his teen years when he built such tableaux; he was also apprenticed to a scenic painter for a time.

By the late 1890s, along with many writers and thinkers in Budapest, he was caught between the old world of traditions and stories, which he understood as powerful and compelling, and the emerging questioning of the direction of human culture. This struggle was far more than a man versus machine concern. The reconciliation of old and new was being played out across the western world. Laban's particular and personal struggles led directly to the evolution of his theories and practice.

Training and studying

Laban entered into officer training for the Austrian–Hungarian army in 1899, into the Military Academy at Wiener Neustadt, near Vienna, at the behest, if not direct order of his father.

His training included riding, social dancing, military maneuvers, fencing, French, German, and "nationalist dogma" (Preston-Dunlop, 1998, p. 6). Within a year and a half, Laban quit, through with the conformist training. He had always been an erratic student – bright but difficult – and the Army of the Emperor found him engaged in the same struggle.

Even as a child, he had been taken with the patterns of military parades, and fencing and social dance patterns also interested him. His intense training in these latter two areas, particularly, informed his personal movement skills. But the parades, large colorful sweeping patterns in which the individual skills of the performers were subsumed, may have been an inspiration for his improvisational choirs later on.

He struggled with both a fascination for the machine, particularly the reliability and discipline that repetitive functional movement and spectacle provided, and for the artistic soul of the individual. He appreciated the particulars of folk dance and the agrarian lifestyle as well as the attractions of high culture and urban life. The academy at Wiener Neustadt afforded him access to all manner of society, but in the end, the desire to live the life of an artist won out.

His father was not pleased with his choice to leave the training academy, but provided support and letters of introduction, as well as financial support for Laban and his new bride, Martha Fricke, to set up household in Munich. It is not clear how Laban and Martha met, but both had aspirations as visual artists and Fricke was already a painter.

Exploring Munich and Paris

Munich in 1898–99 was an up-and-coming center for what would become expressionist art. Art Nouveau was in the ascendancy at the time Laban and Martha arrived, and it was in Munich that he was influenced by Hermann Obrist, a sculptor. Obrist was interested in the modern and the abstract but, more significantly, he worked in many different media forms.

Hermann Obrist (1863–1927) was a German sculptor and part of the Art Nouveau movement. Art Nouveau was popular from about 1880–1914 (World War I) and was a form of design that consisted of curving, flowing, elegant lines, incorporating plants and flowers.

Munich's artists were shifting from romanticism to expressionism. Laban was influenced by all schools and ultimately found himself creating in the spaces between story and abstraction, physicality and expression. He was a man influenced by many sources and he lived in a time when the arts, sciences, psychology and social theories were all converging. Laban began to think about his own path, which had, up to this point, been largely unclear. His barely articulated quest was to find a form of performance that allowed the individual to speak with his/her own voice, to contribute to a greater whole, and that allowed group access to the larger concerns of the human condition.

According to Valerie Preston-Dunlop (Interview, July 3, 2004), Laban started in Munich as a pageant director. He was hired to create a comic carnival piece based on a profession. Given a brief and asked to do it, he came up with the idea of an improvised group dance. Later on, the group work would become far more formalized but even in these early days, he valued both individual and group input.

Laban was deeply concerned with questions about the nature of the individual versus the group. He was developing his philosophy and life choices at the same time that many were reading Marx and Engels, Freud, and anarchists like Michael Bakunin. The very nature of government, of democracy, of capitalism, of culture was being questioned by writers, activists and artists. And the role of the individual within the concerns of the group became a seminal issue of the twentieth century.

Laban loved the mystical, the grotesque and the circus. He knew the sources of play and storytelling as well as the underlying layers of tragedy within those forms. He unpacked the layers readily, and observed as the stories and images that were revealed took form as visual and plastic art.

After he and Martha moved to Paris in 1900, he tried to enroll in various studios and ecoles. It is clear from his subsequent drawings and architectural designs that he did study, but according to Preston-Dunlop (1998, p. 10), his name did not appear on any of the rolls at that time. Martha's did, however. She was enrolled at the Ecole des Beaux Arts School of Architecture in 1903.

Laban and Martha both participated in the café life and the salons. There, the blend of spiritualism and decadence that prevailed led to his early commentaries and works based on this period. The early days in the Paris café scene laid the groundwork for his depth of understanding of the light and dark forces that an artist draws on for creative work. In *A Life for Dance*, he described his attempts, some years later, to capture the dichotomies of the café society that both fascinated and repelled him:

> Has art, so passionately defended as the great provider of happiness and peace, any place amidst this hustle? How can true beauty dwell among the glitter of tattered silk and under the artificial purple lights? How can the soul rejoice amid the rags of the poor and the hollow eyes of hungry children? How utterly remote is the fragrance of the mountains and forests from the air of the slums, so thick with coal-dust and from the deadly smell of the powdered prostitute! Is that the song of man? I wondered in horror.
> *(Laban, 1975, p. 43)*

This somewhat Victorian and judgmental perspective on what was attractive to him as well as repellant did not spring from either an overdose of religiosity or any type of atheism. Laban was highly spiritual but he did not ascribe to any one spiritual practice; he was not a cultist. He was attracted to practices that expanded perception rather than allowing himself to fall under the spell of unexamined beliefs. He was willing to experience the beliefs of any aspect of society and to apply this perspective to his creative work. In the end, his openness was part of his aesthetic, one of his many talents, and later informed the development of his theories.

Laban's journey almost ended, however, when Martha died in 1907, leaving him with two small children. Laban did not soldier on as a single parent. Few men, especially Europeans, would have in those days. The children went to Martha's mother. The next three years of Laban's life are hazy. Rumors place him in Italy for at least part of that time, in Munich, perhaps at a sanitarium. He essentially dropped out of the society in which he had been involved, and left no tracks.

Evolving philosophy/choreosophy

Laban resurfaced in 1910, after having met his second wife, the singer Maya Lederer. They married and moved to Munich. In Munich, Laban found an "island of international culture ... an oasis of anti-authoritarian thought and easy-going tolerance" (Preston-Dunlop, 1998, p. 17). Munich was café-society in its early stages – cabarets, puppet theaters, balls and soirees. The Blaue Reiter group – consisting of the artists Kandinsky, Klee, Franz Marc and others – promoted a more spiritual and expressive approach to abstract art. The composer Arnold Schoenberg was also in Munich at that time, raising questions about what was harmony, harmonic and harmonious.

Munich was a smaller and more intimate city than Paris and the emerging cabaret and café scene provided a locale for writers, artists, musicians and performers to share their concerns about the wealthy and the bourgeoisie. The artists sitting around in cafés were against rigidity of thinking, status-driven success, hypocrisy and complacency. They produced magazines, newspapers, paintings, small theatrical events, vaudeville-like performances, atonal music, and more in the service of the nouveau.

Laban's movement influences during this period also included the body-culture approaches of Bess Mensendieck, Rudolf Bode and Emil Jaques-Dalcroze, all of whom were part of the physical, spiritual and expressive culture-of-the-whole that was prominent in Munich at that time. He studied Noverre's *Letters on Dancing and Ballet*, a text from the eighteenth century in which Noverre recommends privileging the storyline of a ballet over the decorative and technical prowess of the time. Laban was aware of the notation systems used in historical dance forms (especially Feuillet notation, with its swirling pictorial pathways that so well represent Baroque dance). Between Feuillet and Noverre, Schoenberg and Kandinsky, and Dalcroze and Bode, the intertwining of threads into a new dance theory was set to begin. Laban was ready to begin weaving these threads.

Communing in Ascona

It was in the summer of 1913, just before the world changed forever, that the evolving artist/ researcher/visionary/philosopher Rudolf Laban watched a young woman trudge up the hill towards him. She had walked, carrying her suitcase, from the town of Locarno (near the border between Switzerland and Italy) to the village of Ascona. Her name was Mary Wigman, and she was climbing the hill to participate in a community experiment in expressive dance. The hill, called Monte Verità, or the Mountain of Truth, was inhabited by a collection of painters-turned-dancers, singers-turned-actors, dancers-turned-lovers ... in short, what the 1960s labeled "hippies."

Laban had been invited to open up a summer school for the arts in Ascona. He had only recently abandoned his visual art training and identity for that of a dancer/movement artist. Up to this point Laban had not taken an interest in the politics of communal living or anarchy, both of which were of concern to the Asconans. Only the unconventional nature of his relationships with his wife, the singer Maya Lederer, and his mistress, the Dalcroze-trained dance teacher Suzanne Perrottet, indicates a connection to the free-loving founders of the Ascona community. But he understood the mysticism, the triangular balance of Love–Work–Play that had emerged as a cornerstone of the Asconan philosophy.

Ascona is a little village off the beaten path of any of the deep historical struggles in which most of Europe was engaged at the time. It had been re-founded as a utopian and anarchical community in 1900.

According to Martin Green, author of *The Mountain of Truth*:

> At the end of the nineteenth century, intellectual Europe became preoccupied with the problem of its own unhappiness, malaise, or – to use Freud's word – Unbehagen. The favorites of this rich and powerful civilization – the economically and educationally privileged, the most intelligent and imaginative – felt themselves to be unhappier than more primitive peoples. All over Europe ... the Germans and German-speaking ... were moving faster than other peoples to grasp the glittering prize of progress.
>
> (Green, 1986, p. 1)

But the "glittering prize of progress" lost its burnish with the loss of the direct experience of the world. At the same time, a longing for Community had taken over. The Industrial Revolution had separated man from his produce, and had objectified the experience of "making." Therefore, many intellectuals and sociopolitical people felt the need to withdraw from both the industrialization of the workforce and the science-centered empiricism taking over the academy. They divided what was functional from what was expressive. Living a new life together, in a community in which the needs of the individual might be subsumed to the greater good of the whole, had its attractions.

The Asconans were mystical, but not in a gothic sense. The dark relationships among men were not of interest; instead, they focused on a spiritual life-changing approach to work, love and play. They developed small collectives, but the famous figures who came to Ascona were not there to build one large community. Hermann Hesse, D. H. Lawrence, Otto Gross, Gusto Gräser, Mary Wigman and Rudolf Laban were all in Ascona; we do not know which of them may have crossed paths. But whether or not they met in person, their ideas did mingle at the base of the Mountain of Truth, and the basic philosophy resurfaces even today.

Community was an emergent rather than an ideological notion. The cohorts that developed were small and not possessive of ideals or of property. Ascona was a "seed community" in every sense of the word. Growing organically was a metaphor for the way small groups grew up and were reaped and divided and reseeded. These themes played out in the spontaneous dances that arose and were refined during Laban's Ascona period.

Other dancers, in addition to Wigman who came to work with Laban on Monte Verità, included Kathe Wulff, a visual artist; Sophie Tauber, a painter (later married to Jean Arp, the Dadaist artist); Laura Oesterreich, a trained dancer; his wife, the opera singer Maya Lederer; his mistress, Suzanne Perrottet; and a young dark beauty named Betty Baaron Samao (Preston-Dunlop describes her as the children's nanny, but she appears in dance photos and seems to be a lovely dancer). The confluence of various art forms with the ideas of free love, feminism, organic gardening and Freemasonry led to explorations of new forms of creating and sharing dance.

In this maelstrom of influences, Laban evolved methods based on spontaneous processes and an overall sense of design. The result was something he eventually called "Movement Choir." Drawing on improvisational impulses, musical theory and visual design structures, this form was devised and spontaneous, participatory and performative. It was contemporaneous produced and particular folk dance, with contributions from each individual and a resultant communal sense of identity.

Mary Wigman came into this scene after having been disillusioned by the Hellerau (Dalcroze-based) community's emphasis on music over movement. She arrived in time to begin to working with Laban's approach, which she had been told was the dance-centric process she was seeking.

The group's second summer at Ascona, in 1914, began with plans for clarifying the triad of concepts Laban was developing: Tanz, Ton, Wort (Dance, Sound, Word). But weeks into the process, the outbreak of World War I shattered this creative Garden of Eden. It is difficult for us now, looking back after almost a century has passed, to comprehend how devastating it was in the summer of 1914 to have the world (or Europe) rocked by simultaneous declarations of dissolution and nationalism. To the Asconans, whose community was built upon crossing traditional boundaries, and balancing forces of opposition, the loss was devastating. Most returned to their native countries, to try to live within the national boundaries they had tried to transcend. But Laban and Wigman stayed, keeping the Garden of Eden open precariously until October, when the cold weather forced their return to the crumbling civilizations of Europe.

During the war, Laban traveled between Munich, Zurich and, occasionally during summers, Ascona. A good deal of work on the idea of notation happened during this time, and there was much correspondence between Laban and Suzi Perrottet about the theory of movement analysis. Laban drew inspiration from all of the women in his life: Mary Wigman, Maya Lederer and Suzanne Perrottet. In his letters to Suzi, who was often in Zurich while Laban was in Munich or Ascona, he told her what he was experimenting with. "What if I take music away from dance?" he asked.

Wigman had left Hellerau and Dalcroze over the same question. In their work together, Laban and Wigman worked to free dance from music. At one point during the war, he asked Wigman to take over his teaching duties in Zurich while he recuperated from one of his many episodes of illness. Most of these episodes were intestinal, with regular bouts of depression, and he often had to ask students to step into the role of instructor. Wigman moved into a flat above the studio and together they began to derive a curriculum for training dancers. They created a basis for Choreutics (Space Harmony) and Eukinetics (Effort), a theory they developed in order to clarify technique and style and in order to move beyond dance steps into meaningful movement. Together they were laying the groundwork for a new approach to modern dance, one that was expressive of Mother Nature and human nature, that embraced the outer and the inner terrain, and contained the fundamentals of movement: changing, shifting and adapting tensions.

Laban began to write a book (*Die Welt des Tänzers*) and to articulate his vision for a new approach to dance based in theory, practice, experimentation, community and access to basic elements, with dance as an art form in and of itself.

Despite the brutality of the war, Laban held on to some utopian ideals of community and crossing artistic, moral and geographic boundaries. For at least one month (March 1915) Maya, Suzi, Laban and Wigman all lived together in a farmhouse. Maya and Suzi were both pregnant by Laban at the same time. Laban's philosophy of living an essential and organic lifestyle and his generous and bemused approach to the women in his life fostered a sense of the communal over the materialistic. He came and went, from the farmhouse, from Maya's house in Munich and Suzi's in Zurich; he worked with Wigman in Ascona. The art always came first.

Antja Kennedy (Interview, July 8, 2004) pointed out that Laban was an autodidact, keeping his own counsel. No one could tell him he was a bad choreographer or criticize him in any way when he was doing his experiments on the hillside in Ascona. But despite the fact that Munich was a hotbed of experimental art, especially painting and sculpture, it was much tougher to break into the more traditional venues with new ideas about dance. Munich had an opera house, with the standards and traditions that accompany an established artistic domain. In writings at the time, Laban hinted that he did not necessarily want critical eyes observing his early work. After all, movement choirs were made by and for the people who were dancing them, and they were experiments, not products. He was thinking big, and beginning to produce something quite new. The staid opera houses of Europe were not the place for his explorations.

Learning from the world

Evelyn Dörr (Interview, July 9, 2004) described Laban's philosophical explorations during the war and post-war period. "He is looking at ethnology, psychology, physiology, folk, research, philosophy: the symbol of the Creation, nature and Christianity, changing and symbols of the libido, and archetypes." She believes he had questions about Darwinism, wondering if society is based on a hierarchy designed in part by nature. She said that Laban seemed to be developing a new and systematic way for seeking unity in nature and the place of the human in the universe, through the study and practice of dancing.

Other influences on Laban's evolving theory included the then-popular notion of naturally occurring symmetry in both nature and art, and the idea of a shared symbology in dreams, a la Jung. Laban utilized such ideas in developing the early symbols for notation, which were imagistic. Laban attempted the alchemical in his notation system: he was trying to capture the very nature of change.

The revolutionary and evolutionary theory Laban constructed led to dance practice that was the meeting ground for the participatory and the expressive, the inner and the outer experience of the world, the intrinsic and the communicative, thought and action – in short, the field upon which mankind engages with the world of objects and of fantasy, truth and beauty, imagination and experience, and the body moving in space.

Post-war recovering

In the years immediately following World War I, Laban found himself with a number of children (by 1917, he had sired eight), an open marriage, followers, colleagues and a fairly transient lifestyle. Maya and her children were in Munich, Suzanne and their son in Zurich, and his children with Martha Fricke were in Hanover, with her family.

Teaching and lecturing in both Zurich and Munich, he became caught up with the Dadaists and the Cabaret Voltaire scene, and began to make chamber dance works. These works were created in a studio setting (in Zurich), but lacked the short, disconnected, improvised bursts of phrases, repeated over and over, that characterized Dada dance performances. While Wigman had begun her own explorations of dark passions, Laban explored archetypal characters who wandered through movement narratives with unconventional encounters.

However, like the Dadaists, he was searching for new choreography forms from an extreme direction. He wrote that "all the big-headed of the world have sent their main people to Zurich" (Dörr Interview, July 9, 2004). But his revolution was different from theirs. He was a rule breaker, a liberalist, and a positivist, according to Evelyn Dörr, and he was more of a reformer than a nihilist.

Many in post-World War I Europe became fascinated by the emerging sciences and explored the connections between experimental science and philosophical thought, between psychology and art, seeking to unveil the essences of each. Laban, too, was concerned with all of the facets of analysis of the world of objects and visible phenomena, and he was beginning to articulate, even to lecture about a new psychophysical organization of the body in movement, which he understood to be grounded in both rhythm and space.

Laban (1879–1958)

Publishing and theorizing in Stuttgart

After Laban moved to Stuttgart for a time right after the war, he worked further on the analysis of spatial tensions, or pulls, and began to draw symbols for these lines of movement or inclinations off the vertical.

One of the people who came to study at the school in Stuttgart was a young man named Kurt Jooss. Jooss described himself as "entirely unsuited to be a dancer." But, he went on, "from the first moment of being in this new world ... a complete change overtook me. I became deeply involved, my body changed, and my whole being became gradually part of this art" (from the Jooss exhibition catalog, quoted by Partsch-Bergsohn and Bergsohn, 1973, p. 19).

The city of Stuttgart embraced Laban's work and the city of Mannheim followed suit, hiring him as a guest choreographer to make a new production of *Tannhäuser*. He wanted to do well because he needed ongoing work, but he also wanted to reform dance itself, to make the artificial more real. More real meant more organic and less mired in traditional dance steps and techniques. As much as he admired Noverre and the dances of the Baroque era, he wanted at this point to break new ground and produce work appropriate to the rising human spirit of the everyday.

His approach was not procedural or systematic; it was inspired. He wanted to provide accessible egalitarian art that connected human beings to their own mythologies and resolutions. And so he became an active teller of stories through Tanztheater: dance theater stories told as cautionary tales that also contained prescriptions for transcendence and awakenings.

Laban was set back by a bout of the Spanish Influenza in 1919, an episode which only contributed to his long-term health problems and difficulties earning money on a regular basis. As a Hungarian, he was essentially stateless following the changing borders after World War I. In addition, a new relationship with the Russian dancer Dussia Bereska led to the total breakdown of his home life, such as it had been, so he was homeless as well. Although he did not divorce Maya until 1925, after 1918 the marriage was essentially over. Maya was a most understanding ex-wife; Suzi, a most understanding ex-mistress.

Wigman, too, was an understanding ex-pupil, at least for a while. Her work was receiving increasing attention, she was fully German in the eyes of those who cared about such things, and she was a bolder and more singular artist than Laban. While he was interested in the group experience, Wigman was developing her own choreographic voice, primarily as a soloist. Both were leaders and visionaries, but Wigman described Laban at the time as "the worshipped hero." She had to move on and find her own place.

Laban as performance-practitioner

Meanwhile, Laban developed two approaches to creating the type of dance works he was interested in making. On the one hand, he created dance theater works based on archetypes and fantastical stories, using dancers he trained in his global approach to movement. This was the Tanzbühne Laban, the Dance-Theater group, and a smaller version developed in 1923, the Kammertanzbühne Laban, or Chamber Dance Group. He created the first Tanzbühne in 1920, with his new partner, Dussia Bereska, in Stuttgart. He also further developed the communal, improvisational and participatory style of the Movement Choir during the 1920s.

Laban had moved to Stuttgart because the city offered him work, but also because his publisher was there. His book, *Die Welt des Tänzers* (*The World of Dancers*), which he had been working on since 1916, had been ready for publication for most of the war years. But until the war was over, no one was able to gather and edit photographs. The book reveals a great deal about Laban's emerging philosophy of the art form of dance:

> Dancing means overcoming indolence. Thus it does not flatter one of man's basic instincts. Dancing also brings release and I personally believe that man has crossed the threshold where indolence prevails over the desire for freedom and light, everywhere in each individual, but in the majority of people there is a dancer – a dancer who wants to be released.
>
> The final aim. If the result, namely the extinction of a great number of habitually accepted ideas, feelings, and actions is achieved, then there shall be space for knowledge and function which meanwhile has been developing.
>
> Only then shall we be able to speak of the coming transference of the pure reason expressed in the dance to human life.
>
> *(Laban, 1920, translated by Richard Schröder)*

The ideal of "pure reason" expressed through the art of dance permeates Laban's writing and thinking from *Die Welt des Tänzers* forth. He saw himself as both an artist and a researcher (or what we might now think of as a social scientist). Science, philosophy, religion and art were spokes on a wheel, ways of understanding the nature of humanity. Dance reflected all of it and was a part of advancing that understanding.

Laban perceived movement primarily as transformation or change. He was concerned with irregular pulls, constantly shifting sands, crystals, vectors and parabolas, psychology, and mapping constant modifications of movement. His earliest forays at creating a notation system consist of shapes that are reminiscent of vectors in geometry – displacements from the vertical, according to Jeffrey Longstaff, a Laban Movement Analyst in Britain. His wedding of mathematics and art, physics and human movement was both of his time and prescient. By the time the notation system we now know as Labanotation was developed, it was a much more static and simple graphic representation of movement qualities, attitudes and directions. But what Laban was playing with in the late 1910s and early 1920s looks more like something in a paisley design.

The 1920s were a rich period of creative development for Laban. They also revealed some tensions among his followers. He developed the notation system, not as a static plotting of positions of body parts but as a way to capture the shifts off the vertical, the sweeping or coned tracks of movement in ever-changing spatial configurations. He was exploring and attempting to "capture the eternal in time and space" (a description of Laban's work by the psychologist Dr Irene Champerknowne, from notes at the Dartington Archives). He was breaking new ground. Not everyone understood, including the critics. The increasingly differentiated paths of Wigman, Kreutzberg, Jooss, Knust, and others tugged at the German dance world.

In 1921, Laban became the Ballet Master to the national Theater of Mannheim, and he created several works, including *Die Geblendeten*, *Epische Tanzfolge* and the *Orgy of Tannhäuser* by Wagner. He had position and influence in the world of dance. Now he needed the dancers to fulfill his vision.

He began to train his own dancers more methodically by 1923, and set about developing schools and training programs throughout Germany and Switzerland, and eventually, Serbia, Italy and Austria. It was in these schools that the dance and movement choir "curriculum" evolved. Laban was interested in "freie Tanz" – dance that was both expressive and highly evolved. The spiritual part of his thinking led him to begin creating Tanztheater pieces based on mythical stories and mystical themes. These were performed by trained dancers: small ensembles of eclectic performers who had come to believe in the principles and process Laban was evolving for making compelling and innovative work.

According to Valerie Preston-Dunlop, the chamber groups (Tanzbühne) differed from the choirs in several ways. The purpose of the choirs was, in part, to be inclusive and to encourage active participation. The theater works performed by the chamber groups were intended for audiences. The content of the theatrical pieces focused on creating illusion and on social commentary.

Occasionally, the chamber groups and the movement choirs were combined as principles and corps, often for financial reasons: he didn't have to pay the corps. The movement choirs were well-trained bodily, and fulfilled the purpose of supporting the stories with clarity and economy.

In 1923, Laban established the Zentralschule (Central School) Laban and a department for the movement choirs in Hamburg. Among the new dancers who were trained in Hamburg were Ruth Loeser, Sylvia Bodmer, Aino Siimola (later Kurt Jooss' wife), Martin Gleisner and Gertrud Snell.

The choreographic works Laban created between 1923 and 1927 for the Kammertanzbühne Laban include *Der Schwingende Tempel* (*The Swinging Temple*), *Faust Part II*, *Prometheus*, *Die Gaukelei*, *Casanova*, *Don Juan*, *Die Nacht*, *Narrenspiegel* and *Ritterballet*. Specific movement choir works include *Lichtwende*, *Agamemnons Tod*, *Dämmernde Rhythmen* and *The Titan*.

The curriculum of the Hamburg School contained two tracks, one for chamber groups and one for the movement choirs, but both tracks taught Choreutics (Space Harmony) and Eukinetics (later, Effort). The primary difference between the two tracks was that the choir trained in the evening and weekends, while the chamber group (the Kammertanzbühne) trained daily.

The movement choirs were amateur groups, everyday people who came to the training programs to address growing concerns about the human being within the state, the role of spirituality within religion, and the role of the psyche within the forces at play in the 1920s. Adult students took classes that explored expanding and condensing, individual and group consciousness, breath and story, space (Choreutics) and expressivity (Eukinetics).

As the chamber group traveled around, performing such pieces as *The Swinging Temple*, *Orchidee* (a solo by Dussia Bereska), *Don Juan* and a little piece of structured improvisation called *Die Grünen Clowns* (*The Green Clowns*), Laban pulled in the movement choirs in any given town to augment the ensemble. Since he was evolving his notation system at the same time, the vocabulary he was developing for space and body actions was useful in conveying some semblance of structure in advance. Using this language, he could give some directives, to which the choir members would contribute their own continually refined voices, or personal style. When the performances occurred, the result was always specific and unique. In the case of *The Green Clowns*, for example (according to Valerie Preston-Dunlop, who has recreated the work), the sequences and the number of dancers changed from town to town, depending on who was available.

Laban was finding some singular threads, some universality in the ways that people learned, presented and experienced dance. In *A Life for Dance*, he wrote about the movement choirs' simple beginnings, in the small towns of Germany in the 1920s:

> We soon got the impression, which was reinforced by our occasional audiences, that we should show our compositions to the public, for nearly everyone who watched us was stimulated into joining in. Meanwhile, our plays had developed into small choir-works. One of the first was Dawning Light, in which we experienced the change from stepping in subdued sadness to the awakening of the revitalizing capacity which is dormant in the body. I emphasize "experienced" and not "presented" because at this stage we

had no wish to show or convince an audience – although later on a presentation style emerged effortlessly and without our doing. We were solely concerned with experiencing in ourselves and in togetherness the increased vigour of the spiritual-emotional-physical forces which are united in dance. Why? Because we were drawn to it, we benefited from it, and we were inspired by it.

(Laban, 1975, pp. 155–156)

The Tanzbühne group (dance-theater) during the 1920s included Dussia Bereska, with whom Laban had a daughter. (The daughter, named "Little Dussia," was adopted out to a presumably more stable family.) Kurt Jooss, Herta Feig, Jens Keith, Edgar Frank and Albrecht Knust were also a part of the group. The pieces that Laban choreographed in the early 1920s (several of which included the movement choir groups) utilized archetypes and had a mystical flavor. Titles such as *The Fool's Mirror*, *The Crystal*, *Orchidee*, *The Magic Garden*, *The Earth* and *The Titan* reveal Laban's concerns with the imaginative, the socio-political, the natural world, the mythical and the magical.

By the end of the 1920s, Laban and his followers were engaged in coalescing his theories into mutually informing macro and micro concepts. They perceived the union of opposites along a continuum. They connected form and content, individual and cultural style, sweeping huge ideas into personalized dance stories.

His approach to choreography incorporated all of the theory and practice he had developed. He wrote about something he called tanzlogisch (dance logic). In his book *Choreographie* (1926) he laid out (p. 89) a sequence of directions that he called a Reihung, a conglomeration of phrases of movement that built up to a scale, like a musical scale, with logic, interval and pattern. He wrote about Formgebilde (what we might now call shape-shifting), which, when done by the dancer's body, is carried into moving through space and thereby delineates the space. It does not matter which parts are moving in order to create the shape because what is essential is that the shape-changing matches the content and spirit of the dance. A single shape can be a headstand or some other position, but it is the sequencing of shapes that matters to the meaningfulness of the dance. One has to lead into another in order to make sense, and that shifting is tanzlogische.

Laban recommended specifying the first shape or point of departure through his emerging symbol system. To him, a true Tanzdichter (dance-poet) had to determine if it was important that particular parts of the body were used or if any choice was possible, as long as the intention of the movement was fulfilled. He compared choreography to exploring fingering in piano, with the same sense of craft as well as exploration.

In order to clarify the intention of a movement, the choreographer could use an adjective or adverb to modify and make the movement more expressive. Laban was ahead of his time in his understanding of both effortful and harmonic movement. While many of the European choreographers of this period worked with natural breathing rhythms, and ebb and flow, Laban was more of an architect. For him, natural harmony and design superseded technical prowess.

The end of performing

In 1926, Laban fell off the stage while performing *Don Juan*, and severely injured his back. According to Martin Gleisner (*Laban Art of Movement Guild Magazine*), Laban had created the piece to the music of Glück. The choreography was simple, with group passages danced by students of his schools in the localities of the performances. Gleisner made a case for the professional proficiencies of these students, especially the Jena and Weimar movement choirs.

In February and March, Laban came to Jena to prepare the group for his new work. They rehearsed in the evenings, and Laban worked with Gleisner during the day. Gleisner said he later found Laban's notes on *Don Juan*, but these seem to have disappeared.

By 1926, the movement choirs were quite good, although some were seen as too strict and some as too loose. The Jena movement choir Gleisner oversaw was neither, and held up well in reviews of the piece at the time.

Review of *Don Juan* taken from *Die Deutsche Frau*, November 1926 (translation by Richard Schröder)

While there are still doubtful questions concerning the surprising development of physical awareness which at the moment is very popular, a new German art has matured apart from these misunderstood attempts at rejuvenation and renewal. Whoever has observed the course of development of German dance art only during the last three years could have become confused as to the meaning of this artistic event through the many complexities of its development. But now that Rudolf von Laban has reached the peak with a performance of "Don Juan" in Berlin one may in retrospect be pleased at the resoluteness with which this pioneer has proceeded to open up a new door to artistic expression for the German spirit.

The powerful impression of the performance can only be compared with the experience of hearing Mozart's music for the first time, which went far beyond the trifling rococo, beyond the slightly grotesque distortion of the text, and in its devastating sequence of sound illustrated the dramatic power of the story of humanity. To me the most significant thing about this piece of music by Mozart has always seemed to be that it raised the dramatic experience above mere sensuality and emitted a peculiarly active intellectuality, which made the Faust-like insatiable urge for life out of the countless adventures of the Spanish Knight.

In the darkness of the National Stage in the Bülowplatz the same bewitching experience repeated itself in all the wonder of something seen for the first time. The music by Glück, a few borrowed ballet forms by Angolini provided the vibrant framework, then it suddenly became very clear, which had never happened before, that the strict chamber music of Glück can unite with the dance of the present.

And this is not a marvel because the German Baroque is something other than the florid art of other nations and countries. On it is based the tradition of the religious search for form, bursting vitality and the urge for infinite perspective. Certainly this depth in Glück's string orchestra is primly and reservedly confined. But what unfolds there within the scope of the stage causes sparks to fly from these rhythms, and precisely because of the musical background lacks any over-strong accent, the important things are left for the melody of movement which yonder unfolds before the curtains which suggest only a few symbols.

Triflingly sweet, strongly related to the ballet of the Baroque era, the introduction, the four companions of Donna Elvira and then she herself. Then suddenly the knight disguised as a priest, coaxing and blessing the girls, the untouchable virgin retreating from him instinctively.

Quite quickly the wooing and transition take place, the appearance of Comthur, the fight, the outcome and Elvira's lament. The knight takes his victim away from her father's corpse, Donna Elvira, no other, and then after a passionate dialogue, the development of which is entirely incumbent upon the dance figure, holds only a dead woman in his arms.

> And although in these parts of the dance drama entrusted more to the individuals there are moments of compelling greatness, the weight of the artistic experience is felt when the group comes into its own. It now takes over the action of the drama, its powerful ability to express intensified by the varied and yet uniform resoluteness of the movement. It surges in Dionysian pleasure around the dark knight who stays in the midst of this crowd of exuberant admirers, the romantic hero who never gives himself completely but the intellectual who when drinking deep from the intoxicating cup is always master of his passion and master of the one who submits to him. In this wonderful spirited gesture Laban had also as a contrast to the choir surging round him a few quite great moments. A brilliant idea caused him to make the Moor the opponent, he is a creature of habit, instinct, the slave of baser passions and in his grotesque leaps and wild contortions the dark background for the mastery of the hidalgo.
>
> Then comes the third act introduced by a very daring silent scene. The Bacchanal with the knight in the middle storms towards the burial place of the murder victim and behind the palely illuminated crosses rise the shadows of Comthur and his daughter. Here they are met by the loud challenge of Don Juan, here for the first time Comthur grasps the mortal hand, which, however, pulls away from the demonic grip. Only now does the choir change. It becomes a host of hellish messengers, who surround the outlawed one like red waves and drive him from one corner of the proscenium to the other. Still, invincible mortal defiance rebels against the annihilating forces – until once again Comthur appears and pulling the evildoers to him sinks down with him. The choir however, with hands waving triumphantly over their heads, engulfs them like a red glow.
>
> Our pictures have captured a few moments of the play. As good as the performance is it must also be added that the picture can no more do justice to the dance than word can reproduce the expression of the dance because these pictures capture only a second of motionlessness in the course of the movement which actually is not there. The real expression is in the sequence, in the course, in the lively arabesque, in the flow of the line, which in intensification contain the climax, in the greatest degree of force the relaxation. They are means of expression that we are only now learning to use again after they had faded in the last offshoots of the court ballet, which on its way to great art became fixed and finally was only the expression of sensual pleasure. *This newborn German dance spans the whole cycle of life. It is nothing less than the expression of a new universal feeling. It embraces universal heaven and hell and on its horizon is dawning the infinity of all living things.*

The review shows both the level of celebrity Laban had achieved, not only for himself, but for dance in Germany, and the depth of understanding the writer had for what Laban was trying to do in movement and theater. His ideas had come to fruition in noticeable and effective ways, and his creative work had risen to the level of his theoretical work. He moved people.

There are few accounts of what happened on the night he fell. Apparently, Don Juan was supposed to step backwards off the stage and fall onto a mattress. Some accounts say the choir threw him off the stage, missing the mattress completely; others say he simply overshot the mark.

He never performed again, but found ways to continue to lead the dance field through teaching and evolving his theoretically informed artistry. He toured Europe, lecturing and demonstrating his ideas about notation, dance for the layman, dance training and scientific bases for human movement analysis.

Laban (1879–1958)

The approaching nightmare

Laban's work became darker, at least in the case of *Die Nacht*, in 1927. He describes the source of the work as the visits he had made to the stock exchanges of Paris some twenty years earlier:

> I ... watched the excited jobbers pushing and shoving in and out, with fixed stares on their faces, shouting hoarsely and brandishing bits of paper. They would tear these out of each other's hands, career madly about and then collapse in despair in a heap, only to shoot off again, hunting for yet another piece of paper ... I got to know the ugliness of the class struggle ... I went eagerly to meetings ... where I could see waves of hatred being artificially generated and becoming so real that they were almost physically hanging in the air....
>
> A vision took shape within my mind: a dance of the eternally hurrying ones, a dance of the rootless, a dance of the sick cry for the longing of lust, a dance of alluring, seductive women, a dance of greed, a chaotic quivering accompanied by crazy laughter.
> *(Laban, 1975, pp. 41–42)*

The timing of his disquiet is significant; the piece was done as the greed of the 1920s was heading towards its peak, just before the rise of Adolf Hitler. Hitler and the Nazis promised solutions to the dissolute pursuit of money and sex, and that aspect would certainly have appealed to Laban's own concerns.

The work he created in 1927 was not a success, but it was, according to Valerie Preston-Dunlop (1998, pp. 128–129), a shocking piece. Laban explained:

> The play opened with a crowd of mechanically grinning society men and women, followed by all I had experienced and felt when I first met life in the big city.... Greed, covetousness, adoration of three idols: dollars, depravity and deceit ... It is always tragic when people can no longer laugh at the maze in which they are lost. But also in my play the happy ending was missing. Who could have dared to hope for this in those days?
> *(Laban, 1975, pp. 43–45)*

The first Dancer's Congress and Theater Exhibition in Magdeburg also took place in 1927. It was at this event that the growing tensions among the German dance leaders surfaced for all to see.

The Congress revealed a friction among those who valued ballet (Kröller), those who used combined forms (Laban and Jooss) and Wigman, who was decidedly modern.

Heinrich Kröller (1880–1930) was a German ballet master and choreographer.

A secondary conflict was over a proposed high school for dance with subsequent arguments over the content and approach of the school. On the positive side, Laban's notation system was welcomed by all, especially by Jooss. But there was also a lack of communication and organization, described by Valerie Preston-Dunlop as "problematic" (1998, p. 125). The Theater Exhibit was apparently a nightmare of dysfunction. Wigman was not included. She was also given conflicting information about a performance schedule, and she apparently announced at the end of a performance that she was disbanding her company due to financial concerns. While the committee members, who had tried to bring everyone together (including Oskar Schlemmer with his

Bauhaus dances) soldiered on, the tensions were never really resolved. Although the differences among the German "founders" became abundantly clear, and despite the disagreements and financial concerns, the Congress was also another step in Wigman's process of establishing herself as, at the least, Laban's equal, and no longer his pupil.

Advancing mastery

In 1929, Laban was asked to choreograph a festival in Vienna. The situation was already politically charged: the craft guilds that were to be a part of the parade were separate little cultures. The financial situation that year was dire. People were fearful of the future, which caused some consternation among the planners, who were determined to avoid dissension while promoting the industries. The members of the guilds themselves were concerned that the visiting choreographer would have them hopping as they paraded along. They did not want to hop.

Laban set about to learn the movements inherent in each craft. He learned how to shoe horses, how to trim flowers, how to make pottery, etc. He took each of these work-dances and devised short choreographed pieces based on the essential patterns, both functional and expressive, of each guild. The results went far beyond expectations. It was an event that reminds us of the true value of Laban's contributions to dance and to the world. Laban wrote that the performers thanked him, because in the course of performing their work-dances, they had "fallen in love with their work again" (Laban, 1975, p. 143). They each understood what only the masters of the craft knew: that the essence of the movement was the essence of the craft.

In 1929, he was also lecturing, including a series of talks on the "Problems of Dance" (Maletic, 1987, pp. 13–14). Laban laid out the categories to be addressed in dance as separate but interconnected modes of the field. His approach to dance for laymen (the first of the categories) reflected the need for essence and authenticity, even in quotidian play and interactions, while the scientific approach to dance analysis (the second category) included three areas: choreosophy (aesthetics), choreology (analysis of space and time) and choreography (notation). The art of dance, or what had evolved from the Tanztheater and expressive dance works was the third category, and dance pedagogy was the fourth. Such categories did not diminish Laban's understanding of the world of dance, rather, they refined and clarified what he had begun to delineate from the all-encompassing free expressivity of Ascona. But the process of demarcation created yet another tension: his desire to release the human spirit from boundaries of time and place, while teasing apart the characteristics of time and place.

Growing dance theory

By 1930, Laban was feeling the tension between nationalism and socialism that was beginning to increase all around him. His concerns about a loss of human feeling and connection to the work product were not limited to industry. In an article in the journal *Singchor und Tanz* (Mannheim, 15 January, 1929, Vol. II, p. 561), entitled "The Renewal of the Movement in Theater," he wrote about dancing and spirit. He said that theater had abandoned art. He saw a strong attempt to renew or to develop the spiritual part of theater and raised the question: So how can one develop that part?

> It is necessary that every performer master's body and soul. In order to achieve that goal, it's not sufficient to just do rhythmical gymnastics. There has to be an independent dance director in theaters in order to have good results. Young actors/performers should only be allowed to get onstage when they have achieved that mastery in

movement. It cannot be some unrelated form. Gymnastics, sports and fencing can be done; it's OK, but they are just not sufficient to transport the spirit of the dance into the theater.

The director of the movement must understand that it's not ok to just take care of the single performer. In order to serve that spirit of dance, one must serve the whole play. There is no theater that has that kind of director now. It's time and we have to get rid of those obsolete directors.

(p. 561, translated by Sabine Fichter)

In another issue of *Singchor und Tanz*, he directly addressed the dance world in "Choreographie und Theater":

Dance is a serious art form. Dance now requires further development that goes into more depth. Improvising is not enough – it's not really art. The problem for many dancers is that they have been working as soloists and could not have an objective view on what they do. This is a big problem.

(February, 1929, Vol. IV p. 598, translation by Fichter)

Laban proposed that his research-based approach to creating dance meant a new direction for the art form. His space harmony work made it possible to have a more objective view and his notation system took objectivity and the capacity for research even further. Therefore, he wrote that it was possible every dancer would soon be ready to create his/her own dances and so would be able to reflect on what was created, with opportunity to be critical about form, shape, intention, etc. The logical next step would be that dances could be notated and published to a broader audience and followed by exchanges of feedback, reconstruction and refinement of the work. He suggested considering his proposed objective framework, which allowed everyone to interpret movement individually. Laban compared the process to music:

The same will happen to dance as music. In general there will be a distinction between those who create and those who will perform those dances. The possibility of notating dances will be something that will be important throughout history and for the future and will be an important step for this genre. That is a problem with old theater pieces that have been done before; we have no written record. This will change now. Poetry and music have been notated and preserved. Only those things that are notated can be taken seriously.

(February, 1929, p. 598, translation by Fichter)

Laban went on to say that "good directors are movement poets." The director's job is to clarify, humanize and preserve dance movement so it can be replicated and still stay alive.

Tossing and turning

The book *A Life for Dance* was first published in 1935, but Laban wrote it as he struggled with his standing as a choreographer and leader of the German dance world and the hints of coming fascism in Germany. In it, he described his early concerns with class struggles. He asked:

Why care for the satisfied and wealthy, who build such a pathetic illusion of happiness with farthings snatched ruthlessly from the poorest, while their own souls wither and perish among their gilt and opulence? ... How can true beauty dwell among the glitter of tattered silk and under the artificial purple lights? How can the soul rejoice amid the tattered rags of the poor and hollow-eyed children? How utterly remote is the fragrance of the mountains and forests from the air of the slums, so thick with coal dust ... Is that the song of man?

(Laban, 1975, pp. 42–43)

Even as the "song of man" showed early signs of discord, Laban needed income and he sought a position as a ballet-master within the dance world. Many of the ballet companies at that time were affiliated with the opera, and the art form had become stultified. Laban wanted to put his ideas into full practice. When he was appointed to this position, at the Berlin State Opera, in 1930, there was both resistance and curiosity among the dancers. He was not going to support the star system and he was excited about getting the ballet dancers to expand and explore new movement material. Many of the stars of the German ballet companies took exception to his ideas.

The socialist ideals Laban espoused in his book and in his position came up against the Nazis' rise to power in Germany, carried as they were on some of those ideals. Laban was in favor so long as he cooperated with the nationalist agenda.

And he tried to cooperate, for a while. His creative ideals had found support, at least at first. His interest in the mystical and in Wagner's triumphal music has been seen as evidence for his purported manipulative and dictatorial tendencies. Some dance scholars make a case that Laban had a plan for the domination of the world of dance because his work came to be used in a set and stultifying way, in the later Nazi and post-World War II periods.

There is insufficient evidence to support the characterization of Laban as an ambitious tyrant. In fact, the values and behaviors Laban expressed suggest that he was not domineering but seductive; not controlling or rigid but engaged and improvisational. For Laban, dance was the preferred way to address these values. His goal was freedom, light and a new reasoning based on experiencing and interacting dynamically. He was far more interested in the process of opening up and expanding one's personal expressive range than he was in his own personal power or any particular sociopolitical outcome.

Evelyn Dörr put it this way: Laban was focused on themes of being, developing and decomposing/dying. His leitmotif and guiding principles explored symmetry and asymmetry, dynamics, rebounding from sustainment, etc. His work and values went against the Nazi notion of despotism, even if neither he nor they could see the conflict at first. He followed the path of art and humanist movement (Dörr interview, July 9, 2004).

Those who knew Laban best have supported Dörr's contention that Laban was, in essence, naïve. He thought he could influence the Nazis and show them his way was best. The tension he felt was a struggle between his notion of a dance technique that was based in release of ideology, position, or steps, and which he wanted to see housed in a real theater, for audiences to see. The desire to work with the ever-darkening power structures of the Nazis in order to realize his dreams, in contrast with his awareness of the soullessness of any political machine – much less a fascistic one – brings into sharp focus a piece he created in 1927, *The Titan*.

Titan was, in part, a piece that arose from his short visit to the United States in 1926. In *A Life for Dance*, Laban offered up his ethnographic analysis of the melting pot of American dance, although the chapter is sprinkled with what we would now recognize as ignorant racism and sexism. He expressed admiration for the "Red Indian" and was less taken with the African-American culture of Chicago at the time (there is a suggestion that he may have been mugged or ripped off by a prostitute there.) His description of his trip reveals naiveté as well as animosity towards certain ethnic groups, if not a tendency towards over-personalization and projection. But he ends the chapter with this:

> The purpose of life, as I understand it, is a care for the human as opposed to the robot; a call to save mankind from dying out in hideous confusion; an image of the festival of the future, a mass of life in which all the celebrants in communion of thought, feeling, and action, seek the way to a clear goal, namely to enhance their own inner light.
> *(Laban, 1975, p. 137)*

Valerie Preston-Dunlop (1998, p. 127) points out how easily scholars have used Laban's description of the dance-play's "telling of the strength of the common hope which lies in a common will to achieve something better" as evidence of how the Ausdruckstanz (Expressionist Dance) was in tune with Nazism. She goes on to address the concept of the "common," which she points out was a different interpretation of the word from how Laban used it historically. In the movement choir work, there is a common aim – "individual expression through their own light." But that goal does not require a common or regimented approach. Moving together in communion and harmony is not the same thing as marching to a single drummer. And Laban's work required the exercise of the individual artist's mind, body and spirit, in fact demanded a mastery of the discourse of the mind, body and spirit.

In contrast to the Nazi notion of "the Master Race," Laban understood mastery as mastery over self and over mankind's natural indolence. In the end, Laban's definition was too different from that of the Nazis. He understood harmony not as mere structure or regimentation, but as listening, observing and sharing unique aspects, finding common ground that allowed each mover's style to shine and support that of the others.

Waking up

In 1932, Laban's former student Kurt Jooss choreographed his masterwork, *The Green Table*. He created it for the Concours International de Chorégraphie en Souvenir de Jean Borlin, a competition organized by the Archives Internationales de la Danse, held at the Théâtre des Champs-Elysees in Paris, in July 1932. The piece was a huge success. Although he claimed the work was not an anti-war ballet, he was astute enough to see what was happening in Germany. Jooss' wife, Aino, and his composer Fritz Cohen were Jewish and the danger was much clearer to him than it appeared to be to Laban. Jooss warned Laban about the Nazis, and advised him to leave as well. His Jooss Ballet toured for a bit and then settled in southwest England, at an estate called Dartington Hall.

Laban did not leave Germany when Jooss advised him to, and his remaining has led to much speculation and interpretation about the reasons why. There is evidence of cooperation with the National Socialists in regard to delivering lists of Jewish students and in banning, in particular, one Jewish dancer from observing his work in 1934. Those events happened, but we do not know why he cooperated to the extent that he did. Interviews and readings reveal a range of possibilities, from total naiveté, to coercion by the Nazis, to alleged agreement with the Nazi goals.

He did not join the party, and he was not a fascist, although it is equally clear that he was naively racist, in a passive way, from his writings about the "Red Indian" and Negroes in America. He may have stayed in Germany because his work was there, or because he was not so concerned about the racist aspects of the Nazi regime, or he was a little callow about the growing fascism around him.

Nevertheless, by 1936, Laban was getting the idea. He paid as little attention to politics as he could, but he knew what was happening to the voices of individuals under the national socialist framework. In 1936, Laban had position and income, privileges he had not often enjoyed in his life, and that he thought were worth protecting. Nonetheless, in 1936 as a judge at a dance festival, he balked at awarding a prize to a German dance group over other groups, and decided to award prizes to all participants.

Laban was asked to put together a huge movement choir, *Tauwind*, for the opening of a theater in the week leading up to the Berlin Olympics. In the speech he gave at the final dress rehearsal, he praised the uniqueness of the human body moving in concert with others, expressing the very essence of life:

> We do not need to believe in dogmatic explanations, in philosophical systems or in circumstantial calculations to understand the will of life, which fills our whole being. It upsets our natural harmonic condition if we try to find the first source and the final goal outside ourselves ...
>
> What does the faith consist of? What is its essence? We believe in a psycho-physiological way to health and happiness and on this we search for a right functioning of our individual as well as community life. The spiritual vision of the world, and the question of the connection and communication with the life force also finds its natural ground here.
>
> *(Translation by Laban, 1939)*

Joseph Goebbels, the Nazi Minister of Culture and, possibly, Adolf Hitler observed the rehearsal and speech, so Laban's following thought is all the more significant and telling:

> This work demands from us the utmost devotion and great efforts. With these efforts we do not want to cheat or to overreach anybody, we do not want to make a competition and draw external profits. We do not need to fight each other, or envy the other's possession. We carry all we need within ourselves.
>
> *(Laban, 1939)*

What Laban expressed is a clear reference to the Asconan ideals of individual and group interdependence, of the organic unfolding within human institutions of community. Goebbels understood the message very well. In his diary, he commented: "It is all dressed up in our clothes and has nothing whatsoever to do with us" (quoted in Preston-Dunlop, 1998, p. 196). The performance was prohibited. He was accused of homosexuality, a denigration that would have cut deeply. His papers were seized, his travel limited. Laban's career in Germany was over.

He tried to stay, sending a letter to a friend, Marie Lieschke, and asking her to speak to some of the Nazi officials on his behalf, but his fate was sealed.

Eventually, he found his way to Paris, a desperately ill and broken man. He planned to stay with Dussia Bereska who was running a dance school in Paris, but, according to some interviewees, she was drinking quite a bit. He ended up in a dark and damp basement room, where his plight came to be known to Kurt Jooss.

Re-energizing at Dartington

Jooss, his family and his company had found another little jewel of a location in Dartington Hall, Britain, an old estate that had been purchased by Leonard and Dorothy Elmhirst. The Elmhirsts were an intriguing couple: she was an American, a Whitney; he was an idealistic young Brit. They met at Cornell University and devised a dream between his vision and her money. Their home, Dartington Hall, purchased in 1925, became a center for Leonard's experiments in progressive education, rural "reconstruction" (Leonard's word), and, eventually, a refuge for artists.

At Dartington, a number of artists found a home, however briefly, with the Elmhirsts. The list included Mark Tobey, Bernard Leach, Michael Chekhov, Rabindranath Tagore, Cecil Collins, Imogen Holst, Benjamin Britten, Peter Pears, Michael Tippett, the Amadeus String Quartet, Ravi Shankar, Viyhat and Imrat Khan, Stravinsky, Hindemith, Poulenc, Lutoslawski, John Cage – and many more.

Laban arrived at Dartington in 1937, sick and devastated. The students there at the time were told to leave him alone. According to Ann Hutchinson Guest, on occasion he could be spotted in the balcony that overlooked the dance studio, where the Jooss Ballet rehearsed, a figure in shadows.

He might have stayed in those shadows were it not for Lisa Ullmann, one of Jooss' dancers, who became Laban's domestic partner, leading him back into the world, and nurturing both his being and his vision.

It was in his little studio that Laban could be found, studying crystals and thinking about how matter forms itself into beautiful shapes, without consciousness but with a logic based in physics and metaphysics. The swinging scales he had developed some twenty years earlier made sense kinesthetically, allowing the body to fall, as it did, into natural rhythms and directions in space. He began to write and talk about spatial pulls and tensions that lived inside various crystalline forms, and to discover the multi-dimensional ways the human body can transcend gravity and achieve a spicier harmony with nature, one in which movers and environment partner actively and responsibly.

In Ascona, Laban had engaged with the Rosicrucians, the Freemasons and other cult-like groups that also professed openness to seeing the possibilities of human transcendence and a marriage of the spirit and imagination. Laban was not really interested in being part of a cult: he preferred to stand outside and move ideas rather than submit to them. In Southwest England, with time and space galore, he revisited his own thoughts about the myriad ways people are pulled into the farthest reaches of space, orienting themselves to the complexities beyond the vertical pull of gravity. He would sit and turn icosahedra and dodecahedra around and around, finding the center and the possibilities in each. And then he would take long walks around the estate, with its fields and sculptures, cows and medieval tilting yard. In the evenings, he and Leonard Elmhirst might sit and talk about farming and human movement, or Laban and Dorothy Elmhirst might discuss the creative work that was as much a product of the estate as the vegetables.

As at Ascona, the Eden-like existence on the Dartington estate was dissolved by war. Once again nationalism and boundaries between governments mattered. As World War II progressed, all German nationals were moved from the coastal regions and the members of the Jooss Ballet were no exception. The Elmhirsts found a farmhouse in rural Wales for Laban and Lisa, and it was here that a young Betty Meredith-Jones studied with them. Betty was a physical educator; she lived in a caravan (trailer, in the USA), while she and Lisa began to decode the theories Laban was garnering from his crystals. Eventually, Betty came to the United States where she pioneered Laban's work in psychiatry and especially with Parkinson's patients.

F. C. Lawrence was a management consultant when Leonard Elmhurst introduced him to Laban. During and after World War II, Lawrence and Laban blended traditional time – motion study approaches to worker efficiency with Laban's analysis of effort and space. Observing young women throwing around huge tires and pieces of equipment for the war effort gave them opportunities to note the role of personal style in efficiency. Body type and predilections for particular permutations of expression and pathways played a role in the productivity and job satisfaction of the women hired to take over from the men deployed to the war. Laban and Lawrence called their approach "lilt in labour" and it revolutionized industry.

> Few of us realize that our contentment in work and happiness in life, as well as any personal or collective success, is conditioned by the perfect development and use of our individual efforts. We speak about "industrial effort" or "cultural effort", without realizing that each collective action is built up from the mental and manual efforts of individual people.
>
> *(Laban and Lawrence, 1974, p. 1)*

These same notions of individual style became the basis for Marion North's *Personality Assessment through Movement*, a comparative study of the relationship between individual movement style and classroom behaviors in young children. They also underlay the character development work of Geraldine Stephenson, Yat Malmgren and other teachers of Laban-based movement for actors. Individual style analysis became the seeds for the Action Profiling and Movement Pattern Analysis developed by Warren Lamb, who analyzed the decision-making styles of top team planners in industry.

Winding down in Manchester and Surrey

In 1946, Laban and Lisa established a school in Manchester, called the Art of Movement Studio, with funding from the Elmhirsts. It was here that Valerie Preston-Dunlop, Geraldine Stephenson, Warren Lamb and Marion North, among others, found their life's work. One pupil at the school was a young Joan Plowright. It was Laban who suggested that acting, not dance, might be her forte.

Laban did not teach very often at the Studio, but when he did, the old charisma and vision were apparent. Also apparent were his age and ill-health. The remaining years of his life were full of bursts of creative energy and quick insights, and periods of withdrawal and recuperation.

He fostered the application of his work in several fields. He saw it used in actor training, studies of efficiency in industry, an expanded Labanotation system, early dance therapy/psychiatry and education.

Laban kept an eye on all of it, but he rarely interfered, unless it was to redirect, or in many cases, to tutor or just support a young student.

Geraldine Stephenson describes a moment on a train with Laban, sometime in the early 1950s:

> I was on a train with him coming back from several weeks of teaching various workshops for actors. For some reason, he was with me on this particular trip, but really, I had been doing quite a lot of these by myself. I was just exhausted, and I finally turned to him and said, "I do not think I can go on like this. I need a rest."
>
> He looked at me with his fairly piercing demeanor, and said, "Vat you need to do iss a concert." I was horrified! Here he was, suggesting MORE work, when I needed a vacation! But for some reason, I listened to him, went into the studio for weeks and weeks, and created an evening of solos; short effort studies of characters. This was a big success and led into many other opportunities. He was right. I needed to do something for myself.
>
> *(Interview, July 2, 2004)*

Many stories abound of his generosity and exacting standards, of brutal reactions, and warm elegance. His former students spoke of his high expectations, the twinkle in his eye, his dark moods, and his spiritual curiosity. For a man whose creative work had been full of social commentary, his political insight was close to non-existent. He had both democratic and anarchical principles, yet he was a stateless person who found himself engaged with nationalism and fascism, in bewildering and sudden juxtapositions.

Looking backwards and forwards

Rudolf Laban rode along all of the pathways of his times attentively, and with an abiding faith in the nature of the universe to support mankind, even after he saw the limitations and dark nature of mankind. Because he did not plan out his life, or even design his career, he was able to respond to the issues at hand, in the moment, and yet he was also able to avoid taking responsibility for those same issues and in the case of his children, to avoid much more than responsibility. He was an aristocrat who never owned any property, including his own intellectual property, which left his work subject to appropriation, providing a springboard for the careers of others to whom he gave material for further development.

Those who carried the work forward, including Marion North, Valerie Preston-Dunlop, Warren Lamb, Betty Meredith-Jones, Irmgard Bartenieff, Samuel Thornton and so many more, felt empowered to adapt, evolve or augment it in his/her own way. Each adhered to the basic principles of analytic categories, and the basic values of respect for individuality and finding common ground. Interestingly, there was much agreement about those basic principles and values, even though the work looks very different in the hands of those schooled in it by different teachers.

Sam Thornton, who has run summer courses in movement for over thirty years, describes Laban's work with the saying: "We all live in the same world, but we don't all see the same world" (Interview, June 30, 2004).

That statement may best describe Laban's legacy to a world struggling with power, status, greed and war. In terms of politics, while he was not one to comment on government directly or protest policies, he was an astute observer of human conflict.

The Nazi piece is so very tricky however. Artists have historically struggled for approval and funding from those authorized and inclined to provide it. Patronage is a double-edged sword and political hierarchies are real and impact artists. Sometimes the impact is random, sometimes it comes with a vengeance, as in the case of the Nazis, the House Un-American Activities Committee in the 1950s, or the culture wars of the 1990s. The Nazis went after artists for many purported reasons, including a desire to test their loyalties. When Laban's turn to be challenged came, he hastened his exit with the speech he gave before the dress rehearsal of *Tauwind*. He was gone before Kristallnacht as a result of speaking some truth to power. He was not exactly a freedom fighter, but neither was he a despot.

His role was as a social commentator, addressing issues inherently in question during a period of rising fascism. At the same time, he tried to maintain his position within the power structure. In the end, he came face-to-face with bias, unyielding positions, repression and threats, and he chose to escape. For the rest of his life, he struggled with depression and illness, but always came back to the dance itself, for insight, acumen and healing.

In the early 1950s, Laban and Lisa persuaded the Elmhirsts to buy a small estate for the Art of Movement Studio in Addlestone, Surrey. There she taught and he reviewed student work. The studio that was built there was an architectural marvel, and those who studied in it speak of the gardens they helped to nurture alongside their own personal and artistic growth.

Walli Meier, a dance therapist in Britain, tells of her final examination at Addlestone, in which she sat while Laban perused her notations, completed after months of observing psychiatric patients. After turning the pages over and over and scanning, all the while saying "Ja ... Ja ... " he slammed the book shut, chucked it over his shoulder ("All that work!" Walli exclaimed) and looked at her. "Vell, ve know that all, don't ve?" he said. "Now, ve dance!" And so they danced (quoted from a video made by Janet Kaylo and Patrick Lears, May 1996, from the author's private collection).

Laban took walks and spent time with the cat. He reconnected with his and Suzanne Perrottet's son, Allard, and was devastated when the young man committed suicide. He turned crystals around and learned from them. He drew, he pondered; he made no plans. On July 1, 1958, he died. He is buried in Weybridge cemetery, in an obscure corner, under a headstone that says, simply: "A Life for Dance." The dance lives on.

4.2 The Tanztheater and analysis of a work: *Die Grünen Clowns*

At the beginning of the 1920s, the training programs Laban had devised for students all over Europe, including the emerging notation system, the freie Tanz, the movement choirs, and the rest of the curriculum did not yet contain a study of choreosophy (the aesthetics of movement), choreography (which he thought of as the notation of movement) or choreology (the analysis of movement for the purpose of making dances). The rise of the Tanztheater throughout the 1920s clarified the need for more organized and specific training, however. The schools and the curriculum within them had to address a more systematic approach to training as well as a more divergent approach to the creative process.

The Tanztheater, which required specificity of expression, clarity of technique and rampant innovation, provided a laboratory for experimentation in a variety of creative approaches to art making. In this section of the book, we will discover how all of those threads unfolded into one of his works: *Die Grünen Clowns* (*The Green Clowns*).

Tanztheater privileged dance over music and visual components

In the early to mid-1920s, the Tanztheater galvanized the European performance world. Because Laban and Wigman placed movement over music, costume and all external theatrical devices, and through the refinement of physically expressive and spatially clear storytelling, the dance itself became the primary medium. And although music, costume and all external devices were often present and supported the movement, the unfolding of the story happened through the medium of dance.

Laban's approach was in contrast to the music-centric theories and practices of Dalcroze's Eurhythmics work and moved beyond the unrestrained, free flowing movement that Isadora Duncan performed to Chopin and Beethoven. He was after something more specific and dis-cursive. Whereas Duncan's movement was expressive in a general way, she also believed she was channeling the music and the classicism of the ancient Greeks. Dalcroze taught movement as the externalization of the form and expressivity of the movement. But Laban was interested in the movement moment itself, its content, meaning and relationship to the human spirit. He was not concerned with the embodiment of music or a particular aesthetic ideal; he preferred specific and potent movement that was expressive and detailed.

Laban wrote in "Das Tanztheater" in the supplement *Licht - Luft - Leben* in the journal *Die Schönheit: Mit Bildern geschmückte Monatsschrift für Kunst und Leben* (*Beauty: Monthly Journal of Art and Life, with Pictures*) (Dresden, 1924, Vol. XXII) that Tanztheater was a new form of art. In this new genre, the movement itself was the main concern; everything else was secondary. Music could be simple or simply not necessary. Music could even be just noises, or the sound of breathing. The same went for costumes: he used whatever he found or felt might work.

As in all of his writing throughout his life, Laban crossed into the poetic realms, waxing rhapsodically about the art form in "Das Tanztheater": "Dance transports, like a poem or drama. It can be witty; can be humorous, rich and colorful. It's different from music" (Laban, 1924). Laban wrote that there was, for him, a greater degree of relationship between dance and poetry and dance and mimetic drama than there was with music, despite his ongoing comparisons. He understood that dance is not easily put into words and that is why people relate it to music or acting; but in the end, it stands only for itself. He described dance as the Ur-kunst, the Ur-art, or the primary and earliest form of art. Music and drama, he wrote, came later and used elements of dance.

"This new dance theater aims for finding a synthesis of all possibilities of expression and bringing those together again. This synthesis can be dance tragedy, dance ballad (song), dance comedy, or a movement symphony" (Laban, 1924).

Despite his stated belief that dance is less related to music than it is to poetry, analogies to musical form and theory abound in his writing.

> Dance has things to say and express that cannot be said through music or acting, and in a deep way. It is the music of the limbs. The logic of the dance movement has to be harmonic in order to let the dance event be a symbol for a life event that makes us happy or sad, but that touches us.
> *(Laban, 1924, Licht - Luft - Leben, Dresden, Vol. XXII, translated by Sabine Fichter)*

He also questioned how far abstraction could go and decided that good art must maintain a close relationship to life itself. Dance is integral to being alive, to being human. And yet, dance is, in a way, an abstraction. It's both inherent to humanity and a way to be more human. For example, Laban understood the use of masks in dance as both a reflection as well as an extension of human personality. In that sense, dance is a kind of mask that reveals as much as it extends the face of the individual.

Tanztheater drove the need for an analysis and notation system

One of Laban's main concerns was that dance had not yet defined its own language. He made an analogy to the other art forms: music and drama, both of which have conventions, theory, and a textual form. In so doing, he made a case for his notation system, but more than that, he was emancipating dance, at least in his mind, from the other art forms, and providing a means whereby dance could be preserved and recaptured as movement, and therefore maintain value.

Other notation systems existed, and dance had a vocabulary of steps from ballet. But the new dance, freed from those conventions and patterns, required a different way of thinking about how to capture and archive what was essentially ephemeral and inventive.

In developing the notation system, Laban freed dance and captured it again, but he captured it as an ever-changing, context-influenced phenomenon. One can make decisions and do so within a range of choices inherent in the notation system, through an interpretative and synthesizing process. The categories of Body, Space and Effort coexist, inform each other, and transcend the limits of thinking in terms of steps or floor patterns, musical contexts or theatrical terms.

He began to equate movement sequences that occupied the areas of space above the waist as "high dances," equivalent to the songs of the soprano, and dances close to the earth as "low dances," like the songs of the baritone. His comparison of the soprano and the baritone goes beyond the amplitude of the vocal ranges of both. He saw the relationship between space and style as a justification for men performing (an issue he appeared to be deeply concerned about) because, he said, in art, all options have to be present and available and true to life. Just as opera requires the presence of the baritone, men have to be onstage, fulfilling their roles. Such roles and the predilections of men and women differ. Each type of physicality requires different dynamic support.

In an article on anatomy in the supplement *Licht - Luft - Leben* (1924), he wrote about the technique and body training he was beginning to develop. He used the words rising and sinking, descriptors of full body movement that are still used to clarify a particular way of going up and down in space. He wrote about tension and recuperation from tension. He pointed out that the body can widen and narrow, mainly through breathing. For a tiny second, there is a point of rest in breathing, and that moment organizes the one that follows. If a mover wanted to pick up something heavy from the floor, he/she could do this with both quickness and lightness, and then use strong and sustained qualities, which produce complex phrases of meaningful expression. He wrote about movement phrases and that these are not even and unchanging. He believed that the body organizes movement into both evocative and utilitarian segments of differing lengths and emphases.

Imagine playing a character, such as a clown, who enters a space, looks around to take in all of it with a light, quick inhalation that causes a step backwards, with a narrowing of the body shape. Then the character takes a lingering step forwards, reaches down to pick up an object, grabs it, looks at it quickly and then tosses it to the side, turning the head away at the same moment.

Now imagine the exact same sequence as performed by a character such as a heroic knight. Meaning changes with the changing context of the character, but it is still recognizable as meaningful and communicative human movement. Laban's analysis of movement into Body, Effort and Space allows for replicability without the loss of choice and human creativity.

Dancers also must learn to change between stability and mobility, widening and narrowing, expanding and contracting (which he sees as a more general growing and shrinking than widening and narrowing), etc. This exploration of opposites, he wrote, is the origin of beautiful contrasts and all beauty is based on that harmonic change. "This gives a healthy order and structure to our life. And learning about these movement laws, man will be a master of his environment and the dancer will be a master of his space" (Laban, 1926a).

In his 1920 book, *Die Welt des Tänzers*, Laban began to parse the aspects of movement that comprise dance: rhythm (time), space and what he called tensions. He did not see rhythm, for example, as being merely a series of movements proceeding in time, with accents or forces. He understood rhythm to be multidimensional and meaningful. The degree to which movement has force and fluency, tension and release matters to the audience's understanding of the layers of meaning in the dance.

As he further explained in *Choreographie* (1926): "The explanation the world of dance forms must not be confined to an enumeration of rigid states. This world must be considered as undulations (wavings, transformation) alive with constant change" (quoted in Bartenieff et al., 1970, p. 5).

Thus and despite his early enamoration of tableaux vivants, Laban found that the essence of meaning in dance came not from positions or poses, but from evolving and unfolding changes towards and away from points in space and in response to internal and external phenomena.

The period 1928–32 brought another level of development for the notation that Laban was developing with Albrecht Knust and the other dancers. The journal *Schrifttanz* debuted following Laban's presentation of the new notation system at the Second Dancer's Congress, at Essen. The editor, Alfred Schlee, was a young music publisher. At the beginning, the magazine was to be devoted strictly to Labanotation and there were to be four editions per year. The narrow focus was not practical, however, and so the writing expanded to include all types of writing about dance: historical, critical and theoretical analyses.

Schrifttanz was by all accounts a beautifully executed artifact, with covers by Picasso and Schlemmer and an advisory board consisting of luminaries such as Fritz Böhme, the historian, Hans Brandenberg, the critic and writer, Oskar Schlemmer, and Bronislava Nijinska. Notators from all over Europe and the United States were listed, demonstrating that notation was a growing field beyond the borders of Germany.

In 1929, the Tanztheater was represented in the journal by articles about Wigman and Schlemmer, Dussia Bereska in Northern Italy, Harold Kreutzberg and Yvonne Georgi touring the United States, and an announcement of a public meeting with both Laban and Wigman to discuss plans for a State College for Dance, an idea that never came to fruition.

In the January 1929 issue, a section of a small dance piece was notated. The piece was entitled *Die Grünen Clowns* (*The Green Clowns*). The score was from a section entitled "Zeitlupe" (Slow Motion). Dussia Bereska is listed as the choreographer for that section, but the overall work was a Laban creation.

Laban wrote about why the notation was so important to dance at this time:

> Kinetography or movement notation has two objectives, which need to be clearly distinguished.
>
> The first objective is the capturing of movement sequences and dances. The advantages of such a possibility are easy to see; they have been recognized for centuries and have been continually sought, through experiments with varying degrees of success.
>
> The other objective is, from a conceptual point of view, far the more important. It deals with defining the movement process through analysis and thus freeing it from the kind of vagueness which has made the language of dance appear unclear and monotonous.
>
> *(From 1928, "Basic Principles of Movement Notation," Schrifttanz, Vol. I, No. 1, July, p. 32)*

Tanztheater inspired new contexts and form

Laban continued to develop his own exploration of tensions: spatial, relational, social and expressive. Evelyn Dörr describes Laban's work in and around 1928 as a radicalization of the expressionist foundation, drawn out through abstracting tensions inherent in crystalline forms (2003, *Dance Chronicle* article, pp. 1–29). Laban's drawings from this time reflect his understanding of the underlying laws of gravity and form, as well as his aesthetic of interrupting form with something that is human and idiosyncratic. To him, the tension between human and the natural laws is the stuff of art.

How far did Laban feel abstraction could go? Only as far as the movement keeps a close relationship to "life itself," he wrote. "It's in the nature of the dance that there is a necessity to the relationship to being alive, to humanity" (Laban, 1924).

He was fascinated with the spectrum of the familiar to the novel, and part of the tension he describes over and over again in his Tanz-theater writings explores the familiar body-based expressions (gestures) in relation to ever-evolving abstractions of spatial pulls and crystalline forms. Dörr quotes Laban from the 1926 book *Choreographie*: "he describes how a form 'is then dissolved, the process through which it passes into related forms', eventually via related forms reaching less familiar ones" (Dörr, 2003, p. 8).

In *The Green Clowns*, such everyday gestures that extend into the grotesque or novel are both recognizable and tickle the imagination. When a clown drapes herself over another clown, the movement is reminiscent of the human need to reach out for what we need (in this case, support) and to overstate and overreach such needs to the point of absurdity. The draping is repeated throughout one section of the work, as both a comment on and a reflection of a tendency to exaggerate and embellish. The movement is carried into abstraction and evolution, but the meaning is not lost, but rather, universalized.

Tanztheater balanced the abstract and the literal

Laban's approach was not simply to abstract movement from mime or story; he wanted to be sure that the dance always had a relationship to human experiences, feelings, and behaviors. But he also believed dance was inherently an abstraction. Therefore his realm was metaphor, not literality. The specificity and detail in the movement were imagistic and referential, symbolic and often ironic, but also simple and clear.

A simple wave of the hand, as in a gesture of greeting, serves as an example of the dichotomy reconnected. Such a gesture can be performed in many different ways; all refer to the same message of greeting, but one can convey a multitude of nuanced communiqués by clarifying and specifying the details within the wave. An example is the beauty-queen greeting, as she is carried through the streets in a parade, sitting atop a convertible. The direct but general gaze, the even phrasing as the hand turns slightly from side to side, palm revealed to the crowd like a lighthouse beacon, all performed with an unchanging smile, conveys something different from the politician's leap onto a platform with a raised arm that pumps as she waves the entire hand quickly. Both are greetings, but each is specific to the context and to the purpose of the performance.

In *Die Welt des Tänzers* (1920) Laban wrote: "Dance is gesture, i.e. a synthesis of body tension, emotional excitation, and imagining" (Bartenieff et al., 1970, p. 6). Whereas the theorists Dalcroze and Delsarte linked meaning in movement to meaning in other modalities – music and spoken word – and early modern dancers found meaning in cultural references, simple beauty and their own gesture life, Laban tried to unpack meaning from pure elements, as an anthropologist reconstructs meaning directly from artifacts. But as an archeologist of sorts, Laban was also interested in the deeper, human story buried within the movement. And he valued the movement intrinsically, as a manifestation of human spirit or soul. In the examples above, of the beauty queen and the politician, what drives each to the roles they play is something profoundly felt: an identification with a particular way of being in the world that goes deeper than performing a task or communicating a message. Gestures, therefore, can be both universal communications of message as well as specific to identity, role, and culture. Dancers must understand both aspects.

In *Die Welt des Tänzers*, Laban described the process of coming into the profound world of a dancer:

> We hardly see with our eyes, any more than we hear with our ears. To concentrate on the eye: An agglomeration which has arisen from the specially formed harmonic form of uniform infinity is clearly and roughly mirrored by one of our organs, the eye. Clearly in the sense of being explicable, our experience interprets this as a space-claiming agglomeration, a thing. Our research interprets the eye as a darkroom. The process of being and recognizing the nature of the object seen is naturally not explained by this. What sees? The eye? The whole being? ... One evening I go into the woods. Tree branches rise and fall around a patch of empty sky. A strip of clouds passes steeply and obliquely across this patch. Below it, next to it is a star. I am stirred, moved.

> The path leads me to a place where an agglomerate chord, a tension, a thought of god awakes which has always existed but lain dormant within me. I can recall the mathematic aesthetic proportions of the phenomenon; I can be jubilant or tearful according to its effect. I can say to myself, "Tomorrow the weather will be fine." All the same, a thought of god has awoken within me. If I experience this tension fully and if I know how to weave it into my life, then I am dancer.
>
> *(Laban, 1920, Schröder translation)*

The connection of what Laban called "the god within" to deeply felt and detailed expression is recognizable to anyone who practices daily in order to refine performance. To Laban, the execution of each moment was as important as the large ideas behind the pieces he developed. The training for such performances required mastery of body, mind, and soul, and it happened through effort study, spatial analysis and practice, and refinement of skills within the context of story and other meaning-making human experiences. Anyone who danced with him had to experience the tensions fully, and to weave them into and out of his/her own life.

Tanztheater produced a new type of choreographer

In addition to his emerging theories about the categories and characteristics of movement specificity, Laban also had an evolving idea about a new type of "dancing master." Unlike the socially ascendant and advancing of political status effects of the court-based dancing masters' approach to dance training, or the dictatorial and hierarchical attitudes of the ballet masters of the nineteenth century, he preferred the notion of an independent dance director who would support the creative spirit and the deep mastery of technique in each dancer.

Beyond the individual dancer, however, he also understood that the dance director must first and foremost attend to whatever layers of meaning were necessary to serve the larger themes. The dance, he felt, consists of the individual bodies in movement as well as the spirit of the whole piece. A good director attends to both.

Laban was both a generous and an exacting man; he could be encouraging and a little brutal. For him the dance and the often abstract stories the bodies told through movement were as important as the means whereby those stories were being told. Therefore the training his dancers underwent in the 1920s in Germany looked nothing like the ballet classes from the days of the opera's ascendance, nor did they look like the classes at Denishawn or the Martha Graham School, later on. Laban's training was based on both exploration and refinement of the moment, which was a process of creative and divergent investigations along with feedback and discussion about the specificity and clarity of a moment.

As noted in the biographical section, classically trained ballet dancers did not take to his approach easily. His movement process was a great leveler, encouraging depth of feeling rather than virtuosity of execution, and favoring the ensemble over the star system. Daily classes in eukinetics (expression) and choreutics (space harmony, scales, theory and practice together) were taught by Laban and his assistants and experimentation with ideas was encouraged as work was created.

His main assistant in the Tanzbühne classes and performance group was Dussia Bereska, who was also his mistress and the mother of his ninth child (Little Dussia). Bereska was a Russian dancer, trained, and tempestuous by all accounts. Films from the 1920s show a beautiful and clearly expressive dancer, one who was a solo artist by temperament and talent. She could hold the stage with the tiniest of movements; she was so clear. Other dancers may have been better at the large sweeping movements, but Bereska had an elegance that was unique. She was also Laban's partner in running the company. She directed the Kammertanzbühne, or chamber groups, coaching and refining the performances.

Films from the 1920s show her to be specific and clear in her phrasing, and a deeply emotional mover. In *Orchidée* (a short film fragment from the Laban archives at Creekside), for example, a solo in which she sat cross-legged on a platform, nude from the waist up, her arms undulating with a clear connection to her entire torso; movement from the heart and soul. The piece was part of the fascination with "Orientalism" (as Ruth St. Denis also found inspiration), but the piece had a ring of authenticity: the fullness of the undulations and the clarity of expression recalls that Laban had actually spent time studying Dervish dances and had had a Sufi teacher as a boy. Possibly Bereska herself had also been directly exposed to Asian dance, as she was Russian.

Orientalism

The exotic other was often a theme in the arts of the late nineteenth and early twentieth centuries. "Orientalism," a Western view of Near and Far Eastern aesthetics, was prominent in art (the backdrops in Whistler's paintings, Tiffany lamps and countless cigarette advertisements), provided mystery and the thrill of the unknown, and dancers such as Ruth St. Denis drew heavily on their own imaginations, interpreting the snippets of images, myths and cultural memes to which they were exposed during the expanding exotica of the 1900s. Laban himself used the image of Buddha with swinging arms or Siva in several of his Tanz-theater works. Whether or not such uses constitute appropriation, as opposed to recognition or even homage, is the subject of much discussion among historians and theorists.

Bereska also helped to develop the dance technique and curriculum for both the movement choir and the chamber groups. Building on what Laban and Wigman had begun to create and articulate in Stuttgart, she made the specific refinements for clarity in space and quality into the underpinnings of expressionist dance technique. Her role in the development of the creation and execution of all of the Tanztheater works in the early to mid-1920s was significant, especially as a coach for detailed expressive movement.

Laban therefore was a new kind of dance director, one who noted the individual talents of his performers, and who encouraged and empowered others to be part and parcel of the development of the work, both as theory and as practice.

Tanztheater should not be abused!

Laban wrote, in 1924, that the art form of dance ought not to be abused anymore, a lament he was to repeat to some extent for decades. He saw much to complain about with how dance was treated as an art form by the public, but he saved some of his concern for the creators of the art form. Bad dance theater, he stated, is the mime-dramatic copy of life that works with conventional gestures instead of working with space harmony, or Schwingen, as he called the various scales he was deriving at this time. When dancers simply copy rhythmical arabesques and stereotypic exercises, they are missing the aliveness of dance. The dance should not only be controlled by the brain or intellect. One who is a "dance poet" should use the inspiration of those means of expression that are appropriate to convey the specifics of what one intended.

Laban (1879–1958)

In support of the ideals of Ausdruckstanz (expressive dance), the films that still exist of his dance works reveal that, although the movement looks "old-fashioned" in the sense that the vocabulary contains some phrases that have become clichés, it was executed with detailed clarity. The jumpy film of Bereska performing *Orchidée* (1923) reveals characteristic (for the times) "Oriental" movement phrases, but also shows her innate sense of liveliness in the midst of clear spatial con-figurations.

Laban saw the need for theater spaces devoted to the enhancement of the audience's perception of Tanztheater works. But Laban did not have the type of large dance theater to work in (although he was often seen designing such a large space) that he thought was necessary to convey some of his larger, more myth-based works. He did feel that chamber dance, rightly done, could also convey big ideas, however. The solo dancer or small ensemble can be as compelling and moving as a song sung clearly, a sonata, an anecdote, an *aperçu*.

But for such work, Laban felt that neither a well-designed proscenium nor a simple black box theater was enough for the dance pieces he was creating. He sensed that the audience was not used to engaging with dance because most simply were unprepared, having not had the opportunity to see much dance. The audience's eye needed to be trained to see abstract group dance. Without such assistance, audience members see the scope and range but not the specific quality of the movement. Laban felt that the lack of education explained why people saw something merely acrobatic as art, a complaint echoed by dance artists before (Jean-George Noverre in the eighteenth century in his *Letters on Dancing and Ballet*) and since (see TV's *Dancing with the Stars*).

In one rant he said that since the dance theater staff had the task of discovering an appropriate space for the work along with finding an audience willing to really see and be open, a great deal of perspective, education in the discipline of dance performance, and a willingness to solve problems were required.

Tanztheater reflected the political and social issues of the times

The technique developed by Laban and the Tanzbühne fed and informed his socially reflective commentary on everyday life and the populace's growing questions about power, community and violence in the latter half of the 1920s. The cinema, theater and cabarets produced work that was as dark and foreboding as it was wild, bitingly satirical and free-flowing. Fritz Lang's film *Metropolis* (1927) and the Brecht-Weill piece *Die Dreigroschenoper* (*The Threepenny Opera*) (1928) are examples of such work; both call into question capitalist as well as socialist ideals.

Brecht was writing and producing at this time, and even though his greatest fame was still to come, his ideas were part and parcel of the times. He promoted the notion that reason and logic ought to prevail over emotionality. His goal was social change, and in order to charge the audience into considering current circumstances, a certain amount of direct communication, if not detachment from illusion, was needed.

Brecht introduced the notion of epic theater, or theater that distances and objectifies the theatrical experience. In *Die Dreigroschenoper* (*The Threepenny Opera*), which opened in Berlin in 1928, characters commented on the scenes they were in, signage was used as commentary, harsh lighting overly illuminated the dark corners of the world of MacHeath and Jenny. The audience might be both seduced and charmed by MacHeath's cunning and sedition and alienated by them as well. Laban would have been aware of such techniques and used similar approaches to objectify and engage simultaneously.

To take one example, the character of the "Queen of the Night," a recurring archetype in his dance plays, and an ongoing shadow character in his life, was also the symbol for his ambivalence about the café society of the early 1900s and the decay of the 1920s. The model for the "Queen of the Night" came from an old Turkish tale, a story similar to that of both *Cinderella* and the *Sleeping Beauty*. She is the wise fairy who sees what the young heroine needs and who provides ancient knowledge and protection. Laban's sense of the Queen, however, was more complicated and dark. The spirit of creativity and insight, the exploration of the depths of the soul, a concern with human follies and a willingness to intervene prevailed in his interpretation of the myth. But he also saw propensities for self-aggrandizement and narcissism.

The "Queen of the Night" was the all-consuming, larger-than-life, highly decorative, highly acquisitive prima donna. Laban knew that when people are inflated by the world and materiality, they can become grotesque. When such characters are also merely decorative (as opposed to expressive), they can be monsters. The Queens of the Night did not get to flourish by operating from a core of expressivity and good behavior. The archetype does not reflect wrenching self-examination or concern for mistakes made. As in Brecht's plays, and in Laban's *Nacht* (1927) the powerful Queen, represented by a variety of characters both male and female, watches carefully and has years of experience sizing people up quickly for their usefulness and efficacy. Laban used such characters in his dance plays and in so doing, he held up a somewhat ironic mirror of the times. Even in *The Green Clowns*, which was not one of his more somber works, the Club of the Weirdos section must have included such an overpowering reminder of his early days in Paris, when his romantic sensibilities were undercut by the cynical sophistication of the overly decorated denizens of society.

Martin Gleisner, describing Laban's aesthetics some years later, wrote: "To strive too consciously for beauty would only achieve the opposite – ostentatious vanity contradicting the basic conception of the genuine dancer" (Gleisner, 1970, p. 10).

Tanztheater informed and was informed by others creating their own approaches

Ausdruckstanz (Expressionist Dance), and specifically the Tanztheater, valued clarity and specificity: each moment was informed by, if not a linear tale, a decision about meaningfulness and preciseness. The flow of moments from one to the next did not subsume the precision, but allowed breath and life into the work.

One exception to the flow-based expressive movement of the period was the work of Oskar Schlemmer. Schlemmer had been a painter and sculptor-turned-theater artist at the Bauhaus, a school of art and architecture in Weimar and later, Dessau. Schlemmer's *Bauhaus Dances* consisted of dancers encased in costumes that exaggerated the human figure with helmets and rounded rubber suits. The emphasis was on geometry and space rather than flow and expressivity.

Schlemmer complained in a 1931 edition of *Schrifttanz* that his work had been misunderstood and mischaracterized. It was seen as denying the humanity of the dancer and masking the human form. He made the point that at the center of the geometric forms was the man, always. Schlemmer, like Laban, saw that clarity of form and space increased the awareness of individual expressivity, and turned chaos into order.

In another volume of *Schrifttanz* (1930), the editor, Alfred Schlee, addressed the evolution of the Ausdruckstanz, or expressionists, into what he called "the New Dance." He wrote that the expressionists wanted to "raise the banner of art" in a mystical or religious way. But, he wrote, emotional upheaval easily becomes cliché. An awakening of both the human body and the communal can also come out of emotionality, but to reject ballet completely and only deal with the moment and with resulting rituals is a mistake. Both the raising of consciousness and the precision of technique are valuable to dance.

Laban would have argued that he was not sacrificing one for the other. The immediacy of the moment and any intermediacy between inspiration and realization were of value, and clarified the meaning.

Schlee, the editor of *Schrifttanz*, addressed the nationalism of German dance as well and wrote not of Aryan supremacy, but rather, an attempt to define a pan-European basis for the new dance forms. Thus the Tanztheater transcended the national boundaries that were about to come into contention once again, reflecting the desire of the dancers to be artists of the world, as the Asconans had aspired to some twenty years prior. And as the Asconans also discovered, the power-mongering world would not support democratic globalism without clear economic benefits.

The years 1926–30 were personally difficult for Laban, coming after his fall from the stage and the stress of the Dance Congresses. Dussia was a difficult partner, and Laban's various schools were in transition. Dussia moved to Paris to open up a school there, and Laban combined and dissolved various programs as the economic conditions worsened. A somewhat manic darkness had set in to the European community. The most challenging period in western civilization began with chancy, sometimes dangerous activities surfacing in the cabarets and in the streets. What had been liberating and innovative a few years earlier – jazz music, free dance and the like – shifted into a noir sensibility.

The dance was no exception. Mary Wigman's *Totenmal*, a requiem for dead soldiers, based on a poem and in collaboration with Albert Talhoff appeared in 1929. The piece was a large group opus, and Wigman wrote about the work:

> It was no longer a matter of the play of forces with and against one another ... The potential matter of conflict was no longer to be solved within the group itself. What was of concern here was the unification of a group of human beings [that] strove from a unified viewpoint toward a common aim recognized by everyone; a viewpoint which no longer permitted any splitting into single actions ...
>
> In the same way as the choric creation demands its antagonist – whether or not it takes actual shape or takes effect as thematic idea above and beyond the events – in many cases it also asks for a leader [*Anführer*] chosen by the chorus, for the one who conveys the message powerfully, who, supported and carried by the entire chorus, advances the thematic idea and brings it to its final execution.
>
> (Wigman, 1966, pp. 92–93)

Wigman's words are ominous, but make sense within the context of Germany in the late 1920s. Boundaries were being broken regularly on social and artistic levels, and a growing awareness that imposed order might be a relief from the roller coaster economic conditions that began to prevail.

Tanztheater broke old rules and created new ones

Through the entire spectrum of possibilities, Rudolf Laban teased out a new way of creating dance works, a way that embraced seeming contradictions and brought polar ends back together to complete a circle of possibilities. There was no rule that could not be broken, and no dichotomy that could not be mended. In fact, it was always the tensions between and among ideas, points in space, positions, dogmas and expressive moments that made the dance artful.

Laban was, at the core, a craftsman and an explorer of approaches. Because he was at heart an improviser, he liked blasting through boundaries and trying things in new ways. For each piece he created, he devised a vocabulary and style. His process was to begin with an idea, often an archetypal story or setting, then to derive a vocabulary for that time and place. The dancers explored actively, and he selected from their array, much as he did for his 1929 crafts festival in Vienna.

He was also a recycler of material. He was both pragmatic and opportunistic, in the sense of being able to make the best out of a situation. Without needing to adorn, he explored and took what was available, making the best of it. As a keen observer, he saw things that needed to come to fruition, and he was able to tease out the essentials.

Dörr (Interview, July 9, 2004) points out that Tanztheater covered many different genres and styles. "*Don Juan* could be performed by the chamber group alone or with a choir. Laban recycled sections over and over. *Orchidée* may in fact have been derived from a section of *The Swinging Temple*."

Laban added the local movement choir groups (mostly amateur but trained in improvisation) to works if they were appropriate and available. This flexibility was both a financial necessity and part of his choreographic principles.

The Green Clowns/Die Grünen Clowns *as Tanztheater*

Against this complex backdrop, over four years, Laban's work *Die Grünen Clowns* developed. It was described as an ironic comment on human behavior, in contrast to Wigman's *Totenmal*, which was portrayed as a powerful communion of the soul and death. As early as 1926, the artistic differentiation between Laban and Wigman had become evident, leading critics and audiences alike to choose sides. Laban's work, especially following the fall from the stage in *Don Juan* (in 1926) that ended his performing career, moved away from the experimental and toward the epic, but with a sense of irony. Wigman was becoming a well-known artist with particularly trained dancers behind her. Laban's approach allowed for the trained and less-trained dancers to enter into building work with a sense of community.

It is important to remember that in his time, Laban was considered a master choreographer and the "Father of German Modern Dance." Even though none of his works survive in any wholly replicable form, his approach to choreography is precisely how many twenty-first-century contemporary artists work with their dancers. The manipulation of movement into abstract but specifically expressive moments, and the dance director who is more of a guide than a scriptwriter, are both familiar to us now. Laban also learned a great deal from his lovers and dancers, especially Perrottet and Bereska, both more traditionally trained as dancers than he himself was, and both willing to share their own insights into the technical execution of particular movement.

Die Grünen Clowns appears to have begun life as a satiric piece, part of a larger set of such pieces, in 1926. Laban structured it with Dussia Bereska, his muse and partner of that period. It was not in the category of exotic or decorative dances; it was meant to be grotesque, a pantomime depicting Laban and Bereska's observations of contemporary society.

Exotic dances were those that addressed the period's fascination with "Orientalism," as in *Orchidée*. Decorative dances would have been expressive works without deeper meaning; Laban was not interested in such as these.

The grotesque

An agent of transgression, the grotesque is always on the verge of transforming, demanding "the furtive glance rather than the rapacious gaze." He (Remshart) divides the grotesque into "weak" and "strong" categories that depend on the perception of the viewer, his or her cultural and moral assumptions at any given time.

(Robb, 2005, pp. 856–858)

> The grotesque yokes the trivial and the demonic. It establishes "a co-presence of the ludicrous with the monstrous, the disgusting or the horrifying" (Thomson, Philip. *The Grotesque*. London: Methuen, 1972). Exaggeration, hyperbole and excessiveness are fundamental attributes of the grotesque style, according to Bakhtin (Bakhtin, Mikhail, *Rabelais and His World*. Trans. Helen Iswolsky. Bloomington: Indiana UP, 1984, p. 301), who argued that "the central principle of grotesque realism is degradation, that is, the lowering of all that is high, spiritual, ideal."
>
> (Wasserman, 2004, pp. 33–37)

In the sense that grotesque dance is transgressive, or undermining of social expectations, mores and values, Laban's aesthetic for *The Green Clowns* lies firmly in that category. It was a commentary on the society of the time; it was social satire and the creators were not above using the more confrontational style of hyperbole to get the points across.

The relationship between "clown" and "monster" must have been tangible even before the mid-1920s, but by the time *The Green Clowns* made its debut, the connection was present and portended what was to come, in the too-bright cabarets of Berlin and the rise of fascism via a man who was perceived first as a clown and later as a monster. Laban's earlier character of the Queen of the Night fell into the category of the grotesque, and although she did not make an appearance in this work (at least as far as is known), clowns/monsters reminiscent of her did.

One can imagine the work as an exploration of the fine line between the two. One can also imagine that it showed the two as two sides of the same coin, or two facets of contemporary leaders.

The sequence and content changed over the two years (1926–28) that the piece was in the forefront of the Tanzbühne Repertory. At its premiere in 1926 at the Schillertheater Hamburg-Altona, there were ten clowns; that is all we know about it, as there were no reviews. The sections, according to Evelyn Dörr (Interview, July 9, 2004), were as follows:

1 Psychomechanik
2 Verkettungen (connections, chains)
3 Klub der Sonderlinge (Club of the Weirdos)
4 Gedankenflucht (solo – escaping from one's thoughts – daydreaming)
5 Firlefanz (silliness, frivolous stuff – junk, fluffiness, frippery, clowning around)
6 Zeitlupe (slow motion – five clowns)
7 Militarismus (group)
8 Atonale (atonal)

This first sequence of eight sections does not appear to develop an idea or through line so much as present a smorgasbord of shifting rhythms and group sizes. It may be that these were early effort studies, or experiments with qualities. The structure of the piece also suggests that it was designed (to the extent that it was designed) to be performed in a variety of types of spaces. Laban clearly valued the large mythic works that required appropriate stage space, with room for platforms and set pieces, but he also had to solve the challenges of the touring chamber group, and *The Green Clowns* would have been adaptable enough to fit into many spaces that the larger works would not have.

In 1927, Laban gave a new name to the work: *Grotesque in sechs Bewegungen* (*Grotesque in six movements*). The sequence apparently changed and several sections got new names as well:

1   Maschine
2   Romanze in Grün (Green romance)
3   Gedankenflucht (solo – escaping from one's thoughts – daydreaming)

Maschine was another in a long line of Laban statements about the rise of industrialism, and included some nonverbal commentary on the loss of individual enterprise and creativity.

Zeitlupe, Romanze in Grün and Gedankenflucht may have been slower reflections on man's ideals and romantic notions, and the ultimate fatalism of romance. The Klub der Sonderlinge makes sense within the cabaret scene of the time, with its slow descent into darker themes, but it also clearly refers to the grotesque style of undermining the status quo that characterized the clown/monster archetype.

At some point in 1927, a scene called "Spuk" (spook) appeared that consisted of six clowns doing simultaneous movement: one figure facing the audience, with five others with their back to the audience. Press reviews from that time said that scene was "terrific" (from the newspaper NZZ, May 7, 1927). The image is not dissimilar to the line of masked figures moving along in Wigman's *Totenmal* (1930), and has a touch of Brechtian alienation.

By 1928, at the Choreographical Institute Berlin, with music by Erich Itor Kahn, eight sections had emerged, with another new name: *Grotesque mit sechs Clowns* (*Grotesque with Six Clowns*).

It would appear that the clown motif had taken over and become more of the foreground of the through line by this version. The characters of fools, or clowns, trying to get on in a mad world seems to have become the major theme by this time and the question arises as to whether the clowns were perpetrators of the mad world, or victims? The fact that the seventh section, Militarismus, appears only in the early 1926 version, and then disappears from subsequent versions, lends some support to the clown motif taking over from the anti-technology motifs of the earlier version.

Later on in 1928, the sequence changed again; new sections were added:

- Nachtigall (nightingale)
- Gehirnoperation (brain surgery)
- So ist das Leben (That's Life!)
- Five O'clock (a trio, with music by Boris Blacher)

No doubt sections came and went, and versions abounded. The appearance of a new section did not mean that that section was kept, or even performed every time. It may be that Laban added and subtracted sections for many reasons, including who was around to dance that particular performance.

In one version, a dancer brought a little door out onto the stage that he went through, after which he cleaned himself with little brushes. In the Gehirnoperation (brain surgery) section (1928), one dancer mimed screwing off the head of the other and taking the brains out, foreshadowing Marcel Marceau and hundreds of street mimes yet to come. One wonders what might have become of the "brains" in performance, given the context of the grotesque.

According to Dörr (Interview, July 9, 2004), it's also possible that some parts of *Narrenspiegel* (*Fool's Mirror*) were taken and/or given to the *Green Clowns*. Such recycling would have been in keeping with the evolving scenes of clowns or fools trying to negotiate a crazy world, as well as Laban's propensity for improvisation and (by necessity, if not choice) frugality. Press reviews from the time said that all sections, scenery and ideas were grotesque and over the top, which was a positive statement.

Photographs from the period of the piece reveal dancers with a clear sense of space, lots of exaggerated expression, and shaping among the clowns as they are strewn about each other. The grotesque aesthetic Laban espoused did not mean a lack of clarity; on the other hand, it was not realistic movement either. From the photos, not a shred of muddiness or compromise in expression is apparent, in keeping with Laban and Bereska's values of specificity and potency.

Clearly, over time the piece grew, evolved, expanded and shrank; sections were added and others deleted. The piece was alive in temporal, spatial and ever-shifting responsive ways, just like Laban saw human movement itself. The work may have been unique in its fluidity of structure: audiences may have had vastly differing experiences from one night to the next, but it reflected the increasing tensions and sense of dark absurdity of the late 1920s.

As many of his dance-plays were, *The Green Clowns* was a devised work that comprised original moments that formed a specific vocabulary and meaning which served that dance work alone. In this sense, the dance was pure Expressionism, and helped to further define Laban's notion of Tanztheater.

Valerie Preston-Dunlop has set about to recreate the work, using Laban's typical approaches to gleaning movement from the dancers. With only the sketchiest of reviews and photos, and from her memory of working with Laban in the latter half of the 1940s, she managed to derive a full piece that, seemingly, deals with the same issues, themes and approaches to movement as Laban. The piece has the look and feel of a Tanztheater work, and she has captured some of the grotesque aesthetic, especially the attitude of artifice and exaggeration of shape and space.

The process is one of guided improvisation. Dancers need to be trained in Laban-based dance approaches, which would include Effort and Space work, in order to use the "Schwingen" (swinging) and expressive aspects of the work, but once the through line and themes are determined, the movement itself would resemble the photos and descriptions from the times.

It is likely that the aesthetic Laban developed for the piece fed both his systematic approach to movement analysis, providing categories for expressive movement and spatial configurations, and a freewheeling, problem-solving attitude towards the construction of new works that we see in later choreographic processes throughout the twentieth century. From Cunningham to Judson to Pilobolus, each used an approach to choreography that involved solving a problem or defying conventions of one kind or another.

From *The Green Clowns*, twenty-first-century artists can recall and recapitulate the legacies of improvisation, innovation, exaggeration, regeneration and reflection of ever-changing times. The form Laban used of sections of dance-based social commentary became a key element of works that followed, including Kurt Jooss' *The Green Table*.

That work, *The Green Table*, shares more than themes of social commentary with *The Green Clowns*. The color green is significant in several disciplines, the most obvious of which is ecology or environmental studies. The relationship between man and the physical world, or Mother Nature, is dynamic and reciprocal, and the color green appears to have some deep and ancient connection to that relationship.

Green is also the color of gambling and game tables, or platforms for man's follies. Certainly, the notion of the poker table was one of the significant influences on Jooss' title. Laban's use of the color is less obvious, and it seems also to have been mutable. If one goes back to Kandinsky's theories of color, which Laban would have known about, green is a color of restful complacency, hardly adding to the meaning inherent in either work.

But if green is a table or platform and a background color for man's follies, then the choice is intriguing: a cool underpinning for foibles and heartbreak, for madness and absurdity.

Other elements the pieces shared include irony and the use of the grotesque especially to depict characters of power. Jooss' figure of Death, the Gentlemen in Black, and the Profiteer would all be recognizable evolutions of the grotesque clowns in Laban's work, especially those in *The Green Clowns*. Whereas Laban's clowns were not assigned particular roles to play – they were, apparently, just generic clowns – Jooss' grotesque characters took on specific roles and duties. However, all the clown/monster characters in both Laban's and Jooss' work deal with the trivial and the monstrous simultaneously.

The use of tensions, or opposites, in space and expression was also a common mode in both works. In the surviving piece, one can sense the wit and depth of the lost work, for Jooss himself paid homage to Laban's guidance as a director. The coaching of dancers for specificity and clarity of space and expression is a significant part of any restaging of Jooss' masterpiece, and is as apparent in recent reconstructions as the photos of Laban's work from the late 1920s demonstrate.

While *Die Grünen Clowns* was not a piece that remained in memory in the way that *The Green Table* has, and rightly so, the elements and point of view that Laban's work used informed the genre that Jooss was developing at the time, and supported the ingenuity of both men. And there can be little doubt that teacher and student drank from the same wells, and fed each other.

Tanztheater's legacy

The Tanztheater left a lasting legacy. To this day, mature contemporary dance work contains clear and meaningful moments of specific expression, whether the moment be a sideways glance, a throwing motion, a fall to the floor, a sniff at the air, or a turning away from one another. Postural shifts and tiny gestures resonate to the back rows of the audience when effort is clarified and supported by the core of the dancer's body. Movement can be large and stylized and yet detailed and potent. The legacy of the Tanztheater is that generalizations do not carry; delineations communicate.

But all is not literal. In the work Laban created, the idiosyncratic and the abstract played a role. Characters have details as well as unique predilections that can be exploited and even abstracted to a point of unrecognizability and still retain clear focus. Human stories are not necessarily linear or logical, but can still be compelling.

Improvisation yields sometimes-irrational impulses, around which stories of human foibles can be woven and the absurd can be made rational, or at least understandable. Shining light on absurdity is a way of laughing in the light at our all-too-human follies.

And yet, the darker passions of mankind and the dissolution of society that leads in and out of violence are also fodder for the dance theater of today. We have our own stable of grotesque characters and situations to be sure, but such is the richness of human imagination that archetypes are recognizable, no matter what medium they appear in. Contemporary dance work makes good use of the darker side of human souls and issues like war, exploitation and betrayal are still part of the scene.

Materials and ideas are not one-shot deals and just as Laban recycled phrases, costumes and images from one piece to another, contemporary artists embrace the act of retooling older ideas and borrowing images and techniques from one another in order to create truly original versions of the stories we keep telling ourselves. It is a form of sustainability and a shortcut to recognition of pattern.

And finally, audiences in Laban's time began to realize that they had choices about how to take in the work they were seeing and they could engage at personal levels, perhaps even participate. He gave permission for dance to be both virtuosic and accessible; he used pedestrian movement as well as abstract and remote images.

What we appear to have lost, however, is the use of tension and counter-tensions to highlight the internal dramas of human beings. Such angst-ridden movement appears old-fashioned to us nowadays and the value of releasing over containing, of discharging over selecting, has given dancers a virtuosic fierceness but not a richness of scope and depth. Dance training is, all too often, an approaching process rather than a gathering process. The creation process for choreography draws on the eclecticism and improvisation-based approaches Laban developed, but the exploration of dramatic conflicts internally and in social contexts through the movement itself has often been abandoned. The pendulums always swing back, so perhaps his idea of physically negotiating oppositional pulls will return when we decide we need the warmth that friction provides.

> This bold approaching of the dream life is what the artist truly does ... Art is a sublimation and condensation of this piecemeal insertion of the so-called irrational sparks and impulses into all thoughts and actions.
>
> (From *Laban Speaks*, a lecture given in London April 1957, p. 4)

Further reading

Bartenieff, Irmgard and Dori Lewis (2002) *Body Movement: Coping with the Environment*. New York: Routledge.

Bartenieff, Irmgard, Martha Davis and Forrestine Paulay (1970) *Four Adaptations of Effort Theory in Research and Teaching*. New York: Dance Notation Bureau.

Counsell, Colin (2004) *Dancing to Utopia: Modernity, Community, and the Movement Choir*. Edinburgh: Dance Research, 22.2, Winter.

Davies, Eden (2006) *Beyond Dance: Laban's Legacy of Movement Analysis*. New York: Routledge.

Dörr, Evelyn (2003) "Rudolf von Laban: The 'Founding Father' of Expressionist Dance", *Dance Chronicle*, Vol. 26, No. 1, pp. 1–29.

―――― (2004) "Transformation of the Archaic: A Study of the Development and Stylistic History of Modern Dance, 1890–1938", unpublished paper.

Gleisner, Martin (1970) "Movement Choirs", *Laban Art of Movement Guild Magazine*, November, p. 10.

Green, Martin (1986) *The Mountain of Truth: The Counter-Culture Begins, Ascona 1900–1920*. Hanover and London: New England Press.

Hodgson, John (2001) *Mastering Movement: The Life and Work of Rudolf Laban*. New York: Routledge.

Laban, Rudolf (1920, translation date unknown) *Die Welt des Tänzers*. Partially translated by Richard Schröder, in the John Hodgson Collection, University of Leeds, UK.

―――― (1924) "Das Tanztheater", *Licht-Luft-Leben in Die Schönheit: Mit Bildern geschmückte Monatsschrift für Kunst und Leben*. Journal published in Leipzig, Giesecke. Verlag Die Schönheit, Dresden and Leipzig, Vol. 22, translated by Sabine Fichter.

―――― (1926a) "Anatomie", *Licht-Luft-Leben in Die Schönheit: Mit Bildern geschmückte Monatsschrift für Kunst und Leben*. Journal published in Leipzig, Giesecke. Verlag Die Schönheit, Dresden and Leipzig, Vol. 22, No. 1, p. 94, translated by Sabine Fichter.

―――― (1926b) *Choreographie*. Jena: Diederichs (out of print).

―――― (1928) "Basic Principles of Movement Notation", *Schrifttanz*, Vol. 1, No. 1, July, p. 32.

―――― (1929) "The Renewal of the Movement in Theater", *Singchor und Tanz*, Mannheim, 15 January, 1929, Vol. 2, p. 561, translated by Sabine Fichter.

―――― (1939) "Extract from an Address Held by Mr Laban on a Meeting for Community-Dance in 1936". Translated by Laban March 10, 1939. Used with Acknowledgment to the Dartington Hall Trust Archive, T/AD/3/A/5.

—— (1966) *Choreutics*. London: MacDonald and Evans (annotated and edited by Lisa Ullmann).
—— (1971) *The Mastery of Movement*. London: MacDonald and Evans.
—— (1975) *A Life for Dance*. Princeton, NJ: Princeton Books.
—— (date unknown) NRCD Notes. Surrey: National Resource Centre for Dance, University of Surrey.
Laban, Rudolf and F. C. Lawrence (1974) *Effort: Economy in Body Movement*. London: MacDonald and Evans, 2nd edition.
Maletic, Vera (1987) *Body-Space-Expression: The Development of Rudolf Laban's Movement and Dance Concepts*. Berlin, New York, and Amsterdam: Mouton de Gruyter.
Newlove, Jean and John Dalby (2004) *Laban for All*. New York: Routledge.
Partsch-Bergsohn, Isa and Harold Bergsohn (1973) *The Makers of Modern Dance in Germany: Rudolf Laban, Mary Wigman, Kurt Jooss*. Hightstown, NJ: Princeton Books.
Partsch-Bergsohn, Isa and Kurt Jooss (2002) *A Talk with Kurt Jooss and Isa Partsch-Bergsohn* [video recording]. New York: Distributed by Insight Media.
Preston-Dunlop, Valerie (1963) *A Handbook for Modern Educational Dance*. London: MacDonald and Evans.
—— (1998) *Rudolf Laban: An Extraordinary Life*. London: Dance Books.
Preston-Dunlop, Valerie and Susanne Lahusen (1990) *Schrifttanz: A View of German Dance in the Weimar Republic*. London: Dance Books.
Robb, David. (2005) "Staging the Savage God: The Grotesque in Performance", a review, *Modern Drama*, Vol. 48, No. 4, pp. 856–858
Ullmann, Lisa, ed. (1971) *Rudolf Laban Speaks about Movement and Dance*. Addlestone, Surrey: Laban Art of Movement Centre.
Wasserman, Jerry (2004) "Monstrous Clowns: American Grotesques on the Canadian Stage", *Canadian Theatre Review*, Vol. 120, pp. 33–37.
Wigman, Mary (1966) *The Language of Dance*. Middletown, CT: Wesleyan University Press.
Wigman, Mary and Walter Sorell (1973) *The Mary Wigman Book: Her Writings*. Middletown, CT: Wesleyan University Press.

Interviews

June 30, 2004, Sam and Susi Thornton, UK.
July 2, 2004, Geraldine Stephenson, London, UK.
July 3, 2004, Valerie Preston-Dunlop, Blackheath, London, UK.
July 8, 2004, Antja Kennedy, Bremen, Germany.
July 9, 2004, Evelyn Dörr, Leipzig, Germany.

5
WIGMAN (1886–1973)

Mary Anne Santos Newhall

5.1 Mary Wigman: a life in dance

"Strong and convincing art has never arisen from theories."

Mary Wigman

Prologue: why Mary Wigman?

Mary Wigman was the best-known ambassador of German dance during the interwar period, as her touring took her across Europe and to the United States. Promotional literature for those tours sought to educate the public about this new art phenomenon, and critics responded with enthusiasm and keen attention, if not always with praise. When US critic John Martin published 'The Dance' in 1946 he placed Wigman in the highest constellation of dance artists, in part for her artistic creations and especially for how she widened the range and advanced the underlying theories of the art. Following the Second World War, however, Wigman received only fleeting attention in the English-language historiography of modern dance. In fact, the whole of early German *Ausdruckstanz*, or dance of expression, was barely discussed in postwar writing on dance modernism, which centered on the American modern dance pioneers and US dance developments. One later exception was the work of Pina Bausch, whose career began in Germany, continued in the United States and then returned to Germany in the form of *Tanztheater*.

Don McDonagh's *The Rise and Fall and Rise of Modern Dance* (1970) mentions Wigman only in passing. McDonagh's contention was that modern dance "had been created out of the American experience in the same manner in which jazz had been created" (McDonagh 1970: 1). Anti-German sentiment, which ran high during and after the war, offers one explanation of why scholars failed to acknowledge the enormous impact of early modern German dance, and Wigman's work in particular. In *Time and the Dancing Image*, Deborah Jowitt wrote, "quite a few early reviews presuppose some influence from Germany on the major American modernists, if only as a catalyst. . . . it remains a moot point how directly and to what extent [German dancers] may have [influenced the Americans]" (Jowitt 1988: 167–168). Bronner and Kellner claimed, "The role of dance, both as a motif and as a topic of discussion, has not been dealt with in any systematic way in German literary history" (Bronner and Kellner 1983: 351). Fortunately, Walter Sorell assembled and translated some of Wigman's writings in the 1960s and 1970s and

Horst Koegler wrote comprehensively about the period in English and in German. But no one produced an in-depth Wigman biography until 1986, when Hedwig Müller came forward as Wigman's primary biographer. The publication of *Mary Wigman: Leben und Werk der grossen Tanzerin* (Mary Wigman: Life and Work of the Great Dancer) appears definitive and is supported by a great deal of the dancer's own writings. Müller's assiduous research and sensitive reading of Wigman's papers allow insight into her world. Unfortunately, Müller's book has not been translated into English, but such a translation would be a major contribution to the understanding of Wigman's story in the English language.

In 1993, the publication of Susan Manning's *Ecstasy and the Demon: Feminism and Nationalism in the Dances of Mary Wigman* returned Wigman to the scholarly spotlight. Manning's writing drew on a wide range of sources, including Müller's biography. Through analysis of choreographed works, Manning set out to reveal Wigman with a new emphasis. Manning's book sheds much light on Wigman's work. In addition, she sought to question Wigman's accommodations with the National Socialist government. She presents Wigman possibly as a proto-fascist and, if not a willing collaborator, then a less-than-naive participant within the Nazi regime. In *Hitler's Dancers*, Lillian Karina and Marion Kant build on Manning's analysis, citing carefully selected archival evidence to propose reconsidering Wigman, and others, as Nazi sympathizers and thus culpable, particularly in light of her engagement with the *Reichskulturkammer* from 1933 until 1937 under Propaganda Minister Joseph Goebbels.

Acclaimed and accused, Mary Wigman emerges as a genuinely original and multi-faceted human being, one who devoted her life to dance in an era remarkable in its artistic innovation as well as its staggering tragedy. There are no simple answers or clear-cut conclusions in Wigman's story. From the earliest German articles and critiques dedicated to her oeuvre, through the more recent contributions of Karl Toepfer, Michael Huxley, Norbert Servos, Gabriele Fritsch-Vive, Diane Howe, Valerie Preston-Dunlop and Isa Partsch-Bergshon, many have written about this period in German dance history and Mary Wigman's place in that history. In 2014, Kate Elswit published *Watching Weimar Dance* which has contributed a new way of looking at Wigman and her peers in that critical period. Other writings are included in the bibliography accompanying this reissued edition.

In a 2005 review, Marion Kant posed a paradoxical question, "Which modern dancer would not like to trace her training and artistic roots back to Wigman, if only through a summer course?" (Kant 2005: 417). Perhaps, given the ongoing fascination and controversy swirling around Mary Wigman's life and work, another question should be posed, "Why does Mary Wigman still matter?" Are there elements of her work that remain relevant or revelatory for contemporary artists?

Seemingly forgotten by postmodern dancers of the twenty-first century, Wigman's life and work are drawing renewed interest among dance and theater artists in Germany and beyond. Even while modernism by its very nature privileges the new over the past, it seems compelling to consider Wigman's life and work once again. Perhaps enough time has passed since the Second World War to allow objective reflection on the genius and the humanness of Mary Wigman both as an inspiration and as a cautionary tale for our time. Perhaps this reflects an impulse toward a new kind of expressionism for the twenty-first century. And perhaps this is an indication of some commonalities between the *Zeitgeist* of this new millennium and that of the last century. The human body in dance remains a most immediate barometer of the state of the individual body within the world body. And Mary Wigman's life and work offer an exceptional reflection of her world.

The purpose of this book is a simple one. It is meant to serve as a general introduction to Wigman and is organized in four sections. The first section tells the story of her life and the times in which she lived, with highlights of the outstanding moments of her long career. The second section analyzes Wigman's writings with an eye to understanding how her art reveals her philosophy, placing it within related artistic and philosophical movements. The third section focuses on some of her major choreographic works. The final section outlines a series of practical exercises, with particular attention to Wigman's pedagogy. These exercises are intended to give the experimenter a visceral experience of the performance and training elements that appear most crucial to understanding Mary Wigman's perspective. They exercises are in no way meant to recreate Wigman's teaching practice, but are simply intended to provide one contemporary way of experiencing the fundamental elements identified by Wigman as she formulated her deep exploration into the stuff that dance is made of. Certainly, there is much more to analyze, debate and discover about her life and work and this text is written in the hope of encouraging such continued research and creative endeavors.

Introduction

Mary Wigman was born into a middle-class West Prussian family in 1886 and made Germany her home until her death in Berlin in 1973. Her life serves as a prism for viewing the complexity and immense difficulty of her era. She took part in the primary avant-garde art movements of the twentieth century and was eventually a principal founder and transmitter of the *Ausdruckstanz* or expressive dance movement. Wigman's remarkable career spanned the era of the Wilhelmine Empire, the Weimar Republic, the Third Reich and the years of a divided Germany following the Second World War. Not only was she present for the most cataclysmic political changes of her age, but also, as an artistic innovator, she stands as a seminal figure in the conception of what has come to be known as the modern dance.

Ausdruckstanz (expressive dance)

Absoluter tanz (absolute dance) – defined by Wigman as dancing pure and simple, without lights, dance or costume to decorate an idea or conceal its lack. (The origin of the term is attributed to different sources. Apparently it was introduced by Laban or first used by Wigman in a Dada performance art piece with Sophie Tauber. Historically, Absolute was a Hegelian term first used by Fichte.)

Freier tanz (free dance)

Neuer künstlerischer tanz (new artistic dance)

All these terms were renamed German Dance by the Cultural Ministry under the Third Reich.

Her *Ausdruckstanz* was fundamental to the development of dance and theater in Germany and beyond. Her aesthetic ideas were disseminated throughout Europe and traveled to the United States through her touring from 1929–32 and continued with the establishment of the Mary Wigman School in New York City in 1931. The myriad, widespread uses of dance improvisation as a tool for movement development, as a vehicle for performance and even as a method for physical and psychological therapy all have their roots deep in the work of Mary Wigman.

Wigman's work also can be viewed as an assimilation of the major artistic innovations of her time: Romanticism, Symbolism, Primitivism, Expressionism and Dada art, all gathered under the banner of Modernism. Wigman's life can act as a personal guide to these movements and their primary characters. As a child of the rising bourgeoisie of late nineteenth-century Germany, she used her body as a place of resistance against the expectations of her own family and the larger society. Her early years of training were spent with two great twentieth-century systematizers of movement: Emile Jaques-Dalcroze at the garden city of Hellerau and Rudolf von Laban at the utopian community of Monte Verità in Ascona, Switzerland. She was a muse for the Expressionist painters Emil Nolde, Ernst Kirchner, Oskar Schlemmer and others. And she performed alongside the most radical Dada artists at the Cafe Voltaire. Her time as a working artist during the rise and fall of the Third Reich offers a lens through which to view those terrible years and what came after. From her own writing, it is possible to deduce what she might most wish to be remembered for. Throughout her life her focus was on one thing: the dance. In the end, it is her passion for dance and her artistic innovations that endure and also offer tools to reinvigorate contemporary dance and theater. Her innovations are many and include:

- her unique concept of space as an invisible and truly sensual partner in the dance
- her rejection of ballet technique with a fervor equal to that of her fellow dance pioneer Isadora Duncan
- her radical ideas about the relationship between music and the dance
- her use of theatrical elements – notably text – to create a *Gesamtkunstwerk*
- her development of von Laban's ideas for solo works, mass movement and group composition
- her fundamental belief in and demand for a modern emphasis on the transcendent nature and spiritual purpose of dance.

> **Gesamtkunstwerk** – literally "total art work" incorporating technical theatrical elements, text, song, music and dance as integral elements of a total performance. The most prominent practitioner was Richard Wagner; however, Emile Jaques-Dalcroze with Adolf Appia and Laban and Wigman aspired to integrate all these elements into a total work.

Thus Wigman holds many titles in the world of dance and theater. She stands as a trailblazer, a stunning soloist and astute choreographer, a pedagogue and theoretician, an inspiration for many artists who followed, a conflicted figure caught in the political drama of her time, an intellectual, a mystic and the most pragmatic of arts administrators. The complexity of Wigman's persona cannot be overstated, but the real heart of this artist appears in her work as a consummate performer. This, for Wigman, was the moment of transcendence:

> But above the consummation of creation and ambition to succeed in a profession, there emerges something quite colossal and wonderful – a climax of achievement, which comes to you as a glorious gift from the gods. These are the rare moments in which, completely carried beyond yourself and removed from reality, you are the vessel of an idea. In these rare moments you carry the blazing torch which emits the spark jumping from the "I" to the "we," from dancer to spectator. This is the moment of divine consummation, when the fire dances between the two poles, when the personal experience of the creator is communicated to those who watch.
>
> *(Wigman 1973: 170)*

Childhood

Mary Wigman was born Karoline Sofie Marie Wiegmann on 13 November 1886 in Hanover, Germany. Without a doubt, Mary Wigman was a true child of her age who turned her own body into a canvas for the palette of that *Zeitgeist*. She was born a Wilhelmine woman whose parents, Amelie and Heinrich Wiegmann, reaped significant benefits from the expansion that was transforming the German economy. With the unification of Germany in 1871 and the sharp rise of industrialization, a burgeoning middle class was riding a wave of new wealth that also carried the Wiegmann family toward the twentieth century. Heinrich and his brothers, August and Dietrich, built a successful family business selling and repairing bicycles and sewing machines, products that represented the incursion of the machine age into the everyday lives of middle-class Germans. Many families had gone from working class to middle class in a single generation. Mary was the first-born. Her brother Heinrich came along four years later and her younger sister Elisabeth was born in 1894. When Mary was nine years old her father died. Three years later her mother married Dietrich Wiegmann and her uncle became her stepfather. Thus her early life was circumscribed by home and the family business.

> **Karoline Sofie Marie Wiegmann** – birth name of Mary Wigman.

Bright and accomplished at school, Wigman wanted to continue on to *Gymnasium*. Instead, her family sent her brother to secondary school and Mary received lessons in language and music, social dancing and comportment. In 1901, at the age of fourteen, she went to a girls' school at Folkestone on England's south coast for a few months and the following year she traveled to Lausanne, Switzerland. She learned English and French, but the goal of this education was solely to make her an attractive and marriageable *Hausfrau*, one able to contribute to the well-being and upward social mobility of her family. And she would have none of it. She had always identified herself as an adventurous spirit. While at school in England there were stories about a secret passage hidden within the town church. In *The Mary Wigman Book*, she recalls with obvious relish and some pride that she "bought a little hammer and went to tap the walls and listen for a hollow echo" (Wigman 1973: 28). Just as she listened for the echoes in the church walls, Mary Wigman was compelled to turn her attention toward her own inner landscape. Her greatest drive was to express what she described as the stirrings within her.

> *Gymnasium* – secondary school in the German system.

Searching to find an outlet through which to express these inner stirrings, Wigman had thought that she might become a singer. Her singing teacher said, "You have a good voice and you have a way of expression I have never seen before. You could make a career." But her family said no (Wigman 1973: 186). Keeping with their expectations, she was twice formally engaged to marry, only to have both engagements fail. After the second ended she wrote,

> I cried, I begged, and asked my creator to bring me clarity. I didn't know what I should do, I had to break away, I didn't want to continue any longer, I could not. The entire bourgeois life collapsed on to me, you might say.
>
> *(Wigman in Manning 1993: 50)*

Like many youth of her time, Wigman was caught between an old order of prescribed roles and the new world of possibilities that were an outgrowth of economic success. She had traveled and experienced a world far beyond what was available to most women of her mother's generation, yet she was expected to put all of her ambition to the service of her family. She saw hypocrisy in what she considered the superficial bourgeois respectability of her parents' generation and she and many members of her own age group would rebel in a fashion not unlike that seen again in the United States of America and Western Europe in the 1960s and 1970s.

Coming of age in the first decade of the twentieth century, Wigman appeared to have few options available to her. Certainly the life of an artist seemed far from every expectation put upon her by family and society in general. Yet she was swept along by the tide of modern attitudes toward art and life. In 1900 Ezra Pound had challenged the modern artist to "Make it New!" Wigman and her contemporaries responded with a radical change in the very way they fashioned their lives. A life-affirming *Körperkultur* or physical culture arose on both sides of the Atlantic, encouraging fitness and a new sort of bodily expression of emotion. And just as the emancipation of women was being pioneered, Isadora Duncan's introduction of "uncorseted" dance opened new avenues for dancers to follow in her wake. It is important to remember that Mary Wigman came to dance in her late twenties. A ballet career was never a possibility. Nor did she desire one. She and her cohorts indeed had to make the dance art new in order to express the experiences and conflicts of their age.

> **Isadora Duncan** (1877–1927) – great innovator of the free dance. She traveled the Western world sowing the seeds of the barefoot aesthetic dance movement. In 1904 she briefly established a school in Germany, and in 1921 one in Moscow. She introduced a concert dance form that was non-narrative, feminist, but still tightly bound to the music, so much so that she drew scorn from music critics at the time. She remains the progenitor of dance modernism.

The beginning of a life in dance

Following the end of her first engagement in 1905, Mary Wigman was sent to visit her aunt in Amsterdam. There she saw the pupils of Emile Jaques-Dalcroze in a demonstration of *Eurhythmie*, his system designed to wed music and movement through practical experience. His students performed Carl Maria von Weber's *Invitation to the Waltz* and for Wigman it was a revelation of a new way of approaching musical expression through bodily interpretation. Over the next five years, Wigman would return to the dance again and again in her search for a life's path.

> **Emile Jaques-Dalcroze** (1865–1950) – established a dance institute, *Der Bildungsanstalt für Musik und Rhythmus* (Educational Institute for Music and Rhythm), in Hellerau in 1910. Introduced an analytical approach to dance education through a systematic study of the fundamentals of music embodied using codified movement. Collaborated with innovating stage designer Adolphe Appia (1862–1928), who created a new way of designing the stage using "rhythmic spaces" formed by tiered platforms and stairs that added architectural dimension to the space. Appia's ideas traveled to the United States through the work of Arch Lauterer, stage designer for the Bennington choreographers, Graham, Humphrey and Holm.
>
> *Eurhythmie* or *Eurhythmies* – Emile Jaques-Dalcroze's system of linking sound to physical action designed to help in the training of musicians and to facilitate their motor memory. Dalcroze felt that

> rhythm unites the physical body with the spiritual, thus bringing the whole being into harmony. It is one example of the *fin de siècle* propensity to systematize, or to organize or arrange by a system that could be codified. Exemplars include Jaques-Dalcroze, Rudolf von Laban and Arnold Schoenberg. Eurythmy is the name of a separate system developed by anthroposophist Rudolf Steiner.

By 1908 Mary Wigman was twenty-two years old, still living in the family home and plunging toward her family's greatest fear: that she would become an overeducated "Old Maid." She had also ended another engagement and was deeply unhappy. In her memoirs, she describes closing herself in a room and crying in desperation at her situation. And she found that when she cried she made movements with her hands as she paced. During this period of despair, Wigman saw a performance by the three Wiesenthal sisters, Elsa, Berta and Grete. The Wiesenthals were dancing celebrities and Grete, in particular, became well known for her interpretation of the Viennese waltz, representing the elegance, grace and style of *fin de siècle* Vienna. Seeing Grete Wiesenthal's performance of *The Beautiful Blue Danube* at the opera house in Hanover, Wigman felt a new world opening before her. In her memoirs, Wigman appears to have been especially taken by the beauty of Wiesenthal's hands in the dance, as well the range of emotions that the hands could convey. Hedwig Müller describes Wigman as being intoxicated by the movement: "hands that can laugh happily and also express struggle, sadness and the gentleness of the dance" (Müller 1986a: 19). Wigman later wrote that she recognized the cry of her own hands dancing the despair of her heart while she was locked away in the guest room of her family home. Here was the outlet for expression for which she had been searching. She approached the Wiesenthals, hoping to study with them. She was told that at twenty-two she was too old to begin to dance. In her memoirs she reminisced that one teacher advised, "My dear girl, go home and be a *Hausfrau* – you'll be happier . . . You'll never be a dancer" (Wigman 1973: 27). Yet she persisted. She again saw a demonstration of *Eurhythmie* by Dalcroze's students and the way became clear to her. She said, "I want to do the same" (Wigman 1973: 187). Overcoming the resistance of her family and the "whole bourgeois world," she began her life in dance at the age of twenty-seven under the tutelage of Emile Jaques-Dalcroze.

> **Grete Wiesenthal** (1885–1972) – the most famous of the Wiesenthal Sisters performing group, Grete was considered the most important dancer in Vienna during the first two decades of the twentieth century and was said to embody the spirit of the waltz for which that city was famous.

Dalcroze and the Garden City of Hellerau

The beginning of the twentieth century saw many systematizers like Jaques-Dalcroze, theorists who turned to art in order to create an organized system in response to the chaos and uncertainty of the age. While Arnold Schoenberg later would reshape Western music with the twelve-tone scale, cubists Picasso and Braque would dissect and reassemble the familiar human form, and James Joyce would restructure the written word, Jaques-Dalcroze codified a method of applying gesture and movement to corresponding musical elements. Jaques-Dalcroze was considered a leader in art education by 1910, the year he established his school in the planned Garden City of Hellerau situated five miles outside of Dresden. Mary Wigman literally ran away from home to become a member of that community.

> **Garden City movement** – construction of the Garden City of Hellerau was begun in 1908 by the German Garden City Association, founded six years earlier, in cooperation with the *Deutschen Werkstätten* (German Workshops). A consistent feature of the German *Lebensreform* or living reform movement in the early 1900s was the call for cooperatively owned "garden cities." The living reformers, mostly literati and leftist Social Democratic activists, initially envisioned the garden cities as a response to the housing crisis in Wilhelmine-era urban centers.

> **Hellerau** – In 1908, a parcel of urban land in Germany cost up to seven times more than a comparable plot in England. By setting the new town of German industrialist Karl Schmitt (1873–1948) upon the rolling hills outside Dresden, planners could design an entire community from the ground up. The design emphasized low-density building as well as collective housing layouts. The plans conveyed a nostalgia for rural villages of the nineteenth century, as well as a social message that true communities required a firm sense of place, a harmony of interests, and a marriage of livelihood and cultural pursuits. The education of the children of the community was considered equally important as humane working conditions for their parents. Hellerau was conceived as a sort of planning *Gesamtkunstwerk* that integrated many aspects of public and private life.

Many artists were drawn to Hellerau. Due to its proximity to Dresden, members of the Expressionist painters group *Die Brücke* (The Bridge) became part of the Hellerau circle. One member of this group, Emil Nolde, would become a close personal friend of Wigman. Most of Wigman's biographers mention Nolde as the person who introduced her to dance theoretician Rudolf von Laban in 1913; however, the relationship between Nolde's painting and Wigman's choreography warrants greater consideration. In Wigman's autobiography, she describes their artistic relationship:

> My acquaintanceship – I had better say my friendship – with the painter Emil Nolde dated far back . . . Nolde, whenever possible, came to my dance concerts. The managers knew about him and were aware of what was expected from them. They reserved three seats: one for him, one for his tubes and pots of paints, and one for his wife, who stood guard lest he should be disturbed. I don't know what happened to those on-the-scene sketches. The few he gave me were destroyed when Dresden was bombed.
>
> (Wigman 1973: 55)

> **Expressionism** – Expressionism refers to particular German visual art movements of the pre-First World War period. By definition, Expressionism looks within to reveal a world of emotional and psychological states. With Van Gogh, the Fauves, Gauguin and Edvard Munch as points of departure, these painters distorted figures, applied strong colors and exaggerated forms. The Expressionists shared the conviction that art could express an intrinsic human truth and thus restore meaning to people's lives. In its narrowest sense, Expressionism refers to particular German visual art movements of the pre-First World War period. *Die Brücke* and *Der Blaue Reiter* groups housed the best-known

> proponents of the movement. Their development closely parallels Wigman's own, both in philosophical and in aesthetic values.
>
> **Die Brücke** – (The Bridge) *Die Brücke* rejected the classical inheritance and turned to nature and the primal to renew German art. Most of its members moved to Berlin between 1910 and 1914. Members included Erich Heckel, Ernst Ludwig Kirchner, Max Pechstein, Karl Schmidt-Rotluff and briefly Emil Nolde, the group's eldest member.
>
> **Der Blaue Reiter** (The Blue Rider) – *Der Blaue Reiter* group was more overtly mystical and claimed to reveal the spiritual truth hidden within the physical world. These painters, among them Franz Marc and Alexei von Jawlensky, were strongly influenced by the Russian painter Wassily Kandinsky and used a subtler range of colors than did *Die Brücke* artists.
>
> **Emil Nolde** (1867–1956) – German Expressionist painter, member of *Die Brücke* and friend of Mary Wigman. His interest in primitive art prompted him to participate in an expedition from 1913–14 to New Guinea via Russia and China. He was declared a degenerate artist by the Nazis in 1937 although he had been a member of the National Socialist Party.
>
> **Rudolf von Laban** (1879–1958) – born in Bratislava, Austro-Hungary and enrolled in the Military Academy at Vienna Neustadt in 1899 by his father, the military governor of Herzegovina and Bosnia. Before graduation, he left the Academy to pursue the life of an artist. He moved to Munich, then Paris, then Schwabing, stayed in a sanatorium outside Dresden and wound up at Monte Verità in 1912. Laban sought to create a systematic analysis of dance movement based on fundamentals of weight or force, time and space unique to the movement art. He also developed a system of dance notation.

Indeed, *Die Brücke* painters were opposed to the usual practice of drawing static models. They became most interested in capturing physical movement, in the same way that August Rodin had captured movement in his sculpture. The loss of Nolde's sketches of Wigman is regrettable. However, a record of their early relationship does remain in his extant paintings, such as *Dance Around the Golden Calf*, one of many Nolde painted on Biblical subjects. The shapes of the dancers in *The Dance Around the Golden Calf* bear a strong resemblance to Wigman in a photograph of her earliest, 1914 version of the *Hexentanz*. There are obvious similarities in the angles of knees, ankles and elbows and the way that the feet are lifted off the ground while the skirts swirl, in both pictures. The photograph of Wigman and Nolde's painting both capture a sense of wild, abandoned movement, a hallmark of both Expressionist-era painting and dance.

> **August Rodin** (1840–1917) – French sculptor who influenced the art form by the extremely lifelike character of his work, its expressive, light-catching surfaces, its concern with movement and passionate emotion and his treatment of the human body in works such as *The Kiss*, *The Thinker*, *Eternal Springtime* and *The Burghers of Calais*.

Like the Expressionist painters, Wigman and the practitioners of *Ausdruckstanz* were fully conscious of the visible world, but chose to look within and explore and present the mind, spirit and imagination. These artists were aware that humanity inhabits a number of complex, overlapping worlds and that these worlds, which are not seen by the eye, must be explored through the moving body. Their goal was the revealing of a new world of emotion and the mysterious motivations underlying human behavior. And they welcomed Sigmund Freud's identification of the subconscious. Just as Expressionist literature intends to startle the reader with subjective revelations of neurotic, often psychotic, states and just as the clashing dissonances of Expressionist music are intended to arouse rather than soothe the listener, *Ausdruckstanz* sought to produce a finished product that unsettled the viewer while finding a performance mode that took the dancer and her audience to the realm of transcendence and ritual. For Wigman and her cohorts, this flight into archaic rituals seemed at once regressive, progressive and an act of rebellion against their middle-class beginnings. They were joined in this rebellion by other dancers, artists and composers from beyond the borders of Germany.

By a calculated move of the *Ballets Russes* to Paris in 1909, Serge Diaghilev had been freed from the constrictions of the Imperial Ballet, whose repertory reflected the hierarchical social order of the empire, with soloists, demi-soloists and the chorus mirroring the monarchy, the aristocracy and the peasant class. Drawing together a stable of virtuosos, Diaghilev built a company that relied on the market economy instead of royal funding and began to produce ballets that shocked the Parisian art world. In 1913, Diaghilev, Vaslav Nijinsky, Igor Stravinsky and set designer Nicholas Roerich traveled from Paris to Germany while working on a new ballet, *Le Sacre du Printemps*, seeking to make a new myth of Russia by reaching back toward an idealized and imaginary, mythological past. Diaghilev took all of these artists to Hellerau to observe Jaques-Dalcroze's methods and incorporate them into the *Sacre*. Evidence of this influence is obvious, particularly in the second, *Sacrifice* section, where the driving rhythms and pathways in space appear to derive directly from Dalcroze's eurhythmic exercises. Over the span of the twentieth century and into the twenty-first, many dance companies would repeat the theme of the *Sacre*: of primal roots and individual sacrifice for the good of the group. It may well be the unifying myth of the modern age and it certainly has relevance to Mary Wigman's life. More than forty years later, Mary Wigman would set her own *Sacre du Printemps* at the Berlin Opera in 1957, her seventy-first year.

Serge Diaghilev (1872–1929) – impresario and director of the original *Ballets Russes*.

Vaslav Nijinsky (1889–1950) – virtuosic dancer, choreographer of *Afternoon of a Faun* and *The Rite of Spring* for Diaghilev's *Ballets Russes*.

Igor Stravinsky (1882–1971) – influential modern composer. He composed *The Firebird*, *Petrouchka* and *The Rite of Spring* for the *Ballets Russes*.

Nicholas Roerich (1874–1947) – Russian painter, mystic and scenic designer for *The Rite of Spring*.

But Wigman was still only a student at the time of Diaghilev's visit. She was becoming certified to teach the Dalcroze method, but already was growing disillusioned with its pedantic restrictiveness, particularly the way it limited dance in what she perceived as a slavish and subordinate relationship to music. Working alone in her room, Wigman had composed a dance work entitled *Lento* that was done in silence and reveled in the rhythm generated by the moving body itself. She showed the composition to Emil Nolde. He told her that there was another dancer who worked as she did and that she should seek him out. After taking part in Jaques-Dalcroze's preliminary production of C.W. Gluck's *Orpheus and Eurydice*, Wigman journeyed south from Hellerau to another community with a vision even more radically rebellious and emphatically utopian. It was here that Mary Wigman would commit herself to the path of dancer and choreographer.

Return to ritual on the mountain of truth

In 1913, Nolde encouraged Wigman to travel to Ascona, Switzerland, to enroll in Rudolf von Laban's *Schule der Bewegungskunst*, his summer school for the movement arts. Nolde had recognized that Laban's ideas about the possibilities of dance expression reflected Wigman's own. Laban's school flourished in the Alpine community of Monte Verità near Lago Maggiore. Founded as an experiment in the *Lebensreform* or life reform movement, those who sought to create a culture of artistic freedom at Monte Verità also espoused sexual freedom and feminism and rejected conservative ideas of respectability and hierarchical social order.

Martin Green claims that the avant-garde really began in 1900 with the establishment of the Monte Verità community, with the psychiatrist Otto Gross and pacifist Gusto Gräser among the founding figures. Many of those who formed the counterculture of the period between the turn of the century and the end of the First World War came through this commune. The founders of Monte Verità included anarchists, communists, alienists, vegetarians, theosophists and anthroposophists influenced by Rudolf Steiner. At Monte Verità, independent artists such as Paul Klee and Ernst Kirchner, and writers ranging from Dadaist Hugo Ball to Herman Hesse, James Joyce, Rainer Maria Rilke and D.H. Lawrence crossed paths. For the artists of Monte Verità, the act of dancing came to represent an idealized return to the essential and "natural" dimensions of human creative expression. For Mary Wigman it was another revelation. After three weeks of Laban's summer course, the morning post brought her notice of a job teaching the Dalcroze method for which she had recently received her diploma. The job would begin on 1 October. When she told Laban, instead of congratulating her, he replied that it was a shame, that she was a dancer and belonged on the stage. His reply was really an opening to her heart's desire. She chose to stay (Müller 1986a: 43).

Otto Gross and **Gusto Gräser** – founding figures at Monte Verità.

Laban was beginning to work on concepts that would eventually become his well-known theories of Space Harmony, movement analysis and *Kinetographie Laban*, his popular form of dance notation. But in the early years at Monte Verità these ideas were still in their nascent stages. While Laban, with Wigman's assistance, was beginning to trace dance concepts that would eventually become pedagogical, the primary choreographic influences on these dancers were grounded in dance that was chthonic – rooted in nature and ritual. Wigman recalls that the dancers "would camp down in a dell at the foot of a steep rock which I climbed to improvise a wild witch dance" (Wigman 1973: 47). Indeed in 1914, Mary Wigman made her first version of the *Hexentanz* and when Laban gave his approval she recounted jumping around the studio until she sprained her ankle, leaving her unable to dance for a fortnight. Such was the effect of Laban's opinion at that point in her career.

Kinetographie Laban **or Labanotation** – system of recording dance movement through written symbols developed by Rudolf Laban that remains the most widely used system of dance notation.

Combining ideas of *Festival* and *Körperkultur*, the dancers at Monte Verità used dance to bring ceremony and significance to the very shape of the day. Hedwig Müller and Norbert Servos write that such flights into fantasy during the depths of trench warfare appear unsettling in hindsight (Müller and Servos 1982: 15–23). Indeed, the playful naiveté exercised by Laban and company stood in stark contrast with global realities. Monte Verità was a world unto itself until the larger world overtook it. The summer of 1914 brought changes that ruptured even the utopian dream at Monte Verità. On 1 August, Germany declared war on Russia, on 3 August, Germany declared war on France and crossed into Belgium, and the following day Great Britain declared war on the German nation. The beginning of the First World War found the community at Ascona emptying and Mary Wigman and Rudolf von Laban were left to work together. Wigman served as a willing model for Laban's ideas, particularly his development of the swing scales. And the work was grueling for her. In contrast to her dramatic nature, she had to analyze movement without the emphasis on emotion. However, she came to value Laban's more rational process in her own choreographic crafting.

> **Swing scale** – Laban's earliest studies of a codified method of warming the body while exploring dance fundamentals of space, time and effort.

In February of 1914 Mary Wigman had her first public performance in Munich. Ymelda Juliewna Mentelberg, a student of Laban, planned an evening of solo works demonstrating Laban's choreography and she asked Wigman to perform two of her own dances: *Lento* and the *Hexentanz*. It was a humble beginning; the stage was actually a creaky parquet platform in the beautiful old auditorium of the Munich museum. It was in this maiden performance that she first encountered the terrible, trembling stage fright that was to plague her thirty years on stage. But the miracle that would also occur time and again first came to her on that winter night. With the opening dancing gesture, all insecurity fell from her, "as if a magic word had been spoken. Only to have the chance to dance, to be able to dance was bliss" (Wigman 1973: 50). She made the decision to remain with Laban until she had acquired enough technical training to proceed on her own. She stayed with him for four more years.

Dancing Dada

Between summer and winter during the war years, Laban and his students moved between Ascona, Munich and Zurich. Once war had broken out, the neutral territory of Switzerland grew even more appealing and winter found Laban and his stable of acolytes entrenched in the Zurich cafes. Laban and his dancers were not the only ones of the Monte Verità group to relocate. Writer Hugo Ball was a catalyst whose magnetic presence united all the elements that eventually produced Dada. In 1916, Ball founded the Cabaret Voltaire, which came to be the center of the early Dada movement. Hans Richter, another key figure in the developing Dada, claimed that Dada was born in the confluence of poetry, theater, puppetry and dance.

> **Dada** – Dada emerged during the First World War. Shock was a key tactic for Dadaists, who hoped to shake society out of the nationalism and materialism that they felt had led to the carnage of the war. The first Dada manifesto of 1918 claimed that Dadaism was "a new reality" and accused the Expressionists "of sentimental resistance to the times."

> Our celestial headquarters was Laban's ballet school. There we met young dancers of our generation [including] Mary Wigman ... Only at certain fixed times were we allowed into this nunnery, with which we had emotional ties ... These highly personal contacts – and Laban's revolutionary contribution to choreography – finally involved the whole Laban school in the Dada movement ... dancers wearing [Marcel] Janco's abstract masks fluttered like butterflies of Ensor.
>
> *(Richter 1965: 69–70)*

Laban was clearly a man of great personal charisma and particular appeal to the young women who gathered around him as students. Regarding Laban's charm and the appeal of his "nunnery," Dadaist Richard Huelsenbeck reminisced:

> [Laban] would gather the most beautiful girls for his group. I really can't say whether I was drawn more to the beauty of the girls or the newness of the dancing. But since I've never particularly cared for, or understood much about the dance, I tend to think that I was drawn more to the beauty of the girls.
>
> *(Huelsenbeck 1969: 11)*

While the Dada impulse was intentionally full of paradox, it can be seen at its most basic as an attack that used exuberant creativity against a dysfunctional and decaying culture. In the Dada circle, the absurd was celebrated just as the raging of the Great War made an apparent absurdity of civilized existence. Certainly Wigman was drawn to the new and experimental nature of the Dada events. She was happy to claim a role in the inception of Dada.

> By the way do you know that your friend M. W. had an active share in the genesis of Dadaism? What divine feasts we have had in my Zurcher apartment! My friend Sophie Tauber – who later married [Dada artist] Hans Arp – and I sewed ourselves so tightly into our extravagant costumes one day that, for the whole night we could not get out of them. And all the people of the Cafe Voltaire were my daily guests ...
>
> *(Wigman 1973: 141)*

Wigman claimed that she adopted the term Absolute Dance at such a performance with Sophie Tauber. One credo for the Zurich Dadaists was "absolute poetry, absolute art, absolute dance" and Wigman was more than willing to take on that title for her own dance art. Indeed, the Expressionist goal of manifesting "truth" through art implies an acknowledgement of an absolute. In retrospect it seems that the Dada impulse was a transient inclination for Wigman. In truth the Dada manifestos claimed a turning away from the very Expressionist nature that her *Ausdruckstanz* embodied. For the Great Berlin Dada evening in April 1918, Dada artist Huelsenbeck wrote what came to be the first Dada manifesto in the German language.

> What did Expressionism want? It "wanted" something, that much remains characteristic of it. Dada wants nothing, Dada grows. Expressionism wanted inwardness, it conceived of itself as a reaction against the times, while Dadaism is nothing but an expression of the times ... Under the pretext of inwardness the Expressionist [artists] have closed ranks to form a generation which is expectantly looking forward to an honorable appraisal in the histories of art and literature and is aspiring to honors and accolades.
>
> *(Huelsenbeck and Green 1993: 44–45)*

Mary Wigman maintained the Expressionist conviction that art could express an intrinsic human truth and thus restore meaning to people's lives. The Dadaists proclaimed that all extant moral, political and aesthetic beliefs had been destroyed by the war. The coolness and radicalism of the *Neue Sachlichkeit* and Dada developments do manifest themselves in Mary Wigman's use of mask and costume as a way of depersonalizing the performing body. But her themes remained essentially Expressionistic: ecstatic or somber and imbued with mysticism and symbolic imagery. Her primary allegiance to *Ausdruckstanz* would eventually place her at odds not only with Laban but also with larger political and artistic forces within Germany. However, remnants of her time with the Dada artists remained in the theatricality of her performances and the revolutionary way she used the mask and costume in modern concert dance.

> ***Neue Sachlichkeit*** (New Objectivity) – artistic movement that signaled a turn toward realism. It was first applied by museum director, Gustav Hartlaub, in 1923 to an exhibit of paintings grounded in the depiction of reality. *Neue Sachlichkeit* artists included George Grosz and Otto Dix. They aggressively attacked and satirized the evils of society and those in power, demonstrating in harsh imagery the devastating effects of the First World War.

On 18–19 August 1917, Laban and Wigman, along with others from Laban's dance group, returned to the mountains of Ascona. There they presented a twelve-hour, open-air performance of a *Sonnenfest* (Sun Festival). Termed by Laban a "choral play," the spectacle was part of the Congress of the Oriental Order of the Temple or Ordo Templi Orientis. Through studies with OTO founder Theodor Reuss, Laban had been initiated into that branch of Freemasonry and progressed to the highest degree of Reuss's renegade Masonic organization. Laban's stated goal was the "renunciation of all civilizational influences" (Laban 1975: 135). The festival began at 6 a.m. with the *Hymn to the Rising Sun*. The second act of the performance was sited around a fire on a mountaintop at 11 p.m. Involving the entire cast armed with flutes, drums and torches, *The Demons of the Night* section was "a mystical play in which 'witches and demons' were conjured up in masked dances" (ibid.: 22). Following the marathon event, Wigman returned with Laban to Zurich. Then in November she made her own evening, her first dramatic cycle, built of solo dances performed at the Laban School. The six dances that made up the program reflected her fascination with the mystical and the metaphysical. *The Nun*, *The Dancer for Our Blessed Lady*, *Worshiper*, *Sacrifice*, *The Dervish* and *The Temple Dance* did not emerge merely from her experiences with Laban but reveal an atmosphere that permeated the place and time.

> **Ordo Templi Orientis** – secret, mystical fraternity founded around 1902 by Karl Kellner and Theodor Reuss. Rudolf von Laban became a member of Reuss's renegade Masonic organization and brought the OTO to Monte Verità in 1917.

The longing for alternatives to the Western canon took some artists toward alternative spiritual teachings. The yin–yang symbol that stood atop the *Festhalle* at Hellerau represented a larger inquiry into aesthetic practices that similarly guided the work of Wassily Kandinsky, Franz Kafka, W.B. Yeats, T.S. Eliot and Mary Wigman. In film, Paul Wegener presented three versions of the ancient Golem story between 1915 and 1920. In 1919, Robert Weine directed the *Cabinet of Dr. Caligari*, the signature work of Expressionist film and a representation of the darker side of Expressionism through its thematic probing of insanity. The authors intended the tyranny of Dr. Caligari to serve as an allegory against mad authority, but the final version ends with the doctor telling his peers that he can cure his patient now that he understands the root of his own psychosis. Presentation of alternative realities became popular thematic material. For Wigman, such themes came to make a cohesive whole of her life and her work.

Wassily Kandinsky (1866–1944) – Russian abstract painter who was a leader of *Die Blaue Reiter* wing of German expressionism. His influential book *Concerning the Spiritual in Art* appeared in 1911. He became a German citizen upon joining the faculty of the Bauhaus school but was forced to leave the country in 1933 when the school was closed. He became a naturalized French citizen in 1939.

The crisis year

In 1918, Mary Wigman would have her own year of crisis, mental breakdown and self-analysis. The confusion and dissolution at war's end brought defeat, deprivation and desperation to the general population of Germany. Wigman experienced these and also was faced with difficulties in her personal life. In May, her stepfather Dietrich Wiegmann died and her brother Heinrich returned from the war as an amputee. Work at the studio in Zurich ended and Wigman also broke from her relationship with Laban. She found herself physically exhausted and emotionally drained. She went to a sanatorium at Walensee in eastern Switzerland to find some peace. She was also diagnosed with tuberculosis. In those days such a diagnosis could amount to a death sentence. In her writing, she refers to this period as a terrible, wonderful year. She danced alone and created a new series of solos. She also wrote the poetic sketches that were to become her group work *The Seven Dances of Life* (*Die Sieben Tanze des Lebens*) in 1921. Finally, she performed her dances at the sanatorium in Engadin where the audience was made up of shell-shocked veterans, psychiatric patients and local sportsmen (Müller 1986a: 55). She was then ready to enter into a professional life.

After that initial performance, she embarked on a tour of German cities, meeting disappointment at first as audiences were not prepared for her dances depicting the mysterious and the grotesque. What she presented onstage was a far cry from the beauty of ballet or the entertainment of the chorus line. Her first concerts in Berlin and Munich were critical debacles. Newspapers responded with cries of "ridiculous," "idiotic," "mad frenzy," "an imbecilic dislocation of the joints," "the dance without music – unbearable, fatiguing," "the drum and gong accompaniment (was) ear-splitting, torturous" (Dixon 1931: 37). Buffeted by these storms, Wigman did not surrender; nor did she change course. She persisted in her vision of *Ausdruckstanz* and finally in Hamburg the tide turned. She received her first real acclaim from the concert-going public.

When she continued on to Dresden, her audience had been well prepared by art historian and dance aficionado Will Grohmann. With Grohmann's help, Wigman, joined by dancers Berthe Trümpy and Grete Palucca, danced to a sold-out house. On 7 November, six days before her thirty-fifth birthday, newspaper critic Otto Flake wrote, "She realized an idea and fulfilled her task. Dance is for her a religious art" (Müller 1986a: 71). This early success in Dresden was the beginning of a long, fruitful relationship with that city.

> **Berthe Trümpy** (1895–1983) – studied with both Wigman and Laban. She helped finance the first Mary Wigman Schule-Dresden. Trümpy became co-director of the school, teaching and performing with the Chamber Dance Group. In 1926, along with Vera Skoronel, she started the Trümpy/Skoronel school in Berlin.
>
> **Gret Palucca** (1902–93) – was a student at the Dresden Opera House when she saw a Wigman performance. She began to study at the Wigman Schule. Identified by her gift for high jumps, Palucca was considered one of the most talented of Wigman's dance progeny. Palucca stayed in Germany during the Third Reich and gained a favored position even though she was defined under the Nuremberg Laws as *mischlinge ersten Grades*, or half Jewish. Her school in East Germany became an important training ground for postwar German dancers.

Meanwhile, the Weimar government was convulsed in one political upheaval after another. Caught on tour during the Kapp-Putsch and the ensuing general strike, she hitched a ride to Dresden and in many ways her fate was decided there. Wigman writes that in 1920 she was to be engaged by the Dresden State Opera as ballet master. She moved to the Palast Hotel Weber with Trümpy, who had become her assistant, to await her appointment. While there, Wigman began to teach classes in the hotel social room. From a newspaper article, she learned that the position at the Opera had passed her by, awarded to another who had influential romantic connections. Undeterred, Wigman continued to teach in the hotel; many students came but there seemed to be no resolution of Wigman's dream for a center in which to train dancers and from which to take her own creative performance work out into the world. Finally, Berthe Trümpy took action and, using her own Swiss francs, acquired a villa for Wigman in Neustadt-Dresden. It would be the primary home of the Wigman School for the next twenty-two years.

The gilded and tarnished twenties

Later in her life, Wigman would reflect on the 1920s as a "fighting time" of hard and relentless work. But she acknowledged that the end of the First World War brought a surge of creative activity in all of the arts. Much has been written of the inspired swell of innovation that was unleashed in spite of, or perhaps in response to, the ongoing political disarray that plagued the Weimar Republic. Not only was the political situation in flux, but also the economic conditions were equally unsettled. Yet Mary Wigman's school flourished. A roll-call of the students who came to study with Wigman in the 1920s reads like a list of the most important professional dancers of the era. Along with Trümpy, Grete Palucca, Yvonne Georgi, Harald Kreutzberg, Max Terpis, Margarethe Wallmann and Hanya Holm all came to work with Wigman at the house on Bautzner Strasse in the early 1920s. As Wigman's workload grew, she was able to enlist help from several sources.

> **Yvonne Georgi** (1903–75) – born in Leipzig, she attended the Dalcroze school in Hellerau. In 1921 Georgi went to the Wigman school in Dresden. Her successful partnership with Harald Kreutzberg took the duo on tour across Europe and to the United States of America.
>
> **Harald Kreutzberg** (1902–68) – student of Wigman at the Dresden school who became one of the great soloists of his era. Equally renowned as a dancer and actor, he worked with Max Terpis and

> Max Reinhardt. In 1928 he traveled to the United States as a member of Max Reinhardt's theater group and returned to the States for the next seven years with Yvonne Georgi and with American dancer Ruth Page as his partners.
>
> **Max Terpis** (1889–1958) – early student of Mary Wigman, Terpis taught at the Wigman school. He became ballet master in Hanover in 1922.
>
> **Hanya Holm** (1893–1992) – Wigman student who became her teaching assistant and started the American Wigman School. Holm was also a graduate of the Dalcroze Institute. She eventually became a successful Broadway choreographer with such shows as *My Fair Lady*, *Kiss Me Kate* and *Camelot* to her credit.

At age twenty-seven, Mary's sister Elisabeth was still living with their mother in Hanover. In 1921, she came to join Mary's household in Dresden. While their mother had warned her not to take up the dance, she started in Trümpy's evening class for amateurs. Eventually, Elisabeth would take on a great deal of the teaching and day-to-day responsibilities at the school. The same year, the accomplished musician Will Goetz joined the faculty and began to serve as Wigman's collaborator for her dance compositions. With Goetz, she was able to further develop her ideas about the relationship between music and the dance. She also made use of the dancers that she had gathered around her to create group works, including her dance drama *The Seven Dances of Life*. Choreographing that work in 1921, she broke from the solo performances that had defined the previous four years of her career.

As her reputation as a teacher and performer grew, so did the enrollment of her school. Soon students were coming from far beyond Germany to study her new dance. The dressing room has often been described as a place where many languages could be heard. In Germany, *Ausdruckstanz* became popular among the citizens of the Weimar Republic who were hungry for a life-affirming physical culture. Participation in rhythmic gymnastics and *Ausdruckstanz* became a mass movement, alongside the movement choir explorations of Rudolf von Laban and the hiking clubs of the German Youth Movement.

By 1923, Germany was experiencing a measure of economic stability that was mirrored in Wigman's personal life and work. The city of Dresden was able to contribute some financial support to her concert dance group. Her school was flourishing and her choreography was reaching a new level of professionalism. Since her days at Hellerau, Wigman had enjoyed a friendship that grew into a romantic relationship with psychiatrist Hans Prinzhorn. Prinzhorn's work concerned the common ground between psychiatry and art, irrationality and self-expression. In 1922 Prinzhorn published his first and most influential book, *Bildnerei der Geisteskranken* (*Artistry of the Mentally Ill*), richly illustrated with examples from his collection of artwork by mental patients. This book represents one of the first attempts to clinically analyze and value such work. Wigman found that she had many ideas in common with Prinzhorn, who was a strong influence in her philosophical and aesthetic thinking as well as her domestic life. The two remained friends even after the romance ended; after his death in 1933, Wigman kept a death mask of Prinzhorn in her home for many years. And he helped to form that home in ways beyond his lifetime. In his Heidelberg practice, Prinzhorn had employed Anni Hess as assistant and housekeeper. As Wigman's school and performing career flourished, she was able to ask "Hesschen" to manage her domestic affairs. Hess would remain a devoted companion to the dancer from 1923 until Wigman's death in 1973. Indeed, a good portion of the story of Wigman's life lies with the devotion of her housekeeper and companion, Anni Hess.

> **Hans Prinzhorn** (1886–1933) – German psychiatrist and art historian whose work at the University of Heidelberg was concerned with the border between art and psychiatry, self-expression and mental illness. He was Mary Wigman's lover, confidant and companion during her early years in Dresden.

With the assistance of her students, accompanists, sister Elisabeth and Hess, plus financial support from private donors, the city of Dresden, the Saxon state and the federal government, Wigman entered into a period of tremendous productivity. By 1924, she was able to expand her professional group to fourteen dancers. She also became involved with a man fifteen years younger. Herbert Binswanger was from a well-known Swiss family of physicians and psychiatrists. His own specialty was also psychotherapy and he provided a boyish and light-hearted diversion for Wigman, in contrast to her student/pupil role with Prinzhorn. Her time with Binswanger served to further free her as she came into her own as an artist.

> **Herbert Binswanger** (1901–1975) – member of the great family of psychiatrists that founded and operated Bellevue Sanatorium in Kreuzlingen, Switzerland. His uncle Otto had treated Friedrich Nietzsche during his illness. His father Ludwig trained with Jung and had a close relationship with Freud. Ludwig also studied the writings of Heidegger and incorporated these ideas into his branch of existential psychology. Herbert also followed in the family avocation. After her relationship with Prinzhorn, Wigman began a romantic involvement with Herbert. Their correspondence and friendship lasted until her death.

Nearing her fortieth year, Wigman also was reaching a zenith in her creative development. She began to incorporate the use of the mask into her compositions, admitting what she would term an "alien figure" into the choreography. In 1926, she revisited the figure of the witch, donning a mask to craft her second version of *Hexentanz*, a shocking study in female power and the grotesque. Paradoxically, the popularity of *Ausdruckstanz* had unleashed a whole population of earnest, emotive amateurs that threatened to undermine the professionalism of the art form. In the United States of America, Lincoln Kirstein would call Mary Wigman a dangerous woman because she encouraged all young women to dance, whether they had talent or not! The emerging debate between amateur and professional dance would continue into the next decade and would serve as a flash point for the field. As competing camps struggled for philosophical and aesthetic authority over dwindling resources, Wigman entered gamely into the fray.

The First Dancers' Congress

In December 1926, Germany was admitted to the League of Nations and began experiencing a sense of renewal, primarily orchestrated by foreign minister Gustav Stresemann and due partly to the reduction of war reparations under the Treaty of Locarno. Stresemann declared to the Geneva Assembly:

> He will serve humanity best who, firmly rooted in the traditions of his own people, develops his moral and intellectual gifts to the best of his ability, thus reaching out beyond his own national boundaries and serving the whole world.
>
> *(Stresemann in Reinhardt 1962: 666)*

Wigman shared Stresemann's goal of creating a German art that would spread beyond the country's borders. The First Dancers' Congress took place at Magdeburg in May 1927, with the goal of assembling leading German dancers to discuss the most pressing issues of their time. Attendance was modest, around three hundred people, and Laban and his supporters dominated the proceedings. At the Congress, Laban put forward his desire to unite all German dance organizations in a single federation, ostensibly under his own leadership. Wigman and her own disciples stayed away from the primary activities of the conference since Laban had not invited Wigman to participate in the concert performances.

During the Congress, the *Magdeburg Daily News* invited both Laban and Wigman to contribute to a special issue devoted to the German theater. Laban wrote "The Dance as a Work of Art," offering new approaches to movement for the stage in what appeared to be a reconciliation of commercial theater, ballet and opera with his explorations of group performance and movement choirs. With no other platform from which to express her opinion at the Congress, Wigman used her newspaper article as an opportunity to raise issues facing modern dance and the dancer, as well as charges of dilettantism that had been leveled at the *Ausdruckstanz*. On the defensive, Wigman delineated two types of creative dance: the first was her own Absolute concert form that reflected contemporary life and concerns; the second was what she termed "stage dance," which she described as being in a state of confusion and compromise between classical dance and pantomime.

Wigman argued that very few German stages had resident troupes fully trained in the relatively young dance form of *Ausdruckstanz*. She added that the young dancers of the day came from many strata of society rather than those privileged enough to study ballet. In the difficult economic climate of 1927 she asked, "Which dancers can afford to finish their studies?" (Wigman 1973: 114). In comparing the stage choreographer to the musical composer of the day, Wigman declared that very few choreographers had the needed experience to fully employ *Ausdruckstanz* on the theatrical stage. Hers was a plea for patience to allow the development of the art form. In sum, Wigman, Laban and other Congress participants could all agree that a crisis in training had become obvious in the world of professional dance. However, she and Laban would continue to disagree about the prescription to remedy the situation.

The Second Dancers' Congress

The Second Dancers' Congress was held in Essen in 1928. While rivalry had flared between Wigman and Laban at the first Congress, Laban had formed several alliances, most notably with his former student and assistant Kurt Jooss. After leaving Laban, Jooss had established the Folkwang School with Sigurd Leeder in Essen and was emerging as a fine young choreographer. Jooss was also making his own claim as a leader in the German dance and his role as organizer of the Second Congress firmly established this position. Both men called for the integration of classical ballet with the new dance modernism to create a unique theatrical form. Although Wigman was invited to participate in this Second Congress, she remained a rebel against what she termed "hidebound conventional theater." She continued to call for the support of Absolute dance first and foremost as a foundation for more specialized work in theatrical productions. It is crucial to understand that she saw *Ausdruckstanz* as a primary, initiating base of experience for the dance artist. She claimed that it was the only form to assure freedom for individual development through improvisational methods rather than codified technique. Spotlighting the distance between Laban/Jooss and Wigman, the central question appeared to be: Did the future of dance lie with the *Ausdruckstanz*, which repudiated classical ballet altogether, or with the dance-drama which incorporated aspects of ballet as championed by Jooss and Laban's expressive movement methods to create a new entity?

> **Kurt Jooss** (1901–79) – born in a village near Stuttgart to a farming family of landed gentry. Jooss encountered Laban in 1919 as he was working on theories of *Choreutics* and then joined *Tanzbühne Laban*. After traveling to Paris to study ballet, Jooss was awarded the 1932 Paris choreographic prize for his classic *The Green Table*. In 1933 Jooss was forced to flee Germany with his dance company and settled at Dartington Hall in England.

As economic tension grew, the practical possibility of paid work in the opera house or theater informed much of the discussion. For many dancers such work appeared to be the only option for economic sustenance. Notably, a similar debate was a large part of the climate of the US dance community during the Depression as many modern "concert" dancers would turn to what they termed commercial work: entertaining on the Broadway stage or under the auspices of the Works Project Administration. For the German dance world, the Second Congress displayed a discomfort and stagnation that had overtaken the field as well as the paralysis that had overtaken German society as factions battled for control on the political front. Karl Toepfer points out that during the conference very little attention was paid to aesthetic questions; the focus was on pedagogic concerns and career maneuvers. Laban did emerge as the leader once again, mostly based on the strength of his written work as a theoretical foundation for the artists. The press was particularly keen on the introduction of his *Kinetographie Laban* as the most comprehensive form of dance notation to date. Also, dance writer Hans Brandenburg commented that Laban had freed contemporary dance from Wigman's type of "excessive individualism" by choreographing choric works and creating a structure of uniformity through his theoretical writings and notation. To many observers, the Congress appeared long on talk and short on actual performance at the professional level.

However, Mary Wigman did dominate the conference in the one area closest to her own ideals and career goals. If critical reviews are the measure, the performance of her group work *Feier* (Celebration/Ceremony) was by far the best-received dance event of the conference. Using her well-trained group as abstractly stylized, even archetypal figures and rejecting narrative, she reiterated in dance form her belief that the future lay in revival of the ritual origins of dance, not assimilation of ballet or other theatrical forms. Aside from the rhetoric, the performance of *Celebration* solidified her prominence and mastery as a choreographer and supported her claim for the power of *Ausdruckstanz*. As a sad epilogue to the actual performance, Wigman appeared onstage and addressed the audience. She announced that due to financial difficulties she was forced to dissolve her dance group. The performance of *Celebration* was the end of an era.

It also proved to be the beginning of the next phase of her work. Wigman overcame the anxieties over the solvency and management of the school with the entry of industrialist Hanns Benkert into her life. Benkert had been involved romantically with Hanya Holm and through her had a good understanding of the problems facing the Wigman enterprise. An accomplished businessman, Benkert took over management of the school, allowing Wigman to breathe a sigh of relief.

> **Hanns Benkert** (1899–1948) – director of the Society of German Engineers and a leading functionary in munitions production, he became manager of the Siemens Schuckert Works under the Third Reich.

The Third Dancers' Congress

There was no German Dancers' Congress in 1929. As the global Depression began, Wigman had regained her equilibrium in spite of the disappointment that had followed the dissolution of her dance group. Following an idyllic road trip back to the Alps with old flame Binswanger, she returned to the studio to choreograph her solo dance cycle *Shifting Landscape*, which she was soon to premiere during her first tour of the United States. Wigman was assigned the most prominent choreographic project in the Third Dancers' Congress at Munich in 1930. This Congress was held under the auspices of three organizations: *Der Deutsche Tanzerbund* led by Laban and Jooss; *Deutsche Tanzgemeinschaft*, which Wigman established after the slight of the First Dancers' Congress; and the Munich *Chorische Bunde*, organized to supply amateur dancers for the production of Wigman's monumental dance-drama *Totenmal* or *Call of the Dead*. In the midst of economic hardships, the city of Munich renovated a concert hall to house performances, lectures and discussions. The eyes of the Western dance world were turned toward Germany in expectation. International newspapers sent correspondents. Elizabeth Selden's preview expressed the enthusiastic anticipation among US dancers. "For the third time Germany is calling a dance Congress and thereby proclaiming her great interest in the art of motion which is destined like no other, to express the consciousness of our modern age . . ." (Selden 1930: n.p.).

The Congress promised to gather the largest group of dancers ever assembled and more than a thousand came. Many saw the Congress as proof of the profound importance of dance in the modern world. To disciples of the new dance, the magnitude of the event testified how dance had become "a potent factor in the cultural life of the age" (ibid.). The crowning event of the week was to be an open rehearsal of Wigman's *Totenmal*. Designed on a mass scale, *Totenmal* was written and directed by the young Swiss poet Albert Talhoff as a memorial for the dead of the First World War. Selden placed it in the tradition of the grand crucifixion re-enactment produced at Oberammergau. She described *Totenmal* as "the greatest Passion Play of the present, since every spectator here is an actor and has been since 1914 [when the war began]" (ibid.).

In reality, the entire Third Dancers' Congress was judged a disappointment. *New York Times* critic John Martin, the staunchest supporter of the modern dance on both sides of the Atlantic, called it "futile." Not only did he find the performances and presentations unsatisfactory, but also he was shocked at the state of contention within the dance community: "Invective was hurled about promiscuously, scandal was voiced and libel uttered; the private lives of individuals present were attacked and cries of 'Pfui!' and even 'Schwein!' – an epithet of untranslatable venom – filled the air" (Martin 1930a: *New York Times*, 27 July, X6). This is how the Third Dancers' Congress closed: in an unseemly display of deep rifts within the German dance world.

Martin also wrote that the ambitious but flawed *Totenmal* had occupied Wigman to such an extent that she presented "no dancing of her own during the Congress, much to its detriment" (Martin 1930a: *New York Times*, 27 July, X6). To Martin, *Totenmal* was an anomaly or diversion from Wigman's own work. But *Totenmal* was to be performed throughout the summer, with Wigman and her Dresden faculty remaining in residence in Munich.

The high expectations for the *Totenmal* performance reflected the hard-earned prominence that Wigman had gained in a German dance world that had grown increasingly impoverished, contentious and openly hostile. Wigman's own solo performances and touring had always been an important source of professional pride and income. By the end of 1930, she was about to embark on the most important touring cycle of her career.

Coming to the United States

In the early 1930s, the person most responsible for the flowering of international dance in the United States was not a dancer. Sol Hurok was an impresario of the old school who presented acts across the country, most notably the early, exhaustive touring of Anna Pavlova and Isadora Duncan. He redoubled his efforts in the 1930s. The march of US big business in the first decades of the twentieth century also stormed through the field of art and entertainment. Corporations such as the National Broadcasting Company and the Columbia Broadcasting System overtook smaller presenters. Hurok intensified his self-proclaimed mission to remain an independent producer of "the interesting, the exotic, the novel from abroad." The opening of what Hurok came to call the "dance decade" began in 1930 with Mary Wigman (Hurok and Goode 1946: 155).

Certainly, the United States had its own dance ancestry. Isadora Duncan got her start there, as had Loie Fuller and Ruth St. Denis, although all had to travel to the European continent for major artistic success. Martha Graham, Doris Humphrey and Charles Weidman, all the offspring of Denishawn, were beginning to make a mark in the cultural world and by 1930 were the rising stars in the rather small cosmos of American dance modernity. A 1927 New *York Times* article underscores the state of the dance prior to Wigman's arrival. It begins: "The advent of the new German 'physical culture' dancing in to the arena, though yet almost unknown in this country, is causing something to happen in the dance world." The writer goes on to describe a "blood feud" between the advocates and opponents of the ballet. Noting the significance of the fact that the "non-ballet" had not yet acquired a name, the writer tries a few, "esthetic, barefoot, interpretative, rhythmic," arguing that in the dance style itself there is little definitive enough to even bear a name. However, the writer offers hope: "Then, of course, there are the Germans. We have seen almost nothing of them as yet in this country, but Mary Wigman is reported to be headed in our direction." It would be three years before Wigman could make the voyage across the Atlantic. But her reputation preceded her and much preparation for her arrival was made through the work of John Martin. It is telling that the 1927 article bears no byline. This was not unusual. The identification of writer by byline was a fairly new addition to American journalism. There was no staff writer dedicated to the dance art at that time. In 1928, Martin was hired by the *Times* to do just that, launching his decades-long dominance of the field in the United States of America.

Ruth St. Denis (1880–1972) – with Ted Shawn, founded the Denishawn School in Los Angeles in 1915. Known as a striking soloist of "ethnic" styles in the first decade of the twentieth century, St. Denis went on to create "music visualizations" that wedded music to movement, arguably a development of Dalcroze's theories. At Denishawn she taught the American modern dance pioneers Martha Graham, Charles Weidman and Doris Humphrey.

Martha Graham (1894–1991) – seen by many as the founder of American modern dance, Graham codified a unique style and technique for dance which has been transmitted through her school, choreography and company.

Doris Humphrey (1895–1958) – contemporary of Graham and likewise an alumnus of Denishawn, Humphrey along with Charles Weidman (1901–1975) established a strain of American modern dance. Her use of the swing or fall and recovery has remained a mainstay as it has evolved in the art form. She was astute analyst of choreographic principles and her *The Art of Making Dances* (1959) became a bible for modern choreographers. Stricken early in life with debilitating arthritis, Humphrey continued to choreograph for José Limón and his company.

Wigman (1886–1973)

In January 1929, two students of Mary Wigman debuted their work in New York. Harald Kreutzberg and Yvonne Georgi had left the Wigman schools for careers as soloists and were now performing as a duo. They made their way to the United States before their teacher. Following their premiere, Martin was pressed to answer the question, "Is this the new German dance?" (Martin 1929: 29 January, X8). Martin's response displayed his tireless effort to educate the public on the dance revolution that was underway: "It is a complete restatement of physical technique, going back to nature and away from art for its experimentations. It also lays great stress on expressionism" (Martin 1929: 29 January, X8). As correspondent to the Third Dancers' Congress, Martin traveled to Germany in early August 1930. Finally, he was able to write definitively,

> When one comes face to face with Mary Wigman, the truth about the German dance dawns with unexpected suddenness; Mary Wigman is the German dance.... the mystery of the German dance itself clears away in her presence.
> *(Martin 1930b:* New York Times, *3 August, 101)*

Wigman arrived in the United States in November. Hurok had booked her for a "scratch tour." Unsure of her appeal to American audiences, he added concert dates in response to demand. He needn't have worried. With great anticipation, the audiences paid her an unusual tribute. New York's Chanin Theater was completely sold out for her opening performance before she even left Germany! While exciting, this also laid upon her a tremendous sense of responsibility and even anxiety as she considered the task of bringing the "free dance" to an entirely new audience. The stage fright that plagued her all her life came roaring to the fore. Yet, as the curtain opened on that broad New York stage, she was greeted with a thunderous applause, a welcome that she would recall until her death. From her premiere in December, she was met by full houses, along with equal measures of enthusiastic support, perplexity and some outright dismay. Before her first tour, there was rumor that she would be forced to temper her program for consumption by the uninformed American public. Although John Martin pointed out that the homegrown American dancers such as Graham had already struggled mightily to introduce dance modernism, there was some doubt as to the sophistication and depth of the American public when faced with Wigman's unique theatricality. Uncompromising, for her first tour Wigman performed the same program that she had staged in Berlin and Hamburg just prior to her journey.

By her fourth performance, Martin claimed that undoubtedly a new epoch for dancing was beginning in the United States. Comparing the poetry of her movement to the nobility of Homer and the passion of Whitman, he continued, "it matters very little, if at all, that Frau Wigman herself is not possessed of personal beauty ... " (Martin 1931b: *New York Times*, 4 January, X4). Not only was Wigman described as "past her prime," but also her concerts offered works that ruptured the tradition of classic beauty in the dance. Just as the crisis of the First World War brought into question the very relevance of beauty and order in a world radically altered by death and disfigurement, modernism in all of the arts had redefined art itself. Martin observed that Wigman brought to the surface aesthetic differences that had been stirring for years. Unquestionably, the authority and success of Wigman's work smoothed the path for the American moderns. Reflecting the development of a particular kind of Americana based on atavistic themes, Martha Graham choreographed *Primitive Mysteries* and Doris Humphrey made *The Shakers*, both in 1931. That same year interest in the new German dance proved great enough that Hurok backed the establishment of an American Wigman School in New York, headed by Hanya Holm.

When Wigman returned to New York for her second tour in December 1931, Martin observed, "where there was curiosity and shocked surprise; now there is solid enthusiasm based on mutual understanding" (Martin 1931a: *New York Times*, 14 December, X17). Wigman criss-crossed the country, remaining in North America for several months. Her solo dance cycle *Opfer* (*Sacrifice*) anchored her performances. In an interview, Wigman explained that she understood the enormous sacrifices that gripped the American public in the Great Depression. At the climax of the Depression, thirty million were unemployed worldwide, including six million in Germany alone. Wigman also noted that while she herself had not been adversely affected, largely due to the economic success of her American tours, many in her homeland were suffering deprivation. In spite of the economy, she performed for full houses. Hurok was no longer unsure of Wigman's ability to draw a crowd.

She crossed the country to perform for audiences on the West Coast. In San Francisco, young dancer Eve Gentry sat in the audience. Gentry later would join Hanya Holm's original dance group in New York. But for her introduction to Mary Wigman, she was another uninitiated audience member. And her response offers a glimpse of Wigman's impact on the American public. With notebook in hand, Eve recorded her impressions of her first contact with Mary Wigman's *Ausdruckstanz*. She wrote, "I will not let [others] influence me in my reactions, tho' they are over enthusiastic I will not be so until I am sure, sure that I want to give this enthusiasm to Mary Wigman" (Newhall 2000: 36). By the end of the concert, Gentry's restraint dissolved into unabashed admiration.

> I've been sitting on the edge of my seat, my knee quivering. I feel as tho' I just can't sit here longer – I must jump up. I feel as if I have seen a great artist. I have a great deal to think about, a great deal to dance for. I have actually learned things. The audience was riotous. People yelled "Bravo!" "Bravo." I have never been in such an excited place. I have never been so excited it seems. For the first time in my life I wanted to call "Bravo" so much that I actually did scream "Bravo" not only once but a dozen times, I was exhausted, trembling almost crying for joy.
>
> *(Gentry papers)*

Eve Gentry (1909–94) – American modern dancer, born Henrietta Greenhood. Studied with German dancer Ann Mundstock in San Francisco before becoming a member of Hanya Holm's original dance company in 1936. Gentry was also a member of the New Dance Group and was one of Joseph Pilates' chosen representatives.

Der Weg *(The Path)*

Wigman had succeeded in carrying the seeds of *Ausdruckstanz* across Europe and to the United States. She had caused a sensation and furthered her mission to spread the dance that she loved so well. The income and artistic interest generated from her tours allowed her to continue to expand her work and schools. In 1931, the American Wigman School was established with Hanya Holm at its helm. However, when Mary Wigman returned home in 1932, she once again found her German school in financial crisis. In Berlin alone 35,000 businesses were facing bankruptcy. The worldwide depression had thrown many of her students out of work. With massive unemployment, very few could pay tuition for the professional training program and even enrollment in the lay classes dropped precipitously. The struggle for state funds grew even more difficult. She had turned over financial administration of her school to Hanns Benkert whose successful business ventures had him attached to the Siemens Corporation. He was also well connected politically with the rising National Socialist Party, as German industry threw support to the Nazis. For Wigman, his business acumen and political protection became invaluable as she struggled to retain her school and continued a relentless cycle of touring her solo concerts to keep the school afloat.

In July of 1932, Hurok came to Berlin and approached Wigman about a third US tour. The offer appeared a godsend. She hatched a plan to use the tour to raise the profile of her school, employing and thus retaining some of her more advanced students. This could only serve to build future support for her enterprise. She would start a new dance group with these advanced students and create a major new work for them. The new Wigman Dance Group would tour the United States from coast to coast and into Canada. The group would not only be paid for travel and performances, it would also be paid to rehearse, and not in falling Deutschmarks but in solid American dollars, a development that caused much excitement within the Wigman school community (Müller 1986a: 212). She even talked with Hurok about an extended tour to South America.

Once more, Hurok kept all plans contingent on audience enthusiasm, again placing Wigman under extreme pressure to produce. She had less than six months to pull together a group of students who had never performed professionally into an elite troupe equal to an international tour and to make a work that highlighted her own theories of the group dance. She wrote in frustration of the great goodwill of the girls and their equally naive view of the hard work necessary to accomplish such a feat (ibid.). The Group unveiled her new dance cycle *Der Weg* (The Way/Path) on 8 December 1932, in Dresden and performed it again three days later in Berlin (ibid.). They met with sharp disapproval in the press. Leading critics Fritz Bohme and Paul Bloch both challenged Wigman's choice of the group form instead of her own, much stronger solo work. Unaware of the necessities that shaped Wigman's choices, or perhaps in spite of them, Bohme declared it regrettable that this work would represent the current state of German dance and claimed it a greater shame that the work must travel directly to the United States without correction of the problems evident in the German performances. The criticism was surely searing to Wigman, who was feeling pressures from all directions. Perhaps the most painful of all proved to be the assertions that the great Mary Wigman had become artistically and spiritually lost, deserting the values of her homeland (ibid.: 213).

When Wigman arrived for her third US tour in mid-December 1932, she was not alone. Along with accompanists Hanns Hasting and Gretl Curth, she brought those twelve student dancers to perform *Der Weg*. The hurtful claims that dilettantism was making *Ausdruckstanz* obsolete appeared proven. In the case of *Der Weg*, practical necessity prevailed. In the world of concert performance, the proof is what happens onstage. And competition in the United States was heating up. Graham, Humphrey and Weidman all had cast well away from their Denishawn roots. Their own concert aesthetics were evolving and their own schools had growing enrollments.

The American debut of *Der Weg* took place on Christmas Day at the New Yorker Theatre. Wigman was given the opening-night spot of a two-week International Dance Festival. John Martin, ever a champion of Wigman's work, wrote kindly: "Twelve excellently trained dancers, able to alternate between movement and the playing of flutes and percussion instruments, constitute the company" (Martin 1932: *New York Times*, 26 December, 26). He goes on to try to describe the relationship between Wigman and her dancers in the work, "among them Wigman herself moves as the protagonist, though not actually the most important figure." He does concede that "Wigman with a group is not to be compared with Wigman as a solo dancer" (ibid.).

Indeed, Martin and others who had come that evening to see the power of Wigman seemed sorely disappointed that she had made herself an auxiliary of the group, rather than the focus. This was a departure even from her earlier choric staging of *Totenmal*, in which she was the only unmasked, individual figure. Martin claimed that no fault lay in her composition: Wigman was a stickler for clear form, but she had chosen to discard her strongest artistic tool – her own performance personality. Martin saw clearly that:

> Her singular power as an artist lies in her ability to project her highly personal inner experience through movement of sometimes breath-taking originality. When she gives these movements to other dancers, she runs the risk of making them appear manufactured and unconvincing.
>
> *(ibid.)*

In letters, Wigman recorded this difficult beginning of the tour. During the seven New York performances shouts came from the audience, "Mary Wigman Solo!" (Müller 1986a: 214). This certainly didn't aid the confidence of the younger dancers although Wigman did claim a victory in their Chicago performance to a nearly full house (ibid.). The tour was originally planned to take the group by bus and train to Cincinnati, Louisville, Chicago, Winnipeg, Calgary, Vancouver, Seattle, San Francisco, Oakland, Los Angeles, Pasadena, San Diego, Salt Lake City, Denver, Kansas City, Tulsa, Denton, St. Louis, Indianapolis and beyond (ibid.). By the time they reached San Francisco on 15 January, Wigman had inserted solo works from other dance cycles. It appeared an act of desperation, to tear apart the fabric of *Der Weg* with substitutions, sacrificing the subtle sense of the original evening with something that would please the crowd. Martin perceived that, just as Wigman had subordinated herself to the group, she had now been forced "into a mood and style lighter and less vital than her own" (Martin 1933a: *New York Times*, 15 January, X2). Aside from Wigman's valiant attempts to fix the program, the tour had become a fiasco. There would be no South American leg. In fact Hurok declared he had had enough. Never one to back a losing proposition, he suggested that Wigman wait until 1934 or 1935 to return, when the public might be receptive to her work once again. She could no longer envision her future as a "New World" touring artist. By the time that Wigman made it back to New York for her farewell concert on 6 March, she had abandoned *Der Weg*. Instead she danced solo, primarily drawing on dances from the heroic *Opfer* (Sacrifice) cycle, along with *Allegro Arioso* from her *Spanish Suite* and *Monotonie Whirl* from the 1926 group work *Celebration* and *Summer's Dance*, the dances most loved by US audiences in her earlier tours (ibid.). It was a much lighter and more virtuosic program than *Der Weg*.

Perhaps American audiences had grown tired of the heavy expressionism that characterized *Der Weg*, perhaps they were developing a proprietary sense of aesthetic judgement raised by the increasing abilities of their homegrown dancers, or perhaps the young student dancers were just not up to the task. The xenophobia and anti-German sentiment that would come full blown with the rise of the Third Reich may have been partially responsible. When Sol Hurok wrote of that season in his 1946 memoir he put it this way: "One stocky Amazon, providing it was the miraculous Wigman herself, was all right, but a whole group of thick-waisted, thick-legged German girls in wide-skirted bathing suits was too much" (Hurok 1946: 161).

However, for her final US concert there was nothing but praise and admiration for Mary Wigman. Martin deemed her solo performance "of unusual brilliance," even judged by her own high standards (Martin 1933a: *New York Times*, 6 March, 16). The audience filled the New Yorker Theatre to overflowing and "there was in the atmosphere that tension and enthusiasm which mark special occasions" (ibid.). Martin reported the next day that no one moved when the evening was over. Instead "flowers were thrown upon the stage and cheering and applause were maintained for more than a dozen curtain calls" (ibid.). Wigman responded with an encore of her *Gypsy Moods*. But the cheering continued and only an impromptu farewell speech by Wigman satisfied the crowd before the final curtain could fall. In many ways that final curtain call signaled the end of Wigman's brightest years. Hurok recalled:

> Mary Wigman strode down Broadway one evening in 1933 ... It was late, after a performance, and the morning papers were out. That was the day of the last legal election in Germany. Wigman begged for the newspapers, and the lot of them hurried down the steps into Childs Restaurant in the Paramount Building basement to read the election returns. She was happy that night. The Hitler gang had been beaten.
>
> *(Hurok 1946: 162)*

In the elections of 6 November 1932, the National Socialists had lost thirty-five seats in the Reichstag, but this would change in less than three months.

Returning to the new Germany

By the time her boat docked in Germany, Mary Wigman's homeland was in paroxysms of change. She wrote in her daybook, "The new Germany – not simply a change of government but a Revolution – Strange!!! Where is it going?" (Wigman in Müller 1986a: 214). The Weimar government had suffered so many setbacks, creating a politic of instability that spanned economic, social and cultural life. Fear of communism galvanized support for reactionary right-wing elements, including the National Socialists. While Wigman was in the United States, a campaign was mounted to convince aging President von Hindenburg to name Hitler as Chancellor, both as an attempt at unification and to appease conservative elements. Hitler did become Chancellor on 30 January 1933, but he by no means took absolute control at that time. The Nazis promoted the myth of the *Machtergreifung* (seizure of power). However, many still felt that Hitler could be contained and his popular support co-opted. Between 1933 and 1934 he methodically pursued his policy of *Gleichschaltung* (literally, bringing or forcing into line), strengthening his grip on German politics and expanding his reach into all cultural life, particularly the lives of German artists (Fulbrook 1991: 55).

Hitler's art program was not initiated abruptly, nor did it reach its full span all at once. With the gift of hindsight it is natural to question Mary Wigman's accommodations with the new regime. The love of her homeland runs strongly throughout her writings, speeches and creative work. The rise of nationalism was endemic in the twentieth-century West. In the United States, one can point to Martha Graham's promotional material and the choreography of her own Americana as another example of the nationalist impulse. That Wigman did not use her celebrity to speak out against the Third Reich once the evil core of the regime was revealed may represent the most authentic condemnation of her choices. The question of why she chose to stay in Germany remains. Hedwig Müller underscores the fact that Wigman could never desert her homeland. She felt called to bring forth the new German dance with a profundity that equaled the art of Goethe, Schiller and Nietzsche. For her, this was her destiny, the purpose of her life. It was *Schiksal* and *Opfer* – fate and sacrifice.

Historian Hellmut Lehmann-Haupt argues that each revolutionary change favors a brief experimental cooperation of politically and artistically radical forces. Such association seems to rest largely on mutual misunderstanding or hopeful projection, one obvious reason for its brevity. In his speech to open the Reich's Chamber of Culture in April 1933, Joseph Goebbels said, "Every genuine artist is free to experiment." The Depression of the early 1930s had exacerbated an already difficult economic situation. With much work, Wigman had kept her school afloat but most artists held a common conviction that fundamental structural reform of the arts would be required. This conviction underlay the strife within the dance community. Unsatisfactory administrative infrastructure was widely blamed for the lack of professionalism among the schools of dance and for the lack of adequate financial support for the arts or for pensions for artists. Wigman was one of the lucky ones, due to the profits from her American tours. With the less than successful final tour of *Der Weg*, the American source of income appeared closed. The Third Reich came in with a strong message of economic support for the German arts and further support for those great national artists such as Wigman. Those shaping the new Germany quickly grasped the public relations power of international stars like Mary Wigman.

> **Joseph Goebbels** (1897–1945) – Adolf Hitler's Minister of Propaganda and Popular Enlightenment and director of the *Reichskulturkammer*, or Reich Chamber of Culture. He controlled the total output of the German media. He competed for cultural oversight with **Alfred** Rosenberg (1893–1946), who was appointed in 1934 to the "Custodianship of the Entire Intellectual and Spiritual Training and Education of the Party and of All Coordinated Associations." Rosenberg was director of the Office of Racial Politics.

Dancing in Dresden, 1933–1942

Dresden provided a home for Wigman's dance life over the longest period and greatest achievements of her extraordinary career. As the German dance was growing into an institution, Wigman was at the exciting and conflicted forefront of that growth. The contentiousness at the German Dancers' Congresses already reflected a systematic attempt by the Weimar government to regulate dance education even before the advent of the Third Reich. The studio schools were home to these developments, just as government regulation of art education had been going on long before the National Socialists came to power. It took nearly a year for the Saxon Ministry of Economics and the Dresden Board of Education to register Wigman's school as a legitimate vocational institution that could receive financial support and issue diplomas to professional students. And this was under the Weimar Republic. The survival of Wigman's school depended on such official recognition amid growing competition, economic depression and rising costs. Additionally, Wigman had to demonstrate that the school did not need student tuition to survive, that she had sufficient state and city support, as well as adequate income from her touring. Wigman had depended on public grants to support her dance groups, so changes in educational policies and public attitudes affected her school as well. Long merged, the studies of *Gymnastik* and artistic *Tanz* were officially separated by 1930. During the long absences for her international tours from 1930 to 1933, the city of Dresden was beset with rising unemployment and severe cuts in public welfare, school maintenance and other public services.

> ***Gymnastik*** – movement as a means for physical training, relaxation and recreation, in contrast to *Tanz*, movement used for symbolic representation or communication.

Wigman observed the regime change in 1933 when she returned from her last extended American tour. She continued her relationship with Benkert. And while he eventually became prominent in the Nazi Party, Benkert was an established businessman, not a street thug or rabid brownshirt. And Wigman was no longer a young woman. Nearing fifty, she turned to him and he offered a sort of anchor, not unlike the stability of her early upbringing. At this time of crisis in her career and her homeland she returned physically and figuratively to her own roots. No longer the rebel artist, she was now established as the face of the great German dance. Her journal offers some small evidence of her reaction to the new government. Her letters to Hanya Holm during this period reveal even less. Wigman did recognize the Third Reich as a radical change from the beleaguered Weimar Republic, but her focus remained on her German career, particularly after the disappointments of her final overseas tour. She acted decisively to secure the continuation of her primary interests, her school, her dance group, her work.

The Third Reich's mergers of social, technical and political associations put an end to many schools and to the careers of teachers not already licensed. Diplomas from unaccredited schools were not honored, ending any chance of student income. Some schools sought to strengthen their positions as the new status quo took shape. In April 1933 the Law for Restoration of the Professional Civil Service enforced dismissals for those deemed insufficiently educated, politically unreliable or "non-Aryan." The same month, the Gestapo carried out a house search at the Wigman School based on suspicions of "communist machinations." At the same time, the passage of the Law Against Congestion of German Schools excluded Jewish pupils. Wigman fell under suspicion for many reasons. She had traveled abroad frequently and for long periods, she had Jewish dancers in her professional group and Jewish pupils whom she retained in her school, despite the law. The remodeling of her school in 1927 was partly funded by foreign capital and lists of communist party "agitators" included dancers certified by her school. Wigman was taken aback at the intrusion by the authorities. Hedwig Müller points out that in the end it was the detrimental effect of governmental interference upon her work that most outraged Wigman.

In July 1933, following the merger with the Palucca School and the Trümpy School, the *Wigman Schule Gruppe* joined the National Socialist Teachers Federation and opened new branches in Chemnitz, Erfurt, Hamburg, Hanover and Stuttgart. The government prescribed a new dance curriculum as Joseph Goebbels took over leadership of the *Reichskulturkammer*. Wigman appeared as guest lecturer at the *Deutsche Tanzbühne*. But already her motives were under government scrutiny. An anonymous document from the *Bundesarchiv*, dated 16 December 1934, states,

---

Reichskulturkammer – Reich's Chamber of Culture, established in 1933 promptly after Hitler became chancellor, under Joseph Goebbels, the minister of culture and popular enlightenment.

> ... Can one consider a woman truly German, who only two years ago changed her name by deed poll from the good German Marie Wiegmann into the English form Mary Wigman? Besides it is very well known that the teaching personnel ... in the Wigman School in Dresden and in Chemnitz is made up exclusively of communist-Bolsheviks and that the Jews play the main role in the school ...
>
> *(Karina and Kant 2004: 216)*

What does such a letter mean? As an anonymous document, it is difficult to ascertain its direct impact but it does reflect the backbiting and infighting that were encouraged under the *Reichskulturkammer*. It also points to an atmosphere of growing fear and mistrust.

The same day that the accusing letter was filed, 16 December 1934, saw the closing of the German Dance Festival in Berlin. In their analysis of this Festival, David Buch and Hana Worthen point to "the discrepancy between the values embodied in National Socialist discourse and the values represented on the stage" (Buch and Worthen 2007: 216). The parameters of the "new German dance" also appear to have been fluid. Mary Wigman presented her *Frauentanzen* (Women's Dances) both as a new group work and as an excerpted solo within the four-day span of the festival. The sections in the dance suite were all themes that Wigman had addressed in earlier works. Susan Manning analyzes the *Women's Dances* as choreographic proof of Wigman's accommodations with National Socialist ideals. The dance was still essentially Expressionist. Program notes describe the dance as evoking "all five life-spheres of women's experience" and symbolizing her powers: girlish mirth (Wedding Dance), motherhood (Maternal Dance – a solo for Wigman), female capacity for suffering and grief (Lament for the Dead – a familiar theme), prophecy (Dance of the Prophetess) and the final section was a group *Hexentanz* (Witch Dance), subtitled "the abyss." Extant photos show a very animated and smiling group of young women and Wigman with arms akimbo as if throwing a spell outward and delighting in their "witchiness" (ibid.: 236)!

Meanwhile, in the United States Hanya Holm represented the Wigman School as one of the "Big Four" leaders of modern dance – along with Graham, Humphrey and Weidman – when the Bennington College program began in 1934. In parallel, as Roosevelt's economic recovery program established the Federal Theatre Project in the United States, dance in Germany came under the regulation of the Department of Stage in the Reich Theater Chamber. A German dancers' constitution was drafted, including examinations and course guidelines. The 1935 Nuremberg Laws deprived the Jewish population and their spouses of citizenship rights and Wigman's longtime costume designer Elis Griebel was forced to emigrate in response. Wigman remained committed to her representation of the German dance and her first book, *Deutsche Tanzkunst* (1935), shows her determination to support the dance art of her homeland. The distance between Mary Wigman and her international peers had widened into an impassable chasm. Martha Graham declined an invitation to the International Dance Competition in July of 1936, implying that the Jewish members of her company would not be welcome in Germany. Responding to anti-German sentiment, Hanya Holm changed the name of the New York Wigman School to the Hanya Holm School, with Wigman's blessing, in 1936. As alliances formed among nations, they were also played out on a smaller scale among the dance dynasties.

Opening-night ceremonies of the 1936 Olympic Games in Berlin featured a pageant, *Olympic Youth*, produced by Hanns Niedecken-Gebhard. Along with Gret Palucca and Harald Kreutzberg, Mary Wigman danced in the newly constructed Olympic Stadium. Her *Lament for the Dead*, with music composed by Carl Orff, was choreographed and performed by Wigman supported by eighty female dancers (Partsch-Bergsohn 1994: 92). Rudolf von Laban was to contribute a spectacle with a thousand dancers to the Olympic event, but when Joseph Goebbels saw the rehearsal, he was appalled and wrote in his diary:

> Rehearsal of dance work: freely based on Nietzsche, a bad, contrived and affected piece. I forbid a great deal. It is so intellectual. I do not like it. That is because it is dressed up in our clothes and has nothing whatever to do with us.
>
> (Preston-Dunlop 1998: 196)

Carl Orff (1895–1982) – German composer and pedagogue and co-founder of the Guenther School for gymnastics, music and dance in Munich. In 1955, Wigman staged and choreographed productions of Orff's *Carmina Burana* and *Catulli Carmina* for the National Theatre Mannheim.

As the political reins tightened on the artists who had stayed in Germany, many began to realize their perilous state. At the Olympics, Wigman was presented for the last time as Germany's greatest dancer. Her diaries reveal her caught up in the task of that monumental ceremony dedicated to power, prestige and dominance. But soon she came to see that her name was used for a purpose far removed from highlighting the dance art. Within a year her new branch schools were eliminated and the *Wigman Schule Gruppe* was deleted from the National School Registry. She received no further subsidies. Meanwhile her accompanists Hanns Hasting and his wife Gretl Curth expanded their own range of influence within the Nazi Party, benefiting from Wigman's decline even as they remained in her Dresden school.

Wigman had proven too intellectual, too deep and too independent. Ultimately, Goebbels and other Party officials did not welcome her or her *Ausdruckstanz*. Under the National Socialists, dance had to be functional and deemed healthy, meaning angst-free, strong, goal-oriented, happy, *Volkish* and, most importantly, anti-intellectual. Wigman's dances were far from these things. Just as Hitler turned from his devotion to Wagner toward *The Merry Widow* operetta, artistic dance was to become entertainment providing diversion and depicting a particular version of popular history. Art criticism was banned, as was any art outside the Party line. Expressionism, essentially individualistic, unsettling and emotive, was dangerous. And Wigman was seen as a dangerous woman.

It was her artistic autonomy that caused her to hesitate when asked to contribute a dance in honor of Hitler, leading to the break between Wigman and the Party in May 1937. Her performance was to be part of the ceremonies inaugurating Munich's House of German Art, for which Hitler had laid the cornerstone in 1933. As a note, it is telling that the first official construction undertaken by the Nazis was this building dedicated to housing artworks. What became starkly clear by 1937 was that only a particular kind of artwork would be housed there. Albert Talhoff was in charge of the production and he first contacted Wigman. She wrote in her diary:

> The play!? [It is] Talhoff's invention even though there is obviously outside backing. [It is] *Totenmal* over and over again. Also the swinging flags are not absent. What makes me pensive and shaken and dismayed in my deepest being is the fact that the "artistic" [or dance] part of the play is only concerned with the years following the First World War. The new time under the Third Reich should appear symbolically calm …
>
> *(Wigman in Müller 1986a: 244–245)*

Hanns Hasting went as her representative to the initial planning meeting for the event. In her writing Wigman appears hard pressed between her ideals and official demands. Both Benkert and Hasting advised that she could not decline the invitation. She wrote that she had known this immediately with Talhoff's phone call. She likened the demands of this project to "Barbarism – indeed … a decline like that of Greek tragedy, a decline that brought the Roman pantomime. We experience the same decline." Her diary entries reveal a terrible reckoning with the state of affairs:

> My desperation lies in recognizing the bitter facts. For basic things like my dance group, my school my dances, there is no real support. While for the big show everything is procured immediately … Victory of collectivism over the individual! … No living person can avoid it. One is involved in the big fabric. To try to tear it would bring self-destruction.
>
> *(ibid.)*

Hedwig Müller concludes that Wigman did take note of the rising terrorism in daily life. But she did not elaborate in her diaries about the fear and the growing mistrust. Her focus remained on her work: the words "work" and "dance" and the events of her professional life dominate her diary entries and her correspondence. Reading them, one comes to realize that her dance life was her true existence. Every joy or trauma is chronicled primarily in relationship to her art. Müller also concludes that Wigman had become careful. And indeed it was true that one did not know how concealed private life was. Müller writes that Hesschen guarded Wigman's privacy in the home. But ultimately she was a public person by nature of her work. Wigman did attend a planning meeting in Munich on 6 May 1937. Upon her return to Dresden she wrote:

> Confused, broken, hit, smash.... What insanity, I still do not know what approaches me. I have to go into this hell ... as the only woman among the men! Every objection, every doubt is pushed aside as tiresome and questionable.
> *(Wigman in Müller 1986a: 245)*

In the end, Wigman stalled so long that the offer to choreograph for the museum dedication was officially withdrawn. The program went on without her. The day following Hitler's inauguration of the House of German Art, a very different exposition was opened across the street. Nazi exhibitions of *Entartete Kunst* or Degenerate Art made outcasts of the great modern German visual artists, including Wigman's old acquaintances from *Die Brücke*. Even long-time Party member Emile Nolde was ostracized as a degenerate artist in the 1937 cultural purge. Meanwhile, Wigman remained in Dresden, writing.

> Remain quiet – do not allow the nervous shivering to arise. Do not complain ... nobody can take your rich life from you. Your creations may pass, you may be fast forgotten but maybe you have planted a few seeds and maybe the earth was fertile at some places.
> *(Wigman in Müller 1986a: 250)*

Leaving Dresden

The once-fertile dancing ground of Dresden was becoming uninhabitable for Wigman. The city had maintained its reputation as a center for arts and culture during the first years of Nazi dictatorship, but all arts activities were increasingly governed from Berlin. Many cultural institutions began moving from the city of Dresden and Wigman also applied for such a move, to Berlin where Hanns Benkert was residing. In 1937, her application for relocation to Berlin was officially "unapproved" (Karina and Kant 2004: 272–273). There were more than 17,000 trials against Germans who opposed the regime in that year. Mary Wigman choreographed her *Autumnal Dances* in what appeared to be the fading light of her own greatness. Letters from officials reflect an effort to humble Wigman and to bring her into line with Party policy. She had lost her status. Yet she was remembered by some as a national treasure. Her diaries of 1938 reveal that she felt the opportunity for considering immigration had passed. "To go abroad? To the U.S.A.? It is not possible anymore" (Wigman in Müller 1986a: 250). During that same year Martha Graham choreographed *American Document*, placing patriotism and optimism at the center of her work. While the American moderns were developing their own art, much in debt to Wigman and the German innovators, *Ausdruckstanz* was in decline.

On 9 and 10 November 1938, sanctioned violence against Germany's Jewish population was laid bare during the *Krystallnacht*, or the Night of Broken Glass. Jewish synagogues and property were brutally destroyed as officials relentlessly pursued a policy of Aryanization. By 1941, a police regulation required that all Jewish Germans wear the Star of David. The government placed a general ban on dance dramas and anything that did not comply with ballet traditions and National Socialist values. A specific ban of free dance or German expressive dance in public places applied to Wigman's work. But she did continue to perform in venues such as the Theatre Horst-Wesselplatz in Berlin. By 31 March 1940 she was presented in second billing to the students of dance theater there. She had become a political liability to Benkert after more than ten years as business and romantic partner. Traveling to Berlin in 1941 to teach a series of workshops, Wigman arrived at Benkert's house, suitcase in hand. Only then did she learn from Benkert's housekeeper that he had married a woman who was not only younger but who also had Party affiliations more advantageous to his own career.

Loss followed loss, yet Wigman revealed none of them in her extant letters to Hanya Holm in the United States. Only through her poems, letters, diary and her dances can we glimpse the depth of her bereavement, not only for the betrayal by Benkert but also mourning for her own willful allegiances to her nation and to her art. In 1942, the Wigman School, her home for decades, was sold to the city of Dresden. The Dance Academy that had been established within Wigman's school by Gretl Curth-Hasting, Gisela Sonntag and Hanns Hasting was subsumed into the municipal conservatory that ultimately absorbed the Wigman School. Another betrayal, this time by those with whom she had worked for years, added new bitterness to her losses:

> As of today, this, my school, no longer exists. For 22 years, love, effort, care, also joy, beginning, center, expansion, good times, and bad times.
>
> Now it is not only the name on the house that is disappearing; it is also the spirit that is departing.
>
> *(Diary entry: 2 April 1942)*

Mary Wigman presented her final solo concert in 1942, essentially ending her performing career at age fifty-five. By September of 1942, the offensive at Stalingrad was under way and it proved the turning point of the war. In January the Wannsee Conference had secretly laid plans for the "final solution," the systematic extermination of European Jewry. The Reich Propaganda Office further decreed the prohibition of abstract dance and symphonic music.

After 1942, government orders restrained Wigman from performing, but she was not left immobile. She was granted a position as guest teacher in Leipzig through her old friend Hanns Niedecken-Gebhard, who had supported her work as early as 1921 when he produced her *The Seven Dances of Life*. It appears that Goebbels did not want Wigman to hold a full-time position, but Niedecken-Gebhard could make accommodations on her behalf. As a well-positioned Nazi and head of the Department of Dramatic Art at the Music Academy in Leipzig, he was able to help Wigman work under tenuous circumstances, although she was never granted a full-time position there. Under a commission from Niedecken-Gebhard, Wigman worked with composer Carl Orff to stage *Carmina Burana* for a July 1943 performance at the Leipzig Opera House. In February 1944, Allied bombers destroyed the dance building at the Leipzig Music Academy, but Wigman continued to teach a handful of students in her apartment. Her diary reveals that she threw herself intensely into teaching until the declaration of total war in August 1944. At the end of the war, Wigman was left "physically and mentally isolated and exhausted, living under very deprived conditions in the East . . . " (Partsch-Bergsohn 1994: 116). A severe food shortage left Wigman suffering from malnutrition. Annie Hess had managed to keep some food on the table and, with care packages from Wigman's American students and friends, students continued to find refuge at her home. Wigman again opened a school in 1945 but, nearing sixty and in weakened physical condition, her hopes for survival lay in a new start in West Berlin.

To Berlin

In 1942, Wigman began a working relationship and friendship with composer Kurt Schwaen. Schwaen had been imprisoned from 1935 to 1938 as an enemy of the Nazi government, due to his membership in the German Communist Party. Released from prison between 1938 and 1942, he was conscripted in 1943 into the 999th Afrika Brigade, a unit made up of former political prisoners. Letters show that Wigman tried to counsel Schwaen in his unsuccessful efforts to avoid being drafted. Correspondence between Wigman and Schwaen shows her concern for his well-being, as well as her own unsettled position. On 5 November 1943, Wigman wrote to him:

> The heart lies heavy with all that has taken place. Now many men whom I knew personally are suffering at Stalingrad. Also the new regulations lie like a heavy weight around my sphere of activity. Still, nobody knows what shape the occupation [by the Allies] eventually will take.
>
> *(Schwaen 2006: 14)*

These letters starkly show how the focus of her attention, including how she perceived those in her life, revolved around her work and the belief that the work was larger than the chaotic times or the individuals involved. Schwaen was again losing his artistic life under the Nazis and despaired in his diary. He wrote that Wigman could in no way understand what such a conscription meant to him. But later he wrote that he had been wrong about her. Wigman took on Schwaen's wife as her accompanist, thus helping to support her while her husband was conscripted. And Wigman maintained her friendship with the Schwaens for many years.

Wigman continued to live and work in Leipzig under Russian occupation from 1945 to 1946. She directed the staging of Gluck's *Orpheus and Eurydice* at the Leipzig Opera in March 1947, using dancers from the opera house along with her student ensemble. She wrote: "On the surface, one goes on working as if everything was the same. Yesterday's technical rehearsal for *Orpheus* has shown me that the work – in spite of the defective material – could be good" (ibid.). In January 1946 Wigman wrote to Schwaen of the bitter cold in Leipzig.

> I myself work in silence and must do this to be able to exist. I could have it differently if I could join in what one calls Agit-Prop under the KPD [the German Communist Party]. But I want no dependence that obliges or compromises me or lowers the level of my art. I'd rather fight for the penny than stoop to becoming a promotional symbol. I am still curious about the possibility of going to Berlin. Economically, things may prosper here again but culturally it seems dubious to me. Pity!
>
> *(Schwaen 2006: 19)*

Later, in June 1949, Schwaen and his wife helped Wigman gain an invitation to relocate to the Wilmersdorf district of West Berlin. The magistrate of Wilmersdorf offered to support her school for one year, after which she was expected to take over financial responsibility. And international students were again coming to her, many from the United States. American dancer Bill Costanza recalls her all-encompassing grace and ability to communicate in many languages with the students who filled her summer courses. Other German colleagues who had lived through the war were aware of her early work and major contributions to the art form. But the students who populated her Berlin school were of a different generation. Growing up amid the chaos of war and coming of age in a defeated and divided Germany, shamed by the revelations of the Nuremburg trials, these young people felt a calling to their art very different from the calling Wigman had felt. While German dance was utterly disrupted by war, American modern dance had thrived. Merce Cunningham's visit to Germany in 1960 was greeted with enthusiasm, his work hailed as the dance of the present.

> **Merce Cunningham** (1919–2009) – dominant force in Modern dance starting in the 1960s. Graham company member from 1939 to 1945. Founded his own company in 1953. His fruitful collaboration with composer John Cage endured for fifty years.

And Mary Wigman was no longer performing. Brigitta Herrmann began her study with Wigman at the Berlin school in 1957 and continued a long association with Wigman until she emigrated to Philadelphia in 1968. Herrmann said that when one was in the room with Wigman, she always left with the impression of a great artist. After Herrmann's early training in Russian ballet technique, which was the mainstay of the Palucca School, the possibilities of expressive dance at the Wigman School were a revelation. However, Wigman in her seventies could not be an active role model for the young dancers of the new Germany. Many of these students would not come to recognize the strength of her fundamental dance philosophy until later, if at all. And for others of the new generation, her poetic, emotive imagery seemed outdated. Just as the American postmodern dancers had turned away from the psychodrama of Martha Graham, young German dancers were looking for something new to inspire them. Dancer Helmut Gottschild said: "We were the first generation to come to consciousness after the war. The first generation to ask our parents how it could have happened. And suddenly we were confronted with Mary Wigman's pathos . . . " (Gottschild in Manning 1993: 227).

In many ways Wigman had become an outsider within the German nation to which she had dedicated her life and her art. She did continue to stage dance works during her final decades in Berlin. Working closely once again with an accompanist, Ulrich Kessler, she danced with her students in *Choric Studies II* in January 1953. Susan Manning interprets *Choric Studies II* as Wigman's coming to terms with her accommodation to National Socialism (ibid.: 235). Indeed, the intention of *Ausdruckstanz* was an ongoing mining of the depths of individual experience. In this, all her dances were autobiographical in the deepest sense. And the central role of the Prophetess was a natural one for Wigman. But in her diary, she describes her performance of the work as a sort of coming home, a returning to the stage and the transcendent moment when dance and life reach heightened vitality. Dore Hoyer, considered the most talented soloist of her generation, was to have danced the role initially but, when she cancelled, Wigman chose to step into the part. At the Berlin Wigman School it was Hoyer, not Wigman, who became the dancing model for students such as Brigitta Herrmann who were still drawn to the profound nature of *Ausdruckstanz*. And Hoyer was the soloist for Mary Wigman's last great choreographic effort on the concert stage, *The Rite of Spring* (1957). Once again, *Schicksal und Opfer* – Fate and Sacrifice – became the themes of Wigman's choreography as they had anchored the guiding philosophy of her life.

In the end, Mary Wigman allied herself with a music-driven theater that appeared far from the territory of her Absolute Dance. Still, she was able to use her talent to awaken dynamic space on the stage. Between 1954 and 1958 she set Handel's *Saul*, restaged Carl Orff's *Catulli Carmina/Carmina Burana* and Gluck's *Alkestis* for the National Theater in Mannheim. In 1958, she also made one last journey to the United States and met with Martha Graham and Ruth St. Denis, and it appears that the years of competition fell away in their meetings. In 1969, at age eighty-three, she visited Israel with life-long friend Herbert Binswanger, although most of her travel later in life was to Switzerland and the countryside that she had known and loved for so many years. Even though she became nearly blind, she could feel the landscape of those familiar mountains. In 1961, Wigman directed her final work. With Gustav Sellner, she choreographed Gluck's *Orpheus and Eurydice* in Berlin. Through this production her stage life came full circle. Nearly a half of a century had passed since those early, heady days of discovery at Hellerau, where her performing life began with the early study of *Orpheus* by Dalcroze and Adolph Appia. There seems no better myth than Orpheus with which to memorialize Wigman's life and career. The descent and return of Orpheus from Hades represented an ideology of metamorphosis and a metaphor for redemption. Wigman's dance became her own road to emancipation. Steeped in mysticism, Wigman's dance offered a sort of deliverance through ritualized practice and an aesthetic doctrine. As early as 1921, in *The Seven Dances of Life*, it is only through the dance that the character passes through death and attains liberation. The wedding of physical body and inner spirit defined Wigman's work to the end of her life. Mary Wigman continued to teach from 1961 to 1967, when she finally closed her studio. Suffering from failing eyesight and a weak heart, she died in Berlin during the fall of 1973. In April 1973 she wrote to Binswanger:

> Everywhere people are again surrounded by snow despite the fact that snowdrops and crocuses started to flower here too. I only know this from hearsay; for I am living in Hades, in the realm of the shadows, and there everything is in motion . . . it is rather like sinking and being lifted, swaying and tottering . . . I want to resign myself to it. I want to do what I can.
>
> *(Wigman 1973: 200)*

Even close to her death, her description remains rooted in her physical experience. She had made numerous dances in which she grappled with death. Even as she moved toward the end of her life she met her decline with a dancer's sensibility. When she was asked to write her biography in her final years, Wigman responded with a treatise on the dance art itself. She continued to make a case for dance as a profound art form. She broke open structures of movement invention and female objectification, only to be accused of performing madness on the concert stage. In the end she wrote:

> People like my dancing or they think it most terrible . . . It is hard for an artist to tell why her dance method is a success. I have tried to combine emotion with intellect. Some call my art tragic, far removed from sweetness and prettiness. I have tried only to interpret modern man and his fate.
>
> *(Wigman 1973: 149)*

5.2 Mary Wigman as choreographer: choosing the focus

It is a daunting task to choose which works of Mary Wigman best represent her aesthetic practice and philosophy. In order to do this we must consider a career that stretched from her first solo choreography in 1914 to her final production of Stravinsky's *Rite of Spring* in 1957. Over this span of forty-three years, Mary Wigman made more than 170 solo dances and nearly 80 group works. From intimate experience, she knew well that, "in ninety-nine out of a hundred cases the choreographer is author and director in one person" (Wigman 1966: 22). In *The Language of Dance*, she reflects on the inspiration, motivation and "back stories" that gave birth to fifteen of her dances, from the 1927 solo *Ceremonial Figure* to her *Farewell and Thanksgiving* (1942). And in the final chapters, Wigman reminisces about making *Totenmal*, which sparks thoughts on the group dance and the choric dance.

In most of her early works she was also the performer, both visualizing and crafting the work and serving as the vehicle for its realization. In this she was among the pioneering dance soloists who were also the creator-performers of their very individual works. Loie Fuller, Isadora Duncan, Ruth St. Denis, Martha Graham and Doris Humphrey all stand as examples of that unique era of the great choreographer-soloist. Certainly, such soloists came to make group works. As individual techniques developed and were codified, the idiosyncratic expression and charismatic stage persona of the soloist gave way to the unity and uniformity demanded by larger works.

Mary Wigman saw three distinct dance forms as representative of what she termed the "three great complexes of expression and form" of effective dance (Wigman 1966: 22). Of the three forms that she identified – the solo dance, the group dance and the choric dance – Wigman worked primarily in the realm of the solo and the group dance. The choric dance appears as an exceptional manifestation of the 1930s, not unique to Germany. The mid-1930s in the United States also saw experiments in choric or mass dance, carried westward by students who had studied the form in Europe and saw it as appropriate to American populist dance movements. Although Wigman's experience in the true choric form remained limited to her collaboration in the production of *Totenmal* in 1930, she was highly aware of the implications and demands of choric dance. It seems most useful to our inquiry to consider these distinct choreographic forms in choosing works that give a sense of the breadth of her practice. Thus, we will focus on the 1926 solo *Hexentanz*, the small group work *The Seven Dances of Life*, a brief consideration of the specific demands of the choric form as revealed by *Totenmal*, and a glimpse of two solos from her farewell concert in 1942.

Solo as signature: Hexentanz

For each choreographer, one work can be seen as bearing a unique signature through time. This work should be done when the artist's technical and artistic identity has fully matured. It may not necessarily be the final work. In fact, most likely the choreographer will move onward to further develop artistic ideas and values and impart them to others. The "signature work" that I propose is one that comes from an embracing of self, the realization that one's singular human experience can be expressed in a dance that is thoughtfully and meticulously crafted because the ideas and beliefs embedded in the work have been waiting many years to take on a definitive form. Of course this also calls for a maturity that comes with experience and the self-confidence that comes with the acquisition of a set of skills that define a craft.

Hexentanz was such a dance for Wigman. Made in 1914, the original *Hexentanz* was the first dance she created while a student of Rudolf von Laban. What she described as her deepest "stirrings" were realized in dance form, opening the floodgates of artistic expression and pointing a clear direction toward what to do with her life. The social expectations of marriage and identity of *Hausfrau* were banished as she saw her role as dancer solidify. Later, she reminisced about her joy in the creation of the work, giving insight into its place in her development and her long relationship with the dance:

> After Laban had fully approved of the sketch for my first *Hexentanz* I was so overcome with joy that I jumped all over the studio, sprained my ankle, and could not move for a whole unhappy fortnight. But the witch dance was brought to life and continued to

be very much alive. It became part of my first solo program. It had to undergo many changes and pass through many different stages of development until, twelve years later, it received its definite artistic form.

(Wigman 1973: 36)

By the time she made the second version of the *Hexentanz* in 1926, Wigman had been operating her own school, had toured as a solo artist and established her own dance company. Through her teaching, she solidified her approach to dance technique while gaining confidence in her artistic identity through successful performances. This is when *Hexentanz* achieved its final form:

> I believe that *Witch Dance* was the only one among my solo dances which did not make me shake with stage fright before every performance. How I loved it, this growing into the excitement of its expressive world, how intensely I tried in each performance to feel myself back into the original creative condition of *Witch Dance* and to fulfill its stirring form by returning to the very point where it all began!
>
> (Wigman 1966: 42)

The 1926 version of the *Witch Dance* was conceived as the fourth part of a dance cycle she had begun in 1925 with three solos preceding it: *Ceremonial Figure, Veiled Figure* and *Ghost Figure*. Also in 1925, Wigman wrote her article on dance composition. Therein she identified what she called elemental dances as a distinct kind of emotional dance composition. Wigman defined these elemental dances as being the medium and symbol of those forces born of the soil. In her description of beginning the *Hexentanz*, she recalled being drawn again and again back down to "some kind of evil greed I felt in my hands which pressed themselves clawlike into the ground as if they had wanted to take root" (ibid.: 41). In *Ceremonial Figure*, she had begun to incorporate the mask into her performances, thus reintroducing the mask to the modern dance as a tool for metamorphosis. Long recognized as a means of transformation in ritual dance and ancient theater, Wigman reclaimed its sacramental and theatrical roots for the concert stage.

In her role as creator and performer of the *Hexentanz*, Wigman was able to fulfill her desire for metamorphosis through performance. By dancing the *Hexentanz*, she could realize her search for the *Dasein* and *erleben:* the full coming into being or existence that she felt was the heart of the new dance. But she also recognized that "the power, the magnificence of all creative art lie in knowing how to force chaos into form." Yet, she worked well aware that "the original creative urge was neither weakened nor blocked in the process of molding and shaping." In *The Language of Dance*, Wigman recalls the origins of her dance theme:

> Sometimes at night I slipped into the studio and worked myself up into a rhythmic intoxication in order to come closer to the slowly stirring character ... When one night, I returned to my room utterly agitated, I looked into the mirror by chance. What it reflected was the image of one possessed, wild and dissolute, repelling and fascinating. The hair unkempt, the eyes deep in their sockets, the nightgown shifted about, which made the body almost shapeless: there she was – the witch.
>
> (Wigman 1966: 40–41)

The character of the witch allowed the exposure of a part of her personality that she had "never allowed to emerge in such nakedness" (ibid.). She had also mastered the craft of choreographing and thus solidifying such an ephemeral experience, giving definitive form to the physicality and therefore the persona of the Witch. With the addition of the mask she heightened her own experience in performance. Her 1914 Romantic Symbolist representation of a fairy-tale Witch was gone. In its place was a vehicle for genuine change. The desire for an altered state of consciousness in performance was manifested concretely, not theoretically, with the addition of the mask. She wrote of her suffocation within the mask. It sat tightly upon her face, limiting her ability to breathe. The mask also created sensory deprivation by limiting her vision through two narrow eye slits. Orientation in space and balance were both challenged in an extreme way. Through these physical constrictions a new world of possibility for the concert dance was born. In 1933, Rudolph Bach published the definitive reckoning of Wigman's work up to that point. His *Mary Wigman – Werk* placed the *Hexentanz* in the context of her repertory at the height of her career:

> The *Hexentanz* from 1926 can most likely be considered Mary Wigman's most famous work. It truly expresses the summit of her art. Idea, construction of form and interpretation all come together in the *Hexentanz*. It is difficult to decide which dance best exemplifies her art when she has made a steady stream of strong, creative work. Yet the *Hexentanz* emerges as the dance that characterizes the essential elements of her technique.
> *(Bach 1933: 27)*

It is heartening to know that even Mary Wigman's close contemporary Bach was challenged when trying to find a work among the many that defined Wigman's artistic vision. His choice of the *Hexentanz* as such reinforces use of the dance to investigate her practice.

The mask as doorway

Wigman's writings offer a glimpse of what she was looking for when deciding to add the mask to the dance:

> Why should a dancer use a mask? Always when his creative urge causes a split process in him, when his imagination reveals the image of an apparently alien figure which ... compels the dancer to a certain kind of metamorphosis. The mask never can and never ought to be an interesting addition or decoration. It must be an essential part of the dance figure, born in a world of visions and transported as if by magic into reality. The mask extinguishes the human being as a person and makes him submit to the fictive figure of the dance.
> *(Wigman 1973: 124)*

The mask has long been recognized as a tool for transformation, initiating entry into the sacred realm. These ideas of masking, while varied, carry across cultures and geographical location. Dutch theologian Gerardus van der Leeuw tied contemporary use of the mask to older ritual, using words that echo Wigman's dance experience:

> The mask belongs to the *sacer ludus* as the great means of stylization. Through it, all events are reduced to a single event, which is at the same time, divine. The mask removes human differentiation from the realm of the accidental and raises it to the divine, eternal and meaningful world of ritual. Through the mask, human action receives a new dimension. It opens a world in which anarchy and possession lie in wait. Whoever puts on a mask is no longer absolutely certain of himself. It might happen that he asks himself which is his true countenance, the mask or his own face.
> *(van der Leeuw 1963: 84)*

Later in life, Wigman explained to a group of students that she chose to wear the mask in the second version of *Hexentanz* to "overcome the individual sphere in order to connect to the archetype" (Partsch-Bergsohn 1994: 114). She used the mask for transformation from modern dancer to elemental figure. In this case she became the Witch, embodying what she had described as "stirrings" deep within from her Celtic ancestors.

Following her recognition of these early "stirrings," Wigman had joined in Laban's ritualistic experiments at Monte Verità. She had seen Nolde's studies of masks and ritual objects. Following her first version of *Hexentanz* in 1914, she had experienced the Dada performance practice of using mask and costume to transform the body. For her new version of *Hexentanz*, she added a mask made by Viktor Magito, who was studying the masks of Japanese Noh Theater. Wigman herself describes the decision to use a mask: "And there was still left the first and never used mask of the *Ceremonial Figure*, whose features were my own translated into the demonic." She wrote, "I suddenly knew that fabric [of the costume] and mask ... might give the *Witch Dance* its very own stage image" (Wigman 1966: 41).

At this point, Wigman's many influences came together. Because the 1926 solo contains so many of these artistic elements, *Hexentanz* is like a powerful time capsule. *Hexentanz* also shows today's dancer another way of perceiving the world that holds potential for art making in the future. Wigman's addition of the mask clearly undermined the traditional spectator's position. It can be said to reflect the emergence of the *Neue Sachlichkeit* or new objectivity – the dispassioned arts movement that sprung from the general disillusion following the defeats and horrors of the First World War. By adding the mask, Wigman gave the modern dancer a greater degree of control over the performance experience. The masked Wigman chose to objectify herself as the archetype of the witch and, most importantly, become a vessel for transformation. Within the mask she was able to reveal a face and facets of her personality that were not acceptable in the everyday world.

Only a scant fifty seconds of the 1926 version of *Hexentanz* have been preserved on film. Wigman is first seen as a solo, seated figure. Dressed in a costume made of "fantastic," brocaded, metallic fabric, she has arms, back and feet bare. She wears the face mask, which doesn't hide all of her cheeks, nor does it cover her hair. The eyes appear to be downcast. The overall effect of Magito's mask is almost that of a death mask on a body that is very much alive. The costume and mask help to create an aura of otherworldliness in the dancer.

Writers often consider earlier works through contemporary lenses. The dance works of the early moderns have been used as examples of the rising feminist spirit. These modern forebears are easily carried into these analogies because of their gender and the revolutionary times in which they lived. Wigman referenced the female identity when she described the discovery of the character of the witch in *Hexentanz*, asking, "... isn't a bit of a witch hidden in every hundred-percent female, no matter which form its origin may have?" (Wigman 1966: 41). For Wigman, becoming the Witch was a uniquely personal experience, one that placed her in a position of power as a performer, beyond gender, within the realm of shaman and artist.

Hexentanz: *a description*

As the space fills with a hard, white light, Wigman is first seen as a solo, seated figure surrounded by darkness. She sits on the floor directly facing the audience with her feet planted in front of her and knees upright under the fabric of the costume. Her hands cover the masked face as her fingers stretch wide. They grasp the space before the face, pulling apart as if opening an invisible curtain. The tension in the arms and hands is so great as to cause the hands to vibrate as if pressing an invisible wall that separates dancer from audience. From this slow, tensed opening gesture, movement explodes. It begins with a sharp rapping motion of the left hand, as if the dancer were knocking on the door of a forbidden passageway, again, the space between dancer and spectator. The percussive movement of the arms and hands corresponds to the percussive sound of the score. Indeed it is the movement that initiates the sound. Because the movement slightly anticipates each percussive note, it appears to generate the very sound itself.

From this opening percussive movement, tension is released, the hands soften, circling and gathering force in front of the masked face. This conjuring movement is resolved as she places her hands on upright knees. A slow circling of the upper body begins, with each circle resolving in a drawing inward of the body and a sharp look forward, as if a spell is being cast out toward the audience.

The second circling concludes with a downward focus to the center of the dancer. The hands begin to pry the legs open by pressing outward from the inner knees. Here is a source of the Witch's power. The internal focus of Wigman and the slow tempo create a sense of effort and deliberation. Once the knees are opened, she begins a forward, keening ripple that initiates from the center of the abdomen. Circling the upper body over the grounded and opened thighs, each revolution resolves in a sharp thrust of the body, arms and facial focus outward to the right diagonal. There is a sense of increasing urgency as the tempo increases and another sound, the crash of a cymbal, is added to the score.

Then, silence. The right hand slowly, softly circles toward the face and opens out with a reach to the right. The hand returns to the face again, this time nearly caressing the lips and then unfolding, as if performing a benediction or bestowing absolution. For Wigman this gesture carried the hermetic authority of the Sphinx that she referred to, adding the caution to "Keep the secret." The moment of quiet dissolves into mounting tension. The clawed hands reach up together and the focus follows, looking upward as if gathering divine power. Abruptly, the moment is broken as the arms gather toward each other, cross and grasp the knees. Wigman's mastery of time and tension are fully revealed in this moment. The heavy, pregnant tension of the upward reach is ruptured by the lightning movement of the hands and arms. Upward to downward, outward to inward, the dichotomy and contrast of movement qualities is shocking. The silence is broken with a loud crash of cymbals as the hands clasp the knees and the focus shoots directly toward the audience.

The seated figure then begins her assault. Gaining momentum in movement and sound, she shifts from hip to hip, rocking as the hands sequentially reach from knee to knee. The tempo continues to increase as the dancer takes this rocking into a forward locomotion. She strikes out directly toward the audience, reaching with each leg until, grasping both ankles, she pounds her feet on the floor in front of her. With a loud crash, everything stops for a moment. From this brief stillness, the dancer begins to revolve, still seated, while her feet beat out a tattoo as if the floor was the head of a drum. After one eight-count revolution, the pace increases to double time; the feet become a blur and then she suddenly stops with the right leg extended. The final movement that was captured on film is a look over the extended right foot of the dancer that becomes a slow, sweeping gaze.

In *Hexentanz*, the use of sharp, percussive sound punctuates the aggressive movement. The solo figure seems to generate the sound, controlling the environment and all of those within it. Even in the silence filled with a single, slowly fluid gesture, the tension is palpable. The silence is resolved with a percussive slap of sound and movement. From the opening position through the final look toward the audience, Wigman creates a tension that never diminishes in intensity. Even the moments of softening gesture radiate the figure's absolute control over the time and the space. The vocabulary of movement that Wigman created for the dance is unfamiliar and yet specific to the emotions evoked. Power, tension and control are present in each gesture and shape. The construction of this opening of the dance is simple. The dancer never leaves the floor in the first minute of the work. Instead of detracting from the effect, the simplicity adds to the power of the statement. The dancer remains in control of the movement, not carried away by it.

The figure is neither malevolent nor benevolent; it is omnipotent. Throughout *Hexentanz*, sound, movement, mask and costume are unified in intent. The dance presents a mythical creature who has power over those watching. The audience can no longer feel safe. She becomes the Witch and spectators are in danger of becoming bewitched by her. She is a timeless force, embodying pure power. The dance is one of a fully mature woman who recognizes the strength of her sensuality.

In the *Witch Dance*, Wigman was able to synthesize the previous dozen years of her life as a dance artist, including ideas concerning the use or non-use of music in dance that grew from her exposure to Dalcroze's music and movement theories. She crafted carefully, using ideas she had explored with Laban: the paradoxical and synchronous coupling of rational crafting with the flight into the mythic and ritual. Even the Sphinx-like gesture of touching fingers to masked lips crept into the character of the Witch from the Freemasonic practices at Monte Verità. Such imagery is still present in hermetic Masonic texts. Wigman said that the gesture was meant to "keep the secret" – presumably of the Masonic rites and of larger forces. Wigman also drew on masked Dada experiments that distorted the gestalt in performance, and contributed ultimately to the deliberate development of her own distinctive performance persona. Describing the Elemental Dance Composition, she embraced the grotesque and this was a manifestation of "everything apparitional, spectral, whether confined to earthy or released to transcendental experiences" (Wigman 1973: 92). Certainly, she made dances on many themes from the sublime to the anguished, but the potential of the grotesque for danced expression was one of Wigman's most radical visions.

Before Mary Wigman, Isadora Duncan had unleashed such energy in her *Furies*, as had Gluck in his *Orpheus*. *Sleeping Beauty*'s wicked Carabosse had epitomized grotesque and evil forces in the ballet and the narratives of the *Ballets Russes* were filled with unusual heroes and villains. In all of these earlier representations, the grotesque appeared in contrast, diametrically opposed to what was good and beautiful. Wigman's grotesque witch appears somehow more personal, less caricature or literary figure and more immediate. She makes no apologies for allowing herself to revel in the shadow side of human nature – of her own nature. She wrote: "All sensations of anxiety, all chaotic conditions of despair arising from torment, hatred, or fury, grow in this medium of expression up to and beyond the boundaries of the purely human and blend themselves with inhuman, demoniacal violence" (ibid.: 93). The effect was shocking, certainly. But the fact that this aspect of human nature could be revealed and communicated through performance was revolutionary. Wigman spoke about the performance of the *Hexentanz* as possessing her in a profoundly elemental way. She recalled the Witch "with her unrestrained, naked instincts, with her insatiable lust for life, beast and woman at one and the same time" (Wigman 1966: 41). Remembering the emergence of the character, Wigman said, "I shuddered at my own image, at the exposure of this facet of my ego which I had never allowed to emerge in such unashamed nakedness" (ibid.). In this, the *Hexentanz* may be the definitive solo of early *Ausdruckstanz*.

Group dance

Wigman accomplished much as a soloist inside and outside of Germany. But she also aspired to choreograph for an ensemble. Wigman saw the group dance as retaining the essential characteristics of the solo. For the choreographer, the group dance also permitted an amplified use of the formal elements of space, time and energy. Multiple dancing bodies permitted more variety and capacity for change. When she writes of the demands of creating an ensemble work, we hear her own struggles to form a dance group and simultaneously keep the solo dance alive. She described the role of a dancer as twofold: "on the one hand, perfecting the dance personality as an individual; and on the other hand, blending this individuality with an ensemble" (Wigman 1973: 129). She believed that the young dancers of her era had a strong feeling for a common cause that supported ensemble dance. But she also saw that the drive for self-expression must be handled with understanding and patience in order to protect and develop the individual talent. The abilities that group members brought were to be cultivated within the framework of the dances themselves. Thus, self-expression would not come into conflict with the teamwork necessary to work in a dance ensemble.

Dance talent manifests itself in two ways, she said. The first was what she termed the "productive" talent that arises from creative imagination. This talent emerges as having a real mind of its own with which it adapts training to its own original purposes. Along with the ability to modify training material, such talent exerts the power to influence others through initiative and qualities of leadership. From this pool of talent she identified choreographers, managers, composers and soloists. Wigman reflected on these leadership qualities in her 1927 essay "Dance and the Modern Woman," written in English for *The Dancing Times* of London. Her adoption of this *Führer* principle certainly predated the rise of the Third Reich and consolidated as her work with other dancers developed. This progression of choreographic control mirrors the evolution of Martha Graham's leadership role, which solidified in her own dance ensembles and through the codification of her technique. It is worthwhile to consider the development of the innate qualities of the choreographer in the light of Wigman's career. While she could comment on the task of the choreographer from her own experience, she also knew that the so-called choreographic or productive path was not for all dancers.

In contrast or in complement to the productive talent, Wigman termed a second type of dance talent "reproductive." Such talent was innate to those dancers who became ideal instruments for the creative forces and visions of choreographers. And she made it clear that these dancers had gifts all of their own. With the reproductive talent comes the genius for absorbing and carrying to fruition the ideas of others. This requires a critical insight derived from shrewd observation and an intellect capable of penetration into motivations, metaphors and meanings. For these dancers, Wigman saw their professional potential best realized through the challenges of dancing with a group, but not merely as instruments of the choreographer. These artists were called on to use a strength of personality that would be neither subverted nor stifled by working with others.

In 1921, Wigman choreographed her first major-length group work, *The Seven Dances of Life*. Among the dancers rehearsing the work were Berthe Trümpy, Yvonne Georgi and Gret Palucca. Opening night was almost cancelled at the last moment because Palucca suffered a foot injury that required surgery and dancer Birgit Nohr also was injured. New ensemble member Trümpy stepped into Palucca's part and danced alongside Wigman with Hilde Daeves, Lena Hanke and Georgi. Together, they made dance history.

The Seven Dances of Life *(1921)*

On 1 October 1921, Mary Wigman presented a work she had choreographed for producer Hanns Niedecken-Gebhard, a dramaturge interested in expanding the role of the dance within opera performance. He and Wigman had known each other since the days at Monte Verità, and now Wigman's choreography for his production of *The Rose in Love's Garden* firmly established their long friendship. With Palucca, she struggled with the "corseted" dancers at the Stattsopera in Hanover (Müller 1986a: 90). Lured by the idea of theater work, but frustrated by the necessity of working with ballet-trained dancers, Wigman would soon have the opportunity to craft and direct a work that was totally her own. On 14 December 1921, Niedecken-Gebhard produced Wigman's first evening-length performance for her small ensemble. *The Seven Dances of Life* premiered at the Opera House in Frankfurt. The first half of the evening was dedicated to performance of a Mozart operetta, *Basten and Bastienne*. Wigman and her cast took the stage after the intermission.

The Seven Dances of Life may have debuted that evening, but the performance was the culmination of years of analysis, study and self-discovery. In that wonderful, horrible and formative year of 1918–19 Wigman had written the poem that became the libretto for the dance. And her extant sketches for the dance vividly illustrate how she labored over the symbolic content and choreographic form of the work. She undertook this project while recovering from a physical and emotional breakdown. While she was a patient in the tuberculosis sanatorium in the Engadin region of the Swiss Alps, *The Seven Dances of Life* was her creative refuge. It is also a map of her struggle to persist in dedicating her life to dance against all odds. And it is clearly derivative of the experimental works that she had been cast in by Laban.

The year 1918 was the end of her association with Laban. That year he fashioned *The Sultan's Grimace: A Dance Play in Five Scenes*. It was one of the "oriental" fairy-tale pantomimes that he made during his tenure in Zurich. Certainly, many dancers took on "Orientalist" themes, imitating such dance luminaries as Ruth St. Denis and Maud Allen. It has been suggested that Wigman modeled *The Seven Dances of Life* after Allen's work, but Allen's *Salome* had initially made a stir in 1907, more than a decade before Wigman began to work on her *Seven Dances*. It seems likely that Wigman was developing a dramatic piece that had a direct relationship to her final period under Laban's tutelage. The trappings of *The Sultan's Grimace* hold many elements found in *The Seven Dances of Life*. In Laban's work there appeared a Sultan/ruler, a female slave whose dance held the power to save lives, attending dancers, a dervish dancer and an executioner. There was a large throne upon which the Sultan sat as ruler and cloth handkerchiefs that were used as props symbolizing transition and choice. However, where *The Sultan's Grimace* appears as more of a social comedy, in which disguises and mistaken identities drive the plot, Wigman's *The Seven Dances of Life* is earnestly serious and more in the tradition of *Sturm und Drang*, but with an uplifting outcome.

Sturm und Drang movement – literally Storm and Stress, this movement of the late 1700s was the zenith of German romanticism. *Sturm und Drang* writers and artists such as Goethe saw the human quest for perfectibility as impossible, yet the only worthwhile aim for creative genius. The movement can be characterized as a revolt against Enlightenment rationalism and the early stages of industrialization.

By the time that she was to set the work in 1921, many other influences had entered Wigman's creative life. Besides having a group of dancers dedicated to working with her, she had also embarked on a romantic relationship with psychiatrist and art historian Hanns Prinzhorn. She had known Prinzhorn since her days at Hellerau, when he had been engaged to her roommate Erna Hoffman. While Wigman was working with Laban during the years of the First World War, Prinzhorn was gathering and cataloging a unique collection of art works done by patients at psychiatric hospitals. Led by the head of the Psychiatric Department at the University in Heidelberg, he went on to publish a richly illustrated book, *The Artistry of the Mentally Ill*. His groundbreaking book not only documented the art collection but also interpreted and contextualized the artwork. His writing is a phenomenological critique of the prevailing culture that disparaged such "insane art." He argued not only that many of the works therein had genuine artistic quality, but also that the creators of the works deserved a positive re-evaluation in the light of such artistic merit. While his scientific colleagues were reserved in their reaction, artists were enthusiastic. Jean Dubuffet was highly inspired by the works, and coined the term "Outsider Art" to legitimize these artists in the world of aesthetic pursuits. Indeed, for many artists working in the Expressionist style, Prinzhorn's work was a welcome validation of their own artistic impulses and Wigman was among them. Wigman and Prinzhorn saw in each other a kindred spirit with a unique depth of insight into their own pursuits. Extant correspondence between them is passionate and poetic. On 3 March 1921, Prinzhorn began a poem to Wigman with the words "Dance in Holy Life." Equally an Expressionist tome and Romantic love poem, it speaks of the vessel of her body holding the "thousand wild forms that sound the one blessed chord of life," behind which "death stands seething dressed in black yet the body sings of this holy life!" The imagery in Prinzhorn's poem was fully realized through Wigman's dance wherein the Dance of Life follows the Dance of Death (Prinzhorn 1921).

Besides her relationship with Prinzhorn, many other of her early influences were woven into the fabric of *The Seven Dances of Life*. These influences included ideas from Eastern philosophy that she pursued at Hellerau, Laban's experiments in defining the fundamental elements of dance as well as his Freemasonic practices and dramatic theatrical values. The dance also reflects the existential struggle found in Goethe's great epic *Faust* and Wigman's ongoing identification with Goethe's writing. In her biography of Wigman, Hedwig Müller dedicates many pages to facsimiles of Wigman's notes and detailed drawings for the dance, and any deeper analysis would be well served by looking at these pages. They include drawings of the pathways through space done in Wigman's own hand, with detailed description of the costumes and staging. Müller also makes a brilliant case for Wigman's incorporation of Goethe's color theory in her choice of costume color for each section. Such symbolism runs deeply under the surface of Wigman's carefully crafted dance drama. The dance was a mystic composition. When describing the intention of such mystic dances, she clearly stated that she was not creating a tribal or ritual dance, nor representing a singular religious idea. She writes:

> We may call a dance mystic when it is symbolic of cosmic powers in its expression and form, when the personal life experience of the choreographer yields to the dance visualization of the incomprehensible and eternal. The mystic dance presupposes the choreographer's personal maturity.
>
> *(Wigman 1973: 93)*

Johann Wolfgang von Goethe (1749–1832) – one of the greatest thinkers in Western culture; best known as a poet and philosopher, but his scientific, aesthetic and musical ideas were enormously influential. His best-known works were *Sorrows of Young Werther*, *Wilhelm Meister's Apprenticeship* and *Faust*, in which human mortality, the scientific enterprise and the nature of spiritual longing are major themes.

By 1921, Wigman had already choreographed and performed dozens of shorter dances and several dedicated to "oriental" themes, but in *The Seven Dances of Life*, her philosophy is remarkably laid bare. Her skill as a choreographer and performer would continue to develop, yet *The Seven Dances of Life* appears as a manifesto of Wigman's beliefs. It is also reminiscent of a modern morality play, close to the great medieval tradition of performing the spiritual trials of "Everyman," or importantly in this case, of Everywoman. Faced with the obstacles of being a female iconoclast, Wigman naturally identified her life in dance as a calling coming from a higher source. And from that source she could claim cosmic support for her own creative genius and ambitions.

The Seven Dances of Life

Characters in the Dance:

> The Speaker, The Solo Dancer, A Group of Four Female Dancers, Two Drummers.
>
> In *The Mary Wigman Book*, Walter Sorell translated Wigman's description of the opening of the dance drama:

> Music sounds softly, as if coming from afar. The sounds tremble in space … The flute sings wistfully … It dreams of tenderness and love, of happiness and suffering, of ever new desires; then it merges into the singing of the strings, which grows louder and crescendos into a deafening cry of life. – All sounds fade out. Only a single dance rhythm flickers back and forth, lightly and fleetingly … Then there is silence … and the dark space still vibrates [with] the memory of it all.

In the silence,

> A figure steps in front of the curtain; a man wrapped in a huge cape, hardly visible in the half-dark which seems to light up slowly with the sound of his voice. While he speaks, the strings gently accompany him. They whisper like cicadas on the meadows on a hot summer day, a thin, uninterrupted singing sound.
> (Wigman 1973: 72 – *modified from Sorell's translation*)

Mary Wigman's text

The Prologue of the Speaker
The King spoke: "You dance to save your life,
Slave!
And if your dance
Can explain to me
Life's meaning,
Then you will go free."
And the woman danced
the first Dance of Life,
the Dance of unfulfilled Longing
"Loosen her from her shackles,"
said the King.
And the woman

danced the Dance of Love.
"Do not kill her yet,"
shouted the King.
At that the woman danced
the wild Dance of Lust,
breaking out of her shackles
and going beyond all confines.
The King covered his head:
"You will have to die for that,
Woman!"
And the slaves brought
the black veil of death.
But the dancer paid no attention
And danced past them
in the Dance of Suffering.
And then she danced the dark Dance
Of the Demon,
Stirring up all forces
Lying dormant and hidden in life.
And when the dance was done,
she bowed before the King:
"I am ready, my lord."
And she began to dance
The silent Dance of Death.
Again the slaves lifted
The veil of death
to cover her with it forever.
But the King
kissed the dancer's forehead
and said:
"Your dance conquered Life
and it conquered Death.
Now Live and be free!"
   (Wigman in Müller 1986a: 92–93)

[In the following description, quotation marks and block quotes denote translations of selections from Wigman's sketchbook in Müller 1986a and Sorell 1986.]

 At the end of this speech, the orchestra "shouts with joy." The opening lighting is "warm and golden" and reminiscent of the solar imagery found in descriptions of performances at Monte Verità and written in Nietzsche's *Zarathustra*. And, in keeping with her emphatic belief that sound must be integral to the dance, two drummers are crouched in the downstage left and right corners. With their steady blows the action begins, and with the strike of a gong, four female dancers enter. They walk and run with small, precise steps penetrating the space with straight and curved pathways. After a deep bow, they slowly open the curtain revealing a "fantastic figure," a larger-than-life-size effigy of the King. This huge puppet is resplendent, "an idol in gold," and seated on a large, richly carved throne. There is a platform made of three steps that lead to the throne and Mary Wigman is lying stretched along the bottom step. Shining in a silver gown, she rises as "the garment trickles down her limbs like fluid water."

Thus she began the Dance of Longing. Longing for what? With her dance she describes her longing to live life fully, to dance unrestrained and to make a place for her beloved dance in the larger world. Metaphorically, the King had chained her. The figure of the King is not a man or even alive. This effigy appears as an allegorical figure symbolizing all the dominating figures and forces of her past, and perhaps those dominant forces ever present in the world. Wigman used a restrained, wave-like motif that rippled through her body. With her focus turned inward, she danced what she termed a deep yearning that proved her salvation. As the other dancers brought her before the throne, her arms were released as her chains were loosened.

And with more freedom, she began the Dance of Love. Set in 3/4 time, the full orchestra supported her waltzing figure. Described as "cheerful, beaming and warm, with small absurd-humorous movements and some brief sentimentality," the dance builds from a light, floating motif into the "passion of a big swing." In the spoken prelude, this Dance of Love caused the King to shout, "Do not kill her yet!" But then, with a clang of the gong, the scene changes. The Dance of Lust begins. Bright light fills the space. To the sound of beating drums, Wigman rushes around, flying across the stage with wide jumps. Against "wildly rhythmic drumming and howling gongs, the body of the dancer raves and blazes in a self-generating glow." Spiraling through the space and spinning in counter directions she moves from high to low levels in deep turns and high jumps until she pounces into the middle of the stage. With short runs from the corners, the four dancers join her. At the strike of the gong they all run and turn, forming a moving mandala that spirals outward to the four corners of the stage and then condenses by drawing all dancers to the center. This motif is repeated three times and on the fourth repetition the supporting dancers leave, while Wigman slows her spinning and travels to the center. The instruments reach a crescendo – a musical rendering of the King's shout that "You will have to die for that Woman!" In the center of the space she "staggers, reels and falls." In Wigman's scenario, the King and society made no room for such passion, irrationality and abandon especially for a woman, this woman.

So from the Dance of Lust began the Dance of Suffering. Here is Wigman's representation of *Opfer*, the sacrifice required of an individual, which in this case becomes the trials necessary to realize one's destiny. And for Wigman such sacrifice would be made for the dance. Wigman had danced a section entitled *Opfer* (Sacrifice) in her *Ecstatic Dances* of 1917. In 1931, she would devote an entire dance cycle to the theme of *Opfer*, which would become one of her most successful programs. In *The Seven Dances of Life*, grief, suffering and sacrifice are required for her very survival. As the curtain opens on this section, the four supporting dancers enter gravely. They carry a black funerary veil as a symbol of the ultimate limitation that all human beings face. They spread the cloth on the floor and kneel at the edges. The drums are quiet. The drummers cover their faces. Yet Mary Wigman smiles and quietly steps onto the black cloth. With the other dancers as witnesses, she begins to move with "limbs heavy with grief . . . with deep heavy gestures and a slow rotation, with spiraling arms, she sinks slowly to the ground." The dancers embrace the fallen figure. From this silent tableau, a deep ringing fills the room with crystal clear sound. The four girls leave and Wigman is left alone.

The Dance of the Demon begins with a poem by Wigman. It is the first time that the Narrator's voice has been heard – the first text to interrupt the dance action – since the Prologue:

> I was –
> I am, –
> I will be, –
> You became aware of me
> on one day of your life.
> Shapeless, I wafted

Wigman (1886-1973)

through the spheres of
the world.
But you created me,
You gave me the form
In which I now
Dwell in your life.
What could make you
fear me?
[Am I] not that agent
between nothingness and
being?
Why are you frightened
Of the creation of your own
fantasy?
I come to you
in those lost hours
when life is silent.

Wigman remains still. Crouching in the upstage right corner, she seems to wake when the recitation of the *Song of the Demon* dies away. Then she slowly comes to life as if the words have penetrated her dancing body. She gradually rises, creeping along the ground with short rhythmic steps. Then she jumps up and dances. Divided into three distinct sections, most of the dance is done in silence. Her body determines the rhythm. There are abrupt changes from slow to quick time. Accents happen while she is jumping. And these jumps are bound, with the legs tucked into the body and with a sense of being contained and pulled downward rather than releasing upward and outward into the air. The first part of the dance ends as Wigman sinks to the floor, with her body rigid, frozen in stillness while the air fills with the sound of tolling bells and gongs.

The second part of the dance is described as uncanny and grotesque. It is also danced in silence. The dancer moves as if she has sunk deeply into the ground. Time and again she is pulled down "to be reborn time and again, being the same and always different." Finally, the bells sound once again and Wigman returns to the floor.

I carry you through worlds
concealed from the eyes of
man.
I lift you to heights
Which your human eye
can never measure.
I pour
of that life into your veins
of which man must die, if the demon
does not protect him.
You will no longer be without me.
And would you ever want
to miss those dark hours
when your eyes have learned
to see more than can be seen?
When my powers penetrated you

and you became one
with the elements?
Beloved!

The last part of the dance becomes a desperate search. Despairing, by inner conflict, the dancer's steps and movements are huge, and filled with "twitching desire" and distorted beauty. As if a wicked dream, the dance recreates the realm of sleepless nights and dreams and ghostly images.

The smile of horror
around your red lips
makes me thirsty.
I feed
on your warm blood –
Now I am quite close to you!
Do you feel
how the invisible dance
of my limbs holds you embraced? –
I was, –
I am, –
I will be, –
Before you,
with you,
after you, imperishable . . .
(Wigman 1973: 78–79)

At the end, the dancer disappears into the dark side stage as if the ground has swallowed her. She has absorbed the power unleashed in the cycle up to this moment. The space is empty but the music continues to flow through the room in warm waves. The oppression of the previous section lifts.

The music fades and in the silence, Wigman again returns to the stage. She stands alone. She walks with deep and controlled steps as the drummers leave the stage. Wigman opens the curtain to the effigy of the King and bows her head. The four dancers enter with torches lit and place them at the front of the stage. Torchlight is the only light in the room. She dances the Dance of Death with silent resolve. This dance is described as an absolutely solemn ceremony. It ends with Wigman sinking and kneeling before the throne until her forehead touches the ground. The four dancers place the black veil around her shoulders and she is carried off stage.

Yet she enters again. For the final Dance of Life she is clothed in a gleaming golden dress, "shining like the sun." Smiling, she gestures for the other dancers to join her and she flings her arms wide open. The orchestra fills the space with "joyful music" and light floods the stage returning it to the warm glow of the opening scene. Wigman and the dancers respond by opening apart with impetus. Using big, swinging movements they travel in curved pathways. Their high runs are punctuated by turning jumps. They move in unison both in their gestures and in their spatial patterns, using great energy and a joyfulness that reaches toward ecstasy. The dancers come together in a circle. Her notes declare:

Give me your hands. Let us dance together the dance of all dances! Are we not dancers of life? Do we not carry the knowledge of life in ourselves? And do we not carry the full knowledge of life in our dance? Let us sing the dancing beauty of the limbs and of life – the most divine dance, the dance of all dances!

(Sorell 1986: 77)

The Seven Dances of Life still stands as Wigman's own "dance of all dances." As a symbolic rendering of her own life's philosophy, it can offer a window into one important region of the constituent values that guided her life and work.

The King had said:

"Your dance conquered Life
and it conquered Death.
Now Live and be Free!"

Under such a banner of freedom, Wigman pursued her choreographic path. While the pursuit was personal, she had come to realize that, in order to expand her dance repertory, she had to be aware of the larger forces that shaped choreographic processes and greater trends in the dance world at large. Along with solo dances such as the *Hexentanz* and works like *The Seven Dances of Life* in which she incorporated her professional group, the mass choric dance had become an integral part of the dance life of her time.

Choric dance

The principles demanded by the choric dance are born of the needs that arise when moving large numbers of dancing bodies. When considering the choric dance, we can chart a progression from the idiosyncratic movement allowed in the dance solo through the cooperative cohesion of the group dance and the final development of mass unison in the choric. The key feature of the choric dance is that of simplicity of movement. Each dancer's postures and gestures must be pared down to a united expression that creates an impact due to its mass volume rather than technical virtuosity. However, within this form there is room for individual interpretation within the prescribed movement phrases. Demanding group awareness, shared movement qualities and rhythmic unison were vital to the execution of such gestures. While not always the practice of amateurs, the choric dance did lend itself to non-professionals. In 1937, Hanya Holm made her masterwork *Trend* at Bennington College. She carried her experience of working with Wigman to the American stage. Choreographing for thirty-three dancers, many of them students, she imported Wigman's choric methods to make a dance statement of great impact. Following the performance, Alwin Nikolais wrote, "the mass of dancers, just by raising one hand together blew off the whole top of the universe" (Kriegsman 1981: 165).

This is not to say that the choreographer's task in the choric dance is a simple one. Instead of movement invention for individual dancers, the emphasis is placed on the elements of time and spatial structure. Not only does the grouping of dancers in the space create an architecture of bodies but also it reveals dynamic tensions between the groups. Space remains an invisible partner, but one that links groups of dancers rather than the soloist to the cosmos. Expressions of unity or opposition are realized through these spatial relationships. While every individual movement is enlarged through working in union with the group, the rhythmic content is also amplified through use of unison and mass. In theory, Wigman had a mastery of these concepts. In 1930 she was asked to make the concepts into concrete form in the *Totenmal*.

Mary Anne Santos Newhall

Totenmal *(1930)*

Wigman had been approached by Albert Talhoff to choreograph for the cast of more than fifty lay dancers for *Totenmal*. In her attempt to keep up with the trend toward choric works, Wigman took up the challenge. However, her own writing reveals that she viewed her goal not as the creation of mass movement but more as an experiment in uniting dance with the spoken word. Talhoff had anchored the work in his chanted poetry performed by a mass *Sprech-chor* or speaking chorus, which dictated the movements of the dancers along with the shadings of underlying feelings. Wigman saw this undertaking as a natural outgrowth of her mission, not only to create a *Gesamkunstwerk*, but also to prove dance an art form of equal stature to theater. Wigman had cut her pre-professional teeth on opera, performing Gluck's *Orpheus and Eurydice* at the Dalcroze School. Since those early days, she had labored to bring dance to the fore, no longer subordinate to music. But in truth, Wigman lacked the practical experience to direct such a large amateur group. Since those early experiments at Monte Verità and her separation from Laban, she had pursued a professional career distinguished by solos and smaller group works. Given the complexity of making *Totenmal*, Wigman fell back on theories of the movement choir that she had earlier explored with Laban.

While photos allow a glimpse of still shapes from sections in the work, they disguise the overall sweep and style of movement. In keeping with her experiments of the late 1920s, Wigman did employ wooden masks made by Bruno Goldschmitt that gave individual character to members of the women's chorus, comprised primarily of her trained dancers. For the mass of amateur men, the war dead, she used masks that appear individual in countenance yet uniform in effect. Photos reveal her grouping these dancers together architecturally to shape the performance space. The choruses also served to frame and respond to Wigman's solo dance and her struggling duet with a figure that signified the malevolence of war. The dance was to be performed through the summer following the Third Dancers' Congress. After the showing of *Totenmal* in rehearsal, it became clear that the work was a critical failure, despite the collaboration of so many well-known artists and the investment of considerable economic resources. Such extravagance in Germany's desperately depressed economy, coupled with the disappointing outcome of the performance, drew outspoken criticism. *Schrifttanz* editor Alfred Schlee called the performance a sad confirmation of the flood of dilettantism that was destroying the new dance, ironically echoing Wigman's own doubts about the state of dance training.

While the Third Congress and the production of *Totenmal* seemed a failure on many levels, it also appeared that *Ausdruckstanz* was in a state of decline. In truth the entire infrastructure of the German Republic was in chaos and cultural elements such as the German dance reflected the critical state of affairs. Submitting to the choric dance and using amateurs for the performance shows, Wigman was caught amidst desire and necessity, idealism and peer pressure. In her later writing, she appears philosophical about the critical failure of *Totenmal*. She insisted that the entire project was an unprecedented experiment to wed the dance with the spoken word. And it was. For Wigman, the amateurs presented a challenge to be borne for the sake of experimentation. Her company, trained in her own technique, had been disbanded due to lack of funding, leaving only a small core led by Holm to anchor the women's chorus in *Totenmal*.

Susan Manning has proposed *Totenmal* as a prototype for the Nazi spectacles to come. Manning's argument appears particularly concrete in consideration of Talhoff's later commitment to National Socialism and Wigman's work under the regime. However, she allows that "most contemporary spectators considered *Totenmal* a pacifist statement" (Manning 1993: 159). *Totenmal* also can be considered a modernist statement in its pluralism: Talhoff's text included letters from British and French soldiers, as well as Germans. This surprising lack of nationalism, which Elizabeth Selden termed "supranationalism," may be construed as "concealing a highly politicized theater within an apolitical aura" (ibid.: 160). However, it could also be viewed as a statement of solidarity among all combatants and all mourners. No *völkisch*, nature myths appear. Instead, the work reflects a sad sweep of history and the universal misery of warfare. For Wigman, it was a continuation of her mission to use *Ausdruckstanz* to express the human condition. But in truth the human condition was becoming inextricably intertwined with the political order, for such is the nature of totalitarianism.

Final solo concert

Twelve years passed between the experiment of *Totenmal* and Wigman's final solo concert. Since *Totenmal*, she had experienced great successes beyond the borders of Germany and she had choreographed and performed as part of the 1936 nationalist Olympic spectacle. She had also fallen into disillusionment and despair amid personal and professional losses. Wigman had often declared that she would choose to retire from the stage before her performance powers declined. About the same time that she lost her Dresden studio, Wigman presented her final solo concert in February 1942.

As was her practice, the works in this concert grew from improvisatory sessions with her composer at the time, Aleida Montijn. Together they developed the dance themes. The performance included her *Farewell and Thanksgiving*, which was captured on film. In fact, the government supported documentation of this final performance. The film proves that Wigman was still in command of her dancing and also shows her mastery of using motif to build gestural language. She repeats a rippling movement that reverberates through her upper body and along her arm, to the tips of her fingers. Reminiscent of a farewell wave, the gesture is not charged with tension but rather with a sort of yielding, an appreciative acceptance of an inescapable departure. But the movement also speaks of an emotion that was intended to continue beyond that moment of leave taking. Even on film, the surrounding space appears charged and she draws her focus inward in a sort of moving benediction. Then her gaze follows her hand and she looks out beyond the performance space. After one of her last performances, an audience member reportedly approached Wigman, "Mary Wigman, it was more beautiful than ever. But it is dangerous for you. Too many tears have been shed in the audience" (Wigman in Rannow and Stabel 1994: 57).

Isa Partsch-Bergsohn recalls being moved to tears by another dance in Wigman's farewell concert. "*The Dance of Niobe* moved me deeply. It had nothing of the pathos and literalness of the first dance [*The Dance of Brunhilde*] but abstractly condensed desperation . . ." (Partsch-Bergsohn 1994: 112). Wigman was able to dance her own anguish through the character of Niobe. In literature, the earliest mention of Niobe, in Homer, had come to represent a stock form of bereavement. Niobe is the mother forever mourning her slain children. She is a matriarch whose overarching pride left her blind to her own limitations against the infinite power of the gods. In the end, wearied with the shedding of her tears, Niobe was turned to stone. Wigman used her dance theme to express her new reckoning of the political reality. In many ways, Wigman's dances were her children, borne of her calling to prove the dance art a great and profound vehicle of the human spirit. That such a calling could be subverted, co-opted and misguided, and finally rejected had been unimaginable in the cosmology of the young Mary Wigman. However, in her diary she had written, "The unthinkable has become reality; we have war" (Wigman Diary entry, 4 September 1939). After the Battle of Stalingrad, she responded with the new dance:

> I just had to do something about it, maybe only to get rid of my own feelings. So I started this dance, dedicated to women in the war. It started with a haughty feeling,

as if to challenge the gods ... I remember there is a figure in Greek myth who has gone through all this. It was Niobe. The dance begins with a challenge to the gods in the pride of women, then the movements are more quiet, thinking of the wonderful time when the baby was born ... Then it goes back to the challenge; then she gives her children away; then she receives the wound of an arrow through her own heart as she ... mourns over her children; then she [Wigman in the dance] sits again on her stool, emptiness turned into stone as Niobe was turned into stone.

(Wigman 1973: 163)

Further reading

Books and journals

Anonymous ("L.P.M." Probably Louise Martin) (1927) "A Ballet Feud: New Opposition for the Classical School Is Threatened with the Present Invasion of German Physical Culture," *New York Times*, 25 December, X13.

Bach, Rudolf (1933) *Das Mary Wigman Werk*, Dresden: Carl Reissner.

Bell-Kanner, Karen (1991) *The Life and Times of Ellen von Frankenberg*, Chur, Switzerland and New York: Harwood Academic Publishers.

Benjamin, Walter (1968) *Illuminations: Essays and Reflections*, New York: Harcourt Brace Jovanovich.

Bradley, William S. (1986) *Emil Nolde and German Expressionism: A Prophet in His Own Land*, Ann Arbor: University of Michigan Research Press.

Bronner, Stephen E. and Kellner, Douglas (eds.) (1983) *Passion and Rebellion: The Expressionist Heritage*, New York: Columbia University Press.

Buch, David J. and Worthen, Hana (2007) "Ideology in Movement and a Movement in Ideology: The Deutsche Tanzfestspiele 1934 (9–16 December, Berlin)," *Theatre Journal*, 59, 215–239.

Calmoceri, Tanya (2014) "Bodies in Times of War: A Comparison of Hijikata Tatsumi and Mary Wigman's Use of Dance as Political Statement," *Congress on Research in Dance*, September, 32–38.

Cohen, Marshall and Copeland, Roger (eds.) (1983) *What Is Dance? Readings in Theory and Criticism*, New York and Oxford: Oxford University Press.

Cohen, Selma Jeanne (ed.) (1970) "The Shapes of Space: The Art of Mary Wigman and Oskar Schlemmer," *Dance Perspectives*, 41, Spring.

De Mille, Agnes (1991) *Martha: The Life and Work of Martha Graham*, New York: Random House.

Dissanayake, Ellen (1988) *What Is Art For?*, Seattle and London: University of Washington Press.

Dixon, C. Madeleine (1931) "Mary Wigman," *Theatre Arts Monthly*, 15, 1, 37–42.

Elswitt, Kate (2014) *Watching Weimar Dance*, New York: Oxford University Press.

Fraleigh, Sondra (1999) *Dancing into Darkness: Butoh, Zen, and Japan*, Pittsburgh: University of Pittsburgh Press.

Fritsch-Vivie, Gabriele (1999) *Mary Wigman*, Reinbek bei Hamburg: Rowohlt Taschenbuch Verlag.

Fulbrook, Mary (1991) *A Concise History of Germany*, Cambridge and New York: Cambridge University Press.

Gay, Peter (2009) *Modernism: The Lure of Heresy: From Baudelaire to Beckett and Beyond*, New York: Vintage Books.

Gitelman, Claudia (compiler and ed.) (2003) *Liebe Hanya: Mary Wigman's Letters to Hanya Holm*, Madison: University of Wisconsin Press.

Gordon, Terri J. (2002) "Fascism and the Female Form: Performance Art in the Third Reich," *Journal of the History of Sexuality*, 11, 1/2, January/April), 164–200.

Green, Martin (1986) *Mountain of Truth: The Counterculture Begins, Ascona, 1900–1920*, Hanover and London: University Press of New England.

Guilbert, Laure (1999) *Danser avec le Troisieme Reich: Les danseurs modernes et le nazisme*, Brussels: Editions Complexe.

Hardt, Yvonne (2003) *Politische Korper: Ausdruckstanz, Choreographien des Protests und die Arbeiterkulturbewegung in der Weimarer*, Berlin: Lit Verlag.

Heidegger, Martin (1935) "The Origin of the Work of Art," in (ed.) D. Krell, *Basic Writings from Being and Time (1927) to The Task of Thinking (1964)*, San Francisco: Harper Collins, 139–212.

—— (1962) *Being and Time*, New York: Harper and Row.
Holm, Hanya (1992) "The Mary Wigman I Knew," in (ed.) W. Sorell, *The Dance Has Many Faces*, Pennington, NJ: A Capella Books.
Howe, Dianne S. (1987) "The Notion of Mysticism in the Philosophy and Choreography of Mary Wigman, 1914–1931," *Dance Research Journal*, 19, 1, 19–24.
—— (1996) *Individuality and Expression: The Aesthetics of the New German Dance, 1908–1936*, New York: P. Lang.
Huelsenbeck, Richard (1969) *Memoirs of a Dada Drummer*, Berkeley: University of California Press.
Huelsenbeck, Richard and Green, Malcolm R. (eds.) (1993) *The Dada Almanac*, London: Atlas Press.
Humphrey, Doris (1959) *The Art of Making Dances*, New York: Rinehart Press.
Hurok, Sol and Goode, Ruth (1946) *Impresario*, New York: Random House.
Huschka, Sabine (2012) "Pina Bausch, Mary Wigman, and the Aesthetic of 'Being Moved,'" in (eds.) Susan Manning and Lucia Ruprecht, *New German Dance Studies*, 182–199, Urbana-Champaign: University of Illinois Press.
Huxley, Michael (1983) "European Early Modern Dance," in (eds.) Janet Ads-Head-Lansdale and June Layson, *Dance History: An Introduction*, London: Dance Books, Ltd.
Jaques-Dalcroze, Emile (1967) *Rhythm, Music and Education*, trans. Harold F. Rubenstein, London: Dalcroze Society.
Jeschke, Claudia and Vettermann, Gabi (2000) "Germany: Between Institutions and Aesthetics: Choreographing Germanness?," in (eds.) Andree Grau and Stephanie Jordan, *Europe Dancing: Perspectives on Theatre, Dance, and Cultural Identity*, London and New York: Routledge.
Johnson, Robert A. (1987) *Ecstasy: Understanding the Psychology of Joy*, New York: HarperCollins.
Jowitt, Deborah (1988) *Time and the Dancing Image*, New York: W. Morrow.
Kant, Marion (2005) "Book Review: Mary Wigman and Hanya Holm: A Special Relationship: *Liebe Hanya: Mary Wigman's Letters to Hanya Holm*," *Dance Chronicle*, 28, 3, 417–423.
Karina, Lilian and Kant, Marion (2004) *Hitler's Dancers: German Modern Dance and the Third Reich*, New York and Oxford: Berghahn Books.
Kew, Carole (2012) "Mary Wigman's London Performances: A New Dance in Search of a New Audience," *Dance Research: The Journal of the Society for Dance Research*, 30, 1, Summer, 1–21.
Koegler, Horst (1974) "In the Shadow of the Swastika: Dance in Germany, 1927–36," *Dance Perspectives*, 57.
Kolb, Alexandra (2009) *Performing Femininity: Dance and Literature in German Modernism*, Oxford: Peter Lang.
—— (ed.) (2011) *Dance and Politics*, Oxford: Peter Lang.
Kriegsman, Sali Ann (1981) *Modern Dance in America: The Bennington Years*, Boston, MA: G.K. Hall.
Laban, Rudolf von (1975) *A Life for Dance*, trans. Lisa Ullman, New York: Theatre Arts Books.
Lawrence, D.H. (1927) *Mornings in Mexico*, New York: Alfred A. Knopf.
Lehmann-Haupt, Hellmut (1954) *Art Under a Dictatorship*, New York: Oxford University Press.
London, John (ed.) (2000) *Theatre Under the Nazis*, Manchester: Manchester University Press.
Maletic, Vera (1987) *Body-Space-Expression: The Development of Rudolf Laban's Movement and Dance Concepts*, Berlin, New York and Amsterdam: Mouton de Gruyter.
Manning, Susan (1993) *Ecstasy and the Demon: Feminism and Nationalism in the Dances of Mary Wigman*, Berkeley: University of California Press.
Manning, Susan and Ruprecht, Lucia (eds.) (2012) *New German Dance Studies*, Urbana-Champaign: University of Illinois Press.
Martin, John (1929) "Kreutzberg; Brilliant Exponent of German School Transcends It: Current Programs a Misunderstood Movement: Art, Not Propaganda: A School by Himself," *New York Times*, 27 January, X8.
—— (1930a) "A Futile Congress: A Low Level of Achievement, with Much Bitter Dissension, Marks Munich Gathering: A Few Fine Performances," *New York Times*, 27 July, X6.
—— (1930b) "Mary Wigman's Art; Years of Struggle Have Brought Her to the Very Pinnacle of the German Dance Movement, with a Great Following," *New York Times*, 3 August, 101.
—— (1931a) "Cordial Reception for Mary Wigman: A Cycle of Six New Dances Called 'Opfer' Makes Up Most of Her Program: Magnificent Yet Simple Chanin Theatre Is Crowded to Its Capacity: A Warm Welcome Accorded the Artist," *New York Times*, 14 December, X17.
—— (1931b) "Dynamic Art: Mary Wigman's Debut Brings an Insight Into German Movement: New Programs a Theatrical Quality: Music and the Dance," *New York Times*, 4 January, X4.
—— (1932) "Festival of Dance Opened by Wigman: Her Group Makes Its American Debut in Cycle of 8 Numbers Entitled 'Der Weg': Shadows' Seen as Climax One of Dances an Effective Piece of Grotesquerie: Miss Wigman without a Solo Role," *New York Times*, 26 December, 26.

—— (1933a) "Frau Mary Wigman and Her Company: The Deadlock Presented by an Individual and a Group: Programs of the Week," *New York Times*, 15 January, X2.

—— (1933b) "Gala Farewell by Mary Wigman: Dancer Is Recalled a Dozen Times and Finally Has to Make a Speech: To Be Gone Two Years 'Der Feier,' Not Seen Here This Season, Concludes a Performance Unusually Brilliant," *New York Times*, 6 March, 16.

—— (1933c) *The Modern Dance*, Princeton, NJ: Princeton Book Co.; Dance Horizons, 1989 (Republication of original 1933 edn, New York: A.S. Barnes & Co.).

—— (1936) *America Dancing: The Background and Personalities of the Modern Dance*, photographs by Thomas Bouchard, New York: Dodge Publishing Co.

Martin, John and Goldberg, Maurice (1946) "The Dance: Word from Wigman," *New York Times*, 4 August, Sect. 2, 2.

McDonagh, Don (1970) *The Rise and Fall and Rise of Modern Dance*, New York: New American Library.

McNeil, William (1995) *Keeping Together in Time: Dance and Drill in Human History*, Cambridge: Harvard University Press.

Mosse, George L. (1961) "The Mystical Origins of National Socialism," *Journal of the History of Ideas*, 22, 81–96.

—— (1964) *The Crisis of German Ideology: Intellectual Origins of the Third Reich*, New York: Grosset and Dunlap.

—— (1968) *Nazi Culture: Intellectual, Cultural and Social Life in the Third Reich*, New York: Grosset and Dunlap.

Müller, Hedwig (1983) "At the Start of a New Era," *Ballett International*, 6, 12, 6–13.

—— (1986a) *Mary Wigman: Leben und Werk der grossen Tanzerin*, Berlin: Quadragia Verlag.

—— (1986b) "Mary Wigman and the Third Reich," *Ballett International*, November, 18–23.

—— (1987) "Wigman and National Socialism," *Ballet Review*, 15, 1, 65–73.

Müller, Hedwig and Servos, Norbert (1982) "From Isadora Duncan to Leni Riefenstahl," *Ballett International*, 5, 4, 15–23.

Newhall, Mary Anne Santos (2000) "Dancing in Absolute Eden," M.A. thesis: University of New Mexico, Ann Arbor: UMI (UMI Number 1400402).

—— (2002) "Uniform Bodies: Mass Movement and Modern Totalitarianism," *Dance Research Journal*, 34, 1, Summer, 27–50.

Nietzsche, Friedrich (1966) *Thus Spoke Zarathustra*, trans. W. Kaufmann, New York: Viking Press.

Obersteg, Beatrice (2015) *Im Dialog mit Mary Wigmans "Hexentanz": Kunstlerische Recherche zu einer dialogischen Rekonstruktion von Mary Wigmans "Hexentanz"* (1926), Saarbrucken, Germany: AV Akademikerverlag.

Partsch-Bergsohn, Isa (1994) *Modern Dance in Germany and the United States: Crosscurrents and Influences*, Chur, Switzerland: Harwood Academic Publishers.

Partsch-Bergsohn, Isa and Bergsohn, Harold (2003) *The Makers of Modern Dance in Germany: Rudolf Laban, Mary Wigman, Kurt Joos*, Highstown, NJ: Princeton Book Co.

Preston-Dunlop, Valerie (1988) "Laban and the Nazis," *Dance Theatre Journal*, 6, 2, 4–7.

—— (1998) *Rudolf Laban: An Extraordinary Life*, London: Dance Books.

Preston-Dunlop, Valerie and Lahusen, Susanne (eds.) (1990) *Schrifttanz: A View of German Dance in the Weimar Republic*, London: Dance Books, Ltd.

Prevots, Naima (1985) "Zurich Dada and Dance: Formative Ferment," *Dance Research Journal*, 17, 1, 3–8.

Prinzhorn, Hans (1921) *Gedichte Mary Wigman gewidmet* (poems dedicated to Mary Wigman) 15.3.1921, Berlin Archiv.

—— (1972) *Artistry of the Mentally Ill: A Contribution to the Psychology and Psychopathology of Configuration*, New York: Springer-Verlag.

Randall, Tresa (2012) "Hanya Holm and an American *Tanzgemeinschaft*," in (eds.) Susan Manning and Lucia Ruprecht, *New German Dance Studies*, 79–98, Urbana-Champaign: University of Illinois Press.

Rannow, Angela and Stabel, Ralf (1994) *Mary Wigman in Leipzig*, Leipzig: Tanzwissenschaft.

Reinhardt, Kurt F. (1962) *Germany: 2000 Years*, New York: Frederick Ungar Publishing.

Richter, Hans (1965) *Dada: Art and Anti-Art*, New York: McGraw-Hill.

Rousier, Claire (ed.) (2002) *La Danse en solo: Une Figure singuliere de la modernite*, Pantin: CND.

Schlee, Alfred (1931) "Expressionism in the Dance," *Modern Music*, 8, 1, 12–16.

Schwaen, Kurt (2006) *Erinnerungen an die Tanzerin Mary Wigman*, Berlin: Kurt Schwaen-Archiv.

Selden, Elizabeth (1930) "Germany's Dance Congress Marks a Renaissance in the Art of Motion," *New York Evening Post*, 31 May.

Soares, Janet (1992) *Louis Horst: Musician in a Dancer's World*, Durham, NC: Duke University Press.

Sokel, Walter (1964) *The Writer in Extremis: Expressionism in Twentieth-Century German Literature*, New York: McGraw-Hill.
Sorell, Walter (1969) *Hanya Holm: The Biography of an Artist*, Middletown, CT: Wesleyan University Press.
——— (1986) *Mary Wigman: Ein Vermachtnis*, Wilhelmshaven: Florian Noetzel Verlag.
Spotts, Frederic (2003) *Hitler and the Power of Aesthetics*, Woodstock and New York: The Overlook Press.
Steinweis, Alan E. (1993) *Art, Ideology and Economics in Nazi Germany: The Reich Chambers of Music, Theater and the Visual Arts*, Chapel Hill: University of North Carolina Press.
Tallon, Mary Elizabeth (1984) "Appia's Theatre at Hellerau," *Theatre Journal*, 36, 4, December, 495–504.
Thomas, Emma Lewis (2011) "An *'Entre-Guerre'* Phenomenon: The Mary Wigman 'Schule', 1920–1942 [REVIEW: Die Akte Wigman: *Eine Dokumentation der Mary Wigman-Schule-Dresden* by Heide Lazarus]," *Dance Chronicle*, 34, 2, 322–329.
Toepfer, Karl (1992) "Speech and Sexual Difference in Mary Wigmans Dance Aesthetic," in (ed.) L. Senelick, *Gender and Performance*, Hanover, NH: University Press of New England, 260–278.
——— (1997) *Empire of Ecstasy: Nudity and Movement in German Body Culture, 1910–1935*, Berkeley: University of California Press.
Van der Leeuw, Gerardus (1963) *Sacred and Profane Beauty: The Holy in Art*, Nashville, TN and New York: Abingdon Press.
Vanschaik, Eva (1990) "The Mistrust of Life: Relations in Dance Connections between Butoh, Austruckdanz and Dance Theater in Contemporary Experimental Dance" (interview with G. Van der Leeuw), *Ballett Internationale*, 13, 5, 11.
Von Franz, Marie-Luise (1980) *The Psychological Meaning of Redemption Myths in Fairy Tales*, Toronto: Inner City Books.
Wigman, Mary (1927) "Dance and the Modern Woman," *The Dancing Times*, November 1927, 162–163.
——— (1931) "Composition in Pure Movement," *Modern Music*, 8, 2, 20–22.
——— (1935) *Deutsche Tanzkunst*, Dresden: Carl Reissner Verlag.
——— (1963) *Die Sprach des Tanzes*, Stuttgart: Ernst Battenberg Verlag.
——— (1966) *The Language of Dance*, trans. W. Sorell. Middletown, CT: Wesleyan University Press.
——— (1973) *The Mary Wigman Book: Her Writings*, ed. and trans. W. Sorell, Middletown, CT: Wesleyan University Press.
——— (1983a) "My Teacher Laban," in (eds.) Marshall Cohen and Roger Copeland, *What Is Dance? Readings in Theory and Criticism*, New York and Oxford: Oxford University Press, 302–305.
——— (1983b) "The Philosophy of the Modern Dance," in (eds.) Marshall Cohen and Roger Copeland, *What Is Dance? Readings in Theory and Criticism*, New York and Oxford: Oxford University Press, 305–307.

Video

Hanya: Portrait of a Pioneer (1985) Chico, CA: The University Foundation, California State University.
The Makers of Modern Dance in Germany: Rudolph Laban, Mary Wigman, Kurt Jooss (2004) Highstown, NJ: Dance Horizons Video.
Mary Wigman, 1886–1973: When the Fire Dances Between Two Poles (1991) Pennington, NJ: Dance Horizons Video.
Mary Wigman: The Soul of Dance (2014) Berlin: Art Haus.

CD-Rom

Lazarus, Heide (2004) "Die Akte Wigman," Hildesheim (Deutsches Tanzarchiv Koln) Georg Olms Verlag.

6
CHEKHOV (1891–1955)

Franc Chamberlain

6.1 Biography and context

Michael Chekhov, regarded as a phenomenal actor by many who saw him, is one of the key figures in twentieth-century theatre. His ability to transform himself onstage was celebrated by some of the major directors of the century – Stanislavsky, Vakhtangov, Reinhardt and Meyerhold – and his practical advice continues to inspire actors through his writings and through schools devoted to his work in Russia, Lithuania, Holland, Denmark, Germany, Great Britain and the US. His book *To the Actor* is considered one of the best actor training manuals ever published in the European tradition. Yet in spite of this, there have been very few studies of his work published in any language.

Childhood

Mikhail (Michael) Aleksandrovich Chekhov was born in St Petersburg, Russia, on 16 August 1891. His father Aleksandr, the brother of the great playwright, Anton Chekhov, was an eccentric and an inventor. Aleksandr Chekhov was always dreaming up some scheme or experiment, often in order to save money, and involving young Michael in much of the labour. Chekhov respected and admired his father for his intelligence and his creativity, but lamented the time spent helping with his father's experiments when he felt that he should have been playing.

On the positive side, Aleksandr would talk to his young son about a wide range of subjects, including philosophy, natural history, medicine and maths.

One skill that Aleksandr possessed, which gave much delight to his son, was the ability to draw cartoons and capture the essence of a person's character in a few lines (Chekhov, 2005: 21). Michael considered that his own love of cartoons had an important effect on his later development. Cartoon caricatures emphasise a recognisable aspect of a person and exaggerate it until it appears ridiculous. A good caricaturist can make the individual recognisable through this exaggeration and also bring out an aspect of the person which is not usually noticed. Chekhov developed a healthy sense of the ridiculous, or the grotesque, and felt that this was very important for the actor, because it brought a sense of humour and lightheartedness into work that might otherwise have become self-indulgent.

> **Anton Chekhov** (1860–1904): Russian playwright whose major works *The Seagull* (1896), *Uncle Vanya* (1899), *The Three Sisters* (1901) and *The Cherry Orchard* (1904) were all staged by Stanislavsky at the Moscow Art Theatre. Chekhov's plays involve very little action and there is a strong emphasis on mood and atmosphere. Although Chekhov was unhappy with the naturalistic detail of Stanislavsky's productions, it is largely due to the work of the Moscow Art Theatre that these plays have become central to the study of twentieth-century drama.

A major problem in Chekhov's relationship with his father was that Aleksandr was an alcoholic and had an inability to harness his immense energy and talents in any purposeful direction. When Michael was a young man he also became an alcoholic and found himself unable to work systematically. The recollections of his childhood presented in his autobiography, *The Path of the Actor* (1928), suggest the importance of finding a balance between work and play, between spontaneity and discipline. With his father's constant demands that he work, the young Chekhov's life was skewed away from play, and in his young adulthood he swung the other way and emphasised play. This, as we shall see, was to cause him some problems with Stanislavsky at the Moscow Art Theatre.

Performance beginnings

Chekhov's first performances were for his mother and nanny, Aleksandr being much less interested in his son's performances. The self-devised shows often featured the members of this intimate circle as the key figures who would be involved in both realistic and fantastic situations. At this early stage there was no sense that Chekhov would become an actor and he thought that he would become a doctor or a fireman. Later, as he began to perform extracts from Charles Dickens and other authors, with some of his own material incorporated, for his family and guests, he became more aware of the possibility of becoming an actor and joined a local amateur dramatic group before moving on to drama school.

Chekhov at the Maly

From imitation to creation

In 1907, aged sixteen, Chekhov joined the Suvorin Theatre school, which was attached to the famous Maly Suvorinsky Theatre in St Petersburg. Two of his teachers at the Maly, B.S. Glagolin and N.N. Arbatov, were to make an impression on him and influence his later thinking on the theatre, although not necessarily in the way that they intended. Glagolin was a talented actor and it was while watching him in the role of Khlestakov in *The Government Inspector* in 1909 that Chekhov had the insight that:

> Glagolin played Khlestakov *not like everyone else*, although I had actually never seen anyone else in this role before Glagolin. This feeling of 'not like everyone else' arose in me without having any comparisons or analogies, but directly from Glagolin's acting. The unusual *freedom* and originality of his creativity in this role astonished me, and I was not wrong: no-one played Khlestakov in the way Glagolin did.
>
> *(Chekhov, 2005: 39–40)*

What does Chekhov mean by the statement that Glagolin played 'not like everyone else'? In one sense, it is obvious. Any actor necessarily brings personal difference to a role and Mel Gibson's Hamlet is very different from Ethan Hawke's or Laurence Olivier's. Chekhov, however, began to think about why this was. For him it wasn't as simple as answering 'because they're different people'. He was later to put forward the idea of 'creative individuality' as his answer. One of the aspects of creative individuality is a sense of creative freedom and Chekhov was also interested in the freedom with which Glagolin played. Chekhov found Glagolin interesting, because there was no attempt to copy the role as other performers had previously played it.

The tradition within the drama schools at this time was that students would imitate the way that their teachers performed a role. Chekhov later argued that this meant that the students didn't get a grasp of the fundamental principles of the art of acting. That is, they only learned to *imitate* and not to *create*. The lesson Chekhov took from Glagolin's performance, whether it was intended or not, was that the actor doesn't need to be an imitator but can be a *creative artist*. This is an important key to Chekhov's view of the actor.

Artistic freedom and form

One of the fundamental principles that Chekhov thought was lacking in the curricula of the drama schools was an understanding of artistic form. This sense of form is something which is central not only to the art of the actor but to the whole process of staging, from Chekhov's viewpoint. It was Glagolin's colleague, Arbatov, who impressed on Chekhov the importance of this principle. Chekhov was critical of the naturalistic style of Arbatov's productions, claiming that naturalism was the absence of style and therefore of art (Chekhov, 2005: 40). But he valued Arbatov's grasp of form in the overall shape and design of the performance, in his models and even in the arrangement of his study.

Chekhov became critical of the haphazard curricula of the drama schools which failed to educate their students in the basic principles of the art of the theatre. Without an understanding of form and style, Chekhov felt that the actor was either confined to imitating old forms or working without any form at all. Chekhov later described this working without form as being a false freedom. The performer lacks artistic discipline and Chekhov, drawing on his own experience, suggested that a lack of artistic discipline implies a lack of discipline in everyday life; that is, a failure to understand the conditional nature of freedom. Chekhov believed that there were important connections between the actor's life and his or her profession. He was very critical of actors who felt that they didn't have to study even the fundamentals of acting because their natural talent would show them what to do.

He caricatures such actors as believing that study would only stifle their spontaneity. On the other hand, Chekhov only came to this realisation in the 1920s and criticises himself for putting too much emphasis on his own talent and not seeing the value of working systematically to master the craft of acting earlier in his career.

After graduating from the school, Chekhov joined the company of the Maly Suvorinsky Theatre and played a variety of roles, both in performances in St Petersburg and on tour.

Putting on a show

While Chekhov was at the Maly, however, his father's health began to deteriorate and his own inner conflict led to him drinking more and more heavily and performing while drunk. Chekhov described himself during this period as someone who was always 'putting on a show', whether onstage or off (Chekhov, 2005: 27). He was using the theatre as a way of hiding from his personal problems, not least his alcoholism. Hiding from our problems in a fantasy world is not helpful in the long run, even if it brings some temporary relief, because the problems tend not to go away and can often get worse. In terms of the theatre, an actor who is always 'putting on a show' is likely to keep repeating old habits, and to perform just for the approval of the audience. There is also the risk that, if we're hiding from ourselves, we're not really able to make good contact with our fellow performers or the deeper sources of our creativity. In other words, we avoid the challenges to developing the sensitivity necessary for becoming an effective performer. It took several difficult years before Chekhov realised that he had to face his problems.

The Moscow Art Theatre

Meeting Stanislavsky

In Spring 1912, his aunt Olga Knipper-Chekhova, who was visiting St Petersburg with the Moscow Art Theatre, successfully arranged an audition for Chekhov with Konstantin Stanislavsky. Vishnevsky, one of the leading MAT actors, gave Chekhov a preliminary audition and the following day he was auditioned by Stanislavsky himself. Chekhov describes it as a rather traumatic encounter noting that he was always shy and that when he met someone for the first time, 'I can't even say two words' (Beevor, 2005: 22). He was especially nervous to be in the presence of such a celebrated director and was unable to feel at ease. He answered all of Stanislavsky's questions mechanically, then, when he was invited to do his audition speech, his collar suddenly snapped and the edges bit into his cheek. Not surprisingly he was embarrassed and wanted to run away, but froze (Chekhov, 2005: 45). After a few moments, he realised that it couldn't get much worse and was able to relax into his piece. Although we can assume that Stanislavsky wasn't being overly generous because of his connections with Chekhov's family, the audition was a success and Chekhov was invited to join the theatre on 16 June 1912. Stanislavsky's notes after the audition included the comments 'talented, has charm' and 'one of the real hopes for the future' (Benedetti, 1990: 207). In August, Chekhov left his home city of St Petersburg and moved to Moscow.

Olga Knipper-Chekhova (1868–1959): Russian actress who was one of the original members of the Moscow Art Theatre and who married Anton Chekhov in 1901. She played leading roles in all of Anton Chekhov's plays staged at the MAT, as well as major roles in other key productions.

Moscow Art Theatre (MAT): Inspired by small art theatres that had sprung up in Europe during the previous ten years, the MAT quickly became one of the most celebrated theatres in the world.

Konstantin Stanislavsky (1863–1938): Russian actor, teacher, director and founder, with Vladimir Nemirovich-Danchenko (1858–1943), of the Moscow Art Theatre in 1898. Stanislavsky's work is usually associated with realism in both staging and acting, but he also experimented with different styles of theatre.

Looking for a new theatre

Michael Chekhov was only seven years old when Nemirovich-Danchenko and Stanislavsky formed the Moscow Art Theatre in 1898 and included his uncle's play *The Seagull* in their first season. Stanislavsky's approach, at this time, was to attempt to create as detailed an imitation of life onstage as possible. A counter-movement to Stanislavsky's realism was symbolism, which was championed in Russia at this time by such practitioners as Vsevolod Meyerhold. Meyerhold, inspired by the symbolist plays and theories of Maurice Maeterlinck, was interested in the idea of a stylised theatre which emphasised 'atmosphere' or 'mood' over naturalistic detail. It is important to note that Anton Chekhov himself was uncertain of Stanislavsky's approach to his plays (Chamberlain, 2010: 63).

Atmosphere, for Meyerhold, was generated by the actors and, despite his reservations regarding Stanislavsky's production values, he felt that the MAT actors had managed to evoke the appropriate mood of *The Seagull*. Working with these symbolist influences for a decade, Meyerhold attempted several productions of Maeterlinck, searching for a technique which would use movement as 'plastic music' in order to construct an 'external depiction of an inner experience' (Braun, 1978: 36).

The themes of atmosphere, actors' creativity and physicalisation of inner experience, as well as the question of style, which were to become important elements in Michael Chekhov's method, can be seen to have been part of the theatrical milieu for over a decade before 1912 when he joined the MAT.

Realism: an artistic movement which focuses on everyday life and naturalistic detail. Requires a naturalistic and psychological approach to staging/acting.

Symbolism: an artistic movement which emphasised suggestion and atmosphere, attempting to represent the inner world of dreams and imagination rather than everyday 'outer' reality. Requires a stylised approach to staging/acting.

Vsevolod Meyerhold (1874–1940): Russian actor and director who was one of the original members of the MAT but who became opposed to Stanislavsky's realist approach. Meyerhold's creative and imaginative explorations were to lead him beyond symbolism to a rhythmical physical theatre.

Maurice Maeterlinck (1862–1949): Belgian symbolist playwright who was a key figure in the development of a non-naturalistic European theatre. The emphasis on silence, stillness and mysterious dreamlike happenings in his plays required a new kind of staging and acting. His plays are rarely staged nowadays, but he had a major impact on the development away from naturalistic theatre both in text and performance.

Edward Gordon Craig (1872–1966): English actor, designer, director, theorist and artist, whose aim was to create a non-naturalistic theatre. He argued that puppets were more artistic than most live performers, but looked forward to a theatre based on movement which would be created by actor-artists. Author of *On the Art of the Theatre* (1911), a major contribution to twentieth-century theatrical thinking.

Chekhov and Craig

Chekhov's first role at the MAT was as a non-speaking crowd member in the riot scene in the production of *Hamlet* which was a result of the collaboration between Stanislavsky and the great English theatre artist Edward Gordon Craig. Craig was one of the most celebrated and controversial theatre practitioners of the period. He was opposed to naturalism and realism in the theatre, and the collaboration with Stanislavsky was fraught with problems. Craig wanted imagination to replace imitation on the stage and felt that the theatre should have more in common with a dream than a representation of everyday life. Although Craig is often represented as someone who was opposed to actors, he wanted actors to become creative artists in their own right and felt that Stanislavsky didn't give actors sufficient freedom to improvise (Innes, 1998: 49).

Chekhov barely mentions Craig in his writings, but he almost certainly read Craig's *On the Art of the Theatre* and he would have had some insight into Craig's aims through his involvement in *Hamlet*. Craig's interest in improvisation and the actor's creativity, movement and imagination, as well as his interest in the spiritual dimension of theatre, is very much in line with Chekhov's own.

The First Studio

The search for a new approach to acting that would emphasise the creativity of the actor was being undertaken across Europe. Stanislavsky had always aimed to break the fixed habits of actors and to develop acting as a creative art. By the time Michael Chekhov joined the MAT, Stanislavsky was already exploring new directions, and the work with Craig was part of this. The most significant project, however, was the establishment of the experimental First Studio in 1912 under Leopold Sulerzhitsky.

Stanislavsky himself, Leopold Sulerzhitsky and the brilliantly talented Evgeny Vakhtangov carried out teaching at the Studio. Members of the Studio included Chekhov, Boris Sushkevich, Richard Boleslavsky and Maria Ouspenskaya among its members. Boleslavsky decided to undertake a production of Herman Heijermans' *The Wreck of the 'Good Hope'* (1913) and, after several months' work, was encouraged by Stanislavsky to present it before an audience of relatives and friends.

It was in *The Wreck of the 'Good Hope'* that Chekhov first drew critical attention, when he transformed the minor role of Kobe from a stereotypical 'idiot fisherman' into a 'sincere and morbid seeker of the truth' (Gordon, 1987: 119, 1985: 13). When his interpretation of the role was challenged on the grounds that it wasn't what the playwright had intended, Chekhov asserted his creative individuality, claiming that he had found the 'true' character by going beyond both text and author (Gordon, 1985: 13).

Boleslavsky's production was followed by Vakhtangov's of *The Festival of Peace* (1913), the adaptation of Charles Dickens' *The Cricket on the Hearth* (1914) directed by Sushkevich, and Vakhtangov's production of Henning Berger's *The Deluge* (*The Flood*) (1915), creations which established the reputation of the First Studio. Chekhov played significant roles in all three of these productions. In *The Festival of Peace*, he played an alcoholic, Friebe and envisioned him as a man for whom each part of his body was dying a distinct death. This was followed by his interpretation of the role of Caleb, a gentle but frightened toymaker, in *The Cricket on the Hearth* – a performance highly praised by Stanislavsky, among others. Chekhov assisted Sulerzhitsky in making all of the mechanical toys for the production, which gives some indication of the extent of Chekhov's involvement in the Studio. He was, however, plagued by inner conflict and unable to engage with as many of the Studio's activities as he wished. Writing that he was 'unable to understand why on earth all that was being done around me with such love and care was necessary' (2005: 52), Chekhov describes his own state of mind, but also indicates a familiar attitude among young actors who just want to act and do their part and not really be involved in all of the other work that is necessary for the staging of a performance. At the same time, Chekhov obviously had a mental health issue that was preventing him from fully participating in the work – and this is the kind of problem which more and more young people appear to be experiencing in the first quarter of the twenty-first century.

> **Leopold Sulerzhitsky** (1872–1916): a pacifist who was imprisoned in 1896 for refusing military service. Introduced to Stanislavsky in 1900, he had become his personal assistant by 1907, and then the head of the First Studio at its opening in 1912. Sulerzhitsky introduced a form of yoga into Western actor training.
>
> **Evgeny Vakhtangov** (1883–1922): brilliant member of the MAT who attempted to bring together the work of Stanislavsky and Meyerhold in his 'fantastic realism'. Vakhtangov had an incredible period of creativity just before he died, directing Michael Chekhov in one of his greatest roles, Erik XIV, as well as major productions of *Turandot* and *The Dybbuk* (both in 1922).
>
> **Richard Boleslavsky** (1889–1937) and Maria Ouspenskaya (1876–1949): two members of the MAT Studio who remained in the US after a tour in 1923. They became the main teachers at the American Laboratory Theatre, which had considerable impact on the way in which Stanislavsky's teachings developed in America. Both had successful Hollywood careers.

As part of the First Studio, Chekhov developed his skills in the basic elements of Stanislavsky's method: relaxation, concentration, naïvety, imagination, communication and affective memory. Chekhov was eventually to reject Stanislavsky's emphasis on memory, but the other aspects of the Studio's work were to find a place in his own method, although somewhat transformed.

Chekhov and Vakhtangov

In *The Deluge*, Chekhov and Vakhtangov shared the role of Frazer and audiences got the opportunity to compare and contrast the performances of the two most exciting young actors of the Studio in the same role (Malaev-Babel, 2011: 43). Chekhov's performance was criticised in some quarters for being too grotesquely physical, but it was nonetheless an interpretation which also won a considerable number of admirers. However, Vakhtangov, as director, expressed concern about Chekhov's acting during a rehearsal in January 1915 when he noted that Chekhov should 'take out the vaudeville' (Malaev-Babel, 2011: 203). The production opened almost a year later in December 1915 but, by September 1916, Vakhtangov was still expressing concern about Chekhov who 'turns it all into a farce' (Malaev-Babel, 2011: 207). Nonetheless, both actors' reputations were enhanced during the long run, with Chekhov and Vakhtangov alternating in the role until Vakhtangov's untimely death in May 1922.

During his time at the First Studio, Chekhov built a strong friendship with Vakhtangov. There are numerous stories of their friendship, but one which is often repeated is the story of a game they used to play together when they shared a room on tour. It is very similar to a well-known improvisation game called 'Master and Slave', in which the slave has to carry out the master's wishes, whatever they are. Chekhov and Vakhtangov's slave in their version was a monkey. They took it in turns to play the monkey, which had to carry out all of the household chores and whatever else the master wanted him to do. The monkey was to do most things on all fours. If the master was displeased with the monkey, then he could beat him. One day, however, they took it too far and the game ended in a fight in which Chekhov lost a tooth! Chekhov was later to be critical of how actors at the Studio believed that it was necessary to lose themselves in the part and this is a good example of two of the company's leading actors playing it 'for real' (Chekhov, 2005: 66–67). Both Chekhov and Vakhtangov were to become concerned in their work to find an appropriate physical, emotional and psychological balance in performance without losing the sense that they were making theatre.

Chekhov (1891–1955)

Trouble with improvisation

Between 1912 and 1918, Chekhov developed his reputation as a talented actor in a number of roles, despite occasional conflicts with Stanislavsky and some of the other members of the company. Part of the problem appears to have been the expression of his actor's creativity. In one of his earliest roles at the MAT, in *Le Malade imaginaire*, Chekhov was criticised by Stanislavsky for 'having too much fun with the part' (Gordon, 1985: 13) and Chekhov himself describes how the fun, which started out as creative exploration, ended by undermining the performance. A group of actors were given the task of constructing a comic interlude for the play and encouraged to find ways of making the audience laugh; one of their responses was to bet on who would make the audience laugh most during any particular performance. The difficulty arose when the actors began to laugh as well, so Stanislavsky stepped in to stop them experimenting further.

Humour enables us to create a distance from both the work and ourselves, and this enables us to become more objective. Chekhov argued that we need to be objective in order to create good representations on the stage. This sense of humour is, however, to be distinguished from the uncontrolled need to laugh at any opportunity. Chekhov suffered from this defect and records that he was occasionally guilty of bursting into spontaneous laughter in the middle of a performance (what we call 'corpsing'). He came to regard this as an insult to the audience. There is a distinction here between the humour which enables us to represent even the most serious subjects with a light touch, assisting us in going deeper into them, and laughter which undermines the whole process of the performance.

Deepening crisis

The image we get of Chekhov during his time at the Moscow Art Theatre is of an immensely talented actor who is always taking things to extremes. Throughout the years 1912–1918, things got steadily worse.

At the end of his first season at the MAT, Chekhov returned to visit his parents and watched his father die of throat cancer – this led him to some reflections on the representation of death on the stage. He criticised the attempt to merely imitate the physiological processes of dying on stage, because, as we have already noted, he didn't think that naturalism was an art. Chekhov focused on the rhythmical pattern of dying. He suggested that the actor representing a dying person needed to find a way of constructing the rhythm of the role, so that the audience had a sense of time gradually slowing down until there was a complete stop (Chekhov, 2005: 59).

The death of his father, however, intensified Chekhov's personal difficulties and, as he moved deeper into his personal crisis, his work began to suffer. Chekhov was unable to give up drinking and became obsessed by thoughts that his mother was in danger. He became increasingly afraid on her account and this developed into more and more fear in general. What Chekhov was experiencing at this time was the power of the imagination to supply oppressive images and how alcohol abuse can reinforce these negative images. By 1916, Chekhov was moving towards a physical and psychological collapse. He was trapped in a vicious circle of oppressive and destructive fantasies and behaviours, especially his excessive drinking.

The Russian Revolution: Russia was ruled by a hereditary monarchy and moves towards democracy were ruthlessly suppressed. The First World War (1914–1918) caused serious problems and the Tsar was forced to abdicate in March 1917. The provisional government failed to solve the economic

> problems and was overthrown by a communist revolution headed by Lenin. This sparked a civil war in Russia which lasted until 1921, caused many deaths and had a serious impact on the quality of people's lives. In 1923, with the communists victorious, the former Russian Empire became the Union of Soviet Socialist Republics (USSR).

The Russian Revolution of October 1917, which had an immense impact on all aspects of life in Russia and was eventually to lead to Chekhov's exile from his homeland, is hardly mentioned in Chekhov's writings. We know that he was opposed to violent revolution on the grounds that violence only led to more violence and suffering. Certainly, his personal difficulties intensified immediately after the revolution. Chekhov continued to drink heavily and his wife left him taking away their daughter, Ada, on 2 December 1917 (Autant-Mathieu and Meerzon, 2015: 400). Shortly afterwards, on 13 December 1917, Volodya Chekhov, his cousin, committed suicide using Michael's pistol (Beevor, 2005: 47). He was sinking into a suicidal depression and unable to act. Clearly in crisis, Chekhov requested and was granted leave from the theatre and didn't return until October 1918.

Recovery

Interpreting his extreme state as a spiritual crisis, Chekhov began to investigate the anthroposophy, or spiritual science, of Rudolf Steiner, which was attracting the interest of a number of Russian artists, including the poet, novelist and playwright, Andrei Bely, and Wassily Kandinsky. Steiner's relevance to Michael Chekhov is twofold. First, he offered a model of the human being and of spiritual development that was useful to Chekhov, both in his personal life and in his understanding of the art of acting. Second, Steiner developed a set of practices which could be adopted by Chekhov for his theatrical experiments, such as a system of expressive movement, eurythmy and an approach to speech as invisible gesture. Indeed, Steiner and his second wife Marie von Sivers were very much involved in teaching performance skills as well as writing and producing plays.

> **Rudolf Steiner** (1861–1925): Austrian philosopher who stressed the importance of intuitive spiritual knowledge in his system of thought and teaching which he called anthroposophy. Steiner believed that the arts, including theatre, were an important aid to spiritual development. His theories of education led to the foundation of Waldorf schools around the world and the Camp Hill communities for young people with learning difficulties. Steiner was also influential in the development of organic farming and homeopathy.
> **Andrei Bely** (1880–1934): Russian symbolist poet, novelist and playwright whose novel *Petersburg* (1916) is regarded as one of the masterpieces of twentieth-century literature.
> **Wassily Kandinsky** (1866–1944): one of the founders of abstract painting and also a poet, playwright and author of the influential *Concerning the Spiritual in Art* (1912).

Steiner, like others before him, drew a distinction between the everyday self, with which we normally identify, and the 'higher ego' which is our more authentic and creative self. Anthroposophy enabled Chekhov to gain a distance from his personal troubles and to put them in a different perspective, from which he saw himself as a 'drunken egotist' (Gordon, 1987: 124). He began an intense study of Steiner's teachings as a means of liberation from his self-indulgent and self-destructive tendencies. Steiner's theories were to form the basis of Chekhov's personal beliefs and have a significant impact on his theory of the actor.

Against emotion memory

It is after 1918 when Chekhov comes out most strongly against Stanislavsky's use of personal experience and emotion, arguing that this, in effect, binds the actor to the habits of the everyday self, which was not the way to liberate the actor's creativity. Furthermore, Chekhov argued that the emphasis should be on the character's feelings, not the actor's – not 'how would I feel' but 'what does the character feel' – and that this would enable the actor to transform into the character rather than reducing the character to the personality of the actor.

Chekhov gives a very good example of what he means by this. In a scene in which a character's child is ill, the Stanislavskyan actor will behave as if this were their own child. This adapts the character to the actor's life and patterns of feeling and behaviour. The Chekhovian actor, on the other hand, will focus on the character and observe how the character responds to the child and behave in that way. In this case, the actor is adapting to the character. For Chekhov, the Stanislavskyan approach could be called 'subjective' and his own approach termed 'objective'.

Chekhov interpreted Steiner's higher ego as the 'artist in us that stands behind all of our creative processes' (Chekhov, 1991: 16) and believed it was the key to the objective approach. Chekhov eventually identified four ways in which a sensitivity to this higher ego would help the actor's work: (1) it was the source of the actor's 'creative individuality', which explained why different actors played the same role differently, and helped the actor to go beyond the text; (2) it was possessed of an ethical sense which enabled the actor to feel the conflict between 'good' and 'evil' in the play; (3) it enabled a sensitivity to the audience's perspective on the play in performance; and (4) it brought a sense of detachment, compassion and humour into the actor's work by conferring freedom from the 'narrow, selfish ego' (Chekhov, 1991: 24).

Chekhov also drew on Steiner's explorations into movement and speech through eurythmy and on his theories of speech as invisible gesture and these found their way into his system. Once the work of Steiner was added to the influences from the Moscow Art Theatre and his own reflections on the actor's art, Chekhov began to construct a coherent system of training distinct from Stanislavsky's. Between 1918 and 1921, he ran workshops in his flat in Moscow to explore the possibilities opened up by his new interests, although these experiments were only popular with a minority and financial difficulties led to closure. Chekhov's partial recovery from his illness led to his blossoming as an actor and, from 1921 to 1927, he performed a number of major roles at the First Studio (which became the Second Moscow Art Theatre in 1924) and at the MAT which confirmed his exceptional talent.

Eurythmy: (not to be confused with Dalcroze's Eurhythmics): a system of movement developed by Steiner in which sounds are given specific physical postures. In this way, sounds are 'made visible' and poems, for example, could be turned into movement sequences. Steiner's work on speech as invisible gesture is this process in reverse, where the performer in the act of speaking is making an inner gesture.

Discipline and spontaneity

Part of Chekhov's recovery and reorientation included his turn against the idea that natural talent alone was enough for an actor to be successful as a creative artist. The actor had to be willing to work extremely hard in order to develop any apparently 'natural' talent. Any failure to commit to this work would lead to the actor being left behind as the art of the theatre continued to evolve. Talent that wasn't worked on was doomed to fade and die.

That Chekhov should not have come to recognise the importance of the relationship between hard work and spontaneity until after he stopped working with Stanislavsky suggests not only why he had so many difficulties at the MAT, but also something of his talent. Without the change of attitude that occurred after 1918, Chekhov might be remembered just as a promising actor who self-destructed.

Vakhtangov's fantastic realism

Vakhtangov was initially very taken by Stanislavsky's notion of emotion memory, but eventually argued for a combination of Stanislavsky and Meyerhold which he called 'fantastic realism'. Vakhtangov felt that Stanislavsky was too attached to naturalism and missed the significance of theatricality in the theatre, while Meyerhold's fascination with stylised physicality had led him to ignore the importance of feelings; it was necessary to combine both approaches to create a theatre which was both 'live' and 'theatrical' (Cole and Chinoy, 1963: 185–191).

One of Chekhov's major acting triumphs was when he appeared in the leading role in Vakhtangov's production of Strindberg's *Erik XIV* at the First Studio in 1921. *Erik XIV* tells the story of a weak and deranged sixteenth-century Swedish king who imprisons and murders the nobility, is deposed in a rebellion led by his brothers and, after marrying his mistress, attempts to flee the country. Strindberg saw Erik as a Swedish Hamlet and Chekhov's Erik XIV was full of internal conflict which was revealed through sharp contrasts in physical and vocal dynamics. He would, for example, move sharply from a whisper to a loud cry, or from a timid movement to a strong, bold one, but always with a clear sense of rhythm and form that was said to have the clarity of a drawing.

Looking for a physical means to represent the weakness of the character, Chekhov was inspired by Vakhtangov, who visualised Erik trapped within a circle from which he constantly tried to escape. Stretching out his hands beyond the circle in hope, Erik would find nothing and leave his hands dangling in misery. Chekhov felt that the essence of Erik's character was expressed in Vakhtangov's gesture and claimed that, from that moment, he had no difficulty in playing the character, with all of the appropriate nuances, throughout the whole of the play (Chekhov, 1991: 89). Linked to this gesture, for Chekhov, was the image of 'an eagle with a broken wing' (Powers, 2002: xxxii). This condensation of the essence of the character into a single full-body gesture is the prototype of Chekhov's 'Psychological Gesture', and he reports another example from his work with Stanislavsky on Gogol's *The Government Inspector* at the MAT in the same year.

Stanislavsky, Chekhov and The Government Inspector

Stanislavsky was directing Chekhov in the role of Khlestakov and 'suddenly made a lightning-quick movement with his arms and hands, as if throwing them up and at the same time vibrating with his fingers, elbows and even his shoulders' (Chekhov, 1991: 89). Once again Chekhov understood the whole of the role from this condensation. What both of these incidents show is that the idea of expressing the essence of the role in a gesture was familiar to Stanislavsky and Vakhtangov, and that the idea isn't Chekhov's as such. Nonetheless, he was the one who developed the idea of the Psychological Gesture and made it an important aspect of his training as an intuitive rather than an analytical approach to character.

In contrast to the brooding melancholy of Erik, Chekhov's Khlestakov in *The Government Inspector* was light and mischievous. Chekhov imagined that Khlestakov had bedsprings tied to the soles of his feet (Powers, 2002: xxxii). The scene in which Khlestakov improvises fantastic lies in the Mayor's house stunned critics because Chekhov would play it differently each night. Opening to the higher ego involved a means of accessing the creativity and spontaneity that Stanislavsky had been searching for and provided an alternative approach to access a creative state of mind. The problem for Chekhov was that, when creative energy was unleashed, the actor was inclined to overstep necessary boundaries and there was a need to develop a way of ensuring that the limits of the performance were respected. By the time of the performance, Chekhov was able to keep the basic shape of the scene, but earlier in rehearsals he had got so carried away while improvising with an apple that he lost contact with the objective of the scene and the other actors before Stanislavsky called a halt. The ability to improvise within set limits was another aspect of the performer which Chekhov wanted to develop through his teaching (du Prey, 1983: 89).

Chekhov at the Second MAT

Vakhtangov died in 1922 and Chekhov was offered the directorship of the First Studio, which became the Second MAT in 1924. Chekhov continued to act as well as to teach and direct, and in the 1924–1925 season he directed and performed the title role in a critically acclaimed production of *Hamlet*. One of the key moments in the production was the appearance of Hamlet's father's ghost. Chekhov chose not to have another actor play the ghost but to use his imagination to project an image outside of himself and then respond to it – aided by a beam of light and a male chorus that spoke the ghost's text (Senelick, 2015: 150). This strategy was so successful that some members of the audience claimed to be able to see the ghost.

In this way, Chekhov was attempting to solve one of the key problems in non-naturalistic theatre of the late nineteenth and early twentieth centuries: how to stage the supernatural. This had caused great problems for Stanislavsky and his failure to deal successfully with the supernatural elements of Maeterlinck's *The Intruder* resulted in him inviting Meyerhold to attempt a studio production. Meyerhold's production of Maeterlinck's *The Death of Tintagiles* in 1905 was also deemed unsuccessful, and Stanislavsky's attempts to find a way out of naturalism led to his collaboration on *Hamlet* with Craig.

In his collection of essays *On the Art of the Theatre* (1911), Craig had written of the ghosts in Shakespeare's tragedies as the keynote of the performance and was unhappy with the contemporary attempts to stage them. Craig suggested that, while we might feel the presence of the ghosts when we read the plays, we feel nothing when they appear on the stage. Whatever the stage technology used – gauzes, lighting or winches – he felt that the ghosts remained too solid and that a way had to be found to achieve a sense of otherworldliness. Stanislavsky had invited Craig to work with him in 1908, but the production didn't open until 1912 and, despite critical acclaim, neither Craig nor Stanislavsky was satisfied with the results. Vakhtangov had a small part in the Craig/Stanislavsky *Hamlet* and Craig felt that he was one of only two people who really understood his conception of theatre. Chekhov's first stage appearance at the MAT was as a crowd member in the production and this experience, together with his relationship with Vakhtangov, will have contributed to his conception of *Hamlet* and his radical staging of the encounters with the ghost.

Despite the acclaim Chekhov received for *Hamlet*, however, it was the method of staging the ghost and his innovative rehearsal practices which contributed to his reputation as someone with 'mystical tendencies', a dangerous charge in the Soviet Union. In 1927, there was conflict within the Second MAT and sixteen members of the company quit in protest at Chekhov's approach. What were the kinds of things that upset them? That Chekhov had them juggling balls while rehearsing in order to get a sense of rhythm and ensemble, and also that he was conducting experiments with archetypal images in order to approach the character's ego.

The path of the actor

In 1928, at the age of thirty-six, Chekhov published his artistic autobiography entitled *The Path of the Actor*, which describes a sense of disappointment with the state of the theatre in the early 1920s and his personal shame as an actor in participating in what he perceived as a 'great lie'. *The Path of the Actor* was an attempt to look at his life up to 1927 and to cast an eye to the future, towards the direction of his own journey and that which was necessary for the theatre if it was to become an effectively revitalised art.

Chekhov, writing in *The Path of the Actor*, claims that actors have no sense of stage space, nor have they learned to 'draw figures and lines' with their bodies 'in stage space'. He identifies that actors have an impulse to use the space and that this manifests itself in the need to make the occasional expansive and expressive hand gesture, but Chekhov asks 'but why don't they want to make an expansive, fine and expressive gesture with their whole body?' (Chekhov, 2005: 59). He partly answers his own question by claiming that it is 'mimicry' that is at the root of the problem and that this destroys the body's expressiveness. Chekhov argues that this leads to the body becoming stiff and the gesture becoming reduced to a facial gesture, which, in itself, is insufficient on the stage. Furthermore, he claims that the actor's eyes only become fully expressive when the whole body is engaged.

Exile

By 1927, Joseph Stalin's clampdown on experiments in the arts was beginning and Chekhov was accused of being a mystic and a 'sick' actor who would spread corruption. Anthroposophy was banned in the Soviet Union and Chekhov was warned that he was about to be arrested. Therefore, he left Russia in 1928 and his work was discredited in the Soviet Union and not returned to the official curriculum until after 1969. This was a period when the Soviet government was turning its attention towards theatre to ensure that it was serving the needs of the state, and Meyerhold and another experimental theatre practitioner, Aleksandr Tairov, also came under attack. The fate of these three champions of non-naturalistic approaches to theatre indicates something of the dangers of failing to achieve government approval – Chekhov was forced into exile, never to return home; Tairov managed to make peace with the authorities and kept his theatre until his death in 1950; but Meyerhold, after numerous difficulties, was accused of formalism and stripped of his theatre in the early 1930s before being arrested and dying in custody in 1940. Meyerhold's actress wife, Zinaida Raikh, was murdered in their apartment by government agents.

Joseph Stalin (1879–1953): a key figure in the Russian Revolution, Stalin became general secretary of the Communist Party in 1922. He became increasingly dictatorial after 1924. Debate was suppressed, and artists had to conform to a particular kind of realism. The penalty for dissent was imprisonment or death.

> **Aleksandr Tairov** (1885–1950): Russian director who created a dynamic and colourful physical theatre.
> **Formalism**: an artistic movement which puts the emphasis on form rather than content. Opposed by the Soviet authorities after 1927 because it didn't pay enough attention to social content.

Wandering 1928–1935

Chekhov and Max Reinhardt

Chekhov's first port of call when he left the Soviet Union was Berlin, where he hoped to stage *Hamlet*. Unfortunately, he was unable to raise the funds and it was suggested to him that what audiences wanted was entertainment rather than serious drama. Disappointed, Chekhov accepted an invitation from the leading Austrian director, Max Reinhardt, who was at that time director of the Deutsches Theater in Berlin, to take the role of the clown, Skid, in the Vienna run of his production of Watters' and Hopkins' play *Burlesque* (translated into German as *Artisten*), which had opened in Berlin on 9 June 1928. The original Broadway production of the play had run for 327 performances between September 1927 and July 1928. The play is concerned with two burlesque performers, Skid and Bonnie, and their troubled relationship which are mostly caused by Skid's alcoholism. This was the kind of theatre that Reinhardt believed audiences of the time wanted, not Shakespeare.

Although Reinhardt had a reputation as a director who welcomed and encouraged the creative input of his actors, Chekhov was working with his assistant, rather than with the great director himself, and wasn't very happy. Nonetheless, while *Artisten* isn't considered one of Reinhardt's major productions and despite the fact that Chekhov's work on this play isn't even mentioned in a recent study of Reinhardt, Chekhov had an important experience during a performance of the play that affected his future thinking on the art of acting. During a monologue, Chekhov had a strong sense of being separate from the character. The character was in pain, but the actor, Chekhov, had a feeling of ease and calm. This sense of the separation between actor and character, whereby the actor doesn't have to fully feel the emotions of the character, had been discussed in the European theatre since the time of the French philosopher, Denis Diderot, whose essay, 'The Actor's Paradox', was published posthumously in 1830. Stanislavsky's ideas of the actor using his own emotions as the character's appeared to go against this idea of dual consciousness. But Chekhov's experience in the role of Skid went beyond a simple return to Diderot's idea. Chekhov claims that he saw Skid from the outside, as if he were a member of the audience or one of his fellow actors, and that Skid was indicating to Chekhov how he should sit, move and speak (Gordon, 1987: 148; Chekhov, 2005: 144–145). This sense that the character exists outside of the actor is important. Chekhov used this event as further evidence for the existence of a higher ego.

> **Max Reinhardt** (1873–1943): Austrian director who was famous for huge theatrical spectacles which toured Europe. He made a film of *A Midsummer Night's Dream* in Hollywood (1935) and emigrated to the US in 1937 as the situation in Europe deteriorated.
> **Denis Diderot** (1713–1784): French writer and philosopher who argued that the actor must have a part of his consciousness which is always observing and making aesthetic judgements. The actor appears emotionally spontaneous and free but is, in fact, highly disciplined and controlled.

Meeting Stanislavsky in Berlin, Chekhov insisted on the importance of the imagination and attacked Stanislavsky's emphasis on 'emotional recall' for being dangerous (Gordon, 1987: 149). In a lecture during 1941, he repeated his attack and argued for the importance of a divided consciousness:

> When we are possessed by the part and almost kill our partners and break chairs, etc., then we are not free and it is not art but hysterics. At one time in Russia we thought that if we were acting we must forget everything else. Of course, it was wrong. Then some of our actors came to the point where they discovered that real acting was when we could act and be filled with feelings, and yet be able to make jokes with our partners – two consciousnesses.
>
> *(Chekhov, 1985: 102)*

By the time Chekhov gave this lecture, however, Stanislavsky had already acknowledged the significance of the actor's dual consciousness in *An Actor Prepares* (1936). It is unlikely that Chekhov was unaware of Stanislavsky's book, especially as the publisher sent a copy of the prepublication manuscript to Dorothy Elmhirst at Dartington Hall.

Sir John Gielgud (1904–2000): celebrated English actor and director, equally at home in Shakespearean or modern drama, whose professional career on stage and screen lasted almost eighty years.

During 1930, Chekhov continued his studies in anthroposophy and accepted an invitation to direct Habima in *Twelfth Night*. Habima was a Hebrew-speaking theatre, founded in Moscow in 1917, which had received support and teaching from Stanislavsky and international acclaim for its production of *The Dybbuk*, directed by Vakhtangov in 1922. The company had left the USSR in 1926, toured Europe, the US and Palestine and then returned to Germany to raise funds for its own theatre in Tel Aviv. There was considerable mutual respect between Chekhov and Habima because of the group's connections with Vakhtangov and the MAT. Chekhov was able to work in an intense rehearsal process with well-trained actors, and the success of the production as it toured Europe convinced Chekhov that there was an audience for his kind of theatre. The Chekhov/Habima *Twelfth Night* was shown in London in 1932, and Sir John Gielgud judged both direction and acting as 'so extraordinarily inventive' (1937: 32).

Chekhov's short time in Berlin was productive and he appeared in two movies alongside his ex-wife, Olga Chekhova, who had become a successful film actress as well as starting a productive relationship with a young George Shdanoff (1905–1988), who was to later join him in Dartington, Ridgefield and Hollywood.

France, Latvia and Lithuania

Chekhov was dissatisfied with his time in Berlin and Vienna, writing that is was only possible to 'earn' and not 'create' (2005: 220n). In October 1930, he moved to Paris with the aim of setting up a new theatre school. In Spring 1931, he played Khlestakov and Frazer in Riga, Latvia and in June the same year he directed and performed in *Erik XIV*, *Hamlet*, *The Deluge* and *Twelfth Night* at Charles Dullin's Théâtre de l'Atelier in Paris. These productions were then taken on a brief tour in Latvia, Lithuania, Norway, Poland and Czechoslovakia, but the company ran into financial difficulties. Chekhov then staged *The Castle Awakens* an experiment in 'rhythmic drama' (Byckling, 2015: 29) inspired by Russian folklore and experimenting with eurythmy and other ideas from Steiner. *The Castle Awakens* only ran for two performances and was a critical and commercial failure.

Chekhov had hoped that he would find enough support for his work from the large Russian émigré community in Paris, but he was to be disappointed and came to the conclusion that the Russian community in Paris wasn't large enough to support a permanent theatre – and certainly not to support the kind of theatre he wanted to create.

Richard Wagner (1813–1883): an immensely influential German composer, Wagner is known for his operas and his theory of the *Gesamtkunstwerk* ("total work of art"), in which all of the arts are combined in an effective whole.

In 1932, Chekhov accepted an invitation to work in Riga, Latvia where he directed and acted in *Erik XIV* as well as *Hamlet* and *Twelfth Night*. During the same year he was invited to Kaunas, in the neighbouring Baltic state of Lithuania and taught acting classes as well as directing a new production of *Hamlet*. The following year he directed and performed in *The Government Inspector* and *Twelfth Night* in Kaunas as well as beginning rehearsals for a production of Richard Wagner's *Parsifal* and establishing a school in Riga. During a rehearsal of *Parsifal*, in January 1934, Chekhov, just forty-two years old, had his first heart attack. He returned to oversee the final rehearsals of *Parsifal* which opened in March 1934. While he was still recovering, however, there was a military-backed *coup d'état* in Latvia and Chekhov, on the advice of his doctor, moved to Italy to continue his recovery before returning to France.

Chekhov was not the only practitioner, interested in dreams and with a vision of a new theatre, who was finding it hard to get support for his ideas in Paris at this time. The controversial French actor, director, writer and film-maker, Antonin Artaud, was struggling to get funding to set up his visionary Theatre of Cruelty. Artaud had worked with some of the key figures in French theatre and published his 'The Theatre of Cruelty: First Manifesto' in 1932 and the 'Second Manifesto' and his lecture 'Theatre and the Plague' in 1933. Like Chekhov, Artaud believed that the theatre had lost touch with its roots and that it shouldn't be seen as pure entertainment, but as a means to effect personal and social change. Artaud's personal difficulties were even more severe than Chekhov's. Addicted to laudanum rather than alcohol to ease his personal suffering, he was unable to find a means of coming to terms with his inner turbulence and spent most of the last ten years of his short life in psychiatric institutions. Artaud chose to focus on the dark aspect of dreams, believing that theatre should have a direct and violent impact. In fact, Artaud sounds, superficially at least, as if he is encouraging what Chekhov referred to as 'hysterics'. If Chekhov was aware of Artaud's work he makes no reference to it, and by the time Artaud's production of *The Cenci* was staged in 1935, Chekhov had left Paris.

Antonin Artaud (1896–1948): innovative French theatre practitioner who wanted to get away from psychological realism and develop a theatre which used sound, gesture and movement. His influential collection of essays, *The Theatre and Its Double*, was published in 1938.

The Moscow Arts Players and The Group Theatre

In January 1935, after a year's absence from the stage he performed the role of Khlestakov in *The Government Inspector* in Brussels and Paris with a company of exiled Russian actors in preparation for a short US tour. The company, billed as the Moscow Arts Players, played in New York, Philadelphia and Boston with seven plays and an evening of stage adaptations of Anton Chekhov stories. Michael Chekhov also gave a lecture-demonstration to The Group Theatre at the invitation of the actress, Stella Adler. In this lecture-demonstration, Chekhov suggested that when approaching a character, the actor must first identify the archetype on which the character is based. He also outlined his theory of centres and the imaginary body and considered the notion of personal atmosphere (Gordon, 1987: 155–159). The Group Theatre, which modelled itself on the MAT, had been founded in 1931 by Harold Clurman, Cheryl Crawford and Lee Strasberg. In 1934, the company found itself hosting a conflict between Strasberg, who placed his emphasis on the actor's emotional memory, and Adler, who had just returned from visiting Stanislavsky in Paris and put the emphasis on the method of physical actions that Stanislavsky was developing at the time. Adler's conflict with Strasberg continued until his death (and even beyond), and she emphasised the actor's use of the imagination – her teachings suggest the impact of Chekhov as much as of Stanislavsky. Adler and Clurman were among those members of The Group Theatre who were impressed by Chekhov; particularly, by the combination of honesty and truth in his performance – which they associated with Stanislavsky's approach – together with a sense of rhythm, colour and design. Lee Strasberg, on the other hand, was among the unimpressed and suggested that Chekhov should be sent back to the Soviet Union – a strong remark given that Chekhov would have been imprisoned, if not executed, on his return. However, to be fair to Strasberg, not many people in the mid-1930s were aware of the plight of those artists who failed to win the approval of the state.

The Group Theatre (1931–1941): American company inspired by Stanislavsky and the MAT. The Group focused specifically on plays concerned with contemporary social issues by new American playwrights. The Group was founded by the director, teacher and critic, Harold Clurman (1901–1980), Cheryl Crawford (1902–1986), a superb organiser, and Lee Strasberg.

Stella Adler (1903–1992): studied acting with Richard Boleslavsky and Maria Ouspenskaya in the 1920s and joined The Group Theatre in 1931. She established her own school, The Stella Adler Conservatory, in 1949.

Lee Strasberg (1901–1982): acting teacher and director who studied with Boleslavsky and Ouspenskaya. A founder member of The Group Theatre, he taught a version of Stanislavsky's work which became known as 'the Method'. Strasberg's approach emphasised emotion memory as the root of the actor's art.

The studios

Dartington Hall 1935–1938

It was while he was in New York that Chekhov met Beatrice Straight and Deirdre Hurst du Prey. Straight and Hurst du Prey were looking for someone to create a theatre course for the experimental community at Dartington Hall in Devon, and Chekhov was recommended as a possibility. Greatly impressed by Chekhov, Straight contacted her mother, Dorothy Elmhirst, and said that this was the teacher they needed. Dorothy and her husband, Leonard, managed to travel to the US and see Chekhov perform in Philadelphia. Similarly impressed, they invited him to take up the post. Chekhov rejected an alternative invitation to stay in New York with the Group Theatre and accepted the invitation from the Elmhirsts. He moved to Dartington at the end of 1935. Given that du Prey claims that the only English Chekhov knew at this time was 'How do you do?', this was a huge gamble on both sides.

Beatrice Straight (1914–2001): American actress and daughter of Dorothy Elmhirst from an earlier marriage. She was a talented actress and won an Oscar for her performance in the film *Network* (1975).

Deirdre Hurst du Prey (1906–2007): Canadian actress and assistant to Chekhov at both Dartington and Ridgefield, du Prey collected a vast amount of material relating to Chekhov's life and work.

Dartington Hall: Leonard Elmhirst (1893–1972) and Dorothy Whitney Elmhirst (1887–1968) bought the Dartington Estate in Devon, England, in 1925 and set up an experimental school. They were interested in how the arts could be used to transform both the individual and society.

In April 1936, Chekhov began a series of classes with Deirdre Hurst du Prey and Beatrice Straight in order to train them as his assistants. This initial training lasted three months and comprised eighteen lessons. The first lesson was on concentration, and Chekhov predicted that students would become bored and frustrated with work. Rather than trying to find something more 'interesting', however, the teacher must use her concentration to keep the students focused on the difficult tasks. As Chekhov put it:

> It is essential that they have difficult times and find things hard and not to their liking. They must learn to be students.
>
> *(Chekhov, 2000: 16)*

This is a common experience – we begin to learn something new and are excited and full of enthusiasm, but as we continue in our studies we can feel that we're repeating the same things. Nothing seems new anymore and we can't see the point of the repetition. The teacher's task is to help us to recognise that this is a phase we need to go through and to give encouragement. Chekhov wanted there to be a spirit of joy and lightness in the studio, and he realised that his students would have to learn to overcome the dullness and heaviness that could easily dampen their work.

Chekhov had the reputation of being a very gentle teacher who challenged his students but did not torment them or overly criticise them, and some of this attitude he developed from his teachers, such as Leopold Sulerzhitsky. On the other hand, although he had a great deal of respect for Stanislavsky, Chekhov thought that he was a very poor teacher.

The Chekhov Theatre Studio opened with its first class at Dartington on 5 October 1936. There were twenty students, only four of them British, with twelve from the US and Canada. The fees for each student were £150 per year for tuition, food and accommodation. That British students were in a minority says quite a lot about the state of the theatre in Britain at this time, which was lagging behind developments in the rest of Europe. Gielgud, perhaps the leading English actor of his day, lamented the shortage of good schools for actors, but pointed hopefully towards Chekhov's Studio, as well as to Michel St Denis' London Theatre School (Gielgud, 1937: 32). The Chekhov Studio, then, was at the forefront of theatre training in Britain at the end of the 1930s. It is unfortunate that so few British actors were able to take advantage of the opportunity to study with him.

The arrangement at Dartington was ideal for Chekhov, because there were no commercial pressures and he was free to develop his system of training. Chekhov planned a three-year course, which would include the development of concentration and imagination, eurythmy, voice and speech (drawing on Steiner), and musical composition. Folk tales were to be studied, both as a means of freeing the imagination and as the key to understanding a culture, and students would start with short scenes and improvisations, gradually building to longer and more difficult pieces. After completing the three years of training, the students would be eligible to join the school's touring company, which would provide them with their first professional experience. This direct link between training and professional practice demonstrates that Chekhov was always thinking of training in terms of its application within a professional context.

Dartington was an exciting place to be at this time, especially for those interested in developments in modern dance. The choreographer Kurt Jooss (1901–1979), famous for his anti-war piece *The Green Table* (1932), had fled Germany with his company, the Ballets Jooss, and taken up residence at Dartington in 1934. Jooss' former teacher Rudolf Laban (1879–1958) was exiled from Germany in 1938 and moved to Dartington, where he continued to investigate movement as a means of unifying the different art forms. The Indian modern dance pioneer Uday Shankar (1900–1977) also visited Dartington during this period. The possibilities for collaboration and cross-fertilisation were huge, but there was insufficient time for these possibilities to unfold.

Unfortunately, Chekhov's school at Dartington wasn't to last three years because of the worsening situation in Europe. The Second World War didn't start until 1939, but the German occupation of Austria and parts of Czechoslovakia in 1938 and the ongoing Civil War in Spain signalled what was to come. Chekhov decided to move to the US with those who were able to accompany him. Beatrice Straight found an appropriate space at Ridgefield, Connecticut and the new school opened there in December 1938.

Ridgefield (1938–1942)

By this time, the main components of Chekhov's system were in place: 'imagination and concentration', 'higher ego', 'atmospheres and qualities', 'centres', 'imaginary bodies', 'radiance' and 'style'. Chekhov also added what came to be known as the 'four brothers', a series of linked exercises that focused on feelings of 'ease' (to replace Stanislavsky's 'relaxation'), 'form', 'beauty', and 'the whole'.

Unfortunately, there was more financial pressure on Chekhov in Connecticut than there had been in Devon; the school had to be self-sufficient and students were charged fees of $1,200 per year. Chekhov attracted enough students to make the school a going concern and the curriculum was structured into five main areas of work: the technique of acting, training and developing the imagination, speech formation, eurythmy and dramatic studies that involved improvisations and scenes from plays. Both eurythmy and speech formation were based on the work of Rudolf Steiner. In addition to this basic curriculum, students were each required to learn stage design, lighting, set building and make-up. Chekhov was interested in training theatre artists who understood the complete process of theatre production in a practical way.

Chekhov (1891-1955)

With less security at Ridgefield than he'd had at Dartington, although the Elmhirsts still continued their generous patronage, Chekhov was keen to get a production together and have his work seen and acknowledged. He started work on *The Possessed* which opened in New York in October 1939 and ran for a month. This production comprised fifteen scenes based on written episodes (by Shdanoff) and recorded improvisations, in turn based on three novels by the outstanding Russian writer, Fyodor Dostoevsky. The production received significant praise for the quality of the ensemble work, the standard of the characterisation and the clarity of the speech. However, *The Possessed* wasn't as successful as Chekhov hoped it would be and he abandoned the plan to stage a production based on *The Pickwick Papers* by Charles Dickens. Instead, he organised a tour of Shakespeare's *Twelfth Night* and a short play based on Dickens' *The Cricket on the Hearth* to East Coast universities in 1940. The tour was reasonably successful and not only met the aim of providing professional experience for those students selected, but also attracted new students to the school, including Yul Brynner. In 1941, the tour was expanded and included *King Lear* as well as *Twelfth Night* – the latter had a short run at the Little Theatre on Broadway in December that attracted a more generally positive response than had *The Possessed*. Shortly afterwards, in 1942, there was an evening of one-act adaptations of short stories by Anton Chekhov and there were criticisms that the students' performance lacked spontaneity.

Fyodor Dostoevsky (1821–1881): Russian novelist whose novels *Crime and Punishment* (1866) and *The Brothers Karamazov* (1880) are considered among the best ever written. Dostoevsky was imprisoned in a Siberian labour camp for five years for belonging to a socialist circle. His views on the world changed as a result of his experience and he came to believe that individual and social transformation was only possible through suffering and faith.

Yul Brynner (1920–1985): actor who achieved international fame with his performance in the film of *The King and I* (1956). Born in Russia, Brynner worked as a circus performer in France before joining Chekhov in the US in 1941.

It was during this period at Ridgefield that Chekhov began to formulate his ideas on the Psychological Gesture, which had been in the process of gestation since the 1920s.

The Hollywood years

Unfortunately, however, the attack by the Japanese on the American naval base at Pearl Harbor in 1941 precipitated the entry of the US into the Second World War. By 1942, pressures on Chekhov's school were increasing, as rationing restricted the resources available for touring and as some of the male students were drafted into the forces. Chekhov closed the school and moved in 1943 to Los Angeles, where he was hired by MGM and quickly began a film career in Hollywood as well as teaching acting classes and giving lectures on acting and the creative process.

Chekhov made nine films in Hollywood and it was the third, *Spellbound*, which has gained him the most recognition. *Spellbound*, released in 1945, was directed by Sir Alfred Hitchcock and starred Ingrid Bergman and Gregory Peck, both of whom studied privately with Chekhov. In *Spellbound*, Peck plays John Ballantine, a man who is suffering from amnesia and has taken on the identity of a famous psychiatrist, Dr Edwardes. Once the false identity is discovered, Ballantine is suspected of murdering Edwardes and goes on the run, accompanied by Dr Constance Peterson

(Bergman), to try to discover the truth of what happened. Peterson takes Ballantine to her old mentor, played by Michael Chekhov, who, she hopes, will be able to analyse Ballantine's dreams and help him unlock his memory. Chekhov's role is a small one in terms of the amount of time he's on screen, but it's a pivotal role in the film. He gives a finely detailed performance as the old professor, which, although far from the great experimental performances of the 1920s as Erik XIV, Khlestakov and Hamlet, demonstrates his humour and a precise control of physical actions. The quality of his work on this role earned him an Oscar nomination.

Sir Alfred Hitchcock (1899–1980): English director known as 'the master of suspense' and celebrated for films such as *Rear Window* (1954), *Vertigo* (1958), *North by Northwest* (1959) and *Psycho* (1960).

Ingrid Bergman (1925–1982): Swedish film actress whose first Hollywood success was in *Casablanca* (1942).

Gregory Peck (1916–2003): American actor who appeared on Broadway with Stella Adler in a show directed by Max Reinhardt, before moving into films.

Anthony Quinn (1915–2001): Mexican actor whose first film appearance was in 1936. His most famous film role was as Zorba in *Zorba the Greek* (1964).

Jack Palance (1919–2006): American film actor, perhaps best known for his 'bad guy' characterisations in movies from the 1950s.

Marilyn Monroe (1926–1962): perhaps the most famous of all American film actresses, she studied with Lee Strasberg as well as attended classes with Chekhov.

Paul Rogers (1917–2013): English actor and student of Chekhov's at Dartington, Rogers had a long and successful stage and screen career.

Hurd Hatfield (1917–1998): American actor who studied with Chekhov at Dartington and Ridgefield. An extended career in film and television was perhaps overshadowed by an early success as the lead in the film adaptation of *The Picture of Dorian Gray* (1945).

In 1946, Chekhov directed the Laboratory Theatre in *The Government Inspector*, but he was working as a guest director rather than as the director of students trained in his technique. After Ridgefield, Chekhov didn't establish another school or company and he didn't direct another production after *The Government Inspector*. He did, however, continue to lecture and teach acting classes in Hollywood. He often worked with already established Hollywood performers such as Ingrid Bergman, Gregory Peck, Anthony Quinn, Jack Palance and Marilyn Monroe. Monroe described Chekhov as 'the most brilliant man' she'd ever known (Monroe, 2007: 170), and others also had immense respect for his teaching. We must be careful, however, not to attribute the success of these actors to their encounters with Chekhov. It is too easy to see a list of big names and then make assumptions about the effectiveness of his teaching. Chekhov's aim was art, not fame, and he was very aware that, in Hollywood and the commercial theatre, the two don't always go together. Several of those who studied with him for a significant period of time at Dartington, Ridgefield or Hollywood went on to have long and successful careers. Paul Rogers, Hurd Hatfield and Beatrice Straight have perhaps been the most successful of those from Dartington and Ridgefield. Eddy Grove, Joanna Merlin, Mala Powers and Jack Colvin, all active in promoting Chekhov's teaching, began to study with him during his time in Hollywood.

Chekhov's Hollywood career was interrupted by a heart attack during the filming of *Arch of Triumph* in 1948 (Powers, 2002: xli) and, although he continued to teach and act, his health never recovered. On 30 October 1955, Michael Chekhov died after a third heart attack at home with his wife, Xenia.

Eddy Grove (1917–1995): American actor who studied with Chekhov in Hollywood and continued to teach the technique until just before his death.

Joanna Merlin (b. 1931): American actress and casting director who studied with Chekhov in Hollywood and continues to teach the Chekhov technique.

Mala Powers (1931–2007): American actress and executrix of the Chekhov estate. A member of Reinhardt's Junior Workshop in Hollywood, Powers' first film appearance was in 1942. Was active as a teacher of the Michael Chekhov Technique until her death.

Jack Colvin (1934–2005): American film and TV actor who studied with Chekhov in Hollywood and continued to teach the Chekhov technique until his death.

6.2 Chekhov as director

Choosing the focus

Michael Chekhov's career moves through different phases, and one way of looking at these is in terms of the roles of actor, director and teacher. As his career progressed, each of these became more important in turn, although the others didn't disappear altogether. By the time Chekhov moved to Dartington, it was the teacher and director roles which were dominant, and the same was true while the Chekhov Studio was at Ridgefield. Chekhov did consider playing King Lear in the Studio production, but eventually decided against it. By the time he moved to Hollywood, the stage actor had pretty much disappeared, although he enjoyed his film acting. Chekhov the director had also faded, and Chekhov the teacher was very much to the fore. Of course, from Chekhov's perspective, these can all be seen as aspects of Chekhov the artist and as an expression of his creative individuality; we might also add to these roles Chekhov as author, designer and graphic artist.

Which of these roles is most useful for us in understanding Chekhov's practice? Should we be focusing on Chekhov the actor and his great stage roles? Should we be looking in detail at Chekhov's performance as Khlestakov in Stanislavsky's production of *The Government Inspector*? Or at his performance as Erik XIV in Vakhtangov's production? If we take this route, aren't we then only focusing on an individual actor's technique, rather than on the production as a whole?

How do we separate out the work of the director, Stanislavsky or Vakhtangov, from the work of the actor? Then again, what about Chekhov's performance as Hamlet, in which he was both actor and director? This combination of roles was something which he was later to say was too difficult to do and was the main reason he gave for not taking a minor part in *The Possessed*. If we focus on Chekhov the actor, then, we lose the sense of the production as a whole, and that's of vital importance if we're to understand how Chekhov's work pans out in production, rather than just how an individual actor can develop a role within a production.

Would it be better, then, for us to focus on the work of Chekhov the director and analyse one of the productions he did after he left Russia? One of the problems with this approach is that Chekhov was constantly working with actors who weren't trained in his technique and in rehearsal periods that were too short for training them. This inevitably meant that the best Chekhov could do would be to get the outer form of the performance he was after. The work he did with the Habima was, perhaps, an exception to this, as the actors had previously worked with Vakhtangov and had been working together for a number of years by the time Chekhov directed them in *Twelfth Night*. We have already noted that, when Habima brought Chekhov's production of *Twelfth Night* to London in 1932, John Gielgud was greatly impressed. So we know that when he was working with a group of experienced actors, especially those used to working in a manner for which he had great respect, Chekhov was an accomplished director. But we don't have, in the Habima production, the combination of Chekhov as teacher and director; that is, we don't have enough evidence that the two things go together. To focus on this production of *Twelfth Night* wouldn't help us to understand the relationship between Chekhov's teaching and the processes of putting on a play.

The work that comes out of the Chekhov Studio Theatre in Ridgefield does show us Chekhov the director working with a group of performers that he's trained, yet the group doesn't stay together long enough for the ensemble to be fairly compared with any of the other major ensembles of the twentieth century. That is, despite the critical recognition of the Chekhov Theatre Studio's productions of *Twelfth Night* and *King Lear*, the company didn't really mature as a unit, and Chekhov is viewed as a director of classic plays rather than of new work. This is also something worth noting, because, despite Chekhov's vision of a new theatre with new works, his success as a director after leaving Russia is based primarily on his work with the classics. *The Possessed* is an important production because it was the first public production of the Studio, but the members of the company were very inexperienced and not really skilled enough to model Chekhov's method at its full potential; although, as we shall see ahead, the reviews were mixed and sometimes contradictory. Chekhov's adaptation of *The Pickwick Papers* didn't reach the stage, although rehearsals and workshops took place and Chekhov left behind both a draft script and some detailed director's notes. There are also notes, published in Leonard (1984), which refer to Chekhov's 1946 Hollywood production of *The Government Inspector*, but this isn't a document of a single production – more a collection of ideas and reflections on how to approach the direction of the play.

A third approach would be to look at Chekhov the teacher in relation to scenes and short plays worked on in the classes. These are pieces not intended for public presentation. The difficulty here is that, if we focus too much on the teaching, even though it contains the essential ingredients of what Chekhov wanted in public performance, we don't get any sense of how this work is received by an audience. If we stick with studio work, we never get a sense of how our work is received by the wider public and what information this reception gives us about our work. Do people understand what we're doing? Does their criticism demonstrate an understanding of our work which stimulates us to develop it further? Have they missed the point altogether? Are we playing in the right venues? Are we attracting an appropriate audience?

In the circumstances, perhaps the best approach is to examine Chekhov's productions with his students. In these productions, Chekhov the teacher of acting comes together with Chekhov the director, and we can begin to get a sense of how his theories panned out in public performances and how they were received by the critics. The first of these productions after the school moved to Ridgefield was *The Possessed*, which is generally regarded as an artistic and commercial failure.

The Possessed *(1939)*

The Chekhov Theatre Studio production of *The Possessed*, which was scripted by George Shdanoff and directed by Chekhov, opened on Broadway at the Lyceum Theatre on 24 October 1939. Initially, Chekhov had planned to work on *The Possessed* and *Pickwick* simultaneously, but early in 1939 he decided that they must concentrate on *The Possessed* in order to get a production on Broadway as soon as possible. What was the urgency? Chekhov was disappointed with the number and quality of new applicants for the Studio at Ridgefield and wanted to establish his work on Broadway, so that the company's reputation would attract new students. He felt that it wouldn't be possible to run the school on its own without some income from a good run on Broadway. This meant working on the production, even if it led to the work of the school being neglected.

The text

Chekhov and Shdanoff started work on *The Possessed* while the school was still based at Dartington, but the move to Ridgefield interrupted the process. The play, which is based on the writings of Fyodor Dostoevsky and, primarily, the 700-page novel of the same name (but which is also translated as *Demons*), is in fifteen relatively short scenes. Shdanoff had written stage adaptations of other novels by Dostoevsky, including *Crime and Punishment* for Gaston Baty, which ran for two years in Paris. He had also been credited as co-director, with Alexander Trivas, of a German film, *No Man's Land* (1931), which is regarded as one of the best anti-war films ever made.

Chekhov's and Shdanoff's aim wasn't to make a strict adaptation of Dostoevsky's text, but to use Dostoevsky's ideas as a stimulus for 'writing a play which would reflect our modern problems' (Byckling, 1995: 33). This was why, when it was only possible to work on one of his planned productions, Chekhov chose *The Possessed* over *Pickwick*: the material was better suited to dealing with the violence of the contemporary world. Millions had died in Russia and, with the aggressive rise of Hitler and the Nazis in Germany, Chekhov realised that the coming war was going to cause the deaths of millions more.

> **Joanna Merlin** (1885–1952): director credited with introducing expressionist staging to the French theatre.

Devising process

Although there was a text of the play published to accompany the production, it would be a mistake to regard this as a script that pre-existed the rehearsal process. The script itself evolves out of the interactions among writer, director and actors, and as such, *The Possessed* is a form of devised theatre. Shdanoff would write some text as a basis for improvisations and then rewrite in response to what happened in the studio. This was quite an unusual process in the 1930s, but one which, although still relatively uncommon, has become a well-established approach. It is Shdanoff's name which appears as author on the published text, something which seems to downplay the role of the actors in the creation of the text, but this has also become established as part and parcel of this kind of approach to devised work. A good contemporary example would be the work of British writer/director Mike Leigh (b. 1943), whose plays and films are based on the improvisations of actors that he writes down and then publishes under his own name.

This was very much Chekhov and Shdanoff's project, despite the fact that the actors were involved in the development of the script through their engagement in improvisations. The actors were discouraged from reading Dostoevsky's novel (Byckling, 1995: 34), and didn't have the kind of experience of political violence that was all too familiar to Chekhov. They had to bring their imaginations to the actions suggested by the text and the director and not try to make a performance based on their personal experiences of mass violence, which they didn't have, or their experience of Dostoevsky. It's difficult to understand why Chekhov discouraged the actors from reading Dostoevsky, because it would seem to be an appropriate manner of feeding their subconscious with information that would be useful in the rehearsal process. Reading not only *The Possessed* but also other novels of Dostoevsky would have enabled them to get a sense of the atmosphere and style of the novelist's work, including his use of humour and the grotesque. Perhaps Chekhov felt that there was insufficient time with everything else the actors had to absorb. While Chekhov was clear that he wasn't creating a strict adaptation of *The Possessed*, the main storyline and themes of Dostoevsky's novel are clearly in the archived playtext. This suggests that, had the actors read Dostoevsky, it wouldn't have affected their understanding. On the other hand, if the only indication of character the actors were receiving was through the rehearsal process, they couldn't come with a preconception of what the character should be like. In one sense, this helps the actor be free from the text, while in another it leaves the actor at the mercy of the director. A risk here is that the actors might not feel any ownership of the material, and if they are inexperienced, they might be trying too hard to please the director rather than engaging in a dialogue with the director's vision and their own creative individuality.

Why draw attention to this? Because Chekhov, in his books on acting, suggests that everyone should read the text and get to know it thoroughly, allowing their imagination to develop. If the individual actor's vision of the play is different from the director's, then the individual must, according to Chekhov, work to fulfil the director's objectives. But the actors must also be able to find the gaps in the direction to use their own creativity. While Chekhov respected the role of the director, he was very much opposed to the director being a dictator, however benevolent. On the other hand, his desire to work with a writer demonstrated a lack of faith in the actors' ability to develop and organise their own performance material. Perhaps this lack of faith grew out of frustrations with student work at Dartington, where students were required to devise their performances on the basis of short stories and folk tales. Certainly, we know that Chekhov was unhappy with the work achieved at Dartington, feeling that his teaching was too complicated, but also that the students didn't work hard enough to master the technique and would forget what they'd learned in class once they got on the stage. But we must also remember the situation: Chekhov had a group of student actors and he was going to put them on the Broadway stage. It would have been extremely risky to rely on the devising skills of an inexperienced group. Devising on the basis of folk tales in the school with an invited audience is one thing; putting an untried group of actors onstage with a weak text in a mainstream theatre is something else altogether.

The critics and the text

Chekhov was concerned that there was appropriate material for the actors to work with, and he had failed to attract audiences with his production based on a folk tale, *The Castle Awakens*, in Paris. So, there was little chance that this kind of material would be successful in New York, which was much more conservative at this time. But, at the same time, he wanted to work with new material rather than the classics. The irony is that the text of *The Possessed* found very little favour with the New York critics. John Mason Brown of *The New York Post*, for example, felt that the text was so bad that the company couldn't have found a worse one if they'd tried (25 October 1939).

Burns Mantle, in the *Daily News* (25 October 1939), admitted to not really understanding the play – that it seemed to be all about the search for a leader who decided not to lead. But the problem Chekhov was engaging with wasn't if people need leaders, but what kind of leaders were necessary. *The Possessed* puts forward the quite simple idea that those leaders who are 'possessed' by ideas of social transformation and willing to sacrifice the lives of millions to their ideals are not the kinds of leaders that the world needs (then or now). Mantle's difficulty in understanding the play at its simplest level points to the difficulties that any serious new play was going to have on Broadway.

John Anderson in the *New York Journal and American* (25 October 1939) saw the central conflict of the text as being between the Godstates of the European dictators and Buchman's Moral Rearmament. This catches Dostoevsky's idea of man being put in the place of God and the necessary destruction that follows. While this is to simplify too much, Chekhov was an alcoholic and his renewed spiritual perspective on life followed from him accepting his problem and giving up alcohol. Chekhov, like Dostoevsky, was a devout Christian, if a rather unorthodox one.

> **Buchman's Moral Rearmament**: Frank N.D. Buchman was a Christian evangelist who founded the Oxford Group in the 1920s. This group believed in the necessity of moral and spiritual renewal based on what they called 'the four absolutes' (absolute honesty, absolute purity, absolute unselfishness, absolute love). This renewal was what was known as Moral Rearmament and in 1938 MRA was established as an international organization which was both anti-communist and anti-fascist. The MRA owned The Westminster Theatre in London from 1946 to 1997 and used it to stage plays which promoted their ideals (Jenner, 2016).

Dostoevsky, socialist realism and Brecht

Not surprisingly, *The Daily Worker*, an American communist paper, came out strongly against *The Possessed*. This paper aligned itself with the Soviet Union and wouldn't be expected to praise the work of an outcast and 'counter-revolutionary' like Chekhov – remember, Chekhov was considered to be a 'mystic' and therefore a 'sick' artist in Russia when he left in 1928. The state control of the arts and the restrictions on experimentation had increased since Chekhov had left, and socialist realism had become the approved mode for art, including performance, in the Soviet Union and for communists and socialists around the world since 1934. Not all of those artists who regarded themselves as communist or left-wing agreed with this position, and perhaps the most notable example of a communist opposed to socialist realism is Bertolt Brecht. Brecht's *Fear and Misery in the Third Reich*, first performed in Paris in 1938, is, like *The Possessed*, written in short scenes and in a non-naturalistic manner. On the other hand, it is more experimental in form than *The Possessed*, because the scenes are more or less free-standing and don't combine to present a single coherent narrative. Furthermore, while both plays engage with violence in contemporary politics, Brecht is attacking fascism while standing on the side of communism. Chekhov and Shdanoff are anti-fascist, recognising the dangers of Hitler and Mussolini, but are also painfully aware of the violence and destruction of the Russian Revolution.

> **Socialist realism**: the approved mode for all art and literature in the Soviet Union from 1934 to 1991. All art was to be rooted in an optimistic and heroic view of the achievements of the Revolution. This perspective was to be represented through a realistic style, which was free from formalist experiments and from the world of the 'impossible'.

Dostoevsky's novel was inspired by the Nechaev affair. Sergei Nechaev (1847–1882) was a Russian nihilist and anarchist who believed in violent revolution. In November 1869, Nechaev and three other members of his group arranged a meeting in a Moscow park with a former member of their group, Ivan Ivanov. Ivanov had left the Nechaev circle because he felt that Nechaev was becoming too dictatorial. Nechaev and the others were worried that he might turn informer, so they lured him to the park, beat him unconscious, strangled him, shot him in the head and, just to make sure, dropped his body – weighed down with bricks – through a hole in the ice covering the lake. In Dostoevsky's first draft of *The Possessed*, Verkhovensky is called Nechaev, and Dostoevsky's aim is to warn against the dangers of a destructive nihilism which finds it acceptable to kill people in the interests of an ideal – this is picked up in Shdanoff's text. Again, the work of Brecht is worth comparing. Brecht's short 'teaching piece', *The Measures Taken* (1930), is written in short scenes and examines the story of a group of revolutionary agitators who have killed their comrade. The question is: were they correct to do so? Brecht's argument is that they were, and the executed comrade agrees to his own death as being necessary. By getting the character to agree to his death, Brecht avoids the question as to whether or not the killers were morally right. The only question becomes if the killing was justified in terms of the revolution. The agitators acknowledge that 'it is a terrible thing to kill', but at the same time assert that violence is the only way in which the world can be changed. Shdanoff and Chekhov thought that it was this kind of attitude which led to the killing of millions within the Soviet Union. It had almost caused the death of Chekhov himself in 1928, and certainly led to the assassination of Meyerhold and of his wife Zinaida Raikh in 1940.

Brecht would have agreed with the denunciation of Chekhov's work as both mystical and counter-revolutionary, but he was also strongly antagonistic to the doctrine of socialist realism. Had he been writing against socialist realism in the Soviet Union, he would have been at risk himself, and it is instructive that, when he was forced to leave Nazi Germany in 1935, he fled to Western Europe and then the US – regions with strong liberal democratic traditions and values. *The Possessed*, then, is warning of the dangers of a belief in violent revolution and comes out against the view that it is worth killing fifteen million people for future freedom. In *The Measures Taken*, the scale of this revolutionary violence is concealed and it is unclear how many people Brecht thinks it is acceptable to kill in the process of social transformation.

In the light of all of this it is interesting to note that Richard Watts Jr, in the *New York Herald Tribune* (25 October 1939), described the politics of the piece as involving a 'sinister combination of fascism and communism', which was frightening because it appeared that, with the invasion of Poland by both Germany and the Soviet Union in September 1939, Europe was in the process of devising precisely such an amalgam. Once again there is the failure to see that Chekhov and Shdanoff were trying to avoid the extremes of both fascism and communism. The character of The Stranger, who appears in a scene that doesn't come from Dostoevsky, tells a version of the folk tale 'Ivan the Good', in which Ivan tells the people that he doesn't want to rule over them by force; these are key moments in the play which signal clearly the need for consensual government.

Had Chekhov chosen to present a production of *Twelfth Night* for the school's first showing on Broadway, the critics would doubtless have found it easier to understand and could have enjoyed the performances, rather than worrying about the structure and content of the play. But Chekhov had chosen to produce *The Possessed* precisely because it dealt with the difficult issues of the day. Leaving aside discussions of the text and its content, let's look at how the performances by these young students were received and try to get a sense of the performance style from among the various perceptions of the reviewers.

Casting

While Chekhov was auditioning new students for the Ridgefield Studio, he was looking for potential actors to play the key roles of Stavrogin and Pyotr Verkhovensky. Unfortunately, there were no obvious choices to play these two major roles and he considered hiring in a couple of professional actors. This would have been quite a difficult thing to do. The actors would still need to be able to work with the Chekhov technique, even if their basic stagecraft was stronger. In the end, however, he decided to work with two of the students, Woodrow Chambliss as Verkhovensky and Blair Cutting as Stavrogin. Beatrice Straight was to play Liza, Hurd Hatfield, Kirilov and Mary Lou Taylor, Martha. By March 1939, however, while he was happy with Chambliss as Verkhovensky, Cutting had been replaced by John Flynn as Stavrogin and took on the role of Shatov. At this stage, Chekhov still felt that it was important that Dorothy Elmhirst came over from Dartington to play Mrs Stavrogin, in order to give some added weight and experience to the cast. In the end it was Ellen van Volkenburg, a professional actress, who took on the role, but Elmhirst had done a considerable amount of work on it with Shdanoff and commented in a letter to Chekhov that she had a difficulty finding the fiery qualities necessary for the role because she was so quiet herself. This difficulty in being able to transform oneself into a character with different qualities from our everyday selves is at the heart of how the Chekhov technique tries to help the actor. Chambliss found it difficult to transform himself from a soft, charming person into Verkhovensky, but Chekhov was surprised with how far he was able to develop some of the necessary qualities. The ability of the student actors to transform themselves convinced him that the technique, by enabling them to work in a continuous manner and not rely on talent, was effective. Chekhov did, however, hire two other professional actors to play relatively minor roles. Despite requests, especially from Dorothy Elmhirst, that he take on a role himself, he refused on two grounds: first, because of his Russian accent, and second, because he considered it impossible to act and direct at the same time.

The critics and the performance

The ensemble

Despite the reviewers' dislike of the script, there were a considerable number of positive responses to the directing and acting, even though they were often heavily qualified. Mason Brown, for example, disliked the script, and found the performance 'somber' and 'appallingly tortured and confused'; yet he notes that the audience followed the performance in silence and attributes this to the talent of the company as performers and to Chekhov's direction.

One of the key aspects of the acting that critics identified was the strength of the ensemble. This was something that was as important to Chekhov as it had been to his teacher Stanislavsky, and the programme included a note affirming that the Chekhov company did not believe in the idea of 'star' performers and regarded all members of the company as equals, regardless of their role. This was, of course, as unusual for a production on Broadway as it would have been in London's West End, where the star culture dominated and still does to a great extent today. Gielgud, in his review of Stanislavsky's *An Actor Prepares*, doubted whether the ensemble method of acting could possibly work in the West End, with its commercialism based on the star system. To push the message home, there were no cast biographies included in the programme.

This commitment to equality on behalf of the players didn't prevent the critics from picking out the individuals who they felt gave the most interesting performances. Of course, this is always going to happen, and in any performance, some performers are likely to be more successful or have a greater impact than others. The difference between an ensemble and a star vehicle is that, in the latter, the star is always at the centre of the performance and all other actors are only there to support them regardless of the production. An ensemble of the kind represented by the Chekhov company, on the other hand, will have performers who take a leading role in one production and then a smaller one in another so that no one can assume that any particular part belongs to them. This is something that Chekhov took from Stanislavsky: the idea that there are 'no small parts, only small actors'. Beatrice Straight was, perhaps, to take the art of the small part to extremes when she won an Academy Award for the Best Supporting Actress for her role in the movie *Network* (1976). She was on-screen for under six minutes in a film that was over two hours long and with a cast that included Faye Dunaway, Robert Duvall, William Holden and Peter Finch.

Reviewers of *The Possessed* praised the company for working exceptionally well as an ensemble. Brooks Atkinson in *The New York Times* (25 October 1939), however, saw a more sinister dimension to the ensemble work. He described the company as a group of 'muscle-bound actors' who, far from being free and creative artists, performed 'by rote' under the direction of Chekhov, who, he claimed, behaved like a despotic dictator who had destroyed their spirit. Nothing could be further from Chekhov's aims, and Atkinson is aware of the irony, at least in relation to the message of the play. Once again, we see a political reading of the play that's at odds with Chekhov's aims. This time the reading doesn't focus on the content of the play, but on the physicality of the actors. It is as though Atkinson reads the physique of the actors as if they are the embodiment of socialist realist sculpture, or as if the very fact of their working as an ensemble implied a loss of individuality.

Nonetheless, in keeping with other reviewers, he identifies the political meeting scene (which was the longest and most complex in the play) as 'brilliant', possessing the 'genius of theatricality' which filled the theatre with 'sound, movement and frenzy'.

Inexperience and excess tension (trying too hard)

There were a number of problems picked out, however, which will have given Chekhov cause for concern. The first was that a number of critics felt that there was too much tension in the performers. Given that a feeling of ease on the stage was of central importance to Chekhov's work, the criticism that the performers were too tense is a significant one – clearly they weren't yet accomplished enough to carry off a performance in front of a Broadway audience. John Mason Brown identified a problem with the concentration of the performers. It wasn't that their concentration was sloppy or weak, but that they spent so much time showing that they were concentrating, with 'bulging eyes' and 'immovable' stares, and also that they were trying too hard to show that they were listening. For Chekhov, the performers should be concentrating with a feeling of ease. If Mason Brown's assessment is accurate, then we have further evidence that the actors were suffering from excessive tension and this would inevitably have affected the dynamics of the performance. With excess tension, everything begins to flatten out and the actors lose their sense of flow and of rhythm. Brooks Atkinson in *The New York Times* blames the acting style for killing the spontaneity of the actors; that is, the stiffness and tension isn't seen as a result of the actors' nervousness but as a result of the aesthetic choice made by the director.

Connecting with the audience

Another criticism of the actors came from the reviewer of *The Christian Science Monitor*, who didn't feel that there was enough contact between the audience and the performers. It is unlikely that this is a complaint that there was too little direct address, so it is an interesting criticism, given that the co-creativity of the audience is crucial for Chekhov. None of the reviewers commented on the atmosphere of the piece, perhaps because they lacked the vocabulary, but, if Chekhov's theory that the atmosphere unites the audience and the performance works in practice, the audience should feel engaged even if they can't explain why. On the other hand, Mason Brown's comment that the audience members were very quiet during the performance suggests that there was a unifying atmosphere of some kind. It is impossible to know for sure, of course, and the tension in the actors would certainly have affected their ability to build a rapport with an audience. Yet it is important to note that this group of partially trained and inexperienced actors managed to hold the audience – they must have been doing something right!

Characterisation and acting style

Woodrow ('Woody') Chambliss played Pyotr Verkhovensky as a 'super sulphurous slavic Mephistopheles' (John Mason Brown), wearing a brown derby, glasses, large box coat (overcoat) and leather gloves and carrying a small pistol. The costume led some critics to note that Verkhovensky looked like a comic character from Dickens and there was some concern that this was inappropriate in a 'serious' play. One critic caught on that Chekhov saw a 'mischievousness' in Verkhovensky, which made him an almost absurd rather than a conventionally evil villain. Richard Lockridge in *The New York Sun* (25 October 1939) also has a difficulty relating the humour to the piece; for example, he describes Chambliss' Verkhovensky as 'scuttling darkly behind bits of scenery'. This evocative description paints a grotesque image of Verkhovensky, moving with short, hasty steps. If I let my imagination go into this, I get an image of a beetle and think of the story 'Metamorphosis' by Franz Kafka (in which Gregor Samsa awakes to find himself transformed into a gigantic insect) and the subsequent physical theatre adaptation by Steven Berkoff. Whether or not my image of a beetle here is strictly accurate, we can see that, if we're trying to view Chambliss' performance through a naturalistic lens, to assess how 'true to life' it is on a surface level, we'll fail to grasp what's happening. If we read Lockridge's description as accurate, but put his judgement to one side, this appears to be an example of the fantastic realism that Chekhov took from Vakhtangov – a style which incorporates the use of the grotesque.

We can take this further by picking up on the reference to Dickens. Chekhov's admiration for Dickens is well established and his initial objective was to produce *The Possessed* and *Pickwick* simultaneously. Perhaps less well known is Dostoevsky's admiration of Dickens and, in particular, the character of Samuel Pickwick. The two are linked together by their use of exaggeration and the grotesque, although with quite different qualities. Verkhovensky is the chief villain in *The Possessed* and argues that 'freedom is an illusion ... individuality is a lie' and for the importance of 'racial blood'. In this sense, he embodies the 'sinister combination of communism and fascism' that Richard Watts seemed to apply to the whole play. But Chekhov, like Stanislavsky, doesn't want us to see Verkhovensky as completely evil, but as a human being possessed by a destructive idea. The kind of humour to be found in Dickens lightens the representation of Verkhovensky and adds another dimension to the performance. Had Chekhov been able to produce *The Possessed* and *Pickwick* at the same time, then critics might have been able to see the correspondences in style between the two; instead, a number of them found it difficult to understand the style. Lockridge, for example, felt that Verkhovensky's movement around the space became 'funny', but doesn't consider if the humour is part of the characterisation. If we bring back the idea of mischievousness and add to it the image of scuttling darkly, we begin to get a sense of character that's not contained in one description alone.

Franz Kafka (1883–1924): Prague-based author whose works contain nightmare scenarios of individuals trapped within complex bureaucratic and totalitarian systems. His story 'Metamorphosis' was published in 1919, but most of his work, including three major novels – *The Trial*, *The Castle* and *Amerika* – was published after his death.

Steven Berkoff (b. 1937): British physical theatre practitioner and playwright, who adapted three works by Kafka (*The Penal Colony* [1968], *Metamorphosis* [1969], *The Trial* [1970)]. Berkoff's work centres on the actor and requires a high level of physical and vocal flexibility.

Hurd Hatfield's Kirilov, a character who plans to commit suicide to further the cause of the revolution, was angular and slightly camp, with a centre parting. Lockridge described him as an 'awesome character' who spends the first eleven scenes staring straight ahead and then shoots himself. This conjures up a strong image that suggests that Kirilov has no other function in the play. In fact, before he kills himself he betrays Shatov (Blair Cutting), who is killed by Verkhovensky and his cronies. When Lockridge writes that Kirilov is 'comical right from the start', it's not clear whether he finds the characterisation ridiculous; that is, whether he finds it difficult to accept the character or is picking up a sense of humour that, as with Verkhovensky, Chekhov would want to be there as a balance to the intense seriousness.

Other performers received reviews which tell us very little about their presence onstage. Beatrice Straight, for example, is praised for a moment of 'dark beauty and terror', when she realises that the man she loves is nothing more than an 'empty husk' (*Theatre Arts Monthly*, December 1939: 858). This doesn't give us an overall sense of her characterisation, although it does tell us something of the power of her performance. John Flynn, playing Stavrogin, dilated his eyes with 'monotonous frequency', according to the critic of *Women's Wear Daily* (25 October 1939) and, while this hints at a grotesque characterisation, it really isn't enough to go on.

I've been claiming that the critics were somewhat confused about the style of work for which Chekhov was aiming, and this sense of misunderstanding is heightened by the praise given to Ellen van Volkenburg. Playing Mrs Stavrogin, the role she took over from Dorothy Elmhirst, van Volkenburg was considered to be the only actor to create a character who was close to being a human being. I take from this that there was a critical assumption that the characters should appear to be human beings; that is, human beings behaving in a naturalistic, everyday manner. That van Volkenburg should get such praise is interesting, as she joined the cast late on and wasn't even as experienced in Chekhov's methods as the members of the school. Without being able to see a recording of the performance, it is difficult to assess exactly what the critics were seeing, but in the photograph of van Volkenburg and Flynn, it is possible to get a sense of the difference between the styles of the two actors. Flynn's appearance is expressionistic, his eyes are open wide and his left hand has a definite form, whilst van Volkenburg appears very naturalistic. The position of Flynn's hand might suggest excess muscle tension but, as with Hatfield's left hand, it isn't necessarily the case.

As we begin to put together the various comments, it does seem as though the critics were in favour of a naturalistic performance and used the term 'grotesque' as a negative term rather than appreciating that this was very much part of Chekhov's style. The critic of *The Sunday Times* (29 October 1939), for example, considered that the piece was directed in a 'bizarre style of Russian madness'.

The reviewer in *The Daily Worker* attacked the cast for 'overacting' and said that the actors' 'postures, struttings, leaps and bounds make Dostoevsky seem like a marijuana addict's dream' (26 October 1939). Once again, through the negative criticism we can get a glimpse of something else. If the critic was wanting a piece of socialist realism, with a naturalistic acting style, then Chekhov's actors were bound to seem as if they were 'overacting'. The reference to an 'addict's dream' gives further evidence that the piece was in a non-naturalistic style and that the reviewer found this difficult. It is interesting that the strong physicality of the actors, their 'postures, struttings, leaps and bounds', should produce this effect on the communist critic. It suggests a chaotic performance which lacked discipline. On the other hand, we've seen that another critic, Atkinson, also drew attention to the physicality of the actors and used it as evidence for an excess of discipline. The common ground of these two critics is their recognition of the significance of a stylised physicality. They each have a difficulty relating to this physicality. Lockridge also had a difficulty with the physical style of performance, but he connected it to the intense pace of the action. He saw that the theme of the play was important and relevant to what was happening in the world at the time and ought to wake the audience up. Instead of being woken up, however, he felt that the style of the piece was battering the audience into semi-consciousness. He felt there was insufficient control of the play's dynamics with fifteen scenes of 'angry dialogue', and with the company acting 'furiously' and without a 'pause for breath'. Given the importance of the pause for Chekhov, this is quite surprising. Was it the sheer physicality and intensity of the performance that was disturbing? Or is there other evidence to suggest that the problem was a lack of directorial control over the dynamics of the performance?

The dynamics of the production

Chekhov, like any director, was held responsible for the overall dynamics of the piece. For the reviewer in *Theatre Arts Monthly* (December 1939: 857–858), key criticisms were that the performance was overstrained and overdramatic, that it was 'keyed' too high from the beginning and that there was no gradation in the direction. In this sense, it was felt that the audience didn't have time to get into the style of the performance. It was noted that the performance worked best in the 'quieter' scenes, but that there were too few moments of stillness. The mention of 'quieter' scenes indicates that *The Possessed* wasn't performed at a continuously furious pace and that there was at least some variation, and that while the reviewer considers that there was too little stillness, there were at least some moments when the action slowed right down. So, while the overall impression is of an intense physical performance with a blistering pace and loud vocalisation, there are contrasting moments of quietness and stillness. The sense that the performance was 'overstrained' was a more subtle criticism than one which claimed that the actors were overacting. 'Overstrained' suggests that the actors were pushing at their limits and, as the reviewer points out, when a climax might have been reached, the actors had nowhere to go and had exhausted their vocabulary. This hints once again at the inexperience of actors who had not yet mastered their art and suggests that the director, by keying the performance too high, was asking too much of them.

Chekhov saw *The Possessed* as being 'near to tragedy' and wanted the audience to be frightened by it. He saw it as a 'form full of content and ready to break' – this gives us a sense that there was an attempt to signal in the performance that it was the form itself that was 'overstrained' and close to breaking point. Still, we have to return to the fact that, although the form might be overstrained, the actors still needed to communicate this with a sense of lightness and ease, and this doesn't appear to have been the case.

The reviewer in *Theatre Arts Monthly* also described the play as consisting of fifteen scenes of 'extreme violence and tension', which were as 'exhausting to watch as they must have been to perform'. Yet the same reviewer had earlier in the piece described the performance as 'an arresting example of directorial virtuosity'. In what sense could Chekhov's direction of *The Possessed* be described as virtuosic and arresting, while at the same time lacking an appropriate command of theatrical dynamics? Shouldn't the two be mutually exclusive? Certainly, the reviewer signed off by claiming that there was too little variation in acting styles on the Broadway stage, as well as too little experimentation and boldness in direction, and praised the company for its risk-taking. Arthur Pollock in *The Brooklyn Eagle* (25 October 1939) considered that Chekhov had staged the play with 'remarkable suppleness', which, if we add the idea of 'directorial virtuosity', seems to suggest that there was a sense of rhythm and a controlled dynamic in the production, even if this was marred at times by the cast's nervousness and inexperience. Pollock wrote that *The Possessed* was 'something special, something unlike anything to be seen in New York at the moment'.

Praising the detail

This discussion of the overall style and dynamic of the performance and the possible lack of control by the performers might lead us to expect that the individual performances were not quite up to scratch for a Broadway performance, even if the ensemble work was of a high quality. This would be a mistake. The detailed characterisation which was achieved was praised by John Mason Brown, who identified the small gestures that fitted perfectly with the character and that were at a level not even dreamed of by most American companies. This is high praise for a company which is making its first public showing and which is still, at this point, a student group. The reviewers also praised the physical and vocal discipline of the performers. It is important to bear this in mind when reading evaluations of Chekhov's work during this period.

The design

The stage and costume designs were by Mstislav Dobuzhinsky (1875–1957), who designed *A Month in the Country* for Stanislavsky at the Moscow Arts Theatre as well as designing for Diaghilev's Ballets Russes. Dobuzhinsky's set for *The Possessed* consisted of a series of small inset stages against black hangings, with window and sky effects projected on to a backdrop. It was clearly not a set for a naturalistic production, and it had an expressionistic feel that was very much in keeping with the sense of fantastic realism and the grotesque that I've been trying to tease out. Most critics viewed the set positively, although there was some criticism that it created difficulties for the actors with the action seeming too crowded at times. A difficulty here is that it's not possible to know whether the overcrowded moments were an accidental consequence of the design or part of Chekhov's conception.

Chekhov (1891–1955)

Lost humour

We've seen how some critics found it difficult to cope with the production and were unable to find a way of relating to the humour that was implicit in Chekhov's vision of the grotesque. Perhaps part of their difficulty was their stereotyped image of Russian culture.

Sidney B. Whipple, for example, used his review in the *World Telegram* (31 October 1939) to attack Russian culture in general. He described Russians as a 'sour, gloomy and hopeless race', and weighed into Anton Chekhov's *Three Sisters* as an example of this, giving the impression that the American stage would be better off without these imports. As for the Chekhov company, he didn't think that there was a place for them on Broadway.

In spite of his derogatory remarks about Russians, Whipple did, however, make an important observation. He remarked that there was a loss of humour in the adaptation from Dostoevsky, whose writings, particularly *The Possessed*, he considered to be full of grotesque humour. Whipple was not alone in this view – John D. Beaufort in *The Christian Science Monitor* (25 October 1939) also commented that there were too few traces of humour in the production. There is very little, if any, overt humour in Shdanoff's script, but Chekhov's own emphasis on the importance of humour makes this lack surprising. Perhaps the problem here is that the lack of ease in the performance meant that the sense of openness and warmth that accompanies humour was restricted. This might explain why some critics were unsure whether some moments were supposed to be humorous in such a 'serious' play, while others, like Whipple and Beaufort, clearly felt that the humour should have been there but wasn't. On the other hand, Whipple is as inconsistent in his remarks as some of the other critics. He finds the costume comical, for example, but doesn't make the connection to the humour he feels is lacking. What seems to be going on is that the critics are focusing on the script without exploring the relationship between the text and the action and how one comments upon the other.

Summing up

What does all of this add up to? *An exciting piece of physical theatre with detailed characterisation, performed in a style which was not fully grasped by the Broadway critics.* There were some weaknesses in the overall control of the performance, which affected the performance dynamics, but this was a surprisingly accomplished performance by a young company. There might have been some uncertainty as to the wisdom of the choice of text for an initial Broadway performance, but Chekhov's approach to training and directing was relatively successful in artistic terms. The lack of critical understanding of what Chekhov was trying to achieve meant that the reviews came down mostly on what were perceived as the negative aspects of the production, and *The Possessed* was a commercial failure. An uncredited piece in *Variety* on 1 November 1939 gave *The Possessed* the dubious accolade of being the 'first flop' of the Broadway season and reported that *Pickwick*, scheduled to be the company's second production was 'setback because of the war', although it's not quite clear what the war had to do with it.

Chekhov was very disappointed in the reception of *The Possessed*; he was prepared for negative criticism, but he was 'crushed and depressed' by the 'plain, banal, huge and shameless dishonesty' (in a letter to Dorothy Elmhirst shortly after the performance) of the criticism. By exploring the critical response and attempting to get a sense of the performance from both the positive and negative criticisms, we can see that it might be more a case of a lack of understanding rather than dishonesty. The critics weren't equipped to deal effectively with what Chekhov was trying to do in *The Possessed*, but they were sharp enough to realise that it didn't quite work, even though it had many admirable qualities.

Twelfth Night *(1940)*

After the financial disaster of *The Possessed*, Chekhov abandoned his production of *Pickwick* and turned towards two works with which he'd already had success: Shakespeare's *Twelfth Night* (with the Habima) and an adaptation of Dickens' *The Cricket on the Hearth* (with the MAT). These two productions toured New England and some Southern states, playing in university theatres and community centres.

Chekhov felt that the group made 'great strides', and the critical reception of *Twelfth Night* was very positive. Reviewers picked out the production's rhythm, music, harmony and unbroken line. One perceptive writer praised the company's 'joyous and vibrant theatricality', which, he suggested, simultaneously reminded a twentieth-century audience of the 'Ballets Russes and Walt Disney's cartoons'. This suggests precisely the combination of precision and fun that Chekhov admired in Vakhtangov and that was somehow missing from *The Possessed*. There was a strong sense of connection between performer and audience, which critics had also pointed out as lacking in the earlier production. In contrast to the inexperienced group who had appeared in *The Possessed*, the critics now saw a young group who showed a 'maturity beyond their years'.

Chekhov felt that Shakespeare should be edited and rearranged if necessary, to make the plays more suited to the times. *Twelfth Night* was cut from five acts to two plus a prologue, which inevitably sped up the action. The scene changes were done in full view of the audience by members of the cast in period costume, and the tempo of the changes was suited to the mood of the action. This suggests that the actors performing the scene change were effecting a change in atmosphere as much as a change in the arrangement of objects in space. In other words, the scene changes were *psychophysical actions*.

The set was designed by Chekhov, and was appropriately portable for a touring production. It consisted of reversible curtains, a turntable throne, miniature trees made out of coloured wood and a portable door frame and door with an attached balcony. The sense of portability, necessary for a touring production, was woven into the texture of the performance itself with the rhythmic scene changes.

One reviewer, who had the opportunity to observe the company in rehearsal, described Chekhov as a 'quiet-mannered' director who 'understands' the actors' problems and 'gently suggests slight changes' (*Albany Times*, 16 October 1940). This is quite a contrast from the kind of director that appears to have been imagined by the critics of *The Possessed*.

Chekhov's production of *Twelfth Night*, which was also to be well received on Broadway, appears to have improved on much of what was wrong with *The Possessed*. The overall sense was of an ensemble performance that was vibrantly physical, vocally clear, swift moving, imaginative, well characterised and superbly directed. There had been tremendous progress in the ensemble from the first production, but the qualities that were evident in *Twelfth Night* were also there in *The Possessed*. The difference in reception appears to have been partly to do with the intense reaction to the style and subject matter of *The Possessed*. In both productions, we can see that Chekhov's approach to training was having a powerful effect on his students. It may be the case that they were exposed too soon on the Broadway stage, but we have seen that, even at that formative stage, they were producing high-quality performances. In simple terms, Chekhov's approach to actor training was working.

Pickwick

Although there isn't a stage production of *Pickwick* to discuss, it's worth taking some time to look at Chekhov and Henry Lyon Young's script and at Chekhov's rehearsal notes to get some insight into how Chekhov was working at the time of *The Possessed*. Charles Dickens' *The Pickwick*

Papers (1836–1837) is a novel that stretches to over 800 pages and would obviously need considerable cutting to be brought to a manageable size for the stage.

Synopsis of scene one

The opening scene sees Samuel Pickwick announcing to the Pickwick Club that he is about to undertake a journey of discovery with three of his colleagues: Tupman, Snodgrass and Winkle. In the next room, Pickwick's landlady, Mrs Bardell, and her friend, Mrs Cluppins, have paused in the process of drinking their tea to listen to what's happening, while Mrs Bardell's son, Tommy, is spying through the keyhole. At the end of the meeting, Pickwick sees off his guests and Mrs Bardell and Mrs Cluppins have a brief conversation interrupted by Sam Weller, who has come to see Pickwick. When Pickwick returns, he calls Mrs Bardell to his room with the intention of informing her that he's appointing a new manservant, Sam. With Sam waiting outside, and Mrs Cluppins and Tommy listening at the door, Pickwick's rather indirect words are misunderstood by Mrs Bardell, who thinks that he's proposing marriage. She's so overcome with excitement that she faints into his arms. Tommy, not understanding at all, thinks that Pickwick is attacking his mother and springs to her defence, bursting into the room with Mrs Cluppins and Snodgrass, Tupman and Winkle, who have just arrived. Mrs Bardell, in a state of great happiness, is led back to her room, while Pickwick tries to explain what happened to his friends – not having realised that Mrs Bardell thinks that he's proposed to her. Overhearing the conversation, Mrs Bardell and Mrs Cluppins realise that Pickwick has no intention of honouring the proposal, the one very distressed and the other very angry. Meanwhile, Sam has his interview with Pickwick, they agree the terms of the employment and the group sets out for Rochester. Mrs Cluppins goes out to come back with a solicitor, Mr Fogg, and the legal process, which will end in Pickwick's imprisonment for breach of promise, gets under way.

There's quite a lot of action in this short scene, which brings together material that is separated by nearly 200 pages in the novel. Each of the sequences in the novel is considerably longer than the whole scene here, but they are reduced to their essential actions and placed alongside each other. This gives a very clear exposition of the conflict that is at the heart of the novel, but that takes hundreds of pages to take shape. Someone with less experience of adaptation and of the processes of making theatre would create a much more linear text. While they are aware that cuts will be necessary, both in the story and in the dialogue, they won't think to take different scenes from different parts of the story and put them together in order to clarify the major themes.

Making use of the possibility of two related actions occurring simultaneously on the stage, Chekhov and Lyons create a scene that cuts rhythmically between the two rooms, which might as well be two different worlds when it comes to the inhabitants of each room understanding the others' language.

Chekhov's notes on the scene

In his director's notes for the unstaged *Pickwick*, Chekhov (1939) gives clear indication for character, including objectives and inner gestures. The first thing he notes is that we are entering something which is already in process, a moment of change for the Pickwick Club. Because Pickwick is announcing a new adventure, there is a sense of openness, of expansion in the room. By way of contrast, in Mrs Bardell's room there is a sense of contraction. Why is this? Because the occupants of Mrs Bardell's room are spying; they are engaging in a covert, closed activity. They are drawing information into themselves and not giving anything out. Chekhov suggests that the actors see these opposites of expansion and contraction as gestures. We looked at archetypal gestures of expansion and contraction in the previous section, where we had a sense of the action extending out beyond the body. We then considered this in relation to the Psychological Gesture. What Chekhov is asking the actor to do here is to imagine that there is a gesture for the whole room. When I begin to imagine this, I see a large figure in each room, of which all the characters are a part. In one room this large figure is expanding and carrying all the characters with it; in the other room the figure is contracting. In this way I get a sense of all of the characters being a part of something larger than themselves. There are many different ways of imagining this and there is no right or wrong way, as long as you get the sense of the scene in each room having a particular gesture.

This doesn't mean that, onstage, all of the people in one room will be making large, expansive gestures, but that they are part of an expansive atmosphere. Chekhov suggests that the atmosphere in Pickwick's room is that of a 'light, sunny day' together with a sense of 'celebration'.

Chekhov's notes on the characters

Pickwick

This sense of celebration is particularly attached to Pickwick, who keeps his sunny disposition throughout most of the scene, only ruffled when Mrs Bardell approaches him too intimately. Chekhov sees Pickwick as having a quality of 'showing off', coupled with a 'tremendous power of radiation' and large and expansive gestures. His face is quite open, and it is very difficult for him to conceal anything from those around him. In fact, it doesn't occur to him to hide anything, because he is wonderfully naïve. He is a man who knows that others look at him and who recognises that he is charming and well dressed. Throughout the scene, Pickwick has an inner gesture of 'flying up, then down, then up'. Chekhov describes this as a kind of 'buoyancy' and connects it to a 'quality of lifting himself up like a bouncing ball'.

These physical and psychological qualities are also reflected in Chekhov's conception of Pickwick's speech. Pickwick shows off as much in his speech as in his action and he 'loves to make forms and shapes with his speech'. At this moment, Chekhov doesn't discuss the kinds of forms that Pickwick likes to make, but we can see how he does this with his consideration of Mrs Bardell.

Mrs Bardell

The notes on Mrs Bardell, for example, are perhaps even more detailed than they are for Pickwick. Chekhov offers the image that she forms her words 'like little dumplings ... little tasty things'. This is a more specific sense of vocal form than Chekhov has given for Pickwick, but perhaps that in itself is an indication of character. Pickwick is showing off, so enjoys playing with form, whereas Mrs Bardell is less conscious of the forms she makes (although the actor, of course, needs to be very clear about the vocal form as an aspect of characterisation).

Let's look at Chekhov's conception of Mrs Bardell in a little more detail. She is 'flowing like a liquid – always giving herself to everything and everyone' and this is made even more complex:

> When she is listening she is flowing – everything is enveloped in this watery flowing.

And:

> A movement like waves – like a boat – soaring, gliding – coming down she is accepting everything, going up she is embracing everything. Quick psychological power moving very slowly.

(Chekhov, 1939)

At the beginning of the scene, she is listening to everything with a sense of hope, as if it were a 'sermon from Heaven', and then, towards the end of the scene, when she has realised that Pickwick isn't going to marry her after all, she 'falls into a bottomless abyss into which she goes deeper and deeper'. Her Psychological Gesture is 'to receive everything', which is linked to the fact of her 'quietly accepting her destiny'. We can see how this is there, first in her acceptance that Pickwick wants to marry her, then in her acceptance that he doesn't and, finally, in her acceptance of Mrs Cluppins bringing the solicitor. In fact, Chekhov notes that Mrs Cluppins' influence over Mrs Bardell is so great that she acts like a filter between her friend and the world.

Mrs Cluppins

Mrs Cluppins is perhaps the character who provides the strongest contrast to Pickwick in Chekhov's conception of this opening scene. While Pickwick is expansive and drawing attention to himself through his showing off, Mrs Cluppins is 'contracting everything'. She is like a 'lobster' or a 'crab' who is constantly on the look out for 'victims' who she can snatch with her claws. But in their polarities of expansion and contraction, Pickwick and Mrs Cluppins are joined by the fact that they both need to be the centre of attention and pay little heed to the needs of others.

In this discussion of the characters, we can see Chekhov bringing together different aspects of the training into quite complex characterisations, and he does this with the other characters in the scene, as well. The level of detail here is quite difficult to absorb, and Chekhov's notes continue in this vein for the whole of the play. There is a huge amount of information for the actor who's going to be playing the character, but there is also considerable space for their own creativity. A consideration of these notes gives us a sense of the kind of direction Chekhov offered to his actors during this period, and we can imagine this level of information being given to actors during *The Possessed*.

Some thoughts on the rehearsal process

During *The Possessed*, Chekhov did have his actors rehearse scenes in their own words (Byckling, 1995: 34), and we can also imagine explorations that would involve playing the scene without words, just with the actions and inner gestures. Atmosphere was so important to Chekhov that we can imagine him exploring them with the actors for each scene and ensuring that everything fitted together. Because there is such a clear sense of group atmosphere and inner gesture in the opening scene of *Pickwick*, perhaps he would have had the actors construct group sculptures for each atmosphere. Because we don't have a detailed record of the rehearsal process for *The Possessed* and the work on *Pickwick* wasn't developed into performance, we don't know for certain exactly which exercises were used to achieve Chekhov's aims. We can, however, have a sense of the *kinds* of exercises he used and use our imaginations. Deirdre Hurst du Prey published a sample of four classes from July, August and September 1939 that are useful in this respect. The two July classes deal with exercises in the feelings of ease, form, beauty and the whole, although the tone of the class suggests that it wasn't for his regular students. The August class focuses on the rehearsal of some scenes from *Pickwick*; one scene in particular has a quality of 'raging nature' (du Prey, 1982: 25) and, as we might guess, one of the basic exercises is used:

> Imagine the air around you filled with the atmosphere – filled with this raging thing around you. Don't try to squeeze anything out of yourselves – that would be wrong. Everything is in tremendous movement, in you and around you. If you will imagine

this raging atmosphere truly, you will become either as small as a mouse or as big as King Lear. You will merge with it.

(ibid.)

Chekhov then goes on to give instructions which tell the actors how each character responds to this atmosphere. The whole scene is tightly scored in terms of atmospheres and each character's response to the atmosphere is proposed. There is consideration of how scenes fit together and the relationship between them in terms of rhythm. In addition to this, there is consideration of the Psychological Gesture, as we saw in the notes for the first scene.

In the notes to *The Government Inspector* (Leonard, 1984), Chekhov offers a detailed vision of action and characterisation which is quite different from his notes to *Pickwick*. There is clear scoring of atmospheres, marking what the dominant atmosphere is in each section of the play and where it changes into the next, which is also to be found in the notes to *Pickwick*. However, the notes on the characters are far more external. There is nothing to compare with the description of inner gestures of radiating, flying or flowing, or the images we have seen that Chekhov links to these. The notes to *The Government Inspector* aren't written for a group of actors trained in Chekhov's technique, so there is nothing about the Psychological Gesture. Here is a brief example which gives a flavour of the difference:

Artemy's fear and despair about the conditions in his hospital raise his voice in pitch and volume, drawing Anton's attention back to the group still at the door.

(Leonard, 1984: 143–145)

The feelings of the character are clear (fear and despair), as are the causes of the feelings (conditions in hospital), the effect of feelings on his voice (rises in pitch and volume) and the effect of his voice on the other character (draws his attention to the group at the door). But there is no indication as to how the actor might access all of this.

In respect of the score of atmospheres in *The Government Inspector*, Chekhov is very precise. He recommends that the actors all mark their scripts with the atmospheres and where they change, and suggests that the work on the play starts with establishing the first atmosphere. The actors should create the atmosphere, not yet worrying about characterisation, and move in harmony with it. Once they've begun to get a sense of the atmosphere in this way, they should take a line from the text and try to speak it in harmony with the atmosphere. The director should be looking out for the vocal tone, to check whether it sounds in keeping with the atmosphere or not. The next development is to check that both vocal tone and movement quality are in harmony with the atmosphere (Leonard, 1984: 115–117). Taking these suggestions, and information from Chekhov's other writings, we can imagine this kind of exercise being used during the process of rehearsing *The Possessed*, *Twelfth Night*, *The Cricket on the Hearth* and *King Lear*.

Further reading

Books and journals

Anderson, Neil (2011) 'On Rudolf Steiner's Impact on the Training of the Actor' in *Literature & Aesthetics* 21(1): 158–174.

Ashperger, Cynthia (2003) 'Michael Chekhov Association's Conferences 2000–2002' in *Toronto Slavic Quarterly* (4). http://sites.utoronto.ca/tsq/04/ashperger04.shtml (Accessed 10th April 2018).

Ashperger, Cynthia (2008) *The Rhythm of Space and the Sound of Time: Michael Chekhov's Acting Technique in the 21st Century*, Amsterdam and New York: Rodopi.

Autant-Mathieu, Marie-Christine and Meerzon, Yana (eds.) (2015) *The Routledge Companion to Michael Chekhov*, London: Routledge.
Barba, Eugenio (1995) *The Paper Canoe*, London and New York: Routledge.
Beevor, Antony (2005) *The Mystery of Olga Chekhova*, London: Penguin.
Benedetti, Jean (1990) *Stanislavski: A Biography*, London: Methuen.
Black, Lendley (1987) *Mikhail Chekhov as Actor, Director, and Teacher*, Ann Arbor, MI: UMI Research Press.
Braun, Edward (ed.) (1978) *Meyerhold on Theatre*, London: Eyre Methuen.
Bridgmont, Peter (1992) *Liberation of the Actor*, London: Temple Lodge.
Britton, John (ed.) (2013) *Encountering Ensemble*, London: Bloomsbury.
Byckling, Liisa (1995) 'Pages from the Past: *The Possessed* Produced by Michael Chekhov on Broadway in 1939' in *Slavic and East European Performance* 15(2): 32–45.
Byckling, Liisa (2010) 'Michael Chekhov's Production of *Twelfth Night* at the Habimah Theatre' in *Assaph: Studies in the Theatre* 24: 53–74.
Byckling, Liisa (2015) 'Michael Chekhov's Work as Director' in Autant-Mathieu, Marie-Christine and Meerzon, Yana (eds.) *The Routledge Companion to Michael Chekhov*, London: Routledge, pp. 21–39.
Chamberlain, Franc (2003) 'Michael Chekhov: Pedagogy, Spirituality, and the Occult' in *Toronto Slavic Quarterly* (4). http://sites.utoronto.ca/tsq/04/chamberlain04.shtml (Accessed 10th April 2018).
Chamberlain, Franc (2010) 'Michael Chekhov on the Technique of Acting: Was Don Quixote True to Life?' in Hodge, Alison (ed.) *Actor Training*, London: Routledge, pp. 63–80.
Chamberlain, Franc (2013) 'Michael Chekhov's Ensemble Feeling' in Britton, John (ed.) *Encountering Ensemble*, London: Bloomsbury, pp. 78–93.
Chamberlain, Franc (2015) 'Michael Chekhov in England: Outside the Magic Circle' in Autant-Mathieu, Marie-Christine and Meerzon, Yana (eds.) *The Routledge Companion to Michael Chekhov*, London: Routledge, pp. 207–218.
Chamberlain, Franc, Kirillov, Andrei and Pitches, Jonathan (eds.) (2013) *Michael Chekhov: Theatre Dance and Performance Training*, Volume 4, Issue 2, London: Routledge.
Chekhov, Michael (1928) *Put'aktera* [The Path of the Actor], Leningrad: Asadiea. (unpublished translated by Simon Blaxland-Delange (2000)).
Chekhov, Michael (1939) 'Pickwick' (unpublished ms.), Dartington Hall Trust Archive, Dartington, UK.
Chekhov, Michael (1942) 'To the Actor' (unpublished version), Dartington Hall Trust Archive, Dartington, UK.
Chekhov, Michael (1952) 'An Actor Must Have Three Selves' in Senelick, Laurence (ed.) (2008) *Theatre Arts on Acting*, London: Routledge, pp. 267–271.
Chekhov, Michael (1983) 'Chekhov on Acting: A Collection of Unpublished Materials' in *The Drama Review* 27(3): 46–83.
Chekhov, Michael (1985) *Lessons for the Professional Actor*, New York: PAJ Books.
Chekhov, Michael (1988) 'The Golden Age of the Russian Theatre' in *Alarums and Excursions 2*, Los Angeles.
Chekhov, Michael (1991) *On the Technique of Acting*, New York: Harper Perennial.
Chekhov, Michael (2000) *Lessons for Teachers of His Acting Technique* (edited by Deirdre Hurst du Prey), Ottawa: Dovehouse Editions.
Chekhov, Michael (2002) *To the Actor*, London: Routledge.
Chekhov, Michael (2005) *The Path of the Actor* (translated by Simon Blaxland-Delange and David Ball; edited by Bella Merlin and Andrei Kirillov), London: Routledge.
Cole, Toby and Chinoy, Helen Krich (eds.) (1963) *Directors on Directing: A Source Book of the Modern Theatre*, New York: Bobbs-Merrill Company.
Cornford, Tom (2012) 'The English Theatre Studios of Michael Chekhov and Michel Saint-Denis 1935–1965', PhD Thesis, University of Warwick. http://wrap.warwick.ac.uk/57044/ (Accessed 15th December 2016).
Cornford, Tom (2013) 'Beyond Realism: Into the Studio' in *Shakespeare Bulletin* 31(4): 709–718.
Craig, Edward Gordon (2009) *On the Art of the Theatre* (edited and with an introduction by Franc Chamberlain), London: Routledge.
Daboo, Jerri (2007) 'Michael Chekhov and the Embodied Imagination: Higher Self and Non-Self' in *Studies in Theatre and Performance* 27(3): 261–273.
Daboo, Jerri (2012) 'Michael Chekhov and the Studio in Dartington: The Remembering of a Tradition' in Pitches, Jonathan (ed.) *Russians in Britain*, London: Routledge, pp. 62–85.
Dalton, Lisa Loving (2017) *Murder of Talent: How Pop Culture Is Killing 'IT'*, Fort Worth, TX: Peak Performance Living.

The Drama Review (1983) 'Michael Chekhov's Career and Legacy' in *The Drama Review* 27(3): Whole Issue.

du Prey, Deirdre Hurst (1982) *The Training Sessions of Michael Chekhov*, Dartington: Dartington Theatre Papers.

du Prey, Deirdre Hurst (1983) 'Working with Chekhov' in *The Drama Review* 27(3): 84–90.

Fei, Faye Chunfang (2006) 'Huang Zuolin: Michael Chekhov's Link to China's Modern Theatre' in *New Theatre Quarterly* 22(3): 235–248, Cambridge: Cambridge University Press.

Gielgud, John (1937) 'Review of *An Actor Prepares*' in *Theatre Arts Monthly*, January: 31–34.

Gorchakov, Nikolai A. (1957) *The Theater in Soviet Russia*, New York: Columbia University Press.

Gordon, Mel (1985) 'Introduction' in Chekhov, Michael (ed.) *Lessons for the Professional Actor*, New York: PAJ Books, pp. 11–19.

Gordon, Mel (1987) *The Stanislavsky Technique: Russia: A Workbook for Actors*, New York: Applause Books.

Gordon, Mel (1995) '*The Castle Awakens*: Mikhail Chekhov's 1931 Occult Fantasy' in *Performing Arts Journal* 49: 113–120.

Gordon, Mel (2010) *Stanislavsky in America: An Actor's Workbook*, London: Routledge.

Green, Michael (1986) *The Russian Symbolist Theatre: An Anthology of Plays and Critical Texts*, Ann Arbor, MI: Ardis.

Grotowski, Jerzy (1968) *Towards a Poor Theatre*, London: Methuen.

Hodge, Alison (ed.) (2000) *Twentieth-Century Actor Training*, London: Routledge.

Hodge, Alison (ed.) (2010) *Actor Training*, London: Routledge.

Hornby, Richard (1992) *The End of Acting: A Radical View*, New York: Applause Books.

Hutchinson, Anjalee Deshpande (2018) *Acting Exercises for Non-Traditional Staging: Michael Chekhov Reimagined*, New York: Routledge.

Innes, Christopher (1998) *Edward Gordon Craig: A Vision of the Theatre*, Amsterdam: Harwood Academic Press.

Jenner, Pamela Georgina (2016) 'Propaganda Theatre: A Critical and Cultural Examination of the Work of Moral Re-Armament at the Westminster Theatre, London', PhD Thesis, Cambridge: Anglia Ruskin University. http://arro.anglia.ac.uk/702120/1/Jenner_2016.pdf (Accessed 28th March 2018).

Kasponyte, Justina (2012) 'Stanislavski's Directors: Michael Chekhov and the Revolution in Lithuanian Theatre of the 1930s', MPhil Thesis, Glasgow: University of Glasgow. http://theses.gla.ac.uk/3437/1/2011KasponyMPhil.pdf

Kirillov, Andrei (1994) 'Michael Chekhov: Problems of Study' in *Eye of the World* 1, St Petersburg.

Kirillov, Andrei (2006) 'Michael Chekhov and the Search for the "Ideal" Theatre' in *New Theatre Quarterly* 22(3): 227–234, Cambridge: Cambridge University Press.

Langman, Dawn (2014a) *The Art of Acting: Body-Soul-Spirit-Word: A Practical and Spiritual Guide*, Forest Row, UK: Temple Lodge.

Langman, Dawn (2014b) *The Art of Speech: Body-Soul-Spirit-Word: A Practical and Spiritual Guide*, Forest Row, UK: Temple Lodge.

Langman, Dawn (Forthcoming) *The Actor of the Future: Body-Soul-Spirit-Word: A Practical and Spiritual Guide*, Forest Row, UK: Temple Lodge.

Leach, Robert (1997) 'When He Touches Your Heart …: The Revolutionary Theatre of Vsevolod Meyerhold and the Development of Michael Chekhov' in *Contemporary Theatre Review* 7(1): 67–83.

Leonard, Charles (1984) *Michael Chekhov's to the Director and Playwright*, New York: Harper & Row.

Malaev-Babel, Andrei (ed.) (2011) *The Vakhtangov Sourcebook*, London: Routledge.

Marowitz, Charles (2004) *The Other Chekhov: A Biography of Michael Chekhov, the Legendary Actor, Director and Theorist*, New York: Applause Books.

Meerzon, Yana (2003) 'Forgotten Hollywood: Michael Chekhov's Film Figure and the Prague School Theory of Film' in *Toronto Slavic Quarterly* 4. http://sites.utoronto.ca/tsq/04/meerzon04.shtml (Accessed 10th April 2018).

Meerzon, Yana (2005) *The Path of a Character: Michael Chekhov's Inspired Acting and Theatre Semiotics*, Frankfurt am Main: Peter Lang.

Meerzon, Yana (2015) 'Staging the Spectator in Michael Chekhov's Acting Theory' in Autant-Mathieu, Marie-Christine and Meerzon, Yana (eds.) *The Routledge Companion to Michael Chekhov*, London: Routledge, pp. 123–138.

Meerzon, Yana (ed.) (2017) 'Michael Chekhov: Pedagogy Today' in *Critical Stages* 15. www.critical-stages.org/15/essays/ (Accessed 12th April 2018).

Monday, Mark (2017) *Directing with the Michael Chekhov Technique*, London: Methuen.

Monroe, Marilyn (2007) *My Life*, Lanham, MD: Taylor Trade Publishing.

Petit, Lenard (2010) *The Michael Chekhov Handbook for the Actor*, London: Routledge.
Pitches, Jonathan (2006) *Science and the Stanislavsky Tradition of Acting*, London: Routledge.
Pitches, Jonathan (2007) 'Towards a Platonic Paradigm of Performer Training: Michael Chekhov and Anatoly Vasiliev' in *Contemporary Theatre Review* 17(1): 28–40, London: Routledge.
Pitches, Jonathan (ed.) (2012) *Russians in Britain: British Theatre and the Russian Tradition of Acting*, London: Routledge.
Pitches, Jonathan (2013) 'The Technique in Microcosm: Michael Chekhov's Work on the *Fishers*' Scene' in *Theatre, Dance, and Performance Training* 4(2): 219–236.
Pitches, Jonathan and Shrubsall, Anthony (1999) 'Atmosphere, Space, Stasis: Staging Pinter's *Mountain Language* and *A Kind of Alaska* Using the Techniques of Michael Chekhov' in *Studies in Theatre and Performance* 19(1): 36–66.
Powers, Mala (2002) 'The Past, Present and Future of Michael Chekhov' in Chekhov, Michael (ed.) *To the Actor*, London: Routledge, pp. xxv–xlviii.
Raffe, Marjorie, Harwood, Cecil and Lundgren, Marguerite (1974) *Eurythmy and the Impulse of Dance*, London: Rudolf Steiner Press.
Senelick, Laurence (1981) *Russian Dramatic Theory from Pushkin to the Symbolists*, Austin: University of Texas Press.
Senelick, Laurence (1988) 'Review of *Mikhail Chekhov as Actor, Director and Teacher* by Lendley C. Black' in *Theatre Research International* 13(3): 295–297.
Senelick, Laurence (ed.) (2008) *Theatre Arts on Acting*, London: Routledge.
Senelick, Laurence (2009) 'Embodying Emptiness: The Irreality of Mikhail Chekhov's Khlestakov' in *New Theatre Quarterly* 25(3): 224–232, Cambridge: Cambridge University Press.
Senelick, Laurence (ed.) (2014) *Stanislavsky: A Life in Letters*, London: Routledge.
Senelick, Laurence (2015) 'Brief Encounters: Michael Chekhov and Shakespeare' in Autant-Mathieu, Marie-Christine and Meerzon, Yana (eds.) *The Routledge Companion to Michael Chekhov*, London: Routledge, pp. 141–160.
Spoto, Donald (1994) *Marilyn Monroe: The Biography*, London: Arrow Books.
Stanislavsky, Constantin (1980) *An Actor Prepares*, London: Eyre Methuen.
Steiner, Rudolf (1960) *Speech and Drama*, London: Rudolf Steiner Press.
Steiner, Rudolf (1964) *Knowledge of the Higher Worlds and Its Attainment*, Mokelumne Hill, CA: Health Research.
Vakhtangov, Eugene (1922) 'Fantastic Realism' in Cole, Toby and Chinoy, Helen Krich (eds.) (1963) *Directors on Directing: A Source Book of the Modern Theatre*, New York: Bobbs-Merrill Company, pp. 185–191.
Whyman, Rose (2011) *The Stanislavsky System of Acting: Legacy and Influence in Modern Performance*, Cambridge: Cambridge University Press.
Zinder, David (2002) *Body-Voice-Imagination: A Training for the Actor*, New York: Routledge.
Zinder, David (2007) '"The Actor Imagines with His Body": Michael Chekhov: An Examination of the Phenomenon' in *Contemporary Theatre Review* 17(1): 7–14, London: Routledge.

Video

Keeve, Frederick (2002) *From Russia to Hollywood: The 100 Year Odyssey of Chekhov and Shdanoff*, Venice, CA: Keeve Productions.
Mason, Felicity (1993) *The Training Sessions of Michael Chekhov*, Exeter: Arts Documentation Unit.
Merlin, Joanna (2000) *Michael Chekhov's Psychological Gesture*, Exeter: Arts Documentation Unit.
MICHA the Michael Chekhov Association (2007) *Master Classes in the Michael Chekhov Technique* (with Ragnar Freidank, Joanna Merlin, Lenard Petit, Ted Pugh and Fern Sloan), 3 DVDs, London: Routledge.
Sharp, Martin (2002) *Michael Chekhov: The Dartington Years*, Hove: Palomino Films.

Audio

Grove, Eddy (1992) *The Nature and Significance of Michael Chekhov's Contribution to the Theory and Technique of Acting*, New York: Eddy Grove.
Powers, Mala (1992) *Michael Chekhov: On Theatre and the Art of Acting: A Guide to Discovery with Exercises*, New York: Applause Books.

Franc Chamberlain

Useful websites

The Michael Chekhov Association (MICHA). www.michaelchekhov.org
Michael Chekhov School of Acting. https://michaelchekhovschool.org
Michael Chekhov UK. www.michaelchekhov.org.uk
The National Michael Chekhov Association (NMCA). www.michaelchekhov.net

7
BRECHT (1898–1956)

Meg Mumford

7.1 A life in flux

Which Brecht?

Bertolt Brecht (1898–1956) would have been wary of any introduction that presented him as a fixed monolith, rather than acknowledging that there were 'almost as many Brechts as there were people who knew him' (Lyon 1980: 205). For he was an ever-changing lover of flux who came to believe that we are contradictory beings, constantly modified by our interactions with the social and material world, and by the eye of each new beholder. And there have been many beholders, each with their own stance on this contentious subject. Some describe him as Europe's most famous Marxist playwright, director and theatre theorist. Or, Germany's answer to Shakespeare, but with a political twist. Others regard him as a genius who, despite his unfortunate political credo, remained a poet of eternally suffering and enduring humanity. Given that Brecht developed a respect for Marx, Shakespeare and fame he might not have objected to two of these descriptions. But it is this writer's position that Brecht had little time for the idea of eternal suffering.

One of the aims of this section is to capture the changeful nature of Brecht's political attitudes and artistic practice and to locate some of its sources. These include his acute responsiveness to Europe's tumultuous political landscape between the end of the nineteenth century and the beginning of the Cold War. In order not just to survive this upheaval, but also to prosper from it, Brecht had to be constantly on the move. Ironically, the sources of instability in his life played a role in fostering its continuities, especially his passion for experimental learning, collaboration and fighting oppression. Faced with immense social upheaval, Brecht's consistent response was to celebrate and attempt to master change. This book places particular emphasis on that attempt because it seeks to explain why Brecht is still a beacon for political performance makers. It could have told a less flattering or even opposing tale. But in an age like ours, where capitalism threatens to suppress alternative social models, celebrating the insightful practice of a contestatory voice and his collaborators seems a timely and necessary strategy.

Meg Mumford

On the make: from Bavaria to Berlin (1898–1924)

Born by the Lech

'Eugen Berthold Friedrich Brecht' was born in the Bavarian city of Augsburg on 10 February 1898 at 7, Auf dem Rain, in a building flanked by canals of the river Lech. The apartment was noisy, due to the rushing waters and the file cutter's workshop on the ground floor. However tiresome the noise may have been for its inhabitants, its causes – the water and the labourer – provide rich metaphors for a biographer foregrounding Brecht's long-held interest in flux and the cause of the worker. The choice of lodgings probably stemmed from the realities of his father's modest income – Berthold Friedrich was a commercial clerk for the Haindl paper factory. After the birth of Brecht's brother, Walter, the family took up residence in the so-called 'Colony', a group of four-storey houses built by the Haindl founders for the benefit of needy employees. Brecht's father, promoted to company secretary, was in charge of the administration of this social housing, his family privileged with an entire floor to themselves as well as two attic rooms. Unlike the majority of their neighbours, they could afford live-in servants.

The lifestyle of the Brecht family was typical of the bourgeoisie during the reign of Kaiser Wilhelm II (1888–1918), king of Prussia and last emperor of all the states in the German commonwealth. The work ethic and aspirational energy modelled by Brecht senior, who in 1917 became the managing director for Haindl, informed the career attitude of his sons. By his mid teens Brecht junior was already in hot pursuit of fame as a literary figure and his brother would become a professor in the field of paper technology. The patriarchal and class dynamics of the Wilhelminian empire were manifested in the family's strict sexual division of labour – with women relegated to domestic work – and in its observance of class segregation – although the boys played and fought with their working-class neighbours, Brecht's grammar school was an exclusively middle class (and macho) experience. During the exile years in Denmark, he would look back scathingly at his ruling class upbringing:

> I grew up as the son
> Of well-to-do people. My parents put
> A collar round my neck and brought me up
> In the habit of being waited on
> And schooled me in the art of giving orders.
>
> (Brecht 1979c: 316)

When Brecht wrote this poem he had already proved himself a commanding leader, in the best and worst sense. And one whose behaviour throughout his life was characterized by both a condemnation and a continuation of stifling bourgeois habits.

Historicizing interlude

Now, let's stop this biographical flow for a moment. From the 'Born by the Lech' episode, what have you learned about the author's attitude towards her subject matter? Why do you think she selected that material and organized it in that way? How does her telling of the tale reveal her historical context, her worldview, her politics? And why has she sometimes used the rather strange strategy of referring to herself in the third person and past tense? These are the types of questions Brecht asked when reading any type of expression, history texts in particular. And he would have started asking these questions from the word 'go', interrupting the flow of the narrative with analytical commentary.

Had Brecht read the opening section of this biography he would have quickly grasped the point of the third person references to 'the author', for he used the same distancing strategy in many of his own reflective writings. Through this choice of narrative voice he communicated his interest in analytical observation of one's own position, and in treating the self as historical rather than eternally present. He would also have recognized that, rather than telling a tale of inborn genius, the biographer was seeking to demonstrate how his ever-changing material, social and historical circumstances conditioned his thought – an approach in keeping with his own. Brecht would have noted too how she emphasized the material circumstances and associated thoughts and habits of his family, focusing on their relationship to work, to a bourgeois ethos of self-improvement and social mobility and to class and gender division. And he would have understood the Marxist social class terminology:

- bourgeoisie: When Brecht's father became managing director, he joined the ranks of the bourgeoisie, the capitalist owners of merchant, industrial and money capital who in nineteenth-century Europe replaced the land-owning aristocracy as the economic class in control of the bulk of the means of production.
- petite bourgeoisie: Prior to Brecht senior's promotion, he belonged to the group of people, like office workers and professionals, who do not own the means of production but may buy the labour power of others (such as domestic servants) or own small businesses, like the file cutter. Brecht would often apply the term to people who had some economic independence but not much social influence, such as white-collar workers and small shopkeepers.
- proletariat: At the Haindl paper mill, Brecht's father employed and made company profit from wageworkers, members of the proletariat or industrial working class, whose means of livelihood was to sell their labour to property owners.

As you read on, see if you can spot other features of the biographer's position, including the influence of socialist and feminist thought.

War poet: patriot and rebel

Even prior to the outbreak of the First World War (1914), Brecht and his grammar school classmates at Augsburg's Royal Realgymnasium were indoctrinated in a monarchist and militant nationalism. When Germany officially declared war, Brecht was exempted from active duty owing to his heart condition – he suffered heart cramps and palpitations from an early age. Instead, he chose to serve the fatherland through a series of patriotic texts for the local papers. Under the pseudonym 'Berthold Eugen', he praised the Kaiser's leadership, calling for donations to support families who had lost their breadwinner, and eulogizing self-sacrificing German mothers who put their grief for lost sons behind them and devoted themselves to prayers for victory.

Brecht's pathos-laden jingoism was gradually replaced with a sceptical, realist attitude. In keeping with his new, hard-hitting approach, in 1916 he began to use the terse signature 'Bert Brecht'. In June of that year, the critical tone of a school essay brought him close to being expelled. When asked to write about Horace's revered pronouncement *Dulce et decorum est pro patria mori* ('It is sweet and honourable to die for the fatherland'), Brecht replied in combative mode that it was always hard to die, particularly for those in the bloom of their life, and that only the vacuous – and even then, only if they believed themselves far from deaths door – could present self-sacrifice as easy. This was a daring statement in a context where many of Brecht's classmates were being sent to military training or into the heart of the fighting, some never to return and others to be maimed for life. In contrast to his brother and peers, Brecht had no desire to be a hero, managing to avoid military service almost until the end of the war.

After completing school in May 1917, Brecht carried out auxiliary war-worker duties as a cleric and gardener, and was later employed as a private tutor. In October he matriculated at the Ludwig-Maximilians University in Munich, taking courses in literature for two semesters, before suddenly transferring to medical studies. There is little evidence that Brecht applied himself to medicine, and in the summer semester of 1921 he failed to sign up for any lectures. It seems likely that Brecht's transferral arose from a need to ensure that if he were conscripted, it would be as a medical orderly rather than as a soldier. As Brecht said to his life-long friend and future scenographer, Caspar Neher, he would rather collect feet than lose them.

From October 1918 to January 1919 Brecht worked on a venereal disease ward of a military hospital, which, in keeping with the topsy-turvydom of the times, was erected in the playground of an Augsburg primary school. It was during this period that he wrote the famous, politically explosive poem 'Legend of the Dead Soldier', a scathing parody of the heroic grenadier figure in German literary ballads who rises from his grave and nobly steps back into battle. Brecht turned the literary tradition on its head by presenting the soldier as a stinking corpse, who, on the whim of the Kaiser, is 'resurrected' and declared fit for service by an army medical commission. After pouring schnapps down the soldier's throat, painting over his filthy shroud with the black-white-red of the old imperial flag, and hanging two nurses and a half-naked prostitute in his arms, they parade him through the villages. The next day, as he has been taught, he dies a hero's death. The shocking nature of Brecht's attack on idealized heroism was intensified by the contrast between the grotesque imagery of the lyrics and the gentle and sentimental melody, an oppositional technique that would become a trademark of his epic and dialectical theatre. The satirical force of the ballad, often performed by Brecht to guitar accompaniment, was such that in 1923 it earned him fifth place on the Nazi's list of people to be arrested once they were in power.

Brecht's rebellion against authoritarianism indicates an early interest in power structures, a rebellion motivated at this stage more by a concern with his own empowerment than any revolutionary vision of large-scale social change. The desire to be top dog himself would characterize aspects of Brecht's life-long behaviour, in some cases leading to a perpetuation of invidious power relations. For example, his frequently commandeering and proprietorial treatment of women recalled the habits and double standards of his imperial forebears. At the same time that Brecht was convincing Paula Banholzer – the mother in 1919 of his first child, Frank – to break off her engagement with another man and remain loyal to him, he was pursuing the opera singer Marianne Zoff, soon to become his first wife and mother of his daughter Hanne. Brecht's desire to orchestrate and sustain multiple love relationships at any one time bears some relation to 'his delighted, sometimes obsessive engagement with collective activity' as well as his 'tendency to take the lead in such activity' (Thomson, in Thomson and Sacks 1994: 23).

Brecht's simultaneous encouragement of 'think-tank' collectives embodied a relatively egalitarian version of this engagement. In Augsburg these groups consisted of a circle of predominantly male friends who often met in Brecht's attic room, where there would be singing and music making, discussion, reading and reciting. From the mid-1920s onwards, working-class and female members – especially lovers – were increasingly represented as co-workers. Brecht spearheaded and led these collectives – a significant number of his plays, including world-renowned texts like *The Threepenny Opera*, *Mother Courage and Her Children* and *The Caucasian Chalk Circle*, were written and researched in collaboration with others. And it was he who basked most in the fame and royalties they brought. Nevertheless, for the majority of participants who chose to be involved, they were exciting and relatively democratic forums where creative productivity was fostered *en masse*.

A swine and his creature comforts

The post-war period would not have been an easy time to become a breadwinner, especially if your aim was to forge a career as a poet. Brecht's response to a social context riven by hunger, unemployment and hyperinflation was to assert – both in his private life and through his art – the nature and importance of material needs and survival strategies. His increasingly materialist outlook – the philosophical view that everything that really exists is material in nature and that everything mental is a product of phenomena that can be accessed through the senses – was at odds with expressionism, the dominant experimental theatre in the early post-war years. The expressionist movement contained diverse and often contradictory tendencies, but many of the playwrights were idealist in so far as they thought non-material mind and spirit were the prime shaping forces of human experience and the world. Their idealism partly explains the so-called 'New Man' figure found in many of their plays, including Friedrich from Ernst Toller's *The Transformation* (1919), a poet-leader who seeks to change the world through visionary speeches that rejuvenate community spirit.

Brecht's play *Baal* is an expression of his irritation with expressionist idealism and pathos. The first version of the play – it became customary for Brecht to revise or adapt earlier work in the light of new circumstances – was written in the spring of 1918, within a month of the Munich Chamber Theatre production of Hanns Johst's *The Lonely One*. Energized by his love of opposition, Brecht proclaimed that he could write a better play than Johst's expressionist drama, but the resulting counter play was by no means totally oppositional. For example, both texts are episodic presentations of men experiencing social alienation. And as in other expressionist work, *Baal* depicts a journeying, semi-autobiographical protagonist. Brecht's contestatory attitude, as well as his tendency to preserve aspects of the contested model, remained a hallmark feature of his creative approach. Johst presents his protagonist as a lonely playwright genius, misunderstood by the inferior mass. Baal is also a writer, but he is an earthly hedonist who puts drink, food and sex before his poetry. Rather than being a superior and isolated soul, Baal is an insatiable, desiring body who interacts voraciously, guided purely by his own pleasure and greed for sensual experience with men, women and nature. Unlike Toller's poet-leader, his journeying does not lead to heroic self-transformation. Rather, seemingly worn down by rough living and an asocial existence, Baal simply merges with matter: on a stomach full of stolen eggs, he dies alone in the dirt of a forest.

Brecht's vagabond outsider, Baal, embodies a deep dissatisfaction with imperial Germany. Like his favourite playwright at the time, Frank Wedekind, Brecht's shockingly transgressive expressions constituted a rebellion against duty, conformity and suppression of desire. But the revolt was circumscribed by a focus on his own freedom and notoriety, and an unwillingness to commit to any political agenda for change. While Brecht was immersed in *Baal*, and the pleasures of the local fairground, others were choosing the path of martyrdom in defence of the newly proclaimed Bavarian Republic. During the political chaos after the Kaiser's abdication, left-wing activists – including Ernst Toller – seized the opportunity to oust the king of Bavaria and assert a socialist government. It was declared on 9 November 1918 in Munich by Kurt Eisner, who was the poet-leader of Germany's Independent Social Democrat Party (USPD). In an attempt to ensure grass-roots involvement in government, the Republicans instituted workers' and soldiers' councils. Brecht was elected as a representative for the soldiers' council of the Augsburg military hospital, a role involving tasks such as making reports on soldiers' complaints about everyday matters. Brecht would later praise such dialogic approaches to government, but on this occasion his participation was to be short-lived and unremarkable.

The USPD had been established in 1917 by dissatisfied SPD members. From this breakaway group two mythologized revolutionaries, Rosa Luxemburg and Karl Liebknecht, established the Spartacists, who by early 1919 were officially the German Communist Party (KPD). Meanwhile, a provisional national government had been formed in Berlin with the SPD leader, Friedrich Ebert, at its helm. In a bid to establish stability, Ebert made a pact with the *Oberste Heeresleitung* (OHL, Supreme Army Command), which stipulated that the government would not attempt to reform the Army if it promised to protect the government. 'Protection' activities included crushing left-wing dissent with the support of right-wing military forces, such as the *Freikorps* – volunteer units trained by the German Army and made up of demobilized (and disgruntled) officers and soldiers. After the KPD went on the assault, occupying the Berlin newspaper quarter and inciting workers to take up arms against the government, the *Freikorps* were sent in and on 15 January 1919 Luxemburg and Liebknecht were brutally murdered. Hot on the heels of this event, Kurt Eisner was shot dead, and government troops, together with the *Freikorps* and a group called the 'white guard', viciously suppressed the Bavarian Republic in both Augsburg and Munich. Its poet-leaders were either executed or imprisoned. In February, after nationwide elections, the first German republic was declared in the city of Weimar. Until 1933, this so-called Weimar Republic would continue to be dominated by the struggle for power between right- and left-wing forces.

Brecht was by no means uninterested in these political upheavals, but he preferred to remain on the sidelines, operating as a critical – but not yet committed – observer. Taking a stance brought with it the threat of personal danger and the possibility of disconnection from friends and family – Brecht's brother and his friend Otto Müllereisert played an active role in the white guard's activities in Munich. Nevertheless, Brecht did make some left-wing gestures, joining the commemorative marches for Eisner and the KPD leaders, writing theatre reviews for the USPD's newspaper, and harbouring Georg Prem, an important member of the Augsburg workers' and soldiers' council.

One of the ways Brecht grappled with the events of 1919 was through the writing of a shockingly unsentimental soldier-returns-home play set during the Spartacist uprising in Berlin. *Drums in the Night* (originally titled *Spartacus*) presents different responses to the uprising, giving particular prominence to the non-heroic attitude of the protagonist, Kragler, a soldier who has just returned after four years' service in Africa. At the play's finale, the war-weary Kragler faces a dilemma, being urged by the Spartacists to join the fighting. At the same time he discovers his fiancée is pregnant with another man's child. His uncertainty does not last long. The revolution is quickly dismissed as far less attractive than the opportunity to savour some creature comforts: 'Is my flesh to rot in the gutter so that their idea should get into heaven? . . . I am a swine, and the swine's going home' (Brecht 1998a: 114–115). According to the actor who played Kragler in the first production, his character's attitude towards the Spartacist cause echoed Brecht's own scornful treatment of the Revolution in both Munich and Berlin as ridiculously incompetent (McDowell 1976: 105).

Fame in the jungle of two cities

Brecht's sensitivity to a context riddled with violent oppositions and power struggles was reflected in his next play, *In the Jungle* (1922). A dramatization of a fight between two men in the city of Chicago, the play presents the attempt of the Malayan lumber dealer Schlink to take control of George Garga, an impoverished employee of a lending library. When Garga clings to what he calls his freedom, refusing to sell his own opinion of a book, Schlink declares war and a bitter battle ensues in which both protagonists lose their livelihood, Garga his family and lover, and Schlink his life. During a performance of the play on 18 May 1923 at Munich's conservative Residenz Theater, members of the emerging Nazi party staged a protest against its purported glorification of communism by throwing gas bombs into the auditorium. The performance resumed after the smoke had subsided but the production was soon withdrawn. The protestors' interpretation is bemusing, for as Brecht pointed out towards the end of his life, the play 'was meant to deal with this pure enjoyment of fighting' (Brecht 1998a: 438) rather than consciously addressing any struggle between ruling and working class.

The crushing of the Bavarian Republic and the increased presence, during the inflation years, of the Nazis and their henchmen, led members of the intelligentsia, including Brecht, to consider leaving both Munich and the country. Brecht first witnessed Nazi pageantry when he attended a Hitler event in June 1923, together with expressionist playwright and friend Arnolt Bronnen. The event proved stimulating but frightening. According to Bronnen, it inspired a night-long musing on a contemporary mass play that would take place in the circus and deal with hunger, inflation and liberation. And the spectacle of masses of wooden, brown-shirted *petit bourgeois* figures brandishing a red flag prompted Brecht to reflect on the unwelcome advent of a Bavarian society born of anarchy, alcohol and a taste for material comfort and nationalist politics. Bronnen found the advent of 'Mahagonny' – Brecht's name for the philistine utopia yearned for by these marching figures – to be a much more inviting prospect (Ewen 1970: 130). In the late 1920s Brecht would distance himself from Bronnen, who became increasingly involved in right-wing and Nazi circles. Brecht was confronted by Nazi theatrics once again in 1923, when he arrived to direct a rehearsal of his play *Edward the Second* at the Munich Chamber Theatre in November and found the actors talking about Hitler's attempt at a military coup in the city. Brecht cancelled the rehearsal and later that day, at a gathering of Jewish and communist friends, discussed the siege and the issue of whether and how long it was wise to remain in Germany. On this occasion, Hitler's beer-hall putsch proved short-lived and rehearsals continued the next day.

Despite – or perhaps precisely because of – his personal experience of right-wing aggression, Brecht continued to keep his distance from off-stage party politics, immersing himself in the world of the theatre. During his second visit to Berlin in the winter of 1921 his efforts to publicize himself and his work brought dividends when, in November 1922, he was awarded the prestigious Kleist Prize for drama. Brecht also applied himself to learning the trade, observing the work of famous expressionist and post-war directors Karl-Heinz Martin and Leopold Jessner, and gaining entry to rehearsals of August Strindberg's *The Dream Play* under the direction of Max Reinhardt, one of the most prolific and influential impresarios in the German-language theatre. Many of the following performance methods, which Brecht witnessed, would later feature in modified form in his work:

- vivid gestures and diction;
- self-conscious theatricality;
- emblematic use of actors and audio-visual imagery to denote ideas;
- group choreography, tableaux and chorus.

These approaches proved easily transferable to what became his trademark – a theatre concerned with the lucid and critical demonstration of social attitudes and relations.

The cabaret scene in both Munich and Berlin was another formative training ground. Throughout the 1920s Brecht made appearances as a cabaret performer, pretending to be a clarinettist in a sketch called *Orchestra Rehearsal* by the Bavarian folk comedian Karl Valentin and impressing audiences with demonic renditions of songs like 'Legend of the Dead Soldier' at a Berlin cabaret called The Wild Stage. On 30 September 1922 he even tried his hand at organizing a one-off midnight revue called 'The Red Raison', at the Chamber Theatre. This cabaret's 'mix of popular entertainers, stage actors and "authors," all of whom are personal acquaintances performing for the fun of it' was exactly the type of event Brecht loved (Calandra 1974: 87). While Brecht's participation in different types of cabaret came to an end at the close of the 1920s, many of their defining ingredients, outlined below, had an enduring impact on his work:

- an episodic structure characterized by self-contained parts;
- the mixing of 'high' (e.g. poetry) and 'low' (e.g. music hall) art;
- separation of actor from character;
- defamiliarizing parody;
- overt engagement with the audience;
- satirical engagement with society.

His exposure to cabaret and comedic performers, especially Valentin on stage and Charlie Chaplin on screen, certainly strengthened his knowledge of comic devices and their usefulness for puncturing the familiar world and engendering pleasurable critical distance. Valentin also gave Brecht advice about how to help actors become gestural demonstrators, and in this respect Brecht had much to learn.

Like many directors, Brecht began as an authoritarian figure, only gradually moving towards the role of a dialogue partner. His first attempt – a Berlin production of Bronnen's *Vatermord* – came to an abrupt end in April 1922 when the star actors abandoned the project out of frustration with his alienating tendency to forge a new performance mode by simply tearing apart the one they were comfortable with. These actors were well versed in the art of carrying the audience away with their charismatic and passionate performances, and Brecht wanted none of it. But at this stage he did not know how to create the different performance mode he had recently begun to articulate in his diary, one where the spectator 'is not fobbed off with an invitation to feel sympathetically, to fuse with the hero' but enjoys 'a higher type of interest to be got from making comparisons, from whatever is different, amazing, impossible to take in as a whole' (Brecht 1979b: 159). Despite his inexperience, Brecht was given the post of dramaturge and director at the Chamber Theatre in the autumn of 1922. It was during his first assignment as named and independent director of one of his own plays, the *Edward the Second* production of March 1924, that he started to make headway with a new mode of realist performance.

John Fuegi has referred to this performance mode as a mixed or contradictory mimetic style (Fuegi 1987: 36), wherein Brecht would combine careful imitation of social actuality, in the manner of Stanislavsky with a playful, defamiliarizing depiction or distortion. For example, in *Edward*, the actors playing the soldiers who prepare to hang the rebel Gaveston were given a working gallows and instructed to copy the details of a hanging so precisely that they would look as if they regularly carried out such work. They were to perform these actions against an ostentatiously askew and painted canvas backdrop and in 'whiteface' make-up, signifying, perhaps, their state of fear and fatigue during battle (Fuegi 1987: 24, 33). The end product was a tense unity of elements from (a) the late nineteenth-century naturalism that dominated mainstream theatre in Augsburg and even permeated expressionist stagings and (b) popular non-realist forms such as could be found in cabaret and fairground shows. The mixed mimetic staging reflects Brecht's life-long interest in both imitating concrete reality – e.g. the exploited underling henchmen – and making strange their socialized behaviour and its social causes, in this case the soldiers' submission out of habit, fear or exhaustion. The mixing of styles was coupled with a dialogic approach to the creation of both play and production. Not only was *Edward* co-authored with Lion Feuchtwanger, but Brecht encouraged cast, crew and casual spectators to attend the rehearsals and welcomed suggestions, constantly changing his text in the light of the new ideas and bodies before him. Having established the cornerstones of his later directorial style during the 1924 production, Brecht then set off to forge new collectives in Berlin, where he had secured the position of dramaturge at Reinhardt's Deutsches Theater.

Changing the world: Weimar politics (1924–33)

From pugilism to class struggle

During the mid to late 1920s in Berlin, Brecht began to develop a theatre of social commentary and to use the term 'epic' to describe it. Early epic theatre had much in common with the other art forms that accompanied Germany's economic stabilization. Due to events like the rescheduling of war reparation payments in 1924, the country could once again focus on industrial productivity. The obsession with maximizing output encouraged an 'attitude that sought to apply the engineering principles of rationality and streamlining to all aspects of life' (Rosenhaft in Thomson and Sacks 1994: 14). One embodiment of this attitude was *Neue Sachlichkeit* ('New Objectivity' or 'New Sobriety'), a structure of feeling and type of artistic expression characterized by an emphasis on sober observation, utility and clarity. Art forms associated with this aesthetic included documentary-style plays dealing with topical issues; the detective novel (Brecht himself was a fan of the crime thriller); and the clear and satirical representations of corrupt society by the visual artist Georg Grosz, who became a member of Brecht's circle. In the late 1920s Brecht would describe New Objectivity as both a necessary advance and an ultimately reactionary affair (Brecht 1978: 17), presumably because its emphasis on rational argumentation and intensified productivity as the means for alleviating social inequality was not combined with an understanding of the need to dismantle capitalism. However, its treatment of society as an object for critical reflection had a lasting impact on his approach to the issue of how the artist and spectator should look at their work and world.

Throughout the 1920s, Brecht's interest in a critically distanced way of looking was overtly connected with a macho assertion of masterful wit, one that expressed itself in his tough-boy posturing, complete with Caesar haircut, leather jacket and phallic cigar. Inspired by popular cultural events like music hall, where the patrons (often predominantly male) could smoke and drink while watching, Brecht began to promote the image of a smoker's theatre of relaxed and therefore discerning 'cool' spectators who would not be 'carried away' by the on-stage world. He lauded sports events – expansive bright lighting and a lack of mystery and suggestion – as another example of how to set the scene for shrewd spectatorship. Of all the sports that constituted post-war Germany's major entertainment spectacles, it was boxing that most inspired the non-athletic Brecht. One of the members involved in Brecht's next collective venture, the play *Man is Man*, was a proficient boxer who had acted as a second to the heavyweight champion Paul Samson-Körner. Brecht began working on a biography of the champion in early 1926 but it was never completed. Boxing matches contained both a clear demonstration of a skilled struggle for survival and a critical audience. Brecht invoked the boxing model frequently in this period, even using a roped platform recalling the boxing ring in his production of *The Measures Taken* (1930), a play that contains no overt references to the sport. It stages a type of court trial, encouraging both on-and off-stage audiences to judge the behaviour of a Young Comrade, whose tendency to act impulsively in accordance with his emotions endangers the collective. Brecht's treatment of boxing and sport spectator-ship is marked by some intriguing blind spots. For example, he fails to address the passionate and empathetic nature of the onlookers, perhaps a symptom of his tendency at this time to dismiss illusionist theatre as effete, and his longer-term interest in art that minimized emotional enthralment.

The figure of the boxer, a complex icon in Weimar culture, was used to celebrate both the mechanized and trained body, as well as the primitive heroic warrior who fights to reassert himself in the age of the machine and mass living (Bathrick 1990). These contradictory responses reflected an ongoing anxiety about the large-scale shift from rural to industrial city life that dominated the early twentieth century. Urbanization, together with the impact of late nineteenth-century thinkers, such as Darwin, Freud and Marx, intensified debates about the nature of man and the relation of the individual to the collective. Brecht waged a long and unresolved struggle with some of these contemporaneous issues during the copious rewriting and staging of *Man is Man*. Ideas for a play about human identity date back to 1918, but it was not until the formation of the so-called 'Brecht collective' in the mid-1920s – an ever-changing team of artistic collaborators – that the title and overall shape emerged. The version of the grotesque comedy that was premiered in September 1926 uses the image of a trained fighter (a soldier) to explore the malleable nature of man and his exchangeability. Its protagonist, a poor, Chaplinesque Irish dock-porter called Galy Gay, is transformed by a group of British soldiers in a mythical Indian Kilkoa into their missing team mate, Jeriah Jip. After a quick lesson in how to use his weaponry, Gay-cum-Jip becomes a bloodthirsty fighting machine that single-handedly guns down a fortress blocking the British army's pass into Tibet.

In a radio talk of 1927, Brecht suggested that, far from mourning the loss of personality in a technologized mass, *Man is Man* actually celebrated man's malleability and his empowerment through the collective. However, it is hard to reconcile Brecht's positive appraisal of Gay's transformation with the fact that, not only does Galy Gay acquiesce to the lackeys of an imperial army, but his initially fluid self becomes locked in the patterns of a machine-like killer (Schechter in Thomson and Sacks 1994: 73–74). When Brecht directed the play in 1931, the alarming growth in political power of the Nazis spurred him to emphasize the brutality of the collective that his protagonist is all too easily persuaded to join. According to Brecht's friend the Soviet playwright Sergei Tretiakov, the clown-like soldiers were depicted with distinctly sinister overtones, 'armed to the teeth and wearing uniforms caked with lime, blood and excrement', two of them stalking about the stage on stilts and a third padded out in a grotesque manner (Tretiakov, in Brecht 1979a: xiii). When revising the play in 1954, Brecht reinterpreted its theme as 'the false, bad collectivity (the "gang") and its powers of attraction', locating the appeal of Nazism for the *petite bourgeoisie* in their longing for a 'genuinely social collectivity of the workers' (Brecht 1979a: 108).

Meeting Marx

Brecht's understanding of the nature of the individual and the quality of the collective was greatly influenced by his Marxist studies, which began after the Darmstadt premiere of *Man is Man* in autumn 1926. His decision to read Marx's *Capital* was triggered by his difficulties with *Joe Fleischhacker* (1924–9), a play about the demise of a family who leave the country for the big city, only to perish on the streets of Chicago when it is thrown into chaos by the wheat speculations of Fleischhacker. The play embodied Brecht's desire to bring to the stage new and topical subject matter, like stock exchange manoeuvres and economic catastrophes. With the help of Elisabeth Hauptmann, the collaborator and lover working most closely with him at the time, he gathered considerable information. Yet it was not until he began reading *Capital*, Marx's examination of the capitalist mode of production, that the fog surrounding complicated money transactions and the causes of economic crisis began to lift. By the summer of 1927 Brecht was asking the actress Helene Weigel, soon to be his second wife, to send him a stockpile of Marxist literature.

But what became a life-long engagement with a Marxist mode of looking at the world did not translate into a commitment to the German Communist Party. Unlike Hauptmann and Weigel, who joined the KPD in 1929, Brecht never became a card-carrying member. One of his collaborators during the years in America, Hans Viertel, aptly described Brecht's complicated position as that of 'a one-man political party in close coalition with the Communists' (Lyon 1980: 302). Rather than toe the line of a large-scale, pre-established collective, he preferred the role of a supportive but independent observer. Brecht was more at home with smaller-scale think-tanks, like the group who met at his apartment in 1931 to discuss dialectical materialism under the guidance of the ex-KPD dissident Karl Korsch.

The centrality of the dialectical idea that contradictions are the source of change and progressive development was one of the key factors that drew Brecht to Marxism. Not surprisingly, given the strife-ridden and rapidly modernizing context in which Brecht lived, he had long been fascinated by contradiction, oppositions and flux. Marxism added a compelling explanation of the nature and causes of individual and social change, and a vision of progressive movement towards a classless society. Here, impact of Marxist theory is necessary to reflect briefly on its fundamental ideas important to his life work. With regard to the issue of human nature, Marx presented man as both conscious agent and an economically determined object. For Marx, 'humans begin to distinguish themselves from animals as soon as they begin to produce their means of subsistence' and in so doing change themselves and the material world (Marx 1977: 160). However, despite possessing this productive capacity, one that requires consciousness and the ability to cooperate, humans are simultaneously conditioned 'by the social form which exists before they do, which they do not create, which is the product of the preceding generation' (Marx 1977: 192). Following Marx's treatment of determining forces, Brecht's approach to characterization increasingly demonstrated the impact on behaviour of economic class – the roles individuals play in production and in reproductive processes such as childcare and domestic work.

However, while his characters were vividly marked by economic determination, Brecht was wary of presenting them as totally determined or mechanical objects. Brecht's increasing interest in human agency is evident in his teacher-learner characters who transform themselves, such as the revolutionary Pelagea Vlassova, the heroine of *The Mother* (1931), who learns to read and write and then herself becomes a teacher of political intervention. Arguably the most persuasive embodiment of human agency in Brecht's theatre is the practice he developed in the 1930s of an actor who both depicts a character and critically demonstrates that she is a decision-making agent, at any one moment capable of making differing choices. Through the actor-cum-commentator, or 'spectActor' as it will be referred to, Brecht also found a way of reminding audience members that they, too, are capable of conscious intervention.

Marxist analyses of capitalism and class struggle clarified for Brecht the possibility of positive intervention against social injustice. Marx located capitalism as the most recent but by no means final mode of production; one dominated by the creation and private ownership of capital by the bourgeoisie. He argued that the class struggle between capitalists and exploited proletariat would culminate in a revolution and the emergence of a workers' state. By maintaining the best of capitalism, its productive capacity, and replacing its divisive private property relations with collective ownership, this socialist state would forge a classless communist society and itself eventually wither away.

The type of intervention required to kick-start the revolution remained debated. Brecht's declaration in the mid-1930s, that his epic theatre was for philosophers who 'wished not just to explain the world but also to change it', suggests that the cultivation of a revolutionary consciousness was his preferred mode of intervention (Brecht 2014b: 112).

Piscator's documentary theatre and other revolutionary experiments

Of the Berlin practitioners involved in epic art, it was the founder of documentary theatre, Erwin Piscator (1893–1966), who was the most influential in turning Brecht towards an openly political theatre. Piscator's agitational work began with his creation of the Proletarian Theatre in 1920, a no-frills ensemble that toured venues in working-class slums with the aim of developing class consciousness and proletarian solidarity. In 1924 at the Volksbühne he began experiments with new mass-media and narrative forms, translating Alfons Paquet's novel *Flags* into an epic drama by interrupting the flow of action with critical commentary through means such as film, projected texts and direct address to the audience. When Brecht became a member of Piscator's dramaturgical collective in 1927, he gained direct access to the most opulent and technologized phase of Piscator's career, one dependent on a wealthy patron and bourgeois audiences. Brecht also witnessed Piscator's more technologically sparse work when he saw *Paragraph 218*, a touring piece dealing with the contemporary debate concerning the illegality of abortion and aiming to show how the Civil Code oppressed working-class women. In order to animate the audience, Piscator staged semi-improvised dialogues in the auditorium between actors who stood up and spoke about the issues from the point of view of a lawyer, a magistrate, a clergyman and so on, as well as inviting the local doctor to give a speech about the social problems being addressed. Brecht appears to have regarded the show as very successful (Brecht 1978: 66), and no doubt it stimulated his thinking about how to create spectActors in the auditorium as well as on stage.

One of Piscator's innovations was to use the 'living wall' of the film screen and archival voice recordings to tie the events on stage to a wider socio-political reality and to the forces active in history at large. Brecht acknowledged and integrated many of these interruptive and historicizing innovations, particularly in the 1932 production of *The Mother*. Another trademark of Piscator's theatre was his decentralization of the individual and emphasis instead on his relation to society through methods such as:

- large casts and projected images of mass phenomena;
- the use of groups as the units of action;
- the placement of the actor as merely one among many collaborators.

Brecht developed a similar emphasis on the individual's relation to society, as demonstrated in his focus on:

- the events *between* rather than *within* characters;
- his representation of the collective through the use of choir and chorus;
- his arrangement of large-scale groupings that illuminate social power relations.

However, through his development of gestic acting, Brecht would give the actor a much more central role to play in the creation of social commentary. And while Piscator used 'moving' documents and facts about recent history and current affairs, often confronting the audience in a sensational and immediate way, Brecht tended to use characters and events set in more geographically and historically removed contexts so as to encourage comparative and problem-solving responses.

Brecht (1898–1956)

Brecht's love of artistic experimentation and his familiarity, partly through witnessing the work of colleagues like Piscator, with the need to target different audiences and institutional contexts, led him to create a variety of theatre forms. Most of these were *Schaustücke* ('show/showing plays') in that they perpetuated the division between performer and receiver. To varying degrees they also fulfilled the criteria for what Brecht in 1930 defined as 'Minor Pedagogy'. That is, they belonged to the transition period before the prophesied socialist revolution and operated within existing mainstream theatres, seeking to expose the shortcomings of capitalist society and activate the audience to become involved in changing it. The box-office hit *The Threepenny Opera* (1928), a collaboration with Elisabeth Hauptmann and the composer Kurt Weill, is an example of a *Schaustück* that has some features of Minor Pedagogy. Loosely set in the British Victorian era, the operetta plots the business machinations and rivalry of the gangster pimp Macheath ('Mac the Knife') and the beggar king Peachum. Through the depiction of Mac's friendship with the Police Chief, Tiger Brown, it also depicts a symbiotic relationship between the legal system and capitalist business. In a highly entertaining way, the play criticizes the commodification of humans under capitalism, a system that encourages humans to exploit the labour of others and even sell themselves. Yet the play does not fulfil all of the Minor Pedagogy criteria, because it does not clarify *how* or *whether* human bestiality can be changed through social intervention. Weill's integration of popular music forms, such as jazz, and the use of performers from music hall and musical comedy was in part an attempt to use popular forms to create a socially useful art and challenge elitist forms like opera. However, the catchy songs, easily taken out of context and sold as records or used as dance and coffee-house music, ended up serving rather than subverting capitalist commodification.

One of the perks of the *Threepenny* money-spinner was that it gave Brecht the space to experiment with non-commercial forms for different audience strata. The *Lehrstück* ('learning-play') that emerged was a revolutionary experiment 'meant not so much for the spectator as for those who were engaged in the performance. It was, so to speak, art for the producer, not art for the consumer' (Brecht 2014b: 123). In keeping with its name – *Lehre* can mean 'teaching(s)' or 'apprenticeship' – the new text and performance was a type of radical experiential pedagogy. Some of the *Lehrstücke* also came close to meeting Brecht's requirements for a 'Major Pedagogy', a theatre of the socialist future that would remove the divisions between actor and spectator. For example, they were designed to turn receivers into participants within the performance process, and to offer a form of interventionist training. Through copying characters' behaviours – and in some rehearsal situations, correcting behaviour – the participants rehearsed how to think and act rather than how to act a script (Bishop 1986: 274). The *Lehrstücke* were imbued with Marxist philosophy and have often been interpreted – by anti-Marxists in particular – as didactic in a doctrinaire way. Yet Brecht was uneasy with agitational theatre that forced a passive reception of a doctrine, and intended these plays instead to encourage a problem-solving engagement with issues such as the individual's relation to the collective.

The two school operas, *He Who Said Yes* and *He Who Said No* (1930), clarify this approach. The original version of *He Who Said Yes* presents the dilemma posed when a research trip through dangerous terrain is jeopardized by one of its young members. The boy has joined in order to get medicine for his sick mother, but then falls ill himself at a time when the team must negotiate the steep ridge of a cliff face. As it is impossible to carry him through the area, in accordance with custom the boy agrees to his own death. Impressed by a comment from one of the pupils involved in rehearsals at the Karl Marx School in Berlin-Neukölln, that it was not correct simply to follow an old custom, Brecht revised the purpose of the trip. It now became an attempt to secure medicine to combat an epidemic that was threatening both the mother and her township. When the boy says 'Yes' to his death, he is moved by medical necessity, not custom. In accordance with dialectical thinking, Brecht also wrote a counter play, *He Who Said No*, which returns in many respects to the original version of *He Who Said Yes* – where the urgency caused by the epidemic is notably absent – but ends with the boy refusing to sacrifice himself. Instead he asks the group to return with him, on the grounds that their research can wait. Moreover, he asks for the introduction of a new custom – the habit of thinking afresh in each new situation. Brecht intended the plays to be performed together, to offer learners the opportunity to experience the individual's relation to society from very different angles.

The theatre of economic and political crisis

Brecht's assertion of reasoning behaviour through the *Lehrstücke* was itself a counter play to the Nazis' use of emotive rhetoric and physical force during the chaos of the Great Depression. After the Wall Street crash on 29 October 1929, American investors began withdrawing their loans to Germany and the national stock exchanges plummeted, with the result that industry and foreign trade were crippled. During the course of 1930 unemployment rose to three million and, in March of that year, disagreements about the unemployment programme brought the coalition government to its knees. Turmoil in the Weimar government led to the success of its staunchest opponents, the Communists and the Nazis, in the September Reichstag elections. The increased appeal of the KPD lay in their ability to offer an explanation for the Depression and to characterize it as a symptom of the collapse of capitalism. In their powerful play *St Joan of the Stockyards*, the Brecht collective presented a compelling Marxist interpretation of economic crisis. Marx's theory of the recurrent cycle of modern industry and its stages – end of prosperity, overproduction, crisis, stagnation, restoration – is artistically expressed through the play's narration of how the Chicago meat-packer king, Pierpont Mauler, triggers a crash in the stock market (Völker 1979: 152, 156). The play also presents religion and capitalism as partners in crime. Mauler's relationship with the Salvation Army lieutenant, Johanna Dark, shows how the charity aggravates rather than alleviates the plight of the Depression victims it seeks to serve, both by supplying industrial philanthropists with a good name and by giving little people a security blanket that deters them from political revolt. A selection of scenes from *St Joan* was broadcast on radio in April 1932, but during the Weimar Republic it never reached the public domain again, for, despite the acknowledgement of its quality by reputable directors, no theatre establishment dared stage it.

The following month, a heavily censored version of *Kuhle Wampe* was screened in Germany – a semi-documentary film by the Brecht collective on the subject of the Depression. The film is one example of the way the collective depicted both passive and active responses to class oppression in the hope of stimulating a revolutionary consciousness. Set in Berlin and Kuhle Wampe, its peripheral tent city for workers, it deals with the topical issue of how certain working-class groups 'accommodate themselves in a tired and passive way to the "swamp"' (Brecht 2001: 207). To this end it depicted, for example, the suicide of an unemployed youth who 'never finds his way to the workers' militant struggle and who is driven to death by the cutbacks in unemployment assistance'. By contrast, the third part of the film triumphantly depicts workers' athletics competitions that 'take place on a mass scale and are brilliantly organized' (Brecht 2001: 205).

This opposition of negative and positive models *within* a play or film was often also created *between* plays. For example, if *The Measures Taken* provides an instance of a Young Comrade who learns too late how to be a successful revolutionary fighter, its counter play *The Mother* provides an example of an aged, illiterate and politically reactionary mother of a Russian factory worker, who transforms herself into a communist activist, helping pave the way for the 1917 revolution. The Russian setting was designed to assure 'convinced communists by reminding them that revolution was possible' and to encourage 'unaligned spectators to realize the similarities between the Weimar Republic and Tsarist Russia' (Bradley 2006: 31). For example, scene 5's depiction of soldiers opening fire on a peaceful demonstration against wage cuts in 1905 can be read as a thinly veiled reference to the state brutality Brecht witnessed with his own eyes in Berlin on 1 May 1929, when demonstrating workers were shot down by the SPD's police. Brecht's outrage at 'Bloody May' seems to have strengthened his commitment to a partisan theatre for the oppressed, one that seeks to move (and divide) its participants by appealing to both their rational and emotional faculties.

A more humorous act of state oppression took place on 29 February 1932 at a performance of *The Mother* in the working-class district of Moabit. Due to uproar from some quarters over the play's attack on SPD reformist politics and its seeming call for an uprising, the Theatre Department of the Building Police tried to put a stop to the performance claiming, for example, that it constituted an unacceptable fire risk. The company, including Weigel as Vlassova and amateur performers such as Brecht's future collaborator and lover, Margarete Steffin, then decided to perform without set and costumes. The authorities responded by repeatedly interrupting the performance and limiting what the cast could do (Bradley 2006: 54). Apparently the audience found the event very entertaining, possibly because it confirmed the play's political arguments about oppressive state intervention and heroic resistance.

Unfortunately for Brecht and his co-workers, it was the Nazi state that benefited most from the idea of incendiary communists. Although the Nazis lost a considerable number of votes in the elections of November 1932, their political future was secured when President Hindenburg appointed Hitler chancellor on 30 January 1933. After the burning of the Reichstag on 27 February, for which a Dutch communist was – rightly or wrongly – convicted, Hitler seized the opportunity to suspend civil liberties and to arrest communist leaders. The following day Brecht, Weigel and their two children began an orchestrated flight to Vienna, where Brecht was to give a reading of selected works. It would be sixteen years before Brecht returned to live again in Germany.

On the run: exile in Europe and America (1933–47)

Fighting the fear and misery of fascism

For Brecht's family, and many of their friends and collaborators, the long exile years were a period of financial deprivation, isolation and uncertainty. Brecht's experience of the trauma of exile and fascism is movingly expressed in his poem 'To those Born Later' (c. 1937–9):

> You who will emerge from the flood
> In which we have gone under
> Remember
> When you speak of our failings
> The dark time too
> Which you have escaped.
> For we went, changing countries more often than our shoes
> Through the wars of the classes, despairing
> When there was injustice only, and no rebellion.
> (Brecht 1979c: 319–320)

The experience of having to work and live in numerous countries in relatively quick succession – Switzerland, France, Denmark, Sweden, Finland, America – and the need to respond to a diverse range of positions on both European fascism and Soviet communism, strengthened Brecht's strategic ability to create a variety of revolutionary theatre forms for different contexts.

Horrified by the Nazification of their fellow countrymen, and deeply disappointed by Stalin's regime, many émigrés lost their faith in the communist project. By contrast, Brecht remained committed to Marx's idea that, through class struggle, the oppressive capitalist mode of production could and would be replaced. This conviction partly explains why, despite his criticism of Stalin's dictatorship and violent use of force, he continued to praise the Soviet leader for fostering a socialist industry free from private ownership. Brecht's emphasis on economic structures also underpinned his rejection of any essentialist explanations of the Nazi phenomenon, such as the idea that it sprang from eternal barbaric impulses, or that the rise of Hitler demonstrated the inherent servitude of the German people. Instead he interpreted fascism as a type of rule that will occur under monopoly capitalism, one that arises when capitalism reaches a point of crisis and can no longer effectively govern by means of parliamentary democracy. Hence, in the 1934 version of the satirical parable play *Round Heads and Pointed Heads*, the Brecht collective presented Nazi racial theory and warmongering as methods of diverting attention from class division and of stopping the oppressed from uniting in revolt, an interpretation that has been criticized for not fully taking into account the causes and nature of Nazi racism (Ewen 1970: 310). And in the historical farce *The Resistible Rise of Arturo Ui* (1941), Brecht and Steffin drew parallels between the political history of Hitler and the economic history of American gangsters such as Al Capone. For example, they attributed Hitler's seizure of power to the intersection between his *petit bourgeois* aspirations and the willingness of business leaders and landowners to secure market monopolies through gangster terror. The nature of pre-war Nazi terror was expressed vividly by the same authors in *Fear and Misery of the Third Reich* (1938), a loose collection of scenes that movingly demonstrates the atomization of individuals under fascism, the suicidal nature of collusion and the necessity of subversion and mass resistance.

Brecht's attempt to combat fascism by keeping oppositional thoughts alive in difficult circumstances necessitated new modes of operation. For a start, he had to find a substitute for the network of producers he had lost who, literally and figuratively, spoke his own language. On an institutional level this involved making alliances with translators and participating in the founding of ventures such as the anti-fascist German-language journal *Das Wort*, an organ loosely connected with the Soviet-dominated Comintern, an international communist organization dedicated to overthrowing the international bourgeoisie. At the level of creative practice, because his access to theatre institutions was extremely limited, he devoted more time to writing than at any other point of his career, producing a wealth of analytical and lyrical texts and many of the plays canonized in Western theatre, including *Life of Galileo*, *Mother Courage and Her Children*, *The Good Person of Szechwan*, *Puntila and His Servant Matti*, and the play whose spectacular staging is discussed in this book, *The Caucasian Chalk Circle*.

For the first time Brecht's team experimented with work designed primarily to incite immediate political action rather than a long-term change in ways of looking at the world. Thus, in order to make a timely contribution to the united front against fascism, they experimented with theatre methods associated with the bourgeoisie, such as empathetic character–spectator relations. In addition, Brecht grappled with the challenge of engaging audiences that, not unlike contemporary Western spectators, are removed from the type of working-class cultural activism that existed in Weimar Berlin. Brecht's experience of new audiences and their theatre traditions, particularly in America, gave him an understanding – though arguably one he failed sufficiently to act upon – of how aspects of local and commercial theatre could be mobilized to help engage audiences in a foreign political theatre of enlightenment.

Brecht (1898–1956)

Defending experimental realism

Señora Carrar's Rifles (1937) demonstrates how Brecht and Steffin sought to adapt Aristotelian and bourgeois 'dramatic theatre' techniques so that they served immediate revolutionary ends. The play was commissioned by a company of immigrant actors in Paris who sought to inspire the French workers to continue supporting their comrades in the Spanish Civil War and indict the non-involvement policy of the French and British governments. A feature of this policy was the refusal to supply weapons to the defenders of the legally established Republic of Spain against the fascist General Franco and his war partners, Hitler and Mussolini. The danger of neutrality and the importance of weapons are addressed through the depiction of Carrar's dramatic shift in attitude after she learns that the fascists have shot her elder son gratuitously, while he was fishing in the village harbour. Widow of an Andalusian fisherman who died supporting the Republic, she initially tries to stop her family from becoming involved in violent resistance. At the finale, by contrast, she leaves the stage a gun-toting fighter, using her husband's rifles to arm herself and her fellow republicans.

Señora Carrar diverges from Brecht's earlier epic theatre experiments in several ways. For instance, as in Aristotelian drama, the plot events are smoothly dovetailed rather than arranged in montage fashion with interruptive, defamiliarizing inserts. Moreover, epic breadth and multiplicity are replaced by an Aristotelian preservation of the unities of time, space and action: all the events unfold within Carrar's home while the fictional time frame – the approximately 45 minutes that elapse between her placing a loaf of bread in the oven at the opening and her final exit with both the baked loaf and rifles – corresponds to the length of the play's performance. This dramaturgy encourages the audience to experience the world from the characters' perspectives in an uninterrupted present tense, and to become emotionally involved in Carrar's transformation. However, the overt use of emotional arousal is counterbalanced with a thought-provoking presentation of characters' differing approaches to neutrality. This, together with Brecht's comment to director Slatan Dudow about the simple performance style he envisaged for the piece – 'No hysteria, quiet, well thought-out realism' (Brecht 1990: 258) – testifies to the importance for him of maintaining a space for a reasoning analytical attitude. The end result is a drama that encourages interplay between emotional involvement and reflective observation, a dialectical feature that Brecht would increasingly promote, through both his writing and staging.

The play was very popular with anti-fascist theatre groups and their audiences, due in no small part to the accessible nature of its realism. However, *Señora Carrar*'s indebtedness to a nineteenth-century version of the Aristotelian tradition by no means signalled conversion to a particular (or 'more mature') realist style. Indeed, both before and after this play, the Brecht collective created stylistically diverse works that were 'abnormally disunified in every way. even [sic] the genres change constantly. biography, [sic] gestarium, parable, character comedy in the folk vein, historical farce' (Brecht 1993: 145). One of the principles underpinning this diversity was Brecht's idea that the stylistic means of realist art should be variable, according to the dictates of time and place. Theoretical reflections of the late 1930s, during a period when realism was hotly debated in Marxist circles, further clarify his commitment to experimentation and his understanding that realist art was a matter of political attitude rather than form. This is why he rejected the exclusive promotion of specific bourgeois realist forms by Georg Lukács, a key commentator on Marxist aesthetics and contributor to *Das Wort*, but agreed that realist art should demonstrate the connections between ideology, economics and social history (Mumford 2001).

Meg Mumford

From Hollywood to the HUAC inquisition

Brecht's sensitivity to the dictates of time and place is clearly manifest in plays such as *Arturo Ui*, written with half an eye to an audience familiar with American gangster history at a time when he was attempting to secure migration visas to the USA. Threatened by the increasing presence of Nazis and their supporters in Finland, Brecht sought refuge in a country where collaborators such as Piscator, Hauptmann and composer-collaborator Hanns Eisler were already based. The Soviet Union was no longer a viable option, for the failure of the German émigré theatre scene and the purging of innovative artists such as Vsevolod Meyerhold and Brecht's friend Tretiakov was proof positive that Stalin's regime would not be a fruitful environment for his experiments. Moreover, the country was on the verge of becoming deeply embroiled in the war. Fortunately, there was still time for the Brecht collective to escape Europe via Russia's shores. On 13 June 1941 Brecht, Weigel, their children, and Brecht's Danish lover-collaborator, Ruth Berlau, set sail from Vladivostok, spirits very much dampened by the loss of their fellow traveller, Steffin, who had died from tuberculosis in Moscow. They eventually entered the harbour of San Pedro, California, on 21 July, only one day before Hitler's army attacked the Soviet Union.

In many respects they had had a lucky escape from Europe. However, during the greater part of the six-year 'exile in paradise', Brecht suffered from a form of cultural shock that left him feeling anything but fortunate. As an experienced man of the theatre, Brecht had developed the art of 'producing' himself, but while living in American exile from 1941 to 1947 'this "production" failed, and his influence passed almost unnoticed' (Lyon 1980: xi). Based in Santa Monica, Los Angeles, where he hoped to earn his keep through scriptwriting for Hollywood, Brecht unwillingly participated in the world of commercial art, where the artist moulds both self and product to suit the industry bosses and their markets:

> Know that our great showmen
> Are those who show what we want to have shown.
> Dominate by serving us!
> Endure by winning duration for us
> Play our game, we'll share the loot
> Deliver the goods! Be straight with us!
> Deliver the goods.
> When I look into their decomposing faces
> My hunger disappears.
> *(Brecht 1979c: 379)*

In Brecht's eyes, the showmen of his poem 'Deliver the Goods' (1942) were merely an exaggerated version of the type of citizen produced by a young and capitalist nation. In this automobile-oriented society of rootless mobile workers, where 'houses are extensions of garages' (Brecht 1993: 257), money was the measure of man. Brecht's loss of sales in Europe and his inability to create successful film scripts – with the notable exception of *Hangmen Also Die* (Fritz Lang 1943) – meant that it was difficult for him to measure up. Ironically, when his financial reserves were particularly low, Weigel had to shop for household goods and clothing in Salvation Army stores, the very charity he had accused of prolonging rather than alleviating the misery of capitalism. One of the reasons Brecht found himself at a loss in the New World was that it did not regard his revelation of how exploitative capitalist business practice governed interhuman relations as a sensational exposure. In his work journal he briefly mused on a historical reason for this attitude, noting that American democracy, unlike its European counterparts, was founded by bourgeois politicians who openly acknowledged their business interests: 'the representatives of the people do not even symbolically have garments without pockets here, as they did in ancient rome [*sic*]' (Brecht 1993: 198).

Brecht's tendency in America was to impose established methods rather than experiment with the traditions of his target audience. This combative response, perhaps fuelled by ideological disdain and pedagogical fervour, first became visible during a visit to America well prior to the period of exile in the 1940s. In the winter of 1934, Brecht travelled to New York in the hope that he could 'influence' a production of *The Mother* by the Theatre Union. His concerns about the show were first triggered by the script. Instead of an agitational, poetic and episodic text that advocated raising class consciousness, particularly of working-class women, and revolution as the solution to the crisis of the Great Depression, Brecht discovered a cathartic three-act melodrama in a colloquial American register with revenge tragedy elements. Brecht replaced the adaptation with a stilted, near-literal translation, integrated slides and captions, and persuaded the scenographer to abandon his naturalistic design in favour of a plain structure modelled on Neher's sketches for the Berlin premiere. The final production contained a muddled collision of epic text and setting with illusionistic devices such as empathetic acting – most of the actors were trained in the Stanislavsky-inspired methods introduced to America by the Group Theatre. Unfortunately, it proved an artistic and box-office failure from which the company never recovered. In addition to the stylistic confusion, reviewers panned the didactic elements and their inappropriateness for the Theatre Union's typical audience. While agitprop was the official aesthetic of the KPD and a vital tool during the power struggles prior to Hitler's rise, it was not highly regarded in America, where, despite the Depression, the US Communist Party had a relatively minor following and there was no reason to believe revolution was imminent (Bradley 2006: 143). Brecht's involvement in the off-Broadway New York production of *The Private Life of the Master Race* (1945) – an English-language version of *Fear and Misery* – demonstrated a similar lack of inter-cultural dialogue.

By contrast, his approach to the *Life of Galileo* production that premiered in Beverley Hills in July 1947 was characterized by a greater degree of negotiation. One of the factors that made a more dialogic rehearsal process once again possible was the harmonious relationship between the German playwright-director and his leading man, the English actor Charles Laughton. For the first time in America, Brecht was working with a talented performer who, in films such as *The Private Life of Henry VIII* (1933), demonstrated an ability to achieve commentary through gesture. Brecht was particularly fascinated by the scene in the film where Laughton presents the king devouring a chicken, lustily demolishing the bird and throwing the chewed bones behind him, an episode that illuminates, for example, the connection between Henry's material power and his relation to others (his many wives in particular). Laughton was also willing to participate in a lengthy preparation period and a performance that covertly criticized the relationship between contemporary American science and the military.

Midway through their work, America's involvement in the war took a new direction when, in August 1945, atomic bombs were dropped on Hiroshima and Nagasaki. In response, Brecht further sharpened the new emphases that already informed his work with Laughton. The changes had grown out of Brecht's dissatisfaction with the Denmark version of 1938–9, which explored the control of scientific inquiry by the authorities, especially amid a reign of terror, be it the seventeenth-century Catholic Inquisition of Galileo's Italy or Hitler's regime. What the first version lacked was an unequivocal demonstration that Galileo's recantation of his theories about the solar system had robbed the masses of a revolutionary knowledge, one they could have used to dismantle the theology keeping their rulers in power. Thus, the American version attempted to clarify the belief that Galileo's recantation was a criminal failure of the scientist's responsibility to society, comparable to the placement of atomic research in the wrong hands.

Several reviewers were quick to pick up the critique of modern science and many were willing to engage with the unconventional staging. While Brecht regarded the first version of the play text as 'technically a great step backwards' because of its lack of directness, use of interiors, atmosphere and empathy (Brecht 1993: 23), for many in the Hollywood audience this first production was a leap into a new world. For example, reviewers drew attention to the non-illusionist devices, such as the placement before each scene of a verse sung by three choirboys, forecasting the play's events, the use of a boy pulling a gauze sub-curtain across the stage to indicate a change of scene, and the unconcealed movement of props by actors. Despite the fact that other reviewers felt they had been alienated rather than enlightened by the distanciation techniques, Brecht was pleased with the sell-out production.

Shortly after the opening of *Galileo* Brecht was involved in a performance with a very different politics when, on 30 October 1947, he appeared before the US Congressional House Committee on Un-American Activities (HUAC). After the start of the Cold War in 1946, HUAC initiated a notorious investigation into alleged communist infiltration of the film industry. The announcement of public hearings in Washington sent shock waves through Hollywood, where right and left alike feared that the government was making a bid to control the industry. Eerily, a relationship analogous to that between the scientist Galileo and the state-sanctioned Inquisition threatened to rear its head. Of the many prominent figures summoned, staunch conservatives like Ronald Reagan and Walt Disney proved themselves 'friendly' witnesses by testifying that communists were indeed infiltrating Hollywood. Brecht belonged to the 'Hollywood nineteen', a group who opposed the Committee's inquisitional methods and sought to expose HUAC as violating the American Constitution's First Amendment, guaranteeing freedom of speech and belief. To this end they devised a strategy of fudging the question about Communist Party membership, in the expectation that they would then be able to fight HUAC in the courts for transgressing the Constitution.

Unlike most of 'the unfriendly nineteen', Brecht was in the lucky position of being able to declare that he had never been a Communist Party member. He also argued that the difference between their American citizenship and his 'alien' status meant that it was necessary for him to behave as a guest. Reasons such as these – as well as the desire to safeguard the long-planned and imminent departure to Europe – led him to declare to his comrades that, while he commended their fight for freedom, he thought they should answer the party affiliation question truthfully and oppose the authorities through a show of cooperation that concealed their cunning. Brecht was right to question their mode of resistance – after failure in the Supreme Court, ten of his co-fighters would be sentenced to one year in prison. At his own much-publicized hearing, Brecht gave the most successful strategic performance of his life. Prior to the event he had rehearsed the examination scenario with friends. On the actual day, he arrived dressed up in a respectable dark suit – given to him by a tailor who had worn it at his own wedding – smoked cigars throughout in order to ingratiate himself with the cigar-smoking Head of the Committee, and used an interpreter in order to give himself more time to formulate courteous corrections and cleverly deferent answers to an ill-prepared panel. He was deemed a 'good' witness and let free. The next day he boarded a flight for France. Through their blunders, the investigators had unwittingly supported his cause: 'His departure, planned long in advance, now assumed the form of a dramatic escape from an American witch-hunt. One of the greatest dramatists of the century did not miss the cue' (Lyon 1980: 337).

Brecht (1898–1956)

Building a collective: Brecht in the GDR (1947–56)

A controversial figurehead

Despite his communist sympathies, it would be two years before Brecht set foot in the Soviet-administered zone of Germany. Both the increasing heat of the Cold War and his desire to keep doors open to Europe and its German-language theatres made it extremely difficult for him to find the right address. As a stateless person in the FBI's bad books he was unwelcome in the Western part of Germany governed by the Allies. Moving to the Soviet sector could curtail his travel possibilities, while the emphasis in its cultural policy circles on an anti-Formalist aesthetic posed a threat to his experimental practice. After establishing a new network of collaborators in Switzerland, he and his wife successfully bid for Austrian citizenship, a strategic move designed to allow the possibility of residing in the socialist part of Germany without losing their passports to the world.

During Brecht and Weigel's first visit to East Berlin in October 1948 they were warmly welcomed at a banquet attended by Socialist Unity Party (SED) members such as Wilhelm Pieck – future president of the German Democratic Republic (GDR). The Deutsches Theater was put at their disposal and Brecht began preparing *Mother Courage* for a January premiere, with Weigel playing the title role. This fêted production put Brecht on the East German map as a cultural figurehead, while Weigel's high-calibre performance helped to propel forward her negotiations for a major state-funded company. The result was the famous Berliner Ensemble, for which she secured enough subsidy to sustain over sixty performers, more than 250 associates and lengthy rehearsal periods (Ewen 1970: 458). When the Brechts arrived in Berlin the theatre buildings were allocated already, and thus it would be more than four years before the Ensemble was lodged in Brecht's preferred Theater am Schiffbauerdamm. In the interim they lived cheek-by-jowl with Wolfgang Langhoff's company at the Deutsches Theater. Cohabitation proved difficult, but the Ensemble was fortunate to have the luxury of financial independence from its neighbour, an unusual investment that partly reflected officialdom's faith in the propaganda value of the enterprise. This faith was confirmed at events like the International Festival of Dramatic Art in Paris, where, in June 1954, *Mother Courage* was judged best play and best production, thereby becoming a flagship for the young socialist state.

However, *Mother Courage* also established the Ensemble's role as a controversial dissenting voice. The heated discussion that surrounded the 1949 staging, a debate spearheaded by Fritz Erpenbeck, editor of a journal influenced by the Party line, made it the first theatre case in the Formalism conflicts. Although the term 'Formalism' referred to works which experimented with form for its own sake, it was increasingly used by conservatives in left-wing politics to dismiss any art that deviated from Soviet Socialist Realism. The latter, the prescribed artistic practice that emerged from the First Congress of the Union of Soviet Writers in 1934, played a significant role in East Germany during the late 1940s and early 1950s. It was the continuation of the anti-Formalist arguments from the 1930s by former Moscow-based émigrés such as Erpenbeck that helped cement the hegemony of Soviet cultural policy in this period. The features of *Mother Courage* criticized by Erpenbeck included the interruptive songs with their overt didacticism. Erpenbeck was not alone in his wariness of the didactic. Immediately after the war, many who had been bullied or seduced by Nazi propaganda turned their backs on any form of political pedagogy. This response partly explains the prevalent dismissive attitude, at least until late 1954, towards the *Proletkult*, a defamatory term for the revolutionary workers' art traditions during the Weimar Republic, especially agitprop forms and also Brecht's *Lehrstück*.

For the left-conservatives the only traditions that passed muster were nineteenth-century bourgeois realism and an approved group of German classics, starting with Lessing, Goethe and Schiller. These traditions, or so their proponents asserted, were more accessible and familiar to a broader cross section of the population and thus better able to offer reassurance to a traumatized population. The German classics were also lauded as examples of progressive humanism, a communal heritage that could help bring about the peaceful reunification of the divided nation. Uninterrupted illusionism was the usual representational mode of these traditions and it was one preferred by critics like Erpenbeck, who contended that what distinguished theatre from the classroom was its power to create an illusion of real social life happening in the here and now. Socialist Realist dramaturgy utilized many features of these traditions, adding covertly didactic features, such as the hero or heroine with whom the audience could identify and whose actions or virtues paved the way for a collective society. Rather than a unifying aesthetic of identification that helped conceal the theatre's didactic function, *Mother Courage* boldly asserted a counter-model that overtly challenged the bourgeois illusionist tradition and criticized the *petit bourgeois* aspirations that Hitler had appealed to so effectively. Such strategies were a risky business. The lead player in the SED, the First Secretary Walter Ulbricht, remained a staunch supporter of the classics and there were a number of occasions in the early 1950s when the Ensemble had reason to fear it would be dissolved as an independent theatre. Fortunately, events like the triumph in Paris ensured its longevity.

Pedagogue of peace and reconstruction

Brecht's output in the GDR, both his dissenting counter-models and his more orthodox work, was energized by his interpretation of the educational role art should play in the transition to socialism, and then stateless communism. In a country ravaged by fascism and war he believed it imperative that government and artists work together on re-education goals such as:

- exposing the origins and residue of Nazism and capitalist imperialism;
- enhancing public dialogue about socialism and its construction;
- celebrating the GDR's progress.

For Brecht the sobering events of June 1953 – the first workers' strike against a workers' state – confirmed the necessity of such a programme. In his eyes, a significant causal factor behind the strike was the government's 'revolutionary haste'. In a bid to develop heavy industry as rapidly as possible, the government had made the error of imposing, without sufficient dialogue, a number of economic measures that proved detrimental to the workers' living standards. It had also failed to address the diverse background and ideology of the post-war workers who included former bourgeois Nazi Party members ousted from their posts in administration, as well as professional soldiers. The straw that broke the camel's back was the government's decision to raise the output required of industrial workers by 10 per cent. On 16 June miners took to the streets, demonstrating in front of the ministerial building in Berlin. The next day they returned, but this time their ranks were swelled with dissatisfied citizens calling for the end of the government and free elections. By the middle of the day Soviet tanks were rolling into the city centre.

Immediately prior to this military action Brecht had posted letters to three key political figures in which he declared his support for the government, enquired whether the Academy of Arts and Ensemble could be of assistance, and stressed the importance of dialogue with the masses about the tempo of socialist construction. Brecht then went to observe the demonstration first hand. His interpretation of the military defence, as a timely intervention against organized fascist elements intent on using the workers' dissatisfaction to topple the state and take Berlin to the brink of a third world war, was in line with the official SED position (Brecht 2003: 332). However, for him the street performance, with workers singing the *Internationale* (the anthem of international revolutionary socialism) being drowned out by the strength of those chanting 'Deutschland, Deutschland, über alles' (the first line from the banned national anthem, the singing of which was considered an extreme right-wing statement) also expressed the Party's failure thus far to empower the workers against Nazi ideology.

Brecht felt that de-Nazification could not be achieved by a cultural policy that exclusively highlighted the best of Germany's past, and thus he continued to create theatre that addressed problematic aspects of national history and their contemporary relevance. For example, in his 1950 adaptation of J.M.R. Lenz's 1771 tragicomedy, *The Tutor*, Brecht thematized the 'German *misère*', a label applied by left-wing commentators to highlight the repressive nature of the period that marked Germany's transition from a feudal to a bourgeois capitalist society. To Brecht's mind this painful epoch had been unnecessarily prolonged because of the acquiescence of the German bourgeoisie in the ideology of feudal society. Through a satirical depiction of a young tutor trapped in a servile relationship to the aristocracy of the late eighteenth century, he sought to offer a useful critique of the founding moments of the bourgeois education system at a time when educational reform was high on the GDR's agenda (Subiotto 1975: 15–16). Within the ranks of the Ensemble a similar reform was under way. Convinced that the GDR had inherited the Hitler Youth, 'educated to destroy the world, but not educated to live in a world that has been destroyed' (BBA 66/45 trans. Speirs 1982: 179), he had company members study Marxist-Leninist texts on a weekly basis. Brecht and Weigel's approach to casting also ensured that their young actors had access to experienced performers who had not absorbed the emotive charismatic style popular under Hitler's regime, including those who worked in leftist theatre during the Weimar Republic, former émigrés, and guests from the Zurich Schauspielhaus.

On the related subject of imperialist warfare, productions like Brecht's *Trumpets and Drums* (1955) supported the Party line against Western imperialism. An adaptation of George Farquhar's *The Recruiting Officer* (1706), Brecht's satirical play complemented the Party's criticism of recent Cold War developments. These included the remilitarization of West Germany and its mooted entry into the North Atlantic Treaty Organization (NATO), a military defence alliance of North American and European countries. But the staging of *Trumpets and Drums* also foregrounded the connection between imperialism and the ubiquitous socialization of men as colonizers, particularly in the army and law. In doing so it implicitly spoke against imperialist conditioning within any country. Through features such as the way the female drag role was staged – in order to be with her beloved Captain Plume, Victoria Balance dresses as Squire Wilful, enters the army, and successfully metamorphoses into the soldier Sergeant Wilful – the production demonstrated how militaristic masculinity was not innate so much as learned within a particular type of society (Mumford 1998: 247).

Moved by both his experience of two world wars and his dread of resurgent Nazism, Brecht maintained a vigilant stance against warmongering and territorialist machismo, both of which he associated with capitalism, a stance forcefully expressed in his poem 'To my Countrymen' (1948):

> You men, reach for the spade and not the knife.
> You'd sit in safety under roofs today
> Had you not used the knife to make your way
> And under roofs one leads a better life.
> I beg you, take the spade and not the knife.
>
> *(Brecht 1979c: 417)*

In addition to anti-war plays, he prepared letters and declarations and spoke at congresses in support of Germany's peaceful reunification. In recognition of his contribution, he was awarded the International Stalin Peace Prize on 22 May 1955, an event met with consternation from many quarters on the other side of the border.

Brecht's satirical treatments of the 'German *misère*' and imperialism continued his long-established practice of estranging capitalist society. However, he acknowledged that socialist reconstruction also required a theatre that could inform its audience about the nature and achievements of revolutionary change. Through productions like *Katzgraben* (1953), Brecht sought to develop new practices that would meet this need. Erwin Strittmatter's Socialist Realist *Katzgraben* was the first and only contemporary East German play Brecht directed. Strittmatter was a farmer's son, and for Brecht the fact that the author had become a writer at all – and in Brecht's eyes a good one – was testimony to the success of the GDR's dismantling of the bourgeois monopoly on education. The text also addressed what he had consistently lauded in public and in private as the genuine achievements of the GDR, land reform after the expulsion of the Junker squires and schooling for proletarian youth (Philpotts 2003: 63–66). For instance, its *Fabel* – 'the plot of the play told as a sequence of interactions' (Weber, in Thomson and Sacks 1994: 181) – outlines the victory of small farmers against larger landowners. Their success results from a combination of individual enterprise, sympathetic leadership and help from the Party in the form of tractors and scientific education.

Having mastered the art of defamiliarizing the known, Brecht now experimented with familiarization strategies in order to give his city audience access to the 'foreign' world of rural life. These strategies included:

- an emphasis on detailed observation, exemplified in the documentary-style set and costumes based on a field trip to the village area where the play is set;
- individualistic characterization, to which end Strittmatter composed character *résumés* for the actors, with an emphasis on social background, and the production programme incorporated diary extracts and letters supposedly composed by the characters.

Brecht also encouraged actors to develop an empathetic relationship with their character wherever it served the social commentary of the *Fabel* of *Katzgraben*. For example, concerned that Erwin Geschonneck's ridicule of the wealthy farmer Herr Grossmann actually undermined the farmer's credibility as a threatening opponent in the class struggle, Brecht urged the actor to subjectively justify his character by thinking of him as an intelligent man, only overturned by the new situation. An empathetic approach to a character's emotional state of being was also used to help introduce unfamiliar progressive elements such as the humanized socialist figure Steinert, miner and local Party Secretary. An antidote to the poker-faced stoic type of hero, what Brecht described as the ideal capitalist in disguise, Steinert presented a new male role model who did not conceal his feelings of uncertainty and helplessness. As Brecht put it, the 'human face under socialism must again be a mirror for feelings' (Brecht, in Mumford 1995: 254).

Katzgraben coincided with the peak both of Brecht's Stanislavsky studies and of the Stanislavsky wave in the GDR. At the First German Stanislavsky Conference in April 1953, only one month before the staging of *Katzgraben*, the Russian's methods were vigorously promoted as the best means to realize Socialist Realism. Brecht's engagement with Stanislavsky during *Katzgraben* was no doubt influenced by the pressure to conform to cultural policy. However, just as the choice of Strittmatter's play expressed a sustained commitment to social reform, the Stanislavsky studies reflected a genuine desire to equip a young company with the range of tools necessary both to defend and to constructively criticize such reform. Assisted by the publication flurry that accompanied the Stanislavsky wave, Brecht gained greater access to Stanislavsky's period of work after the Russian Revolution, particularly his everyday training and rehearsal practices. It was here in particular that he found approaches that could be readily modified to suit his materialist *Fabel*-oriented theatre:

- attention to contradictions and concrete historical detail;
- organization of crowd scenes;
- analytical segmentation of the action;
- attention to physical actions and the play's super-objective.

Whereas in the 1930s Brecht had rejected Stanislavsky's emphasis on empathetic relations with the character, he now adapted techniques like emotion memory and *résumés* to facilitate complex contradictory characterizations, and to create a dialectic between demonstration and experience. However, Brecht continued to view Stanislavsky's interpretive practice as non-Marxist, and to counter his emphasis on emotional truth with an insistence on critical demonstration informed by social truth.

While minute taking was not new at the Ensemble, the extensive nature of the rehearsal notes written by Brecht and his crew of assistants during *Katzgraben* testifies both to the influence of Stanislavsky and to the depth of Brecht's commitment. In addition to their important function as a means of recording performance, Brecht often used the documentation for pedagogical purposes. The existence of a bound volume of selected notes and photos from the staging suggests he was hoping to publish his practical experiments in an instructive format similar to the so-called *Modellbuch* ('modelbook'). A practice initiated by Berlau, each modelbook contained a sequence of photos with captions, detailing significant gestures, positions, groupings and turning points in a particular production. One of their functions was to inform future theatre practitioners of Brecht's Marxist art of 'scenic writing' (Weber in Thomson and Sacks 1994: 181), a form of storytelling typified by socially significant comportment, *Arrangements* and tableaux. Brecht involved his cohort of young, contracted assistants in the production of these books, not only as a cost-cutting measure, but because he believed the task of selecting and glueing the production photos would improve their critical eye. The male assistants in particular were not enamoured of this teaching method, and found the collaborative work on rehearsals a more fruitful training ground. Here Brecht would seat himself in the stalls at a point where he could assess the choreography, and actively seek input and solutions from the collaborators, assistants and curious onlookers around him as well as the actors on stage. At last Brecht was able to rekindle the dialogic rehearsal practice he had so enjoyed prior to the exile years.

For the pleasure of the river-dwellers

Like a children's nursery on a sunny day, these rehearsals were usually characterized by an atmosphere of playful experimentation, humour and relaxation. Brecht had long insisted that the labour of art should be fun, but in the context of a new society that promised to remove exploitation and divisions between work and enjoyment, the issue of pleasurable production acquired a new relevance. In his *Short Organon for the Theatre* (1948), an exposition designed to provide an up-to-date introduction to his theatre aesthetic and written prior to his first trip to the Soviet zone, Brecht called for the sister arts of dramatic art to recall that their task 'is to entertain the children of the scientific age, and to do so with sensuousness and humour'. To this end he advocated a theatre of pleasurable analysis, invention and intervention. A theatre that emancipated because its representation of 'events involving human beings' gave the pleasure of insight and an enjoyable experience of changing the world for the better (Brecht 2014b: 254, 233). Here spectators had the opportunity both to witness the flow of life's river and to learn a productive critical attitude that could help them regulate it for the common good:

> We produce our representations of the way people live together for river engineers, fruit farmers, vehicle designers and social revolutionaries, whom we invite into our theatres and whom we ask not to forget their cheerful interests when they are with us, while we hand the world over to their brains and hearts for them to change as they see fit.
>
> (Brecht 2014b: 235)

Thanks to the resources put at Brecht's disposal in the GDR, he was able to realize the type of sensuous entertainment he advocated. Brecht also began to elaborate on his aesthetic of the naive, of producing pleasurably lucid and concentrated expressions of contradictory reality. The paintings of late medieval Flemish artist Pieter Brueghel – landscapes populated by peasants and rich with pictorial contrasts – and scientific expressions like physicist Isaac Newton's third law of motion – 'for each action there is an equal and opposite reaction' – exemplify the quality of intelligent simplicity that Brecht increasingly promoted. To enhance the GDR's experimental cultural playground he also applied himself to the development of German comedy and comedic performance, a reflection of his understanding that humour – in both its satirical and cheerful modes – was an important emancipatory force.

Equipped with his own apparatus and in the midst of a society aiming to achieve social production – by and for the people rather than for private profit – Brecht experienced the most intense period of collective creativity in his life. Unfortunately his health did not keep pace with his enthusiasm for productive assent and dissent, be it in the form of staging, adaptation, teaching, theorizing, cultural policy or poetry. Due to his deteriorating health, a new production of *Galileo* had to be postponed. He was never to see the final version. On 14 August 1956, after a prolonged struggle with a heart condition, Brecht died of a coronary thrombosis. In accordance with his wishes, he was buried in the Dorotheen Cemetery neighbouring his Berlin apartment. Here Brecht's grave joined that of G.W.F. Hegel, the early nineteenth-century idealist whose dialectical philosophy Marx had challenged and reworked for his materialist agenda. In this staging of the graveyard scene, Brecht once again proved himself a man who took great pleasure in 'the wit of contradictory circumstances' and 'the possibilities of change in all things' (Brecht 2014b: 257, 252).

Brecht today?

In light of the momentous political and environmental changes that have taken place since Brecht's death it has become more difficult to share his optimistic vision of progress towards a world beyond exploitation and class division. The Cold War has abated, but the victor has been global capitalism rather than international communism. Germany has been reunified, but little remains of the socialist republic. Scientific technology has greatly increased our productive capacities, but it has exacerbated rather than resolved world poverty. In such a context, Brecht's diagnosis of the ills of capitalist society, including its misuse of science, continues to resonate. But his odes to progressive river-dwellers, tractors and scientific education can seem quaint and dusty. What, then, does Brecht offer contemporary artists and teacher-learners interested in representing, or even changing, society? This book responds to that question by exploring his revolutionary methods for challenging the way we create and imagine the social world and ourselves. While Brecht's

Marxist narrative is in need of revision, he can still help us to know the interpretive frameworks within which we operate, to transform our oppressive positions, and to develop what it takes to master the complex art of pleasurable production.

7.2 *The Caucasian Chalk Circle*: a production model

Prologue: a model

The Berliner Ensemble's 1954 staging of *The Caucasian Chalk* Circle in East Berlin was a spectacular embodiment of Brecht's passion for collective creativity. One of the last productions of his own work that Brecht undertook, it vividly demonstrated what had become his trademarks, especially his Marxist approach to text and *mise-en-scène*. Like all his stagings it was characterized both by the consolidation of earlier innovations and by new departures that marked his receptiveness to the immediate political context and love of artistic experimentation. Not only did the production continue his technique of expressing contradictory reality by combining divergent modes of performance, but it also ushered in a new experiment with mixed genre. The *Chalk Circle* is an intriguingly hybrid form, bringing together Brecht's established practice of satirizing class-based society with what for him was the relatively unfamiliar strategy of modifying 'happy ending' traditions in order to celebrate the pathway to a just and communitarian society.

Like none other of his productions, this one showcased Brecht's delight in mixing old and new artistry in order to make a social point. Here Brechtian epic theatre collided with Aristotelian dramatic techniques, and ancient Greek and Asian, medieval and folk art were brought into dialogue with various forms of contemporary realist performance. While the play contains numerous clues about the type of dialectical staging Brecht envisaged, many interpreters emphasize its dramatic theatre features without considering their relation to antithetical elements or to Brecht's transformative politics. As a result, this much-performed text is often read and staged as a melodrama in which justice and love appear 'dependent on the quirks of fortune' rather than on social change brought about by human agency (White 1978: 158). In this section I offer an alternative interpretation that demonstrates why Brecht regarded his political performance strategies as embedded in the text – an opinion he expressed early in rehearsals when everything seemed to be running of its own accord, leading him to exclaim that the only possible way of staging it was implicit in the play (BBA 944/17). Of course Brecht was aware that his work could and would be interpreted in diverse ways, but he was clearly surprised at how readily it lent itself to the ethos and methods of the Ensemble. As this company's practice is still not widely understood, I shall try to show how the Brecht collective carefully and playfully animated the text in accordance with their politics.

That Brecht regarded the production as an exemplary experiment is evident from the fact that he commissioned Hans Bunge, and many other directorial assistants, to create a *Modellbuch* ('modelbook'). When reading this section it is important to keep in mind that for Brecht a model was not a definitive 'classic' to be slavishly and eternally imitated. Rather, it was a clarifying example of his company's experimental methods and their relation to a particular historical moment, a guide whose wisdom should be tested afresh in each new circumstance. While the model book was never finalized, the extensive documentation of the staging through rehearsal notes, recordings and photographs offers us an invaluable insight into why and how Brecht and his numerous collaborators – assistant director Manfred Wekwerth, scenographer Karl von Appen, costume and mask designer Kurt Palm, composer Paul Dessau, actors, dramaturges and other spectActors on and off stage – created a production rich with socially significant gestures and groupings. In our own political environments it is likely that some of the Ensemble's strategies will no longer be appropriate tools for resisting oppression and forging new types of community. But in order to make that judgement we first have to understand the old wisdom.

Source materials

There are a number of ways of getting to know the *Chalk Circle* model. Given that Brecht was a playwright-director, versions of the play text are an important source. The first drafts, which he wrote in collaboration primarily with Ruth Berlau, were completed during his American exile in 1944. He made (mainly stylistic) changes throughout the rest of his life, publishing different editions, including a 1954 text directly influenced by his experiences in directing the play. For English-language readers the best-known and readily accessible translations are:

1   Revised translation by James and Tania Stern with W.H. Auden, with commentary and notes by Hugh Rorrison, London: Methuen, 1984, 2005.
2   Revised English version by Eric Bentley, Minneapolis: University of Minnesota Press, 1999.

In this section I will be quoting from the Stern and Auden translation – a reworking of their 1944–6 version – partly because it is clearly informed by Brecht's work on the text in the light of the Ensemble production. Moreover, Brecht was much enamoured of poet W.H. Auden's rendering of the lyrics, which to my mind powerfully convey the artistry of the original's poetry. For better or worse, Brecht also had considerable input into this translation. While he was dissatisfied with the prose sections, later encouraging Eric Bentley and Maya Apelman to attempt a new translation, James Stern did carry out the changes suggested by Brecht before the first Stern and Auden version went to print (Lyon 1980: 128–129).

Whichever copy of the play you are able to locate, it is worth checking the year of the German version it is based on and whether it contains the opening 'Prologue', which Brecht renamed 'The Struggle for the Valley' shortly before his death. By creating a new title, and by numbering it the first of six scenes, Brecht clearly indicated that he wanted this utopian presentation of Georgian agricultural collectives building a socialist future in the wake of the Second World War to be treated as an integral part of the play. For political and historical reasons this frame play has often been omitted, both in print and on stage. On some rare occasions Brecht himself authorized its omission, a judgement made in order to ensure both his own survival and the public dissemination of his work during the Cold War. For example, Eric Bentley states (1999: viii) that Brecht advised him not to include the Prologue in the first printing of Bentley's own English translation of the play in 1948. This was a time of increased anti-Communist sentiment in the US which Brecht had experienced very directly when he was called to appear before the House Committee on Un-American Activities the previous ye. In 1955 Brecht explained that he had accepted the decision of West German theatres to remove the Prologue because otherwise the artistic directors of these state-authorized institutions would not have been able to stage the play (Brecht 1998b: 357). Despite such concessions, Brecht's extant comments about the valley scene suggest he regarded it as crucial to the play's vision of social change.

Methuen's 1984 edition of the preferred translation contains both the 'Prologue' and politically astute commentary from Hugh Rorrison, which is clearly informed by a close acquaintance with rehearsal documents, as well as a helpful collection of production photos. Alfred D. White (1978) presents an equally insightful interpretation of German-language materials on the production, while John Fuegi (1987) offers very helpful information and translations from key primary sources. Here, these guides are supplemented with my own research at the Bertolt Brecht Archive (BBA) into the numerous firsthand accounts made by Bunge and his colleagues. I also draw on Brecht's notes about the text, which appear in translation in volume 7 of the *Collected Plays* (Brecht 1976), and on two German volumes about the production edited by Werner Hecht (1966, 1985). The latter includes reviews, as well as commentaries from collaborators such as the actress Angelika Hurwicz, who played Grusha, the play's heroine. Even if you do not read German, Hecht's volumes are valuable for their numerous photographs, sketches and set and costume designs. Further helpful visual material on the production can be found in the book Hurwicz produced together with photographer Gerda Goedhart (1964), the pictorial Brecht biography by Ernst and Renate Schumacher (1981) and Friedrich Dieckmann's richly illustrated volume on Karl von Appen's scenographic work at the Ensemble (1971).

This section not only reconstructs the production from archive materials, but it also interprets them very differently from writers such as Fuegi. While Fuegi reminds us that many of the source materials surrounding the production are or could be edited records, tidied up for posterity, his interpretation of these records and the additional information he has discovered is underpinned by assumptions that lead him to dismiss Brecht's politics. Consequently Fuegi sees Brecht as an innate genius as well as a contradictory and cruel psychosexual entity, whose 'essential self', rather than his passion for social change, was the shaping force for his art. This assumption explains why Fuegi treats Brecht's interest in contradiction as primarily the product of an ingrained emotional volatility, evidenced supposedly by Brecht's sudden mood changes during rehearsal, and by a major shift in his sexual affections during the production. A further assumption informing Fuegi's commentary is the belief that dramatic theatre – one that prioritizes action over narration, encouraging identification, empathy and emotional stimulation – is mature theatre. For him the presence of dramatic elements in the *Chalk Circle* production makes it 'the lovely butterfly of dramatic art' rather than the plain caterpillar of Brecht's early epic theatre (Fuegi 1987: 149–150; 167). In contrast to Fuegi's emphasis on the *Chalk Circle*'s dramatic elements, this section considers their dialogue with epic demonstration and how they served Brecht's social(ist) agenda in a particular historical moment.

Plotting new models of productivity

A model of dialectical art, the 1954 staging also presented Brecht's preferred model of economic production. A brief overview of the play's plot makes apparent that this theatre event addressed the issue of how we can create ways of producing ourselves and our society that are more empowering and just for all. The opening frame play, set in a decimated Caucasian village in the aftermath of the Second World War, depicts a meeting between delegates of the Galinsk goat-breeding kolchos (or collective farm) and delegates from the neighbouring Rosa Luxemburg fruit-growing kolchos. They discuss the settlement and use of a valley previously farmed by the Galinsk members and located in the Caucasus, a range of mountains between the Black Sea and the Caspian Sea. We learn that during Hitler's invasion the goat-herders were forced to move further east and the fruit-growers had to become fighters, moving to the hills to defend the terrain. Now the Galinsk kolchos wish to resettle the beloved homeland where they have lived for centuries. According to the old laws, the land is theirs. However, in a bid to make the defended homeland even more fertile, the Rosa Luxemburg kolchos have devised an irrigation project that will increase 'their' orchards tenfold and even make possible the introduction of vineyards – but only if the disputed valley is included. After a peaceful debate presided over by an Expert from the Reconstruction Commission, including a cheese-tasting moment that confirms the goat-herders are still producing a calibre product even in their new homeland, all delegates agree to the orchard plan.

To celebrate the visit of their former neighbours, in the evening the fruit-growers and the epic singer Arkadi Cheidze stage 'The Chalk Circle', a play directly relevant to their earlier debate about ownership and justice. Despite the many demands of post-war reconstruction, the farmers put aside considerable time and resources for the performance. The state representative is encouraged to pay the same respect to art. When the busy Expert enquires whether the play can be shortened, the Singer answers with a firm 'No'. Ironically, for the Berlin production Brecht did shorten his play, aware that nearly four hours' running time would have made the public transport logistics a nightmare for his audience. Even the edited version demanded a serious commitment of time, from both the live audiences that witnessed it in East Berlin, London and Moscow, and the practitioners whose 125 rehearsals were spread from November 1953 to the premiere on 7 October 1954. In addition, the production demanded a serious financial commitment from the East German government, as it required a cast of about sixty performers to play approximately 150 roles as well as needing musicians and elaborate scenography. The Singer's response to the Expert offers a strategic reminder that theatre itself is an important productive activity that can demonstrate how the collective management of ideas, materials and human relations is able to produce a garden in bloom for all.

Introduced by the Singer as an old legend 'derived from the Chinese' (8), 'The Chalk Circle' is set in Grusinia, medieval Georgia. It has musical accompaniment, contains epic songs and is performed with the help of the old masks supplied by Arkadi Cheidze and his travelling musical troupe. The play comprises two fictional stories that both take place in the wake of a palace uprising, instigated by a group of princes who overthrow the Grand Duke and his Governor. The first story, which starts in scene 2, depicts the downfall and beheading of Governor Georgi Abashvili, as well as his wife Natella's hasty departure from the city of Nukha – so hasty she leaves her only child behind. Baby Michael is discovered by Grusha Vachnadze, a palace kitchen-maid, just after her fiance, soldier Simon Chachawa, has been ordered to accompany Natella on her flight. After much reflection, Grusha decides to rescue the child and flees with it into the country. In scene 3, after an unsuccessful attempt to leave Michael with a peasant couple, and with soldiers in hot pursuit, at considerable risk to herself she decides to become his parent, continuing the dangerous journey to her brother's farm in the northern mountains. In scene 4, to secure a roof over their head she agrees to a planned marriage with a dying farmer, Yussup. When the Grand Duke is restored, just over two years after the uprising, Natella employs mercenary soldiers, so-called 'ironshirts', to track down her son, who is the heir to her former husband's estate. Michael is discovered and taken to Nukha where a court trial is scheduled to determine the true mother of the child.

At this point the second story takes over and scene 5 begins. We return to the Easter Sunday of the palace revolt and are introduced to the village clerk, Azdak, who discovers a fugitive in the woods and takes him home to his hut for a meal. When he later discovers the fugitive was none other than the Grand Duke himself, Azdak hands himself over to the Court of Justice in Nukha, in the belief that a new social order has begun and he will receive a proper public trial. However, he is mistaken: one oppressive oligarchy is simply being replaced by another. Arriving at the court, Azdak stumbles upon a scene of chaos. The Judge is hanging dead from a pillar, drunken ironshirts are talking about how they have beaten the rebellious carpet weavers to a pulp, and their new employer, Fat Prince Kazbeki, is hoping they will agree to the election of his nephew as the new Judge. Emboldened by the fact that, with the Grand Duke and Michael still alive, Kazbeki needs their support to maintain his precarious hold on power, the ironshirts mischievously decide to appoint Azdak rather than the nephew. In his new role Azdak proves a carnivalesque Robin Hood figure, taking his travelling court to the people and judging in favour of the poor at the expense of the rich. However, Azdak continues to put his own needs first, forcing bribes from all parties and making some dubious rulings in pursuit of his own survival and pleasure.

When the old regime returns, Azdak fears for his life and unsuccessfully attempts to flee, only then to be reinstalled in scene 6 as Judge by the Grand Duke himself. His next task is to preside over two trials: one is to determine Michael's future and the other is to decide whether an old married couple will be granted the divorce they long for. After hearing Natella on the bonds of blood, her lawyers on the importance of securing the estate, and Grusha on how she has 'brought up the child to be friendly with everyone' and 'taught him to work as well as he could' (88), Azdak institutes the famous chalk circle test: 'The true mother is she who has the strength to pull the child out of the circle, towards herself' (94). Two tests are conducted, and Grusha's refusal to pull Michael for fear he will be torn to pieces convinces Azdak that she is 'the true mother'. Instead of signing the divorce papers for the old couple, he annuls the marriage between Grusha and Yussup, freeing Grusha to live with Simon and advising her not to stay in town with Michael. He also legislates that the Abashvili estates be turned into a public playground.

Laying aside the robes that have become too hot for him, Azdak invites all court attendants to a farewell dance, disappearing behind the dancing couples as Arkadi Cheidze sings a brief epilogue:

> But you, who have listened to the story of the Chalk Circle
> Take note of the meaning of the ancient song:
> That what there is shall belong to those who are good for it, thus
> The children to the maternal, that they thrive;
> The carriages to good drivers, that they are driven well;
> And the valley to the waterers, that it shall bear fruit.
>
> (97)

This song invites us to consider the many relations between the teachings of the frame and those of the inner play. In the opening commune plot, the farmers' decisions validate the idea that land and any other means of production should belong to all and be put to use by those who can best make them serve the common good. Their dialogue demonstrates the workings of an egalitarian legal system, one made possible by new social arrangements, such as collective farms and socialist government, and new forces of production, including agricultural technology and scientific thinking. In medieval Grusinia, by contrast, we see how justice and prosperity for all is made impossible by a private property and class system in which ownership is determined by the ruling elite through their soldiers and law courts. In such circumstances, the Golden Age of Azdak's rule can only be short-lived. However, the subversive actions of Grusinia's kitchen-maid and clerk contribute to the history of resistance and the models of revolutionary practice it can provide. The ruling in favour of the foster mother, who will teach the child friendliness and how to work, rather than the biological mother, who will make sure he 'wears the shoes of gold/ Tramples on the weak and old' (93), constitutes a provocative child-care suggestion both for the kolchos members and the off-stage spectators. Not only the production of wine, law and art, but also the education or (re)production of humans must be changed if we want a fairer world.

A historicizing epic

Historicization on page and stage

In a journal entry of 9 November 1949 Brecht described *The Caucasian Chalk Circle* as one of the 'few real repertoire pieces' by a German author, a play that could be performed at almost any time period because it dealt with general or common themes (Brecht 1993: 423). He does not elaborate, but, as the plot makes clear, the play certainly explores the nature of law and identity and the defence of kin and property, recurrent topics in the history of human culture. However, the label 'repertoire piece' was not meant to imply that his treatment of such issues was valid for all peoples at all times. As the play's genesis, its chalk circle imagery and the staging demonstrate, Brecht's approach to content and form was shaped both by specific historical contexts and his desire to respond to them in a historicizing rather than a generalizing manner.

Brecht first used chalk circle imagery in 'The Elephant Calf', a ludicrous interlude in his 1925 version of *Man is Man*. One source for the motherhood test was the Old Testament account of Solomon's threat to resolve a similar dispute by slicing the child in half with a sword (I Kings 3, 16–28). Another source was the adaptation by the contemporary German poet Klabund (Alfred Henschke) of Li Xingdao's thirteenth-century 'Chalk Circle' play. In both Klabund and the Bible it is the biological mother who is judged the true parent. In *Man is Man* Brecht inverts the test and makes the would-be child, Elephant Calf (played by docker Galy Gay transformed into soldier Jeriah Jip), be the one who must pull the mother (played by soldier Uriah) out of the circle. This parodic trail highlights the 'man-made' and fluid nature of identity at a time when Brecht was responding to the upheaval of renewal and intensified modernization after the First World War by celebrating man's transformability in a technologized mass.

Brecht redeployed the chalk circle imagery in *The Augsburg Chalk Circle*, a short story he wrote in Denmark in 1940 when in exile from the Nazis. The historical circumstances had thrown up a new issue, man's malleability in the hands of a fascist collective. Now, while the child is reinstated as the object of dispute, the foster mother replaces the biological mother as the true parent. This new inversion can be read in part as a forceful challenge to the Nazis' organization of society around ties of blood and racial purity. Written four years later, *The Caucasian Chalk Circle* continues this challenge. In addition, the 'Prologue' also attacks another cornerstone of Nazi ideology – the emphasis on old ties and emotional attachments to territory which were used to justify the expansion of the Third Reich through warfare (White 1978: 163). Written at a time of hope and uncertainty, when Hitler's armies were being vanquished on all fronts, this frame play and the inner play both warn against a divisive post-war settlement and further imperialist territorialism in Europe.

Against imperialism Brecht pits examples of communitarian society and behaviour, situating them symbolically in the Caucasus, the first Soviet territory to be freed from the German invaders. Originally he chose a 1934 pre-war Soviet setting for his 'Prologue', but soon changed the setting for the valley dispute to a badly shelled village in the Republic of Georgia *after* the exodus of Hitler's army. This enabled him to demonstrate both his interest in post-war reconstruction and his vision of how a new communist society could be forged. That vision was both celebratory and critical of the Soviet past. Brecht's admiration for the modernization of agriculture under Soviet communism, and the encouragement of female leadership in the field, led him to depict characters such as the girl tractor driver and the female agronomist who support the irrigation plan, types commonly found in Soviet-inspired Socialist Realism. However, the portrayal in the frame play of the resolution of a dispute through humorous negotiation, with minimal intervention from the state's representative, enacts a forceful correction to Stalin's bureaucratic dictatorship with its infamous 'show trials'. A parallel corrective force animates the inner play, which, through its depiction of Azdak's disappointment at the brutal crushing of Grusinia's carpet weavers and the reassertion of an oligarchy, warns against the transformation of revolutionary energy into totalitarian regimes.

The hybrid form of the *Chalk Circle* is attributable not only to Socialist Realist art but also to the American stage and screen of the early 1940s. Initially conceived in part as a vehicle for the Academy Award-winning actress Luise Rainer, who had helped Brecht obtain a Broadway contract for the play before he had written a word of it, the play was influenced both by the need to address an American audience and by Brecht's interest in experimenting with local commercial and popular culture. One aspect that caught his experimental eye was the use of suspense in Chaplin's films and the 'shows' and burlesques of American popular theatre. In his 1944 notes to the play he cited, as a source of inspiration, their use of tension 'focused not merely on the progress of the plot … but more on the question "How?"'(Brecht 1976: 299). Long wary of dramaturgy that used suspense merely to draw attention to *what* was going to happen next, here he praised the way it was used to generate a consideration of *why* and *how* things happen. This said, Brecht was not averse to using suspense in a conventional fashion. Some episodes in scene 3, particularly Grusha and Michael's narrow escape from the palace soldiers after crossing a frayed rope bridge over a precipice, owe more to the influence of the Hollywood Westerns, gangster films and 'action flicks' that Brecht the movie-buff saw in Los Angeles than to any experimental use of suspense. However, as the musicians make clear at the opening of scene 3, when they sing 'How will the merciful escape the merciless/The bloodhounds, the trappers?' (25), what is at stake in the scene as a whole is not *whether* Grusha will escape, but *how* in her social context she will manage it.

According to Brecht the play's structure was also conditioned by a negative response to his host culture, particularly a 'revulsion against the commercialized dramaturgy of Broadway' (Brecht 1976: 299). During the play's gestation, Hollywood and Broadway repertoire was characterized by a high percentage of upbeat musicals and escapist comedies, an antidote to the sombre mood produced by nearly three years' involvement in war (Lyon 1999: 242). Often Brecht managed the difficult task of trying to appeal to and re-educate a new target audience, comfortable with art he found repellent, by subversively appropriating commercial forms. Take, for example, the way the *Chalk Circle* plays with the ingredients of a commercial happy ending. Loose ends are neatly tied up, but only through coincidences – such as the timely reinstatement of the Grand Duke and Judge Azdak – that are glaringly artificial. The lovers are reunited, but instead of the boy getting the girl and settling down, the kitchen-maid foster mother gets the noble child, a divorce and a new man, but must soon take flight, for Nukha is once again governed by ruling-class law. A ritualistic dance finale in the play, replaced in the production by a procession to the dance, celebrates the triumph of justice and productive nurture. But when Azdak removes his robes and disappears behind the dancers, an air of uncertainty and loss troubles the revelry, an air accentuated in the staging by the notable absence from the procession of not only Azdak, but also Grusha and her family. Is this an unequivocally joyous and closed ending? Was it so for the 1954 GDR audience, which knew that the progressive step towards the Golden Age concretized on stage in scene 1 had yet to be realized off stage?

The Ensemble production was staged at a time when the shadows of both Hitler and Stalin and the start of the Cold War were threatening the advent of a Golden Age. Only a few months before rehearsals began, East German workers had taken to the streets in the strike of June 1953, many of them frustrated with their government's Stalinesque attempt to force the pace of modernization through dictate rather than dialogue. In his letters to key political figures at this moment of crisis, and in the *Chalk Circle* production, Brecht promoted the idea of collaboration, urging government and artists to work together to enhance public discussion about communism and its construction. That Brecht believed theatre should be used to help publicize and rehearse new ways of resolving dispute, distinct from the combative legal proceedings of the Nazis and other imperialists in European history, was particularly evident in the way he directed the actors in the valley scene. Steering them away from their tendency to make the discussion formal, as if in parliament, or wild and tumultuous in the manner of freedom fighters from a heroic Schillerian drama, he suggested they play with dry and light spontaneity. As Bunge noted, the aim was to model unfamiliar behaviour, and to highlight the extraordinary fact that, for these farmers in a semi-mythical socialist society, such behaviour was completely ordinary (Hecht 1966: 80).

The staging of the valley scene demonstrates clearly how Brecht the historicist sought to provoke both a celebratory and a questioning attitude towards the contemporary GDR by comparing it not simply with the past but also with an imagined future society. On the one hand, he reminded the performers that they must take a more historically specific approach to their portrayal of the farmers, criticizing their tendency to erase any differences between life at the end of the Second World War and their own experiences in a more prosperous environment nearly a decade later. Partly for this reason he corrected their casual treatment of the moment when the goat-herders present their cheese for inspection, reminding them that in the wake of war such a commodity was a precious rarity. To help build the episode into a historical moment, he swiftly replaced the rehearsal prop they were using – a piece of bread wrapped in paper – with an enormous round cheese, suggesting that it could be carefully unwrapped and distributed to all (BBA 945/34). Brecht's love of cheese was not the only culinary issue at stake here. Performing the cheese offering in this ceremonial way provided the GDR audience with an opportunity to remember the material and social developments in their country since the war. On the other hand, Brecht also asked the performers to create behaviour, such as the way the farmers managed dispute, which was inspired more by a vision of *possible* rather than by actual socialist practice. Through a defamiliarizing comparison with both the past and a potential future, and the use of a setting that mixed actual history with myth, Brecht encouraged reflection on the achievements and shortcomings of his contemporary GDR, a reflection designed to stir all participants in his theatre to action in the present.

Epic demonstration and dramatic experience

One related defamiliarizing strategy that characterized the staging was an emphasis on *demonstrating* the 'pastness' and artificial nature of the characters and situations being re-enacted. In a more varied manner than any other Ensemble staging, the *Chalk Circle* foregrounded the epic act of telling something about a historical and mythical past, and the rehearsed and socially critical nature of that telling. Pieces of business like the cheese ceremony exemplify the more subtle and embedded epic acts in Brecht's theatre. In addition, this production contained numerous overt methods of epic demonstration, such as when the Singer informs the spectators in the frame play that he, his musicians and the host villagers are going to present an ancient tale. The villagers' use of masks, the demonstrational acting, and the Singer's narrative interjections constantly reminded the spectators of the inner play's constructed and partisan nature. The epilogue, addressed directly to both the on-and off-stage audiences, is another overt epic device. Many of Brecht's plays use prologues and epilogues to encourage the spectator to engage with the contemporary relevance of their lessons from the past, a strategy I playfully echo in this chapter.

A further defamiliarizing element in the production was the sustained friction between epic demonstration and dramatic illustration. In dialectical fashion, epic elements were juxtaposed no less overtly with dramatic theatre elements, such as melodramatic scenes that encouraged emotional involvement in the here-and-now of the stage world. In this section I not only introduce you to the multiple modes of demonstration employed in the production, but also illustrate how and why demonstration involved an interplay between the analytic and emotive, between present-tense drama and its interruption through the use of defamiliarization techniques.

Like ancient Greek epic poems, the *Chalk Circle* contains episodic tales about national history and legend, and the greater part of its narrative sections are to be performed by a master of recitation and song. The musically accompanied ancient epic was a source of inspiration for Brecht, leading him to request for the production a kind of music which would permit the delivery of a lengthy text. Meeting this request required Dessau to compose forty-eight separate pieces of music, including forty-one songs. However, Brecht's text diverges from its ancient counterpart, particularly in the way it places marginalized voices (such as farmers, clerks and kitchen-maids) centre-stage. Moreover, as Arkadi Cheidze tells the Reconstruction Expert, on this occasion solo recitation is to be replaced by a play with songs performed collaboratively with his fellow musicians, and almost the entire Rosa Luxemburg kolchos, who have been rehearsing under his tutelage.

In the Ensemble staging of this new musical theatre, particular emphasis was given to the fact that the Singer had scripted, and was now orchestrating, the kolchos performance. Positioned alongside the nine singers and instrumentalists, who were seated both on the stage and in a side-box of the Theater am Schiffbauerdamm stage right (on the left-hand side from the audience's point of view), he peered through prominent spectacles at a well-thumbed script with slips of paper in it, thereby drawing attention to the rehearsed nature of the proceedings. His two female co-singers also used books, the act of reading helping to disrupt the illusion of spontaneity. In early rehearsals Brecht and his scenographer sought to shatter this illusion even more forcefully by experimenting with configurations in which the Singer's ensemble performed simultaneously to the kolchos farmers positioned upstage behind them – either live actors or a painted backdrop depicting the kolchos members – and the 1954 spectators before them in the auditorium (Fuegi 1987: 139). This idea was soon abandoned, in part because it required a type of acting that had yet to be developed in Western theatre (Hecht 1966: 97). In the production itself the performers simply played to the auditorium, thereby turning the theatre audience into attentive Caucasian farmers.

Introduced as a Soviet comrade and artist, the Singer repeatedly alerted the audience not only to the fabricated nature of his tale, but also to the fact that it was a Marxist telling. His partisanship was further emphasized by the way his lyrics expressed support for the disenfranchised and a commitment to social change. The casting of Ernst Busch, a star familiar to the German audience as a dedicated communist with a proletarian and activist background, further underlined the politics of the Singer's poetry. Like the ancient Greek chorus, the Singer was also a key contributor to the production's combination of epic and dramatic elements. In addition to announcing entries and exits, he anticipated, commented on and summarized events. These interventions highlighted the action's status as fictional drama, while at the same time encouraging a socially engaged attitude towards the on-and off-stage worlds. The Singer also helped link the actions in each episode and externalized some characters' unspoken thoughts and emotions, helping to create present-tense action. Whether contributing to narration, commentary or drama, the Singer appealed to both the intellectual and emotional faculties of the audience, as well as their senses, encouraging them to adopt a critical attitude similar to his own.

As the Singer's commentary on the downfall of Georgi Abashvili illuminates, this complex appeal was established at the very beginning of the inner play. As the arrested Governor is led away, the Singer not only informs the audience that he will be executed but also comments on the social significance of his death:

> When the houses of the great collapse
> Many little people are slain.
> Those who had no share in the fortunes of the mighty
> Often have a share in their misfortunes. The plunging wain
> Drags the sweating beasts with it into the abyss.
>
> *(16)*

This narrative discourages the kinds of emotions that are created by the suspense of not knowing *what* will happen to the Governor or his subjects, and instead encourages reflection on *why* the palace revolution will bring no relief. It also reminds us that feudal ruler Abashvili is a social type scripted by the Singer, one similar to a stock character from medieval drama. However, Cheidze's description of a dehumanizing class structure is emotive, inviting the audience to share his attitudes towards the 'plunging wain' and 'sweating beasts'.

Even in expressive moments such as the lovers' 'reunion' at the end of scene 4, a complex mix of analytical and empathetic responses was sustained. When Simon finds Grusha in the northern mountains after the war, the physical barrier of a stream, Simon's shock at her marriage and motherhood, and Grusha's justified fear that a truthful explanation of Michael's ancestry will be overheard, all combine to bring their ability to communicate to a standstill. In Brecht's staging the two lovers stood silently facing each other across the stylized representation of a stream – two parallel ground-rows of rushes placed on the diagonal – while the Singer narrated what Simon wanted to say about the horrors of war and Grusha about Michael's adoption. According to Hurwicz, Brecht directed the Singer not to narrate Simon's accusatory thoughts in the usual detached manner, but to express anger and reproach (Hecht 1966: 63). At the same time, the actors playing the lovers were to accompany the Singer's lyrics with finely modulated facial movements, expressing attitudes like distrust and disappointment.

This depiction of the lovers' attitudes certainly invited empathetic and sympathetic responses to each individual's situation. Yet the content of their narratives made it clear that social warfare had shaped their situation. Moreover, the presentation of each character simultaneously by two different means – aurally by the Singer and his musicians, and visually by the miming actors – was a reminder that these flesh-and-blood characters were also artistic signs. In this adaptation of techniques from Japanese and Chinese theatre, fruitful tension was generated between responses caused by emotional involvement and present-tense flow and those aroused by analytical commentary and the interruption of a spontaneous here and now. While Brecht's theatre had long been characterized by this tension, it was in the 'Appendices to the *Short Organon*', written in the same year as the production and influenced by the recent translation of Mao Tse-tung's article 'On Contradiction', that Brecht first clearly articulated his dialectical interest in this complex interplay.

Ernst Busch's doubling of the roles of Singer and Azdak opened up another layer of dialogue between demonstration and experience. While Brecht's text does not specify such casting, a reduction of the Singer's part in Azdak's story, particularly in the final trial scene, makes doubling possible. The Singer becomes less prominent at the moment when the articulate Azdak enters and begins to assume the role of ironic social commentator. That the Ensemble production wanted to connect these characters was indicated not only by the casting but also by the suggestion at an early *Arrangement* rehearsal that the first transformation of the Singer into Azdak should be emphasized by carrying it out in front of the curtain (BBA 944/13). In the opening stages of Azdak's story the Singer continues to make frequent interjections, requiring Busch to make quick and explicit shifts between the two characters and thereby transgress the conventions of illusionism. In scene 6, where the Singer's role is minimal, this sort of transgression was reduced and the present-tense drama progressed with far less interruption. However, though the intensity of the role doubling and sung narrative might have changed, other modes of demonstration were still in force, for scene 6 is a court trial rich in demonstrational features – such as public narration of past events, presentation of argument and evidence, overt social role play and calls for judgement. Not surprisingly, the courtroom trial was one of Brecht's favourite models for epic theatre.

Brecht (1898–1956)

A Berliner ensemble show

Telling the Fabel through scenic writing

The way the Singer and his team carried out their storytelling – laying bare the social significance of its events and the social attitudes and interpretive approach of their participants – in many ways echoed Brecht's work during rehearsals. Operating as a playwright-director, he made his starting and finishing point the so-called *Fabel*, the plot of the play 'as retold on stage from a specific point of view' (Kinzer 1991: 27). Here 'plot' is to be understood as a sequence of both interactions between characters and individual gests, developed in accordance with a Marxist attention to contradictions. Brecht was particularly keen for the *Fabel* to be communicated through visual means such as scenography and *Arrangement* (the configuration and movements of the actors), often stating that even if the spectators were deaf, or forced to watch through a glass wall blocking the sound, they should be able to follow the *Fabel*. As directorial assistant Carl Weber notes, 'the term "scenic writing" may best convey what Brecht was aiming for' (Weber, in Thomson and Sacks 1994: 181).

Right at the outset on 17 November 1953, Brecht indicated that for him the point of rehearsals was to experiment collaboratively with ways of telling the *Fabel*. His dialectical and analytical approach to the play text was crucial to this experimentation. Brecht encouraged a unique awareness of the text and its staging as a unified whole. While it was common in his day for actors just to have a copy of their own lines and dialogue and to attend rehearsals only where their characters were involved, each Ensemble actor was given the entire text and was encouraged to come to every rehearsal. At the same time, however, by not conducting a read-through rehearsal and not choreographing the play chronologically from scene 1 to scene 6, he disrupted the actors' experience of the text as a sequence of interconnected scenes. Moreover, he often rehearsed a particular episode as a self-contained unit, almost as if the play consisted only of this one segment.

This preference for analytical segmentation and episodic structure ('each scene for itself') also informed Brecht's use of the prompter. He urged his actors to work without the script, receiving each line like he did from the prompter, and then to present it through a full, bodily expression of the character's comportment. This sentence-by-sentence procedure was one of many methods that helped create a surprised and questioning attitude towards the development of the action and inhibited actors from being content with prematurely fixed renditions. Others included:

- withholding any overt statement of a directorial concept at the first rehearsal;
- directing by posing questions rather than giving commands;
- resisting actors' requests for run-throughs, the uninterrupted playing of a scene which might make it easier for them to memorize actions and words;
- giving directorial assistants frequent opportunities to test their own suggestions.

By these means, and his 'Who wrote this play?' attitude, Brecht strove for an environment that encouraged dialogue and was open to change.

A key dialogue partner in the telling of the *Fabel* was the scenographer Karl von Appen. Rather than give von Appen a detailed description of how he visualized the production well in advance, Brecht made some brief comments at the beginning of the rehearsal period, and added the hint, 'Cribs, crib figures' (Hecht 1966: 95). Out of this cryptic remark, Brecht and von Appen developed a look for the inner play that was modelled on European nativity scenes and other folk art – particularly that of Brecht's own southern Germany. This aesthetic helped clarify not only how the inner play was told but *why* and *from what perspective*. For example, it accentuated the play's secular reworking of events and figures from the Old and New Testaments. If the Grusha story echoes the archetype of the Holy Family, replete with virgin mother, an exalted child, and an official father called 'Yussup' (recalling 'Joseph'), it also secularizes the story by, for instance, not making the virgin mother the blood mother and thereby rendering the Holy Spirit superfluous (Nussbaum 1993: 43). And if Azdak is a clown-like Christ figure, journeying through the country with the sacrament of a new Law and being beaten, stripped and almost strung up by soldiers (Suvin 1989: 168), his actions are directed towards social change in the here and now and the establishment of a secular Garden of Eden.

One formal aspect of nativity art adopted by the Ensemble was its non-illusionist artifice and open display of the makers' labour. For example, Brecht sought to reproduce the visibility of the stitched seams in crib-figure costumes, exposing them even further on a stage bathed in bright, cool lighting. The scenography also captured the naive quality as well as the overladen, gaudy splendour of nativity scenes. In scene 2, the palace and church were metonymically represented just by two ornate, door-like facades. Made of *papier mâché* covered with copper and silver foil to give the impression of costly, beaten metal, and connected by a curving red carpet, these facades recalled the inauthentic, mobile and allegorical nature of the crib sets. The Ensemble also adopted the 'stationary' staging techniques employed in medieval theatre. During the 'Flight into the Northern Mountains', as Grusha trudged with Michael on her back against a revolve, the various stations on her journey were represented by simple and easily constructed set pieces that emerged from behind a drop-cloth and travelled towards her. Brecht's allegory, unlike that of nativity and other medieval plays, had a Marxist inflection. For example, the red carpet in scene 2 signposted a direct link between the church and the ruling class. The Marxist perspective was also implicit in a visual code that differentiated characters according to class, the feudal rulers characterized by copper, silver, steel and silk materials, the people by coarse linen. It is important to remember that black-and-white photographs of this and other Brecht productions are a form of documentation that cannot fully capture the allegorical and richly sensuous nature of scenography at the Ensemble.

The production's constant audio-visual reworking of folk, medieval and ancient art not only increased its quotational quality, but also served as an embodiment of the perspective that both dialogue with the past and innovation are crucial to social change. Take, for example, the reference to Chinese art in the white silk drop-cloths against which the action was played – Caucasian mountains in the valley scene, a beehive town of box-like houses for the palace and trial scenes, and gnarled trees, precipices and landscapes to situate scenes set in the northern mountains and to accompany Azdak's travels. Painted in black in the style of Chinese ink drawings, and suspended without battens so that they fluttered like flags, these beautiful backdrops were a reminder of the tale's roots in an ancient Chinese legend. They also functioned as a celebration of contemporary China at a time when the GDR's relationship with the People's Republic was strong, and Brecht was looking to the country as a promising model of how old and new practices could be combined to bring about progressive change (Berg-Pan 1975: 215). The image of the flags' instability and their juxtaposition with the technology of the revolving stage generated a sense of the old art's openness to modification and the value of combining it with modernizing wisdom. The emphasis on cultural dialogue and innovation was also supported by composer Dessau's mixing of folk and modernist art music from Eastern and Western Europe, and his invention of a new instrument called the *Gongspiel*, which combined a set of metal gongs reminiscent of ancient Chinese music with a hammer action and pedals similar to a piano. In echoing the play text's montage of ancient and modern tales and dramaturgy, the production's audio-visual design helped to promote a dialectical perspective towards cultural traditions and heritage.

Brecht (1898–1956)

Orchestrating oppositional Arrangements

As well as accentuating Brecht's juxtaposition of art forms, von Appen also helped to create the *Arrangements* that clarified the *Fabel*. The two men used a model set with figurines to experiment with composition and choreography, and von Appen also worked independently on numerous *Arrangement* sketches. After the staging had been established, he completed a beautiful series of colour images that vividly convey the lucid and oppositional nature of the Ensemble's *Arrangement*. His image of the episode in scene 2 where the Fat Prince feigns a warm and respectful greeting to the Governor before he enters the church and production photos of the same moment (see, for example, Hecht 1985: 114), also demonstrates the great extent to which the Ensemble staging was governed by a tableau aesthetic of carefully organized groupings. However, while the model set experiments and sketches provided a crucial springboard for the stage *Arrangements*, they did not set them in stone. After the initial *Stellproben* ('position' rehearsals) for each scene were complete, Brecht turned his attention to individual actions and episodes, altering the *Arrangement* in the light of this work.

Brecht's work on the scene 2 pivot point, which in Bunge's rehearsal notes is given the gestic title 'The Governor's Wife leaves her child behind', illustrates exactly how detailed and experimental his approach was. Considerable time was given to pondering and trying out the different types of gestural complex which could be used to present the abandonment. At a rehearsal in April 1954, Brecht argued that it was relatively unimportant whether Natella fled of her own initiative or was carried away by the Adjutant after fainting, even though this latter behaviour would minimize her responsibility for abandoning Michael, because, for him, the *Fabel* was not a moral tale about the punishment of a bad mother but was designed to show that a child should be kept by the mother who is better for it (BBA 944/98). Three weeks later he suggested that the fainting option was preferable: by placing less emphasis on the guilt of the Governor's Wife, Azdak's decision to award the child to Grusha was made more unexpected and interesting. However, as Bunge disappointedly notes, Brecht again changed his mind, finally opting for the gesture of flight (BBA 945/18–19). An important element of surprise was sacrificed, but Brecht's final choice of gesture not only challenged the notion that female nurturing behaviour is innate, but also extended the criticism of Natella's class-based individualistic behaviour.

As the visual documents and Hurwicz's description of the meeting between the Governor and the Fat Prince clarify, the *Fabel* revealed Brecht's fascination with dynamic, conflict-laden sociological pictures, and his willingness to deviate from his own text in order to establish them. The staging of this meeting lends far greater emphasis than either the text or von Appen's sketch do to the intimate relationship between Natella and Shalva, the Adjutant who later supports her bid to regain Michael and, through him, her right to dispose of her deceased husband's estates. By placing Shalva behind Natella – an arrangement repeated whenever the couple appeared – and by visually linking them in this episode through the suggestive flow of her long train in his direction, the production drew attention to the way the feudal legal apparatus bolstered the ruling class. The inclusion of Kazbeki's Nephew in this scene, and his placement close behind the conspirator uncle, listening attentively to the ambiguous conversation and aping his uncle's movements, served a similar purpose. In the text the Nephew first appears *after* his uncle has successfully overthrown the Governor and wants to install his young protégé as the new judge. The introduction of the Nephew *before* the downfall not only underlined the nepotism of the aristocracy and its manipulation of the legal apparatus, but also established an opposition between the comfortable incumbents and the would-be usurpers, thereby laying bare the constant state of warfare within the ruling class.

Arrangements such as these show how Brecht used spatial opposition to express social division (Evenden 1986: 136–137). In the scene 4 wedding different types of both spatial and temporal contrast helped convey another social conflict – the division of the sexes through marriage. The most eloquent spatial opposition was that created by the depiction of groom Yussup's farmhouse as two adjoining, but sharply juxtaposed, rooms. The cramped conditions spoke of his family's poverty, and helped explain his mother's desperate decision to marry her dying son in exchange for cash and Grusha's free domestic labour. In addition to this, Brecht used the division to heighten the uneasy mix of wedding and funeral imagery that contributed to the scene's criticism of patriarchal marriage. The contrast between the room on the right – where wedding-cum-funeral guests, musicians and the monk ravenously feasted, made merry and prayed – and the room on the left, where Yussup lay behind a shroud-like curtain, provided an ominous reminder of the marriage's proximity to mourning.

This proximity was further highlighted by the staging of the episode's main pivot point, the moment when Yussup, after hearing the guests talk about the war and danger of conscription being over, sits bolt upright in bed and proves he is *not* dying *but* simply feigning illness in order to ensure his survival. Brecht paid great attention to the creation of temporal oppositions through pivot points, interruptive moments at which a scene is given a change of direction and/or a character is given a change of behaviour, using them to create puzzles that could be resolved through social analysis. For example, Yussup's extreme ruse is the product of his social situation as an impoverished farmer who can easily be exploited as cannon fodder. On this occasion Brecht heightened the impact of the pivot point by instructing Hurwicz to bring about an equally shocking opposition in Grusha's comportment. To prepare for it, she was *not* to present Grusha as sad about being treated as a commodity, *but* as confident that the marriage would help her to conceal and support Michael without cutting her off from Simon (BBA 945/78). From the moment of Yussup's 'resurrection', however, her whole attitude was to change. Now the marriage had become a potential entombment, something made even clearer moments later when, in frustration at her unwillingness to scrub his back or give him his other conjugal rights, Yussup reminded her that 'Woman hoes the fields and parts her legs. That's what our almanac says' (56). Through the use of oppositions over space and time the production exposed Grusha's marriage contract as an oppressive economic exchange firmly related to patriarchal property law.

Fixing the 'not-but' and contradictory comportments

The staging of this pivot point demonstrates how – and why – Brecht used strategies, such as 'fixing the "not-but"' and juxtaposing comportments, to create each character as an unstable unity of opposites. First, to show that humans are ever-changing entities, constantly shaped by and contributing to the flux of their physical and social environments. And second, to alert attention to contradictory behaviour that is the symptom of an oppressive society in need of change. When Hurwicz demonstrated that Grusha was pleased rather than sad about the marriage, she showed that her character had made a decision to adopt a particular attitude and that she could have made it very differently. Her sudden change in comportment clarified how an alteration in social circumstances leads to a marked shift in attitude, and the fact that as a single mother in a feudal – or indeed capitalist – landscape it is difficult for her to make decisions conducive to her happiness. By developing such instances of contradictory behaviour, Brecht underscored what he described in 1954 as the play's main contradictions:

> The more Grusha does to save the child's life, the more she endangers her own; her productivity tends to her own destruction. That is how things are, given the conditions

of war, the law as it is, and her isolation and poverty. In the law's eyes the rescuer is a thief. Her poverty is a threat to the child, and the child adds to it. For the child's sake she needs a husband, but she is in danger of losing one on its account.

(Brecht 1976: 304)

His notes and directorial suggestions clarify how he engaged with the *Fabel* in a dialectical way, bringing out 'the contradictions in people and their relationships' and the determinants under which they develop (Brecht, in Rouse 1989: 29).

Brecht's work on the exchange in scene 3, where a peasant farmer charges Grusha an exorbitant price for the milk she must buy for Michael, illuminates how he encouraged a historicizing and dialectical attitude by modelling one himself. According to Bunge's notes, rather than tell the actors what to do, Brecht initially let them play the scene in a conventional way (Hecht 1985: 96). The actors presented an exchange between an essentially or 'naturally' motherly person who is willing to make every sacrifice for her child, and an essentially evil farmer who throws every obstacle in her way. He then provided questions and statements to help the actor playing the farmer observe his character as a historically specific entity, rather than a conglomeration of fixed characteristics. For example, he asked:

- Why does the farmer charge an exorbitant amount?
- Is it because he is a bad character?
- Is the price of milk determined by a person's character?
- Should we doubt that he is capable of being more generous simply because *right now* he is not?

In addition, he suggested why the farmer was being so tough and mistrustful: his hut was on an army road during war and hungry soldiers had stolen goats, his main source of milk. He then asked the actor and Hurwicz to find gests and interactions that would create a contradictory mix of wariness and interested concern towards Grusha, while also hinting at how the peasant might behave if he were in a less hostile world. To this end, Brecht suggested later that when Grusha was struggling to take off her pack, the farmer should lend a helping hand. When the actor expressed concern that this sudden change in behaviour from mistrust to helpfulness was unjustified, Brecht asked why the farmer should have only one side, and pointed out that people are inclined to dispense kindness when it costs them nothing (BBA 945/100). Showing that the farmer was exploitative *and* friendly drew attention to the economic reasons for his contradictory behaviour. And in a more subtle way it also revealed the interpretive activity of the actor and director, reminding the spectator that while we are economically determined we are also capable of changing these determinants.

Gestic rather than psychologizing characterization

It is evident from the milk-buying episode that Brecht's actors had to adapt to 'a primary concentration on the sociological, behavioral aspects of characterization' (Rouse 1989: 40). Although Brecht acknowledged that there were behavioural elements outside those linked to social class, he believed it was imperative to understand the elements that *were* connected if society was to be changed. While protagonists like Grusha and Azdak displayed multiple attributes, including seemingly 'inborn' characteristics, Brecht focused on the way even these traits were shaped by their social class and circumstances rather than by innate psychological forces. The result was a gestic theatre where rhetorical 'gestures' – the movements, positions and vocal activities of the performer/character's body, as well as gestural extensions such as costumes, props, make-up and masks – externalized the thinking body's socially conditioned relation to time, space and people.

When redrafting the play in 1944, Brecht strove to characterize Grusha as a beast of burden who, by being 'stubborn and not rebellious, submissive and not good, long-suffering and not incorruptible' wears 'the backwardness of her class openly like a badge' (Brecht 1993: 319). His interest in social determination was particularly evident in his treatment of her relationship with Michael. Brecht regarded Grusha's decision to rescue the child as indeed based on certain predispositions, including her tendency to be what he called a 'sucker' (American slang for a person easily fooled), her maternal instinct, and her willingness and ability to be productive (Brecht 1976: 301). However, he also presented these attributes as shaped by the character's role in the mode of production. For example, by contrasting Grusha's activities as a kitchen-maid, used to preparing the Easter Sunday feast, with the utter dependency of the Governor's Wife on her servants when the time comes to pack her trunks, he connected the protagonist's interest and skill in nurturing with her social enculturation. By linking Grusha to the problem-solving agronomist in the valley scene through casting Hurwicz in both roles, Brecht further underscored her social usefulness.

Not only did Brecht present Grusha's behaviour as socially derived, but he repeatedly sought to avoid the presentation of her character as a fixed entity. For example, by foregrounding Grusha's long hesitation before taking the abandoned child he interrupted the idea that her decision was a spontaneous impulse born of an eternally honourable character. In his eyes, the hesitation confirmed her suitability as parent *precisely because* it displayed a class-specific practical bent rather than impulsiveness, a clear-eyed awareness of what might be involved in caring for an infant, with a price on his head, during wartime. His antipathy to essentialist characterization also informed his dialogue with Hurwicz about the depiction of Grusha's bundle during her journey. When Brecht discovered that Hurwicz had been making the bundle smaller and smaller, so as to indicate her character's increasingly pressured economic situation, he commented that such a solution was based on an assumption that it was not in Grusha's nature to steal. His suggestion that perhaps the bundle could become increasingly heavy stemmed from a desire to replace any hint of a fixed noble or 'sucker' character with a subtle reminder of her fluid nature, changed both by circumstances and by her willingness to adopt even anti-social behaviours to survive in an alienating world (Brecht in Fuegi 1987: 157–158). The enlarged bundle also continued the 'beast of burden' imagery, a notion partly inspired by Brueghel's *Dulle Griet* ('Mad Meg' c. 1562), in which a peasant woman, brandishing a sword at the mouth of hell in a chaotic war scene and laden with domestic loot, carries a similar burden. Brecht has stated that any actress who plays Grusha should study the beauty of this painting (Brecht 1976: 299), advice that tells us much about the way he nurtured the actors' understanding of social struggle and ability to express it pictorially.

Brecht's development of Grusha's hesitant comportment and visible burden also helped him to externalize the tension she experiences between her interest in the child and her interest in self, and to identify class-based society as its cause. Grusha's contradiction is only temporarily resolved by the carnivalesque Judge, who himself is troubled by a similar conflict. Described by Brecht as 'a disappointed revolutionary posing as a human wreck, like Shakespeare's wise men who act the fool' (Brecht 1976: 302), Azdak was presented as a type of intellectual who sympathizes with the poor but ultimately puts his own self-interest first. Rather than depict Azdak's 'selfish, amoral, parasitic features' as inborn, Brecht attributed them to his social awareness that the new rulers were simply going to reinstate the old status quo (Brecht 1993: 311). When Azdak first enters the court at Nukha, in chains and dragging the policeman Shauva behind him, his fundamental *Gestus* is that of a defiant man willing to reverse the usual order of things in order to deliver himself up to the judgement of the people. However, once he realizes the golden age of the people's court has not come, he rapidly adopts a *Gestus* of submission, bowing down to the ruling class and its law enforcers in order to save his skin. Throughout the production, Azdak's contradictory comportments not only expressed his fluid and socially determined nature but also his inability, in the given context, to reconcile his interest in serving the oppressed with his own self-preservation and pleasure.

Azdak's self-indulgent attitudes were signposted by means such as the representation of his judge's seat. Brecht arranged for Azdak to be carried by the ironshirts like a sultan in his throne, but suggested that, as his journey progressed, the appearance of the chair should change, becoming increasingly adorned with ornamental altar mats and other precious objects, together with the sausages, ham and wineskins that he had received as bribes or taken at the hearings. As well as expressing his venality, by making the seat into a magnificent processional object Brecht hoped to develop the chair as a witty paradox, a dignified throne being occupied by an undignified judge (BBA 944/72). However, in the chalk-circle trial, Busch presented Azdak not as self serving, but as a revolutionary arbiter for the people who watches the emotional performance of the Governor's Wife, as she tries to persuade him of her rights to the child, with the mistrustful attitude of an experienced trade unionist listening to the 'humane' apologies of the capitalists as they justify a pay cut (Hecht 1966: 85).

The performance of Azdak's appetites also demonstrated Brecht's view of the way in which biological determinants are shaped by class and gender politics. Azdak's transformation of his desire for Ludovica, the voluptuous and well-fed defendant in a rape case, into an exploitative act of conquest is informed both by a class-based desire for revenge and a patriarchal assertion of power. Brecht's rehearsal of the scene between Grusha's brother, Lavrenti, and his wife Aniko, who grudgingly offer her shelter during the first winter in the mountains, provided an even more extensive commentary on the way sexual desire and gender relations express or are dominated by economic structures. For example, he insisted that Lavrenti's subservience to Aniko should not be regarded either as the result of innate determinants, such as weakness and cowardliness, or as fundamentally determined by sexual attraction. Instead, its primary cause was her economic superiority as the original owner of their farm and livestock. That he worked hard for Aniko was to be written in the way he conversed, his tired hands resting on his knees rather than gesticulating. In turn, Aniko was to be represented as pleased by and dependent on Lavrenti because of his efficiency as a farmer. Her cultivation of a softly voluptuous image, plus the way she gave him more space at table and the best pieces of meat, guaranteed his dedication and their success as an economic unit (BBA 976/65; 945/73, 87; 944/87).

Brecht's work with socialized gesture in this scene also exemplified his trademark attention to the way a character's thoughts and body were moulded by their role in the mode of production. The function of the play's many soldiers to act as physically powerful and violent defenders of the Establishment's social power and property interests was presented by Brecht as a major source of their crude behaviour and thinking. Thus, he had the ironshirts on guard during the court hearings be depicted as only interested in questions of inheritance and pornographic issues, and as totally lacking in social concern (Hecht 1985: 93). In distinguishing them from other subordinates by giving them full-size masks, like their superiors – with the notable exception of Simon whose masculine beard hinted at his vocational identity (White 1978: 170) – he emphasized both their aspiration to be the masters and a tendency towards the rigid behaviour of men who are trained to take and give orders. Occasionally compared during rehearsal to Hitler's SS, their long, heavy and stiff tabards gave the soldiers a lumbering, tank-like clumsiness, helping to create a fundamental *Gestus* of dull subservience. Here, Brecht's gestic experimentation was clearly tied to his social criticism of the *petite bourgeoisie*, particularly its susceptibility to fascist regimes.

Gestic masks and stylized naturalness

The masks and costume of the soldiers provided an ideal vehicle for the vivid display of social inscription. They also helped Brecht replace a theatre of psychological realism, oriented around facial expression, with a type of socialist realist performance centred on comportment. As the design and use of the masks in the production make clear, Brecht's realist aesthetic was characterized by the interplay of literal imitation and the playful manipulation of form. This interplay reflected not only Brecht's taste for oppositions, but also his belief that, in order to reveal society's causal complex, a realist artist must be concrete and enable abstraction. That is, she must be socio-historically specific, and carefully observe material actuality and the contradictory flux of the real. At the same time, she must be analytical and make legible social causality and the socially significant, i.e. those humans, events and contradictions which are most decisive for the progress of humankind. The artistic means Brecht employed to fulfil this agenda was the combination of literal representation (e.g. the soldiers' behaviour during Azdak's hearings) with defamiliarizing, non-literal representation (e.g. the soldiers' striking tabards). Brecht often described this unity of the diverse as a bringing together of naturalness and realist stylization.

While the use of masks was a pragmatic solution to the problem of a large-cast play – role-doubling enabling the complex *Fabel* to be told without any loss of clarity – Brecht also ensured that they became a gestic vehicle for displaying socialized comportment. His insistence that the masks should capture the play's multiplicity of social types, rather than blurring them through a fixed schema, such as 'rich people – masks, poor people – none', testifies both to his anti-Formalist position and to his attention to the unity of naturalness and stylization. Not only members of the ruling class but also some servants wore masks. Moreover, different degrees of behavioural rigidity were indicated by different sizes, and each mask was individualized and recognizably human. Thus the Governor, the Fat Prince and the soldiers had almost full-sized masks. The Governor's Wife was given only a half-mask in order to ensure that her mouth be kept free for smiling at the Adjutant, a gesture which demonstrated their flirtatious relationship. Noticeably smaller and less rigid masks distinguished the professionals, such as the Adjutant, Advocates and Doctors, from the rulers to whom they had sold themselves. The palace servants wore small masks, each particularized according to the behaviour of its wearer. A number of characters – the major protagonists, Michael, Simon, Lavrenti and his wife, peasants and many other figures in the northern mountains – remained unmasked. Arguably, even this differentiated mask design erred on the side of the schematic: all those who directly perpetuate a ruling class – masks, all those who do not – none. Nevertheless, the attempt to depict the complexity and flux of the concrete is evident (Mumford 2001: 160–164).

By encouraging a presentational body language in keeping with their stylized nature, the masks also enhanced the demonstrational quality of the acting and the play's nativity scene imagery. At the very first rehearsal Brecht cited the nativity play as the mode of performance he was looking for, later characterizing its acting as similar to the exaggerated and jerky behaviour of circus clowns (BBA 946/31). The masks helped the actors achieve this performance mode by obliging them to use exaggerated gesture. The resulting mime-like style was matched by a forceful vocal delivery, the product of the actors' attempt to match the production's music, which, inspired by music such as folk dance from Azerbaijan and composers like Bartók, was often loud, percussive and full of movement (Fuegi 1987: 148). The simplification and reduction of movements dictated by the masks also helped to isolate and intensify significant comportments. For example, once the actor playing the Fat Prince began rehearsing with his mask it became obvious that his continual fanning movement was not required and that Kazbeki should instead only fan himself at the one moment when he becomes really hot – when the Rider from the capital city arrives, filling him with anxiety that the uprising against the Grand Duke and his governors, and consequently his own plot to murder Abashvili, will be revealed. Here the mask helped to effect the transition from more naturalistic detail to a single, telegraphic piece of business that underlined the power politics of the play.

Even in episodes where there were no characters with masks, such as the one where an exhausted Grusha first sets foot in her brother's home, naturalistic detail was combined with a defamiliarizing demonstration of the socially significant. Scenographic elements, such as the spacious nature of the quarters, the oven, and the sheepskin cover on the table bench, established the relative wealth of the farmhouse. Against its material warmth Brecht carefully built up a frosty social configuration. He set the estrangement process in motion by first transforming the actors' initial agitated manner when playing the episode, one loaded with anger at Grusha's condition, into a more analytical approach by having them add 'the man said', 'the woman said', to the spoken text, thereby helping them to treat their characters as observable objects (Fuegi 1987: 145–146). Slowed by this device, the actors were then in a better position to study the episode's conflictual social relations. The groupings and gestures that ultimately emerged, particularly the uncomfortably sustained separation of Grusha from the couple, made these conflicts graphic. When, for example, a pale Grusha entered the room stage left, supported by a stableman, interrupting Lavrenti and Aniko as they sat sharing a large bowl of soup stage right, rather than rushing to assist his frozen sister obviously on the verge of collapse, Lavrenti remained fixed at his wife's side until her first exit. Such unexpected *Arrangements* and comportments helped to make legible the material and ideological reasons for the couple's unfriendly reception of Grusha. If Aniko is concerned that a relative who seems to be in ill-health and a single mother to boot could undermine her financial and social position, Lavrenti is loath to lose his creature comforts by displeasing his wife.

Scenography, props and pieces of business were also governed by a principle of stylized naturalness. Brecht used authentic objects like the sheepskin in the farmhouse, rather than abstractions or symbols, to indicate something about the owner's social context and material circumstances. However, he and von Appen worked in a metonymic way with the set pieces, carefully choosing a few key segments which supplied the outlines of an environment and contributed to the *Fabel*'s commentary. His assistants undertook extensive cultural history research into cultural objects, situations and customs in the Caucasus and medieval Georgia, using their findings when they helped to propel the gist of the *Fabel*. Thus, the Caucasian custom of breaking large, flat loaves of bread by hand was incorporated into the wedding scene, Grusha and her mother-in-law dividing large, flat cakes to feed the starving guests in a secular echo of Christ's miracle with the loaves and fishes. This activity both conveyed the hand-to-mouth nature of their existence and emphasized their need for material rather than spiritual transformation (Fuegi 1987: 147). Both the metonymic use of selected authentic objects and customs and their combination with obviously crafted elements, such as the drop-cloths and masks, provided a reminder that the human world was a constructed entity open to change through the hands and imaginations of men and women.

Epilogue: 'the proof of the pudding is in the eating'

Animated by a playwright-director dedicated to the progressive reconstruction of theatre and society, the *Chalk Circle* production was both a celebratory and questioning performance, unique in its dialectical unity of the diverse. A testimony to the Brecht collective's mastery of popular and pleasurable entertainment, it achieved success abroad at the International Theatre Festival in Paris in July 1955 and during its tours to London in 1956 and Moscow the following year. The production remained prominent in the Ensemble repertory until the end of 1958, by which time it had been performed about 175 times. But did this richly dialectical pudding actually challenge the culinary tastes and preferences of its historical audiences? And can Brecht's play and staging methods still provide a useful challenge to the way we produce and artistically represent our social world?

The initial reception of the production by the East and West German presses, at least until it began to win accolades in Paris, suggests that it had considerable force as an aesthetic and ideological provocation. After the previews in Berlin, the show quickly became contentious in the East, arousing heated cultural debate, yet being pointedly ignored by the Party newspaper. Much of the negative commentary was fuelled by the association of epic theatre with decadent art that deviated from the artistic tenets of Soviet Socialist Realism. Many critics accused the dramaturgy of inappropriately adopting novelistic conventions which jeopardized the play's unity. They referred especially to its lack of a central conflict and resolution, its episodic nature and length, and what were deemed the inadequately established links between the kolchos and chalk circle plots. A key figure in the debates was Fritz Erpenbeck, the editor who five years earlier had turned the Ensemble's *Mother Courage and Her Children* into the first theatre case in the GDR's Formalism conflicts. Erpenbeck claimed that the artistic unity of the production was also compromised by its failure to reconcile moving dramatic action and realist performance with narrative commentary. For similar reasons he criticized the interiors brought in on the revolve stage in act 3 for being a stylistic break from the more subtly suggestive signs like the palace and church facades and the painted city on the silk drop-cloth. In a fragmentary riposte published posthumously, Brecht defended his experimentation by arguing that the unexpected and unusual were typical and pleasurable components of theatre, and by asking that less attention be paid to the form of his artistic means and more to their social purpose.

Ironically, while the East German arbiters of taste mainly concerned themselves with its formal features, the Western critics focused on its Marxist underpinnings. Scornfully referring to it as a thesis play, they repeatedly singled out the 'Prologue' as a source of tedious didacticism, one commentator describing the valley scene as an attempt to make the entire play more palatable to the East German cultural functionaries (Brecht 1992: 473). In fact, the Party-line Eastern press was also sceptical about the play's overtly didactic elements, though it was concerned more with epic elements such as the masks and narrative commentary. Critics from both sides of Germany also expressed concern about the presentation of motherhood as a social rather than a primarily biological process. The ideological nature of the Western response was particularly illuminated by the controversy surrounding the West German premiere of the play in April 1955 at the Frankfurt Schauspielhaus, a production directed by Harry Buckwitz and over-seen by Brecht, with the Ensemble actress Käthe Reichel as Grusha. Angered by what they understood to be Brecht's support for the East German government during the first workers' strike of June 1953, Christian Democratic Union city councillors tried to prevent the premiere. While the production nevertheless went ahead, as a concession to the political environment Brecht authorized the omission of the frame play. Not only did Brecht's art confront the aesthetic preferences of its spectators, but there were also, clearly, occasions when the politics of its audience threatened to overwhelm his art.

Today, after the fall of communism in Europe, Brecht's Soviet setting in the 'Prologue' has become an even more problematic vehicle for his utopian vision of egalitarian law and collective productivity. While in our current landscape of ongoing violent territorialism and intensified battles for material resources, oil in particular, the need for a counter-model has become arguably even more pressing, it may be necessary to follow Brecht's historicist approach and find ways to embody his vision that better suit our particular time and place. One is to create a frame play that foregrounds the relevance of the inner play to a contemporary world. This is the path director Heinz-Uwe Haus pursued in his 1992 University of Delaware production, when he scripted a new scene 1 that depicted the plight of children from the world's trouble spots and their discovery of an old storybook of the Chalk Circle. For those of us interested in the alterable causes of our devastating struggles for land and power, and in ways of better nurturing the future, that story remains both thought provoking and socially relevant.

If it matters to us that productions of *Chalk Circle* are not reduced to hackneyed melodrama about the quirks of fortune, we would do well to learn from the Ensemble's staging. Their pictorial crystallization of class and gender conflict demonstrates how the inner play can be read and presented both as a forceful criticism of the way humans produce and reproduce in class-based societies, and as a celebration of our ability to change invidious habits of ownership. Understanding how the Ensemble approached Grusha and Azdak's stories better equips us to make theatre that questions the large-scale colonization and consumption practices that dominate our landscape, while also modelling a more fruitful stewardship of children and society. Furthermore, the 1954 production shows us how Hollywood-style psychological realism might be supplemented (or even replaced?), and a *Gestus*-based performance developed, in which socialized behaviour is theatrically foregrounded.

The Ensemble's version of gestic theatre was guided by an aesthetic of stylized naturalness, which, in its day, was a revolutionary breakthrough to a more lifelike performance, as Kenneth Tynan's review of their London tour memorably records:

> When the house-lights went up at the end of *The Caucasian Chalk Circle*, the audience looked to me like a serried congress of tailor's dummies. I probably looked the same to them. By contrast with the blinding sincerity of the Berliner Ensemble, we all seemed unreal and stagey. Many of us must have felt cheated. Brecht's actors do not behave like Western actors; they neither bludgeon us with personality nor woo us with charm; they look shockingly like people – real potato-faced people such as one might meet in a bus-queue.
>
> (Tynan 1976: 196)

Brecht's blend of familiarizing imitation and defamiliarizing stylization is a unique political aesthetic. However, in an age when resemblance to everyday reality is the rule rather than the exception in much cultural performance, particularly in the West, we may need to reconsider the use of naturalist imitation. However, any revisions we undertake should be informed by an appreciation of how Brecht and his collective pursued the goal of making the dialectical mode of considering things a pleasure, as they did in model productions like the groundbreaking *Caucasian Chalk Circle* of 1954.

Further reading

Bathrick, David (1990) 'Max Schmeling on the Canvas: Boxing as an Icon of Weimar Culture', *New German Critique* 51, pp. 113–136.

Berg-Pan, Renata (1975) 'Mixing Old and New Wisdom: The "Chinese" Sources of Brecht's *Kaukasischer Kreidekreis* and Other Works', *German Quarterly* 48, pp. 204–228.

Bishop, Philip E. (1986) 'Brecht, Hegel, Lacan: Brecht's Theory of Gest and the Problem of the Subject', *Studies in Twentieth Century Literature* 10: 2, pp. 267–288.

Bradley, Laura (2006) *Brecht and Political Theatre: The Mother on Stage*, Oxford: Clarendon.

Brecht, Bertolt (1964) 'Notes on Stanislavski', trans. Carl R. Mueller, *Tulane Drama Review* 9: 2, pp. 155–166.

—— (1967) 'BB's Rehearsal Scenes: Estranging Shakespeare', *The Drama Review* 12: 1, pp. 108–111.

—— (1972) *Collected Plays*, vol. 5, eds. Ralph Manheim and John Willett, New York: Vintage.
—— (1976) *Collected Plays*, vol. 7, eds. John Willett and Ralph Manheim, London: Eyre Methuen.
—— (1978) *Brecht on Theatre: The Development of an Aesthetic*, ed. and trans. John Willett, New York: Hill and Wang; London: Methuen.
—— (1979a) *Collected Plays*, vol. 2i, eds. and trans. John Willett and Ralph Manheim, London: Eyre Methuen.
—— (1979b) *Diaries 1920–22*, ed. Herta Ramthun, trans. John Willett, London: Eyre Methuen.
—— (1979c) *Poems*, ed. and trans. John Willett and Ralph Manheim, 2nd edn, London: Eyre Methuen.
—— (1984, 2005) *The Caucasian Chalk Circle*, trans. James and Tania Stern with W.H. Auden, London: Methuen.
—— (1986) *Life of Galileo*, trans. John Willett, London: Methuen.
—— (1990) *Letters 1913–1956* ed. John Willett, trans. Ralph Manheim, London: Methuen.
—— (1991) *Werke: Große kommentierte Berliner und Frankfurter Ausgabe*, vol. 24, eds. Peter Kraft et al., Berlin and Frankfurt am Main: Aufbau and Suhrkamp.
—— (1992) *Werke: Große kommentierte Berliner und Frankfurter Ausgabe*, vol. 8, eds. Klaus-Detlef Müller, Berlin and Frankfurt am Main: Aufbau and Suhrkamp.
—— (1993) *Journals*, ed. John Willett, trans. Hugh Rorrison, London: Methuen.
—— (1998a) *Collected Plays*, vol. 1, eds. John Willett and Ralph Manheim, London: Methuen.
—— (1998b) *Werke: Große kommentierte Berliner und Frankfurter Ausgabe*, vol. 30, eds. Werner Hecht et al., Berlin and Frankfurt am Main: Aufbau und Suhrkamp.
—— (1999) *The Caucasian Chalk Circle*, English version by Eric Bentley, Minneapolis: The University of Minnesota Press.
—— (2001) *Brecht on Film and Radio*, ed. and trans. Marc Silberman, London: Methuen.
—— (2003) *Brecht on Art and Politics*, eds. Tom Kuhn and Steve Giles, London: Methuen.
—— (2014a) *Brecht on Performance: Messingkauf and Modelbooks*, eds. Tom Kuhn, Steve Giles and Marc Silberman, trans. Charlotte Ryland et al., London: Bloomsbury/Methuen Drama.
—— (2014b) *Brecht on Theatre [BT]*, 3rd edn, eds. Marc Silberman, Steve Giles and Tom Kuhn, trans. Jack Davis et al., London: Bloomsbury/Methuen Drama.
Brooker, Peter (1988) *Bertolt Brecht: Dialectics, Poetry and Politics*, London: Croom Helm.
Bryant-Bertail, Sarah (2000) *Space and Time in Epic Theater: The Brechtian Legacy*, New York: Camden.
Calandra, Denis (1974) 'Karl Valentin and Bertolt Brecht', *The Drama Review* 18: 1, pp. 86–98.
Dickson, Keith (1978) *Towards Utopia: A Study of Brecht*, Oxford: Clarendon.
Dieckmann, Friedrich (ed.) (1971) *Karl von Appens Bühnenbilder am Berliner Ensemble*, Berlin: Henschel, Kunst und Gesellschaft.
Eddershaw, Margaret (1991) 'Echt Brecht? "Mother Courage" at the Citizens, 1990', *New Theatre Quarterly* 7: 28, pp. 303–314.
Evenden, Michael (1986) 'Beyond Verfremdung: Notes Toward a Brecht "Theaterturgy"' in *Before His Eyes: Essays in Honor of Stanley Kauffmann*, ed. Bert Cardullo, Lanham, MD: University Press of America.
Ewen, Frederic (1970) *Bertolt Brecht: His Life, His Art and His Times*, London: Calder and Boyars.
Fogg, Derek (1991) '*Mother Courage and Her Children*, by Bertolt Brecht' in *The Citizens' Theatre Season: Glasgow 1990*, eds. Jan McDonald and Claude Schumacher, Glasgow: Theatre Studies Publications.
Fuegi, John (1987) *Bertolt Brecht: Chaos, According to Plan*, Cambridge: Cambridge University Press.
Giles, Steve (1997) *Bertolt Brecht and Critical Theory: Marxism, Modernity and the Threepenny Lawsuit*, Bern: Peter Lang.
Hecht, Werner (1966) *Materialien zu Brechts 'Der Kaukasische Kreidekreis'*, Frankfurt am Main: Suhrkamp.
—— (ed.) (1985) *Brechts Theaterarbeit. Seine Inszenierung des 'Kaukasischen Kreidekreises' 1954*, Frankfurt am Main: Suhrkamp.
Hurwicz, Angelika (1964) *Brecht inszeniert: Der kaukasische Kreidekreis*, photos by Gerda Goedhart, Velber bei Hannover: Erhard Friedrich.
Jones, David Richard (1986) *Great Directors at Work: Stanislavsky, Brecht, Kazan, Brook*, Berkeley: University of California Press.
Kinzer, Craig (1991) 'Brecht, the "Fabel", and the Teaching of Directing', *The Brecht Yearbook* 16, pp. 25–37.
Lang, Frits (dir. 1943) *Hangmen Also Die!*, Hollywood CA: Pressburger Films.
Leach, Robert (2004) *Makers of Modern Theatre: An Introduction*, London and New York: Routledge.
Lennox, Sara (1978) 'Women in Brecht's Works', *New German Critique* 14, pp. 83–96.
Lyon, James K. (1980) *Bertolt Brecht in America*, London: Methuen.

—— (1999) 'Elements of American Theatre and Film in Brecht's *Caucasian Chalk Circle*', *Modern Drama* 42: 2, pp. 238–246.
Martin, Carol (2000) 'Brecht, Feminism, and Chinese Theatre', in *Brecht Source-Book*, eds. Carol Martin and Henry Bial, London: Routledge, pp. 228–236.
Marx, Karl (1977) *Selected Writings*, ed. D. McLellan, Oxford: Oxford University Press.
McDowell, W. Stuart (1976) 'Actors on Brecht: The Munich Years', *The Drama Review* 20: 3, pp. 101–116.
Mitter, Shomit (1992) *Systems of Rehearsal: Stanislavsky, Brecht, Grotowski and Brook*, London and New York: Routledge.
Mumford, Meg (1995) 'Brecht Studies Stanislavski: Just a Tactical Move?', *New Theatre Quarterly* 11: 43, pp. 241–258.
—— (1998) '"Dragging Brecht's Gestus Onwards": A Feminist Challenge', in *Bertolt Brecht: Centenary Essays*, eds. Steve Giles and Rodney Livingstone, Amsterdam: Rodopi, pp. 240–257.
—— (2001) 'Gestic Masks in Brecht's Theater: A Testimony to the Contradictions and Parameters of a Realist Aesthetic', *The Brecht Yearbook* 26, pp. 143–171.
—— (2003) 'Verfremdung', in *The Oxford Encyclopedia of Theatre and Performance*, vol. 2, ed. Dennis Kennedy, Oxford: Oxford University Press, pp. 1404–1405.
Nussbaum, Laureen (1993) 'Brecht's Revised Version of Genesis 1 and 2: A Subtext of the Caucasian Chalk Circle', *Communications from the International Brecht Society* 22: 1, pp. 41–50.
Philpotts, Matthew (2003) '"Aus so prosaischen Dingen wie Kartoffeln, Straßen, Traktoren werden poetische Dinge!": Brecht, *Sinn und Form*, and Strittmatter's *Katzgraben*', *German Life and Letters* 56: 1, pp. 56–71.
Ramthun, Herta (ed.) (1969–73) *Bertolt-Brecht-Archiv: Bestandsverzeichnis des literarischen Nachlasses*, 4 vols., Berlin and Weimar: Aufbau.
Rouse, John (1984) 'Brecht and the Contradictory Actor', *Theatre Journal* 36: 1, pp. 25–41.
—— (1989) *Brecht and the West German Theatre: The Practice and Politics of Interpretation*, Ann Arbor, MI: U.M.I. Research Press.
Schumacher, Ernst and Renate Schumacher (1981) *Leben Brechts in Wort und Bild*, Berlin: Henschel.
Speirs, Ronald (1982) 'Brecht in the German Democratic Republic', in *Brecht in Perspective*, eds. Graham Bartram and Anthony Waine, London: Longman, pp. 175–189.
Subiotto, Arrigo (1975) *Bertolt Brecht's Adaptations for the Berliner Ensemble*, London: MHRA.
Suvin, Darko (1989) 'Brecht's *Caucasian Chalk Circle* and Marxist Figuralism: Open Dramaturgy as Open History', in *Critical Essays on Bertolt Brecht*, ed. Siegfried Mews, Boston, MA: G.K. Hall.
Taylor, Ronald (ed.) (1977) *Aesthetics and Politics*, London: NLB.
Thomson, Peter and Glendyr Sacks (eds.) (1994) *The Cambridge Companion to Brecht*, Cambridge: Cambridge University Press.
Tynan, Kenneth (1976/1956) '*The Caucasian Chalk Circle, Mother Courage* and *Trumpets and Drums* at the Palace', in *A View of the English Stage*, ed. Kenneth Tynan, Frogmore, St Albans, Herts: Paladin.
Völker, Klaus (1979) *Brecht: A Biography*, trans. John Newell, London: Calder and Boyars.
Weber, Carl (1967) 'Brecht as Director', *The Drama Review* 12: 1, pp. 101–107.
White, Alfred D. (1978) *Bertolt Brecht's Great Plays*, London and Basingstoke: Macmillan.
Willett, John (1977) *The Theatre of Bertolt Brecht: A Study from Eight Aspects*, rev. edn, London: Methuen.

8
DECROUX (1898–1991)

Thomas Leabhart

8.1 A Promethean life

Introduction

From my daily work with him over a four-year period, and subsequent visits during more than a decade, I know first-hand of Etienne Decroux's deep and abiding belief in what he called the Cathedral of Corporeal Mime, a project he imagined would consume, like the great cathedrals of France, the lifetimes of many workers. I know too that he pursued his mission single-mindedly with what some saw as a religious fervor. As one who believed his sincerity, admired his genius, and apprenticed in his atelier (not as an impartial observer, if such a thing could exist), I have tried to tell, in the measure possible, Decroux's story as I imagine he would have wanted it told. With the same information, arranged differently, another writer could depict a misfit and sometimes a buffoon, a megalomaniac, a man with pre-feminist French views of women, and one who wittingly and unwittingly alienated many while reveling in his outsider status.

Having known Decroux and his penchants – his strongly pronounced tastes and his volatile temperament – I surmise he would have chosen tragedy as the genre for recounting his life, rather than melodrama, farce, or Theatre of the Absurd. And yet, in this story of a Promethean "man who preferred to stand," as he identified himself, we might glimpse an agile, masked, and cavorting *commedia dell'arte* actor (though never a pantomime!) skittering around the edges of these otherwise serious pages.

His appearance in the Performance Practitioners Series places Decroux accurately in a line of influential twentieth-century theatre reformers, helping to rescue him from years of oblivion and benign neglect.

When I mentioned to Italian theatre historian Nicola Savarese that Decroux had died in 1991, he replied with astonishment: "In theatre history terms, the body is not yet cold in the grave!" Truly one might say that the body of Decroux's work lives on vibrantly today through his students and their students in schools including those in London, Paris, Toulouse, Rome, Naples, Madrid, Barcelona, Montreal, Vancouver, Spring Green, WI, and Claremont, CA, to name a few. Graduate students in Italy, France, and Spain regularly select areas of Decroux's work as thesis or dissertation topics, several important publications in French and in English have appeared in recent years, and Decroux's book *Paroles sur le mime* has been translated into five languages.

These encouraging indicators suggest that Decroux will not remain an idiosyncratically colorful footnote to twentieth-century theatre history, but will increasingly take his place among his better-known colleagues.

The life of Etienne Decroux

Childhood

Etienne Decroux's father, Marie-Edouard, a mason, walked 400 miles (644 kilometers) from his native Haute Savoie (eastern France, bordering Switzerland and Italy) to Paris, where he married the cook in a household which had employed him as *maître d'hôtel* (Benhaïm 2003: 241). Decroux, born July 19, 1898, spoke affectionately of both parents, yet saw his father as the decisive figure in his early life. He not only built houses but also cooked meals, bathed his son, nursed him through illnesses, cut his hair, took him every Monday to the *café-concert*, a kind of music hall, where he discovered musicians, singers, comedians and pantomimes. His father's voice "caress[ed] the heart" of his disappointed son, found secretly crying after the departure of the first circus he had ever seen (Leabhart and Chamberlain: 49). Father and son visited a family of Italian sculptors, where, joining art with ethics and political commitment, they held "prolonged conversations on justice and injustice. In our neighborhood, he was the only person thinking as he did"; he "read verse to me in a restrained manner . . . I looked at my father as one looks at a moving statue" (Decroux 1950: 2). Later he wrote: "Thanks to him, for me, there is nothing higher than a political sense. I have . . . remained impressed with what one could call political lyricism" (Decroux 2003: 57). Thus, in his early life, the strands of familial love interweave with politics and art.

An apprentice butcher at thirteen, Decroux later worked as a dishwasher, painter, plumber, mason, roofer, day laborer, dockworker, farmer, and in a factory repairing wagons; he placed hermetic seals on iceboxes; he was a nurse (Decroux 1985: ii); and served in the military for three years. In 1920, Georges Carpentier became the boxing champion of the world, combining a strength and grace that would influence Decroux's subsequent endeavors: "In sport I saw the origin of dramatic art. I had for it an almost dazed admiration" (Decroux 1950: 3). He later explained, "These things, seen and experienced first hand, gradually moved into the back of my mind, down the back of my arms, and finally down to my fingertips where they modified the fingerprints" (Decroux 1985: ii).

In the first years of Decroux's life, themes appear that he developed throughout his career. In his love of the circus, we see his later preference for energetic and highly trained actors on an empty stage. Decroux's early reverence for sculpture and his vision of his father as a "moving statue" adumbrate Mobile Statuary, one of the primary categories of Decroux's Corporeal Mime technique.

At the *café-concert*, Decroux saw the last gasps of nineteenth-century pantomime, the only art he frankly "detested," and from which his Corporeal Mime technique radically departed. Recent scholarship (see Martinez 2008) depicts a complex and variegated landscape of nineteenth-century French pantomime, reminding us that Decroux knew and responded negatively to only some of its many aspects: charming and entertaining vignettes presented primarily through facial expressions and use of the hands. Corporeal Mime as he conceived it began in the deepest parts of the body (inside the biceps and the buttocks, and from the abdomen below the navel), and did not primarily aim at entertainment (see Table 1.1).

While, in later years, Decroux perceived a clear dichotomy between nineteenth-century pantomime and twentieth-century Corporeal Mime, the situation in theatres and music halls

Table 1.1 A comparison of Corporeal Mime and pantomime

Corporeal Mime (Etienne Decroux)	Pantomime (Charles Deburau)
Twentieth-century modernist	Mid-nineteenth-century Romantic
Non-narrative (symbolic or abstract)	Storytelling (linear)
Often tragic	Often comic
Emphasis on articulated trunk	Emphasis on expressive face and hands
Body uncovered, masked face	Body covered, face exposed
Physical causality replaces plot	Traditional beginning, middle, end
Gestures exist for themselves	Gestures replace words or show emotion (for G. Wague)
Lower center of gravity	Higher center of gravity

throughout Paris at that time was more nuanced. In fact, he did not mark a clear distinction before working with his early collaborator Jean-Louis Barrault on the film *The Children of Paradise*. Until then he often used the words "pantomime" and "mime" interchangeably to describe his art (Martinez 2008: 265). And, as an examination of his creations reveals, not all were modernist. In New York, for example, in the late 1950s, he performed a variation of the Pygmalion myth in which the sculpture comes to life and strangles her sculptor. In later years, however, he rarely created anecdotal entertainment, for reasons that we will discover.

How did Decroux, a young, working-class, politically engaged idealist, transform himself into one of twentieth-century theatre's most original thinkers and doers? Decroux's first consequential professional encounter – with the visionary Jacques Copeau – changed the course of his life.

Chez Copeau: the Chapel, the laboratory, the school

At age twenty-five, having spent a decade as a manual laborer, Decroux had saved enough money to live for a year without working. Desiring a less physically exhausting life, he imagined that an acting career would allow him the time and energy to pursue political interests. However, in politics as in theatre, his pronounced working-class accent needed correcting; and, in an age without electronic amplification, he had to master articulation and projection. Decroux, entering Jacques Copeau's school to study voice, discovered instead the expressive body. Copeau and his associate Suzanne Bing cultivated in Decroux a spark that would, over the course of his career, burst into the flame of Corporeal Mime.

"Give me a bare stage!"

Jacques Copeau (1879–1949), born to a family of manufacturers and salespeople, worked, before founding a theatre, as a writer, editor, and critic. In 1913, at age thirty-three, without previous practical experience and with only his intuition to guide him, Copeau founded (with actors Charles Dullin, Blanche Albane, Suzanne Bing, and Louis Jouvet) the Théâtre du Vieux-Colombier.

Copeau modeled his theatre's stage after those historical spaces he admired: the Greek theatre, the Noh stage, the *commedia dell'arte* platform, the Elizabethan "Wooden O," and the circus ring. All had open, uncluttered performing areas, practically unknown when Copeau leased and renovated what would become the Théâtre du Vieux-Colombier prior to World War I.

Finding actors who could fill such spaces proved more difficult than merely implementing architectural changes. Copeau wrote: "On an empty stage I see how important the actor becomes. His stature, his acting, his *quality*" (Copeau 2000: 182). Although Copeau recognized the need for a school to help actors develop this quality, administrative responsibilities initially kept him from founding one.

With most of his actors conscripted during World War I, Copeau closed the theatre. Unable to serve because of illness, and in order to focus his thought on actor training, he visited Edward Gordon Craig (1872–1966), Emile Jaques-Dalcroze (1865–1950), and Adolphe Appia (1862–1928). These encounters confirmed Copeau's initial intuitions that movement and improvisation must predominate in the training of new actors.

Edward Gordon Craig (1872–1966), the son of actress Ellen Terry and architect Edward William Godwin, acted (with his mother) in Henry Irving's company at the Lyceum Theatre in London from 1885 to 1897. In the early 1900s he renounced acting, developing instead his career as a stage and costume designer, theoretician, and printmaker. Devising his own revolutionary approach to moveable architectural staging, he published *On the Art of the Theatre* in 1911.

Editor of *The Mask* (1908–1929), in which he published his famous essay on the Übermarionette, Craig sought to abolish the Victorian trappings of realism and sentimentality and to replace them with a more open and symbolic space (influenced by Greek theatre and the *commedia dell'arte* stage). Copeau and Decroux learned important lessons from Craig, who admired Asian performance and advocated total theatre incorporating symbolist set designs, masks, verse, and dance.

Craig's influence moved Copeau to include theatre crafts, *commedia dell'arte*, and Asian theatre concepts in his plans for a school. Seeing Craig's masks, for example, led Copeau to experiment with covering the face in actor training exercises and, to a more limited degree, in performance (Leigh 1979: 12).

At first, guardedly enthusiastic about Dalcroze's rhythmic gymnastics, called Eurhythmics, Copeau imagined incorporating modified versions into his curriculum. Later he found the gymnastics of Lt. Hébert more appropriate: rather than Eurhythmics, in which one responds to musical accompaniment, Copeau preferred Hébert's lifting real weights, traversing real obstacles, and relating to the material world.

Navy Lieutenant Georges Hébert (1875–1957), as captain of the last sailing ship in the French navy, observed harmonious human bodies working and playing outdoors. Throwing, running, jumping, carrying, and swimming were essential activities for people in the less industrialized ports of call, as well as for sailors in the masts and rigging of the ship he commanded. Hébert advocated following one's own work rhythms according to individual abilities while as lightly clothed as possible; overcoming natural obstacles (rocks, logs, uneven terrain); using natural and useful gestures (carrying, pushing, pulling); balancing on one foot, walking on hands and feet; sustained effort to develop endurance and breath, but with an alternation of contrasting efforts. He opposed competitive athletics, practiced in stadiums to entertain and to break records, as contrasted with his more natural and organic method of physical education.

More lasting influences on Copeau came from Dalcroze's exercises in which students evolved from silence and immobility to movement, sound, and finally words. This progression, adopted by Copeau, later permeated Decroux's work (Leigh 1979: 13). Suzanne Bing, Copeau's most important collaborator, also noticed that Dalcroze's Eurhythmics with its predilection for a conditioned response to external music, impeded improvisers' attempts to listen to internal "music" or impulses (Copeau 2000: 114). The ability to perceive and respond to these *internal* impulses, essential to Copeau, would later constitute the basis of Decroux's work in improvisation and creation.

An observation in Copeau's notebook reveals the basis of Decroux's teaching:

> I have already noticed, especially with Dalcroze, that the student, as soon as you call upon an emotion (fatigue, joy, sadness, etc.) to provoke a movement, . . . right away, and perhaps unconsciously, out of necessity, he allows the intellectual element to predominate in his action, facial expression. This is an open door to literature and to ham acting.
> *(Copeau 2000: 101)*

Copeau's nephew and assistant Michel Saint-Denis remembers how Copeau closed this "open door" at the Vieux Colombier Theatre when a young actress prevented a rehearsal from moving forward because of her inability to overcome self-consciousness. Weary from waiting for her to relax, Copeau spontaneously "threw a handkerchief over her face and made her repeat the scene." This impromptu mask improved her performance while furthering Copeau's influential actor-training experiments that involved covering the face (Saint-Denis 1982: 169–170).

Copeau's erasure of facial expression in favor of larger physical movement, especially in the trunk, became a significant plank in Decroux's theatrical platform and a primary concept in the creation of Corporeal Mime.

After these decisive visits, Copeau spent the remainder of the war years in New York, where, with a troupe of French actors, he produced an ambitious program of plays each season, intending to sway American public opinion to side with France in the war. During these challenging times, as a cure for the stilted and dishonest acting he observed in his troupe, Copeau returned to animal observation and imitation, an idea about which he had written as early as 1915. In the spring of 1918, Copeau recorded his fascination with a red-breasted robin, which reminded him of the power of clearly isolated, relaxed, and focused movement, qualities he had encouraged in his exiled French actors (Copeau 1991: 87).

In addition to his keen interest in the movement of animals, Copeau admired the skill of craftsmen who "use an economy of gesture so that everything seems in its rightful place. That comes from their really doing something, that they do what they do and do it well, knowing the reason, absorbing themselves in it" (Copeau in Leigh 1979: 19). For Decroux, respect of *craft*, knowhow that comes only with experience – what the French call *métier* – became throughout his career a point of departure for movement studies like his signature compositions *The Washerwoman* and *The Carpenter*. No doubt he acquired this taste during ten years of manual labor and in his self-identification as a socialist/anarchist and proud son of working-class parents. Ironically, Copeau, who came from a privileged background and who had never labored manually in his life, nonetheless recognized, in the work of craftsmen, "a point of departure" for all movement, "a kind of purity of integrity of the individual, a state of calm, of naturalness, of relaxation" (Copeau in Leigh 1979: 19), which in turn became central to Decroux's work.

Copeau's theatre reopened in Paris in February 1920, a period in which he increasingly used the term "laboratories" for both theatre and school. In 1921, the (newly inaugurated theatre) engaged a staff to assist Copeau, Bing, Jouvet, and Copeau's daughter, Marie-Hélène, in their ground-breaking actor-training experiments. In 1923, by then a legendary theatre director, Jacques Copeau auditioned and subsequently admitted the impassioned young Decroux as an observer of classes at the Ecole du Vieux-Colombier.

Copeau's new chapter

In the spring of 1924, despite glimmers of brilliance in the school activities, Copeau experienced a crisis provoked by his recent conversion to Catholicism, dissension among his supporters, accumulated fatigue, and ongoing problems funding his theatre experiments. Closing the Vieux Colombier, he retreated to a château near Beaune, accompanied by family, students, and colleagues. Decroux joined them in October 1924 but left, along with ten others, in February 1925 as Copeau's uncertain venture faltered. This, despite Copeau's unceasing and valiant efforts to support his project financially through public lectures and spellbinding readings of plays throughout France, Switzerland, and Belgium.

Copeau and Decroux, who shared artistic sensibility, differed greatly: Copeau, a bourgeois (upper-middle-class) Protestant who converted to Catholicism in midlife, lived comfortably from family money and leaned right politically; Decroux, a proletarian agnostic, leaned left. Both were first-class dreamers who worked zealously to realize their visions. What did Decroux experience *chez* Copeau that ignited his imagination and kept it burning for the next sixty years?

1. Decroux audited Suzanne Bing's classes in silent improvisation named *corporeal mime* (or, alternatively, *The Mask*) where minimally clad students with faces covered by veils or inexpressive masks discovered a wide world of expressive movement. Even though Decroux remained an observer, he embraced these experiments and in fact never abandoned the lessons learned from them.
2. In March of 1924, Decroux witnessed a dress rehearsal for the Noh play *Kantan*, directed by Suzanne Bing. Although only a first-year observer and therefore unable to participate as an actor, Decroux retained the vivid memory of this rehearsal throughout his life.
3. Decroux saw a final student presentation on May 13, 1924 that consisted of vignettes, many without text, which opened his thoughts to the possibilities of actor-centered and collectively created performance.

After Copeau: "those of us who left took fire with us"

After leaving Copeau, Decroux returned to Paris, where, acting briefly with Gaston Baty (1885–1952) and Louis Jouvet (1887–1951), he spent eight years, beginning in 1926, with Charles Dullin (1885–1949), acting in his Atelier Theatre and teaching in his school (De Marinis 2015: 39).

Concurrently, Decroux frequented the anarchist milieu until 1929. There he met Suzanne Lodieu, also a political activist, who worked as a shoemaker's apprentice; they married in 1930. In 1931, the Decrouxs performed *Primitive Life* in the Salle Lancry in Paris (Lorelle 1974: 107); the same year, Decroux formed his own theatre troupe, A Seed, to which he devoted seven years. This anti-capitalist and anti-Stanislavskyan group produced movement and choral works for leftist organizations, but never for communist groups (Benhaïm 2003: 247).

Jean-Louis Barrault

If Jacques Copeau, Decroux's senior, proved the first great influence in Decroux's professional life, the younger Jean-Louis Barrault became the second. They met in 1931, when twenty-year-old Jean-Louis began studying at Charles Dullin's Théâtre de l'Atelier, where Decroux acted in the troupe and taught in the school. A chemistry between Barrault and Decroux, nurtured by hours of practical exploration, resulted in consequential discoveries leading to the development of Corporeal Mime. Barrault remembers Decroux as an eccentric who stylized his roles to the point of dancing them, and whose friends spoke of him with a sidelong smile. Decroux, at that time a "puritan revolutionary" who "cultivated the more-than-perfect" (Barrault 1951: 21, 23), solicited people to continue the corporeal research he had begun at the Vieux Colombier. Decroux (despite speaking rudely to him at first) won over Barrault, who became his first disciple and principal collaborator.

Vegetarians, nudists, and physical culturists, they bounced off the walls of the Atelier basement while the other actors played cards. Decroux, his wife Suzanne, and Barrault presented *Medieval Life* at the Atelier in 1931, continuing the cycle begun with the performance of *Primitive Life* earlier in the year at the Salle Lancry.

After two years of intense collaboration, they performed *Ancient Combat* for Dullin, who marveled at their technical abilities that he considered equal to that of Japanese actors (Barrault 1972: 72). Dullin's vision and generosity made the Atelier one of the few Parisian theatres that welcomed such avant-garde experimentation.

Two years of partnership revealed to Barrault what many students afterward remarked: Decroux's uncompromising passion for art and his rigorous devotion often made a long-term association impossible. His explosive temperament extended onto the stage where he would abruptly stop and then restart a show to rectify a less than perfect performance (Epstein and Fried 2015: 86) or at the hint of an audience's inappropriate laughter. "We must continuously insult the audience," declared the perfectionist known to rehearse a piece for months or even years (Decroux 2001: 31).

In creating and performing three ground-breaking presentations using mime, mask, and minimal text (*Autour d'une Mère*, 1935; *Numance* 1937; and *La Faim* 1939), Barrault effectively abandoned Decroux and his research. Despite Decroux's entreaties that he remain a mime, Barrault went on to become a perennial *enfant terrible*, popular movie star, and – with his wife, the renowned actress Madeline Renaud – the director of one of Europe's most important theatre companies. In addition to regular Paris seasons, the Compagnie Renaud-Barrault (1946–1987) often toured internationally, promoting French culture.

1789 and The Extravagant Captain Smith

In 1937, A Seed disbanded. Two of his previous company members joined Decroux and his wife to form a new group called 1789 that performed existing repertoire and new mime pieces entitled *The Carpenter* and *The Machine*. One critic wrote of 1789: "While they perform, one believes oneself to be in a laboratory, in a temple, and in a workshop. It is research, it is soul, and it is work" (in Benhaïm 2003: 248). In 1938, Decroux performed one hundred times in his dining room for audiences of two or three. The group 1789 lasted one year; at the outbreak of the war in 1939, Decroux ceased all overtly political activity, Corporeal Mime becoming his only and all-absorbing interest. For most of the rest of his life, he existed on two parallel tracks, earning his living from theatre, films, and radio while devoting his spare time to the development of this new theatrical form, Corporeal Mime. He played over sixty-five roles in works by Aristophanes, Ruzzante, Shakespeare, Ben Jonson, Molière, Tolstoy, Strindberg, Pirandello, Marcel Achard, and Jules Romains. His directors were, among others, Jacques Copeau, Gaston Baty, Louis Jouvet, Charles Dullin, Antonin Artaud, and Marcel Herrand (Decroux 1985: i). The most commercially successful theatrical work of his prewar career was the eponymous leading role in the play *The Extravagant Captain Smith* in 1938 and 1939 (Benhaïm 2003: 250). Decroux also especially enjoyed performing Trotsky in *Tsar Lénine*, and Tchernozium in *Le Quadrature du Cercle* (Decroux 1950: 4).

In 1940, during the dark days of the Occupation, Decroux continued perfecting *The Machine, The Carpenter, The Washing* (renamed *The Washerwoman* in 1973), and *Character Walks in Place*, performing them another hundred times for audiences of three or four spectators at a time. Then, as he looked down from his apartment window at parading Nazi soldiers, he imagined how he might turn that violent goose step inside out to create a beautifully vulnerable Poet's Walk. In 1941, Decroux opened his school on rue de la Néva and gave one performance of his first large composition, *Camping*, at the Comédie des Champs-Elysées. Decroux presented *Passage of Men Across the Earth* and other pieces ten times in public and one hundred times for invited audiences in his school. In 1942, Decroux performed at the Salon d'Automne and the Théâtre des Ambassadeurs, as well as giving sixty private performances (Veinstein in Decroux 1985: ii).

During his career, Decroux acted in twenty films, the best known being Marcel Carné's celebrated *Children of Paradise* (1943). This project touched the lives of its actors in powerful and unexpected ways and, in particular, proved pivotal for the careers of Etienne Decroux and Jean-Louis Barrault and in the development of Corporeal Mime.

Children of Paradise

In 1943, Jacques Prévert, at Barrault's suggestion, wrote the scenario for a three-hour film based on the life of the nineteenth-century pantomime, Jean-Gaspard Deburau, who performed silently to circumvent government regulations limiting the number and genre of Paris theatres in the 1840s. German occupation forces similarly censored French theatre, giving Deburau's story resonance in 1943–1944. Marcel Carné directed the film amid shortages of electricity, costume materials, wood, plaster, and motion-picture film stock. The title, *Children of Paradise*, refers to the poor but enthusiastic audience far up in the balconies (in "the gods") of theatres of the time. These establishments lined the Boulevard du Temple, called the "Boulevard du Crime" in the time of Louis-Philippe (king of France from 1830 to 1848) because of the bloody subject matter of their melodramatic plays. Film star Arletty played the role of Garance, a great beauty whose four suitors were historical figures in nineteenth-century Paris: the mime Deburau (played by Jean-Louis Barrault); Fréderick Lemaître, a melodrama actor (Pierre Brasseur); the killer known to all Paris, Pierre-François Lacenaire (Marcel Herrand); and the aristocrat protector of Garance, Edouard de Montray (Louis Salou). Decroux created the role of Anselme Deburau, Jean-Gaspard's father.

Jean-Gaspard Deburau (1796–1846), born into an itinerant French circus family in Bohemia, performed with his family in a tent. Tightrope walker, trapeze artist, acrobat, juggler, magician, and (most notably) pantomime at the Théâtre des Funambules, where as Baptiste – his own refashioning of Pierrot – he garnered spectacular popularity. The film *Children of Paradise* recounts his life.

One of the most successful French films of all time, *Children of Paradise* appeared when the new modernist tendencies in mime had taken root only tentatively. While years of professional activity had established Decroux's role as master teacher and innovator, his antipathy to most audiences and his love of research made him almost invisible to a general public. If modern mime were to appear outside Decroux's atelier, a brilliant student would have to bring it out. Barrault's first performances as a mime in a modernist vein had impressed Antonin Artaud and received critical if not popular success; as Barrault later wrote, "there were so few people who really understood it [modern mime]. Hardly anyone appreciated it then" (Barrault 1951: 29). What might have happened had Barrault remained allied with Decroux while continuing to develop his own experiments, or if audiences had not been so seduced by *Children of Paradise*, with its soft-focus images of charming and romantic nineteenth-century pantomime? As it happened, Decroux and his brilliant collaborator unintentionally revived nineteenth-century pantomime's popularity, despite having dedicated themselves for years to the evolution of its antithesis: their Corporeal Mime aimed not to recreate a recognizable reality or evoke a yearned-for past, but rather to explore movement possibilities and, in some cases, "pure" drama independent of plot.

As Decroux and Barrault researched nineteenth-century pantomime for their performances in the film *Children of Paradise*, perhaps they reduced their adversary (*pantomime ancienne*) to a "straw man," to which they then contrasted their new mime (*mime corporel*). Ariane Martinez (2008: 256) points out that Decroux and Barrault conflated the work of the two Deburaus (Jean-Gaspard and Charles) with George Wague and Séverin. In so doing, they invented a composite figure in much the way that film director Marcel Carné conflated characters and situations from different times in nineteenth-century Paris, creating an imagined rather than an historically accurate backdrop. And just as this "homogenized" version of Paris had never existed, even so the new *mime corporel* was not a binary opposite of their imagined *pantomime ancienne*; Decroux's mime had within it many (sometimes divergent) tendencies ranging from pure abstraction (*Méditation*, *Trees*) to vignettes which could have easily been performed as popular entertainment (*The Mischievous Spirit*, *The Statue*).

In 1944, Decroux and his students gave private showings for ten to fifty people in the Foyer des Beaux Arts. Also in 1944, while teaching for Dullin at the Théâtre Sarah-Bernhardt, he met the student Marcel Marceau (Lorelle 1974: 114), whose singular career would, in subsequent years, help to define and shape Decroux's own development.

Marcel Marceau

> To us, [Chaplin] was a god. As a boy I sat entranced in motion picture houses, watching those shining images unfold before me. It was then that I determined to become a pantomimist.
>
> *(Marceau 1958: 59)*

After the war, during which he worked heroically for the Resistance and in which his father perished at Auschwitz, Marcel Mangel became Marcel Marceau and moved to Paris. While teaching theatre in a children's school in Sèvres, he met Eliane Guyon, then Decroux's leading student. Beginning in 1944, Marceau studied with Decroux for three years in Dullin's school. Soon after, Marceau built upon some pantomimic elements gleaned from Decroux's teaching as well as the silent film acting of Chaplin to establish himself as a solo performer of white-faced pantomime. He toured the world to great acclaim reviving the art invented by Jean-Gaspard Deburau in the previous century. For fifty years, Marceau's name was synonymous with mime; on street corners and at birthday parties, innumerable imitators performed his signature vignettes of a man struggling within a vice-like box, or of a carver trapped behind his firmly affixed mask, among other sketches.

Despite Marceau's exceptional talent, Decroux expressed disappointment in his student's popular performance style, which, to his mind, owed more to entertainment, driven by storytelling and obvious narrative, than it did to Decroux's often formalist and demanding experiments.

Decroux eschewed these narrative aspects of Marceau's work to the point of abandoning the term "pantomime" in reference to his own work. Henceforth he adopted, almost exclusively, the term "Corporeal Mime."

The divide between them became evident when Marceau performed in New York City in the early 1960s at a large theatre to sold-out houses while Decroux taught daily classes in a small walk-up flat. Italian *commedia dell'arte* actor and teacher Carlo Mazzone-Clementi, recounted that Decroux, when asked if he knew of Marceau's successful Broadway engagement, replied: "Ah yes. The Pope is in St. Peter's and Jesus Christ is still in the catacombs!"

We see here Decroux's sense of humor as well as his passionate, quasi-religious commitment to modern mime. Marceau's meteoric career, in which he once performed for forty million television viewers (Veinstein in Decroux: i), strengthened Decroux's innate preference for research. Mazzone-Clementi's story reveals Decroux's disdain for anyone, even an excellent former student, reluctant to join his "search for the absolute" – anyone less than *militant.* This word takes on special importance given Decroux's background as an anarchist and socialist for whom a performer's desire to please an audience, to win them over, betrayed not only a lack of taste but also of courage, or even a moral or spiritual failure. He dismissed pantomime, saying: "I detested this form which seemed to me comic even before one knew what it was about" (Decroux 2003: 61). Decroux once taught me the famous "walk in place," as performed by both Marceau and Barrault, on the condition that I never show it anyone. "People would think we're pantomimes!" he protested. It is true, as mentioned earlier, that Decroux referred to his own work as pantomime or Corporeal Mime interchangeably until 1943 (Martinez 2008: 242). Indeed, his project included pantomime early on, but only briefly and never exclusively. Nonetheless, some continue to describe him as a pantomime, owing to the celebrity of his first collaborators, Barrault and Marceau.

Two of Decroux's most talented early students, thus, triumphed in what Decroux considered a retrograde theatre form: Marceau, in his version of white-faced, illusionistic pantomime, created a character named Bip; Barrault resurrected Deburau's Baptiste. Ironically, Barrault and Marceau helped Decroux define, by reversal, his modernist investigations that one scholar identified as Decroux's "most advanced experimentation ... the true culmination of his efforts" (Veinstein in Decroux 1985: ii–iii).

When a former student visited the school after some months away, Decroux fixed his penetrating gaze on him and probed: "*Toujours militant?* [Still militant?]." Had the student succumbed to what Decroux considered malevolent forces at work in commercial theatre, or did he still subscribe to Decroux's ascetic doctrines of art for art's sake?

Painting with a broad brush, we could say that Marceau's vast commercial success as a solo performer, following the triumph of *Children of Paradise*, caused Decroux to become even more uncompromising in his demanding path and increasingly chary of crowd-pleasing. One student remembers Decroux's animated remark, "Success is the death of creativity," and Madame Decroux's response, "But Etienne, maybe just a *little* success would be alright?" (Loui: 106).

Performance at la Maison de la Chimie

In 1945, the film *Children of Paradise* was released in France. That same year, Decroux and Barrault (temporarily reunited) performed *Ancient Combat* as part of *Antony and Cleopatra* at the Comédie Française. According to Decroux, who spoke about it years later, it proved an unsuccessful marriage of "rich" text and "rich" movement, as the choreographed combat stopped the forward movement of Shakespeare's play. Later, based on this and other experiences, he preached a doctrine of "rich" text with "poor" movement, and "poor" text requiring "rich" movement.

The most consequential mime event of this period, however, occurred, not at France's national theatre, but, on June 27, 1945 at the Maison de la Chimie, where an audience of more than a thousand attended a performance by Decroux, Barrault, Eliane Guyon, and Jean Dorcy (master of ceremonies), in the presence of Edward Gordon Craig (guest of honor). Dorcy's description of the event could guide one's encounter with any modern art:

> With corporeal mime, we no longer read known forms, we decode, reassemble, and appreciate according to our knowledge and our emotional state: the passive observer becomes active. Could one dream of a more fecund meeting of actor and audience?
> *(Dorcy 1945)*

Dorcy's use of the word "decode" does not suggest that Decroux created guessing games requiring the audience to uncover the verbal equivalents for the performer's gestures. Instead, Decroux proceeded by analogy and by metaphor: for Decroux, "when I see the body rise up, I feel as if it's humanity that's rising up" (Decroux 1978: 10). Dorcy's "decoding," thus, differs remarkably from an audience guessing, for example, that an actor rising onto his toes while holding his fist above his head translates as "man lifted up by helium balloon."

Dorcy continues:

> Let us understand that the corporeal mime wants a bare stage, nude actors, and no variation in lighting. For once, the theatre is no longer a cross-roads of all the arts, but the triumph of one art only: that of the body in motion.
> *(Dorcy 1945)*

When filtered through Decroux's working-class background, this love of purity – a legacy of Copeau and Craig – contributed something new to the Western actor art: a muscular aesthetic.

As a modernist and formalist, Decroux shares more with contemporaneous artists such as Dutch Neo-Plasticist painter Piet Mondrian (1872–1944) and Romanian abstract sculptor Constantin Brancusi (1876–1957) than he does with the storytelling of nineteenth-century history painters or the soft focus and painterly beauty of their successors, the Impressionists. Decroux finds an ally in Mondrian's geometric purity and fertile limitations as in some of the latter's best-known work. Brancusi's *Bird in Space*, by erasing feathers, beak, and claws, reduced the representation of the animal to the evocation of its airborne trajectory via a vertically aligned, smooth, curvilinear form. This sculptor chose heavy matter (metal, stone) instead of lighter materials to evoke flight, airiness. The Corporeal Mime uses a relatively light human body to evoke, through rigorous training, sculptural density, gravitas, weight, and, thus, the Promethean struggle. Despite the fundamental difference between sculpture – a static creation – and a Corporeal Mime composition, the spirit of these artists' projects remains analogous.

According to the program, the June 27 presentation highlighted these doctrinal links from Craig to Copeau, from Copeau to Decroux, from Decroux to Barrault, evoking along the way the work of Appia. The performance consisted of eight pieces, the first of which, *Evocation of Concrete Actions*, included three parts: *The Carpenter*, *The Washing*, and *The Machine*. In first two, Decroux performed simplified and amplified work movements: sawing, planing, hammering, and other actions associated with carpentry; and washing, rinsing, wringing, hanging out to dry, and mending laundry. Here, again, Decroux sought "evocation" rather than "depiction," "reproduction," or "representation." Whereas the titles can inform and assuage a mystified observer in the same way that identifying labels on Cubist paintings do, the artistic project, in both cases, thrives on its own. Decroux's transposition of quotidian objects or actions into surprising progressions of fragmented and superimposed planes constitutes the drama, the subject.

Likewise, as some twentieth- and twenty-first-century music rejected "common practice melody," Decroux abstained from traditional notions of character and plot apart from the logical sequence of the work actions themselves.

> ### One can't "pretend" a counterweight – a detour
>
> Decroux's intersecting of manual labor and art, *métier* with imagination, requires the mastery of accurate counterweights in which the performer expends an energy matching that of the real worker. The key element in a successful counterweight is a properly situated and fixed fulcrum point. A failure to achieve this level of accuracy blurs the movement and produces a "decorative art" rather than an efficiently elegant and utilitarian one. Without a correctly placed and fixed point, the artistic project crumbles as the actual task would in real-life, physical work.
>
> Since he eliminated plot from his theatre, "story" in much of Decroux's work does not derive from the *what*, but instead, from the *how*. A human body at work, Decroux allowed, inherently reflects drama, since work provokes an intra-corporeal struggle or play. In making art, the Corporeal Mime makes trial-and-error selection from among compositional elements such as lines of force, changes in plane, rhythm, pauses, variations in weight, resistance, hesitation, and surprise. The real-life manual worker has arrived at a movement sequence based on economy, precision, and intention, embodying movement in a honed and repeatable manner to get the job done most efficiently. From this, as Copeau and Decroux witnessed in seasoned artisans and manual workers, a kinesthetic poetry emerged. Decroux's Corporeal Mime, thus, strove to stay true to the task even while sometimes extending the lines of force already present in quotidian actions, other times cutting them off abruptly. He explored the body's limits in negotiating changes of plane, hesitations, and sudden bursts of movement that are both musical and, for a laborer, functional. Thus, Decroux explored design elements but always within the framework of authentic work movements, even though he might amplify or reduce them, changing their speed or weight. All of his classroom studies examining work movements translated to the stage. Decroux's shift to a poetic terrain – to "evocation" – preserves the acquired internal music of a real working body, that of an experienced and able laborer. The Corporeal Mime's true-to-the-work training creates art that remains "a doing" and not "a pretending-to-do." The compositional process involves exploring where these interior movement generators, never abandoned, might lead. Pretending a counterweight is like lying under oath.

The third part of the opening, *The Machine*, evoked a favored subject for graphic arts, theatre, dance, cinema (Chaplin's *Modern Times*), and mime in these Futurist years, reflecting a society radically changed by machines and trying, often unsuccessfully, to adjust to new relationships to speed, weight, effort, and space. Corporeal Mime reminds us that, in real life, the person operating a machine is also operated by it, involuntarily taking on mechanical, linear, and sometimes abrupt, sometimes slow motion, movements.

These *études* of human and mechanical work preceded *A Counterweight Study* performed by Decroux's students. His counterweight exercises carefully analyzed pushing, pulling, carrying, or otherwise displacing objects of varying sizes, shapes, and weights.

Decroux then performed *The Boxer, The Wrestler, The Bureaucrat,* and *Some Passers-by*. While he probably portrayed the boxer and wrestler in a noble way, like classical statues and concentrating on the dynamics of these sports, Decroux's sharp wit and taste for satire doubtless delighted in skewering and deflating affectations in the bureaucrat and the passers-by.

This suite preceded a symbolist mime chorus. Earlier, Decroux had staged speaking choruses for radical socialist and anarchist events. The idea of many voices blending together to articulate a single idea kindled his imagination. On this occasion, however, the "chorus" consisted of only three actors (Decroux, Barrault, and Eliane Guyon), who performed, probably without using their voices, *Passage of Men Across the Earth*. The piece, revived in the 1950s for Decroux's New York company, evokes famine, mass movement of populations, revolution, and, finally, peace. Without overt story line or attempt at traditional characterization, and with actors often masked, the piece uses symbolic collage to evoke incidents taken from current events. In a manner similar to Picasso and Braque, who pasted real newspaper cuttings into some of their two-dimensional works of art, Decroux, working in three dimensions, assembled disparate actions in the style of a cinema newsreel montage.

Decroux and Guyon next performed a work-in-progress (but for Decroux almost everything was in-progress!) entitled *Materials for a Biblical Piece*, subtitled *Juxtaposed Figures Without Dramatic Connection*. Decroux's aversion to traditional plotline shows up in every composition, and this title reminds the spectator not to bother searching for one.

Barrault next performed an extract from his 1935 adaptation of William Faulkner's *As I Lay Dying*, renamed, for copyright reasons, *About a Mother*. Barrault performed *Illness, Suffering, Death*, in addition to his brilliant horse-taming sequence which preceded the evening's sublime summit, Decroux's *Mobile Statuary With Covered Face: Differences Between Admiration–Adoration–Veneration* "both in the same theme: Will." Decroux signals his self-consciously Promethean approach: he and his hardest-working apprentices knew the sacrifice of pleasures and comfort required by the daily discipline of Corporeal Mime, the true cost of bringing fire to his audience. Decroux placed this purest and most abstract expression of Corporeal Mime just before the crowd-pleasing *Ancient Combat*, which crowned the performance.

The program indicates that the evening ended with Decroux lecturing on the differences between pantomime and Corporeal Mime. While Dorcy found it inappropriate to have mere words follow the livelier parts of the program, Decroux the orator, the student of French literature, the politician, felt compelled to provide a commentary, an explication of the "movement text" that the audience had just seen.

Craig, reviewing the performance in a newspaper article entitled "At Last a Creator in the Theatre, of the Theatre," places Decroux at the forefront of postwar European work.

> I am tempted to believe that Mr. Decroux possesses genius, but that he is a very suspicious man. He does not dare count on it entirely. He mistrusts it. He prefers to help his genius rather than to possess it and enjoy it. They say he will be seen as the master of mime. I consider that the title already belongs to him.
>
> *(Craig 2001: 97)*

In 1946, Decroux reprised the role of Captain Smith and, in his parallel life with his students, presented *The Factory, The Trees,* and *The Mischievous Spirit* at the Théâtre d'Iéna in Paris. Decroux and a small company toured Belgium, Switzerland, Holland, Israel, and England, and performed occasionally in Paris in the following years, during which he also created *Little Soldiers* (his only full-length mime play), *Making Contact, Checkers* and *Party*. Meanwhile, his school in Paris became well-known, drawing students from Europe and America.

According to Maximilien Decroux, his father's astringent, unyielding personality often made these tours and rehearsals difficult, nettling his student actors as well as audiences. "Etienne Decroux," Dorcy wrote, "was hostile to those he was supposed to win over: he disliked his public; and worse still, he had no respect for it. It often seemed as though he took malicious pleasure in antagonizing the audience" (Dorcy 1975: 49).

New York years

In October of 1957, Decroux began teaching, lecturing, directing, and performing in the United States. After short stints at Lee Strasberg's and Elia Kazan's Actor's Studio, at Saul Colin and Stella Adler's Dramatic Workshop, at New York University, and at The New School, he returned to Paris briefly before regaining New York in January 1959. There he offered morning and evening classes in a small apartment on 8th Avenue and 55th Street, training actors who later performed with him at the Kaufmann Concert Hall, Carnegie Hall, and the Cricket Theatre.

The performance repertoire consisted of *The Factory*, *The Trees*, *All the City Works*, *Mischievous Spirit*, Decroux's solos, and a new duet entitled *The Statue*, with Decroux playing the sculptor. Student actors at the time included Lucy Becque, John Casey, Michael Coerver, Roger Dresler, Abby Imber, Sterling Jensen, Gina Lalli, Jerry Pantzer, Sonia Pearlman, Vivian Schindler, Leslie Snow, Demoiselle Snowden, Sunja Svendsen, Nell Taylor, Marjorie Walker (née Oplatka), Jewel Walker, and Solomon and Mina Yakim. Decroux also performed solo lecture-demonstrations and taught short workshops at Tufts University in Medford, MA, and Baylor University in Waco, TX, aided by his American translator and assistant Mark Epstein (Loui: 105).

Last years in Boulogne-Billancourt

Decroux returned to France in 1962. There he lived in the little brick cottage built with his father's hands at the back of a garden, 85 avenue Edouard Vaillant, in Boulogne-Billancourt, a working-class suburb of Paris. To transform the basement with its low ceiling into a mime studio, the Decrouxs, over a period of six months, excavated bucket loads of gravel, which they surreptitiously distributed, like prisoners needing to avoid detection, one shipment at a time, in the daily trash collection (Fogal 2017). There he taught six days a week, almost never taking a vacation, until March 1987 – an astonishingly long run for this basement laboratory/school. In 1963, André Veinstein edited and Gallimard published a collection of Decroux's essays entitled *Paroles sur le mime* [*Words on Mime*], considered "one of the fundamental texts for the theatre culture of the twentieth century" (De Marinis 2015: 40). He continued to "perform" in class, but his already diminished interest in placing himself or his students before uncomprehending and uninitiated audiences weakened even further. However, his basement school flourished, attracting students from around the world. Their number varied from as few as six or eight to as many as one hundred, spread over three classes each day, which he taught with the help of his assistants-translators and, at times, his son Maximilien. Students who often came from abroad to study at better-known mime schools (Marceau's, Lecoq's, Ella Jaroszewicz's) sometimes found their way to Decroux's cottage basement, where he offered the least expensive, but among the most challenging, lessons in Paris. Although Decroux required singular allegiance to his course of study, immediately expelling any offenders, some ambitious students secretly continued concurrently with one of those other teachers.

For some he was a charismatic teacher; others saw him as a despot, and many considered him an eccentric who sometimes taught in flannel pajamas, a terry cloth bathrobe and bedroom slippers. He seemed happily at home as his teaching blossomed. To Suzanne, who sang in the kitchen as she cooked, he might shout up the narrow blue stairs: "They're making progress, you know!" Likewise, she wouldn't hesitate to call down to him, to temper what seemed a threatening tone of voice, "Don't lose your cool, Etienne!"

The next three paragraphs detail one of his favorite *lazzi* ("jokes") that played out in this setting.

The telephone in his ground floor study rings loudly. In the basement classroom, all activity instantly ceases as we conspiratorially anticipate Decroux's coming interjection. Before Madame can answer the phone, Monsieur merrily calls up the stairs, "If it's the Paris Opera, I'm not interested!" This joke made us proud of our unheralded teacher's clear preference for his marginal, working class milieu. We were only a few Metro stops from the center of Parisian cultural elitism – the Opera – but we savored the absurdity of even imagining that one could bridge such an immense gap.

In his teaching, Decroux was whimsical, insulting, witty, charming, angry, brilliant, seductive, and prophetic, often in one class. He sang, told jokes, made bilingual puns, and taught exercises that, in their poetic conception and athletic execution, took the breath away, literally and figuratively.

When we were giddily adolescent, he reprimanded us: "Mime is not an amusement. It is a religion!" and when we took him too seriously, he implored: "Don't look so glum. This is only a way to fill the time between breakfast and lunch." Despite his frequent good humor, he did not hesitate to escort to the door hapless students who seemed insufficiently respectful; this lesson demonstrated, to those who remained, the necessity for an underlying gravitas in our daily work.

Decroux's "underground" school

Decroux, like Copeau before him, recognized the establishment of a school as the precondition of a new theatre. But, while Copeau produced plays successfully with actors trained by others, Decroux's Corporeal Mime needed actors proficient in a new physical language, one taught exclusively by Decroux. Whereas mainstream theatre in twentieth-century France selected actors mostly by type, without necessarily requiring extensive previous study, Decroux demanded that actors train as thoroughly as musicians, for whom instruction and skill are paramount. Actors, he thought, should be able to supersede their physical type to portray, potentially, characters of a different sex, age, or body type, as do Noh actors. He imagined the preposterousness of a symphony conductor addressing a stranger on the street: "You look like a violinist. We are just about to have a concert. Here is the violin, and here is the music. Begin!"

Decroux's underground school, where he trained actors for his new theatre, compelled him to remain in one place, working daily on himself and his students. Though he sometimes left Paris to teach – almost never for a vacation – Decroux spent decades closed inside a workroom, carefully gardening the landscape of the body, mapping its expressive articulations, preferring to work in pajamas or in black boxer's shorts. He found his workroom in Amsterdam, Tel Aviv, Milan, Stockholm, Zurich, Oslo, Innsbruck, New York, Waco (Texas), but usually in Paris ("Even if I never go out, I like knowing that the Eiffel Tower is there," he once said.) No matter the physical location, he occupied the basement figuratively, if not literally. That is to say, he worked "on the margins" and, with a few notable exceptions, invisible to the public eye.

Here are a few of the things that obsessed him during these extended periods of concentration, discovery, trial and error, and creation of new performance pieces. A word of warning: no number of words on mime can elucidate what the new student can only hope to grasp in person, with demonstration. No text can bridge that gap. For insiders, a written explanation becomes, with time, blindingly simple and may even seem insufficiently detailed. For the uninitiated, and despite my best efforts at a clear prose style, the technique described here may well seem abstruse precisely because a description cannot replace the doing of it: the physical experience.

In Decroux's lexicon, one may move the spine in three ways: "Bar," "Chain," and "Accordion."

- *Bar* indicates movement in straight lines: head, hammer (head and neck together), bust (head, neck, and chest together), etc. These "bar" articulations can then move in relation to each other in myriad combinations of translation, inclination, contradiction, and rotation.
- *Chain* indicates movement in curved lines as in segmented movements, undulations, compensations, re-establishment, contradictions, and many other combinations.
- *Accordion* indicates the spine alternately collapsing upon itself and expanding away from the center, like the bellows of an accordion.

Against this general background, we see more specific details.

Scales: The actor can create a keyboard with the body, articulating each segment, allowing an infinite number of subsequent movements: articulations forward, back, side, in rotation, in rotation on an inclined plane, and in any one of eight triple designs. One can perform a triple design, made of two inclinations and a rotation, with the head, the bust, the trunk, and the Eiffel Tower (the whole body). One can produce four- or five-part designs by adding translations[1] to inclinations and rotations.

Mobile statuary: The art of moving the body as if it were a classical statue, inside a glass sphere (remember Decroux's vision of his father as a "moving statue"), Decroux named Mobile Statuary. Many types of segmented movements come under this heading and could as well be listed under "Scales." Undulations, compensations (parts of the body moving in opposite directions simultaneously), reestablishments (one inclined element and one vertical element reestablishing on the oblique, or two inclined elements reestablishing on the vertical), and all their related categories constitute mobile statuary.

Walks: One might say that Decroux spent his life in search of the ideal walk. He thought people unwittingly revealed their true selves in daily activities – in handwriting, in walking, and in the unconscious manipulation of objects. Hence, his constructed, artificial, and artistic handwriting (often produced with a quill pen dipped into India ink), and his studied ways of walking, handling objects, or of opening a door, all reflected his desire to achieve an artistic, articulated, and artificial construction in life as in art. Decroux's repertoire included about forty walks (Asselin 2017) at various times in his career, variations on perhaps ten basic ones. For example, the "Walk of the Poet" constituted a turning inside out of the Nazi goose step that he had witnessed during the German occupation of Paris. Since this despised march involved forcefully extending arms and legs forward while leaving the trunk behind, Decroux's antithetical "Walk of the Poet" advocated a risky and courageous translation forward of the trunk as arms and legs remained behind. Thus, the Poet fearlessly exposed his vulnerable trunk and organs to attack.

The Poet, he observed, believed in the goodness of human nature while the Nazi ignored it. Decroux often explained that he had invented nothing but only moved things from the street into his studio; the elaboration of the Poet's walk exemplifies his method of creation.

Figures of style: These include brief etudes such as "The Prayer," "Salute to the Dawn," and "O, Walt Whitman," as well as longer sequences such as "The Shepherd Picks a Flower for the Princess" or "The Princess Accepts the Flower." The titles for these figures changed from year to year as the figures themselves evolved. Decroux fashioned these pedagogical mini-compositions from his technical repertoire in much the same way that a ballet class will progress from discrete elements at the beginning of a class (*pliés* and *tendus*) to more elaborated combinations performed mostly in place (*adagio, petit allegro*) or across the floor (*enchaînements*).

Counterweights: This area of Decroux's work comes directly from his years of manual labor and observation of Hébert gymnastics at the Ecole du Vieux-Colombier. Decroux, like Lecoq (see Murray 2003: 85), made the radical statement that all acting could be reduced to some form of pushing and pulling: moving people, objects, and even ideas nearer or further away constitutes the actor's primary occupation. In Decroux's classroom, the eyes could push or pull as expressively as the hands.

The categories of *counterweights* and *walks* overlap, since, according to Decroux, walking entails counterweights. The upright body is constructed to move vertically – up and down – by bending joints. In order to survive, we must be able to go somewhere else. We must, thus, convert this purely vertical movement, a movement up and down in place, to the horizontal plane. The upright body's transition from merely standing to walking is the biped's first counterweight. In order to take that first step, the two parts of the leg, upper and lower, which are arranged vertically when we stand with straight legs, must shift (one leg at a time) to a diagonal orientation by bending at the hip, the knee and the ankle, while the bottom of the leg (the foot) moves forward, transferring weight onto that bent leg in front of us and straightening it. This "reestablishment of two elements on the diagonal" (of both legs successively)[2] propels the body into forward displacement, which, when repeated, becomes a walk.

Decroux often spoke of the omnipresence of counterweights in the workaday world prior to the invention of the steam engine and later, the internal combustion engine. Before the mid-1800s, people were dependent entirely upon themselves and domesticated animals to accomplish work, aided only by water and wind power harnessed by mills and sails.

Improvisation: Some of Decroux's former students tell me that he taught for years on end without introducing improvisation. Yet he taught it regularly in the years 1968–1972. For the first year or two, I couldn't fathom what Decroux required during these stressful and intimidating experiences held on Friday evenings after his weekly lecture. He would ask individuals or small groups to stand at one end of the basement studio in a pool of what he called, with a flourish of his large worker's hands and with mocking vocal affectation, "artistic lighting." His guidelines for improvisations differed strikingly from those his students might have encountered in other drama schools. He admonished: "Portray a thinker. After a while, you will become Thought. Emotion leads to motion, whereas Thought begets immobility. Begin!" These enigmatic instructions intensified rather than dispelled our uneasiness as we struggled with this movement/immobility conundrum, making us think that, in these improvisations, we were damned if we moved and damned if we did not.

After years, tears, and frequent and profound discouragement, most students eventually understood that state of being relaxed yet alert, poised on the razor's edge separating movement from immobility. Until then, neither our movements nor our immobilities partook enough of their opposite qualities, provoking Decroux to thunder, in heavily accented English, his worst criticism: "Human, too much human!" When students had not sufficiently "evicted the tenants from the apartment," he knew it, and "God could not come to live there." These startling words from the avowed atheist meant that one had to silence voices habitually filling thought with self-conscious concerns; only after completing this process of emptying out could we experience being "struck with a thought." Being taken over by an exterior force, yet still lucidly aware and alert, actors achieved vibrant immobility, usually followed by movement imbued with that immobility. After being struck with a thought, one became a "*thinker*," working in the area of mime technique known as Man in the Drawing Room (*triple designs* of head and bust; mostly upright torso). Further into the improvisation, with enough experience, one became what Decroux called "*pure Thought*," fully engaging the body in the domain of Mobile Statuary, using all levels of the space, including lying on the floor.

For these improvisations, Decroux insisted upon inexpressive, mask-like, noble, and beatific faces. The present-yet-absent state which accompanied such a face seemed difficult or impossible to achieve, and mysterious. But we students knew who had succeeded and who had not: the first looked larger than life, radiant, almost possessed, while the latter looked uncomfortable, small, and petty. Those who succeeded looked as if they had attained a different world, whereas the others, by trying too hard, remained firmly in this one.

What Decroux accomplished

Through occasional success and relative obscurity, Decroux remained militant. He died in 1991 in the brick house his father had built; students from over the world flocked there in his last decades. Its basement-studio, "underground" literally and metaphorically, represented many things for Decroux, who joked, "Never forget! The first Christians worshiped in catacombs!" Digging Simplon's Tunnel (a metaphor Decroux appropriated) took years and cost lives, but finally connected France with Italy, under the Alps. Decroux dug toward "a new day" and slowly undermined established ways of doing things. He knew that precious things require persistence: the militant works slowly, subterraneously, biding his time, removing the gravel one bucketload at a time.

Decroux's name conjures many varied images. A central figure in modern mime, everyone in the field has heard of him and many studied briefly with him. But because of his unusual aversion to performing, few, even among specialists, saw him onstage. For the general public, the highly visible and perennially popular Marcel Marceau embodied mime, while his teacher, Decroux, *not* pantomime and *not* Marceau, made from this double negative a positive: Corporeal Mime.

Thanks to the international mime festivals held in the US (directed by Michael Pedretti, Reid Gilbert and Lou Campbell), in Canada (Giuseppe Condello, Jean Asselin, and Denise Boulanger), in France (Peter Bu and others) and in England (Joseph Seelig and Helen Lannaghan), along with the efforts of Eugenio Barba and ISTA (International School of Theatre Anthropology), scholars have begun researching and writing about Decroux. In this series on Performance Practitioners, Decroux appears for the first time in the company of his contemporaries – Stanislavsky, Copeau, Meyerhold, and other major twentieth-century explorers.

Decroux's work, like Picasso's, comprises numerous styles over a long career. For Decroux, as for Picasso, Cubism constituted one of several particularly fertile approaches. With a painter, the stylistic differences become apparent when works from different periods hang side by side; we cannot as easily evaluate Decroux's ephemeral compositions, seen by small audiences and then erased.

In the scrapbooks of press clippings in the Bibliothèque Nationale's Fonds Decroux, one frequently encounters phrases such as "magnificent ardour" to describe Decroux's approach. Journalists call him a "zealot of mime" and "a curious man, with fixed and fevered eyes . . . a high priest." They saw Decroux's actors as "young Egyptian gods, participating in the rites of this strange religion" and a "priestess of a mysterious cult." An especially vivid article concludes: "Etienne Decroux, who resembles a prehistoric man, plays his body as one plays a violin."

Eric Bentley's article from 1950, "The Purism of Etienne Decroux," continues in this vein:

> Decroux – his baleful eyes set in his tragic mask of a face, his magniloquent language pouring out in his sinuous, wistful voice – is above all a person and a presence. A presence, one might say, and an absence.
>
> He is courteous and warm, and to that extent present, but his eyes betoken distance and an ulterior purpose. The tone of voice is gentle, but there is steel behind the velvet, an insistence, a certitude, a sense of mission. In this presence one has no doubt that all that occurs is important.
>
> *(Bentley 1953: 186–187)*

Bentley describes *Ancient Combat* as the

> expression of a personal vision. Although one can admire every leaf and bough, the supreme fact is that the bush burns. The work breathes a fanatic spirit. The reverberations quiver and repeat; then comes the shock, rude, shattering – but it is the old religious fanaticism, which can bide its time before it springs.
>
> *(Bentley 1953: 188)*

In describing *Little Soldiers,* he especially notes the "humorless wit, the dark fantasy, and unearthly, tremulous joy of Decroux."

Bentley finishes his essay by writing that "[e]ven if his work does not turn out to be the principal, central theatrical work of our time, it can resemble the work of some small, strict holy order from which the whole church profits" (Bentley 1953: 195). French mime Pinok calls studying with Decroux "some secret initiation" (p. 64) and his house as "a place out of time where secret ceremonies unfolded" (p. 66). Another student wrote she felt "part of a holy order" describing Decroux as "of another age ... medieval ... mystical ... in which there was a belief in the transformative power of art" (Wylie 1993: 110).

These writers describe Decroux and his work with a special, highly charged, vocabulary – a language of spirituality and religion, of ritual and of shamanism used in the service of art. Deidre Sklar wrote:

> Corporeal Mime is not a secret study, yet it has never been a popular form. Decroux's "puritan revolutionary" personality discourages the merely curious, and his art seems esoteric to many. Decroux's "small, strict holy order" remains outside the mainstream because he is less concerned with entertaining spectators than with transforming students – mind and body – into his image of the Promethean actor or ideal Everyman. This ideal is achieved through mastery of the physical technique of Corporeal Mime and through assimilating its theoretical principles. Students who remain with Decroux long enough to master the system have undergone a deconstruction and reconstruction process that more closely resembles ritual initiation than theatre.
>
> *(Sklar 1985: 75)*

While some wrote of him as a "high priest," and descriptions of his teaching and technique often stress the mystery and ceremony that surrounded his work, in his own writing, Decroux declared his "pronounced taste for ... public things – politics and religion," and on the same page admits "hostility toward the mysterious" (Decroux 1948: 1).

Paul Bellugue (1892–1955), professor of anatomy at the Ecole des Beaux Arts in Paris from 1936 to 1955, took art students to sports stadiums and invited athletes, dancers, music hall performers, and mimes into the drawing studio to optimize study of the living, moving human figure. His posthumously published *A propos de forme et de mouvement* [*About Form and Movement*] (1963) chronicles Bellugue's lively interest in sport, dance, posture through the ages, Cambodian dance and sculpture, and antique statuary and classicism. Decroux often assisted Bellugue in lecture-demonstrations and, with his collaboration, Decroux defined an aesthetic well grounded in art history and anatomy.

Eugenio Barba noted that Decroux "did not merely teach the 'scientific' principles of acting, but a way to *position oneself* which from posture and movement radiated to an all-embracing ethical and spiritual stance" (Barba 1997: 8). In Decroux's own words: "One must busy one's self with mime as the first Christians did with Christianity, as the first Socialists did with Socialism. We need militants" (Decroux 2003: 73).

Decroux and Asian theatre

Leonard Pronko's *Theatre East and West* (1967) documents how Asian forms revitalized twentieth-century European theatre practice, not only for Copeau and Decroux, but for many others as well. The Asian strand in Decroux's work finds its origin in a version of a Noh play, *Kantan*, which, when performed by students at the Ecole du Vieux-Colombier, touched Decroux deeply. Although far from achieving an accurate reconstruction, these French students, under Suzanne Bing's direction, found a quality, an essential value that strongly marked Decroux's early aesthetic development (Pronko 1967: 92). Bing started with the text, aspiring to the qualities it contained: judging by descriptions of the performance, the collaborators achieved an austere aesthetic incorporating dynamically charged immobilities (Leigh 1979: 47).

This aesthetic, these charged immobilities, set Decroux and his work apart from his peers. Of the twentieth-century reformers, perhaps Decroux alone left not only a philosophy, an aesthetic, and a repertory, but a vocabulary, a specific technique of moving and being on the stage, a way of achieving presence. Eugenio Barba contends that Corporeal Mime encompasses a "knowledge of the actor's pre-expressive level, how to build up presence, and how to articulate the transformation of energy, [that] is unequalled in Western theatre history" (Barba 1997: 12).

Like Zeami Motokiyo (1363–1443), founder of the Japanese Noh theatre, and Jerzy Grotowski, Decroux worked assiduously on voice and text, although he considered one lifetime insufficient to realize "vocal mime" as well as Corporeal Mime. At age fifty-five, Decroux remained committed to his personal development.

> I took my first diction lesson thirty-one years ago and the last one this morning. I took my first classical dance lesson thirty-one years ago, and the last one yesterday morning. Since I left Copeau, I have done speaking theatre as a stop-gap measure and, as for movement theatre, I have thought of it incessantly without ever [daring to] dream of it, and I've abandoned all else to add deed to thought.
>
> *(Decroux 1953: 27)*

Some of his contemporaries considered Decroux's insistence on training, similar to that required in Asian theatre and martial arts, sterilizing for Western actors. He, however, compared mime study to technical learning in music or dance where performers find freedom of expression through discipline. Eugenio Barba wrote: "the actor who works within a network of codified rules has a greater liberty than he who – like the Occidental actor – is a prisoner of arbitrariness and an absence of rules." Barba goes on to compare Decroux's teachings to those of Asian techniques.

> [I]n the same way that a Kabuki actor can ignore the best "secrets" of Noh, it is symptomatic that Etienne Decroux, perhaps the only European master to have elaborated a system of rules comparable to that of an Oriental tradition, seeks to transmit to his students the same rigorous closedness to theatre forms different from his own.
>
> *(Barba and Savarese 1991: 8)*

Correspondingly, American director and teacher Anne Bogart writes: "To allow for emotional freedom, you pay attention to form. If you embrace the notion of containers or *katas*, then your task is to set a fire, a human fire, inside these containers and start to burn" (Bogart 2001: 103). Decroux's compositions resemble *kata*, often containing fire. The uninitiated think technique turns performers into sterile robots, while the opposite ideology governs, to varying degrees, the work of Decroux, Barba, and Bogart.

Decroux and Grotowski

In late 1968, I stood on line in the rain for what seemed like hours, in a remote Parisian suburb, before gaining admittance to a makeshift theatre where *Akropolis*, the work of a then little-known Polish director, was to be performed. I was one of the lucky few to obtain a seat. Then, in 1976 I saw a performance of *Apocalypsis cum Figuris*, by the same, now better-known, director, late at night, in an unmarked building in an unlighted street in Wroclaw, Poland, still behind the Iron Curtain. Not until Eugenio Barba's ISTA (International School of Theatre Anthropology) Tenth Meeting in Copenhagen (May 1996) did I hear the legendary Jerzy Grotowski speak; certain expressions, identical word for word, like "the actor must be as relaxed as an old peasant," and others which had strong echoes, like "the only spectator is God," reminded me of Decroux. Although the style was different – Decroux's oracular thundering contrasting Grotowski's gently diffused meanderings – something about Grotowski's uncompromising presence recalled Decroux. Later in the summer of 1996, in Pontedera, Italy, I witnessed Grotowski's collaboration with his long-time American disciple and successor Thomas Richards. Although different in its outer manifestations, something in the intensity, the commitment, the clarity, echoed Decroux.

Decroux, Grotowski, and the audience

The nature of the event that Grotowski created, and not only his words, evoked Decroux. Unlike ordinary public performances open to anyone with a ticket, each audience member for Decroux's or Grotowski's events was chosen or in some way specially prepared.

At Decroux's home in Paris, one entered first through the kitchen, and went to a simple basement studio, both workroom and "theatre." On rare occasions, Decroux invited a limited number of initiated spectators (students in his school, a trusted neighbor, old friends) for readings he gave of Victor Hugo and Baudelaire or for a performance by his students. Decroux briefed the selected audience members beforehand, suggesting to them what they might look for. If they did not belong to his immediate circle, he tried with his earnest arguments to "convert" them to his unique vision.

At Pontedera, a comparable formula held. First, in a small, scrubbed kitchen (similar to Decroux's in its monastic simplicity) a senior student-actor told us (an already pre-screened group of nine artists, academics and others sympathetic to the work) the rules: no foot tapping, singing, laughing, clapping, or other overt participation. He then let us read the texts used in the presentation from sheets of paper that he reclaimed before we left the kitchen. Most importantly, he admonished us to not look for a plot or try to "understand." (This frame of mind, Grotowski said in his Copenhagen ISTA lectures earlier that summer, would only make us blocked and unresponsive.)

Then, leaving behind coats, bags or anything that could fall or make noise, we went to the adjoining workroom where the event unfolded.

From superficial evidence, one could say that Decroux and Grotowski, with time, lost interest in the audience. However, one might argue contrariwise that individual spectators became more and more important even as their numbers diminished. As Decroux and Grotowski aged, each valued the experience, treating it more carefully, preparing the spectator and actor more profoundly. Have actors and directors ever before in the history of theatre given the audience lessons in etiquette prior to a performance? Have Western actors ever been more thoroughly trained through years of intensive study and rehearsal? Finally, for Decroux and Grotowski, the ideal theatre became the home studio, where they each closely controlled conditions. During a certain period, Decroux performed in his dining room for not more than ten people at a time, since, for him, people in larger groups lost their individual free will and, thus, their ability to discern. After his return from New York to Paris in 1962, mentioned above, Decroux usually chose not to perform outside his basement workroom, except for two trips that I made with him while still a student at his school: in 1970, we gave a lecture demonstration in Rennes at the Maison des Jeunes et de la Culture; in 1971, in Copenhagen, we did two or three work demonstrations. Before the presentation in Rennes, where I performed *The Carpenter* and he demonstrated arm and hand movements, our only "warm-up" occurred when he walked me back and forth across the stage behind the closed curtain. As we strolled arm in arm, he assured me I needn't worry, that it wouldn't matter if I performed well or not, since everyone in the audience (as they had not yet been "converted") was an "imbecile" and incapable of understanding what they were about to see.

Once he said: "Experimental theatre! If they want to try a *real* experiment, let them get rid of the audience!" Decroux went to great lengths, as did Grotowski, to diminish the audience's authority. While Decroux may never have gotten rid of the audience completely, he reduced their number and their influence on the event, while maximizing the potential effect of the performance on each spectator (or "witness," Grotowski's preferred terminology).

In a lecture in Paris, Grotowski told the story of an old Peking Opera actor who performed better than his young son because the former was not so eager to please the audience. He also spoke of a Russian actor whose work took on a greater depth and who no longer sought to please the audience after learning that his onstage exertions could prove fatal. Decroux, like Grotowski, considered playing to the audience as a kind of prostitution of a sacred art. I hear Grotowski's voice: "The only spectator is God."

Consider Decroux's best words on the topic of the audience:

> [L]et's continue to do what we like, what we understand, and if that does not succeed for a while, don't change anything. The more we change to please the public, the less they will understand . . . We must think of people's respect; to be respected, one must not lower oneself to the audience. We must wait for them to come up to us.
>
> (Decroux 2001: 33)

Grotowski's view of Decroux's work

In 1997, the prestigious Collège de France created the Chair of Theatre Anthropology for Grotowski. In his early lectures, Grotowski repeatedly mentioned having seen Decroux's work, which clearly impressed him significantly. In his inaugural lecture at Peter Brook's Bouffes du Nord theatre, for example, Grotowski remarked that Decroux looked for "laws of life which flow, and which finally, in an advanced phase of the work, became organized, structured, and perceptible by another." He compared this to things in nature that are expressive without trying to be so: the movement of the ocean, or a tree, for example. He contrasted Decroux's theatrical method with a more conventional way of working which had the audience in mind from the start (Grotowski 1997b). In a 1946 newspaper interview, Decroux describes his way of working for himself rather than for the audience:

> Beauty is like happiness, one must find it by the by, without looking for it. I make mime pieces first for my own pleasure. I learn afterwards that they also interest my friends, some workers, my concierge and the fireman on duty.
>
> *(Decroux 2001: 57)*

In a later lecture, Grotowski spoke of an inner power, something we might call spiritual strength, radiating from Decroux despite his advanced years: an "illuminated purity in a ruined body" (Grotowski 1997a).

The vibrato and dynamic immobility in Decroux's work

Grotowski subsequently used the example of Decroux to show that a performer could reach a high level of "inner work" without following the same path that he himself had. Grotowski long advocated singing traditional songs, which function effectively because of their "vibratory quality," influencing the singers as well as their audience. Grotowski could not have known how important vibratory quality was to Decroux, whose favorite musical instrument was the violin. When he demonstrated an exercise, Decroux played his muscles like a violin, every movement originating from a sustained vibrato in the deepest parts of the body.

Decroux told stories to illustrate this quiet vibratory quality. I paraphrase, from memory:

> *Story Number 1*: Look at our teacher the cat! How he waits for the mouse: the body completely still, yet inside an almost imperceptible quivering, a high-pitched vibration, comes from moving yet not moving, wanting to go forward yet holding back. Then, suddenly, at the right moment, a lunge of stunning efficiency and clarity: the paw darts forward and claws ensnare the mouse.
>
> *Story Number 2*: A woman has purchased expensive cloth and meticulously pinned the pattern to it. After careful reflection and repeated verification, she lifts the scissors, opens them, and waits. At this point of no return – before cutting – the silence is icy hot.
>
> *Story Number 3*: The attentively alert and vigilant soccer goalkeeper watches in all directions. Not wanting, himself, to do something, he wants, instead, to prevent something from being done. Relaxed yet concentrated, weight equally distributed on two expectantly bent knees, ready to respond, he exemplifies the biblical citation "No one knows when the thief will come."

In *Words on Mime*, Decroux calls this quality

> mobile immobility, the pressure of water on the dike, the hovering of a fly stopped by the window pane, the delayed fall of the leaning tower which remains standing. Then similar to the way we stretch a bow before taking aim, man implodes yet again.
>
> *(Decroux 1985: 51)*

Decroux, almost never silent when teaching, spoke and sang constantly; he whistled, hummed, breathed loudly and buzzed as he demonstrated movements. Perhaps Grotowski did not know that Decroux taught by singing, that one of his "jokes" had him teaching singing (*enchanter*, he reminded us, meant "singing within"), while the singing school down the street taught mime (Fogal 1993: 31).

Decroux (1898–1991)

Deidre Sklar wrote that she is

> a person attuned to dynamo-rhythm [dynamic quality], which is the way the universe expresses and experiences itself. In my mind, I "sing" a reverberation of people's movement expressions with the "tocs" and vibratos I learned to think with in Decroux's basement, and, though I sometimes protest it, the *maître* stands behind me, humming in my ear.
>
> (Sklar and Cohen-Cruz 1993: 78)

Internalized singing (muscular respiration) lies at the heart of Decroux's work. A sometimes subtle, almost invisible, alternating of tense and relaxed muscles in quick succession informs Corporeal Mime. This vibration of muscles evokes the Promethean struggle that Decroux saw as the innately dramatic human condition, illustrated by the three stories above, and by one that dancer Gina Lalli remembers, below.

Whereas Decroux used vibratory quality, he also mastered dynamic immobility, a striking example of which Lalli witnessed in his midnight performance on February 3, 1958 at the Morosco Theatre in New York City:

> He talked about the principles of mime for about ten minutes. As the time passed, the audience sensed something extraordinary was happening or, perhaps, was not happening. Decroux was standing completely still, looking straight ahead. There was no gesture, no shifting of weight; only his lips were moving ... The audience was also compelled to be still and hardly breathed. At the end of this lecture, Decroux's left hand shot out and he swooped the heavy microphone stand overhead, in a triumphal gesture, and carried it offstage. The dramatic effect was not lost on the audience. In one gesture he had won them over. They had seen the power of the corporeal mime.
>
> (Lalli 1993: 41)

Many of us experienced something similar in his classes when, suddenly, the atmosphere became charged as Decroux performed a simple movement with arresting clarity and punctuated with startling immobilities. In his demonstrations of presence-in-absence, and the contrary, Decroux reminded us that we spend a lifetime studying movement in order to remain immobile while retaining the audience's interest.

Transmission: patience is a long passion

Once in rehearsal Decroux said to me: "Now we are working on plumbing, not very exciting. But someday you will have hot steam running through those pipes." This and other stories prepared students for a lengthy process. "All great art is anonymous," he said. "Who is the architect of Chartres Cathedral? It will take centuries and many workers to build the Cathedral of Corporeal Mime." He attracted idealistic people to his school using charm, wit, and eloquence to "convert" them to this "Great Project." Without transmission through his students, his life work remains unfulfilled and he a mere footnote in twentieth-century theatre history.

Within his lifetime, and unlike most of his contemporaries, Decroux repositioned the actor at the center of the theatrical endeavor, making the actor the *sine qua non* instead of the "last hired and first fired." Thus, Decroux challenged the predominance of playwrights and text, a paradigm that, except for *commedia dell'arte*, had prevailed since Aristotle. In the 1996 Copenhagen ISTA,

Grotowski opined that the actor must do other than merely "say the author's words and make appropriate gestures," a sentiment that Decroux would have shared.

Transmission of what?

Decroux continuously reinvented himself through his work, which changed according to students' abilities or lack of them. The Decroux that Barrault and Marceau knew differed from the later Decroux and his work. What one saw in the 1950s (the time of Dutch artists Will Spoor and Frits Vogels, and French performers Raymond Devos and Marise Flach) varied from what another experienced in the early 1960s (the time of Alvin Epstein, Sterling Jensen, and Jewel Walker); what one witnessed in the late 1960s (Yves Lebreton, Ingemar Lindh, Leonard Pitt) contrasted with what another lived in the 1970s (Jean Asslin, Denise Boulanger, Claire Heggen, Yves Marc, George Molnar) or in the 1980s (Corinne Soum, Daniel Stein, Steven Wasson). Decroux postulated, "Memory is the first artist" – memory which selects, arranges, highlights, obscures, filters. A student's memory of Decroux will be shaped by her nature, her individual experience with him and her life's subsequent development – by the person she has become. Thus, one's current memory, inevitably subject to this filtering process, differs not only from the memories of other students but even from one's own earlier mental record.

Was Decroux a purist who spent sixty years developing esoteric forms? A man who, in the early 1920s, gave shelter to Russian anarchist Nestor Makhno (Benhaïm 2003: 90)? A large worker who dressed in stylish women's clothes and an expensive wig to parody, at Leftist political meetings in the mid-1930s, a philanthropic member of the *haute bourgeoisie*? Like his crystal paperweight, a cherished gift from the New York students, Decroux's life and work were multifaceted. Which Decrouxs should we remember? All of them, and from all periods, matter, as all will prove essential in establishing the foundations of the Cathedral of Corporeal Mime.

"If corporeal mime survives, the world will survive"

In 1972, Decroux wrote a dedication for me in his *Paroles sur le mime*:

> One does not modernize a monument in order to conserve it. One must therefore conserve the body, which was strong, skillful, ascetic. What will conserve it? Sport is not one of the fine arts. One gives oneself to it only to vanquish others. Dance is not a portrait of struggle. Old-fashioned pantomime is not an art of the body. Corporeal mime is more than a diversion. If it survives, the world will survive.
>
> *(Decroux 1972)*

A documentary film that Grotowski showed during his Paris lectures illuminates, to my mind, this passage. In footage from southern Italy in the 1950s, we saw women dancing the tarantella as a cure for the tarantula spider's poisonous bite. The dancers bounded unbridled to the musicians frenetic playing and singing, not to impress viewers but to wrest themselves and others from death. The music's strongly vibratory qualities (tambourine and violin) heightened the women's trembling. Their expert dancing and playing, Grotowski surmised, elicited a cure. Speaking of the tarantella, seemingly unrelated to Decroux's Corporeal Mime, Grotowski conjectured that Decroux could go beyond himself, could move for God, because of his competence and aspiration toward something surpassing spectacle. Decroux implied as much in the inscription, "Corporeal Mime is more than a diversion."

In writing "If [Corporeal Mime] survives, the world will survive," did Decroux consider his movement research a tarantella to save humanity? Did he imagine Corporeal Mime a cure for a world bitten by laziness, apathy, and passivity induced by mass media and increasing mechanization? He imagined that, one day, people would attend mime performances solely to witness people exerting themselves, since machines would have supplanted all other human physical endeavor.

Neither Decroux nor Grotowski considered theatre a "diversion." But Grotowski wondered, in his tarantella lecture, if Decroux had consciously developed spiritual aspects of his work. Many of us know Decroux as the atheist or agnostic who nonetheless created figures entitled "God Fishes Man" and "The Prayer." He often used religious metaphors and quoted the Bible regularly; he sang "He rests in the arms of God" while performing arm exercises based on vibrations of the biceps. I consider Decroux a spiritual person rather than a religious one. Through metaphors, he admonished students to suppress nagging voices, doubts, fears, and preoccupations – mental clutter – that would prevent effective performance. He chose a vocabulary that mentioned not only evicting negative influences, but welcoming positive ones. His birthday inscription for me in his gift of Bergson's *On Laughter* reads: "Paris was far. God guided you" (Decroux 1971).

Without direct reference to traditional Indian chakras, spiritual energy centers used in Indian meditation, medicine, and theatre, Decroux made similar poetic references: a sunburst between the shoulders, the sap rising in the body as in a tree, and the fire in the belly. Like Grotowski, Decroux acted "as if" the chakras existed. Grotowski suggested, for example, that one might awaken the sleeping serpent at the base of the spine (Slowiak and Cuesta, 2007: 77, 124). And Decroux started every class with such an exercise – one in which the spine itself became an awakened serpent. In Decroux's work, this "aroused" spine had to accompany an "expressionless" face, like those in deep meditation on statues from the Temple at Angkor.

The great project

Decroux wrote in *Words on Mime*; "I shall die a young man in the first stage of the Great Project" (Decroux 1985: 108). Does his Great Project exist today, or did it live solely as a figment of Decroux's monomaniacal imagination? One of my students reported that, at the definitive closing of the school, Decroux seemed disoriented, shook his head, and murmured, "I have found nothing, I have discovered nothing." What did he, in fact, find? What did he discover?

For Decroux, the Great Project, Corporeal Mime, hovered between diction and classical ballet (Decroux 1953: 27). While Decroux's ideal theatre need not be silent necessarily, a silent phase of reconquering the body – key to reestablishing the actor's centrality – had to precede the reintroduction of the voice and text to the theatre. Like Zeami Motokiyo (1363–1443), founder of the Japanese Noh theatre, and like Grotowski, Decroux based his theories firmly on the physical practice of theatre rather than on literature primarily.

At the first stage of his Great Project, Decroux chased principles into his students' bodies and minds, to inspire in them the will to persevere in the development of this Cathedral of Corporeal Mime, a project requiring ardent workers over generations. His work, demanding prolonged self-sacrifice, contradicted twentieth-century visions of instant wealth and glory, facile fame and fortune. His teaching, as political as it was artistic, engaged the whole person and not the performer alone.

Often his pedagogical approach, a relentless honing, used both audible and silent vibrations created by singing or by moving muscles in alternating currents of tension and relaxation. Often he placed parts of students' bodies where they should go, with an urgent insistence and vibratory quality; like the teacher of Noh drama, he pulled back against an arm or a leg to show how much resistance one had to offer to movement. He pronounced the word "*résistance*" with an especially incisive diction, allowing no misunderstanding. The resistance he taught was as much moral as physical.

Can Decroux's teaching continue if assimilated into mainstream theatre? Does Corporeal Mime exist as a separate entity, or only as one more "movement-for-actors" tool, only as a support for traditional Western theatre practice? Decroux, haunted by these questions, addressed them in many Friday-night lectures. While theatre, superficially influenced by Decroux's teaching, might exist, what about this daily Corporeal Mime classwork with serious students over a long period, and the ongoing teaching and performance of Decroux's repertoire? In other words, what about the Decrouvian project in itself? Now we must carefully watch the second generation, students of Decroux's students, to see how the Great Project progresses.

Others will judge whether Decroux's technique has aspects of inner work comparable to the Noh actor's or Grotowski's. History will determine whether to make of him a twentieth-century Zeami, founder of a new theatre whose repertoire will continue for generations, and whose various schools will naturally pass down different versions of it. If, however, Decroux's discoveries merely acculturate to the hundreds of other existing "movement-for-actors" possibilities, work on the Great Project might have to continue elsewhere, unadulterated. After all, the history of Corporeal Mime from its inception has been one of alternating periods of analysis (pure research) and synthesis (divers practical applications in theatre and cinema).

8.2 Decroux as director/creator: how did Decroux make a performance?

Banishing text

When most directors ask "What play shall I produce?" or "What work of literature shall I adapt for the stage?" their primary job becomes the interpretation, elucidation, or elaboration of that text. Decroux, on the other hand, expelling literature from the theatre to develop exclusively the "actor art," began with the actor on a bare stage. With the exception of two plays that he prepared in 1941, in a failed attempt to gain government subsidy (Benhaïm 2003: 252), Decroux always began without text. The author, he contended, lived in a "sitting down world" whose limited expectations could only inhibit the actor-citizen of the "standing up world." Whereas the author works exclusively with words, the actor acts with words, without them, or, usually, in spite of them.

Decroux wanted to banish from the theatre what he called the "alien arts." One could say that he wanted to drive the author further away than the other theatre collaborators, since the author had become for Decroux the theatre's chief oppressor or colonizer. When we speak of Etienne Decroux as a twentieth-century theatre revolutionary, we note that in this select company he and Jacques Lecoq alone proposed a paradigm shift which questioned the primacy of theatre's historically established relationship with text.

Only during the heyday of *commedia dell'arte*, he found, had Western actors broken free of the author's chains. Decroux took on the mission of proclaiming the actor's freedom for our time.

Making performances from improvisation

Without pre-existing text, but instead with the actor's collaboration, Decroux initiated a series of guided improvisations that he described as a "petri dish" (Decroux 2003: 59). He allowed the actor's random or unconscious movements to grow, and subsequently edited and built upon this growth, or expunged it and began afresh. Corinne Soum describes improvising as the first steps toward the creation of a piece with Decroux:

> From time to time Decroux conjured up the traces of a theme to help us, but more often threw at me, with a joyous voice, "Go on, do something!" Or he declared, with a serious voice, "It's beautiful to be mystical" or yet again "This morning I saw a sparrow taking a bath." Out of the question, of course, to "mime" these statements, but one had to use them as a kind of terrain of sensations, a storehouse of impressions.
>
> (Soum 1999: 62–63)

Soum reminds us that it was never a question of literally reproducing Decroux's remarks, but instead of using these "traces of a theme" as a metaphorical springboard to suggest ways of moving through space and ways of being still that might result in the creation of a phrase and, perhaps eventually, a composition.

In my work with him, Decroux told me to follow the body's "naturally asymmetrical tendencies," to lean in whatever direction my body wanted to go on that particular day, and to continue until I met an exterior limitation (the wall, the floor) or an internal one (e.g., the knee will only bend so far; the arm has raised to its maximum). Along the way, he wanted me to begin to hear what he described as an "internal music," a sort of non-rhythmic series of sounds – more vibrations or impulses, really – that resembled articulated speech rather than music. Since these eluded me at first, he sang – sometimes quite forcefully – what they sounded like to him. When improvising successfully, the actor's body entered a special world, a metaphorical one, in which it created these inaudible but very real, internal sounds (like depth-charges exploding in the psyche's undersea) and simultaneously followed their reverberations.

If the reader has trouble envisioning what kinds of movements the body as a "consequence and prolongation of thought" (Soum 1999: 62) might make, rest assured that his students found it equally difficult. But after some time – more or less, depending upon the aptitude of the improviser for nonlinear understanding – the quotidian movements of a person deeply lost in thought became a possible terrain on which to build. These movements (because of their ordinariness), if made in public, might not engage an observer. But the actor's training in Corporeal Mime allowed him to continue certain lines of force (leaning pensively forward; turning suddenly away as if repelled by an idea) into a logically satisfying configuration of movements which departed significantly, yet logically, from their original quotidian source.

Every day for most of 1971, Zoe Noyes Maistre and I stood in front of Decroux and improvised for the better part of an hour. He offered suggestions, interrupting our attempts with praise or with censure, but guided us mostly with the sheer silent power of his presence and his piercing regard. One had the feeling of having never really been seen before. Little sequences, more or less complete in themselves, figures based on protecting, cradling, being attracted to, or pushing away from, slowly emerged from these improvisations. (Years later I would realize that the attraction, repulsion, or stillness that Zoe and I manifested were but smaller versions – yet not necessarily less powerful ones – of the counterweights manifested in *The Carpenter* or *The Washerwoman*.) We rehearsed these figures, to which he assigned poetic and evocative titles like "rising sap" or "sunshine on your back," in varying orders until he settled upon one that he preferred. Decroux, who never knew what he was looking for until he found it, encapsulated his strategy for creating a piece through improvisation:

> First, one must improvise without even knowing the theme upon which one is improvising.
>
> Thus, one finds a theme, then a second, then a third.

You must therefore move in order to think.

In placing in a logical order the ideas one finds in moving, a play composes itself without words ever breaking the silence.

We find the usefulness of words by doing without them.

(Decroux 1950: 7)

This time-consuming practice of letting the "play compose itself" required patience from both director and actors; one could not feel hurried, as anything less than complete surrender to the process would sabotage it. He often said that "patience is a long passion" to fortify us when we tired (he never seemed to), or told the humorous story of a British gentleman who says to his chauffeur: "Drive slowly, we're late!" Decroux's themes were never literary ideas, but always poetic and metaphoric physical explorations – discoveries of the way the body related to space, to props, and to other bodies. The "how" mattered more than the "what," and conflated with it.

To explain his method of working, Decroux delighted in telling a story about a necklace of potatoes: "If I give you a string of potatoes and ask you to imagine a string of pearls, you might have some difficulty. But if I give you one exquisite pearl and ask you to imagine a necklace of them, you will have a better chance." Decroux's inexhaustible appetite for detail, crafting individual "pearls" (figures or phrases) for what could seem a frustratingly long time, dismayed many apprentices. Decroux rallied them by citing the seventeenth-century French poet Nicolas Boileau's *The Art of Poetry:* "Hâtez-vous lentement; et, sans perdre courage, Vingt fois sur le métier remettez votre ouvrage . . . " ("Hasten slowly; and without losing heart, twenty times upon the loom, go at your handiwork . . . "). After creation of an individual movement phrase through improvisation, there followed extended examination and reworking, refining, and polishing. Only then would he reluctantly move on to another "pearl," and another; at last, he arranged these carefully honed movement phrases into a felicitous order, a process he often called "jewelry making." Before he could string the necklace, however, the actors had sometimes left the school, either out of a desire (premature in Decroux's opinion) to perform, or through the material necessity of doing something that could eventually earn them a living. Decroux took refuge from this constant source of disappointment by redoubling his efforts to create something enduring; somehow, he finally succeeded on his own terms.

While Decroux foresaw the eventual reintegration of text into the theatrical event, this required, to his mind, that the actor expel, at least for a time, "colonizers" from other fields. However, his own work (with few exceptions) did not include text even in a secondary role, and he warned his students against taking shelter under great literary names (Decroux 1985: 32).

Decroux's actor

During his lifetime, only Decroux and a few advanced disciples could provide the rigorous and transformative training in Corporeal Mime required of his actors. Hence, Decroux the director inevitably fused with Decroux the teacher/creator. From this already small group of trained performers, Decroux carefully selected individuals whom he could trust. He had to feel empathy, a seriousness of purpose, a certain possibility in the actor. Being asked to rehearse with him outside of regular class hours was an honor, usually bestowed upon his teaching assistants only, but sometimes on a special few others for whom he felt an affinity.

Nicole Pinaud, one of the last to work with him in this privileged way, describes the symbiotic relationship between Decroux and the actor:

> I think I was like all those who lent their bodies to him to create – unconscious matter which corresponded to his universe. But he also corresponded to mine. In that, he was not only a Pygmalion, he also revealed my own dreams to me.
> There was an echo, resonance between us. Or love.
>
> *(Pinaud 2003: 510–511)*

Marcel Marceau, who worked with Decroux just after World War II, spoke poignantly, in an interview he gave on the occasion of Decroux's death in 1991, of the "kind of deep friendship based on mutual respect ... I had [for him] a kind of spiritual love" (Marceau 1991: 12). And, while not everyone working with Decroux felt what Pinaud and Marceau describe as love, everyone whom I have met has described it as an attachment of corresponding strength.

Funding for performances

How could Decroux afford to create such labor-intensive theatre and almost never sell it to a paying public? He underwrote his own work from the beginning with a combination of stage, film, radio, and television acting. From 1962 onward, upon his return to Paris, he taught in the basement of his small house and lived modestly. He had some income from retirement pensions, as well as rental income from an apartment and a café at the same address as his house. He took no vacations, never owned a car, never flew in an airplane, and rarely ate in restaurants; books were his only luxury. The basement workroom and Decroux's study took primary focus in his house; the miniature kitchen, bath, bedroom, and upstairs changing room seemed afterthoughts. He produced his private art to please himself and a few others and, like a Renaissance prince, but on a reduced scale, he subsidized it from his own funds. As Eugenio Barba once said, Decroux succeeded in creating "an island of freedom" which, while small, provided him the liberty to create (Barba 1997: 12).

His student-actors, too, had to subsidize their mime apprenticeship from which they almost never had earnings. The cost of Decroux's lessons, already the least expensive in Paris, Decroux reduced or completely waived for teaching assistants, translators, or those who worked with him on a performance. The student actor did not pay with money, but instead in regular daily attendance and unquestioning devotion to the requirements of the work – and this not for a month or two, but for a period of years. Many held jobs such as teaching English or babysitting; parents supported the more fortunate ones. In exceptional cases, apprentices did receive a windfall: in 1971, Decroux's friend, documentary filmmaker Frédéric Rossif, convinced him to leave his basement for an afternoon, accompanied by two of his more advanced students, in order to create film footage that might be woven among interviews and documentation about French action painter Georges Mathieu (1921–2012) for a program entitled *Georges Mathieu ou la fureur d'être* (*Georges Mathieu or the Fury of Being*). On this occasion, while most of the mimes' performance ended up on the cutting-room floor, they nonetheless earned in an afternoon what they might have made in a month of English teaching.

After many public performances with his New York company, Decroux returned, as we noted above, in 1962 to Paris, where he performed rarely and almost exclusively in his basement classroom equipped with one white theatrical light, white curtains, and folding canvas stools for the audience. He charged no admission and did not publicize his presentations, although he sometimes sent postcards to friends inviting them to the aforementioned poetry readings he gave of Victor Hugo and Baudelaire. In reducing the theatrical event to its basic elements, it became a priceless gift for a precious few.

The number of audience members for mime presentations or readings never exceeded twenty, and might include: the concierge (for the larger building adjacent to Decroux's brick cottage) and her bus-driver husband; former and current students; and longtime friends of Monsieur and Madame Decroux. Thus continued a long tradition of performances at home that he had begun at the start of his career.

The other "alien arts"

Along with text, Decroux banished what he called "artistic lighting" in favor of the white unchanging light, simulating what one would find in outdoor performances. He insisted that the actor alone, rather than lighting effects, provide the phrasing and changes in focus.

He also largely rejected costumes, preferring, first, an almost nude body and, later, tights and leotards to conceal the body's imperfections while still revealing its myriad movement possibilities. Masks or veiled faces, vital in an earlier phase, almost completely disappeared, giving place to the inexpressive face. Whereas the actors in *The Little Soldiers* wore simple costumes and limited make-up, these elements were rare and never figured prominently in the totality of his work.

Decroux adamantly refused music, as well, until he later welcomed it as the one necessary alien art, an "alcohol" which he maintained could transform the fruit juice of life into the exquisite liqueur of art.

The movement itself: counterweights

Now that we have examined the unique context in which Decroux created and performed his experiments, what were they exactly?

He created two works early in his career which he continued to hone until the end of his life: *The Carpenter* and *The Washing* (renamed, from 1973, *The Washerwoman*). While other pieces appeared and disappeared from his repertoire, he returned periodically to these touchstones, part of the category of work that he called Artisanal Life. Decroux describes this historical period as one in which the artisan accomplished his tasks without the help of extra-animal power (steam, electricity, etc.). For Decroux, this era represented a kind of paradise lost, a golden age before human bodies atrophied from lack of use or became deformed from imbalanced and stressful labor. Decroux's work presented metaphoric counterweights (for example, a person pushing away an idea with the same expenditure of energy that he would use to displace an object) and use of real counterweights, as he employed them in *The Carpenter* and *The Washerwoman*:

> In life we make certain expressive gestures that complete our words, or augment their force. We do them with such spontaneity that they must be really ancient. I believe that one of the dominant things in prehistoric man was the [use of] counterweights. It was almost his daily regimen. And the use of counterweights as a dominant activity lasted well after the prehistoric period with the slaves of antiquity, the serfs of the Middle Ages or with the artisan.
>
> *(Decroux 2003: 130)*

Decroux remarked that, to function effectively, a skilled worker lacking great innate strength needed counterweights in their four major and myriad, minor, applied forms: "removing the support," "jumping to fall on the head," "the wool-carding machine," and "reestablishment of two elements on the oblique" describe specific categories used in The Carpenter, The Washerwoman, and other work-based figures and études. (As verbal descriptions cannot fully explain these complex maneuvers, you will eventually need a live demonstration from an exponent of this art. Until then, the words below attempt to give you some notions.)

1   *Removing the support*: The actor, quickly withdrawing his leg and foot from a second position, falls with his upper body upon the object he wishes to move. The leg that remains planted in the ground becomes the fixed point against which the body transforms vertical (falling) movement into horizontal (pushing or pulling) movement. The actor might pull instead of push by placing the object he wishes to displace on the other side of the fulcrum.
2   *Jumping to fall on the head*: In this counterweight, the actor jumps into the air and, while falling to the ground, redirects his body's weight from a vertical fall to a horizontal push around the central axle (fulcrum point) in the pelvis. The pelvis traces an upside-down J shape in the space above the horizon line.
3   *The wool-carding machine*: The image of this implement stayed with Decroux from his early adulthood. In the mime exercise, the body traces an arc that resembles the path followed by the machine's two intermeshing curved forks. The previous two counterweights push or pull along the horizontal line, whereas the wool-carding machine lifts weight. The lifting activity occurs when the cord of the body's arc moves backward around a fixed central point (a fulcrum). As in "Jumping to fall on the head," the pelvis traces a J shape. Here, however, the mime moves down and under the weight to be moved, rather than up and over it.
4   *Reestablishment of two elements on the oblique* ("*sissonne*" in ballet terminology): This counterweight provides the underpinnings of a human being's most basic work: displacement in walking. Decroux explained that the leg's two parts (one below and one above the knee) straighten to form one straight line. If they do so *vertically*, the person remains in place, able only, for example, to take fruit from trees by jumping. In order to go to the next tree, the person must reestablish the two parts of the leg onto the *oblique* line, causing a small fall forward that he then repeats; the repetition becomes walking. He often quoted Charles Gide: "Production comes down to displacement."

(Decroux 1985: 109)

These counterweights move the work from the periphery (hands) to the center of the actor's body, 3 inches (7 centimeters) below the navel. Even if the hands did sometimes, of necessity, occupy space away from the center of the body, they needed strong energetic links to that center. While the hands hold the tool – often close to the center of the body – the body does the work. Counterweights alter the intra-corporeal and inter-spatial relationships between center and surface. According to Decroux, a pantomime might begin superficially and never connect to the center, running the risk of insufficient continuous inner connection from hands to the body's center through the energetic links cultivated by the manual laborer and the Corporeal Mime.

The dynamic construction – "dynamo-rhythm"

Snap. Glide. Crackle. Veer. Pop. Implode. Accelerate. Careen. Swoop. A verbal description, even one accompanied by drawings, cannot give the reader a correct idea of the rhythmic complexity of *The Carpenter* and *The Washerwoman*; in Decroux's mind, Corporeal Mime performances had to satisfy through variation of phrasing, as does poetry or music. He invented the word "dynamo-rhythm" to describe a combination of three elements: trajectory of the movement; its speed; and its weight or resistance. He counted on dynamo-rhythm to "slap the audience to keep them awake." For example, whenever the actor moved an arm along a predetermined pathway, it frequently had to press on through difficulties or speed up unexpectedly, since Decroux insisted that one must anticipate the audience's boredom and change dynamic quality, or shift suddenly to the next movement before their attention strayed. He called this "killing the gesture before it dies," or "editing out" its completion, or "splicing in" the next movement without transition.

This cubistic cutting, shaping, and even sometimes rearranging of sequences, like quick cuts in film, might give the compositions a shattered and jittery surface or, in the case of rounder, slower sequences, a seamless veneer. The Corporeal Mime might accomplish a grouping of four or five smaller movements with a percussive and implosive rhythm, or a larger movement with a steady slow-motion quality; or surprisingly, he might perform these movements with their opposite dynamo-rhythm. Decroux constantly refined qualities of a composition – soft or hard, heavy or light, with or without attack, accelerating or decelerating, with beginning, ending, or median "tocs." These "tocs" – sudden bursts of energy – function as punctuation that stop, start, or alter the movements in which they occur. In the same way that he constantly edited the dynamo-rhythm of his compositions, Decroux never tired of refining or enhancing the shape of the movement itself. Sirlei Alaniz describes his approach to dynamo-rhythm:

> Corporeal mime never imposes a metrical rhythmic structure. Historically, it is founded on rhythms of work, of crafts, of physical actions of man in his environment. These include accelerations, pauses, quick changes of movement, and slowing down, which are necessities.
>
> *(Alaniz 2004: 19)*

These work movements often led to more subjective moments of pure acting which alternated with work: "It's the rhythm of man who works, who thinks, and who, while thinking, doubts, stops, speeds up, resists, gives space for the unexpected, never follows predictable cadences" (Alaniz 2004: 20).

Decroux evolved a vast number of what he called "causalities" – ways of defining how a movement began (e.g., imperceptibly, as when triggered by an electric eye; brusquely, as when un-sticking from a surface; or as the consequence of another body part beginning the movement and pulling or pushing the second part). He defined ways of ending a movement, suddenly, as when hitting an immoveable object, or with a light internal "toc" which marked its arrival at an imaginary finish line.

Of causalities in his new mime, Decroux once said that as a young man he believed that causalities could replace plot completely. He often assigned them evocative names, helping the actor play them imaginatively: "snail's antennae," "tug-boat," "spider web," "electric eye," and many others (see Asselin 2013).

The Corporeal Mime always engages in a struggle with weight and inertia (his own and that of others; of the tools he manipulates; of the inanimate matter he struggles to shape; of his own or another's thought). He constantly pushes, pulls, carves, and twists both his own body and the matter he manipulates or wrestles with, as one mirrors the other.

We might imagine the Corporeal Mime, trained to extend or to cut lines of force, as a person attached to the earth with invisible elastic bands of variable lengths and resistance. Moving his hand through space to lift a glass of water, moving a foot forward in order to walk, turning the head quickly or slowly – all these quotidian movements require more energy, more struggle, and hence have higher dramatic value and visibility, than their equivalents in real life. The Corporeal Mime constantly negotiates these difficulties, plays with these variable weights and resistances, anticipating the culmination of his task. Sometimes it seems the Corporeal Mime moves through different poetic zones and climates, with differing temperatures, flora and fauna, or through imaginary substances, like molasses or water, or across different surfaces of silk or sandpaper. When the Corporeal Mime so generously celebrates the "how," the "what" certainly has to take second place, or disappear entirely.

Material actions suggest mental states

In the contrasting activities of *The Carpenter* and *The Washerwoman*, the actor's body, the spine especially, takes on the qualities of the objects used and the activities mimed. Handling wood differs fundamentally from manipulating cloth and, while counterweights used in the pieces may seem the same, each study requires a different agility, dynamism, and range of movement. The actor, in learning to play these roles, schools her body in a wide range of dynamo-rhythms that suggest multifarious states of thought. For Decroux, matter formed the basis for everything immaterial: thought, spirit, emotion, dreams. He wrote: "I am what you could call a spiritual-materialist. That's to say the spiritual influences me when it gives form to the material" (Decroux 2003: 57). Thus the exploration of various kinds of matter – in different situations, with different weights – became a primary focus of his research.

> Not everything is round, but everything weighs. Not everything is pointed, but everything weighs. Not everything is hot, but everything weighs. Not everything is tender, but everything weighs. And it's astonishing that when I realized that everything weighed, the idea didn't come to me to rely on the simple fact that the earth attracts bodies and it's because the earth attracts bodies that everything weighs. You see the importance of what we call counterweights.
>
> *(Decroux 2003: 131)*

Constant effort, as the actor falls toward the earth or pulls away from it, lies at the heart of each of Decroux's compositions. This struggle with gravity manifests itself especially in *The Carpenter* and *The Washerwoman*, where the character's relationship with weight, dynamo-rhythm, and states of thought form the basis of action. In these compositions, Decroux demonstrates the nobility of honest labor, accomplished with commitment (implying struggle), acquired skill (implying patience, perseverance), and reverence (implying integrity, a higher purpose) for the task. Drama ensues when things don't follow as expected: the jar lid remains stuck; the rusty compass requires extra effort to open; the screwdriver is just out of reach. These unforeseen circumstances require a dexterity of mind and body, *métier*, character, and adaptability. Decroux's love of word origins made him explain to us that "virtuosity" comes from the accumulation of virtue, from systematic, daily work, implying the close alliance between the actor's and the carpenter's craft. Here again, he noted, the origin of the French word "*menuisier*" (carpenter) means to make small, to articulate, to detail – for both carpenter and actor.

> Basically, when man thinks, he struggles against ideas, like we struggle against the material. Because we don't see ideas, because we don't see thoughts, because we don't have a direct hold on thought, the best thing is to do a material job that implies intelligence and of which the gestures are like echoes of our intelligence.
>
> *(Decroux 2003: 77)*

One might argue that abstract mime never existed before Decroux and Barrault imagined it. Their study of weight and movement quality, counterweights and dynamo-rhythm took the actor into the realm of conflict and struggle – not only with real objects, but also with thought, into the world of metaphysical or phantom counterweights and abstract or subjective mime.

Thus, Decroux's work differed radically from his nineteenth-century predecessors and from his early twentieth-century contemporaries. For example, Oskar Schlemmer's (1888–1943) Bauhaus experiments in three-dimensional, moving constructivist images used costumes and masks that limited the actor's movements while simultaneously creating unforgettable geometric designs. Schlemmer's Triadic Ballet explored abstracted bodies in space, but, unlike Decroux's experiments, Schlemmer's figures have little dramatic weight or resistance. They contained none of Decroux's counterweights or dynamo-rhythm, which the complex construction and weight of Schlemmer's body masks would have prevented or obscured. Decroux's varied articulations of the spine from occiput to sacrum ran counter to Schlemmer's necessarily rigid balletic trunk.

Decroux's approach also differed from that of Russian director Vsevolod Meyerhold (1874–1940), whose movement *études* served to illustrate or extend a dramatic text into performance, but which, without the playwright, existed primarily as actor training exercises.

The Carpenter

Decroux read Jean-Jacques Rousseau's *Emile* only after beginning his fifty-year project (Decroux 2003: 76) and thus did not count Rousseau's ideal son as a literary antecedent. This fictional craftsman, however, assumed tremendous proportions in Decroux's imagination: the woodworker who fells the tree, drags it to his atelier, removes the bark, saws the wood into rough planks, imagines and draws an object that he wishes to produce, and cuts the planks into smaller pieces, joining individual elements into a whole, sanding and applying the appropriate finish to a utilitarian object.

> The carpenter has contact with wood, which is a beautiful material, a friendly material, an almost living material. The carpenter is a man who knows botany a little. He has to distinguish among trees; the trees have their specificities. When it's about building furniture, some of them, like the ash, are a little too flexible. He also has to know how wood should be treated, because he is going to need to let it dry a long time and he is going to bend it. What a story! There's no world like that of the carpenter. Having seen how this activity is general, how it is dramatic, because it deals with all the moral phenomena – hesitation, confidence, retrospective examination – has he made a mistake or not? Should he risk it? – we are necessarily disposed to consider it a beautiful subject.
> *(Decroux 2003: 76)*

A chair, a desk or a building, Decroux said, does not signify a thing, it *is* that thing. Corporeal Mimes do not *pretend*, Madame Decroux reminded me, as I passed through the kitchen one day, they *do*. One could not overstate Decroux's insistence that thought manifests itself in matter, that the thinker should not remain a talking head but become instead a dancing philosopher. The Carpenter made his thought visible. "So, precision, minutia, hard work: that's a complete man. We have to ask ourselves what's missing. It's the flowering of all human faculties, and as Jean Jacques Rousseau observed, it's a clean job" (Decroux 2003: 76).

As shown in the first paragraphs of this section, improvisation played a key role in the creation of most of Decroux's works. In the case of *The Carpenter* and *The Washerwoman*, however, Decroux was reconstructing pieces he had first made in the 1930s and had revived several times over the years. An actor could suggest solutions to problems encountered along the way, and surely the actor's limitations or abilities shaped each version. But the sequence and basic scheme of the work remained unchanged from previous versions.

What happens in *The Carpenter*? Removing plot or anecdote, a mere succession of actions remains. Traditional suspense – "What will happen next?" – does not manifest itself across the performance as a whole; rather, suspense of a different sort exists within the performance of each action, in the moments of pause, weight, resistance, hesitation, and surprise, before the Carpenter begins or completes an action or a gesture. The importance attributed to the traditional or anecdotal "what" adjusts as the "how" becomes preeminent; an "unblocked" spectator's focus shifts from story to actor, from plot to presence. Decroux said of the Carpenter's work: "It's almost abstract. It's like a perfume coming from a concrete action" (Soum 1999: 18). He considered the Carpenter a generality, nearly an abstraction: "We've encountered *a* horse, but not *the* horse. We've never seen *the* Frenchman, we've seen *a* Frenchman. And it's like that with everything. We've never seen *the* carpenter, either" (Decroux 2003: 77).

Decroux had worked with film director Pierre Prévert and stage director and author Antonin Artaud (1898–1948), both of whom also were anti-realistic in their approaches. He observed that

> there are people in this vast movement who are anti-realistic in literature, painting, and sculpture, but when it comes to the actor – finished! They fall back into a kind of realism that reminds us of the period of Antoine and Stanislavsky.
>
> *(Decroux 2003: 189)*

Decroux's compositions, as they pushed the limits of theatre, risked alienating audiences by not "falling back into a kind of realism": "There are people who are happy to see a body that moves without them knowing what it means. Then, there are others who aren't interested by that. You can't make concessions in this sphere" (Decroux 2003: 92).

The Carpenter: *the "what"*

1. Introduction. The person becomes an actor who, in turn, becomes a carpenter.
2. He planes a plank of wood and puts the plane away.
3. He reaches for a drill, drills a hole in the wood, and puts the drill away.
4. He takes a compass from the counter in front of him, inscribes a circle onto the wood, and returns the compass back to the counter.
5. He reaches up to a shelf to take down a jar. After unscrewing the jar lid, he places the lid on the shelf. He searches in the jar for a screw of just the right size, finds it, and returns the jar to the shelf. He holds the screw vertical in relation to the plank of wood, looks for and finds a hammer, and gives the screw head a light tap, which plants its tip into the wood. He looks for and finds a screwdriver that he uses to tighten the screw. At one point during this activity, thinking he hears his wife (the Washerwoman) call to him, he looks over his shoulder but decides he was mistaken. He returns to his work, completes it, and returns the screwdriver to the counter top.
6. He looks for and finds a pencil stuck behind his right ear. He takes it out and places its point on the surface of the plank. He traces a figure eight on the wood plank. He puts the pencil back behind his ear.
7. He takes a box of gouges from the shelf and looks into the box to find just the right one. He takes it out and tests its sharpness. When satisfied it will do the job, he begins to gouge the wood. When finished with this activity, he sees a knothole in the wood, which he removes with the gouge. He leaves the gouge stuck in the wood.
8. To finish, he brushes the sweat from his forehead, and caresses the wood.

Thomas Leabhart

The Carpenter: *the "how"*

This sequence is hardly realistic; our carpenter would end up with a plank, a hole drilled into it, a circle traced onto it, a screw planted in the middle of it, a figure eight drawn on it, and bits of wood gouged out of it. Decroux obviously ordered these activities for other than literal reasons. The play is about the work movements themselves, heightened to reveal their lines of force, ordinarily hidden, but now visible in the actor's body.

> *The Carpenter*, in particular, made certain gestures with a certain violence, and, like [things moving] in water, these gestures call out for continuation. In practical, everyday life, the gesture is stopped. We have the impression that actions are like hairs – they ask to grow, but social life, or even other necessities, oblige you to cut them close to the head. So close that we don't understand the whole truth, all the "power" of things. We see what they are, but not what they want to be. So, in *The Carpenter*, lots of movements are the continuation of something that, of habit, is normally cut with social scissors.
> (Decroux 2003: 78)

ANALYSIS: A NOTE ON THE METHOD

The Carpenter begins with a person facing upstage, seated on a white kitchen chair, downstage left. This opening play within a play, in the tradition of self-conscious art, presents a person preparing to perform a piece, in this case, Decroux's *The Carpenter*. The subsequent standing up and first few steps of walking constitute an artistic – artificial – rendering of an ordinary person (a non-actor), grappling with his immanent transformation from a quotidian being into an articulated one who manifests an extraordinary state of mind and body. Decroux displays three phases of what is usually safely hidden backstage: (1) an ordinary being who (2) transforms into an actor who (3) becomes a character, in this case the Carpenter. Dealing with the question of characterization, Decroux's actor may embody the ideal of a carpenter while not attempting to become a specific carpenter of a specific age who "wants something" in contemporary acting terms. (Only once in four years did Decroux offer any personal information about the Carpenter, and he did so smiling lightheartedly: the Carpenter married the Washerwoman – no mention of children – and they lived in a stone cottage surrounded by fields of lavender in the south of France, where the sun shone more frequently than in Paris.) Resistance posed by the inertia of his own body; challenges posed by the picture inside his head of the object he wishes to create; the weight and resistance of the materials with which he works – the person-as-actor-as-carpenter's work consists of overcoming these concrete obstacles rather than psychological ones. Decroux did not give credence to modern psychology or psychiatry. He opposed Freud before it became popular to do so and believed only in thought made visible through action.

Decroux, like Lecoq, believed that all acting consists of pushing and pulling (I pull you toward me, I push you from me) as his Carpenter pushes and pulls against great physical and spiritual weights. The Carpenter, Decroux's Hamlet (another character from an age before psychiatry), embodied the pause, weight, resistance, hesitation, and surprise that we find between the ellipsis points of "to be . . . or not to be."

1 THE PERSON BECOMES THE ACTOR, WHO BECOMES THE CHARACTER

As mentioned above, a person (not yet an actor, not yet a character) dressed in tights and a leotard sits on a white wooden kitchen chair, downstage left, facing upstage. He (a woman could just as easily play the role) is simply himself, having "slept well or poorly, having had a good breakfast or not," as Decroux said. He begins shifting his weight forward, and as he stands on his right foot he swings his left foot forward and walks two or three steps, stopping with heels together and feet slightly turned out. As right heel touches left ankle, the impact creates a current that passes through the body, straightening it, changing him from Person into Actor.

No longer himself, but now an Actor, he walks upstage three steps (a gliding, idealized walk which took months to learn), turns an eighth of a turn toward the back corner, takes another step, and then shifts again one quarter of a turn toward the front corner. While remaining standing, he "wilts" and his center of gravity falls backward, then surges forward again and moves directly front to center stage. These forward surges and relaxations backward, microcosmic portraits of the actor's giving in to, and then overcoming, inertia and fatigue, prepare him, somewhat reluctantly, to assume the role.

Opening an imaginary drapery and passing through, our performer completes the transformation from Actor to Character. An observer might not recognize this gesture as opening a curtain – in fact, spectators need not divine the concrete basis of this or any subsequent gestures in *The Carpenter*, no matter how clearly based on reality. Whereas a pantomime offering indecipherable gestures disappoints his audience members, hungry for plot, Decroux's goal remained evocation rather than depiction. Indeed, he often asked his handpicked spectators to forget the "what" in order to enjoy the "how." As a modernist, Decroux intended to lure his viewers into an alternate reality where laws of design and of poetry, rather than physical laws, held the upper hand, and where, as in Cubist and Surrealist paintings, one might see inside a woman's head or fly over the moon for the sheer beauty of movement for movement's sake. This was perhaps why, Decroux noticed, the "first people to have understood our art were visual artists and musicians" (Decroux 2001: 31).

As if entering from another world, hands part this invisible curtain followed by a staccato one-two step forward into relevé. His magnetized heels then pull toward the earth. He resists this powerful downward pull by an upward surge of energy through the vertebrae, which allows his descent to proceed gradually, slowly. Snapping (sternum "tocs" upward, heels draw down precipitously) to a vibrant verticality, he becomes, in that instant, the Carpenter. His hands grasp and hold the invisible plane, in resonance from the shock of feet sucked to the ground, rearrange themselves: he becomes the Character only as he undertakes the Character's work. (I am providing only an abbreviated description, as the level of detail in the choreography, every bit of which contributes to the magical effect of the whole, becomes tedious, trying the patience of writer and reader alike, when translated into words.)

2 THE PLANE

The Carpenter, now downstage center, planes an imaginary plank of wood using an old-fashioned tool: a rectangular wooden box, containing a sharpened blade, adjusted to protrude at just the desired angle from the box's bottom, to control the amount of wood shaved during each pass. The Carpenter's whole body simplifies and amplifies the gesture, revealing the importance of counterweights – only the entire being can realize the work, as the hands and arms lack strength to do so on their own.

In planing the wood, the head and chest enter into a left/left/front design (bust rotated left, inclined left, inclined forward). When the actual gesture of planing begins an imaginary plumb line (attached to the point between the actor's legs) moves forward to traverse the left ankle. If the plumb line falls short of the ankle, no real physical work seems to have taken place. One finds this engaged attitude, forward gravity, in classical sculpture and in the activities of manual laborers. As the Carpenter prepares to plane, he performs a movement from the Corporeal Mime technical repertoire that Decroux called "jumping to fall on the head", in which the body gathers downward momentum that is then converted by the wooden plank into horizontal energy, providing the main force enabling the planing. He labors, first in profile to the audience as if emerging from the surface of a medallion and later, body facing the audience, as he planes a different part of the wooden plank.

Then, the plane blade catches on a knothole. This catching (like other bits of resistance we see later, such as the reluctant opening of a rusty compass, the stuck jar lid, the gouge encountering a knothole) adds an element of surprise and provides the equivalent of a "plot twist."

Twice, the Carpenter empties the plane of wood shavings, his hands and arms miming their airborne curlicue trajectory that unfurls lines of force through space. The first time, the long, fat wood shavings curve voluminously, while, in the second, one long delicate wood strand creates mimetic correspondences in the worker's body as he digs it from the plane's body to drop it to the floor. Then, in a surprising sequence of conical inclinations and rotations of the whole body, the Carpenter – holding the plane in his left hand – maneuvers around the workbench and caresses the wood to determine its degree of smoothness.

3 THE DRILL

This old drill, vastly different from electric ones used today, has two wooden "eggs," one for each hand, moving in opposition. This contrary movement serves first to drill into the wood, and then, with a change of direction, to unscrew the drill bit from the plank. These circular movements of hands and arms guide the tool's trajectory, while the whole body weight, as if suspended from a point one inch below the navel, provides the counterweight in a "jumping for falling on the head" required to pierce the wood with the steel bit.

4 THE COMPASS

Decroux's metal compass – not one for drawing but, rather, for engraving – has two sharp points that carve into the surface of the wood. The Carpenter finds the compass on his workbench. The search requires that his body twist into triple designs, the arm and bust alternating causalities. With a bit of juggling, he throws the compass into the air and catches it, then opens it. (Decroux often observed the juggling that workmen perform in handling their tools; or barmen, in mixing drinks.) An old rusty tool, the compass resists the Carpenter's first efforts to open it, this resistance adding to the drama. The Carpenter implants the two points into the surface of the plank, and proceeds to turn the compass inscribing a circle, the body making appropriate compensatory movements – carving horizontal curves into the space around him with the side-bending sweep of his ribcage. When he finishes the work, the Carpenter closes the compass, again juggles to transfer it from two hands to one, and replaces it on the surface of the workbench.

The real interest of this section, the composition of half-circles, involves turning the head (in triple design) against bust (usually in opposing triple designs), hands and arms working in complex causalities with the bust, a formidable interplay of fixed and moving points. The machine-like precision with which the Carpenter works in this section contrasts with other more poetic sections, or with transitions that show his fatigue, his joy, or his reverie.

5 THE JAR AND SCREWDRIVER

Above the Carpenter's worktable, a shelf supports a glass jar with a metal screw-on top. In a series of right-angled lines, the Carpenter reaches up, removes the jar from the shelf, lowers it to the center of his body (where most work activity occurs, Decroux remarked, as if we had only one arm and hand, coming from the body's center). The Carpenter then unscrews the jar lid with some difficulty, as it is stuck. This brief moment of resistance (an important word in mime) forces the Carpenter to alter his dynamo-rhythm. He places the freed lid back on the high shelf, retracing with his hand the linear right-angled path.

His fluttering fingers look for and, after several seconds of suspense, find just the right-sized screw that he carefully extracts from the jar, then swiftly replaces the jar on the wooden shelf. He picks up a small hammer, and with one deft blow, plants the screw vertically into the plank. Then, by gently skimming the tabletop (employing one of Decroux's oft-quoted maxims, "Do without looking, look without doing"), he searches for and eventually finds the screwdriver, which, as he leans forward, he lines up with the groove in the screw head. After several effortful turns, the wood yields to the screw's incising turns. These words don't begin to describe adequately the complex series of triple designs of the bust that either initiate or respond to movements in the hands and arms while making a simplified and amplified portrait of manual labor: a precariously far reach of the torso; a figure-eight swirl of the hands; fluttering of fingers in the hollow formed by a domed bust, to give just a few examples. Suddenly, the Carpenter imagines that he hears the Washerwoman calling from the house (he is in the workshop); one hand holds the screwdriver vertical as he turns the body away from that fixed point and, when he realizes that he has been mistaken (she has not called), he comes back to the workbench and to the last turn of the screwdriver. Once he has replaced the screwdriver into the box, an ensuing chain of causalities concludes one section and bridges into the next: the pencil. These few words describe what happens and a bit more of how; but the complex and unexpected trajectory, speed, and weight render the "what" musical, poetic, and cubistically shattered, hence probably unidentifiable to an average audience.

6 THE PENCIL

Now the Carpenter tentatively searches in his hair for a pencil, finding it behind his right ear. The dart-like diagonal movement of his hand and arm with which he removes the pencil, and the matching oppositional movement of his head and torso, set his whole body rocking side to side, like a cardboard cut-out (not unlike the quality of a finger's gesture that would set a pendulum in motion). When the rocking stops, he lowers the pencil along the central axis of the body. His right hand, now positioned at waist level, traces a figure eight on the board as the body responds in corresponding triple designs. To finish the design, the Carpenter pulls the pencil in a straight line, the body lunging to stage left, the free left hand and arm acting as a kind of barometer that describes the pressure of the work of the right hand and arm.

7 THE GOUGE

In a lively cubistic dance, the Carpenter takes a rectangular wooden box from the shelf above the worktable, moving it away from that surface, and then back. This displacement serves only to explore the possibilities of lateral motion, the body maintaining its shape, moving in advance of, or slower than, the box. The Carpenter pulls it along, or is pulled by it, exaggerating its weight to emphasize its significance as a "dancing partner." After reaching his hands into the box three times to search for the appropriate gouge (the Carpenter's fingertips respond to the sharpness of the various tools with "snail antennae" shock-resonance), he selects one, grasping it by its wooden handle. During rehearsal I once grasped the gouge in the box directly in front of me. Decroux questioned why I was taking it from the box, insisting instead that I seize it from *outside* the box, an inconvenient stretch away. "We are not slaves of realism!" he roared. In hindsight, I recognize that this inconvenient and illogical stretch created a beautifully demanding and daring movement, resulting in an unusual and risky forward-leaning attitude on relevé.

Now in a complex series of movements, the gouge shifting briskly from hand to hand, the Carpenter tests the sharpness of the blade. Using his whole body for leverage, the Carpenter sculpts the plank horizontally and vertically, encountering another knot (remember the one encountered in planing). His gouge rebounds three times. Changing tactics, he inserts the blade into the wood just below the knot and, twisting it, expels the knot, following it with eyes and head.

8 WIPING THE SWEAT FROM HIS BROW: REVERIE

Now the Carpenter wipes the sweat from his brow, and caresses (again, "doing without looking") the plank, in this moment that Decroux described as "retrospective reflection." Here the fatigued worker asks himself if he has done well what he set out to do. The nobility of manual labor and the Carpenter's intrinsically poetic nature appear simultaneously in this final sensitive contact between fingertips and wood. He has engaged a Promethean struggle with weight, resistance, and inertia, and has triumphed, at least for today. Tomorrow he will begin again.

Even in this cursory description of the "what" and the "how," we necessarily encounter Decroux's convictions and tastes:

1 The "how" is more important than the "what."
2 Manual labor is noble and ennobling.
3 The Carpenter is a poet, but one standing up and working in three dimensions, unlike the seated writer.
4 Counterweights mean something more than displacing heavy objects, but they must first do that accurately.
5 The abstract is the flower of the concrete.

The Washerwoman

Decroux first created *The Washing* in 1931; he did not call it *The Washerwoman* until 1973, when he added a woman's mask, gloves and a long-sleeved costume that included a little skirt, a kerchief over the head, and a padded bodice.

The Washerwoman: *the "what"*

1 Beginning. Testing the water. The Washerwoman begins by standing at stage center. In an opening protocol, she begins by testing the temperature of the water by touching it lightly with the fingertips of both hands.
2 Defining the washtub and washboard.
3 Lifting the bed sheet and placing it on to the washboard.
4 Grasping the soap and projecting it onto the sheet on the washboard. Soaping the sheet, and placing the soap back on the table.
5 Washing the sheet.
6 Scraping the sheet from the washboard, wringing it out, and placing it into a basket.
7 Emptying water from the tub.
8 Transition to stage right, and pumping fresh water into the tub.
9 Transition back to stage left, picking up the basket, and placing the sheet into the water.

10 Transition back to stage right. Rinsing the sheet.
11 Wringing out the sheet and carefully placing it onto a clothes line.
12 Transition to upstage left to find a dry sheet. Transition to downstage center for the ironing.
13 Ironing and folding the sheet.
14 Darning a hole in the sheet. Moment of retrospection.
15 Exit, drawn up to heaven.

The Washerwoman: *the "how"*

1 BEGINNING

The Washerwoman begins at stage center, facing the audience. Decroux called her first movements simply an "opening protocol," as they are completely abstract, seemingly designed to get the body moving gradually. In this sequence, the Washerwoman first inclines the bust to the right, a movement that unsticks the arms from their position along the sides of the body. The arms, responding to this unsticking movement, curve into parenthesis shapes, the fingertips sliding up the sides of the legs. Then the arms, abruptly moved by the bust snapping back into vertical position, project the arms on to the House Top (one of three possible levels for arms: the V, the Water Level, and the House Top). The forearms then drop, elbows remaining fixed, the hands becoming the motor, flinging themselves downward; when they hit their nadir, they rebound upward, pulling the arms with them, and finally pulling the bust as well into a right inclination with the hands together over the head. These abstract gestures now end, as the hands begin a trajectory downward, toward the tub of water, in order to test the water temperature. The two hands in "palette position," one in front of the other, lower slowly toward the water. When the fingers touch and pull backwards suddenly and sharply (a snail antennae causality, indicating that the water is hot), they separate, and when the Washerwoman flings the water droplets from her fingertips, the arms rebound upward. Again, they pass through some abstract (but very specifically designed) forms before lowering.

This whole sequence is a series of causalities, the arm movements causing bust movements, the bust movements causing the arm movements, the hands joining in this ballet of cause-and-effect, each movement varying dynamo-rhythm.

Considering it like a ballet or a wrestling match could help us imagine the movement. Instead of a stage full of dancers or a ring full of wrestlers, however, each body part becomes a separate dancer or fighter, provoking the movement of another by pushing or pulling, by slapping or responding to a blow.

2 THE WASHTUB AND THE WASHBOARD

As her hands lower, she defines the wooden tub, thumbs inside the tub and her hands outside. She traces the interior of the tub twice, her thumbs sticking on calcium residue around the interior water line. She now repeats the two-part circling, sticking on the same calcium deposits, this time with the whole hand inside the tub. Quick, small vibrations of the actor's biceps create this illusion of sticking on a rough surface. (These same vibratos can project the arm into space or, when the vibrato occurs in the buttock, can displace the leg.) Then her hands come to rest on the washboard, which she caresses using the same rhythm.

She now confirms the presence of the washboard, continuing the same rhythmic phrase. The small vibrations, which had indicated the calcium deposits along the inside of the tub's rim, now echo the washboard's small grooves.

3 LIFTING THE SHEET AND PLACING IT ON THE WASHBOARD

The Washerwoman, having worked until now in first position, in a surprising moment leans quickly from side to side, into second position with bent knees, her body opening laterally like a compass, the legs sticking into the floor like compass points. Using a counterweight known as "wool-carding machine" she lowers her body in a J shape to insert her weight between the sheet and the floor. Then, in order to project her weight onto the washboard, she uses a corresponding counterweight called "jumping for falling on the head" in triple design (right/right/back changing to left/left/forward). After she places the sheet on the washboard, she gives it two taps that provide a coda to the rhythmic phrase created by lifting and projecting. This challenging sequence combines two complex counterweights, in triple design, within a tight rhythmic phrase.

4 THE SOAP

The soap, a large square of *savon de Marseille*, rests on a low table, stage right of the tub. Using a combination of "doing away with the support" in the lower half of the body, and a large arm circle that provokes a right/right/forward bust design in the upper body, the Washerwoman leans over the soap. Her whole trunk curves to mirror the shape of her hand cupped around the soap. Then, as she tightens the body to mime the tightening of her hand around the soap in an attempt to lift it, she pulls the upper body toward stage left; the plumb line, which had cut the right ankle, now moves toward the left. The soap, however, remains firmly stuck to the table. This movement perfectly reflects Decroux's counterweight theories: the soap itself has almost no weight, and the Washerwoman can, in reality, move it easily without counterweights. However, this kind of movement – banal and without "drama" – Decroux preferred to heighten or amplify with the use of counterweights, imagining the soap as much heavier, and the Washerwoman much weaker, dramatizing the conflict between the two.

With a second effort, pulling again toward stage left, the soap at last un-sticks and the Washerwoman's body changes from a curve left (left/left/forward bust design) to a high left/right/forward bust design which, as the legs change under it, becomes a right/right/forward bust design, the body in a curve with the cord of the arc inclined to stage left. Here the Washerwoman, unable to guide the soap without this help, thrusts her right hip against her right elbow, projecting the soap – still in her hand – on a long upward diagonal. After moving in opposition to the body's forward bend, the soap, held in the palm, changes direction with a downward flip of the wrist at the top of its trajectory. The Washerwoman then lowers it slowly to the washboard, her body reestablishing its balance on two feet, facing front.

The Washerwoman now soaps the sheet.

Decroux uses all of the maneuvers with the soap in order to explore "lines of force" which, he explained, are trajectories that people, objects and events would follow if not limited by lack of strength or social pressures. For example, any event, like yawning or putting on a jacket, could take place in a restricted space (an elevator) or in an unrestricted space (a large garden). A shy person's desire to remain inconspicuous and discreet or, in the absence of spectators, an individual's lack of inhibition, would limit or free the movements according to the circumstances. In following a line of force, one might allow the gesture to attain an amplitude unknown in polite society, revealing a deeper truth that oftentimes remains unexpressed in quotidian life.

5 WASHING THE SHEET

The Washerwoman now inclines her entire body (Eiffel Tower) from left to right, vigorously propelling her right hand back and forth across the sheet on the diagonal washboard (the washboard here represented by the left hand in "palette" shape). This movement design stands out all the more in that the whole body remains stabilized against the sweeping metronomic arcs of the right forearm. As she continues her work, the forearm's movements accelerate while decreasing their range and further build to a crescendo with the addition of rapid-fire, staccato movements of the bust instigated by her discovery of a spot that she must scrub from the sheet. In the midst of this controlled kinesthetic frenzy, a curious thing happens. The Washerwoman stops abruptly, believing that the Carpenter is calling to her. Arching back into a right-leaning spiral, she reproduces the pattern similar to the one made by her husband, the Carpenter, at the moment that he too listened for his wife's call. This moment of "intertextuality" finished (she was mistaken; he had not called), she completes the sequence by removing the stain with short quick movements, returning then to her Eiffel Tower inclination to the left.

6 SCRAPING THE SHEET FROM THE WASHBOARD

The Washerwoman now scrapes the sheet from the washboard (using a hand design, appropriate for the maneuver: the Salamander), wrings it out, and tosses it into a wicker basket. The whole body participates in the wringing as the body wraps itself into a densely compacted sphere that squeezes out the last drops of moisture. Again, the Washerwoman uses her hips to project this tightly packed sheet into the basket. As the hips initiate the movement, the arms and the rest of the body follow sequentially. This tying and untying, tightening and loosening of the intermingled sheet-as-body, creates a strikingly curvilinear design, beautiful in its truthfulness to the action portrayed.

7 EMPTYING OUT THE TUB

The Washerwoman's previous gestures have propelled her to stage left. She now turns abruptly into profile, facing stage right. In one of the most spectacular counterweights of the piece, she drops down and fits both hands under the bottom of the massive, water-filled wooden tub. She then elevates one end of the tub far enough to allow her to change her symmetrical grip to an asymmetrical one. Continuing her struggle, she uses her pelvis again, this time as a prop for her left elbow in order to further raise the tub. With great effort, she succeeds in upending the tub, emptying the last drop of water. The last moments of the pouring out are accomplished in an arabesque *penché*, the supporting foot momentarily in *relevé*. By tipping the tub forward and emptying the water out, she rendered the tub progressively lighter and the lifting process less and less arduous. The tub now completely empty, the Washerwoman manages this still relatively heavy container with less agonizing effort. It has become, comparatively speaking, almost a toy. From a great height, she lets the weighty tub drop, then scoops her body quickly backward, arms flying up, to escape its fall.

8 TRANSITION TO STAGE RIGHT AND PUMPING FRESH WATER INTO THE TUB

The Washerwoman now circles halfway around the washtub from left to right, her bowed body reflecting the shape of the tub that she faces while circumnavigating it. Her feet slide in small, staccato movements, one heel knocking into and displacing the other in quick succession. She arrives on the other side of the tub, grasps the pump handle, and begins to lift and lower it. These initial movements, sometimes called "priming the pump," unstick the vertical pump handle and lift it abruptly upward; her arm and hand manifest the dry, wheezing gasps the pumping makes, until water eventually rises in the pipe. The subsequent movements flow more graciously as water pours from the spout. Once the tub has filled with water, she depresses the pump handle completely, expelling the last drop of water from the pipe, her rising left arm and hand imitating the water flowing from the spout. An actor who had never pumped water from a rusty iron pump might find it beneficial to do so as a preparation for this study.

9 TRANSITION BACK TO STAGE LEFT, PICKING UP THE BASKET, AND PLACING THE SHEET IN THE CLEAR WATER

After arriving at stage left, having retraced with small sliding steps the half-circle around the washtub, the Washerwoman must lean forward to pick up the basket. She accomplishes this by performing an *attitude penchée*, lifting the bent back leg higher and higher which tips her precariously further and further forward onto the bent front leg to grasp and lift the wicker basket to a braced position against her body. Here, but only from the viewpoint of nineteenth-century pantomime, the logic of the composition breaks down, since the laws governing Decroux's Corporeal Mime universe – this new paradigm – follow the requirements of accurate counterweights, of design and of rhythm rather than the literal depiction of an event: the Washerwoman removes several clumps of laundry from the basket despite having placed only one item into it – the tightly wrung sheet. Doubtless, this repetition adds rhythmic interest to the sequence. The whole upper body – head, neck, and chest – work together with the right arm and hand to form a large mechanical crane-like structure to close around the compacted spheres of wet cloth, to lift them, transport them, and drop them into the recently pumped water. The contraction of the upper body and right arm occurs against the immobile left arm and hand, holding the wicker basket balanced upon the left hip. She then takes the handle of the basket, braced against her left pelvis, into her right hand, and again passing through a precarious balance in *attitude*, lowers the now empty hamper to the ground.

10 TRANSITION BACK TO STAGE RIGHT AND RINSING THE CLOTHES

Returning the basket to the floor, she turns her body inside out and, facing the opposite direction, now reassumes the shape that will take her on the half-circle return trip around the upstage side of the curved washtub (see 8 above). Once there, and with a small percussive step, she jumps sharply into profile to rinse the sheet in the clear water. She uses two hands to submerge the cloth several times, inclining backward into a half-Eiffel as a counterweight; the sheet gradually becomes more fluid in the water, allowing her to shift her grasp of it to one hand, which she accomplishes by a quarter-turn of her body. Here an undulating movement, beginning with an alternation of tension and relaxation in the actor's right biceps, creates the illusion that the sheet is unfurling into the water. Then the actor, with the right hand, pulls the sheet through a trough created by the left.

11 WRINGING OUT THE SHEET AND PLACING IT ON THE CLOTHES LINE

She then begins to wring the sheet, and passes through a series of movements that often provoke laughter. Here the wet and flexible sheet for a few brief seconds becomes a rifle and the Washerwoman becomes a soldier standing at attention, performing choreographed maneuvers with the rifle. Next the Washerwoman opens the sheet and through an unexpected series of movements parallel to the audience and parallel to a clothesline which "appears" along the proscenium line, she projects the wet sheet on to the line and affixes it with clothespins.

12 TRANSITION TO UPSTAGE LEFT TO FIND A DRY SHEET

Now we imagine that a second sheet, which she had earlier hung on a different line, upstage, has dried. She turns upstage and there embraces the dried puffy sheet, removes the clothespins, and, turning downstage, unfurls it. As she manipulates the voluminous cloth, The Washerwoman's movements themselves become billowy, like the dry sheet on a warm breezy day. Allowing the air to catch under the sheet, she finally extends it on an ironing table.

13 IRONING AND FOLDING THE SHEETS

The Washerwoman uses the type of old-fashioned iron that one heats on a coal stove. She lifts the iron and approaches it cautiously toward the side of her face, testing the warmth by making a translation of the head toward the iron, then quickly pulling back in response to the heat as she confirms the temperature. Decroux named this movement "the snail antennae," because of its slow approach and sudden recoil. The whole body then engages in the counterweight of ironing by becoming a large iron. The action of pushing through the body serves as the pressure which, combined with heat, removes the wrinkles from the sheet. She irons first in one direction, then in another; between heavy, angular sequences, she lightly folds the sheet this way and that, scooping out the body to make room for the circular smoothing motion of the hand and sheet. She finally pulls it from the table as the whole body glides backward with smooth, practiced efficiency.

14 DARNING A HOLE IN THE SHEET – MOMENT OF RETROSPECTION

Now a darning egg – an egg-shaped wooden or ceramic support for cloth used while reweaving holes – appears in one hand, as does a large needle and thread in the other. The Washerwoman begins to darn the sheet. Never mind that it has been neatly folded on the table. Without reopening the sheet, she begins to reweave the fabric, first in one direction, and then at right angles. After four such cross-hatchings (performed to the rhythm of a section of *Swan Lake* playing in the actor's mind but not heard by the audience, the Washerwoman makes a step upstage (while still facing the audience) and begins a fifth stitch. This stitch, however, becomes much larger, the thread impossibly long, and carries the Washerwoman's body into designs that fully explore the lines of force that had remained latent during the first four stitches. Decroux said that in realistic theatre the longer one sews, the shorter the thread gets, while in his theatre the reverse can happen. At the end of the fifth stitch, the Washerwoman replaces the darning needle in her apron strap, and looks back over her morning's work.

15 EXIT AND "ASCENDING"

As she (still rather hesitatingly) walks on a long diagonal upstage left, the Washerwoman pauses, her body balloons forward and upward from the sternum, and seems to ascend into the clouds, having fully and beautifully accomplished her work.

Summary

These two works, certainly among the most unusual theatre pieces of the twentieth century, attempt to redefine theatre practice, as well as to implement a new art form. Their weighted, purposeful movements clearly employ a vocabulary derived from work rather than dance. They exist without written text, and in their first productions, Decroux, the actor-creator, performed them. In subsequent incarnations, Decroux as director taught the movements he had originally created for himself to successive generations of actors. Video documentation exists of first-generation performers Steven Wasson, Corinne Soum, and Thomas Leabhart.

Decroux at one time added Bach's Brandenburg Concerto No. 5 in B Major as a support for *The Carpenter*, and Ravel's *Bolero* for *The Washerwoman*. As, in both cases, the musical composition lasts longer than the mime performance, in a gesture that irks musicians, he simply faded out the music at the end of the mime piece. He insisted on what he called a "music of repetition" – one with a clearly defined rhythm (readily discernible in each of these compositions). However, Decroux wanted the actor himself to embody *irregular* rhythm – pause, weight, resistance, hesitation, and surprise – reflecting the movement of thought and work, and usually contrasting the regular rhythms of these two musical compositions, creating a tension between the audible and the visible.

For a filming in 1973, Decroux added white mask, hood, body suit, and gloves to completely conceal the actor, making him an archetype in both compositions – a kind of marionette. This costume for *The Washerwoman* included a headscarf, padded bodice, short white skirt, and a woman's mask.

Although these two early solo pieces represent only a small part of Decroux's impressive accomplishment of nearly one hundred works, they epitomize the highly technical and complex rhythmic approach that enthralled him throughout his career. Despite variation in length and in number of performers, all of his works had in common a challenging rigor for actor and audience alike. Comedy's notable absence from Decroux's work reflected his belief that an art must first be serious, and only later and secondarily permit itself to entertain. His *Mischievous Spirit* comes closest to comedy, in whose creation Maximilien Decroux claimed a strong hand, affirming that his father had no talent for staging comedy (Decroux 2001: 79). Decroux's work however, not ponderous or grave, could evoke laughter without a comic subject through surprising juxtapositions of movements and shapes, and their unforeseen combinations and dynamic qualities, creating a sense of delight by visually "tickling" the spectator. Freed from a desire to communicate the quotidian or a narrative in the conventional sense, Decroux mastered the absurdly incongruous in both movement and words.

Notes

1 One can easily imagine inclining or rotating the head, or some other part of the body. A translation of one part, however, requires the next lower part to incline: for example, as the head remains vertical and *translates* to the right, the neck will *incline* to the right.
2 "Re-establishment of two elements on the oblique" is a technical designation involving a series of movements that brings two aligned vertical elements, one on top of the other (two parts of the body, for example, the head and the neck, or the hand and the forearm) towards a new oblique alignment of the same two elements: (1) the upper element inclines so that the top of it comes to rest on an imaginary inclined plane running from the top of the top element – now inclined – down to the bottom of the bottom – still vertical – element; (2) as the lower, still vertical, element moves toward the diagonal line, the upper element joins it by decreasing its oblique angle as the lower element increases, to the same degree, its oblique angle. The two elements thus align with each other on the oblique that the upper element had previously only touched with the uppermost part. Or, two inclined elements can align onto the verticality, the top part of the top element, and the bottom part of the bottom element touching the vertical line at the inception of the movement.

Further reading

Alaniz, Leela. (2013) "The Dynamo-Rhythm of Etienne Decroux and His Successors," *Mime Journal* 24(2): 1–50. doi:10.5642/mimejournal.20132401.01.

Alaniz, Sirlei (2004) "La Notion de dynamo-rythme chez Etienne Decroux et ses successeurs," Mémoire, University of Paris 8.

Asselin, Jean. (2013) "Encyclopédie sur l'art du mime: Les Marches," *Omnibus*. 2017 December 2. www.mimeomnibus.qc.ca/encyclopedie/chapitre/chapitre-2-socle-agent-d-expression-et-transporteur-tronc.

Barba, Eugenio (1997) "The Hidden Master," *Words on Decroux II*, Claremont, CA: Mime Journal.

Barba, Eugenio, and Savarese, Nicola (eds.) (1991) *A Dictionary of Theatre Anthropology: The Secret Art of the Performer*, trans. Richard Fowler, New York: Routledge.

Barrault, Jean-Louis (1951) *Reflections on the Theatre*, trans. Barbara Wall, London: Rockliff.

——— (1972) *Souvenirs pour demain*, Paris: Seuil.
Barthes, Roland (1977) *Image, Music, Text*, trans. Stephen Heath, New York: Hill and Wang.
——— (1986) *A Barthes Reader*, New York: Hill and Wang.
Bellugue, Paul (1967) *À propos d'art, de forme et de movement*, Paris: Librairie Maloine.
Benhaïm, Guy (2003) "Etienne Decroux, ou la chronique d'un siècle," *Etienne Decroux, Mime Corporel*, ed. Patrick Pezin, Saint-Jean-de-Védas: L'Entretemps édition.
Bentley, Eric (1953) "The Purism of Etienne Decroux," *In Search of Theatre*, New York: Alfred A. Knopf.
Bogart, Anne (2001) *A Director Prepares*, New York: Routledge.
Cole, David (1977) *The Theatrical Event*, Middletown, CT: Wesleyan University Press.
Copeau, Jacques (1931) *Souvenirs du Vieux Colombier*, Paris: Les Nouvelle Editions Latines.
——— (1990) *Texts on Theatre*, ed. and trans. John Rudlin and Norman H. Paul, New York: Routledge.
——— (1991) *Journal 1916–1948*, vol. 2, ed. Claude Sicard, Paris: Seghers.
——— (2000) *Registres VI: L'Ecole du Vieux Colombier*, Paris: Gallimard.
Craig, Edward Gordon (2001) "At Last a Creator in the Theatre, from the Theatre," *An Etienne Decroux Album*, Claremont, CA: Mime Journal.
Decroux, Etienne (1942) "Copeau ne peut plus maîtriser le mime qu'il a déchainé," Unpublished Manuscript, Box 1 (No. 75), Fonds Decroux, Bibliothèque Nationale de France.
——— (1948) "De la personnalité d'Etienne Decroux," Unpublished Manuscript, Box 2 (No. 76), Fonds Decroux, Bibliothèque Nationale de France.
——— (1950) "Autobiographie d'Etienne Decroux," Unpublished Manuscript, Box 2 (No. 76), Fonds Decroux, Bibliothèque Nationale de France.
——— (1953) "Mai 1953," Unpublished Manuscript, Box 2 (No. 57), Fonds Decroux, Bibliothèque Nationale de France.
——— (1971) Inscription Dated October 25 in Henri Bergson's *Le Rire*.
——— (1972) Inscription Dated July 16 in *Paroles sur le mime*.
——— (1978) *Etienne Decroux 80th Birthday Issue*, Claremont, CA: Mime Journal.
——— (1985) *Words on Mime*, trans. Mark Piper, Claremont, CA: Mime Journal.
——— (2001) "Insulting the Audience," *An Etienne Decroux Album*, Claremont, CA: Mime Journal.
——— (2003) "L'Interview imaginaire," *Etienne Decroux, Mime Corporel*, ed. Patrick Pezin, Saint-Jean-de-Védas: L'Entretemps édition.
De Marinis, Marco (2015) *Etienne Decroux and His Theatre Laboratory*, New York: Routledge.
Dorcy, Jean (1945) Unidentified newspaper clipping, Fonds Decroux, Bibliothèque Nationale de France.
——— (1975) *The Mime*, New York: Robert Speller and Sons Ltd.
Epstein, Alvin, and Fried, Jonathan (2015) *Dressing Room Stories: The Making of an Artist*, Blurb.
Fogal, Dean (1993) "Etienne Decroux: Outside Paris Proper," *Words on Decroux*, Claremont, CA: Mime Journal.
——— (2017) *Email to Author*, 8 May.
Grotowski, Jerzy (1997a) "La 'Ligne organique' au théâtre et dans le rituel" ["The Organic Line in Theatre and Ritual"], at the Théâtre de l'Odeon – Paris, Villefranche-du-Périgord: Le livre qui parle, June 2.
——— (1997b) "La 'Ligne organique' au théâtre et dans le rituel" ["The Organic Line in Theatre and Ritual"], inaugural lecture at the Théâtre des Bouffes du Nord – Paris, Villefranche-du-Périgord: Le livre qui parle, March 24.
——— (2002) *Towards a Poor Theatre*, ed. Eugenio Barba, New York: Routledge.
Kusler, Barbara Anne (1974) "Jacques Copeau's Theatre School: L'Ecole du Vieux-Colombier, 1920–1929," Dissertation, University of Wisconsin.
Lalli, Gina (1993) "Amazing Moments with Etienne Decroux," *Words on Decroux*, Claremont, CA: Mime Journal.
Leabhart, Thomas (1997) "An Interview with Maximilien Decroux," *Words on Decroux 2*, Claremont, CA: Mime Journal.
Leabhart, Thomas, and Chamberlain, Franc (eds.) (2008) *The Etienne Decroux Sourcebook*, New York: Routledge.
Lecoq, Jacques (1983) Personal interview.
Lehmann, Hans-Thies (2006) *Postdramatic Theatre*, New York: Routledge.
Leigh, Barbara Kusler (1979) *Jacques Copeau's School for Actors*, Allendale, MI: Mime Journal.
Lorelle, Yves (1974) *L'Expression corporelle: du mime sacré au mime de théâtre*, Paris: la Renaissance du Livre.
Loui, Annie (2001) "An Interview with Mark Epstein," in *An Etienne Decroux Album*, Claremont, CA: Mime Journal.
Marceau, Marcel (1958) "The Language of the Heart," *Theatre Arts*, March, 58–70.

—— (1991) "Paroles pour un mime," *Télex-Danse* 38(June): 12.
Martinez, Ariane (2008) *La Pantomime théâtre en mineur 1880–1945*, Paris: Presses Sorbonne Nouvelle.
Mitchell, W. J. T. (1995) "Representation," *Critical Terms for Literary Study*, ed. Frank Lentricchia and Thomas McLaughlin, Chicago, IL: University of Chicago Press.
Murray, Simon (2003) *Jacques Lecoq*, London: Routledge.
Pinaud, Nicole (2003) "Le Minotaure," *Etienne Decroux, Mime Corporeal*, ed. Patrick Pezin, Saint-Jean-de-Védas: L'Entretemps édition.
Pronko, Leonard (1967) *Theatre East and West, Perspectives toward a Total Theatre*, Berkeley: University of California Press.
Rudlin, John (1986) *Jacques Copeau*, Cambridge: Cambridge University Press.
Saint-Denis, Michel (1982) *Training for the Theatre*, New York: Theatre Arts Books.
Shawn, Ted (1974) *Every Little Movement: A Book about François Delsarte*, New York: Dance Horizons.
Sklar, Deidre (1985) "Etienne Decroux's Promethean Mime," *The Drama Review* 29(4): 64–75.
Sklar, Deidre, and Cohen-Cruz, Jan (1993) "Chez Decroux Circa 1968," *Words on Decroux*, Claremont, CA: Mime Journal.
Slowiak, James, and Cuesta, Jairo (2007) *Jerzy Grotowski*, New York: Routledge.
Soum, Corinne (1999) "A Little History of a Great Transmission or Simplon's Tunnel," *Transmission*, Claremont, CA: Mime Journal.
Souriau, Paul (1983) *The Aesthetics of Movement*, trans. and ed. Manon Souriau, Amherst: University of Massachusetts Press.
Thody, Philip (1977) *Roland Barthes: A Conservative Estimate*, Chicago, IL: University of Chicago Press.
White, Hayden (1987) *The Content of the Form*, Baltimore, MD: Johns Hopkins University Press.
Wylie, Kathryn (1993) "The Body Politic of Corporeal Mime," *Words on Decroux*, Claremont, CA: Mime Journal.

9
OHNO (1906–2010) AND HIJIKATA (1928–1986)

Sondra Fraleigh and Tamah Nakamura

Note on names

For Japanese names we have chosen the Japanese convention of using the last name first. Thus Hijikata Tatsumi appears with the surname first and the personal name second. English language names retain the familiar form of first name followed by surname.

Butoh in its genesis has interesting ties to European dance, theater, and visual arts, as well as other cultural sources. Several aesthetic and literary movements having their origins in the nineteenth and early twentieth century are involved, such as surrealism, existentialism, and expressionism.

9.1 Butoh shapeshifters

Kaze Daruma: *the origins of butoh*

We begin with a definition: In Japan, a Daruma *is a limbless figure (or doll) weighted so that it bounces back when knocked over. It is a symbol of persistence leading to success.* Daruma *is also an abbreviation for* Bodhidharma, *a mythical Middle Eastern priest said to have carried Buddhist practice and teachings to China about 500 BC. From there, the teachings traveled to Korea in AD 372 and eventually to Japan. Prince Shōtoku proclaimed it the state religion of Japan in AD 594.*

In February of 1985, the night before the Tokyo *Butoh Festival 85* and one year before his death, Hijikata Tatsumi gave a lecture at Asahi Hall called *Kaze Daruma* (Wind Daruma), quoting an ancient Buddhist priest, Kyogai, and then telling stories of harsh winters in his homeland of Akita where *darumas* come rolling in the wind with their bones on fire. When the *Wind Daruma* stands at the door and goes into the parlor, "this is already *butoh*," Hijikata says. He remembers how as a child in the country of snow and mud he was made to eat pieces of half-burnt coal, which were supposed to cure him of "peevishness." Then he spoke about *Showa* the third [1928], the year of his birth and harbinger to war "when the Asian sky was gradually, eerily becoming overcast" (Hijikata 2000d: 74). The *Showa* period of Japanese history [1926–1988] coincides with Hijikata's life span [1928–1986]. The Japanese era designation indicating an emperor's life span started in 645, and is used in conjunction with the Christian calendar.

In his lifetime, Hijikata witnessed Japan's military build up preceding World War II and its post-war Westernization. He experienced Japan's defeat and drastic changes in political and social values – growing to extremes in the 1960s. No area of Japanese life was immune to the political shifts taking place around the world at this time. In 1968, the year of Hijikata's dance *Revolt of the Flesh*, Japanese youths, like those in America and Europe, took to the streets in unprecedented numbers. Hijikata's theatrical revolution, while not a declared movement of The New Left, nevertheless resembled the politics of public protest. Meanwhile, under American protectionism after the war, economic growth incomparable in world history placed Japan as one of the world's major economic powers.

This is the historical crucible that tested Hijikata and marked his butoh. During the war, he languished as a lonely adolescent in a house with a lot of empty rooms with his five older brothers off in the army (2000d: 73). He began his study of modern dance in 1946 during the difficult aftermath of occupation, as Japan recovered from near collapse with America's fire bombing of Tokyo claiming as many lives as the atomic bombs dropped on Hiroshima and Nagasaki; at least 300,000 were killed, and that many more were doomed. Hijikata would eventually originate a radically new form of dance theater, *Ankoku Butoh* (darkness dance), gestating in the early post-war era and finally coming to attention during the global upheavals and political riots of the 1960s. His dance, now known simply as *butoh* (dance step), flourished underground in Tokyo, and eventually resounded around the globe in dance, theater, visual art, and photography.

Rustic and contemporary, as Western as it is Eastern, the butoh legacy of Hijikata spans cultural divides. Honed from personal and inter-cultural resources, butoh mines identity, even as it reaches beyond its local beginnings. Retention of identity amid synthesis has been the Japanese way for centuries. Likewise, it is a butoh strategy – growing at first from Hijikata's dissatisfaction with Western ballet. He finally understood in the 1950s after studying ballet for several years that his own body was not suited to this Western form. He was not innately plastic and flowing in ballet, but rather bow-legged and tense. In time, he was to turn this liability into an asset, creating out of the well of his frustration; turning first to the Japan of his rural roots, Hijikata began to work with the givens of his own body.

He also developed an absurdist, surrealist philosophy that flaunted societal taboos. His first experiment in butoh, *Kinjiki*, performed for the Japanese Dance Association 'New Face Performance' in 1959 in Tokyo, was based on the homoerotic novel *Kinjiki* (Forbidden Colors) by Mishima Yukio (1951) and featured a chicken being squeezed between the legs of Ohno Yoshito, the very young son of Ohno Kazuo (b. 1906). The elder Ohno later became a butoh icon and one of the most treasured Japanese performers of the twentieth century. The stage was dark and the dance was short, but its sexual message shocked the All Japan Art Dance Association (the name was later changed to Japan Dance Association). Some accounts say Hijikata was expelled from the association over this dance, but in fact he voluntarily resigned along with Ohno and their friend Tsuda. Hijikata's early subversive themes were drawn from the writings of Jean Genet that he read in the mid-1950s – *The Thief's Journal* (1949) and *Our Lady of Flowers* (1944) – just translated into Japanese. He even performed for a while under the stage name of Hijikata Genet. In his one program note for *Kinjiki*, Hijikata says, "I studied under Ando Mitsuko, consider Ohno Kazuo a brother, and adore Saint Genet" (Hijikata 1959).

Goda Nario wrote of *Kinjiki*:

> It made those of us who watched it to the end shudder, but once the shudder passed through our bodies, it resulted in a refreshing sense of release. Perhaps there was a darkness concealed within our bodies similar to that found in *Forbidden Colors* and which therefore responded to it with a feeling of liberation.
>
> *(Goda 1983: unpaginated)*

Hijikata's work eventually gained audiences in the Tokyo avant-garde, as he drew inspiration from such diverse sources as the films of Kurosawa Akira – *Yoidore Tenshi* (The Drunken Angel) – and European surrealist writers.

Hijikata's butoh

In 1968, Hijikata choreographed one of his most quoted works – *Hijikata Tatsumi to nihon-jin: Nikutai no hanran* (Hijikata Tatsumi and the Japanese: Rebellion of the Body). This work, also known as *Revolt of the Flesh*, marks Hijikata's shamanistic descent to darkness and clearly establishes a new form of dance rooted in his memories of Tohoku, the rustic landscape of his childhood in a poor district of Japan. In *Revolt*, Hijikata casts spells as his body morphs through shocking juxtapositions, twitching trance-like in a G-string beside a dangling rabbit on a pole. He gyrates and provokes with a large strapped-on golden penis, dances in a dress, swings on a rope with white cloth trailing and wrapping his hips, then surrenders himself, Christ-like, in crucifixion. Over ten years on the fringes of Tokyo's postwar modernization, Hijikata creates a radically new form of Dance Theater, merging the universal spectacle of the naked human body, stooped postures of old people in his homeland, the pain of his childhood, and his distrust of Western ways as they enter Japan through the American occupation after World War II (see Fraleigh 2005: 328). "One thing for sure," he writes in 'To Prison' in 1961, "I will no longer be cheated by a bad check called democracy.... Is there any greater misery than entrusting a dream to a reality from which one will sometime have to wake?" (2000b: 43).

Butoh gained a following in Japan and internationally as Hijikata's repertoire and his collaborators expanded. Through his association with Ohno Kazuo and his female protégé, Ashikawa Yoko, butoh moved from a phallocentric aesthetic to a full spectrum dance form with permeable boundaries. In 1954 the young Hijikata began lifetime collaboration with Ohno who was already middle-aged and a leader of modern dance in Japan. Ohno had studied with Eguchi Takaya who in turn was a pupil of Mary Wigman in Dresden, Germany before World War II, but Ohno turned away from Western modern dance through his work with Hijikata. Through his world tours and generous nature, Ohno won international audiences while assimilating the other, dancing *Admiring La Argentina* in a flamenco style and French painter Monet's *Water Lilies* in an impressionist one. Ohno performed his poetic butoh around the world. Hijikata never left Japan (Fraleigh 2005: 328).

Ashikawa became the third founder of butoh through her work with Hijikata beginning in 1966. Exploring the watery soma of infancy and bodily discovery, she flowed through Hijikata's word imagery in poetic streams, pouring her body through Hijikata's profuse kinesthetic images – his *butoh-fu*. He numbered and classified these; thus, while butoh remains a poetic, intuitive form of theater, it also has structure through Hijikata's imagistic and verbal notation for motivating dance (see Stewart on structure of butoh, 1998: 45–48). Today there are continuing themes of butoh, reminders of Hijikata, scattered around the globe.

Nature, mud, and butoh morphology

Tsuchi kara umareta (I come from the mud).

Hijikata Tatsumi

Butoh can be traced to at least three major sources: Hijikata's memorial to mud and wind in his published speech '*Kaze Daruma*' outlines his somatic intimacy with nature, and casts butoh first as a unique type of performed ecological knowledge with agricultural roots. Secondly, Hijikata's development of butoh in the East/West atmosphere of Tokyo as it modernized after the war lends his dance political, cross-cultural, and urban juxtapositions (Fraleigh 2005: 327). Thirdly, Hijikata's butoh connects to the Japanese traditional arts, especially early Kabuki of the *Edo* period, in which social outcasts were believed to have special access to magic and the world of the dead. He often spoke of his desire to create a Tohoku Kabuki, reinstating the raw power of the bawdy beginnings of Kabuki while it was still a reactive art close to the folk and not yet cleaned-up for the West. White rice-powder painting of the face and body create ghostly appearances in butoh aesthetics as evolved in the work of Hijikata's disciples, subliminal reminders of the ghosts of Kabuki and Noh Theater, even though we know that Hijikata distanced himself from traditional and classical theater, both East and West. White faces and bodies link to Japan's traditional aesthetics, but in butoh these come paradoxically in the guise of darkness. Perhaps the best-known contemporary butoh company in this respect is the polished and popular Sankai Juku, grounded spiritually in the pre-history of the body, as conceived by choreographer Amagatsu Ushio.

Today's butoh dancers are still plastered with mud or offset with chalky white, as they were in Hijikata's day. The same bodies can also shine in glowing theatrical metamorphosis. Butoh can be plain and simple: still, slow, and stark. As Japan's most prominent performance export, butoh is deconstructive in its own way: "The body that becomes" is the ontic, metamorphic signature of butoh aesthetics, recently sustaining new permutations like MoBu – blending modern dance with butoh stylizations. Butoh's deconstructive tendencies can be wild in ways the West does not often associate with the East – free and uninhibited, nude and raw. Butoh can also be understated and smooth, cultivating small details of movement in facial expressions that move and melt sublimely (Ibid.: 337). The refractive imagery of butoh does not idealize nature, nor does it present human nature as such. Rather butoh dancers expose multiple natures as they become insects, or struggle to stand upright and pass through states of dissolution as in Hijikata's famous "Ash Pillar" process. As pillars of ash, dancers enter the paradox of themselves, struggling for presence while disintegrating.

Contradicting the balanced essence of ballet, butoh plies the excitement of being off-balance, and the psychic path of shaking and plodding. Its somatic subtly goes to hair-splitting extremes. Takeuchi Mika and Morita Itto who base their butoh therapy in the movement work of Noguchi Michizo teach that what you experience depends upon how well you discern "hair-splitting" minute differences. Characterized by subtle change, butoh is not one thing: Morphing faces, states of limbo and contradiction, mark its beautiful ugliness. A dance film made in the 1960s by Hosoe Eikoh featuring Hijikata and his wife Motofuji Akiko, *Heso to Genbaku* (Navel and Atomic Bomb) is an early example of butoh metamorphosis or "the body that becomes," also grasped in the irreconcilable poetics of Hijikata as "the nature that bleeds." Morphing, melting figures permeate butoh. Their meaning is not literal but ongoing and open to interpretation.

Although Hijikata disavowed religion, the irrational non-doing of Zen, deeply embedded in the quietude of Japan, is subtext in much butoh. In his final workshop, Hijikata encouraged students to disperse into "nothingness" – quite a Buddhist ruse. Kasai Akira, who danced with Hijikata in the formative years of butoh, states that surrealism and the theater of the absurd influenced Hijikata early in his career (Fraleigh 1999: 232). Hijikata's search for a Japanese identity resulted in surreal (or disorienting) aesthetic features of butoh techniques. The butoh aesthetic loops historically from Japan to the West, and goes back to Japan. More recently it reaches out internationally toward a "community body" of floating and gravitational powers in the work of Kasai (Ibid.: 247–249), while the *Jinen Butoh* of Takenouchi Atsushi approaches the aura of death chambers and the far-reaching effects of nuclear fallout – dancing on the killing fields of war.

Ohno (1906–2010) and Hijikata (1928–1986)

Butoh alchemy in global circulation

As their butoh grew through the latter part of the twentieth century, Hijikata and Ohno rejected the theater dance of their time, whether modern or traditional – American, European, or Japanese. It is possible, nevertheless, to trace butoh's influences back to the original expressionist "stew" of modern dance in the 1920s and 1930s, and to discern traditional Japanese aesthetics in butoh as well: from the theatrical flair of Kabuki and inscrutable slowness of Noh to the exaggerations of physique and stylized facial expressions in Ukiyo-e color prints. Butoh is based on individual experiment, the same faith in intuitively derived movement and improvisatory exploration that fueled the expressionist beginnings of modern dance. But butoh differs from earlier dance experiments through its inclusive return to Japanese folk roots, while at the same time exposing a postmodern jumble of cross-cultural currents, just as Tokyo itself meshes East and West in its post-war culture, and throughout Japan, one can find amazing aesthetic assimilation: ornate Chinese temples, Indian yoga, religious practices from around the world, European fashions, kimonos and Western business suits in the streets, expensive Swiss-like ski resorts with outdoor Japanese baths, American popular culture everywhere, Disneyland and Zen amidst the celebrations of Christmas (Fraleigh 2005: 327).

Hijikata and Ohno, studied with proponents of German Expressionism – as expressionist creativity probing a collective unconscious spread to Japan and other countries. Dalcroze Technique and German *Neue Tanz* were imported to Japan through Yamada Kosaku and sustained in the influential teaching of Ishii Baku. Eguchi Takaya who studied with Mary Wigman imported the creative experiments and developmental physical techniques of *Neue Tanz*. Eguchi's teaching spread two ways in Japan: toward the growth of lyric and dramatic modern dance through such contemporary artists as Kanai Fumie (who became his assistant), and also toward the more gestural and raw dance of butoh through Ohno and Hijikata. Ohno studied with Ishii in 1933 and Eguchi in 1936, and Hijikata first studied German-style modern dance as a young man in rural Akita under Masumura Katsuko, a student of Eguchi. Later he studied with Ando Mitsuko a disciple of Eguchi. Ohno and Hijikata met through Ando sometime between 1952 and 1954. Ohno's six page vita and biography notes his experience of seeing expressionist Harald Kreutzberg, a student of Wigman, dance in 1934; this inspired him to study with Eguchi and his wife, Miya Misako, who had studied with Wigman and returned to Japan to teach the new German dance.

Cultural assimilation was not a one-way street, however. Before Japanese dancers began to study the emerging modern dance abroad, the expressively stylized and much admired Japanese Ukiyo-e woodblock color prints were popular in America and Germany. Aesthetic exchange between Japan and the West developed from world trade and travel after Japan opened its doors to foreigners in 1868 at the end of the *Edo* period and fifteen generations of Tokugawa Shoguns during this period from about 1615 to 1868. *Edo* is the original name for modern Tokyo, and it also designates a period in Japan's history that brought peace – an end of internecine warfare and a flourishing of the arts under the authority of the shoguns. As the economic power of the bourgeoisie grew, it undermined the shogunate's artistic hegemony, leading to a sharing of cultural values and pluralism in the arts that transcended class in shaping a national identity (Guth 1996: 1–11, 168).

Ukiyo-e color prints, originating in the latter half of the seventeenth century and developing throughout the *Edo* period, had become wildly fashionable in Europe and the United States by the late nineteenth century and in the early twentieth century. Scholars and collectors became connoisseurs. The French impressionists Edouard Manet, Edgar Degas, Henri de Toulouse-Lautrec, Paul Gauguin, and American Mary Cassat shared an admiration of the Ukiyo-e woodcuts

(Ives 1974). Ukiyo-e included depictions of the "rough stuff" or dynamic *aragoto* acting style of the early Kabuki Theater that audiences in *Edo* found so appealing. Long before the emergence of stylized emotional dancing in German expressionism and butoh, Ukiyo-e displayed distorted and ferocious dancing figures in a kind of *aragoto* dance theater painting if you will. Ukiyo-e artist Torii Kiyonobu who began working in *Edo* in 1687 developed a stereotypical figural style depicting rough style *aragoto* actor-dancers with "legs shaped like inverted gourds and wriggling-worm contours" (Guth 1996: 100). Butoh, likewise, cultivates stooped and bow-legged postures, wild sweeps of movement, and wriggling contours. So much so that some of the first Japanese audiences for butoh, even though they could appreciate highly stylized traditional versions of bodily distortions, choreographed awkwardness, wrathful and pathetic figures in the Kabuki Theater, wondered why butoh dancers moved as if "crazy" or "handicapped." A friend of Hijikata's, the poet Yoshioka Minoru, wrote that Hijikata's inspiration for the 1972 series known as "Tohoku Kabuki," *Shiki no tame no nijushichiban*, came from *Nishiki-e*, multi-colored Ukiyo-e (Yoshioka 1987: 56–57).

Early expressionism in Germany also stylized raw expression and frenzied emotion, especially Wigman's *Witch Dance* of 1926, springing from features of Japanese and Javanese cultures. Wigman has described how easy it was to throw herself into fits of emotion in her improvisational work with Rudolph von Laban and in preparing her dances. At the same time, she emphasized the bond between form and expression in classes that Sondra Fraleigh took with her from 1965 through 1966. Wigman, a key teacher of early pioneers in Japanese modern dance, was herself influenced by Eastern aesthetics. Ernst Scheyer writes that in Dresden in the middle twenties Wigman's interest in the East was reinforced by her contact with the Dresden Ethnological Museum and with Felix Tikotin who exhibited his full collection of Oriental art in the Gallery Arnold in 1923. Victor Magito, a mask carver who had experimented with Japanese Noh masks, created the mask for Wigman's *Ceremonial Figure* in 1925 (Scheyer 1970: 20). Dance in the United States during the first decade of the twentieth century also incorporated the East – often through trite Oriental imitations in ballet, the interpretive dance of the Denishawn School, and Delsarte Orientalism. The dance world seemed intoxicated with exotic and Oriental stereotypes, especially the Ballets Russes.

Now, with butoh's international proliferation and renewals of expressionism through Pina Bausch and others, the expressionist origins of modern dance, once repressed by the American postmodern dance of the 1960s and the objective dance of Merce Cunningham, returns, but with a difference. Butoh presents special challenges in this regard. It is very expressive, but in a unique postmodern way. "The Hanging Body" (Laage 1993) with the dead weight of the head or limbs hanging from taut points of focus in the dancing gesture, and ghostly figures in surrealist costumes, white powder, gothic painting, or mixed message dressing, are aesthetic signatures in butoh. Cross-gender dressing, cross-cultural dressing, and use of music from around the globe attest butoh's postmodern eclecticism and East–West amalgamations.

Butoh dancers contrast these external complications with simple gestures of striving and longing, or minimize theatrical show with diminutive kinaesthetic awakenings that grow and quickly fade before maturing. Butoh techniques include blunt and wild motifs thrown into space, like Waguri Yukio's, or rhythmic gyrations of the torso that flail through the limbs, like Mikami Kayo's. At the other extreme, dancers may pause suddenly in silence and shift to embryonic floating, like Ohno Kazuo, or develop eternally slow and grounded walking, falling down lightly without making a sound, seeming empty, like Ashikawa Yoko. At times dancers like Kasai Akira incorporate technical dance movement from other forms. His butoh includes inspiration from the dance of Isadora Duncan and Mary Wigman, and he also uses eurythmy, a dance like form of body training founded by the mystic philosopher Rudolph Steiner in 1921 that he studied in Germany in 1979. Some current butoh dancers like Yamada Setsuko even incorporate the sheer lightness of ballet and the sculpting of modern dance in their butoh, blending these with the lowered center of gravity found in tai chi. (Fraleigh 1999 provides full descriptions of the works of the foregoing artists.) Indeed, butoh draws the witness into an emotional space through its reach into the dark soul. Still more, through its ability to transform negatives into positives, it empties a place in the mind for spiritual recognition. Butoh has an improvisatory basis, but it also cultivates structured choreography with a significant change from early expressionism. Ohno Kazuo states the difference: "As long as the body maintains an existence marked by social experience, it cannot express the soul with purity" (Viala and Sekine 1988: 94). Like characters in calligraphy, butoh characters are signs and transparencies. The butoh dancer's manner of shedding the social body is immediate.

Life in a speck of dust, dance in a drop of sweat: butoh has taken surprising directions. *I-ki*, Yoshioka Yumiko's butoh installation of 2003 in collaboration with Joachim Manger, is a daredevil escape from a labyrinth of plastic tubes. Wet with the sweat of dare, the dancer makes her way through the plastic, barely breathing, carrying a knife in her pocket (just in case): danger, dance, or game of suffocation? Yoshioka bases her work in Germany and performs in Europe, Canada, and the United States. Non-Japanese butoh artists also perform internationally. These include Su-En, aka Susanna Akerlund from Sweden who was given her butoh name by her teacher Ashikawa Yoko, and Ledoh, a dancer from Burma with his butoh company *Salt Farm* based in San Francisco. Circling back to Hijikata's influence, *Harupin-ha*, a dance company in Berkeley California formed by Tamano Koichi and his wife, Hiroko, has performed on world tours with the popular contemporary musician Kitaro. In Japan, Tamano's teacher Hijikata anointed him the "bow-legged Nijinsky." Recent Japanese butohists who perform internationally and hark back to Hijikata and Ohno for their inspiration are Katsura Kan, Endo Tadashi, and the all female company of Kawamoto Yuko.

Hijikata: a corpse standing desperately upright

Hijikata grew up in rural Tohoku in the rustic Akita prefecture of the northern region of Japan's main island of Honshu. He died of liver disease at the age of fifty-seven, having dedicated his life to dance. He had created not only a new form of dance, but also a wide circle of artistic associates with whom he enjoyed a lively social life, and he had inspired a generation of students who remained fiercely dedicated to him. Hijikata first became exposed to Western culture at age eighteen when he began studying *Neue Tanz*, the German dance movement that began early in the twentieth century with the work of Laban and Wigman among others. Eventually, he came into contact with Western surrealist literature and poetry and the techniques of classical ballet. Through his discontent with ballet, he began to search for his own style of expression. Mikami Kayo writes that Hijikata's development as an artist through modernization provides a prototype for the discontent of modern Japanese artists since the Meiji restoration of 1868, and the growing encroachment of Western values. She sees that Japanese artists have experienced two stages since then, first turning to the West for new models, then facing East, looking back into their own identity (1993: 38–40). In this regard Hijikata was no exception. He followed in the wake of many Japanese artists after the *Meiji* period, but an ancestral path marked his search for originality. Looking back, Hijikata embodied the pain of his childhood and connected with his Japanese heritage.

Japan was forced into the modern era in 1853 when Admiral Commodore Mathew C. Perry of the American Navy sailed into Tokyo's harbor and ordered Japan open to commerce. The *Meiji* era began in 1868 with Japan's new relationship to the world outside. Since 1945 and Japan's defeat by the United States in World War II, Westernization had accelerated. It reached a high point in the 1960s. This was also a time of struggle over the renewal of the US–Japan Security Treaty forged at the end of the war. Inevitably, the ways of the West were questioned in Japan. In the fields of theater and dance, artists sought to rescue the Japanese body from Western dualism. The Western effacement of the Japanese body is examined brilliantly by Noguchi Hiroyuki (2004) in 'The Idea of the Body in Japanese Culture and its Dismantlement'. It was in the 1960s that Hijikata reached a turning point; he questioned the West's logic, its split of body and spirit in refusal of the flesh. Thus his seminal work – *Revolt of the Flesh* (1968) – initiating *Ankoku Butoh* – darkness dance.

Yoneyama Kunio

Hijikata Tatsumi (born Yoneyama Kunio) was the sixth son and tenth child of eleven. His parents were farmers and owned a buckwheat noodle (*soba*) shop. Hijikata himself pointed out the relationship between his birthplace of Akita and *Ankoku Butoh* – his dance of utter darkness. In his speech '*Kaze Daruma*' (1985), he describes a link between butoh's signature physiology, shrinking arms and legs, and the physicality of people in the country. The folded-up legs of infants kept in rice preservers, Hijikata said, inspired his butoh. He used features such as bowlegs and muddy feet in rice fields to teach the physicality of butoh, which contrasts with the verticality of Western dance, and he created improvisational processes like the "Mold-Ambulation" and "Bug-Ambulation" from his memories of rural life. Butoh teacher and performer Yoshioka Yumiko believes Hijikata used his sense of place as a universal metaphor: "There is a Tohoku in England," he said, and "Northeast is everywhere" (Yoshioka, Interview in Fraleigh 1999: 245–246).

He also based his public image on his poor-farmer family background, but his father was in fact the son of a village mayor, and Hijikata sometimes wore Western clothes. While fortunate in some ways, he nevertheless writes in a 1969 article, 'From Being Jealous of a Dog's Vein', of childhood terrors and endless days of soggy rice crackers. No doubt the poverty surrounding Hijikata in pre-war Tohoku shaped his early development; as he often complained: "What Tohoku exports are horses, women, soldiers, and rice." In his '*Kaze Daruma*' speech of 1985, he talks of the disturbing feelings and movements of three-year-old babies as he observes them tied to posts and left alone in their farmhouses. They probably felt themselves to be *other* he says: "Their bodies were not their own. . . . What I learned from those toddlers has greatly influenced my body." He also speculates about the limitations of his own body as he speaks of babies placed in *izume*, a rice-warming basket, while their parents worked in the rice paddies. The children were tied down and "bawled endlessly" as Hijikata remembers: "In the damp open sky a gluttonous wind swallows the children's screams" (2000d: 74–78). Hijikata reflects on human symbiosis and remembrance of place. But we should also notice that his Tohoku is emblematic, a primal landscape of Japan that is now lost.

Studying Neue Tanz

In 1945 at the age of seventeen, Hijikata graduated from Akita Prefecture Technical High School and went to work for the Akita Steel Company. The next year he started taking lessons in *Neue Tanz*, the German modern dance movement, at the Masumura Katsuko Dance School in the lineage of Eguchi Takaya. (Eguchi and his wife Miya Misako, both from Tohoku region, studied with Wigman from 1931 to 1933, and returned as influential teachers of *Neue Tanz*.) Hijikata toured rural farming villages with his first teacher, Masumura, and eventually wrote in a 1960 article, 'Inner Material/Material', about the circumstances of his first dance studies:

> I became a disciple of a woman dance teacher in my hometown. I was fond of the phrase 'to become a disciple,' so I put on new underpants and went through the gate to the teacher's house. Because the term 'foreign dance,' however, makes me vaguely anxious, I hesitantly asked her what kind it was, while at the same time thinking I would just quit if it were not what I wanted. When she told me it was German dance, I immediately took steps to become a disciple. I figured that since Germany was hard, its dance too would be hard.
>
> (2000a: 36)

Hijikata was considerably affected by seeing the Hitler *Jugend* (Youth) marching during a tour of Japan. He found the blond boys in uniforms impressive, and feared his female schoolmates might be kidnapped by those grand and orderly young boys. Butoh scholar Kurihara Nanako says Hijikata gained the impression that "things German were impenetrable." She believes this contributed to his notion of male beauty as "a phallic fortress – stark, invincible, immediate, tense, stiff, bare, impenetrable, clear-cut, and acute" (Kurihara 1996: 61). Here we sense the climate of the pre-war military aesthetic in Japan and Europe seen in marching. It is all the more interesting then that as Hijikata's work developed his dancers moved so minimally. "They seemed rather to be protecting something vulnerable inside rather than attacking outward," Kurihara says. She reports that Hijikata desired to make his dancer into a "dreaming murder weapon" (Ibid.). His butoh eventually developed the tough militant outside or yang qualities of phallic male eroticism, countering this with a vulnerable liquid *yin* essence on the inside, leaving an eerie impression unlike anything seen in modern dance, except perhaps the controlled frenzy of Wigman's *Hexentanz* (Witch Dance 1926). Wearing a mask of her own face made by Japanese Noh mask maker Victor Magito, Wigman sat and turned in a hunched-over minimal pattern, pounding the floor percussively with her feet, while her hands morphed from tense claws to delicate flutters grazing the still mask.

Modern dance grew throughout the twentieth century as a discovery form of dance focusing on creative and personal resources in contrast to the stylizations of classical ballet. Ishii, Eguchi, and others who studied in Europe and America in the second and third decades of the twentieth century introduced it to Japan, as we saw. The mainstream modern dance in Japan before World War II was German Expressionism, or *Neue Tanz*: Sometimes termed "Poison Dance" because of its expressive extremes and inclusion of grotesque gestures. The liberating essence of this new dance sparked Hijikata's originality; admitting his body and pushing extremes, he overturned previous styles. In a country where community takes precedence over the individual, his breakthrough inventiveness is all the more amazing.

The drug of Ohno

During a visit to Tokyo in 1948–1949, the twenty-one-year-old Hijikata saw a dance recital given by Ohno Kazuo at *Kanda Kodo Kyoritsu* Hall that moved him profoundly. This was after Ohno's return home from nine years as a soldier in World War II, the last two years spent as a prisoner of war in New Guinea. In 'Inner Material/Material', Hijikata recalls his encounter with Ohno who later became his partner in the development of butoh:

> In the fall of 1948 in Tokyo, I saw a wonderful dance performance, overflowing with lyricism, by a man wearing a chemise. Cutting the air again and again with his chin, he

made a lasting impression on me. For years this drug dance stayed in my memory. That dance has now been transformed into a deadly poison, and one spoonful of it contains all that is needed to paralyze me.

(2000a: 36)

Ohno, who had studied with modern dancers Eguchi and Ishii early in his life, felt dissatisfied with the established style of dance expression in Japan, and was searching for his own style. He was forty-three by 1949, and just beginning to develop his dance career after the war; Hijikata later named Ohno's dance "Poison Dance."

Tokyo

In 1952, Hijikata moved to Tokyo to study dance at the age of twenty-four. He wanted to be a part of the urban art scene, but was in the beginning just a country boy with a quaint dialect adrift in a large city. In 1953 Hijikata entered the Ando Mitsuko Dance Institute. He and Ohno met through Ando. Under Ohno's influence, Hijikata also acquired various styles of Western dance including Spanish, jazz, and ballroom. He started associating with Tokyo's circle of artists as can be seen from his writing, 'Inner Material/Material'. "Rimbaud" was the password for the club. But romance with the fellows who liked Rimbaud gradually faded, as Hijikata admitted: "We welcomed the misery provided by alcohol. The club went downhill when someone who played with guns joined it" (2000a: 38).

In his early days in Tokyo, Hijikata copied the fashions he saw in Hollywood movies and wore his hair like his hero James Dean. He gradually assimilated city life through his association with artists and writers as well as prostitutes. His survival was difficult on the margins of Tokyo society. Although he is not explicit, his writings (ever difficult to decode) refer to trouble with the police in his early days in Tokyo. (In later life, he would operate a nightclub to make ends meet, where members of his company danced nude, and he once again had occasions to dodge the police.) As his work matured, Hijikata let his hair grow long, and achieved a guru status among his followers.

Hijikata's life in Tokyo in the 1950s revolved first around theater and dance; he also worked in a laundry, as a warehouse keeper and longshoreman, and at one time he lived in a flophouse. During this time he met a group of artists who would later become prominent figures of modern Japanese art – Kawara On, Shinohara Ushio, and the set designer Kanamori Kaoru. He spent time drinking sake with them, and talking about art and theater.

Meanwhile, Motofuji Akiko, an accomplished ballet dancer whom Hijikata later married, established her dance school between 1950 and 1952. This would later become Hijikata's Asbestos-kan (Asbestos Hall theater) school and butoh company. Hijikata's mother died in 1954 the same year that he and Ohno also appeared in their first joint performance *Crow* with the stage artist Okamoto Taro and choreography by Ando, their modern dance teacher.

New names

In 1958, a year before his first radical butoh, *Kinjiki* (1959), Yoneyama Kunio took the stage name of Hijikata Tatsumi. A year after this performance, Hijikata began to further formulate his subversive view of dance. His idea for his first recital DANCE EXPERIENCE *no kai* in July of 1960 arose when he realized that he could not accomplish his own dance in the image of the West. The works on this recital included *Hanatachi* (Flowers), *Shorijo* (Disposal Place), *Shushi* (Seeds), and *Diviinu sho* (Divine), which was a solo for Ohno Kazuo.

While associating with male prostitutes in Ueno-Kurumazaka, Hijikata came up with the idea expressed in 'Inner Material' that he would have to make dances from the material at hand: "I even dreamed of a dance about hair that as a matter of course examines a skinny belly." He thought seriously about "the art of impotence," he says in the same passage, "when a general image of life hit me with unbearable speed.... I was completely impotent. All my seeds were cut off. That was when the springs in my legs weakened in the 'dance of sterilization.' Swaying legs are now a technique of my dance. Violence of course had to hit me from without" (Hijikata 2000a: 39). One has the impression of layers upon layers in Hijikata's development of butoh. He finally rejects the "Tokyo spirit" which places the artist above everyone else under the name of art – a spirit without wound or bleeding. Against arts of capitalist production and the "Tokyo spirit," Hijikata casts his "Imitation Arts," "Impotent Arts," and "Terror Dance."

He married Motofuji in 1968 and took her last name, changing his legal name to Motofuji Kunio. This was the same year that he choreographed his signature work *Revolt of the Flesh* as harbinger to *Ankoku Butoh*. His last performance before beginning to choreograph extensively for others was *Summer Storm* in 1973; by then his work had matured considerably and he had established his dance company. In October of 1974, he choreographed *Ankoku butoh ebisuya ocho* (The Utter Darkness butoh Ocho at House of Ebisu) for the formal opening of Asbestos Hall Theater, named in dubious honor of Motofuji's father, whose business was selling asbestos (another kind of poison). *Ankoku* was taken from popular French movies at the time – the "film noir," which is *Ankoku Eiga* (Black Film) in Japanese. Hijikata named his new form of dance *Ankoku Butoh*.

Motofuji and Hijikata had two daughters; eventually she gave up her career to support his work and take care of their children, and in later years, she managed his nightclub. More recently, until her death in 2003, she and Hijikata's daughters oversaw the archives dedicated to his life and work. Meanwhile, she also became a butoh training master and officially the managing director of the Hijikata Tatsumi Memorial Asbestos Studio. It is increasingly clear that Motofuji is one of butoh's unsung heroes, initiating the endeavors of butoh with Hijikata, and also explaining them through her book *Together with Hijikata Tatsumi* (*Hijikata Tatsumi to tomo ni*) (1990). Among Hijikata and Motofuji's early dances together are *Roses for Emily* and *Aerial Garden*. After his death, she choreographed *Mandara* (1993), *A Letter to Abakanowicz* (1994), and *Heaven: We Walk on Eternity* (1997), combining butoh innovatively with ballet and *Neue Tanz* in a sweeping style of expression. Motofuji also directed *Theoria of Mirrors* in 1997 and performed together with Ohno Kazuo and Yoshito for the first time in thirty years, furthering possibilities of the butoh form. At her death, dancers held a memorial performance in honor of Motofuji.

Dancing life: Ohno Kazuo

> A fetus walked along a snow-covered path. It cleared a path by spreading its clothes upon the snow after removing them one by one as in a secret cosmic ceremony. Then it peeled off its skin and laid that upon the path. A whirlwind of snow surrounded it, but the fetus continued, wrapped in this whirlwind. The white bones danced, enveloped by an immaculate cloak. This dance of the fetus, which moved along as if carried by the whirlwind of snow, seemed to be transparent.
>
> (Ohno Kazuo in Holborn 1987: 36)

As aesthetic associates, Hijikata and Ohno represent two opposites of a yin/yang magnetic polarity. While Hijikata celebrates the negative in his themes of death and sacrifice, in ugly beauty, and in mud, Ohno also spirals downward, but with a fluid spirituality. For Ohno, the sacred is dynamic and organic, belonging to the embryo in the mother's womb, and to the dance, just as his classes often revolve around spiritual matters. Ohno was already a mature and skillful modern dancer when the young Hijikata saw him dance in a dress to lyrical poetry by the German poet Rilke: "flower, flower let's bloom – in the summer there will be a great harvest" (Ohno and Ohno 2004: 181). This would have been the first of five modern dance recitals Ohno performed in Tokyo between 1949 and 1959 (Chronology of Public Appearances, Ohno and Ohno 2004: 315). (Hijikata remembers the performance as 1948 in 'Inner Material/Material'.)

Ohno was born in Hakodate City, Hokkaido, in 1906. Upon graduation from the Japan Athletic College, he began working as a physical education teacher at *Kanto Gakuin* High School, a private Christian school for girls in Yokohama. After seeing a performance in 1928 by the Spanish dancer Antonia Mercé known as La Argentina, he was so impressed that he decided to dedicate his life to dance. He began training with two of Japan's modern dance pioneers, Ishii Baku and Eguchi Takaya. His interest in this period was in modern expressionist dance. Ohno's conversion to Christianity was a major influence in his life and on his dances with their recurring themes of life, death, and rebirth. Even before being drafted into the military, he converted to and became a follower of the Baptist faith influenced by Sakata Tasuke, the principal of *Kanto Gakuin* High School where he first taught (Ohno and Ohno 2004: 112–114). "When I became a Christian in 1930," he says, "I expected some significant change in my life, but nothing happened. It takes time to understand and incarnate an idea." Ohno appears to have thought deeply into Christian issues, for instance the concept of judgment: "I have thought, why did Judas hang himself even though he was forgiven?" (Slater 1986: 7–8).

Equally important were his beliefs as a non-church pacifist, nearly a decade of experiences in World War II, and the influence of his mother and other defining women in his life. Such motivating forces were portrayed in his dances – *Jellyfish Dance* (1949), *Admiring La Argentina* (1977), and *My Mother* (1981). Ohno's accounts of the war are fragmented, but this is what we do know. In 1938 he was called up for military service and spent the following nine years in active service in China and New Guinea; his final two years in the military were spent as a prisoner of war in the jungles of New Guinea. Out of eight thousand prisoners he was among the two thousand few who survived. Ohno rarely talks about the war, except when he speaks generally in his workshops about how "many people die in wars to serve the living," and that we who survive carry the dead within our bodies. For himself, he says: "I carry all the dead with me" (Fraleigh 1999: 57). Yoshito feels his father's experiences as a soldier must have been horrifying, and he thinks that Ohno "talks" about his experiences through his dances. *Jellyfish Dance* in 1949, his first public performance after returning home in 1946, is thought to depict the burials at sea he witnessed on the crowded ship carrying repatriated prisoners of war home to Japan (Ohno and Ohno 2004: 85, 110).

Yoshito provides us with an account of his father through the eyes of a son who practiced and danced with him from a young age, first performing under his father's watchful eye in Hijikata's very controversial *Kinjiki* when he was just twenty. In a video production of Ohno's life, *96 Years Old: Lifelong Butohist, Dancing in My Hometown*, one sees the complete dedication and respect that Yoshito has toward his father in his old age, and how he so tenderly takes care of him (ETV 2003). Ohno gets constant attention and love from his wife and family, especially his son and dancing partner, and he continues to participate in dance by being present in the classes that Yoshito teaches in their now famous Yokohama studio carrying on his father's work. Students acknowledge Ohno as they bask in his presence, and sometimes he performs for them in his wheelchair. Ohno is seen performing in *Hakodate tokubetsu koen: Waga haha no oshie tamaishi uta* (Special Performance in Hakodate: The Song My Mother Taught Me); Yoshito wheels him up the aisle where a full house greets him, then onto the stage where he continues to live through the sensitive gestures of his spontaneous dance. Audiences are certainly aware that Ohno will reach his 100th birthday in 2006, and they celebrate every movement as golden.

Ohno and Yoshito have been father-son dance partners for over forty years. Their first joint performance was in *The Old Man and the Sea* in 1959 at Ohno's fifth recital. They complement each other in this work, as the younger Ohno's minimal slow movement diagonally across the stage grounds the space–time frame of the scene, while the older Ohno flies around in waltzes and expressive gestures processing body–time. This is the same partnering technique still used in *Suiren* (Water Lilies) in 1987. Ohno bases this dance on Monet's painting of the same name with Yoshito appearing as a tense, blocky masculine figure in the first scene, against his father's soft delicate dance with a parasol, both figures in transit to later images as Yoshito becomes the lily (the lotus goddess) and Ohno mimes and dances freely in a black suit. The audience senses a mutual respect and symbiosis between them. Yoshito – an unassuming butoh hero from the very beginning – is a constant assistant and collaborator in the work of his father and Hijikata.

Ohno's life is dance and performance. In his quiet way, he is always "on." Yoshito says that the father he knows on stage is more of a real father than in day-to-day life, showing great love and emotion that he rarely expresses openly when not performing. His dances in the early years before collaboration with Hijikata were about life (*sei*), expressing the feeling of someone who is full of life. "Life comes from the mother," Ohno says in his workshops: "Go back to the womb and feel how your embryo self moves" (Ohno in Fraleigh 2004: 255). For Ohno, dance takes shape only if there is spiritual content, and form is a flowing expression of body that projects "the inner voice" (Ohno and Ohno 2004: 18). Ohno's very expressive face and extremely large hands rivet audiences. His inner world unfolds through an expressive use of the mouth, what he thinks of as "the eyes of the body," the listening ears of the soul, and even the back of the body felt by the audience – as we see in a chapter of Yoshito's book that describes his father's dance methods (Ohno and Ohno 2004: 9–40). Bearing humanity with him, Ohno falls off his feet into another boundless world that takes the audience beyond the floor to a limitless universe (Ohno and Ohno 2004: 41).

Born to dance

> I simply received all things that moved me as they were, and I try to pass them to you.
> (*Ohno Kazuo in Slater 1986: 7*)

Hijikata's anti-social courage gave birth to the theater dance movement that he called Ankoku Butoh. However, it was Hijikata and Ohno's interactive collaborations that projected butoh into a living dance genre. Hijikata admired Ohno, and even when directing Ohno's dances treated him with fatherly respect. Ohno's theater performances, never simply for show, were always genuine, as thousands experienced through his international tours. One day, at the apartment of dancers Eiko and Koma in New York City, he responded to Richard Schechner's question about how he cools down after a particularly moving performance:

OHNO: Me, I never cool down. A good performance is like going to a doctor and getting good medicine. I feel great.
KOMA: Actually, I think he is always excited like this.
OHNO: At the age of nearly 80, there is no more "stage" and "daily life."
EIKO: He doesn't commute.

(*Schechner 1986: 169*)

In being himself, albeit through the guise of amazing theatricality, Ohno often leaves audiences in tears. His extraordinary physical gifts and gentle mind, as also his childlike innocence in improvisation, move them deeply. Gestating over long periods and appealing to multinational audiences, his panoramic dances are never arbitrary. Ohno carried his vision of the flamenco dancer La Argentina with him for fifty years before he danced in her memory. The vision returned, he said, now and again: "But no matter if I called her or cried for her, she never appeared in front of me again, though she hid deep in my soul" (Ohno in Holborn 1987: 38). Hijikata carried his dead sister inside his body: A Flamenco dancer possessed Ohno. What a pair!

Ohno was born to dance, and also a superb actor, able to excavate great depths of emotion through his agile body and compassionate facial expressions. On the historical world stage, he can be compared with Isadora Duncan through the generous spirit of his dance and his power to move audiences. In *Suiren* (Water Lilies), there is a sense of pathos that follows in the wake of Ohno's motions, traces of body memory as he trades his body for ours, dancing sometimes as an old woman, and at others like a lithe Fred Astaire (without the taps). Ohno doesn't show emotion nearly so much as he becomes it, with pain and love pervading every gesture, no matter what the theme of the dance.

Yoshito says that when his father isn't dancing he gets bored, but let someone ask him to dance, or even mention it, and Ohno comes to life. Likewise as a teacher in his studio in Yokohama, Ohno is alive to the moment, mischievous sometimes, and a chameleon; he is butoh morphology personified. But Ohno is more than butoh; he is himself, always. This is clear in his approach to dance when he speaks of his work *Admiring La Argentina*, voicing his admiration for the real Argentina:

> The dance of La Argentina invited people to a sea of excitement. She embodied dance, literature, music, and art, and furthermore she represented love and pain in real life. She would have said, 'It was not my art that moved people. I simply received all things that moved me as they were, and I try to pass them to you. I am simply a servant conveying these things to you'.
>
> *(Ohno in Holborn 1987: 38)*

The very sensitive Ohno, a Christian pacifist, experienced serious pain through his forced participation in the war. Hijikata recognized something of this in Ohno when he saw him dance, sensing his connection with an inner resource he himself was trying to release, though perhaps not so transparently as Ohno. Like the Greek satyrs and comic actors with their harnessed-on exaggerated *phalloi* (Cahill 2003: 130, 134, 209), Hijikata, an enormous bronzed erection strapped to his body, belongs to the word of form; Ohno, who can break your heart with longing and hope for an unseen presence, belongs to the world of spirit. He and Hijikata eventually develop divergent philosophies of form in dance. Hijikata believes that "life catches up with form" so that when there is structure, content will naturally follow. Ohno, however, feels that "form comes by itself," if initially there is spiritual content (Ohno and Ohno 2004: 94). In his workshop words he says:

> Spirit comes first when you dance. When you walk, do you think about your feet? There isn't anyone who thinks about their feet. When a mother calls to her child, 'Come here,' the child responds, 'Mother.' Life is always like that. It doesn't remain still.
>
> *(Ohno 1997: 83)*

To cast the chemistry of their partnership widely from East to West: Ohno, "the poison dancer" by Hijikata's account, delivers "the scorpion sting," an image that pre-Socratic Greek philosopher

Heraclitus uses for moments of recognition that break through the universal continuum of time. Ohno's acute expression of life is a "wake up call" that piques Hijikata's desire to arrest the forms of his pain. In an interview with Susan Klein, Ohno said that he and Hijikata had personalities on opposite ends of the spectrum (Klein 1988: 6). The polarized extremes of Ohno and Hijikata released the stunning energy that produced the original *Ankoku Butoh*.

Together and apart

Just prior to their 1960–1968 period of close collaboration in creating DANCE EXPERIENCE, both Hijikata and Ohno appeared in *Crow* choreographed by Ando at the Ando Mitsuko Dance Institute. It was 1954 and Hijikata's first public performance in Tokyo. Hijikata later served as stage director for Ohno's Fifth Modern Dance Recital in 1959. Ohno was attracted to Hijikata's experimental approach to dance. After Hijikata and Ohno started working closely together, Ohno's dance radically changed. His dances had been full of life (*sei*) but soon he began reflecting on the question of death (*shi*), which became the focus for his creative process.

Shi to sei (death and life) become the two prominent themes around which Ohno's performances evolve. In 1960, just one year after his first work *Kinjiki*, Hijikata choreographs *Diviinu sho* (Divine) for Ohno, a solo inspired by Divine the hero/ine of Genet's novel *Our Lady of the Flowers*. In the opening scene of *Divine* (Divine's Death), Ohno portrays the dying moments of an elderly male prostitute. In the second scene, "Rebirth as a Young Girl," a different person is born in the place where the prostitute died. Ohno recalls his early collaborative encounters with Hijikata as the time he came face to face with his soul, dancing *Divine*:

> This was my first encounter with Genet, my encounter with Hijikata, my encounter with myself. My dance encounter is with Mankind, an encounter with Life.
> *(Ohno in Viala and Sekine 1988: 26)*

The production of *Divine* marked the beginning of an intense working relationship between Ohno and Hijikata that lasted eight years. Then they parted company for about ten years from 1968 until 1977 when Hijikata again directed Ohno, this time in the performance of *Admiring La Argentina*, one of Ohno's signature works. Yoshito says the hiatus was not out of animosity, and that their work together naturally came to a close in this phase. Each of them went through a period of inner reflection. Hijikata's *Ankoku butoh-ha* group performed for the last time in 1966. Then he undertook a three-year groundbreaking project with photographer Hosoe Eikoh. Returning home to look for their common roots in Tohoku, Hijikata and Hosoe sought to capture the spirit of the *kamaitachi*, literally sickle-weasel, also referring to a cut on the skin caused by a mythical whirlwind that creates a vacuum of air. In this sharp illusive animal image, the photographer conjures the wounded dancer/magician of a forgotten past, seen not on stage but by local witnesses as a phantom flashing by. Hosoe, who had lived in northern Tohoku as a child, won the 1970 Ministry of Education Arts Encouragement Prize for *Kamaitachi* (1969), his book of photographs of Hijikata, immortalizing butoh in compelling outdoor portraits of the dancer in the rustic fields Tohoku. Since the late 1990s, Hosoe has been working on a book of photographs of Ohno.

Ohno went through an identity crisis filled with self-searching during this hiatus and could not perform in front of an audience. He starred in a series of films directed by Nagano Chiaki, called *The Trilogy of Mr O*: "The Portrait of Mr O" (1969), "Mandala of Mr O" (1971) and "Mr O's Book of the Dead" (1973). "Mandala of Mr O" echoes Ohno's voyage of self-discovery. The emotional turmoil in these films proved cathartic. Fascinated by such things as pig squalor and filth, Ohno incorporated the ugly underbelly of beauty in Nagano's films, thinking nothing of falling to the ground and sucking a sow's teat. He may never have gone back to dancing if he had not had time for exploration, synthesis, and healing. In a chance visit to an art gallery, he saw an abstract painting of geometrical curves painted on a zinc sheet by Nakanishi Natsuyuki that inspired him to make a dance dedicated to Antonia Mercé – a Spanish dancer born in 1890 in Buenos Aires and known as La Argentina. As a young man of about twenty-three, Ohno saw her dance at the Imperial Theater in Tokyo. "I could feel her presence," Ohno said on remembering her through the painting, "I could see her there dancing among those flowing curves." This inspiration brought him back to the stage in an intimate autobiographical dance, connecting his own life to Argentina's through the music of Ikeda Mitsuo's seven-member tango orchestra. (The tango was also one of the favored rhythms of *Neue Tanz*; Ohno had performed this Latin form in his studies with Miya and Eguchi who popularized the tango in Japan.) He dedicated his comeback performance to La Argentina's memory in *Admiring La Argentina* (1977). On a visit in 1980 to her grave in Neuilly, a suburb of Paris, Ohno wept and realized "the price she paid to live." He clung to her tombstone he says, "not wanting to leave her ... ever" (*Admiring La Argentina* program notes, trans. Barrett 1988).

Together again

Beginning with Hijikata's direction of *Admiring La Argentina*, Ohno became an even greater dancer in the decade in which he and Hijikata reconnected. The renaissance that Ohno experienced in his early seventies blossomed into a collaboration with Hijikata from 1977 to 1986 in which they choreographed dances that could be recreated on stage. This was a shift from their former experimental "Dance Experiences" (as they called them) that were ephemeral one-time performances created in the moment. Most of the dances that became part of Ohno's repertoire were from this late period of collaboration – with the younger Hijikata as director and the elder Ohno as dancer. Ohno sometimes spoke of his attraction to Hijikata's dance methods: "The most important thing that I received from Mr. Hijikata was the power and strength of eroticism; he could show that it was so exquisite, something so strong that people were afraid of it" (Ohno in Slater 1986: 8).

In his working relationship with Hijikata, Ohno also encountered death again, not so literally as he had in war, but in the dances of death that Hijikata created. It is far from surprising then that in Ohno's return to the stage after almost a decade of self-reflection he would choose once again to collaborate with the man who had brought him face to face with himself. Their dance, *The Dead Sea*, premiered at the *Tokyo Butoh Festival* in February 1985, and was to be the last collaboration of Ohno, Yoshito, and Hijikata. This was also the occasion of Hijikata's famous speech *Kaze Daruma*, declaring the childhood source of his butoh in the mud and wind of Tohoku, and just one year before his death.

Ohno's international stage

Ohno is butoh's ambassador:

> Butoh's best moment is the moment of extreme weariness when we make a supreme effort to overcome exhaustion. That reminds me of my show in Caracas. I was covered in sweat. My body had grown old and I was working like a rickety old car, but I was happy. Is that what we call wearing oneself out for glory?
>
> (Ohno Kazuo in Slater 1986: 8)

Ohno (1906–2010) and Hijikata (1928–1986)

Achieving world renown at the age of seventy-four, a time when most dancers have long since retired, Ohno became the leading international representative of butoh. While the 1985 *Tokyo Butoh Festival* introduced butoh to the mainstream in Japan, Ohno had already introduced it to the world outside. After Ohno premiered his comeback performance, *La Argentina Sho* (Admiring La Argentina) in 1977 in Japan, he performed this same work in 1980 at the *14th International Theatre Festival* in Nancy, France. Even though Sankai Juku and other butoh performers were part of the festival, as primogeniture, Ohno's performance represented butoh's introduction to the world stage. He continued his international tour at this time with performances in Strasbourg, London, Stuttgart, Paris and Stockholm. With Hijikata directing, he created two more major works, *My Mother* (1981) and *The Dead Sea* (1985) performed with Yoshito; both of these dances he subsequently performed abroad. Other repertoire works that follow include *Suiren* (Water Lilies 1987), *Ka Cho Fu Getsu* (Flowers and Birds, Wind and Moon 1990), *Oguri Hangan* (A White Lotus Blossom 1992), and *Terute Hime* (Princess Terute 1992). *Tendo Chido* (The Road in Heaven, The Road in Earth 1995) was initially presented in Indonesia. As one of the most significant international butoh performers, Ohno toured throughout Europe, North and South America, Australia and Asia. Well into old age, Ohno performed in Hong Kong, Korea, Singapore, Taiwan, Indonesia, France, Spain, Denmark, Poland, Canada and the United States.

Ohno's contribution to dance is recognized both in Japan and internationally as evidenced by his many public awards – signaling endeavors that go beyond the original reactive underground movement of butoh. Among his recognitions, Ohno earned the Dance Critic's Circle Award for his acclaimed performance of *La Argentina*, a cultural award from Kanagawa Prefecture in 1993, a cultural award from Yokohama city in 1998, the Michelangelo Antonioni Award for the Arts in 1999, and the Asahi Performing Arts Award in 2002.

Ohno is a bridge

> The body in butoh is already the universe dancing on the borders of life and death.
> *(Ohno Kazuo with Dopfer and Tangerding (in conversation) 1994: 55)*

Ohno's philosophy of dance is grounded in the belief that if we do not go beneath the surface of our everyday lives, then we cannot call what we are doing "dance." His ontological and spiritual concerns grounded in bodily experiences of birth, maturation, and death cross national and cultural boundaries. Such universals are not limited to time and place, even if their representation often is. Ohno embodies the image he dances, not so much symbolizing or representing it. Ever young and old, his body is by now marked and wrinkled by the human affections he communicates. Ohno's stage is the world, and he consciously draws other cultures into himself. His work *The Dead Sea* is inspired by themes of mortality spurred by an on-site visit, relaying his continuing theme of life and death in the mother:

> In the stark ecology of the desert there is an absolute relatedness of the rodent to the landscape. The rodent feeds on the dying landscape much like the fetus consumes the nourishment of the mother's body.
> *(Ohno in McGee 1986: 49)*

Because of Ohno's birth in the culturally rich port city of Hakodate, he is acquainted with foreign influences from a very young age. There he encounters the West through the American and British embassies. At home his mother creates an international ambience through her love of Western music, French cooking and literature. As the eldest boy and second child in a family of ten, Ohno, reputedly his mother's favorite, loves to listen to her read aloud the ghost stories of Lafcadio Hearn, a Western resident of Japan and writer of things Japanese in the late 1800s. We also know that Ohno first encounters dance styles through German expressionism and American modern dance. The butoh he finally exports from Japan has incorporated the multicultural scenes of his life, even as his dancing becomes increasingly more layered through his travels abroad. We see this cultural matrix in Ohno's costumes – from masculine tuxedos, to Victorian gowns, and antique Japanese kimonos; as also in one of his favorite encores, he prances to Elvis Presley's songs (or waves his arms to the music from his wheelchair), transporting audiences across time and space – from Japan's premier butohist to America's popular icon.

Ohno's global appeal is beyond the boundaries of race and gender as he assimilates the feminine and the cultural other. He is furthermore a bridge between modern dance and butoh, moving past them in the end. Nakamura Fumiaki (1993), a butoh critic in his conversation with Yoshito, helps us understand Ohno's dance as beyond modern, beyond butoh. Yoshito tells him about a conversation he had with Hijikata:

> When Hijikata asked me what I thought of my father's dance, I answered with certainty that his dance is *modaan dansu* (modern dance). Hijikata nodded in total agreement with me. Ohno Kazuo's dance doesn't have to be butoh. His dance cannot be called Japanese aging beauty or *wabi sabi*. Ohno Kazuo has to be lively forever. He has to be *modaan*.

This is not to say that Ohno's dance is within the frame of the existing modern dance, Nakamura cautions. He explains that Ohno has lived through the history of Japanese modern dance represented by Ishii Baku, Eguchi Takaya and Miya Misako. Ohno's body carries the history of Japanese modern and contemporary dance including the history of butoh. What Yoshito means by *modaan* is a free zone that is beyond the frame of existing dance genres:

> What Hijikata Tatsumi saw in Ohno Kazuo's body is *shigen* [natural resource], something he had never seen in any stage art but something he had seen in his own body. Hijikata called what he saw in Ohno Kazuo's body *Ankoku Butoh*.

Hijikata and Yoshito confirm that Ohno embodies the power of life, a vital *shigen* that all dances have internally. *Shigen* is like a vein of gold ore. Of course trinkets can be made from this, and gold can also be ornamental, but the essence that people see in Ohno's dance is pure gold, not artifice (Nakamura 1993: 32–33).

Butoh, community, and healing

The butoh that Hijikata and Ohno initiated proliferates, often in unpredicted ways, as it is studied and practiced around the globe. Writers focus on the historical, political, and economic conditions that provide the context for the emergence of butoh as a reactionary form (Klein 1988; Kurihara 1996). Butoh performances have been viewed as psychological expression of consciousness through improvisation rather than technical dance (Fisher 1987). Joan Laage, an American butoh dancer and scholar, studied the use and meaning of the body in the theatrical performance of butoh (Laage 1993). Sondra Fraleigh wrote a personal ethnology including accounts of experiences with butoh and Zen in Japan, which includes performance reviews from a philosophical perspective (Fraleigh 1999), and her book *Dancing Identity* examines butoh in context of World War II (Fraleigh 2004). Recent studies by butoh dancers explore butoh as a method of movement therapy (Kasai and Takeuchi 2001). In an ethnographic and sociological approach, Tamah Nakamura looks at butoh as a context for relationship and community building beyond the performance arena (Nakamura 2006).

Butoh performers have taken their own directions. Takenouchi Atsushi, working in the light of Hijikata and Ohno, but with his own personal stamp, uses nature as an overarching paradigm for his work, dancing outdoors in every corner of Japan, in Thailand, Cambodia, Europe, and in North and South America, circling the globe. Strongly influenced by Ohno Kazuo, Takenouchi sometimes moves by himself, dancing like a shaman to heal the earth where people have died in great masses. Like many other butoh artists today, he includes elderly people in the fabric of his dances, and especially integrates handicapped people (Takenouchi, Interview with Fraleigh, 2003). The seeds for this inclusiveness were certainly evident in Hijikata and Ohno. The values of communal life have been a butoh hallmark, even if sometimes cultish as with Hijikata and Ashikawa's early efforts to form dance companies in the image of family. Tanaka Min has experimented with communal living also, inviting dancers to live, dance, and work in the Japanese countryside at his *Body Weather Farm* in Hakushu, Yamanashi Prefecture.

The *Seiryukai* dance group in Fukuoka, Japan is establishing a new forum for butoh dancers to build a sustaining, healing community. Harada Nobuo organized Butoh *Seiryukai* in 1994. His former teacher, Kasai Akira, who danced with Hijikata, believes that butoh can heal what he calls "the community body" (Kasai Interview, in Fraleigh 1999). Kasai sees that butoh can renew the participant and the society through its relational essence. His butoh explorations increase self-awareness and connections between dancers. He teaches that dance can connect us to others and to the past, and that community is more important than individualism. Kasai says that we are not dancing truly if we are not dancing the community body. He reminds us that butoh is dance and not principally an ecological or political movement, but that it also includes all things in nature, not just the human community. The person grows within the community, and through rites that were once the province of magic, can dance toward healing (Ibid.). Harada's concept of "butoh for the people through community building" expands Kasai's view. Harada addresses the social issue of helping young people:

> Most of the young people don't come to dance. They come because they hear about butoh, or see a poster and think it looks different. They come searching for something different. The basic grounding and bonding of human energy used to be expressed through community festivals and other community events in which everyone participated. These events have changed focus so that a few perform while most watch. *Seiryukai* offers a space for a kind of community dance festival.
>
> (Harada Nobuo, Interview with Nakamura July 6, 2001)

Harada reminds us of the early impetus of butoh, dancing like a shaman in his workshops, inspiring magical transformations with his spirit, and not putting theater performance before the local development of community and dance. He is a good example of what Hijikata talked about when he said he never wanted butoh to become a commercial success. Harada has produced two notable works in this regard, *Hiraku* (Awakening) for children with Down's Syndrome and adults with psycho logical disorders, and *Keiko no kotoba* (Workshop Words) for the community at large. Developing butoh as therapy, Morita Itto, a butoh performer and practicing psychologist, and Takeuchi Mika, who performs with him, have opened a *Takeuchi Mika Butoh Institute* in Sapporo, Japan that offers butoh classes and stress reduction techniques through their Butoh Dance Therapy Method. In Göttingen, Germany, Endo Tadashi includes people with disabilities in his workshops, mainstreaming them with experienced dancers.

Butoh continues to diversify its means from performance to healing, from the Mexican ritual butoh of Diego Pignon to the evolutionary dance theater of *Sankai Juku*, architecting the pre-history of the body in sandy mystical tones. Probing the dark spot of consciousness, butoh foreshadows wounded healers, shifting shapes in perpetuity: from Hijikata's sacrificial *Ankoku Butoh* to Ohno's haiku poetry in dances that push the boundaries of birth and death. Hijikata's revival of surrealism is marked by profuse imagination, erotic, poetic, and non-rational subject matter, and by resistance to the notion of progress espoused by political and social forces of capitalist democracies. The dance legacy of Hijikata and Ohno is descendant in its general direction. In contrast to Western ballet with its upward ascent, butoh descends to what Hijikata called "the frog's position," drawing up human concerns for the preservation of community in all its diversity, and inspiring personal transformation. Ohno, who makes the whole world his friend, puts the descendant message of butoh this way: "We cannot turn away from the messy refuse of life" (Interview with Fraleigh 1986).

9.2 Dances of death, sacrifice, and spirit

Sacrifice is the source of all work and every dancer is an illegitimate child set free to experience that very quality.

(Hijikata Tatsumi, Inner Material/Material (2000a: 39))

Two butohists: why they dance the way they do

Japan, like many regions of Asia and the "melting pots" of the West, has developed diverse aesthetic and political/religious configurations, and in many cases has welcomed change. Hijikata himself, while decrying the Western colonization of Japan, used the creativity he garnered from German *Neue Tanz* and European surrealism to invent his "Body in Crisis." Theater dance in today's Japan is diverse, ranging from the traditions of Kabuki and Noh to Japanese development of Western ballet and modern dance – and still the continuing evolution of butoh. Dance critic Tachiki Akiko says that butoh often slides into the work of other new dance in Japan (Daiwa International Butoh Festival, London, 2005). So how do we know butoh when we see it in the twenty-first century, and does it still bear a relationship to butoh founders, Hijikata Tatsumi and Ohno Kazuo? Nakamura Fumiaki (1993) calls the current, new performers of butoh "butoh dancers" because they emphasize the beauty of butoh as choreographed performance. However, those who maintain the spirit of Hijikata and Ohno's butoh, Nakamura terms "butoh-ists."

Clearly, Hijikata and Ohno provide the term "butohist" its original meaning and restive force. From the very beginning, Hijikata and Ohno intrigue audiences as much as they baffle them. In several ways their butoh is like all dance in this regard. Dances don't tell stories, except in the tales of ballet and in narrative forms, and even then the stories are seldom literal or linear. Narrative in dance, as in the early modern dances of Martha Graham, is cast in metaphors and symbols that peak the body's deep responsiveness to kinetic images. To dance is to explore human consciousness through bodily means.

Hijikata and Ohno invert consciousness, however, sublimating the body while extending its liminal states, as we explore in analyzing five of their dances in this section. These men are not narrative or symbolist modern dancers; neither are they neutrally postmodern. As butohists, they move past modern categories altogether. One does not so much read their butoh works to find meaning there; rather, one enters into morphing states of awareness through the performances. There is a difference between metaphoric and metamorphic imagery; butoh does not ride on metaphor, but rather on change and an *ethos* of becoming. As the root word of ethics, *ethos*, points to a matrix of values, attitudes, habits, and beliefs. Here we refer to a cultural disposition that appreciates the ongoing nature of life and the life/death/life cycle, never-ending in solid form, because it comes from emptiness, itself not really empty, but in process of emptying and filling, like the process of breathing.

Meaning in butoh comes through one's *experience* of the dance, and not from deciphering a message or choreographic intent. Surely there is an element of subjective reflection in being an audience for any kind of dance, but Hijikata and Ohno are the first to proffer wholly experiential avenues for relating to dance. *Hijikata's offering comes in the form of sacrifice; Ohno's comes through reverence for life and the healing of trauma.* Hijikata dances his darkness, constructs his body of pain and absurdity, and the audience morphs through these aspects of themselves. As for Ohno, people feel better in his presence and through the spirituality of his performances. The audience for butoh is offered an experience of theater that is not distanced – filtered through centuries of movement styles and character development – as in Kabuki and Noh, or even Western ballet. As Japan's first butohists, Hijikata and Ohno circumvent the abstractions of modern dance and transcend the neutral pose of Western postmodernism.

Now students of dance have access to an experience of Hijikata's butoh through his *butoh-fu* (his notation) and can learn how to work with metamorphic imagery in a similar vein. Seeking a direct route to butoh experience, dancers and actors from around the world still come to Ohno's workshops in Yokohama, even as his son Yoshito now teaches them with Ohno approaching his 100th year and in a wheelchair. Some say they make the pilgrimage to Yokohama simply to be in Ohno's presence – as these authors learned through speaking with several of Ohno's students and in taking his workshops. (For Fraleigh's accounts of taking Ohno's workshops, see 1999: 57–64, 164–165).

Dance as experience: shedding the social body

Experience, as such, guides Hijikata and Ohno. They dance human experience in broad strokes as they connect to life and death. In their shapeshifting, they become other creatures and explore elements of nature, even as they poke holes in the political world stage they inhabit. It will become apparent, as we look into their dance works that they are searching for something underneath the human skin of society – Hijikata through his challenge of social conventions and connections to his childhood, and Ohno through his spiritual brand of depth psychology.

We do not examine their works for symbolic content and meaning, but rather for their personal, social, and political context, and their dark/light reversible structures. Hijikata's *Ankoku Butoh*, as initiated during the rebellious atmosphere of the 1960s, is admittedly political, and it can also be described as a globally oriented social movement. Emerging first in Japan through Hijikata's *Dance Experience Recitals*, as a criticism of Western culture and political dominance at a time of violent social protests against the Japan–US Security Treaty (AMPO: *Nichibei Anzen Hosho Joyaku*) and the Vietnam War, this early butoh is referred to as *gishiki* (ritual) in Japanese media reports of the time. The early butoh of Hijikata and Ohno can be interpreted on one level as an anti-social resistance movement effected through a deconstruction of the social body. Hijikata and Ohno were certainly aware of the social issues of their time and how the body is culturally conditioned or constructed. Their dance attempts to question, deconstruct, shed, or deform the body's cultural conditioning – to excavate experiences of the native human body, also called in butoh "the body that has not been robbed."

There are other interrelated perspectives on the body that are important in butoh. These come from the idea of representing the trauma of the war and its resulting social memory through the body (Igarashi 2000: 168–169) and from considering the performance of desire through "physical nostalgia" in an experimental form (Sas 1999: 176). Such readings of the butoh body through trauma and desire extend beyond those of violent rebellion, anti-social behavior, and bodily deconstruction. Butoh is not the product of a single event, nor can it be reasoned through a single social lens; it can be explained less reductively as a form of dance experience and a social movement emerging through two talented men in the opportune environment of creative freedom. Even as we focus on Hijikata and Ohno, it becomes increasingly clear that Ohno's son Yoshito, Waguri Yukio and three important women – Motofuji Akiko, Ashikawa Yoko and Nakajima Natsu – also contributed to the founding and perpetuation of butoh.

The presentation of the butoh body as a form of social rebellion converged with an aesthetic tendency toward Obsessional Art in 1960s Japan. Revivals of surrealism, neo-dadaism, expressionism, existentialism, post-war social upheaval, and demonstrations against American political and economic hegemony all played a part (Kuniyoshi 1990). Japanese art after World War II derived from action and developed around issues of the body and place. Physical and site-specific works examined the relationship of the appropriate body expression with the elements of place and environment (Osaki 1998; Munroe 1994). Like Jackson Pollock's modern art in America in which he threw paint on the canvas to get his body viscerally involved, the anti-social movement and art in Japan were action-oriented, placing importance on the temporal process of experience. Underground street theater or *Shogekijo* (Little Theater) developed at the same time in response to the perceived need for expression of social issues by and for the people. These itinerant groups performed in tents and small theaters in an attempt to recapture the popular entertainment of pre-canonized Noh and Kabuki Theater. Influential groups included *Aka Tento* – Red Tent, and *Jokyo Gekijo* – Situation Theater; *Tenjo Sajiki* – The Gallery; *Kuro Tento* – Black Tent and *Waseda Sho-gekijo* – *Waseda* Little Theater.

Thus, avant-garde art and theater opened a social gap for Hijikata to create a new form of "ethnic dance" through his *Ankoku Butoh*. Dance historian and butoh critic Kuniyoshi Kazuko sees that Hijikata's butoh stems from a concept of the body called *suijakutai*, literally "weakened body," or the body that you sense living in your body other than your present self (Kuniyoshi 2002: 64). Hijikata says that his dead sister lives inside his body, scratching away the darkness inside him when he dances (2000d: 77). For him *suijakutai* confirms the existence of the origin of self farthest from modernism (Kuniyoshi 2004a). New is not necessarily better; the movement of old people, introverted and slow tempos can all be beautiful. Western dance celebrates youth; while in contrast, Hijikata and Ohno reveal a full spectrum of human experience, not just the Japanese experience. Their dance figures are empathetic and openly affective, not perfect.

Challenging modernization

Hijikata wanted to create what he called Tohoku Kabuki, in restoring the original, local intent of Kabuki before the Westernization of Japan. The social context for the emergence of butoh through Hijikata and Ohno had its antecedent in the history of Kabuki, particularly the movement to reform Kabuki as the influence of the West expanded in the *Meiji* period beginning in 1868. With the aim of rejuvenating the Kabuki tradition, 'civilization and enlightenment' (*Bunmei Kaika*) became guiding principles for the theater reform movement in the early *Meiji* period (Tschudin 1999: 83). The establishment of the Ministry of Religious Affairs effectively placed all actors and entertainers in government service as teachers to educate the masses and to 'encourage virtue and chastise vice' (Tschudin 1999: 84). Kabuki gradually became monopolized and institutionalized by large corporations. European artistic techniques and radical political ideas produced actors who were no longer suited for the Kabuki stage. *Shingeki* (New Theater) was then created as a stage for expression of multinational theater ideas and by 1960 was dominant in Japanese modern theater (Lee 2002: 377).

The *Seinen Geijutsu Gekijo* (Youth Art Theater) was formed in 1959 when *Shingeki*, which was really Western-inspired theater serving a dominant text, itself became establishment theater, and could not respond to the perspectives of young people. One of the early underground dramatists, Kara Juro, leader of *Jokyo Gekijo* (Situation Theater), developed his group as a pre-modern Kabuki troupe of itinerant actors producing a bawdy vaudeville act (Goodman 1971: 163). Transcendence of the modern age was one of the concepts of contemporary Japanese theater out of which Hijikata's butoh was born. To challenge and revolutionize modernization, a new language was needed that recognized and shifted the fallacies of established policies and laws. Thus butoh was fundamentally political. As an example of one of the new aesthetic languages, butoh also exhibited characteristics of the original Kabuki's folk appeal as well as Kabuki's representation of the dark side of social life (Klein 1988: 16–18).

Butoh has been described quite differently from classical and modern forms in Japan and abroad. Western and Japanese discourses in the English and Japanese media over the past forty-five years have held butoh in an image of resistance through deconstruction, death, and grotesque body forms. In Japanese performance reviews over four decades (1961–2003), butoh is described using terms such as *ankoku* (darkness), *zen-ei* (avant-garde), *waizatsu* (chaotic, vulgar), *angura* (underground), *kimi no warusa* (creepy), *kitanasa* (dirty), *boryoku-sei* (violent), *erotisizumu* (erotic), *konton* (chaotic), *anaakii* (anarchistic), *kikei* (deformed), *igyo* (uncanny), *tosaku-teki* (transvestite), *keiren* (trembling), *shinpiteki* (mysterious). Butoh reviews first began appearing in the *New York Times* around 1984 after groups such as *Sankai Juku* and *Dai Rakuda Kan* performed abroad. Butoh is commonly described in the *New York Times* and other US-based newspapers as grotesque, hallucinatory, painful, decaying, startling, destructive, insane, and dislocating. These authors believe such partial valuations interpret only the surface look of butoh. A close look at dances of Hijikata and Ohno will take us more deeply into the subjects and experiential approach of butoh, as we describe and analyze five works in chronological order, including an extensive note on a recent film of Hijikata's *Summer Storm*. Our own experience of these dances informs the text where possible, and we include experiences of others that are available to us through published accounts.

Kinjiki *(Forbidden Colors, 1959)*

Hijikata dared to go against the safely coded lyric and dramatic modern dance that developed in Japan through the influence of the West. In so doing, he ushered in Japan's postmodern dance in stark dramatic tones. In his first dance, *Kinjiki*, performed for the Japanese Dance Association in Tokyo, Hijikata surrenders to what analytical psychologist Carl Jung calls the shadow side of life. In *Kinjiki*, as in later work, Hijikata is interested in looking death and forbidden feelings in the face, acknowledging the experiences these stir in him, and transferring the experience directly to his audiences. *Kinjiki* was controversial in this respect. Some audience members attested their release of dark emotions and a therapeutic connection to the dance, as Goda Nario remembered (Goda 1983), while others were disgusted. Through this dance, Hijikata eventually left the Japanese Dance Association.

Forbidden Colors is the English title for *Kinjiki*. We have only been able to mention that Hijikata's inspiration for this dance was the Japanese literary master Mishima Yukio and his book *Kinjiki* with homosexuality as one of its themes. After 1970, the year of Mishima's suicide, Hijikata's work shifted to a new register, completing its liberation from Western dance movement altogether and finding a unique notational vocabulary based on pictorial and verbal imagery that he called *butoh-fu*. By then, Hijikata was learning how to dance the various selves and hidden images of his subconscious, excavating his sister there and admitting his childhood terrors. He also began to choreograph extensively for others, consciously including women and feminine energy in his work.

In its raw beginnings, at the dawn of the politically driven 1960s, Hijikata's *Kinjiki* was exclusively masculine with its forbidden theme of homosexuality and referred to bestiality as well, though audience accounts were not in agreement about this aspect. The chicken squeezed between Ohno Yoshito's thighs was later sacrificed in the dance. The cruelty, however shocking, might have seemed mild to Hijikata at that time, in light of the chaotic, defeated world of post-apocalyptic Japan. What the audience is left to sort out *in their experience* of *Kinjiki* is the same question that American playwright Edward Albee explores in *The Goat, or Who is Sylvia?* – his Tony winning play of 2002, where the main character falls in love with (guess what) a goat! In love with a goat? This is the rub! And why allude to bestiality on stage? Albee was born in 1928, the same year as Hijikata, and although American, he writes in the same surrealist, political vein as the European authors who inspired Hijikata, Samuel Beckett and Jean Genet with whom Albee is often compared.

Now we ask, is Hijikata just a country bumpkin who blindly fraternizes with farm animals? Or is he an artist who is often in agony about his relationship to the land and his ethnicity? The latter implies one's relationship to country, land, people, race, and the human body, even as animals are represented there. Certainly he is aware of the strong societal taboo against bestiality. In his characteristic, intentionally crazy surrealist stance, he tests the audience in this regard. These authors also believe that Hijikata's pre-occupation with chickens and animal imagery *per se* is emblematic of his search for identity in the midst of the spiritual crisis of Japan after the war. Death and life were large issues then, perennial ones in any case, and Hijikata was a man in search of his identity. When he performed *Kinjiki*, he was thirty-one years old, poor, and still adjusting to Tokyo in post-war Japan. In staging a totem animal sacrifice, he proceeded much as shamans have often done, moving toward the dark regions of subconscious life, projecting this into visible performance. It is clear at this time, that he is not seeking admiration for his dancing, rather he seems to be taking upon himself the mantle of the dancer-shaman, harking back to his childhood roots and testing social boundaries. His intent to shock his audience awake is apparent.

Kinjiki is a dance of darkness in several ways. The stage itself is darkened: Yoshito, Ohno's young son, dances in dim light with Hijikata, and they mime sexual attraction at points – looking deeply into each other's eyes. Kurihara Nanako, who interviewed Nario Goda about the work, describes it briefly from his account of seeing the dance and his article about it (Goda 1987: 41–42). He describes the dance as a ritual sacrifice. Hijikata portrays *Man* with bell-bottom trousers and a shaved head, using black grease on his face and upper body. As the *Boy*, Yoshito wears a black scarf around his neck and lemon-colored shorts. They dance barefoot. After the boy appears on stage, the man, holding a chicken, enters and runs in a circle. The boy stiffens, and walks to a narrow illuminated area center stage, where the man is waiting in the darkness. Breathing hard, they face each other, and the man thrusts the chicken into the light with the white wings fluttering "stunningly." The boy accepts the chicken, turns his head, and holds it to his chest. Then placing the chicken between his thighs, he slowly sinks into a squat, squeezing it to death while the man watches from the darkness. (Not everyone believes the chicken dies.) The boy stands in shock, and the audience is outraged. When they see the chicken lying at the boy's feet, they gasp. Black out (Kurihara 1996: 54–55).

In the second half, as Goda remembers, the dancers perform in total darkness with the audience hearing sounds of breathing and moaning. The boy runs, and the man chases him. Toward the end Yasuda Shugo plays bluesy jazz on a harmonica, and the stage brightens slightly. "The boy walks away, dragging his feet and holding the chicken in his arms" (Ibid.: 55–56). This partial description aims to capture the costumes, movement on stage, and the physical sounds of the dance. *Kinjiki* has been interpreted in different ways: as dark, masochistic, abusive, homoerotic, ritualistic, sacrificial, strong, quiet, stiff, withheld, and as both beautiful and ugly. Perhaps all of these apply in view of personal perception and differences in audience perspectives. Hijikata is never simply linear or obvious. He textures *Kinjiki* with *pathos* and the complexities of masculinity, as also in subsequent work, he becomes increasingly more able to exhume from his own body a theater of hope and misery, stemming from his childhood with a tyrannical alcoholic father who beat his mother.

Hijikata ran, he says, chasing after his mother as she tried to escape these violent episodes. He felt helpless, and eventually dissociated by visualizing his home as a "theater" (Ibid.: 23). One senses this sublimated anguish in Hijikata's portrayal of "Leprosy" (a section of *Summer Storm*, 1973) with its trembling emotional shading and quiet forbearance. *Kinjiki*, as Hijikata's first butoh, also paints a tremulous inner landscape – though perhaps not as skillfully articulated as "Leprosy" – where Hijikata's subtle body shifts seem to transform the very space around him. This incredible power of Hijikata as a performer cannot be captured in a photograph or verbal description, and it seems to have been there from the beginning – with *Kinjiki*.

Many who see Hijikata perform report how he viscerally enthralls them. Motofuji, who later becomes Hijikata's wife, and is in the audience for *Kinjiki*, says she feels "electricity run through her body." Dance writer Miura Masashi reports in his article, '*Hijikata Tatsumi no kyofu*' (Fear of Hijikata Tatsumi), that Hijikata's performances make him "tremble" and his hands sweat (Ibid.: 43, 58). At the same time, Hijikata's works offer the audience a space to texture emotional engagement – even as his exploitation of fear is mollified by bitter sweet and tender contrasts. There are beautiful episodes of slow restrained movement in *Kinjiki*. Eternally slow continuously morphing movement – not unknown in Japanese traditional forms such as Noh Theater and the spare aesthetics of Zen meditation – eventually mark a butoh signature, surfacing, paradoxically, in Hijikata's first choreography.

The chicken, however, is most remembered in accounts of *Kinjiki*. The dancers' attitude toward the chicken displays both the experience of love and violence. Hunger is perhaps the over-riding theme. The wary chicken, playing its part as an object of hunger, crosses over categories of food, sexual hunger, and spiritual longing. This is a famous chicken: *Kinjiki* with its three performers, Hijikata, Yoshito, and the chicken, separates Hijikata from the then known dance world in Japan – and also the 1960s postmodern dance in the West, which turns increasingly toward neutral, unemotional pedestrian forms. There is nothing else like *Kinjiki*, and for the rest of his life Hijikata continues to develop the archetype of the rebel in butoh.

Barairo Dansu *(Rose Colored Dance, 1965)*

In November 1965, Hijikata and Ohno performed *Barairo dansu: A LA MAISON DE M. CIVECAWA* (Rose Colored Dance: To Mr. Shibusawa's House) at *Sennichidani Kokaido*. This is a group dance choreographed by Hijikata with a duet section for himself and Ohno – also featuring Ohno Yoshito, Ishii Mitsutaka, Tamano Koichi, and Kasai Akira. Nakanishi Natsuyuki, a well-known painter, and Yokoo Tadanori, an accomplished graphic artist, also collaborated in this performance. The stage scenery of this dance is vivid and morphs considerably – from a fortune telling chart in front of which a dancer fences in full attire, to a scene with a vagina painted on the back of dancer Tamano. This realistically painted image opening the outer lips and folds to expose the inner design of female sexuality covers Tamano's entire back. Hijikata is more often identified with the erect phallus he later wore in *Rebellion of the Body* (1968), a costume also copied by other butoh dancers, but here he reverses his sex and gender glance. In *Rose Colored Dance*, the stage is decorated with drawings of human internal organs and female genitals drawn in graphic detail.

There is also a pedestrian scene with a barber cutting hair on stage, as three men sit in a row of chairs wrapped in large striped towels, much as one might find in a Tanztheater work of Pina Bausch. Ohno Yoshito and Kasai Akira are in the dance. They perform wearing briefs, their nude bodies spattered with muddy chalk, as they dance with plastic tubes, blowing and looking through them, wrapping up in them, and creating striking shapes with their preoccupation.

Hijikata and Ohno dance a satirical duet in white dresses, their dance caught in photographs now widely published. Hijikata sometimes emulates Ohno's movements and they indulge suggestions of intimacy. We know that in their daily life, however, their relationship was not intimate but rather formal, and Hijikata deferred to Ohno's maturity as elders are respected in Japan. As artists they were exploratory; in *Rose Colored Dance* they performed in playful embrace, smelled each other's feet, and roiled in mischief, rolling on top of each other. They were in effect *experiencing* each other, not in the physically neutral manner of contact improvisation as it developed in the West, but directly, through touch, smell, and intentional association. Their dance while not overtly sexual was rebellious in flaunting taboos of sexuality and the body, but it was still somewhat under the influence of movements from the lyric modern dance they both had studied.

Incomplete videos and films of the dance show its irony and edgy playfulness. Hijikata and Ohno wear matching white Western style gowns, simply cut with scoop necklines and sewn with gathers around a drop waistline. They dance unassumingly in the dresses, not to parody women, but simply to be themselves, moving together and apart, foregrounding each other's movement, and tangling at points. Ohno Yoshito states that this dance fulfilled a wish of Hijikata's to dance with Ohno in a similar costume and to share his movement (Ohno and Ohno 2004: 134). Hijikata writes of Ohno's contribution to his dance: "Mr. O. [Ono Kazuo], a dancer of deadly poison and a pioneer in experiential dance, an awe-inspiring teacher and a friend, helped carry my dance works to the theater. He is both a cabinetmaker and a poet who, with a fond gaze, singles out every work of unhappy heartburn" (2000a: 39).

Hijikata explains the sacrificial impulse behind *Rose Colored Dance* when he revisits his failed efforts at Western dance techniques, and vows to prepare an antidote – "a dance of terrorism," his way of demolishing dance for display. In technique classes he endures "the jockstraps and Chopin" of Western dance, and throughout it all "the diarrhea of misery." In spite of his negative feelings, Hijikata reports that he continues to go to the theater in his early days in Tokyo, and that it gradually dawns on him from this position that "audiences pay money to enjoy evil." He conceives *Rose Colored Dance* to compensate for that. We can see this in his comparison of the "rosy" and "dark" sides of his work:

> Both the "rose colored dance" and the "dance of darkness" must spout blood in the name of the experience of evil. A body that has kept the tradition of mysterious crisis is prepared for that. Sacrifice is the source of all work and every dancer is an illegitimate child set free to experience that very quality. Because they bear that obligation, all dancers must first of all be pilloried. Dance for display must be totally abolished. Being looked at, patted, licked, knocked down. A striptease is nothing to laugh at.
>
> *(2000a: 39–40)*

Ohno (1906–2010) and Hijikata (1928–1986)

Nikutai no hanran *(Rebellion of the Body, 1968)*

In 1968, Hijikata choreographs the work that marks *Ankoku Butoh* as a new genre. His dance *Hijikata Tatsumi to Nihonjin: Nikutai no hanran* (Hijikata Tatsumi and the Japanese: Rebellion of the Body), also known as *Rebellion of the Body* and sometimes *Revolt of the Flesh*, is performed at *Nihon Seinen Kan Hall*. This shamanist dance, signaling Hijikata's maturity as a surrealist and his further embrace of the subconscious, is symptomatic of the inner turmoil through which he is living; his preoccupation with personal identity as a native son of Japan from the remote Tohoku region finally explodes. His concern for explicating culture has been building. In June of 1968, he performs in *Ojune sho* (Excerpts from Genet), a recital given by his student Ishii Mitsutaka. Hijikata dances *Hanayome (neko)* (Bride [Cat]) in a kimono. He also dances *Kirisuto* (Christ), and later develops these dances into episodes of *Rebellion of the Body* in October that same year.

Antonin Artaud's *The Theater and its Double* was translated into Japanese in 1965 and had a profound influence on a new generation of Japanese directors and performers including Hijikata. This is evident in the directly experiential aspects of his work and the anarchy of *Rebellion of the Body*. In this work, Hijikata under the influence of Artaud and still in the thrall of Jean Genet, enters the stage through the audience, borne on a palanquin, a long kimono covering his naked body, and in his hand he holds a golden phallus – as in Artaud's *From Heliogabalus, or The Anarchic Crowned*. Hijikata transforms episodically through several scenes in this concert length work, morphing from the demonic to the satiric, waving a large strapped-on golden penis, dancing as a man in a gown, and binding himself with ropes in crucifixion, his sleek and browned body wrapped in swaths of white cloth. The wildness of his long hair and beard seem to mock the short pink dress and ankle socks he wears in a particularly absurd scene. In another, he dances violently in a long heavy gown, his movements reminiscent of the waltz and tango. Western and Japanese elements coexist in clashing collage and spasmodic movement. It is through this work, performed nearly a decade after his first radical experiment *Kinjiki* (1959) that Hijikata's butoh is gradually understood as a new form of dance born of his memories of the poverty and mysticism of Tohoku.

But he in no way returns to a simple past; rather he fastens on the present indelibly by scattering Western costumes and dance styles along the path of descent to his own Japanese roots. Sondra Fraleigh saw an installation film presentation of *Rebellion of the Body* at the Asian Museum in San Francisco in the summer of 1996. Hijikata's costumes for the dance were part of the installation. She remembers watching people come and go, and that she and her husband were the only audience members to stay for the entire performance. People seemed baffled by what they saw, unprepared for the surrealist tactics of Hijikata and the raw energy of his dance. Many covered their eyes or mouths, or looked at the floor.

One of the most startling images of the dance that appears so often as an image in books of butoh photography is that of Hijikata, an erect metallic penis strapped to his groin as his only costume, reaching his arms around his head to enclose a sideward glance. Characteristically, he sucks in his abdomen – all the more to expose the bony structure of his emaciated rib cage. We know that he prepared himself for this dance through fasting and tanning his body under artificial light, leaving his skinny body shining like a dagger with mystery and daring. When Hijikata criticizes the "lethargic fat" society of Tokyo, he says, "in such a case the penis will never become a radiant dagger" (2000a: 40–41).

What is he trying to say to us through this phallic dance, audiences have wondered and critics pondered? Does he himself seek some revelation? Some healing transformative secret to unravel? Or is he simply provoking us, as artists will, to experience our bodies more sharply? If we consider precedents in the West, especially the Greeks through Dionysus and the horny satyr, we see, without any trouble, several related explanations for Hijikata's strapped-on penis and those phallic dances of Tanaka Min and others who followed Hijikata in butoh. The exaggerated phallus, represented in Greek plays by comic actors and satyrs, is also admired and feared in the God Dionysus, who was always a pesky outsider in the Apollonian, Platonic world of perfect form. In other words, Dionysus is the *Other*, not necessarily the male other in terms of gender, but the sensuous other, as a deeply feminine and flawed God imported from the East. Historian Thomas Cahill in *Why the Greeks Matter* tells us that "Dionysus, almost certainly a homegrown Greek god going back to earliest times – but also the epitome of Otherness – was always spoken of as a foreigner, an intromission from the effete East" (Cahill 2003: 202).

As a challenge to social mores of the Japanese, Hijikata (as satyr) acts satirically – even as the Greek god Dionysus would – to enliven the sight and soul of forgotten otherness in his audience; and through the subconscious region of darkness that is also Dionysian, he probes rejected shadows of erotic vitality. Now this is not necessarily to embrace evil, even though Hijikata says he wants to "go to prison" in a rebellious turn of mind, to be caught "smack in the middle of a mistake" (2000b: 45). More it is to ward off evil, by staring it in the eye, as was also the function of the satyr. There is a not-so-fine-line between the vital desires that compel people in love, fear, and conquest, and the crossover into evil doing. Hijikata apparently understood this, and he wanted to blur the line, so as to make the darkness more evident. He was certainly willing to risk being *Other*, the social outcast, in the name of his dance.

His most immediate model for this was the original bawdy Kabuki before it was purged of folk vulgarity for Western audiences, but we know that Hijikata also studied the West. He admired German author Friedrich Nietzsche's writing from the nineteenth century and understood the Dionysian and Apollonian values interlacing Nietzsche's *Birth of Tragedy*, harbinger to twentieth century European existentialism. In 'To Prison', Hijikata quotes Nietzsche's view of work: "My work is to reanimate with vitality a skeleton pieced together from the consciousness of being a victim. I am a man of simple sensual passion. The sense of the tragic increases and declines with sensuousness." In the next breath, Hijikata quotes German born American philosopher and political theorist Herbert Marcuse in *Eros and Civilization*, also on the subject of work: "Work is *a priori* power and provocation in struggle with nature; it is the overcoming of resistance." Hijikata's provocation he says in his own words is "dance." His goal in dance is an existential answer to Nietzsche (whose philosophy had already borrowed a great deal from the East) and Marcuse (a thinker who also transcended Western categories). Cast in assimilation of their language, Hijikata's goal in dance is, as he says:

> ... to open up the current situation with hands that hold a chalk eraser which wipes out signs of an impotent future, of that culture of mournful cries which exist in the skeleton of victim consciousness. I am placing in the body of my work an altar similar to asceticism in front of a human body purged of impurities.
>
> *(2000b: 47)*

Hijikata's *Rebellion of the Body* can be understood in terms of East and West, and how he synthesizes them in surrealist dance. He maps his semi-starved erotic body in the process, becoming the forgotten other, but not to forget his childhood terrors and Japanese "earthbody" in the wake of Western technocracy and domestication of the body. He says after the war, and twelve years of living in Tokyo:

> I am chewing on cries and the profundity of esoteric gestures by gazing closely and unceasingly at the mundane. I am inventing a walk molded of the present from atop the

dark earth where dancing and jumping could not be united. In boyhood the dark earth of Japan was my teacher in various ways of fainting. I must bring to the theater that sense of treading. I am a naked volunteer soldier who forces this treading to confront the handling of legs that have been domesticated by floors.

(2000b: 48)

Hijikata's dance assimilates archetypal human experiences of the dancer shaman, the cheated victim, the rebel, the satyr, the crucified martyr, and the wounded child, bearing his audience finally toward an experience of the impeccable, naked political warrior, fighting with righteous indignation for a life of simple sensual passions. Of the latter, he says: "My work is to remove toy weapons from the limbs of today's youth, who developed in barren circumstances, and to finish them as naked soldiers, as a naked culture." One is reminded of an earlier time and the naked beginnings of modern dance in Hijikata's statement – that Rudolph von Laban at the foundations of *Neue Tanz* in Germany advocates dancing nude in nature for benefits of health and the recovery of human expression. Hijikata's nudity, however, comes in the guise of combat.

Note on Natsu No Arashi *(Summer Storm, 1973)*

Arai Misao brings Hijikata's *Summer Storm* to light in a 2003 film and DVD of a 1973 performance at Kyoto University in Japan (Arai 2003). The footage of *Summer Storm* that Arai took in 1973 sat in a can for thirty years, he said, until he looked at the dance again, realizing that there were few complete records of Hijikata's dancing and choreography. He didn't want to interfere with the integrity of the dance by editing it. He did however commission new music by YAS-KAZ to respect Hijikata's style, also showing city scenes of Tokyo to introduce the dance, and at the end summer snow (Arai in conversation with Fraleigh). As the film finishes, pulling away from the dance and snow in sunshine, it fades gently to the sea and land of Japan, shooting Tohoku from the air in stunning views.

The film captures one of Hijikata's last performances in public and his incredible embodiment of "Leprosy" in two sections. It is also important as a record of one of Hijikata's most mature works as a performer and choreographer, showing clearly delineated movement and compositional structures. As a concert length work, *Summer Storm* develops episodically and is choreographed by Hijikata for his company members, all of whom have carried his butoh legacy forward as choreographers and performers: Ashikawa Yoko, Kobayashi Saga, Tamano Koichi, Waguri Yukio, and Hanagami Naoto.

As a dance of prayer, *Summer Storm* is a gift from Hijikata's poverty – a haunting, mesmerizing work of quiet struggle and compassion, its somber tones also offset with playful skittering elements, as in the scene: "Young Girls Picking Herbs." Significantly, *Summer Storm* lays to rest questions about the influence of war in Hijikata's choreography. It is clearly anti-war, addressing death through the names of places where many died in World War II in a section called: "Dreams of the Dead, the Sleep, the War." Hijikata narrates this part, speaking over the dance in his poetic way, such lines as: "Sleep oh Sleep . . . Iwo Jima . . . The sea of Midway." (The battle of Iwo Jima was one of the most costly battles of the Pacific campaign of World War II – about 6,000 American marines died and 21,000 Japanese – and the Pacific battle off Midway Island is one of the most famous naval battles in history). "The world tilts. . . . I offer this votive candle to the God of Oki. . . . " (Oki Islands are a group of small Japanese islands in the southern part of the Sea of Japan.) "War is the dripping of blood. . . . From Oki, let us find a favorable wind with one thousand days of sunshine and peace."

Sondra Fraleigh and Tamah Nakamura

La Argentina Sho *(Admiring La Argentina, 1977)*

By the time of Ohno Kazuo's famous dance *Admiring La Argentina*, Hijikata was defining himself more as a choreographer and director than a performer. In November of 1977, Ohno premiers *Admiring La Argentina*, directed by Hijikata Tatsumi at the *Dai-ichi Sei Mei* Hall, a dance for which he receives the Dance Critics' Circle Award. "Death and life in that order are the predominant themes in the opening scenes of *Admiring La Argentina*, in which Kazuo poignantly portrays Genet's prostitute's last moments" (Ohno and Ohno 2004: 76). Kazuo climbs onto the stage from the audience, leaving life behind, later to return to the same spot reborn as a young girl. Death in this dance unearths a more profound existence.

The performance of *Admiring La Argentina* serves as a rebirth for Ohno from the introspective 'death' during his ten-year absence from dance and the stage. He is seventy-one years old. The entire performance is a tribute to Antonia Mercé, a Spanish dancer known as La Argentina whom he had seen dance fifty years earlier. The only full-length videotape of the performance is in the Ohno Archives in Yokohama, which is not yet open to the public. In addition to a few film clips in collections of Ohno's works (Ohno 2001), written accounts describe it as a two-part performance, *Self-Portrait* and *La Argentina* (Ohno and Ohno 2004: 150–169). *Self-Portrait*, a series of four scenes, symbolizes the cycle of life of Ohno Kazuo. In "Divine's Death," he portrays a dying male prostitute inspired by Genet's character, *Divine*. Walking from a seat in the audience and up the aisle, he climbs the stairs to sink to the stage floor as he dies in deep suffering. In "Rebirth of a Young Girl," Ohno, now wearing a white chemise with a paper flower in his hair, appears after a brief blackout at the spot where the prostitute died. In the third scene "Daily Bread," he is clad in black trunks, appearing as himself in a physical expression of the body. In "The Marriage of Heaven and Earth," the final scene of the first act, Ohno stands, still wearing the black trunks, "crucified" against a grand piano, head thrown back and arms outstretched. This series of dances deals with death and rebirth and the nourishment of spiritual needs.

In the second act, the two scenes of "Flower and Bird" open with tango music. Ohno evokes the spirit of *La Argentina*: dancing in a dark green dress, changing to a flowing gown, and finally into a white ruffled gown. In contrast to Western stage and drama in which a man wearing a dress potentially denotes cross-dressing, Ohno is not conscious that he is dressed as a woman. A metamorphosis takes place in which Argentina takes bodily form in his dance. Ohno and Argentina merge until Ohno becomes La Argentina. He offers homage to Argentina by sharing his experience of her through his embodiment of her; that is, he dances for her and with her.

Yoshito looks back on the events that caused Ohno to break out of his introspective phase through his reconnection with Argentina. In the interview below with Tamah Nakamura, March 19, 2005 in Yokohama, Yoshito describes this period of discovery:

Discovering Argentina:
For about ten years it was difficult for Kazuo to be on stage. He continued to get experience at small places and he taught Hijikata's students for two years or so at Hijikata's request. After that Kazuo made three movies in about four years. We, his family, didn't know what he was doing. He sometimes disappeared somewhere. I knew he was making movies but I really didn't know where he was making movies or what he was doing. He even shot a movie near here. When I look back, I think he was looking again at what he was through those movies. He was reflecting on his origin. He really looked at himself closely – even to the point of being with pigs and being smeared with dirt.

One day when he went to an art exhibition, he was so excited: "I saw Argentina," he said. I asked him: "What is Argentina?" He explained that he had seen Argentina, a

Spanish dancer, when he was young, and that he saw her again today. "I was so moved," He said aloud: "Maybe I can dance." The picture he saw wasn't a photograph or a painted picture of the image of a woman. It was almost milky white and not much was painted clearly. *(The picture was an abstract painting of geometrical curves painted on a zinc sheet by Nakanishi Natsuyuki.)* It looked like a cow or like a bull fighting. There was almost nothing literally drawn in the picture. It was very wondrous. Certainly I could see how Kazuo recalled Argentina, when I saw the picture.

Two or three days after he saw Argentina at the art museum, Kazuo received various books on Argentina from Eiko and Koma, dancers and his students in New York. He was surprised and got so excited. He said he wanted to produce a stage performance. I asked him, "What kind of music did she dance to?" He said, "Well, she danced with modern music of that time." But there was no information left, and we had no idea what kind of music it was. Since she was born in Argentina, in Buenos Aires, she was called Argentina. She was originally from Spain and was named Antonia Mercé, so she went back to Spain and became a dancer. Since she was born in Argentina, we decided to dance with Argentine Tango. There was the most famous Argentine tango musician, Hayakawa Shinpei and his wife was Fujisawa Ranko. I looked for him, and finally found his apartment. "Well, Ohno-san," he said, "I am sorry but I no longer play. Argentine Tango requires a very high level of technique and skill." So I asked him, "Well Sensei, I believe you have something like records." He said, "I got rid of them all, but I will introduce you to one of my students, Ikeda." Ikeda was with a student band and performing at a festival. I asked him to come to our place and see my father's dance. After seeing my father's dance, Ikeda said, "I will do my best to play music for you; I really want to."

It was a few years before the 200th anniversary celebration of tango that Ohno performed Argentina. I think that was good timing, because if it had been later after tango got popular again, we could not have used tango for the Argentina performance. La Argentina was unique, since no one was using tango music at that time.

The performance of *Admiring La Argentina* is a pivotal stage for Ohno and for butoh for several reasons. It heralds the return to dancing and stage performance for Ohno after a hiatus of ten years of self-imposed reflection. Perhaps more significantly, the performance highlights Ohno as a star solo dancer. Further, the *La Argentina* performance creates a new relationship between Ohno and Hijikata, with Hijikata in a non-performance, advisory capacity. This new collaboration ensures the longevity of butoh beyond the earlier *Dance Experience* works, which could not be reproduced and restaged through the creation of deliberately structured forms. In a global perspective, from this period onward, Ohno's international repertoire grows extensively through restaging of his performances beyond Japan to twenty-nine countries. His successful performance of *La Argentina* at the Nancy Festival, France in 1980 launches his dance worldwide.

From there Argentina is reborn in Yokohama: A young Brazilian modern dancer, Antonio Fuerio, saw Ohno dance at the Nancy Festival. He was greatly impressed with Ohno's butoh rendition of *La Argentina*. Subsequently, he choreographed *Carmen Miranda: Homage to Kazuo Ohno* with his dance troupe, *Grupo de Teatro Macunaima* and performed it in March of 2005 in Yokohama, Japan. Fuerio's homage performance conjures a Brazilian Ohno dressed in a white suit with red rose in pocket, white bow tie, straw hat with black band – and a searching, wistful, soul.

There is an interesting historical trace here: In the beginning, Ohno's memory of Antonia Mercé's performance was a catalyst fifty years later for his *Admiring La Argentina* performance in Nancy, France. Ohno's dance had lived in Fuerio's memory for twenty-five years when he brought his *Homage to Ohno* back to Yokohama, Japan from Brazil. In *Admiring La Argentina*,

Ohno Kazuo built an international bridge through the feet of three dancers from two different world climates, combining the cool temperament of Japan with the heat of Argentina and Brazil.

Suiren *(Water Lilies, 1987)*

(In this section, we refer to the two Ohnos of *Water Lilies*, Kazuo and Yoshito, using their first names to avoid confusion.) Kazuo's performances, nuanced through a conscious construction of his dancing body, are also true to his natural body – large hands, expressive face, and limberness. He is aware, as his son Yoshito says, of eyes all over his body, and the expressive power of the back of the body, never dissociating the front and the back (Ohno and Ohno 2004: 37–40). Nowhere is this integral sense of the dancing body more evident than in Kazuo's duet with Yoshito – *Suiren* (Water Lilies 1987) – based on Claude Monet's *Water Lilies*, forty-eight highly successful landscape paintings the French impressionist artist explored from 1897 to 1900 and painted between 1904 and 1906. As in *La Argentina*, Kazuo draws inspiration from sources outside his native Japan, using images of great power and beauty to position the themes and characteristics of his dance. Behind *Suiren*, one senses the transparency and spiritual luminosity of Monet's work, the surface of the water, motionless or gently rippling, emerging through the flat leaves of the Water Lilies, and floating flowers in repose like the lotus lilies of Buddhist tranquility.

Kazuo, like Monet, gives the illusion of movement through calm and serenity, cultivating a feminine presence that one also finds in Monet, especially his reflective handling of water and light in his exquisite waterlily paintings. Kazuo's suave, flowing lines in *Suiren* remind us that Monet is one of the impressionist painters strongly influenced by the Japanese masters of Ukiyo-e, also called "Pictures of the Floating World" (Fraleigh 1999: 9–11). In choosing Monet, Kazuo incorporates a part of Japan's aesthetic history, whether consciously or not. (We explained the influence of Japanese Ukiyo-e on the French Impressionists in section 9.1.) Monet's idea for painting varied images of his pond garden at Giverny in several temporal planes came through Hokusai's *Hundred Views of Mount Fuji* and Hiroshige's *Hundred Views of Edo*. He saw these works at Samuel Bing's Paris gallery in 1888 and at the *Exposition Universelle* in 1889. Eventually Monet collected Ukiyo-e colored wood-cut prints by Hokusai, Hiroshige, and Utamaro, some of which were displayed in the dining room of his home at Giverny, a small village northwest of Paris (Sagner-Duchting 1999: 34).

Hokusai foreshadowed impressionism at its source: part of Monet's inspiration for the Water Lily paintings (dating from about 1897) came from Hokusai's detailed woodcut *Chrysanthemum and Bee* that he had owned since 1896 (Ibid.: 57). Monet's work marked impressionism as an aesthetic movement, and it borrowed liberally from the artistry of Japan. In time, Monet's friendly relations with Japanese art collectors and dealers Hayashi Tadamasu and Matsukata Kojiro who admired his work and introduced it to Japan, aided the symbiosis of Ukiyo-e and impressionist painting (Ibid.: 34).

Kazuo problematizes impressionism and the great canvases of Monet in *Suiren;* he is not simply imitating them. In Monet's original paintings, flowers and leaves appear on reflecting water as viewed from above (like Ukiyo-e without horizon, and seemingly without limits), showing different seasons of the year and times of day in his garden under a Japanese bridge. Monet's cool and soothing scenes are devoid of people, and in their idealization of nature, cut off from narrative human themes. His is a beautiful, uninterrupted vision of warm, marshy, undisturbed water, with flowers symbolic of feminine fertility and interiors of the soul. Kazuo departs from the idealized surface of Monet and also from the illusions of French Impressionism in his juxtaposition of Yoshito with his own luminous dances in *Suiren*, telescoping him away from the shimmering surface, as though focused intensively through a broken mirror. Even as Kazuo's dances can elevate nature in the same open indeterminate way as Monet, they also break the static surface of contemplative perception, moving in the dark and messy places that trouble still waters.

Yoshito and Kazuo both transform thematically in this dance, moving neither without horizon nor along parallel lines, but together and apart, alive to their separate spheres. As in Kazuo's works in general, everything is alive to the moment, and each moment is an opportunity to peek through to another reality, to dream and reflect, yes, but also to grieve and change. Yoshito says of dancing with his father that as a twosome they transcend their separate identities and opposite approaches to performance, merging into a larger whole, even while maintaining separate voices (Ohno and Ohno 2004: 96). As in much butoh, white make up assists the blend. In *Suiren*, Kazuo and Yoshito wear *shiro-nuri*, the typical white make up of butoh, to erase individual personality and private history. Kazuo also applies thick black eye liner to accentuate his eyes. Indeed, he seems to use make up for both illusion and disappearance of personal features, so that his dance becomes more numinous, allowing a wide identification with the audience. He can be a woman in a frilly gown, as he is in the beginning of *Suiren*, or an old man leaning on a crooked stick trailing a long yellow kimono, a character he develops through the middle of the dance. Wearing the same white face with exaggerated eyes, he can also morph into more robust figures as he does at the end of *Suiren*, dancing in Western black formal attire, casually, the white shirt unbuttoned at the top, with his arms and hands telling short stories, summarizing life (as a pond) in transition.

Less flowering than Kazuo, Yoshito begins the dance as a blocky, tightly strung man in a suit. For a long time, he seethes inwardly with just a veneer of visible shaking, eventually exploding in short violent jump-starts that settle quickly back into taut oblivion. Yoshito holds an electric charge in this opening scene that these authors have seldom seen in theater, completely focused, percussively broken and riveting, and with such minimal means. Kazuo enters the stage quite unobtrusively in the beginning, almost like a whisper. The light gradually picks up his delicate, slowly moving presence and the gently ruffled gown that he wears as a second skin. He carries a parasol, sweetly feminine and old-fashioned, like the ones women in southern Japan use to block the sun on hot days, or the ones Monet used to protect his out-of-doors paintings at Giverny.

Kazuo inches along, his large eyes shining with tenderness in the glow of his white face. He captures our gaze from the beginning, like the exaggerated eyes and aging beauty of American movie icon Gloria Swanson whom Kazuo admired. The stark contrast between Kazuo and Yoshito opens a space in the mind, readying it for another condition.

The audience is invited to share in the flowering metamorphosis of the dance as it develops. Yoshito tells us that in Kazuo's world, flowers are cited as the most ideal form of existence; his physical presence must at all times be flowerlike (Ohno and Ohno 2004: 89). *Suiren* invites us to join Kazuo's world in this respect, finally making an explicit identification with nature. Kazuo's use of flowers appeared early on in his 1981 work *My Mother*. Yoshito comments on Kazuo's embodiment of flowers:

> By becoming an integral part of the body's nervous system, a flower functions much in the same way an insect's antennae do: constantly palpating the air. Not only does it receive and respond to incoming stimuli, it also acts as a natural extension of the hand, and, in doing so, becomes a point of contact with the outside world. It functions independently as though it were an external eye detached from the trunk of the body. In that respect it exists both as an autonomous entity and as a sensory organ.
>
> *(Ibid.)*

As a metamorphic signature dance of Kazuo with his son Yoshito, *Suiren* shifts magically through several stages (or canvases) from its opening scene, juxtaposing Kazuo's extended entrance in a fragile gown with Yoshito dancing to the music of *Pink Floyd* in his blocky-man suit. In view of the dance's impressionistic pulse, this is the pond as cosmos, seen in the dawning light (Kazuo) and shattering surfaces (Yoshito) of morning. The light fades up to midday, featuring Kazuo's solo in a long yellow kimono at the pond's zenith. Here he dances in glowing gestures that eventually wane, as he trails the kimono behind his almost nude and aging body, and leans on his gnarled walking staff through various incarnations. The dance gradually gathers an evening atmosphere, the pond at twilight and the birth of Yoshito as a White Lotus Goddess in a long white robe, crowned with a magnificent Buddhist lotus, also a lily. In the chakra system of Asian yoga, the lotus opens the seventh energy system of the body at the crown of the head, extending the body into pure spirit.

It would, however, be trite and predictable to finish with this climax, and Kazuo, ever unpredictable, seeks another end, one more earthy in his black suit and white shirt, even casually postmodern, meeting us where we are for the night, settled there in our own black attire, or blue jeans, while he communicates not of other worlds but of this one here and now tonight, his gestures drawing us intimately into the enclosure of his storied hands. When he bows, we get this message over again, as he embraces us whole in one flowing movement that gathers in the heart chakra. No wonder there are few dry eyes. Kazuo, as many audiences around the world know, can make you cry.

Interview with Yoshito Ohno – on Suiren – Tamah Nakamura, March 19, 2005

TAMAH: What is your memory of dancing with your father in *Suiren*?

YOSHITO: This was Kazuo's first work after Hijikata's death. I performed *Suiren* with my father at the opening of a drama festival in Stuttgart, Germany. This was its first performance. On our return to Japan, we performed *Suiren* for the butoh festival held in *Ginza* in Tokyo.

TAMAH: It was the first performance without Hijikata.

YOSHITO: Yes, that's right.

TAMAH: How did that affect your performance?

YOSHITO: Since we had depended pretty much on Hijikata, I was worried at that time and felt insecure. Well, I was very worried, but in Stuttgart there was a large party hosted by the drama festival after the performance.

TAMAH: Ohno-sensei is very international!

YOSHITO: Yes, people were pleased with the performance very much. And when the first performance was held at *Saison* in *Ginza*, Hijikata's friend, Minoru Yoshioka-sensei, at a party after the performance praised the performance highly. His wife also said to me, "You did an amazing thing." I was surprised; it made me feel I wanted to continue to perform from that moment on. She encouraged me very much.

TAMAH: Did you and Kazuo make *Suiren* between the two of you?

YOSHITO: Together. Yes.

TAMAH: In *Suiren* you also danced with your father as an equal for the first time.

YOSHITO: Yes, that's right. That was the first time I had to create my own part. It was an awesome experience. I was really worried and didn't know what to dance until the last minute.

TAMAH: What were the connections between you and Kazuo afterwards?

YOSHITO: Well, the core work in *Suiren*, "Portrait," the scene of "Portrait," ah, in that I danced my own dance and Kazuo did the dance he created. But I felt something was missing, something that connected my dance and Kazuo's with Hijikata. I thought we needed one, just one water lily to give to Hijikata. That's the most important thing. When we thought of that we were connected. Our minds bonded. At that time, Kazuo was still dancing, but now I have to dance for Hijikata. I want to dance and give one flower to Hijikata. I still have that thought now that he is gone. But it has not been achieved yet. It is not easy.

The future of Butoh

Dance forms, to survive, must change and evolve in new contexts. Definitions of dance, as of art in general, are temporal and situated; they also evolve. Some of the institutions and activities available in Japan for advancing understanding of butoh through Hijikata and Ohno are: the Taro Okamoto Museum of Art, Kawasaki City with its *2003 Exhibition of "Tatsumi Hijikata's Butoh"*; the Keio Art Center Hijikata Archive, Keio University, Tokyo; the Ohno Dance Studio Archives, Yokohama, a private collection on Ohno, seeking an exhibition home; and an academic project in process at the Hijikata Archive to do an extensive evaluation of Hijikata's *butoh-fu*, sixteen bound scrapbooks of collections of his writings and images for dances from the early 1970s to 1985.

Further reading

Arai, Masio (2003) *Hijikata Tatsumi Natsu-no arashi 2003, Hangi-daitohkan* (Hijikata Tatsumi, Summer Storm) Film and DVD, Tokyo: Daguerro Press.

Argentina Sho (Admiring La Argentina, 1977) choreographed and performed by Ohno Kazuo. Program notes translated by Barrett in 1988, Ohno Archives.

Baird, Bruce (2005) 'Buto and the Burden of History: Hijikata Tatsumi and *Nihonjin*' (Japan), unpublished doctoral dissertation, Philadelphia, PA: University of Pennsylvania.

Cahill, Thomas (2003) *Sailing the Wine-Dark Sea: Why the Greeks Matter*, New York: Anchor Books.

Esslin, Martin (1961) *The Theater of the Absurd*, Garden City, New York: Anchor Books, Double Day.

ETV Educational Television (2003) *96 Years Old: Lifelong Butohist, Dancing in My Hometown*, Tokyo: ETV Production, NHK.

Fisher, Elizabeth (1987) 'Butoh: The Secretly Perceived Made Visible', unpublished master's thesis, New York: New York University.

Fraleigh, Sondra (1986) 'Interview with Ohno Kazuo', Yokohama, Japan, August 17, 1986.

—— (1987) *Dance and the Lived Body*, Pittsburgh, PA: University of Pittsburgh Press.

—— (1999) *Dancing into Darkness: Butoh, Zen, and Japan*, Pittsburgh, PA: University of Pittsburgh Press.

—— (2003) 'Interview with Takenouchi Atsushi', Broellin Castle, Broellin, Germany, *EXIT Butoh Festival*, August 15.

—— (2004) *Dancing Identity: Metaphysics in Motion*, Pittsburgh, PA: University of Pittsburgh Press.

—— (2005) 'Spacetime and Mud in Butoh', in *Performing Nature: Explorations in Ecology and the Arts*, edited by Gabriella Giannachi and Nigel Stewart, Oxford: Peter Lang, 327–344.

Fumiaki, Nakamura (1993) 'Butoh no oshie' (Teachings of butoh), in *Ten-nin keraku: Ohno Kazuo no sekai* (Ten-nin keraku: The World of Ohno Kazuo), edited by Takashi Tachiki, Tokyo: Seikyusha, 11–41.

Genet, Jean (1969) *The Thief's Journal*, translated by Bernard Frechtman, New York: Grove Press.

Goda, Nario (1983) 'Ankoku Buto ni Tsuite' (on Ankoku Buto), in *Butoh*, edited by Hanaga Mitsutoshi, Tokyo: Gendaishokan, unpaginated.

—— (1987) 'Hijikata butoh sakuhin noto 2' (Hijikata Butoh Work Notes 2), *Asubesutokan tsushin* 5, October: 41–42.

Goodman, David (1971) 'New Japanese Theatre', *The Drama Review* 15: 154–168.

Guth, Christine (1996) *Japanese Art of the Edo Period*, London: Weidenfeld and Nicolson.

Hijikata, Tatsumi (1959) *Program Notes for Kinjiki, 1959 Zen'nihon buyo kyokai shinjin koen* (All Japan Dance Association New Face Performance).

—— (1984) Letter to Natsu Nakajima, "To My Comrade," Fraleigh's private collection.

—— (2000a) 'Inner Material/Material' (*Naka no sozai/sozai*, 1960), in Kurihara Nanako (ed.), 'Hijikata Tatsumi: The Words of Butoh', translated by Jacqueline S. Ruyak and Kurihara Nanako, *The Drama Review* (Spring) 44, 1: 36–42. Article originally published in July of 1960 as '*Naka no sozai/sozai*', a pamphlet for Hijikata Dance Experience *no kai* (recital).

405

—— (2000b) 'To Prison' (*Keimusho e*, 1961), in Kurihara Nanako (ed.), 'Hijikata Tatsumi: The Words of Butoh', translated by Jacqueline S. Ruyak and Kurihara Nanako, *The Drama Review* (Spring) 44, 1: 43–48. Article originally published in January of 1961 as '*Keimusho e*' in *Mita Bungaku* (The Mita Literature): 45–49.

—— (2000c) 'From Being Jealous of a Dog's Vein' (*Inu*, 1969), in Kurihara Nanako (ed.), 'Hijikata Tatsumi: The Words of Butoh', translated by Jacqueline S. Ruyak and Kurihara Nanako, *The Drama Review* (Spring) 44, 1: 56–59. Article originally published in May of 1969 as '*Inu no jomyakuni shitto suru koto kara*' in *Bijutsu Techo*.

—— (2000d) 'Wind Daruma' (*Kaze daruma*, 1985), in Kurihara Nanako (ed.), 'Hijikata Tatsumi: The Words of Butoh', translated by Jacqueline S. Ruyak and Kurihara Nanako, *The Drama Review* (Spring) 44, 1: 71–79. Originally published as '*Kaze daruma*', in *Gendaishi techo* in May of 1985. Hijikata's *Kaze daruma* is a speech originally titled '*Suijakutai no saishu*' (Collection of Emaciated Body), given the night before the Butoh Festival in February of 1985.

—— (2000e) 'Fragments of Glass: A Conversation between Hijikata, Tatsumi and Suzuki Tadashi', in Kurihara Nanako (ed.), 'Hijikata Tatsumi: The Words of Butoh', translated by Jacqueline S. Ruyak and Kurihara Nanako, *The Drama Review* (Spring) 44, 1: 62–70. Article originally published in April 1977 as '*Ketsujo to shite no gengo-Shintai no kasetsu*' (Language as Lack and Temporary construction of the Body) in Gendaishi Techo.

Hijikata, Tatsumi Archives (2000) *Hijikata Tatsumi butoh shiryōshū dai ippo* (Hijikata Tatsumi Butoh Materials), Tokyo: Research Center for Arts & Arts Administration, Keio University.

Holborn, Mark and Hoffman, Ethan (eds.) (1987) *Butoh: Dance of the Dark Soul*, New York: Aperture.

Hosoe, Eikoh (1969) *Kamaitachi* (Sickle-Weasel), Tokyo: Gendaishichosha.

Igarashi, Yoshikuni (2000) *Bodies of Memory: Narratives of War in Postwar Japanese Culture, 1945–1970*, Princeton, NJ: Princeton University Press.

Ives, Colta (1974) *The Great Wave: The Influence of Japanese Woodcuts on French Prints*, New York: Metropolitan Museum of Art.

Kasai, Toshiharu (1999) 'A Butoh Dance Method for Psychosomatic Exploration', *Memoirs of the Hokkaido Institute of Technology* 27: 309–316.

Kasai, Toshiharu and Takeuchi, Mika (2001) 'Mind: Body Learning by the Butoh Dance Method', *Proceedings from the 36th Annual Conference of American Dance Therapy Association*, Raleigh, NC, October 11–14.

Klein, Susan (1988) *Ankoku Butoh: The Premodern and Postmodern Influences on the Dance of Utter Darkness*, Ithaca, NY: Cornell University Press.

Kuniyoshi, Kazuko (1990) *Performing Arts in Japan Now: Butoh in the Late 1980s*, Tokyo: The Japan Foundation.

—— (2000) *Ichikawa Miyabi: Mirukoto no kyori, dansu no kiseki* (Ichikawa Miyabi: The Perception of Distance in Dance), Tokyo: Shinshokan.

—— (2002) *Yume no ishō: Kioku no tsubo* (Dance and Modernism), Tokyo: Shinshokan.

—— (2004a) *Contemporary Dance in Japan: New Wave in Dance and Butoh after the 1990s*, Tokyo: Arts Midwest.

—— (2004b) 'Hijikata Tatsumi to ankoku butoh: Miidasareta nikutai' (Hijikata Tatsumi and his Ankoku Butoh: Dance of Darkness – The Retrieved Bodies), in *Taro Okamoto Museum of Arts*, edited by Keio University Research Center for the Arts and Arts Administration, Tokyo: Keiogiju-kudaigakushuppankai.

Kurihara, Nanako (1996) 'The Most Remote Thing in the Universe: Critical Analysis of Hijikata Tatsumi's Butoh Dance', unpublished doctoral dissertation, New York: New York University.

—— (2000) 'Hijikata Tatsumi: The Words of Butoh', *The Drama Review* (Spring) 44, 1: 12–33.

Laage, Joan (1993) 'Embodying the Spirit: The Significance of the Body in the Contemporary Japanese Dance Movement of Butoh', unpublished doctoral dissertation, Denton, TX: Texas Woman's University.

Lee, William (2002) 'Kabuki as National Culture: A Critical Survey of Japanese Kabuki Scholarship', in *A Kabuki Reader: History and Performance*, edited by Samuel Leiter, London: M.E. Sharpe.

Matsubara, Saika and other commentators (1998) 'Hijikata Tatsumi: The Compassionate Soul Bird Comes to Unfurl Its Rustling Skeletal Wings', Tape and Booklet, ARIA Disques in Japan, Tape and booklet based on Hijikata's original spoken monologue in 1976.

McGee, Micki (1986) 'An Avant-Garde Becomes an Institution', *High Performance* 33: 49.

Mikami, Kayo (1993) *Utsuwa to shite no shintai* (Body as Vessel), Tokyo: NamishobM.

Motofuji, Akiko (1990) *Hijikata Tatsumi to tomo ni* (With Hijikata Tatsumi), Tokyo: Chikumashobō.

Munroe, Alexandra (1994) *Scream against the Sky: Japanese Art after 1945*, New York: Harry N. Abrams.

Nakajima, Natsu (1997) 'Ankoku Butoh', *Speech at Fu Jen University Decade Conference, Feminine Spirituality in Theatre, Opera, and Dance*, Taipei (October 1997), translated by Lee Chee-Keng in 1997, revised by Elizabeth Langley in 2002.

Nakamura, Tamah (2001) 'Interview with Harada Nobuo', Fukuoka, Japan, July 6.

—— (2005) 'Interview with Ohno Yoshito', Yokohama, Japan, March 19.

—— (2006) 'Beyond Performance in Japanese Butoh Dance: Embodying Re-Creation of Self and Social Identities', unpublished doctoral dissertation, Santa Barbara, CA: Fielding Graduate University.

Hiroyuki, Noguchi (2004) 'The Idea of the Body in Japanese Culture and Its Dismantlement', *International Journal of Sport and Health Science* 2: 8–24.

Noguchi, Michizo (1996) *Genshoseimeitai to shiteno ningen: Noguchitaiso no riron* (The Theory of Noguchi Exercises: Humans as the Agent of Life), Tokyo: Iwanamishoten.

Ohno, Kazuo (1986) 'Selections from the Prose of Ohno Kazuo', *The Drama Review* 30, 2: 156–162.

—— (1992a) *Dessin*, Kushiro, Hokkaido: Ryokugeisha.

—— (1992b) *Ohno Kazuo butoh fu: Goten sora o tobu* (Ohno Kazuo on Butoh: The Palace Soars Through the Sky), Tokyo: Shichōsha.

—— (1997) *Keiko no kotoba* (Words of Workshop), Tokyo: Firumuātosha.

—— (2001) *Beauty and Strength*. NHK Video Software.

—— (2002) *Ishikari no hanamagari* (The Ishikari River's Hooked-Nose Salmon). Kyoto: Karinsha.

Ohno, Kazuo, Dopfer, Ulrike and Tangerding, Axel (1994) 'The Body Is Already the Universe: Dance on the Borderlines of Death: A Conversation with Kazuo Ohno in Yokohama in March 1994', *Ballet International* 8, 9: 52–55.

Ohno, Kazuo and Ohno, Yoshito (2004) *Kazuo Ohno's World from within and without*, translated by John Barrett, Wesleyan, CT: Wesleyan University Press.

Ohno, Yoshito (1999) *Ohno Kazuo: Tamashii no kate* (Ohno Kazuo: Bread/Food for the Soul), Tokyo: Firumuātosha.

Osaki, Shinichiro (1998) 'Body and Place: Action in Postwar Art in Japan', in *Out of Actions: Between Performance and the Object 1949–1979*, edited by Paul Schimmel, New York: Thames and Hudson.

Ozawa-De Silva, Chikako (2002) 'Beyond the Body/Mind? Japanese Contemporary Thinkers on Alternative Sociologies of the Body', *Body and Society* 8, 2: 21–38.

Sagner-Duchting, Karin (1999) *Monet at Giverny*, Munich: Prestel Verlag.

Sakurai, Keisuke, Itoh, Seiko and Oshikiri, Shin-ichi (1998) *Nishiazabu dansu kyōshitsu* (Seminar of Dance at Nishiazabu), Tokyo: Hakusuisha.

Sas, Miryam (1999) *Fault Lines, Cultural Memory and Japanese Surrealism*, Stanford, CA: Stanford University Press.

Schechner, Richard (1986) 'Interview with Kazuo Ohno', *The Drama Review* 30, 2: 163–169.

Scheyer, Ernst (1970) 'The Shapes of Space: The Art of Mary Wigman and Oskar Schlemmer', in *Dance Perspectives* 41, New York: Dance Perspectives Foundation.

Senda, Akihiko (1977) 'Fragments of Glass: A Conversation between Hijikata Tatsumi and Suzuki Tadashi', *The Drama Review*: 62–70.

Slater, Lizzie (1986) 'The Dead Begin to Run: Kazuo Ohno and Butoh Dance', *Dance Theatre Journal* (Winter): 6–10.

Stewart, Nigel (1998) 'Re-Languaging the Body: Phenomeno-Logical Description and the Dance Image', *Performance Research*, 'On Place' (Summer) 3, 2: 42–53.

Strom, Kirsten (2004) '"Avant-Garde of What?": Surrealism Reconceived as Political Culture', *The Journal of Aesthetics and Art Criticism* (Winter) 62, 1: 37–49.

Tachiki, Takashi (1993) *Ten-nin keraku: Ohno Kazuo no sekai* (Ten-nin keraku: The World of Ohno Kazuo), Tokyo: Seikyusha.

Tanizaki, Junichiro (1977) *In Praise of Shadows*, translated by Thomas J. Harper and Edward G. Seidensticker, Foreword by Charles Moore, Stony Creek, CT: Leete's Island Books.

Taro Okamoto Museum of Art, Kawasaki City and Keio University Research Center for the Arts and Arts Administration, Tokyo (eds.) (2004) *Hijikata Tatsumi no butoh: Nikutai no shururearizumu shintai no ontoroji* (Tatsumi Hijikata's Butoh: Surrealism of the Flesh, Ontology of the Body), Tokyo: Keio Gijukudaigakushuppankai.

Toland, John (1970) *The Rising Sun: The Decline and Fall of the Japanese Empire 1936–1945*, New York: Penguin.

Tschudin, Jean-Jacques (1999) '*Danjuro's Katsureki-geki* "Realistic Theatre" and the Meiji Theatre Reform Movement', *Japan Forum* 11, 1: 83–94.

Viala, Jean and Sekine, Nourit Masson (1988) *Butoh: Shades of Darkness*, Tokyo: Shufunotomo.
Waguri, Yukio (1998) *Butoh-Kaden*, CD-Rom and booklet, Tokushima: Justsystem.
Wurmli, Kurt (2004) 'Images of Dance and the Dance of Images: A Research Report on Hijikata Tatsumi's Butoh', commissioned by Keio University, Tokyo, unpublished manuscript.
Yoshioka, Minoru (1987) *Hijikata Tatsumi ko* (On Hijikata Tatsumi), Tokyo: Chikumashobo.
Yuasa, Yasuo (1987) *The Body: Toward an Eastern Mind-Body Theory*, New York: State University of New York Press.

10
LITTLEWOOD (1914–2002)

Nadine Holdsworth

10.1 Biography in political, social and artistic context

Introduction

During the mid-twentieth century, Joan Littlewood was one of the foremost directors of her generation. Her imagination, originality, theatrical chutzpah and lively representations of working-class life stood out when compared to the rather bland British theatre available at the time. As a person, she also stood out in relation to the domesticated, subordinate role assigned to women during this period and the genteel culture of the male-dominated arts industry. Littlewood was a maverick associated with anti-establishment views. She had a fiery temperament and bluntly refused to respect authority for its own sake. Carving out a varied career that more often than not captured the spirit of the times, she wanted to create theatre that had the capacity to be as exciting and all-consuming as the cinema whilst keeping the immediacy of direct contact with an audience. She was a pioneer of the creative ensemble, devised performance, improvisation and for a theatre that moved beyond a polite regurgitation of middle-class life to capture the exuberance, wit and poetry of working-class lives and communities. She showed how theatre could be simultaneously thought-provoking and pleasurable; exuberant and serious; playful and highly skilled. A cultural and artistic innovator, Littlewood's widespread impact can be seen in the many performers and directors with whom she worked, those who were influenced by productions she created or received their training at the East 15 theatre school established to promote her working methods. This book will outline key aspects of Littlewood's career, approach and theatrical output by asking the following questions: What influenced Littlewood? What did she reject about traditional theatre practice? How did her outlook on the world affect the working methods she used? What was so radical about her approach for the time? How and why did her work change and develop?

Before we begin to uncover Littlewood's ideas, theories and practical approach to theatre-making, it is important to issue a few provisos to the material presented in this book. It is a feature of series such as these that the focus is on the work of an individual. However, this approach can mask the fact that theatre-making is a collaborative process that relies not on the vision of one person but the creative engagement of many: performers, designers, technicians, playwrights, producers and the people who make the event of theatre possible: theatre managers, box office staff and cleaners, for example. During her career, Littlewood was unusual in her insistence that her work relied on discussion and creative explorations with other people. She worked closely with performers, writers, choreographers, designers, architects and community activists to develop their practice as part and parcel of her creative output, but it is difficult to pin down exactly what the nature and extent of that input was. As such, there are points in this book when it is tricky to distinguish exactly what Littlewood was responsible for as her tentacles stretched far beyond the parameters traditionally associated with the director figure. Sometimes it is only possible to write about the broader conditions for working that she championed rather than the detail, but I hope that this information itself will illuminate the work of a visionary 'theatre person' who variously turned her hand to teaching, play writing, acting, choreographing and directing, sometimes by financial necessity and sometimes as a natural extension of the directorial role and function. It is also important to accept that, unlike some practitioners covered in this series, Littlewood did not propose a definitive method or style of theatre in the same way that Konstantin Stanislavsky (1863–1938) was associated with naturalism or Bertolt Brecht (1898–1956) with 'epic' theatre. She was a theatrical magpie who stole ideas, adapted them and through this process generated an approach that evolved, developed and turned back on itself as she rejected or returned to ideas. Above all, she never stood still and was variously associated with the experimental avant-garde, radical interpretations of classics, new writing, musical theatre, rousing comedies and large-scale community initiatives.

This chapter will chronologically document Littlewood's development as a theatre practitioner and situate her changing practice in relation to wider social, political and cultural events, movements and debates. Following a brief overview of her origins and early life, the chapter will focus on four key stages in her career. The first section will explore the intersection between politics and innovative practice that characterised Littlewood's early work with Ewan MacColl (1915–1989) in Manchester during the run up to the Second World War. Following discussion of this early work, I will examine the formation of Theatre Workshop following the Second World War and the seven-year period Littlewood spent developing her skills as a director whilst establishing a highly trained ensemble to tour an eclectic repertoire of revitalised classics, modern European texts and original plays by MacColl. The next section will concentrate on the period following the relocation of Theatre Workshop to the Theatre Royal, Stratford East in 1953. From this point Littlewood achieved notoriety for her lively interpretations of the classics and widespread critical acclaim for groundbreaking productions of *The Quare Fellow* (1956), *A Taste of Honey* (1958) and *Oh What a Lovely War* (1963). The final section turns to the 1960s and early 1970s, which found Littlewood increasingly preoccupied with community initiatives and the Fun Palace project. Drawing on widespread concerns with access to and participation in the arts, Littlewood pioneered a series of small and large-scale projects that combined entertainment, communication and learning. These projects form the central focus of this final section although I also document the final shows Littlewood produced at the Theatre Royal before her decision to retire from theatre-making in the mid-1970s.

Early life

Born on 6 October 1914, Joan Littlewood lived with her mother grandparents in Stockwell in South London. Unusually for a girl from a working-class background, she continued her education beyond the age of fourteen after a local convent school recognised her academic potential and awarded her a scholarship. There she continued to develop a love of books, as well as interests in the arts and politics. Throughout her formative years, Littlewood was aware of the advent and consequences of a world-wide economic crisis. In Britain, whilst many people prospered from rising standards of living and the growth of affluent suburbia, class divisions widened as many working-class communities suffered a period of extreme physical, social and economic deprivation as unemployment rose rapidly when coalmining, textile and steel industries declined, the Means Test took hold and the housing crisis deepened. However, rather than suffering quietly, members of the desperate working class began to show their discontent by demonstrating, a move best exemplified by the 1926 General Strike and Hunger Marches that took place across Britain in the 1920s and 1930s. Despite being young, these events politicised Littlewood, as did events closer to home such as the death of her Aunt Carrie from tuberculosis and her own relative poverty compared with her peers at school.

> **General Strike**: on 1st May 1926, a conference of the Trades Union Congress announced a General Strike in defence of miners' wages and hours. The strike involved key industries and a significant proportion of the adult male population as dockers, printers, steelworkers and railwaymen came out on strike for nine days.
> **Hunger Marches**: a series of regional and national marches, organised by the National Unemployed Workers' Movement during the early 1930s, to protest against the poor living conditions of the unemployed.
> **Means Test**: in 1931, the Government restricted access to the employment insurance fund and introduced the 'means test', a humiliating appraisal of all sources of personal and family income before sanctioning assistance.

Littlewood discovered theatre after seeing a production of Shakespeare's *The Merchant of Venice* and secured a place and a scholarship to train at RADA in 1932, but she soon grew frustrated by the type of people she met and the limited learning environment she encountered. She hated the concentration on classics, classical verse speaking and drawing room comedies that bore little relation to the 'real' world and her experience growing up in London. The prospect of a theatre capable of contributing to the widespread calls for social change excited Littlewood and she did not find these represented at RADA. Despondent, she left early in 1933 and, after a brief spell in Paris, decided to walk to Manchester, an industrial heartland far from the elite atmosphere of RADA. As she remembered:

> I loved the northern city at first sight. No Horse Guards, no South Kensington accents, no sir and madam stuff. The wind from the Pennines which swept through the Manchester streets had blown them away . . . This was the Classic Soil of Communism.
> *(Littlewood 1994: 75)*

After contacting Archie Harding, a BBC producer who awarded her First Prize for verse speaking whilst she was still at RADA and cast her as Cleopatra in a BBC Overseas Service programme, *Scenes from Shakespeare*, Littlewood secured irregular work reading poetry, acting and helping pioneer regional documentaries for the BBC. It was here that she met her artistic collaborator, fellow Communist and husband to be, MacColl, then known as Jimmy Miller, in 1934.

Early career: 'theatre as a weapon': Theatre of Action and Theatre Union (1935-1945)

In MacColl, she met someone with strikingly similar goals and together they made a formidable pairing. MacColl was already active in the Workers' Theatre Movement (WTM) a movement associated with the Communist Party that aimed to use 'theatre as a weapon' in the political struggles of the day. With groups such as the Red Megaphones, MacColl took topical, flexible and portable agit-prop theatre to the streets that consisted of short didactic sketches, satirical songs, mass declamation and, more often than not, information or appeals for money on behalf of a particular cause or strike. However, following the rise of Hitler in Germany and the rapid spread of Fascism throughout Europe, it became clear that the changing political climate required more sophisticated, discursive analysis than street theatre could provide so in 1934 MacColl formed Theatre of Action. Littlewood became involved as they rehearsed a variety show that included *Newsboy* (1934), some songs by Brecht and Hanns Eisler (1898–1962), an anti-war sketch and a recitation of *The Fire Sermon*, a poem by Sol Funaroff (1911–1942). During this time, Littlewood also worked at the Rusholme Repertory Theatre as an Assistant Stage Manager, who played small roles. Here, Littlewood worked with the exiled German dramatist, Ernst Toller (1893–1939), when he came to supervise a production of his play *Draw the Fires*. However, this was not typical of the Rusholme Repertory Theatre's usual theatrical diet of staid thrillers and limp comedies. Committed to theatrical exploration and working with socially committed subject matter, Littlewood resigned shortly after working with Toller, to join MacColl full-time to research, develop and 'create a theatre which would be more dynamic, truthful and adventurous than anything the bourgeois theatre could produce' (MacColl 1990: 211). They wanted freedom to experiment as they formulated their own distinct training methods and theatrical vocabulary that placed movement at its centre and drew on their research into leading continental practitioners such as Stanislavsky, Brecht, Rudolph Laban (1879–1958), Vsevolod Meyerhold (1874–1940) and Erwin Piscator (1893–1966), alongside popular cultural forms such as music hall, films and street entertainers. Their pursuit of knowledge was extraordinary and their research continually expanded their theatrical frame of reference and desire to experiment.

During the summer of 1934, Littlewood and MacColl attended a WTM Conference in London, where they saw the anti-war play *Slickers* (1934), a left-leaning well-made play. Despite being appalled at the sub-West End style of production and acting, this show provided source material for a new Theatre of Action production called *John Bullion* (1934), which offered commentary on the capitalist pursuit of war for material gain. During this period, the peace movement was at its height. The Peace Pledge Union formed in 1934 and the League of Nations released the results of its Peace Ballot in 1935, which showed overwhelming support for the League of Nations, the prohibition of private arms sales and a move against rearmament. Whilst the content of *John Bullion* chimed with this mood of pacifism, its mode of expression was highly controversial. The 1931 publication of Leon Moussinac's *The New Movement in the Theatre* disseminated information about seminal works by directors such as Piscator and Meyerhold, but also, more importantly, provided a wealth of images from which to glean a sense of the growing influence of constructivism, expressionism and the application of new technologies. Described as a 'satirical ballet' (Littlewood 1994: 100), *John Bullion* combines agit-prop techniques with a constructivist set on three levels, with symbolic lighting, sound and action. A man in a mask performs a dance symbolising the modern war for profits, the sound of heavy artillery fire intrudes as businessmen buy shares in an armaments manufacturer and three mannequins in swimsuits and gas masks appear as the threat of war gets ever closer. Despite the political credentials of the subject matter, the form radically departed from the Communist Party's support for Soviet socialist realism and, at a series of meetings, Littlewood and MacColl faced accusations of individualism and putting art before politics. Eventually, the local Communist Party branch expelled them.

> The **Workers' Theatre Movement** (WTM): emerged in 1926 and responded to the political climate by taking theatre to the streets, outside factory gates, alongside dole queues and to political rallies. This was an international movement and groups from all over Europe, Russia and America shared scripts and information, culminating in the International Olympiad of Workers' Theatres held in Moscow during October 1932. The WTM ended in 1936, as the rising threat of Fascism called for a broad alliance of 'popular front' politics rather than a class versus class emphasis.
>
> **Agit-prop** (agitational propaganda): is the term used to describe the style of short, topical and provocative sketches performed by the WTM.

In late 1935, the Moscow Academy of Theatre and Cinema granted MacColl and Littlewood study scholarships. However, after a short period in London waiting for visas and spending the meagre travel grant they had managed to scrape together with the help of friends, they temporarily formed a theatre school where they gave lectures on key theatre movements, practitioners and ran practical workshops. By the time visas came through, they could no longer afford to get to Moscow and accepted an offer from the Manchester branch of the Peace Pledge Union to produce Hans Schlumberg's anti-war play *Miracle at Verdun* (1930). After a two-week run at the Lesser Free Trade Hall that secured the group its largest audience and a core of like-minded participants and supporters, Littlewood and MacColl called a meeting of all those who had taken part. They proposed a new inter-disciplinary group, Theatre Union, consisting of actors, artists, technicians, tradesmen and writers who were committed to training, as well as producing socially relevant and theatrically engaging material. A heady whirl of researching, planning, talking, training, rehearsing and performing followed. To aid their quest to reach the broadest possible working-class audience they appealed to Trades Unions and to all groups engaged in political struggle to affiliate with this new organisation in order to build up a network of supporters who could promote shows in their local community and/or workplace. Theatre Union declared its ambitious theatrical aims and broad frame of reference in the following manifesto:

> The Theatre must face up to the problems of its time: it cannot ignore the poverty and human suffering which increases every day. It cannot, with sincerity, close its eyes to the disasters of its time. Means Test suicides, wars, fascism and the million sordid accidents reported in the daily press. If the theatre of to-day would reach the heights achieved four thousand years ago in Greece and four hundred years ago in Elizabethan England it must face up to such problems. To those who say that such affairs are not the concern of the theatre or that the theatre should confine itself to treading in the paths of 'beauty' and 'dignity', we would say 'Read Shakespeare, Marlowe, Webster, Sophocles, Aeschylus, Aristophanes, Calderon, Moliere, Lope de Vega, Schiller and the rest.' The Theatre Union says that in facing up to the problems of our time and by intensifying our efforts to get at the essence of reality, we are also attempting to solve our own theatrical problems both technical and ideological. By doing this we are ensuring the future of the theatre, a future which will not be born in the genteel atmosphere of retirement and seclusion, but rather in the clash and turmoil of the battles between the oppressors and the oppressed.
>
> *(MacColl 1986: vix)*

> **Naturalism**: emerged through the work of French novelist, Emile Zola (1840–1902). Naturalists stress the importance of heredity and environment in determining behaviour and therefore imitate the *real world* as a means of locating fictional characters as products of their background and upbringing. In the theatre, the movement is principally associated with Konstantin Stanislavsky's productions of Anton Chekhov's plays such as *Three Sisters* (1901) and *The Cherry Orchard* (1903).
>
> **Socialist Realism**: has formal similarities with naturalism, but stresses the importance of social factors such as environment over heredity. It views people as products of society, but able to intervene in their own destiny and to enact change.
>
> **Constructivism**: an artistic movement that grew out of the modernist avant-garde in the early part of the twentieth century in Russia. As opposed to concerns with the individual and the subjective, constructivists used new technologies, abstraction and geometric design to convey universal meanings.
>
> **Expressionism**: an artistic movement originating in Germany in the early part of the twentieth century. The preoccupation of the Expressionists was to find a way of representing reality as subjective experience as opposed to reflecting external reality.

The Spanish Civil War (1936–1939) prompted the newly formed company to produce pageants and sketches at 'Aid for Spain' meetings and anti-fascist demonstrations. They also mounted a full-scale production of Lope de Vega's *Fuente Ovejuna* (1612–1614) to promote solidarity with the International Brigade's struggle against fascism and the forces of Franco, as well as raising money for medical aid. Telling the story of revolt against a tyrannous feudal overlord, the play called for large crowd scenes where people fought, danced and sang songs, as well as intimate scenes and overall the play marked a stylistic advance for Littlewood and MacColl as they tackled their first classical production. The first British production of *The Good Soldier Schweik*, which Littlewood and MacColl translated from Piscator's 1928 version of Hasek's famous novel, and a version of Aristophanes' *Lysistrata* (411 BC) followed. Both extended Theatre Union's theatrical range and vocabulary. For *Schweik*, the company drew on their knowledge of Piscator's original production and experimented with a back-projector designed and built for them by four engineering research scientists from Metropolitan-Vickers, alongside agit-prop techniques, an episodic structure, knockabout comedy and comic dance-interludes. Alternatively, *Lysistrata* employed burlesque style comedy to tell the famous story of women standing up against the ravages of male-dominated war. Theatre Union mounted the production during the immediate run-up to the Second World War, a time of appeasement, the Munich Pact and the relinquishing of Czechoslovakia to Hitler. The threat of Fascism across Europe and the growing strength of the British Union of Fascists formed by Oswald Mosley in 1932, made it clear that a more urgent and topical response was required.

> It wasn't a matter of having less art and more politics but of having more clearly stated politics and more powerful art. The better the politics, we reasoned, the better the art and the nearer we would be to achieving our goal of a truly popular theatre.
> *(MacColl 1986: xliv)*

This sense of political urgency became even more acute following the outbreak of the Second World War in September 1939. Deciding that they could no longer justify producing classic plays to obliquely comment on contemporary events, the group began working on a large-scale living newspaper project inspired by the American Federal Theatre's *Triple A Ploughed Under* (1935) and *One Third of a Nation* (1938). Performed in March 1940, *Last Edition* made extensive use of documentary material from libraries, government papers and newspaper items as a basis for sketches about the Spanish Civil War, unemployment, the hunger marches, the Gresford pit disaster and the outbreak of the Second World War. Whilst the piece promoted the fight against fascism, it also presented a blatant critique of the politics of compromise evident in the run up to War and a call for the working class to unite across Europe and fight the forces of capitalism. Whereas Littlewood and MacColl had functioned inter-dependently on previous productions, from this point there was a far clearer division of labour as MacColl concentrated on writing and Littlewood devoted her attention to staging and direction. In addition to the central stage area, she employed two platforms that ran down each side of the auditorium so that the eclectic, variety-style mix of sketches, song and dance would confront and engulf the audience as they played simultaneously or in carefully orchestrated counter-point. She also pulled together all of the techniques previously experimented with as MacColl remembers it:

> the mass-declamatory form, the satirical comedy style of agit-prop, the dance-drama of *Newsboy*, the simulated public meetings of *Still Talking* and *Waiting for Lefty*, the constructivism of *John Bullion*, the expressionism of *Miracle at Verdun*, the burlesque comedy of *Lysistrata*, the juxtaposition of song and actuality from the Spanish Civil War pageants and the fast-moving episodic style of *The Good Soldier Schweik*.
>
> *(1986: xliv)*

In order to get this controversial show past the Lord Chamberlain's censorship, the company decided to run it as a club performance, a familiar strategy whereby the audience enrolled for club membership before admittance to the show. Nonetheless, during the run, the police arrested Littlewood and MacColl, the courts bound them over for two years and they had to withdraw the production. Shortly afterwards, they were blacklisted from the BBC for their communist sympathies and lost their only secure source of income.

In the early years of the War, the group continued their training regime and classes, which focused on Laban-based movement exercises and vocal training, but eventually call-ups, blackouts and bombings made it impossible to sustain the company and Theatre Union disbanded in 1942. Agreeing to reunite after the War, Littlewood and MacColl urged members to keep in touch and gave them reading lists so they could continue their education. To make ends meet, Littlewood turned her hand to freelance journalism and during 1942 wrote a series *Front Line Family* with Marjorie Banks, a producer at the BBC who managed to get around Littlewood's BBC ban with a temporary pass. By the end of 1942, the BBC removed her name from the blacklist as it became far too complicated to ban somebody for their communist sympathies as the Soviets were by now allies in the Second World War. With the ban removed, Littlewood spent the next couple of years making BBC radio documentaries charting the lives of ordinary people in their everyday environments. However, her first love was theatre and as soon as the War ended, she started another venture.

Communism: a political ideology based on the teachings of Karl Marx (1818–1883) in the *Communist Manifesto* (1848) and *Das Kapital* (1867), which offered a critical analysis of the economic organisation of capitalist societies. Marx argued that the state secured ruling class domination by

> supporting private capital and suppressing the mass of the population through institutions such as religion and culture. However, he argued that capitalism was inherently unstable and subject to crises that would eventually lead to revolution and the working class establishing a communist society based on shared ownership and the abolition of class distinctions. Marx's writings underpinned the many communist parties that emerged across the world in the early part of the twentieth century and specifically following the Russian Revolution of 1917 that appeared to show Marx's theory in practice. The Communist Party of Great Britain formed in 1920 through the merger of various left-wing groups.
>
> **Fascism**: the Italian dictator Benito Mussolini (1883–1945) founded the Fascist movement in 1919. Profiting from economic and political instability in the inter-war period, Fascism based itself on aggressive nationalist sentiments, militarism, a hatred of socialism, rejection of democratic and liberal institutions and the presence of a single charismatic leader. A Fascist totalitarian regime headed by Mussolini came to power in Italy in 1929 and exerted influence during the Spanish Civil War (1936–1939) when the 'Republicans' fought 'Nationalist' insurgents under the leadership of General Franco. Nazism was an extreme manifestation of fascism that arose under Adolf Hitler in Germany during the 1920s and 1930s.
>
> **Lord Chamberlain's censorship**: in accordance with the Theatres Act of 1843, all theatre scripts had to be submitted to the Lord Chamberlain for scrutiny before a licence for performance would be granted in Britain. The 1968 Theatres Act abolished this censorship.

On the road: the creative ensemble (1945–1952)

Filled with post-war optimism, Littlewood, MacColl, Bunny Bowen, who first appeared in *Newsboy*, Rosalie Williams and Howard Goorney, who joined for *Schweik*, and Gerry Raffles, who performed in *Last Edition* and became Littlewood's life partner, re-formed as Theatre Workshop. The new name signalled a growing concern with making theatre as an on-going process that grew out of research, training and collaboration. Living and working as part of a collective, Littlewood spent the next few years establishing an ensemble through regular movement, voice and actor's training. A spirit of invention characterised this period as the group experimented with all aspects of theatre from developing their physical skills to constructing cheap sound and lighting equipment and over the next two years, they established a repertoire of plays including original works by MacColl and European classics. Developing a distinctive, energised theatrical style, Littlewood rejected the more familiar text-driven approach of the English tradition in favour of an eclectic, textured, European aesthetic that drew on her earlier agit-prop work, alongside *commedia dell'arte*, burlesque and revue forms that combined drama and dance, verse and stylised movement, song and direct address, together with satire and emotive sequences. Imaginative sets and stark, atmospheric lighting influenced by the work of Swiss scenic designer, Adolphe Appia (1862–1928) equally characterised these early Theatre Workshop productions.

In terms of content, the company remained aligned to a left-wing perspective and used theatre to offer social commentary on the complexity of modern life in the immediate post-war period. The social misery and political unrest of the 1930s initiated a widespread call for change when the War ended. This popular mood for fresh ideas saw Labour sweep to victory in the 1945 general election and prompted attempts to tackle various social problems through the introduction of the Welfare State. Unfortunately, the euphoric mood of optimism waned and post-war disillusionment set in as people lived with the reality of rationing, a devalued pound, the decline of Empire, the increasing prominence of America, the threat of atomic war, the ushering in of the Cold War and the awareness that large social divisions still remained despite the successes of the Welfare State. Theatre Workshop explored these issues and the fight for a more egalitarian and humanitarian society in the work they produced between 1945 and 1952.

> *Commedia dell'arte*: originates in sixteenth-century Italy and refers to a form of popular improvised comedy based on stock scenarios and characters such as Pantalone and Harlequin. Most of the characters wore masks and the material had a strong physical element as it included mime and slapstick. *Commedia* has had a significant influence on comic theatre in Europe ever since.

Littlewood dreamed of creating a cultural centre where she could research, train her company, run workshops to disseminate her ideas and be free to rehearse and create work that would revolutionise British theatre and re-connect with a large working-class audience. She believed those who had experienced war would want a rich cultural life that valued the forces of creativity, civilisation and humanity rather than the forces of destruction and had every faith that an audience would be forthcoming if Theatre Workshop created appropriate and stimulating work. Unfortunately, the next eight years were to disabuse her of this notion. Despite widespread critical praise, the company faced a constant fight against poverty, homelessness and a largely uninterested public.

> The **Welfare State**: was fully implemented after the Second World War to tackle social inequality as the state took responsibility for the provision of basic welfare for its citizens. The principle aim of the Welfare State is to use tax and national insurance to fund free education, health care, social housing and pensions. The Beveridge Report instigated a new national insurance scheme to protect those blighted by loss of wages from unemployment or illness. The Butler Report initiated free compulsory secondary education for all and to ensure investment in an industrial infrastructure crucial for an effective economy, the Government set about nationalising key industries such as coal and steel.
>
> The **Cold War** refers to the mistrustful relationship that developed between the East and West, largely dominated by the USSR and America, after the Second World War. Both sides lacked respect for the other's approach to social organisation – capitalism in the West and communism in the East. The Cold War dominated international affairs and involved several major crises such as the Cuban Missile Crisis and the Vietnam War. For many, the most worrying aspect related to the growth of weapons of mass destruction that meant the consequences of any escalation of violence between these superpowers was unthinkable.

With no public subsidy, the company lived a hand to mouth existence touring the north of England and Scotland playing often ill-conceived, one-night stands and short bookings in out of season theatres. Without a permanent base, the company survived on short-term digs, communal living, minimal wages and regular periods of disbandment whilst Littlewood and Raffles sought appropriate financial and physical resources. Despite these hardships, it was a period of intense commitment, exciting collaboration and rigorous creative practices. There were also several highlights including regular appearances at the Edinburgh People's Festival and successful tours of Sweden and Czechoslovakia during September and October 1948.

To launch Theatre Workshop, the company decided on a double bill of MacColl's ballad opera *Johnny Noble* (1945) and a *commedia dell'arte* inspired adaptation of Molière's *The Flying Doctor* (1649–1650) that employed broad physical and vocal caricature alongside stylised movement. Theatre Workshop built a small, manually operated revolving stage for *The Flying Doctor* that consisted of two halves representing a domestic interior and the street. In stark contrast, *Johnny Noble* played in front of black drapes, with no set or props. The company identified transitions and different settings through an ambitious use of light and recorded sound of artillery, aeroplanes, ships' engines, factory noise and the street played through new portable switchboards and a sound unit consisting of six turntables, built by the company. The play charts the life of a north-east coast fisherman through recorded sound, live narration, folk song, poetry, naturalistic scenes and movement material ranging from a stylised depiction of a gun crew loading and firing weaponry to a joyous jig celebrating Mary and Johnny's engagement. This conventional love story is off-set by recent political events and ends on a topical note of post-war disillusionment illustrated by Johnny's cry, 'we fought for something better' (Goorney and MacColl 1986: 65). These first two productions, one a classic piece of popular theatre and, the other, a multi-dimensional theatrical experience dealing with contemporary political issues, set the tone for Theatre Workshop's repertoire and were quickly joined by a British premiere of Federico García Lorca's *Don Perlimplin* (1931). *Johnny Noble* received considerable praise for its treatment of contemporary themes, alongside the energy and originality of the production. Typical is a review in the *Penrith Observer* that hailed it as 'something new, something vital. A simple story told by the clever orchestration of song, dance and dramatic interlude – an unforgettable theatrical experience' (Anon 1945: 2). Despite lacklustre public support, faith in their aims, gritty determination and youthful exuberance compelled the group to continue and soon events took a positive turn. After seeing *Don Perlimplin* at St John's Hall, Middles-borough in May 1946, Colonel and Mrs Pennyman invited them to stay at Ormesby Hall where they had access to facilities to rehearse and run training classes and summer schools co-organised with local authorities. Unfortunately, personal relationships prompted the company to withdraw from Ormesby Hall in 1947.

Shortly after arriving in Kendal, the official Smythe Report appeared, a document detailing the development of atomic weaponry and the bombing of Hiroshima and Nagasaki. Two new recruits with scientific backgrounds, Bill Davidson and Verity Smith, urged Theatre Workshop to develop a piece about the horrific implications and widespread anxieties generated by the discovery of atomic energy. For many on the Left, it was clear that British political, economic and intellectual life, 'had been transformed by wartime participation in the development of the atomic bomb, and by the decision – taken in secret by the first post-war Labour government – to establish an independent nuclear force' (Davies and Saunders 1983: 31). With the help of Davidson and Smith, MacColl set about learning the history of atomic energy. At first glance, the subject does not suggest the makings of a scintillating evening's entertainment, but the result was the thematically, theatrically and technically ambitious *Uranium 235* (1946). Adopting a fast-paced, episodic structure of fifteen scenes containing fifty-seven characters, in many ways, *Uranium 235* harks back to the agit-prop days of Theatre of Action and Theatre Union with its use of audience plants, microphone voices, actors as narrators and direct address. Yet, it is much more than this. The central scientist figure encounters a chorus of dancing alchemists and expressionistic figures of the Puppet Master, his secretary and servant, Death. A waltz inter-cut with verse explains the scientific discoveries of Marie and Pierre Curie before Death removes them from the stage and Albert Einstein, together with his sidekicks, Nils Bohr and Max Planck, are knock-about comedians who enact the processes of atomic fission through an 'atomic ballet'. The central theme pits the forces of humanity and civilisation against the forces of destruction as MacColl puts science on trial for generating the means to destroy the human race in the pursuit of profit and power. A generation who once had faith in science to alleviate, if not cure, the problems of mankind, now faced the daunting reality that science enabled the manufacture of sophisticated killing machines, poisonous gas, ovens capable of murder on an unimaginable scale and atomic warfare. One moment in the piece encapsulates the sense of outrage that permeates the work and the ideological and moral struggles explored in the play; an inmate of Auschwitz confronts the scientist and declares, 'You are accused of conspiring against the world, of betraying mankind to war and wretchedness, of using the brain to do the work of death' (Goorney and MacColl 1986: 124).

First performed as a short play at the Newcastle People's Theatre in 1946 and developed into a two-hour version first staged at the Community Theatre, Blackburn on 24th April 1946, over the years, *Uranium 235* played numerous venues including the Library Theatre, Manchester and a famous week at Butlin's Holiday Camp in Filey, alongside tours of South Wales in late 1950, Scandinavia in February and March 1951 and a week-long run at the Edinburgh Festival in August 1951. The company achieved great success in Scotland and a group called the Friends of Theatre Workshop formed to promote their work. In the programme accompanying their sponsorship of *Uranium 235* at St Andrew's Hall in Glasgow 24–25th March 1952, the Chair of the group, Morris Linden explained the impact of the company:

> The state of British theatre to-day is unquestionably very low. Standards over the years have gradually become debased. The West End theatre is largely a closed shop; theatres everywhere, with few exceptions, are in the hands of small groups of impresarios. While we have many good actors, producers generally seem to lack originality. Because the box-office must come first, the emphasis in productions has been on spectacle and on the star system, and rarely on originality of thought, or of experiment.
>
> ... It was in this atmosphere of frustration that members of this committee first encountered THEATRE WORKSHOP at the Edinburgh Festival three years ago. It was an exciting experience. By comparison, the offerings of some of the other, famous, companies seemed to be stiff-jointed and inarticulate. It was with a jolt that one realised how much one's standards had been reduced by the general lack of virility in present-day British theatre. But in THEATRE WORKSHOP we found a group of dedicated players, led by a producer of genius. Here was something fresh, delightful and stimulating. The old techniques of Stanislavsky, Eisenstein and of the *commedia dell'arte* had been revived, and all the elements of artistic creation excitingly fused into one.
>
> *(Theatre Royal Stratford East Archive; hereafter TRSE Archive)*

In 1947, the company added Chekhov's *The Proposal* (1888–1889), Irwin Shaw's *The Gentle People* (1939) and *Operation Olive Branch*, MacColl's free adaptation of Aristophanes' *Lysistrata*, to the repertoire. Nonetheless, with mounting debts, the company temporarily disbanded before settling in a shared house in Manchester during March 1948. At this time some of the company worked at other jobs to earn a living, many took classes at the Art of Movement Studio run by Laban associates and rehearsals took place for MacColl's *The Other Animals*, which opened at the Library Theatre on 5 July 1948. The production proved an excellent example of the complex theatrical vision Littlewood was developing with MacColl. It was a far more abstract, philosophical piece than the group had worked on previously. Adopting an episodic structure and a fluid approach to time and space, the play depicts Robert Hanau, a political prisoner who has been in solitary confinement for three years and suffered abuse at the hands of his captors and the prison doctor to the point that he slips between consciousness and delirium. Whilst not as overtly topical or political as earlier work, all the prisoners declared insane have attempted to disrupt the status quo: a woman who refuses to bear children in a war-obsessed society and a labourer who commits himself to the class war, for example. Drawing on European expressionism, particularly Lorca's *Blood Wedding* (1933), the characters include the Moon, Death as an Old Woman and Morning as a Young Girl and the piece calls for song, dance, heightened poetic speech, choral speaking, dream sequences, stylised lighting and an intricate musical score. Littlewood recognised the play's potential obscurity but welcomed the theatrical challenge and the critics applauded her results. The reviewer for the *Manchester Guardian* argued that the company should be seen not only 'because they give new ideas of theatre's potentialities but because they were unique in this country' (J.W 1948: 3). At last, Littlewood was receiving credit for her careful manipulation of experimental theatre techniques.

Unfortunately, financial constraints began to take hold once more and after MacColl produced two rather uninspiring pieces for the company, *The Rogues Gallery*, performed at Manchester's Library theatre in July 1949, and *Landscape with Chimneys* (later renamed *Paradise Street*), which received a South Wales tour in January 1951, Littlewood became increasingly pragmatic. For example, she adapted versions of Shakespeare's *Twelfth Night*, *As You Like It*, *A Midsummer Night's Dream* and *Henry IV* to raise money on schools tours of Manchester and Glasgow between 1949 and 1952. At the time, there were few theatre-in-education companies so schools welcomed the opportunity for children to experience a live performance in their own environment. Less successfully, in December 1949 the company also rehearsed Littlewood's adaptation of Lewis Carroll's classic children's stories *Alice's Adventures in Wonderland* (1865) and *Through the Looking Glass* (1871) to take advantage of the Christmas family market. However, the company's decision to replace the traditional pantomime format with Carroll's vivid and surreal fantasy left many audiences flummoxed. In 1951, Littlewood collaborated with Raffles to write *The Long Shift*, a piece evocatively described as follows:

> A tale of five miners in a Lancashire pit – how they laughed and joked, spat and cursed their way through the day.
> The tale of 'Plodder Seam' the wickedest seam in Lancashire. Only 60ft to go, then 'Plodder's finished' – But 'Plodder' won't be finished . . .
> Suddenly the roof caves in – the men are trapped between two bad falls. Four pit props between them and a mile and a quarter of the earth's crust.
> How long will their bit of roof hold?
>
> *(TRSE Archive)*

This story of a working-class community's bravery and camaraderie in adversity preceded MacColl's *The Travellers*, which opened at the Oddfellows Hall in Edinburgh during the 1952 festival. Preparations for *The Travellers* provide an excellent illustration of the company's hand to mouth existence during this period. Without a permanent base, the company rehearsed in a barn, slept in tents in Tom Driberg's grounds and raised money for food, travel and production expenses by working as farm labourers when not rehearsing. The ambitious set of a simulated train complete with compartments, guard's van and platform transpired after an enthusiastic response greeted an appeal in a local Glasgow paper for help with materials, construction and space to work. Help was also forthcoming from a furniture manufacturer after Harry Greene traded his drawing skills for material and the help of an upholsterer. The play itself marked a return to a broader political canvas as, once again, the company tackled the subject of war. Carrying passengers from many nations, an American train hurtles towards an unknown destination, but to a certain war. MacColl represents the West having learnt little from experience and there is a growing sense of America as a new assertive, arrogant, and brutal superpower blighted by ignorance and prejudice. A battle of wills ensues between the warmongers, individuals driven by their own desire for success in the land of opportunity and those who want to promote collectivism, peace and post-war prosperity for all. The conscientious objectors, who recognise the imminent perils of war, win out and collective action stops the train in its tracks. Whilst accusing the play of blatant Communist propaganda, the reviewer for the *Scotsman* praised the strength of the production and Littlewood for proving 'once again her masterly handling of grouping and movement' (Anon 1952: 6). Littlewood used sound and motion to convey the rhythm of the train and the audience were intimately involved in the action as they sat either side of the elaborate set, which extended from the stage to the hall's entrance. Despite being a great success, *The Travellers* ironically marked the end of touring for Theatre Workshop. Exhausted by lack of money, poor digs, small audiences and unable to find a permanent base in Manchester or Glasgow, the company voted on whether to relocate to a dilapidated Victorian theatre in the East End of London. Founding figure and primary dramatist, MacColl refused to make the move, as he feared a London setting and reliance on critical acclaim would undermine the ideological basis of the company's work. However, a majority voted to try a permanent base and a new chapter for Littlewood and Theatre Workshop opened at the Theatre Royal, Stratford East in January 1953.

Popular theatre/critical success (1953–1963)

During the next decade, radical interpretations of classics, vibrant new writing, popular theatre forms, avant-garde experiment, theatrical inventiveness and groundbreaking representations of working-class life, earned Theatre Workshop a reputation for invigorating the British stage and Littlewood established herself as one of Europe's most critically acclaimed and influential directors. Nonetheless, without Arts Council support, the company struggled to survive and financial worries placed continual pressure on the company. Unfortunately, in the climate of the Cold War, Littlewood and Theatre Workshop's left-wing perspective and communist sympathies made them incompatible with the ethos and prevailing cultural conservatism of the Arts Council, which was more concerned to disseminate high culture then to foster artistic experimentation. However, in the wider cultural sphere of the 1950s, challenges to post-war consensus politics emerged from a generation who benefited from the progressive policies that inaugurated the Welfare State, but who resented the failure of the Labour government to enact significant changes to the status quo. A stasis emphasised by the maintenance of Labour's post-war legislation following Conservative election victories in 1951, 1955 and 1959. As a growing economy, low unemployment rates, increased standards of living and rampant consumerism encouraged Prime Minister Harold Macmillan to proclaim 'you've never had it so good' in 1959, there also developed the embourgeoisment thesis, which argued that class divisions were being eroded as the working class adopted the lifestyle and voting patterns of the middle class. Social theorists, alongside novelists, filmmakers and playwrights, began to re-evaluate and represent issues of class, metropolitan dominance over the regions and popular culture. With its defiant rejection of cultural elitism, desire to establish a local working-class audience, preference for subject matter that placed the working class at its centre and its inventive use of popular cultural forms, regional dialects and colloquial speech, Theatre Workshop keyed into many of these post-war concerns. Moreover, their work stood in direct contrast to the prevalent theatrical diet of middle-class intrigue, drawing-room comedies and Shakespearean star-vehicles. Littlewood's emphasis on creative collaboration, the ensemble and improvisation also placed her at odds with the hierarchical structure of British theatre and the Lord Chamberlain's censorship during this period.

Arriving with no money, the company worked and lived in the cold, damp and seriously run-down Theatre Royal as they attempted to overhaul the décor at the same time as developing their opening programme of fortnightly repertory theatre. A fortnightly turnaround meant far less time for research, training and discussion, but Littlewood initially benefited from working with a long-standing ensemble familiar with her methods. Raffles took responsibility for theatre management and in 1955 acquired the money to buy the theatre, a change that marked a significant shift in the company's organisational structure and decision-making process as whilst the company still nominally operated as a cooperative, Raffles held the purse strings and Littlewood concentrated on the selection and production of scripts. As key members of the ensemble such as Harry Corbett, George Cooper and Joby Blanshard left in the mid-1950s to pursue careers elsewhere, new actors joined but, according to Goorney, the atmosphere and creative ethos changed radically as 'the emphasis was now on learning from Joan rather than on learning together as previously' (1981: 103). As the years passed, the cult of 'Joan' ensued, as she became the central artistic focus rather than the collective ensemble, a change that proved devastating for Littlewood's working practice.

Directing classics

In the first few years at Stratford East, Littlewood performed in a number of productions, directed an ambitious repertoire of historical and contemporary classics including Molière's *The Imaginary Invalid* (1673) and Sean O'Casey's *Juno and the Paycock* (1924) and adapted works by novelists such as Charles Dickens and Mark Twain. Despite playing to small audiences, the company received immediate support from the local press who praised Theatre Workshop's commitment, willingness to experiment, tenacity and theatrical vitality in the face of physical exhaustion, financial struggle and a lacklustre reception. In these early years, Theatre Workshop relied on this local support because minimal attention was forthcoming from the national press, although all this was about to change with events that emerged in 1955. In January 1955, Littlewood staged Shakespeare's *Richard II* to coincide with a production of the same play at the Old Vic. The national critics flocked to compare two very different productions. Whereas the Old Vic emphasised pomp and ceremony, Littlewood offered a stripped back production. Even the critic Harold Hobson, who had reservations about Corbett's portrayal of the king as an effeminate man struggling to keep a grip of his mental faculties, admitted that 'of the two, it is more interesting, controversial and subtle' (1955: 11) because it offered an interpretation of the play rather than providing a predictable vehicle for a bravura performance of poetic verse; an interpretation that has been highly influential for subsequent productions of the play. In May, following an invitation by the organisers, Theatre Workshop represented Britain at the Théâtre des Nations in Paris, alongside the Peking Opera, the Berliner Ensemble and the Abbey Theatre, Dublin. Regardless of the fact that the company arrived with no subsidy or official support, the performances of *Arden of Faversham* (1592) by an unknown Elizabethan dramatist and Ben Jonson's *Volpone* (1606) were acclaimed for their energy and originality. In July, Littlewood directed and played the title role in *Mother Courage*, the first professional production of a Brecht play in Britain following a recommendation from Oscar Lewenstein, a long-time supporter of the company. These events put Theatre Workshop firmly on the theatrical map and Littlewood continued to raise the profile of herself and Theatre Workshop by acquiring a reputation for lively, experimental productions of neglected classics such as John Marston's *The Dutch Courtesan* (1605). In her direction of classics, Littlewood was never interested in poetry or trying to preserve museum pieces, instead she wanted to see the works with fresh eyes, to concentrate on the action as well as the verse and, above all, to bring out their contemporary relevance. These productions also gained a reputation for their sets by John Bury (1925–2000), who had taken responsibility for lighting and stage design. Employing minimal resources such as scaffolding and planks, his austere angles of ramps, stairs and textured surfaces provided ideal subjects for atmospheric, cinematic side lighting used to create the effect of pools, shafts and shadows, as opposed to the painted backdrops and realistic settings seen in the West End. For example, at the beginning of 1956, Littlewood produced Christopher Marlowe's *Edward II* (1594) ingeniously set on a ramp covered in a vast map of England, with a singular elongated throne that converted into a stained glass window and tombstone with lighting changes that also created shadowy areas for plots to unfold.

New writing/improvisation

The 8th May 1956 is indelibly etched on the theatrical consciousness as the premiere of John Osborne's *Look Back in Anger*, a play widely credited with revolutionising the content, if not the form, of British theatre and sparking the 'Angry Young Man' movement. As Osborne's character, Jimmy Porter, indiscriminately railed against the establishment and the contemporary state of England in a Birmingham bed-sitter, commentators welcomed the voice of a generation and theatre, once again, became a fashionable pastime for the young and socially conscious after decades of trite comedy and bland drawing-room dramas. When Brendan Behan's *The Quare Fellow* opened two weeks later on 24th May 1956, another radical theatre voice was born, and a new chapter in Theatre Workshop's history began. Whereas Littlewood had secured a reputation for fresh interpretations of classics, over the next five years she became renowned for working with emerging theatre writers to create vibrant depictions of life on the fringes of society that captured the public's imagination and the interest of West End producers keen to capitalise on a successful product. The theatre text had never been sacred to Littlewood but she now began looking for texts with a spark of life, an original subject matter or grasp of everyday speech patterns from which the company could improvise and flesh out the details of dialogue, relationships, atmosphere and stage business. Because of this eccentric approach, Littlewood developed the reputation of a 'miracle worker' capable of conjuring exciting theatre from minimal resources. Legend has it that Littlewood read the first five pages of Behan's unsolicited text before telegramming her acceptance and invitation for him to come to England to help her tighten and produce his script about twenty-four hours before an execution of a prison inmate. In rehearsal, with Behan's approval, Littlewood started cutting and honing his text to find the best way to theatricalise the tragic and comic elements of this hermetically sealed environment, the robust language, popular song, gallows humour and wry look at the darker recesses of humanity. In particular, she used improvisation to generate a realistic atmosphere and an intricate depiction of the individuals, relationships, habitual actions and tensions that are part and parcel of prison life as the characters share banter, jokes and observations on life and death as the tension builds to the horror of execution. Critics welcomed Behan's exuberant text brought alive by Littlewood's theatrical vision and after a four-week run at the Theatre Royal, the production settled in for a three-month run in the West End, followed by a short regional tour.

Littlewood added to her reputation for courting controversy with Henry Chapman's *You Won't Always be on Top* (1957), a naturalistic portrayal of a day in the life of a building site. The attempt at verisimilitude was helped by an impressive set by Bury that included a three-storey building in the process of construction and a wall built from scratch every night. Offering a faithful depiction of men at work, the authentic dialogue benefited from Chapman's experience as a building worker and, more unusually, from the help received from local bricklayers, who trained, watched and criticised the performers at Littlewood's request. Littlewood wanted the performance to come across as *real* as possible and for her this entailed going to the source – the building site – to authenticate the action; it also meant using improvisation to develop dialogue and to keep the show fresh and in the moment of performance. However, this approach ensured that the show changed, in some aspect, every night, which resulted in a high profile court case as Raffles, Littlewood, Bury, Chapman, and the actor Richard Harris faced prosecution by the Lord Chamberlain for presenting unauthorised material. The whole incident achieved masses of publicity as it became central to a wider debate on and campaign against censorship in British theatre. For Littlewood, the case further secured her reputation as a maverick unafraid to confront head-on British theatre practice and received modes of working.

Littlewood's unconventional approach to text and production struck gold once more with Shelagh Delaney's *A Taste of Honey* (1958). A study of dysfunctional family life in a grotty Salford bed-sit, Delaney was a nineteen-year-old factory worker and cinema usherette when she sent Littlewood her unsolicited script, but Littlewood recognised an original voice in the rich, earthy northern dialogue, finely drawn characters and chaotic relationships. Through some judicious cutting and improvisation, Littlewood shaped Delaney's text. In performance, she avoided sentimental mawkishness by investing it with music-hall style theatricality as direct address, quick-paced banter and a live jazz trio burst through the fourth wall. This dynamic combination excited critics including Lindsay Anderson who declared he had found 'a work of complete, exhilarating originality ... [that] has all the strength, and none of the weaknesses of a pronounced, authentic local accent' (1958: 42). After *A Taste of Honey*, Littlewood produced Behan's *The Hostage* (1958), a loosely structured, vaudevillian follow up to *The Quare Fellow*. As Behan struggled with alcoholism and greater desire for the conviviality of the bar, rather than putting his art for storytelling and witty dialogue on the page, Littlewood received only small sections of text to work with. Hence, she developed *The Hostage* in a haphazard way using Behan's text as a basis, bolstered by noting, and having others note, Behan's drunken anecdotes and vast repertoire of original, folk and music-hall songs and by filling gaps through improvisation. The result was a freewheeling tragi-comedy populated by eccentrics, prostitutes, pimps, a secret agent, religious zealot and IRA sympathisers who share their songs, stories and coarse banter with the audience. The critics loved the production and Hobson best exemplifies their enthusiasm:

> ... it made on me the impression of a masterpiece ... It crowds in tragedy and comedy, bitterness and love, caricature and portrayal, ribaldry and eloquence, patriotism and cynicism, symbolism and music-hall songs all on top of one another, apparently higgledy-piggledy, and yet wonderfully combining into a spiritual unity ... It is an honour to our theatre.
>
> *(1958: 21)*

The Hostage received similar accolades when it represented Britain, with support from the British Council, at the Paris International Festival in April 1959 and during a transfer to the West End later the same year. Littlewood's next new writing project, a musical *Fings Ain't Wot They Used T'Be*, written by Frank Norman with music and lyrics by Lionel Bart, similarly made it into the West End. Littlewood had become deeply fashionable and the West End impresarios were not going to miss the chance of making some money on the back of her reputation. Despite being criticised for having a meandering plot, a lack of purpose and only minimal entertainment value, *Fings Ain't Wot They Used T'Be* won the *Evening Standard* Award for the Best Musical of 1960 and received praise for Littlewood's 'slap-up, street-party production' (Brien 1959: 289). The latter description pinpoints a significant shift in Littlewood's output. Gone were the serious-minded interrogations of contemporary political questions, which during this period could have dealt with the consequences of the ever-deepening Cold War, the Suez crisis, the decline of Britain's imperial power and the increasing global power of America. Instead, Littlewood replaced Theatre Workshop's earlier political and social agenda with a rousing knockabout East End 'knees up' style of theatre that owed a great debt to popular variety entertainment.

Despite the emphasis on music-hall style banter and raucous comedy on-stage, behind the scenes things were taking a toll on Littlewood. Critics largely dismissed attempts to move away from the 'knees-up' aesthetic and Littlewood, due to a lack of public subsidy, found herself forced back to a winning formula. However, by the time she produced an improvised version of Marvin Kane's television play *We're Just Not Practical* in 1961, there was a general feeling that 'what began as a highly original and altogether stimulating method on the part of Miss Littlewood has now degenerated into something of a stale formula that is beginning to fail to inspire either the producer or the players' (Roberts 1961: 13). After a six-month break from producing work at the Theatre Royal when she went to work and live in Berlin, Littlewood directed James Goldman's fantasy *They Might Be Giants* (1961). Littlewood produced the play in association with Robert E. Griffith and Harold S. Prince, American impresarios who achieved success with *West Side Story* and now wanted Littlewood to provide a Broadway hit. The opening night boasted the presence of Princess Margaret and large numbers of press, but the show was barely ready and received a damning response. Upset by the critics' reception and frustrated by financial pressures that meant minimal rehearsal time and the constant pressure to generate West End transfers that ultimately broke up her ensemble, Littlewood withdrew from the Theatre Royal declaring, 'when you have to live by exporting bowdlerized versions of your shows as light entertainments for sophisticated West End audiences you're through' (1961: 5). During the next two years, Littlewood travelled extensively, tried to get a film of Wole Soyinka's *The Lion and the Jewel* (1959) off the ground, read numerous unsolicited scripts and devoted much of her energy to plans for a Fun Palace. She returned to the Theatre Royal in early 1963 to create the politically charged and theatrically adventurous *Oh What a Lovely War*, a satirical dissection of the capitalist imperatives, power-brokering, class relations and devastating human consequences of the Great War, a 'War To End All Wars', re-interpreted in the long shadow of the Second World War and the widespread political fall-out of the very present Cold War. The impetus, rehearsal process, production and influence of this piece will receive detailed attention in Section 10.2.

> **Suez Crisis** (1956): a political crisis focused on the Suez Canal in Egypt following intensive re-armament by Egypt, the nationalisation of the Suez Canal and a plot by Egypt, Syria and Jordan to isolate Israel. In October 1956, Israel launched a pre-emptive strike in the area which prompted Britain and France to request all sides to withdraw from the Canal Zone and agree to temporary occupation. When Egypt refused, Britain and France invaded, but the USSR and USA forced them to withdraw following diplomatic action, a defining moment in Britain's imperial decline and the rise of the two superpowers.

Community initiatives (1963–1975)

The fun palace

During the mid-1960s and early 1970s, Littlewood increasingly withdrew from making theatre and threw herself into ambitious plans to democratise the arts and to animate community-based activity and values. In particular, she developed and promoted ideas for a Fun Palace, which harked back to traditional forms of popular entertainment such as the Vauxhall Pleasure Gardens, whilst also utilising all the advantages of the new technological age. Littlewood's plans for a centre of cultural, educational and technological activity situated in the East End were echoed in the ill-fated Millennium Dome but, in many ways, Littlewood's plans were far more ambitious. Her visionary project was inextricably tied to the spirit of the times as speculation arose about how much extra leisure time people would have as computers or robots took over the bulk of the manufacturing process and domestic labour-saving devices freed people from time-consuming domestic chores. Writing in the *New Scientist*, Littlewood proposed that:

> Those who at present work in factories, mines and offices will quite soon be able to live as only a few people now can: choosing their own congenial work, doing as much or as little of it as they like, and filling their leisure with whatever delights them.
>
> *(1964: 432)*

Littlewood and the architect Cedric Price's plans for a Fun Palace aimed to meet these new demands. Described as both a 'university of the streets' and 'a laboratory of pleasure', Littlewood envisaged the Fun Palace as a multi-use space housing a series of short-term, frequently-updated activities dedicated to pleasure, entertainment, communication and learning. During the 1950s and 1960s, social and cultural theorists such as Richard Hoggart and Raymond Williams were concerned that Welfare State educational and cultural policies, alongside American-dominated commercially-produced consumer culture and mass-media communications, were resulting in passive audiences. In contrast, Littlewood wanted to provide opportunities to learn and experience culture beyond the commercial market place and hierarchical institutions such as the BBC and education system. By providing numerous types of activity, Littlewood hoped to encourage people to make active decisions about what inspired them, gave pleasure and stimulated their imagination, regardless of whether that involved high art, popular culture, direct participation or casual observation. Alongside opportunities for activities, cultural encounters, eating, drinking and socialising, Littlewood also wanted a space akin to the great parks that facilitated strolling and a chance to watch the world go by.

Littlewood wanted her Fun Palace to draw on the latest scientific gadgets, technological systems and groundbreaking ideas. A 'science playground' holding illustrated lecture-demonstrations by day, by night was to become a space for sharing new theories and ideas. An interactive 'fun arcade' would include games for people to test their knowledge, spatial awareness and physical skills, alongside tests to explore character traits, moral dilemmas and contemporary social themes. A 'plastic area' would enable people to experiment in woodwork, clay, textiles, painting and metalwork. The idea being that somebody could pick up an activity and discard it in a day or return to develop skills and techniques over a longer period. Similarly, a 'music area' would provide access to instruments, free instruction, recording facilities, a music library and places to listen during the day, followed by jamming sessions, music festivals and dancing in the evening. An 'acting area' dedicated to drama therapy formed an important and exciting part of Littlewood's vision. Rather than performing to an audience, she proposed a theatre of everyday life in which people would use theatre to explore ideas, events and dilemmas that directly affected them.

> Men and women from factories, shops, and offices, bored with their daily routine, will be able to re-enact incidents from their own experience in burlesque and mime and gossip, so that they no longer accept passively whatever happens to them but wake to a critical awareness of reality, act out their sub-conscious fears and taboos, and perhaps are stimulated to social research.
>
> *(Banham 1964: 191)*

Littlewood's intention to use enactment and discussion to activate personal and political awareness of relationships and social structures was later developed through Augusto Boal's notion of the spect-actor and his work developing theatre to help liberate people from restrictive, exploitative situations by offering them alternative ways of seeing and responding. Even when more traditional theatre events were proposed, Littlewood planned mechanisms to enable audience participation such as a backstage computer to calculate and relay audience input and responses. In another forward-thinking move, Littlewood proposed an extensive use of large screens to transmit local and national news as well as popular events including concerts, Cup Finals and state occasions such as weddings and funerals. She also anticipated the current cultural obsession with reality television and fly-on-the-wall observation in her plans for closed-circuit television that would capture and transmit unedited images of people going about their daily business in and around London or in the complex itself.

Littlewood developed her ideas with Price, whom she met in 1961. Like Littlewood, he was happy to fly in the face of convention and together they produced groundbreaking plans for a modern, non-permanent, multi-functional arena, which completely opposed the post-war obsession with permanent structures such as new housing estates, universities and municipal buildings. Price believed in innovation over conservation and re-conceived a building's worth not in terms of its durability or the quality of its construction material, but in terms of its use and social value. He proposed a physical network of zones housing numerous adjustable units that could range from small workshop spaces to large volume enclosures for rallies, concerts and major exhibitions. Exploiting the potential of technology to revolutionise architectural practice, Price used cutting-edge technology to maximise accessibility, control climatic conditions and to divide the spaces in new and exciting ways. The emphasis on flexibility, consumer choice, impermanence, pleasure and technological solutions connected to the wider social and cultural context of the 1960s. In particular, the Fun Palace provided a cultural response to Labour Prime Minister Harold Wilson's claim that the 1960s were characterised by the 'white heat of technological change', exemplified by experiments in space travel and satellite communication systems.

Throughout the 1960s, Littlewood battled to raise awareness of, interest in and financial support for the Fun Palace. She assembled a board of high profile trustees comprising R. Buckminster Fuller, Lord Ritchie Calder, The Earl of Harewood and Yehudi Menuhin, to lend weight and credibility to the project. She wrote articles, spoke at conferences and delivered lectures, as well as lobbying local councils, arts organisations and residential associations. To generate funds she made TV commercials, directed a film of *Sparrers Can't Sing* (1963) and agreed to direct *Twang!* (1965) in the West End. There was a general sense that support for the arts would increase during the 1960s as local authorities made use of the provision made in the Local Government Act of 1948 for cultural activities and the Arts Council received more central funding from government. Unfortunately, no organisation was prepared to back such a radical, untested project and whenever Littlewood and Price identified a potential site, the Fun Palace got caught in a vicious administrative cycle of plans, proposals, feasibility studies, council meetings, local resident groups, muted support and eventual rejection. The project was way before its time and demanded a leap of faith and imagination from potential funders, local councils, town planners and local residents that few were able to meet and, unfortunately, the Fun Palace never materialised.

Local redevelopment and the playground projects

Between the mid-1960s and early 1970s, the immediate area around the Theatre Royal was subject to extensive redevelopment. The Council were determined to replace the rows of Victorian Terraces, the street market, small local shops and a local school with an office and shopping complex, car parks and low-rise flats. Newham Council wanted the theatre demolished as part of this process but, typically defiant, Raffles responded by having the theatre designated a listed building by the Historic Buildings Council in 1972. However, Raffles and Littlewood's concern stretched beyond the theatre as they feared children, teenagers and adults, with nowhere to go and nothing to do in the evenings and weekends, would become increasingly socially alienated. To remedy this situation, Raffles proposed that Newham Council build an entertainment complex around the Theatre Royal with a cinema, disco and restaurants. Newham Council declined. Undeterred, Littlewood approached the immediate problem of local demolition creatively and set about animating environments blighted by destruction. Erecting temporary structures on sites cleared by volunteers and using the theatre itself, at various points between 1967 and 1975, Littlewood arranged drama activities, playgrounds, gardens, a city farm, educational and recreational classes and pony rides for local children and teenagers. She also gave the children freedom to organise their own events such as mock trials and 'posh nights' on the Theatre Royal stage. To help transform the area, local firms donated turf, scaffolding, tools, paint and toys. Teenagers painted the shop fronts around Angel Lane a multitude of colours, children helped lay crazy paving, volunteers lay turf and trees to replace all the lost gardens and, in all, five sites were cleared and transformed. Writing to potential backers, Littlewood explained her rationale:

> Everywhere land is becoming temporarily derelict while local authorities wait for the go-ahead on new building schemes. There is insufficient money for schools, nurseries, modern youth clubs and clubs for people of all ages. At the same time, talented people are prepared to give their time and skill to direct practical solutions of (*sic*) this problem.
>
> Pleasant, temporary structures to house these activities can be erected on the old debris instead of giving it over to dumping and dirt. When rebuilding starts, the structure can be moved on.
>
> Meanwhile, we may find out how to enjoy ourselves and even enrich ourselves a bit more. The talent, which in the old days seemed to belong only to the 'stars' in society, is in each child. It just needs cherishing.
>
> *(TRSE Archive)*

In 1969, activists for the Theatre Royal Club, led by Christine Jackson, together with children, teachers and helpers took over, cleaned and decorated a disused factory so that is could be used for classes, games and drama therapy. In 1974, Littlewood gave the children responsibility for organising a Grand Easter Fair in an old National Car Park site and established a Zoological Garden for the Easter holidays. Heavily subsidised by Littlewood and Raffles, all these activities came under the auspices of the Fun Palace Trust.

The final productions

Littlewood directed less than twenty shows at the Theatre Royal between 1964 and 1973 as her creative energies were devoted to the Fun Palace. With *Oh What a Lovely War* in the West End, in March 1964 Littlewood directed Norman's follow-up to *Fings Ain't Wot They Us'ed T'Be* called *A Kayf Up West*. Critics were unanimous in their disappointment with this pale imitation of Norman's previous success and complained about a lack of authenticity, clichéd characters and an absence of theatrical vitality. A strained relationship with the critics continued with Littlewood's modern adaptation of parts one and two of *Henry IV* into a single piece that premiered at the Edinburgh Festival in August 1964. Frustrated, Littlewood retreated from making theatre at the Theatre Royal for another two years. During this period, *Oh What a Lovely War* went to America; she directed two Summer Schools with students from all over the world in Hammamet, Tunisia, and focused her attention on raising funds for the Fun Palace by directing *Twang!*, a satirical musical based on the Robin Hood legend. The writer and composer Lionel Bart envisaged a spectacular extravaganza that combined Theatre Workshop techniques with all the trappings of commercial theatre. The combination was a disaster and Littlewood resigned on the opening night of the pre-London run in Manchester. Many held Littlewood responsible for the failures of *Twang!* The honeymoon period of the mid- to late 1950s and early 1960s was definitely over.

Littlewood returned to the Theatre Royal in April 1967 to direct four shows and expectations ran high as she re-assembled several Theatre Workshop regulars. Barbara Garson's *Macbird* (1966) opened as a Theatre Royal Club production after the Lord Chamberlain refused to issue a licence for a play that put two American presidents, John F. Kennedy and Lyndon B. Johnston, at the heart of a parody of *Macbeth* and American political power-brokering. Transforming Garson's text from a biting satire to a vaudeville romp, critics accused Littlewood, once again, of riding roughshod over an existing text. Based on the satirical magazine, *Private Eye*'s column that explored national and international events through the eyes of the Prime Minister's wife, Littlewood's production of Richard Ingrams' and John Wells' *Mrs Wilson's Diary* (1967) marked a significant precedent in British theatre censorship as living politicians and, specifically the Prime Minister, were held up for topical ridicule. Political satire had become popular on the cultural circuit in the early 1960s with *Beyond the Fringe* in the theatre, *That Was the Week That Was* (TW3) on television and *Private Eye*. The growth of satire signalled a wider social shift, specifically a decline in social deference as the working class became successful in all walks-of-life and events such as the Profumo Affair revealed the fallibility of people in authority.

Akin to an extended revue sketch with songs and comic turns, *Mrs Wilson's Diary* presents the Wilsons as ridiculous, tasteless figures, who put gnomes in the No. 10 Downing Street Garden, eat paste sandwiches and send off for the Dalek competition advertised on the back of Frosti-puff cereal packets. Its affectionate lampooning of authority figures proved hugely popular and the show transferred to The Criterion in the West End for an eight-month run. Daniel Farson and Harry Moore's *The Marie Lloyd Story* (1967), an old-fashioned musical based on the life, loves and songs of the East End music-hall entertainer Marie Lloyd, starred Avis Bunnage. In nineteen scenes announced like music-hall turns, Littlewood emphasised the shifts between realistic scenes of backstage life, the personal tragedy of a very public star and the highly theatrical music-hall songs, sexual innuendo and banter to the audience. Several critics hailed a return to form for Littlewood, but the Theatre Royal was still struggling financially and, once again, she withdrew from making theatre for several years.

> **The Profumo Affair**: named after the Conservative MP John Profumo, who resigned as Secretary of State for War in 1963 after he deceived the House of Commons about his relationship with Christine Keeler, who was also involved with a Soviet diplomat. The high-profile scandal at the height of the Cold War rocked the establishment and the Prime Minister, Harold Macmillan, resigned shortly after the publication of Lord Denning's report into the events.

When Littlewood returned to directing she complemented the community-orientated work outside the theatre with the productions *Forward Up Your End* (1970), *The Projector* (1970) and *The Londoners* (1972), which tackled local politics, particularly 'the erasing of communities in the name of bureaucratic progress' (Ansorge 1972: 20). For instance, *The Projector*, billed as a newly unearthed work by the eighteenth-century playwright William Rufus Chetwood, offered a humorously satirical treatment of the 1968 collapse of a residential tower block at Ronan Point. Threatened with legal action if she pursued her original plan to produce a drama documentary based on the inquiry into the Ronan Point disaster, Littlewood and Wells concocted the story of Chetwood's non-existent play, *The Mock Mason*, centred on a crooked Dutch property developer, Van Clysterpump, who bribes and dodges his way through a series of deals and mishaps including the collapse of one of his buildings. Evoking the song spiel style of *The Beggar's Opera* and the biting wit of Hogarth's paintings, the vaudeville style revue was populated by Theatre Workshop's familiar band of prostitutes, hucksters and social misfits, who introduce an atmosphere of amoral lasciviousness to accompany the political intrigue surrounding the Ronan Point incident. After another break, Littlewood returned to the Theatre Royal in early 1972 with two revivals: a musical version of Lewis' *Sparrers Can't Sing* called *The Londoners* and a new version of Behan's *The Hostage* with eight members of the original cast. With music by Bart played by Bob Kerr's Whoopee Band, *The Londoners* heralded a return of the East End knees-up first seen with *Fings Ain't Wot They Us'ed T'Be*. Nonetheless, its depiction of the inhabitants of a condemned slum terrace and their rumbustious community spirit also spoke volumes in the context of the loss of two thousand such homes in the immediate vicinity of the Theatre Royal. Behan's *The Hostage* had similarly acquired significant contemporary relevance owing to the violent escalation of 'the troubles' in Ireland, Northern Ireland and mainland Britain.

Littlewood's final productions in 1972 and 1973 increasingly resembled end-of-pier entertainments with their saucy postcard-style humour. Reminiscent of the hugely popular Carry On genre of films, Frank Norman's *Costa Packet* (1972) even had an accompanying series of risqué postcards produced by the cartoonist Larry, who also created the set. Unfortunately, these productions simply did not reflect the spirit of 1970s Britain during a period of fervent political, social and industrial unrest. The work seemed frivolous in comparison with the burgeoning alternative theatre movement that attempted to attract non-theatre going audiences with a progressive approach to subject matter and performance strategies. Ironically, this movement drew on Theatre of Action's agit-prop and Theatre Workshop's creative approach in its attempt to revolutionise theatrical process and product, but, in the light of this new aesthetic and political radicalism, Theatre Workshop appeared populist, commercial, and even reactionary.

Littlewood and Raffles battled to keep the theatre going for twenty years without any significant subsidy from the Arts Council or the local authorities and, by the time revenue funding was finally allocated in 1972, Littlewood was too disillusioned to take advantage of it. There was a remarkable shift in the Arts Council's culture during the early 1970s that reflected an economic boom and an atmosphere of social and political upheaval. A new generation of Arts Council employees and panel members such as Philip Hedley, who eventually took over as Artistic Director of the Theatre Royal in 1979, recognised Littlewood's contribution to British theatre, but despite offers of increased funding, it was not enough to run the building efficiently or effectively. Raffles resigned as theatre manager in April 1974. A year later he died. Littlewood's grief and her subsequent decision to move to France put an end to her work at the Theatre Royal. She established an advisory council to discuss artistic proposals and handed over to a new generation headed by Maxwell Shaw, a long-standing Theatre Workshop actor. In 1975 Littlewood announced her intention to give the Theatre Royal to Newham through the Fun Palace Trust and from this point she had very little to do with the theatre. After 1975, Littlewood lived a nomadic existence staying in a small apartment and enjoying the hospitality of friends. She spent her time writing letters, established a long-term friendship with Baron de Philippe Rothschild, whose autobiography she edited, and wrote her entertaining, if highly selective, autobiography, *Joan's Book*, before her death in London in 2002.

10.2 Description and analysis of *Oh What a Lovely War*

Introduction

Ironically, the production that secured Littlewood's reputation as one of the great twentieth-century directors was not her idea, but that of Raffles. On 21st February 1962, he listened to a radio broadcast by Charles Chilton called *A Long Long Trail*, in which Bud Flanagan narrated a history of the Western Front from an ordinary soldier's point of view, interspersed with popular songs from the First World War. Raffles was convinced that the songs would make a strong basis for a theatre piece so he acquired a copy of the broadcast and commissioned Chilton, as well as playwrights Gwyn Thomas and Ted Allan, to come up with theatre scripts. Raffles took this decision without any consultation with Littlewood who was absent from the Theatre Royal at the time. Chilton failed to produce a play and the playwrights' first attempts received a lukewarm reception because they tried to represent the War in naturalistic terms. When Littlewood returned and experienced a read-through of one of the submitted plays, she was adamant she could do better and came up with a rough structure sketching out some key events, quotes and production ideas. After assembling the nucleus of a company, Raffles and Littlewood called a meeting with them at the Theatre Royal attended by Chilton, alongside the Musical Director and choir who performed the songs from the original broadcast. The actors were decidedly under-whelmed; Victor Spinetti and Griffith Davies made their dislike of the sentimental songs very clear and Littlewood recalled being taken back to her childhood, 'red, white and blue bunting, photos of dead soldiers in silver frames, medals in a forgotten drawer, and that look as family and friends sang the songs of eventide' (Littlewood 1994: 676). Despite reservations and no script, the show went into production with Littlewood as director and the result became a widely recognised theatrical landmark that premiered at the Theatre Royal, Stratford East on 19th March 1963.

1963: political and cultural context

In many ways, it is not surprising that a seminal piece of theatre should emerge in 1963, as this was an extraordinary year in many respects. It was a year full of high profile events and audacious challenges to authority and the established order. In America, the assassination of President John F. Kennedy shocked the world. The Civil Rights movement reached new heights when 250,000 people marched on Washington to demand equal rights and Martin Luther King delivered his famous 'I have a dream' speech. In Britain, the Profumo sex and security scandal involving the minister for war, John Profumo, and Christine Keeler came to light. For many, these revelations not only confirmed the presence of corruption at the heart of government, but also exposed the hypocrisy of those in high office. In addition to unease with domestic, defence and foreign policy, the 'Profumo Affair' was another reason cited for the declining faith in Conservative rule that lead to Harold Macmillan's resignation in October 1963 and the first Conservative defeat since 1951 when Harold Wilson became Prime Minister in 1964. Wilson marked a significant shift in British politics as he 'stepped forward to present the country with a fresh self-image' (Hewison 1986: 39) that drew on the modern age of technological change and scientific development. With a distinct Yorkshire accent and 'an extraordinary ability to project a working-class and anti-establishment image' (Sked and Cook 1984: 185), Wilson signalled a more egalitarian impulse in Britain and a move away from the traditional political hierarchy epitomised by the new Conservative leader, Sir Alec Douglas-Home. Cultural producers were equally challenging hierarchies in the cultural field. Whilst the National Theatre staged its inaugural production of *Hamlet* played by Peter O'Toole and directed by Laurence Olivier; John Arden and Margaretta D'Arcy held a 'festival of anarchy' in Kirbymoorside in Yorkshire, which included films, plays, poetry readings and concerts. The Beatles launched their rise to international stardom after releasing *Please, Please Me* and the television show *That Was the Week That Was* continued to grab headlines with its satirical treatment of authority figures after its launch in November 1962.

The war game

Oh What a Lovely War captures a spirit of oppositional defiance and as Paget points out 'The play's essential line of argument (which is to attack upper-class incompetence, insensitivity and hypocrisy) will always tell us something important about the time in which it was written' (Paget 1990b: 119). At the same time, *Oh What a Lovely War* is the last in a long continuum of works in which Theatre Workshop and its predecessor Theatre Union, characterise war as inextricably tied up in capitalist profiteering, imperialism and the exploitation of the working classes. In terms of the wider political climate, *Oh What a Lovely War* clearly engaged with the prominent Campaign for Nuclear Disarmament (CND) that arose in the late 1950s supported by many Theatre Workshop members, including Littlewood. The Second World War proved those in power had not learnt lessons from the mass destruction of the First World War; whilst the continuing presence of the Cold War and the threat of nuclear war, brought chillingly home by the Cuban Missile Crisis, fuelled a widely supported campaign for unilateral disarmament. The campaign took the position that following the decline of Empire Britain no longer had status as a world power and urged it instead to be 'a great moral rather than a military influence in the world' (Sinfield 1983: 31). Debates raged about the futility of war, the economic imperatives that drive war and the humanitarian and environmental damage proposed and implemented through nuclear testing, let alone the prospect of *actual* nuclear war. In the current climate, it is difficult to imagine how real the threat of nuclear war seemed to be at this time, but this generation lived through the unthinkable events that occurred in Nagasaki and Hiroshima during the Second World War – for them nuclear war was a very real and present danger.

Oh What a Lovely War also responded to, and coincided with, wider cultural interest in and attempts to uncover the everyday 'truth' of the First World War, the first truly modern, industrialised and mechanised war that caused unimaginable scales of death and trauma as it was played out across land, sea and air. The early 1960s saw numerous works about the First World War thrust into the public arena: autobiographies and biographies of leading figures, radio programmes, anthologies of poetry and BBC2 ran a six-month documentary series, *The Great War*, in 1964. This material ignited a renewed sense of loss, waste and anger that found expression in CND, as well as a broader questioning of the values and wisdom of the establishment. The long-held suspicion that the War was ill-conceived and ill-managed by a brutal and incompetent upper-class elite that stayed well away from the danger zones of the front line was by now widespread and Theatre Workshop gave voice to this view. In order to provide counter-narratives to the official versions of history written by those in positions of power and in line with concerns to recuperate working-class histories, there was also a move to discover the front line soldier's role in the War. From the start, the aim of *Oh What a Lovely War* was to provide a collective voice for the many ordinary soldiers who had lost their lives and been reduced to nameless and faceless statistics. For instance, like many people, Chilton was keen to make sense of his personal history and the loss of his father in the War. As the programme for *Oh What a Lovely War* explains, in 1958 he visited Arras to photograph his father's grave, but found no grave and just a list of '35,942 officers and men of the Forces of the British Empire who fell in the battle of Arras and who have no known graves'. He writes:

> What could have possibly happened to a man that rendered his burial impossible? What horror could have taken place that rendered the burial of 35,942 men impossible and all in one relatively small area?
>
> The search for the answer to this question has finally led to this production, in the sincere hope that such an epitaph will never have to be written upon any man's memorial again.
>
> *(TRSE Archive)*

Cuban Missile Crisis (1962): a defining moment of the Cold War when the USA discovered Soviet nuclear missile sites in Cuba. Military confrontation was only avoided when Soviet leader Nikita Khrushchev agreed to President John F. Kennedy's demands for the base to be dismantled in return for the withdrawal of US missiles from Turkey.

Hence, a major impetus behind *Oh What a Lovely War* was an attempt to record and honour the experiences of these men, to celebrate their lives and to make them the stars of the show, whilst simultaneously questioning the legitimacy and management of the War that brutally claimed their lives.

> Having been in the production, it is quite clear to me that *Lovely War* is a celebration of human resourcefulness in the face of the most appalling catastrophic conditions. So Joan celebrates courage, humour, comradeship, the triumph of life over death and the international solidarity between soldiers.
>
> *(Barker, cited in Goorney 1981: 126)*

Barker's last point is worth further consideration. Another notable characteristic of *Oh What a Lovely War* is its international perspective and universal respect for the common soldier, regardless of their country of origin. There is a sense that all the soldiers, whether British, French or German, are pawns in a war driven by capitalist profiteering, imperialism and power-hungry generals.

Theatricality

The most striking aspect of Littlewood's 1963 production of *Oh What a Lovely War* was the sheer audacity, confidence and variety of her theatrical vision. In this one production, she successfully combined all the theatrical elements she had previously experimented with from her early days producing politically motivated sketches in the 1930s to the creation of what John Russell Taylor refers to as 'magnified realism' in productions such as *A Taste of Honey*. For *Oh What a Lovely War* she put together a framework of exuberant, parodic, comic and poignant First World War songs on which she hung a collage of antithetical theatrical styles. The traditions of popular entertainment – the seaside pierrot show, music-hall, comic turns – sat alongside huge projected slides of recruiting posters and photographic evidence of trench life and war casualties, whilst a 'ticker-tape' newspanel flashed contextual information, official death tolls and statistics of battles fought, won and lost. These living newspaper techniques functioned in dynamic interplay with multi-faceted live action: a Master of Ceremonies' jocular interjections and actors performing satirical sketches, vaudevillian acts and realistic scenes of trench life. The acting styles were drawn from agit-prop, music-hall, expressionist and naturalistic traditions and demanded great flexibility from the actors as they tackled a variety of roles and modes of delivery. In constructing the piece, Littlewood constantly played with the order of scenes, information, songs and slides to find the most potent combination. She stressed the importance of dialogue between the scenes and in *Joan's Book* argued that the success of the piece is 'all a question of juxtaposition' (Littlewood 1994: 682). Paget has identified the theatrical lineage of European innovators such as Meyerhold, Piscator and Brecht in the creation of this 'collision montage' technique and throughout *Oh What a Lovely War* it is possible to see the impact of scenes coming up against each other to generate ironic counterpoint, bitter commentary, comedy and radical shifts in tone and atmosphere. The formal complexity of the show ensures that the audience has to remain alert to shifts and subtle combinations of material. Thus, 'the active calling of the spectator's attention to technique shifts more of the burden of construction of meaning on to the audience' (Paget 1990a: 61), a process that has led the show to be referred to as an example of Brechtian theory in practice. The overall result was a show that succeeded in being at once 'epic and intimate, elegantly stylized and grimly realistic; comic and tragic-comic' (Marowitz 1965: 231), didactic and entertaining, educational and pleasurable, uproarious and deeply moving.

> Joan Littlewood performed a miracle of integration, not by ironing out the discontinuities but by emphasising them. The preposterousness of the stylistic mixture has been imitated so often since 1963 that it is hard to recall the impact it made then, but style was inseparable from substance in the resultant exposure of historical falsifications. Ruthlessness, mindlessness, and inefficiency had been disguised as recklessness, patriotism, and courageous disregard for actualities. In the fighting itself there had been elements of farce as well as mass slaughter; reducing the slaughter to statistics, the production focused on the anomalies. Most ingenious and most influential of all were the transitions which Joan Littlewood contrived, a series of giddying jolts as hilarity faded into pathos or solemnity was replaced by obscenity.
>
> *(Hayman 1979: 136)*

Developing the show

Constructed through collectivist principles of sharing knowledge, discussion, exploring possibilities and theatrical experiment, work to develop *Oh What a Lovely War* completely rejected theatrical hierarchy. The generation of material occurred through creative collaboration, argument, trial, error and Littlewood trusting her instincts that what she witnessed emerging on the stage through improvisation could amount to a unified whole when all the elements were fused together. Littlewood was keen to emphasis this collaborative creative impulse in her assessment of the project:

> Part of the good that has come out of this show is the way which a group of young people have worked together. Each brought a different point of view. They hated some of those songs. They didn't want to do propaganda, so they argued their way through each scene, and you've got, in the piece, the points of view of many people. This has been splendid. What you see is not a piece of direction by a producer. There were no rehearsals as they are known. There was a collection of individuals, more of an

anti-group than a group, working on ideas, on songs, on settings, on facts. And if you get a few people with a sense of humour and brains together, you'll get theatre.

(cited in Goorney 1981: 126–127)

In the first instance, detailed research fed into the subject matter of the show. Littlewood presented the whole company with a mandatory reading list and organised lectures to help foster intellectual engagement, interest and identification with the material under discussion as the company reached decisions about the inclusion of key bits of information and the theatricalisation of real life events. As the programme to the show and the published edition of the text acknowledge, multiple documentary sources such as books, newspapers, military despatches, regimental histories and oral testimonies informed the political stance, subject matter and dialogue of the show. In particular, Paget identifies that three texts provided crucial source material: Leon Wolff's *In Flanders Field* (1959), Alan Clark's *The Donkeys* (1961) and Barbara Tuchman's *August 1914* (1962) (for a detailed analysis of these sources see Paget 1990b). The company also had access to Chilton's research files, material brought in by the actor, George Sewell, who was an avid collector of First World War memorabilia, and Raymond Fletcher, who receives a credit as a military advisor. Scenes arose from this research in a variety of ways and extensive improvisation gradually built up the detail, characters and interaction that brought the piece to life. Alongside the scenes suggested by Littlewood in her rough plan, Chilton also developed scripts that Littlewood employed to kick-start improvisation. As Chilton recalls:

I'd work on a scene, I might work two or three days on it, and I'd take it up to Stratford. Then Joan would get me to go and write another one. Meanwhile she'd take what I'd written to the cast and get them to read it. Then she'd say, 'Right, throw the script away, and play your own!' And what they thought was worth keeping they kept in their minds.

(Paget 1990c: 249)

Littlewood spent many rehearsals exploring how best to convey information about historical events, individuals and the complex manoeuvrings that characterised the relations between people, organisations and countries during the War. Hence, scenes such as the circus parade and the grouse shooting party emerged, which provided potent theatrical metaphors for the ways in which countries vied for positions of power and influence. This experimental approach was praised by Marowitz, who argued that this is 'the *healthiest* kind of experiment because it is not exploring, in the abstract, questions of technique and style, but devising forms to suit the practical need of conveying its intentions' (1965: 233). Mind you, evidence suggests that this was not always easy. For instance, the 'war profiteers scene' caused considerable difficulty as the company strove to theatricalise material drawn from Raffles and Littlewood's documentary sources that included H. C. Engelbrecht and F. C. Hanighen's *Merchants of Death* (1934) and *The Private Manufacture of Armaments* (1936) by P. Noel-Baker. As Brian Murphy, an original member of the cast, remembers:

We had to get so much in the way of 'facts and figures' over, but in a way that would make the point and also hold the attention. And, let's face it, entertain. We worked on it, changed it – we always worked on it, it seemed to me, always. We were forever working on that scene!

(cited in Paget 1990c: 255)

Littlewood also used extensive improvisation to develop the right atmosphere, rhythm and tone of sections – the boredom of the trenches, the fear caused by bombardment, the exhaustion experienced by the soldiers and the camaraderie forged amongst men forced to live in close proximity and in such dangerous circumstances. Littlewood would often suggest a scenario and invite the actors to respond by immersing themselves in the moment of improvisation:

> Imagine there's a trench running across the stage, you're in it, protected from the enemy by a wall of sandbags. A bombardment, which has been going on for two days, has just died down. Can you put yourself in that situation?
>
> *(Littlewood 1994: 677)*

From these scenarios, individual characters, relationships and details evolved as Murphy recalls of the Christmas 1914 scene:

> We first improvised being stuck in trenches, out of which we had to find some kind of character. So somebody would take on the role of being the witty one, or somebody would play cards, or somebody would just want to play a mouth organ.
>
> *(cited in Paget 1990c: 252)*

The dialogue for this scene owed much to the spoof newspapers generated by troops in the Ypres sector during 1916 that the company reproduced in the programme for the show. Littlewood's faith in her ensemble, alongside the dynamic combination of detailed research, documentary actuality and the chance encounters that originate during improvisation characterised the development of *Oh What a Lovely War* and the creation of a seminal piece of theatre that could never have been pre-planned. The result, according to Richard Eyre, 'was political theatre that, unlike most of the genre, neither patronised its audience, nor tried to reprimand of reform them. It sought to inform and to entertain, and it broke your heart in the process' (2000: 269). Nevertheless, Littlewood's eclectic approach sat uncomfortably with the more familiar divisions of labour and classic hierarchical structures seen in the theatre industry. Whilst the ensemble gathered for *Oh What a Lovely War* were familiar with Littlewood's methods from prior collaborations, people new to this mode of working experienced some difficulties, particularly when it came to issues of authorship. Ronald Hayman recognised that 'it may never become clear how credit should be apportioned either for the concept or for the text' (1979: 134) and there have certainly been several expressions of dismay from Allan and Chilton that they did not receive due credit for their contributions to the production.

The pierrot show

Littlewood refused to have actors depicting events from the War through a sustained realistic narrative and instead created a multiple theatrical experience that utilised numerous elements to bring the causes, character and consequences of the War to life. Rejecting Raffles' plans for authentic khaki costumes and sandbags, Littlewood decided on the format of a music hall style pierrot show driven by a Master of Ceremonies who, with a ringmaster's whip, directly addresses the audience, tells jokes and introduces scenes. The seaside, end-of-pier, pierrot show not only drew on the medieval Italian *commedia dell'arte* tradition that Littlewood returned to throughout her career, it also specifically referenced a form of British entertainment contemporaneous with the First World War. In fact, the Master of Ceremonies refers to the performers as 'The Merry Roosters', appropriating the name of a troupe that existed during this period.

Therefore, Littlewood deliberately placed *Oh What a Lovely War* as part of a long continuum of popular entertainment perpetrated by strolling players who existed outside of traditional theatre structures. Arguing that 'the pierrot imagery is more decorative than functional' (1985: 130), Joel Schechter suggests that the pierrot costumes were solely about establishing historical precedent and referencing a music-hall style rather than serving any specific political or theatrical purpose. However, this is a rather limited assessment. In theatrical terms, the pierrot costumes become stark Brechtian alienating devices that constantly remind the audience that they are watching actors playing pierrots playing soldiers or representing real-life military personnel. Right from the outset it is also clear from the stage directions that the pierrots are 'one of us', they are associated with the audience as they enter and watch the newspanel, just as the audience would be doing, before beginning the first scene. Dressed in loose, shiny, white satin pierrot costumes with traditional black ruffs and pompoms, the actors are dressed in a neutralising uniform of sorts, which stresses their collectivity in a similar way to the army uniform. The costumes undergo rapid emblematic transformation through the addition of hats, belts, cloaks and other more specific props, but the underlying clown imagery never goes away. Equally the setting of a traditional seaside entertainment, complete with red, white and blue fairy lights and highly coloured circus tubs, remains throughout the action. Together with the costumes, the set serves as a signifier of a more frivolous, innocent time corrupted by the brutal machinations of war or, as Littlewood put it, a satirical reminder that 'war is only for clowns' (Littlewood 1994: 675). Hence, Littlewood places the content's emphasis on military blunders, war profiteering and mass slaughter in complex dialogue with the form of the show as the documentation of death is juxtaposed with seemingly light-hearted banter, popular songs and the affectionate depiction of pierrots.

Documentary material/the 'technological actor'

According to Schechter, 'The pierrot show framework serves largely to stress the past tense of events' (1985: 131); in direct contrast to this historical signification, *Oh What a Lovely War* employed cutting-edge new technologies. This strategy connects the show to Piscator's ambitious attempts, in the 1920s and 1930s, to use technology (principally film) to bring the outside world on to the stage. The multi-media environment and ability to 'cut' between elements similarly aligns the piece to a new sophisticated 'technological age' in which televisions and even rudimentary computers were becoming part of everyday life. According to Paget, the modernist 'technological actor' and documentary elements of the production were 'used subtly, dialogically, both to illuminate and to throw into relief the activities of the production's human agents, the actors' (2003: 72). As such, technology enables a dialogue to take place between the historical period of the First World War and Theatre Workshop's theatrical treatment of it using dramatic scenes as well as a mixture of existing, adapted and hired lighting, sound and projection equipment including a large screen capable of moving in and out of the space quickly and silently, two projectors, a tickertape newpanel supported by scaffolding and a complex sound system. All required meticulous timing to achieve maximum impact during the production and throughout rehearsals Littlewood and several technicians played with the choice, timing and volume of sound effects, the order and speed of slides and the placement of newspanel facts and figures, as well as practical ways of ensuring good sightlines and avoiding image distortion and spill. According to Ivor Dykes, a technician at the Theatre Royal, 'Theatre Workshop productions at Stratford NEVER had formal lighting, plotting or exotic things like technical rehearsals' (1998: 4), instead technical elements were part of the wider creative process and subject to continual revision.

The newspanel was inspired by one Littlewood had seen over the Friedrichstrasse in East Berlin and sourced by Raffles, who had an uncanny knack of acquiring things that Littlewood wanted. Raffles took responsibility for 'assembling and collating the facts and figures which would flicker across the panel at a relentless speed while living, breathing men and women held the stage. The dead only appeared as numbers' (Littlewood 1994: 683). Relaying information from documentary sources meant the newspanel acquired 'imperious authority' (Paget 2003: 72), particularly given the signification of the newspanel as a conveyor of facts. The technical team were intricately aware of the power of the words and statistics being ushered across the stage and played with the speed and timing to ensure maximum impact. 'Words were accelerated and decelerated in their travel across the proscenium, and they were highlighted for emphasis' (ibid.: 74). Hence, no matter what happens on stage, or the theatricality of any given moment, the piece draws the audience back to the actuality of the First World War through the stark record of facts and figures, as well as the large-scale posters and photographic images projected to tower above the actors. These slides underlined the human dimension; these were not just nameless and faceless figures but men with histories, families, friends and futures. 'Joan was insistent that we get away from the idea that these people were old dim photographs long dead. These are young men and women full of life and ideals, they do not know they are to be wasted!' (Dykes, undated manuscript, TRSE Archive). It is they, and the millions more they stand in for, who reside at the heart of this piece and technology makes their presence possible. As Paget describes, 'This theatre tradition, too, testifies to the twentieth century's faith in the ability of the photograph to represent reality and to capture and preserve significant historical experiences' (1996: 94). In its powerful combination of text and image, the documentary material translated through technology, authenticates the stage action, asserts its credibility and provides a potent multi-dimensional agent in the cognitive and emotive impact of *Oh What a Lovely War*.

The songs

Littlewood maintained the music-hall quality of the show through the dominant presence of songs from the First World War that appeared in the original BBC broadcast, as well as a few additions. However, Littlewood was adamant that *Oh What a Lovely War* would not adopt the nostalgic mood and sentimental atmosphere that pervaded *A Long, Long Trail*. She wanted to 'shed the schmaltz' (Littlewood 1994: 679) and asked her actors to tackle the songs 'as if you were talking to someone' (ibid.: 678) rather than trying to offer a beautiful rendering. Throughout the show, the songs serve multiple purposes such as period authenticity; comic interludes; examples of propaganda; bitter commentary; gallows humour and ironic critique. The show opens with an overture of songs that from the patriotic *Land of Hope and Glory* and English national anthem, to the rousing *Oh It's a Lovely War* and the resigned mood of *Goodbye-ee* and *Pack Up Your Troubles*, capture a sense of the shifting mood and atmosphere that characterises the show. The overture ends with *I Do Like to Be Beside the Seaside*, which sets the mood for the light-hearted pierrot show beginning that continues with *Row, Row, Row*, a gentle story of Johnny Jones and his girlfriend Flo as they kiss and cuddle on his 'cute little boat'. However, this age of innocence has been well and truly disrupted by the assassination of Archduke Ferdinand and Germany's invasion of Belgium by the next song *Belgium Put the Kibosh on the Kaiser*, a hopelessly upbeat, jingoistic song that celebrates British victory and the humiliation of Germany. The next big number, *I'll Make a Man of You*, is pure music hall with a woman delivering a mixture of sexual innuendo and comedy as she contributes to the recruitment drive. The music-hall style emphasised in the grand costuming of a long sequinned dress complete with an oversize hat covered in white feather plumes. The songs in the first act reflect the optimism exhibited in the early period of the War, but the mood shifts abruptly at the close of the act when a low-key rendition of *Goodbye-ee*, is drowned out by the sound effect of a shell exploding and an ironic newspanel declaring 'welcome 1915 ... happy year that will bring victory and peace' (p. 54). A sombre mood continues throughout the second act with songs depicting trench warfare, such as *Gassed Last Night* and *Hush, Here Comes a Whizzbang*, alongside the dark humour of *I Don't Want To Be a Soldier* and the defeated tone of *If You Want the Old Battalion*. Roger Gellert found that:

> In the context of history the Tommies' songs have a crushing pathos the original singers can't have guessed at, and after being informed, quite unsentimentally, that 13,000 men died in three hours at Passchendaele for a net gain of 100 yards, it is heart-breaking to hear '*Keep the Home Fires Burning*'.
>
> *(1963: 470)*

Towards the end of Act Two, bitter parodies of hymns including *Onward Christian Soldiers* and *What a Friend we have in Jesus*, depict anger towards the army commanders, resentment against the church and a sense of anguish and purposelessness. A shift that characterises the trajectory of the play from the Act One focus on the beginnings of the War in 1914 and the optimism, jingoism and patriotism for the cause; to the second Act, which compresses the final years of the War and deals with the scale of death, destruction and maiming on the Western Front.

Act one

The opening style and mood is that of a variety night with a Master of Ceremonies (MC) welcoming the audience, telling jokes and generally lulling the audience into a false sense of security as he declares 'We've got some songs for you, a few battles and some jokes' (p. 12). The mood is light, jovial and conceals the seriousness of the material, just as the title, *Oh What a Lovely War*, is tainted with irony by the end of the show. From the outset, it is clear that the production abandons any pretence of a fourth wall and refuses to present the illusion of 'truth'. This is a theatrical event that openly acknowledges itself as such as the MC embarks on a three-way conversation with the audience and actors as pierrots. The audience play an active part in the proceedings and their presence is crucial to activate the live interaction between stage and auditorium. After the pierrots sing their light-hearted period piece, *Row, Row, Row*, the MC introduces the beginning of the 'War Game' and the opening Circus Parade.

The beginnings of war: the Circus Parade and Promenade

The theatrical device of the Circus Parade and Promenade can be traced back to Meyerhold, who 'used exercises based on the traditional circus "parade" opening' (Leach 1989: 73) and even staged one in his 1924 production of *The Forest*. Taking inspiration from Meyerhold's practice, the pierrots enter in the stylised national dress of France, Britain, Germany, Austria and Russia and engage in a circular parade of the stage. Introduced by a band playing the national music of their various countries each representative unit provides a brief outline of how other nations view them. For example, Britain is presented as a rather arrogant nation protecting its colonies and Empire; France as a centre of civilisation, culture and love and Germany as 'disciplined, moral, industrious' (p. 13), but with the hint of an inferiority complex. There is a sense of the build up to war as the nations express imperialist and nationalist ambitions, vie for position, eye up their competitors and deny the possibility of war. A stance that quickly dissolves into bravado as the nations talk up their military power and strategic planning after eavesdropping on the Kaiser and General Moltke discussing their scheme to pursue world domination and the 1914 Schiefflen plan. During this scene, the first slides come into play depicting a map of Germany's plan to invade Belgium before attacking Paris, a map of France's plan for a counter attack and images of the Russian infantry and a British battleship. As occurs throughout *Oh What a Lovely War*, these images pre-empt what is to come and provide a stark reminder of the historical actuality of the events depicted.

Moving the action along with regular blows on his whistle, the MC figure introduces the next section entitled 'Find the Anarchist', which portrays the assassination of Archduke Ferdinand in Sarajevo. The pierrots embark on a jolly promenade before the action is brutally interrupted by a pistol shot. An innocent scene of strolling, chatting and flirting is harshly disrupted by the event that triggers the War. Littlewood used 'Living Newspaper' techniques of short exchanges between newsboys, girls and businessmen to convey the confusion and rumour that accompanies the onset of war, until Germany makes a formal declaration of mobilisation and invades Luxembourg and Belgium. Following this scene of frantic exchanges the stage directions indicate: 'Explosion. The lights go out. Full stage lighting flashes on. The whole company is standing in a semicircle grinning and clapping wildly but soundlessly. The band plays a line of the National Anthem. All the pierrots stand to attention' (p. 22). This expressionistic image of the predominately white pierrots grinning and soundlessly clapping the onset of war is eerily suggestive of the many ghosts that will be created as the brutality of war takes its course. To break the mood following the pierrots slow exit, the MC ushers in the projection screen to show images of civilians waving flags, cheering military parades and recruiting as the band plays a chorus of 'We Don't Want to Lose You'. During the last chorus, a slide of General Kitchener with the caption 'Your Country Needs You' appears and the pierrots replace their pierrot hats for uniform caps, kiss the girls goodbye and march off saluting to their unknown fate. The optimistic newspanel 'COURAGE WILL BRING US VICTORY' (p. 24) and the confident cry of 'Pour la gloire' as the French officers charge is rapidly undermined by the sound of machine gun fire, the sight of men collapsing and the newpanel simply announcing the fall of Brussels. This sharp change consolidated in speeches by French and German Officers that emphasis the parity of the soldier's experience regardless of their country of origin:

> FRENCH OFFICER: The battlefield is unbelievable; heaps of corpses, French and German, lying everywhere, rifles in hand. Thousands of dead lying in rows on top of each other in an ascending arc from the horizontal to an angle of sixty degrees. The guns recoil at each shot; night is falling and they look like old men sticking out their tongues and spitting fire. The rain has started, shells are bursting and screaming; artillery fire is the worst. I lay all night listening to the wounded groaning. The cannonading goes on; whenever it stops we hear the wounded crying from all over the woods. Two or three men go mad every day.
>
> *(p. 27)*

The simple, present tense observational narrative is deeply moving and provides a jolt to the audience as it appears directly after the music-hall jollity and cartoon-like imagery of 'Belgium Put the Kibosh on the Kaiser'. However, the tone shifts again for the bayonet drill sequence.

The bayonet drill

According to Littlewood, the drill sergeant's scene emerged after Raffles invited a serving sergeant to come and help the actors with their portrayal of soldiers. The resulting torrent of abuse, chaos and scenes of 'lunging and stabbing and twisting imaginary bayonets in the imagined enemy's guts' (Littlewood 1994: 681) was unintentionally funny. Moreover, when the others left Melvin blowing his nose whilst they charged at the audience with blood-curdling cries and Griffith Davies jumped down into the auditorium and chased the cleaner, Littlewood knew she had the makings of a great scene. However, it was only when Spinetti offered to play the drill sergeant as an incomprehensible Welshman that Littlewood was convinced they would be able to get the scene past the censors. As it transpired, the harsh language remained implied rather than actual and the comedy arose through the sheer speed of Spinetti's delivery as he cajoled four inept pierrot recruits to be aggressive with walking sticks instead of rifles. The recruits' failure further fuels the comedy as the distance increases between the sergeant's instructions and the recruits' ability to fulfil his demands, as rifles are lost, dropped and pathetically handled. This highly comic scene of male incompetence is juxtaposed with the song 'I'll Make a Man of You' and slides of 1914 recruitment posters appealing to male bravado and pride.

Communication breakdown

The next scene centres on a meeting between British army commanders, Field Marshall Sir John French and Field Marshall Sir Henry Wilson and French leader General Lanrezac and Belgium leader General de Moranneville. It introduces the dominant theme of the British army commanders' arrogance, class prejudice and incompetence. For example, French's refusal to take Wilson's advice or to allow an interpreter to aid the conversation is indicative of his blind faith in his own abilities. The resulting conversation at crossed purposes is comical, but has much deeper implications. As General Moranneville reminds French and Lanrezac, if there had been 'Decisive action by Britain and France, while my troops were holding Liège [then] the war would have been over by now' (p. 38). Instead, the generals are more concerned with protecting their own interests and self-congratulation, a fact theatrically symbolised by the opulent exchange of medals in the midst of military confusion. Once again, there is no attempt to give a naturalistic portrayal of these men, they are satirical caricatures; alternatively, the emphasis is on conveying information about the character of men in charge of the War, it is about establishing their failings and an attitude towards them.

The soldiers take centre stage

Theatre Workshop revealed the chilling consequences of the British commanders' incompetence and the ingrained hierarchical class structure of the War in the next scene. The newspanel introduces the scene: 'AUG 25 RETREAT FROM MONS. AUG 30 FIRST BRITISH WOUNDED ARRIVE AT WATERLOO' (p. 40). Rather than the flags and heroes welcome the soldiers expect; their superiors have stranded them without ambulances as they have only arranged transport for officers. In an awkward exchange between an officer and soldier, the reality of the men's function as front-line fodder is highlighted when the officer departs saying he'll see the men back at the front, a sentiment reiterated by a nurse who informs a soldier on a stretcher that she will have him swiftly back to the front. The soldier's collective anonymity is emphasised by the gradual build-up to their singing 'We're 'ere because we're 'ere, because we're 'ere, because we're 'ere' (p. 41) over and over until the Sergeant curtails them. The sense of working-class solidarity is further underlined when local lorry drivers volunteer to transport the wounded soldiers in their lunch break – a small act that tells a big story about Littlewood and Theatre Workshop's class-based sympathies.

Following a newspanel imparting the information that there were 300,000 Allied casualties during August alone and ironic slides depicting adverts for health remedies such as Beechams, Carter's Little Liver Pills and Phosphorine, all useless in the face of men blinded, maimed and suffering from shell shock, is one of the most powerful scenes of *Oh What a Lovely War*. Offering a moving portrait of the camaraderie, resilience and black humour exhibited by men engaged in trench warfare, the Christmas 1914 scene offers a master-class in how to create naturalistic dialogue, quick-fire banter, dramatic tension and a compelling vision of collective humanity. As Paget informs us:

> Arguably, one of the reasons why *Lovely War* was so successful was that its collectivity was so manifest in performance, offering a potent theatrical emblem for another sense of collectivity – that which helped sustain the 'ordinary' soldier of the Great War.
>
> *(Paget 1990a: 67)*

As in the previous Waterloo scene, the emphasis is on the soldiers who, by being nameless, are representative of all the soldiers who fought in the War. From the outset, the pierrot soldiers are seen co-existing as they establish the scene with humorous signposts proclaiming 'Piccadilly' and 'Conducted tours of the German trenches'. The actors employed appropriate movement to convey cramped conditions and the physical discomfort of chilblains, corns and infestation, as well as creating the rhythms and atmosphere of habitual familiarity as they settled down in their shared space. Moreover, collectivity is not only exhibited by British soldiers as they share banter, talk of their loves back home and ways of coping with the boredom of trench life such as playing a harmonica, writing for a satirical magazine or composing letters, but also between the British and German soldiers as they enact the famous Christmas meeting in 'No Man's Land'. The fact it is German soldiers who initiate the connection, signals Theatre Workshop's desire to present the 'enemy' in a sympathetic light that transgressed the common perception of a cold, autocratic and unfeeling German character. As the men share greetings, gifts, drinks and songs, it becomes abundantly clear that all these men are stranded in a trench on the Western Front during Christmas and that they have far more in common than that which divides them. This scene of everyday connections between human beings freezes on a newspanel statistic giving the casualty figures for the first year of the War, a grim shift in tone lightened temporarily by the gentle rendering of the song 'Goodbye-ee' and the optimistic newspanel 'WELCOME 1915 ... HAPPY YEAR THAT WILL BRING VICTORY AND PEACE', both cut off by the sound of a shell exploding.

> Such a 'final number' runs deliberately counter to theatrical folk-lore about musical entertainments – that is, that the interval song should be upbeat in order to lift the audience's spirits. Here, ironies surrounding the idea of 'goodbye' (Brother Bertie's cheeriness about it, contrasted with the fact of its likely finality), coalesce as the song rather lamely (from a theatrical-musical point of view) 'grows fainter', as the stage direction instructs. The final optimistic newspanel is then undercut by the shriek of a shell.
>
> *(Paget 1990c: 251)*

Rather than leaving the audience with a rousing number, Littlewood gave a Brechtian-style indicator of the shift to a pessimistic appraisal of the realities of war in the second act.

Act two

Act Two begins with a newspanel, giving details of extensive British losses at the Battle of Ypres, Aubers Ridge and Loos, whilst also announcing the first German use of poison gas. Sombre material ironically undercut by the upbeat song *Oh It's a Lovely War*, sung by the whole company.

The tone jumps again straight away when the MC informs the audience that after the Conscription Act '51,000 able-bodied men left home without leaving any forwarding addresses ... and that's in West Ham alone' (p. 56). This statement brought the material right back down to earth from the rather romantic vision of British and German soldiers holding hands across the divide. This was a war that caused immense suffering and death and the following scenes set about attributing blame and culpability.

The war game Part II: find the biggest profiteer

In the first scene after the interval, *Oh What a Lovely War* tackles the role of capitalism in generating and fuelling the War. Echoing the concerns of Brecht's *Mother Courage* (1939), which Littlewood produced in 1955, the scene emphasises the economic and political ramifications of war through a cartoonish, agit-prop style representation of arms manufacturers from Britain, France, Germany and America, alongside a Swiss banker, joined for a grouse shoot in the Scottish Highlands. These highly caricatured men will go no where near the front line and instead spend their time developing and selling weapons to the highest bidder with not the slightest hint of guilt that German fuses are being used in British grenades or that the French purchased German barbed wire to ensnare German troops. The scene deftly communicates the principle of profit over patriotism. As they shoot grouse, cry with delight and count their dead birds, they congratulate each other on their business acumen, success and profitability. The dead grouse offer potent symbols of all the dead men shot down with similar ease on the front line; whilst the squeals of delight underline the fact that every spent bullet equals profit for the arms manufacturers. Whilst the scene points the finger at all profiteers, the newspanel framing the scene states, '21,000 AMERICANS BECAME MILLIONAIRES DURING WAR' (p. 57), highlighting fears about American imperialism. Equally, the scene is full of dark humour as the profiteers discuss the inconvenience of blockades disrupting the free-flow of trade and they voice their fears that a peaceful resolution will damage their profits, share prices and the world's stock markets. However, critics were specifically damning of the scene and accused it of lifelessness, over-simplicity and failing to find the form to convey the content. Criticisms that perhaps hark back to the difficulties encountered during rehearsals.

The consequences of the war profiteers' callous actions in the name of profit are brought chillingly to the fore by off-stage voices singing *Gassed Last Night*, whilst slides depict actuality images of French, German and British infantrymen facing gas attacks, soldiers with bandaged eyes following gas explosions and soldiers up to their knees in mud. In accordance with the 'collision montage' style, these provocative images are juxtaposed with a scene of black comedy when a Commanding Officer (CO) visits a trench to congratulate men who have survived in the face of snipers, shells and bombs, as well as having their own gas blown back at them following a change in the wind's direction. The upper-class CO's ignorance of the conditions the men face is quickly established and climaxes with the discovery of a German soldier's leg. The following music-hall style exchange reveals mordant humour and the level of desensitisation the soldiers are forced to muster:

> LIEUTENANT: Hardcastle. Remove the offending limb.
> SERGEANT: Well, we can't do that, sir; it's holding up the parapet. We've just consolidated the position.
> LIEUTENANT: Well, get a shovel and hack it off; and then dismiss the men.
> *He goes off.*

SERGEANT: Right, sir. What the bloody hell am I going to hang my equipment on now. All right, lads, get back, get yourselves some char. Heads, trunks, blood all over the place, and all he's worried about is a damned leg.

(p. 67)

The 'palm court' scene and Sir Douglas Haig

After the pierrot soldiers depart, the stage is set for a plush official reception. A sense of a bygone age is evoked by a couple singing *Roses of Picardy* before forming 'a static tableau, as for a period photograph' (p. 67). A waltz is played and a comic anti-naturalistic device is inserted as an actor formally announces the guests whilst standing with a jardinière containing pampas-grass on his head. As the Commanding Officers of the British army, Sir John French, Sir Douglas Haig, Sir Henry Wilson and Sir William Robertson arrive with their partners, Littlewood created a filmic style fading in and out of focus as the characters danced around the space before delivering their lines downstage. The scene marks the audience's introduction to Haig, who plays a pivotal role in Act Two. New in post, the others are suspicious of his ability to overcome failed staff college entrance examinations, quick ascent to power and origins in 'trade', which for some makes him unfit to hold a post in high office. Indeed, the entire scene is devoted to uncovering social hierarchies, power brokering, nepotism, petty squabbles, jealousy and gossip in high office. Rather than figures deserving of their positions and respect, an impression is given of childish games of one-up-man-ship as Robertson is publicly snubbed, Haig reveals French's weakness for unsuitable women and Haig is portrayed as a humourless individual driven by personal ambition. As Paget recalled, 'George Sewell presented a dried-out, repressed husk of a man – convinced of and blinkered by his own righteousness' (2003: 84). An interpretation that fuels the scene following further large-scale images of dead soldiers of several nations, a French soldier on burial duty and a field of white wooden crosses that accompanies the song, *Hush, Here Comes a Whizzbang* sung off-stage. The fact the song comes from off-stage is important, as it means that the actuality images are the only things on stage, the portraits of soldiers and those implied by the burial sites are the central focus for the audience and this vision of multiple corpses is held directly next to a scene presenting Haig's blind faith, arrogance and brutal disregard for the lives of his men. As a slide depicts men advancing across no-man's-land to almost certain death and a man slowly sings *There's a Long, Long Trail*, Haig delivers an impassioned oration:

Complete victory . . . the destruction of German militarism . . . victory march on Berlin . . . slow deliberate fire is being maintained on the enemy positions . . . at this moment my men are advancing across no-man's-land in full pack, dressing from left to right; the men are forbidden under pain of court-martial to take cover in any shell-hole or dugout . . . their magnificent morale will cause the enemy to flee in confusion . . . the attack will be driven home with the bayonet . . . I feel that every step I take is guided by divine will.

(p. 77)

The combination of image, song and speech is deeply chilling and curtailed by the sound of heavy bombardment and a newspanel that reads: 'FEBRUARY . . . VERDUN . . . TOTAL LOSS ONE AND A HALF MILLION MEN' (p. 77). Haig's speech is not just empty rhetoric it has unimaginable human consequences. A fact hammered home in the next scene when Haig orders a newly arrived unit from Ireland, who have gone without food for forty-eight hours, to make a fresh assault across no-man's-land. Expressionistically abstracting their attack as a spirited Irish jig, Littlewood juxtaposed this highly theatrical approach with down-to-earth naturalistic dialogue as the soldiers advance only to find themselves under attack from their own side. As the men protest, their comrades shoot them as enemy and the scene dissolves from naturalism into expressionism once more.

Mrs Pankhurst

As Mrs Pankhurst delivers her speech on a typical 'speaker's corner' style platform, Theatre Workshop insert the first openly pacifist voices in a typical agit-prop style scene that attempts to simplistically present a two-way pro- and anti-war argument. After reading an eloquent letter from George Bernard Shaw denouncing the War as the folly of capitalists, politicians and all those lusting after power, Pankhurst charges the leaders with war-mongering, failing to enter into peace negotiations and threatening civilisation. Playing to a hostile crowd who heckle her as a traitor for over-intellectualising the war effort and undermining the cause that their husbands are fighting for, Pankhurst retorts by suggesting the ordinary men and women have been seduced by misplaced patriotism and duped by duplicitous politicians and media propaganda. The strength of her convictions and degree of cynicism is powerfully conveyed, but so too is the faith the un-named men and women have in war and their refusal to accept dissenting voices. As the newpanel ushers in the information that 60,000 men died on the first day of the Battle of the Somme, the crowd affirms their support for the War and drown Pankhurst's objections with the rousing jingoistic anthem *Rule Britannia*. However, the patriotic fervour exhibited by those relatively safe at home is comically undercut by two drunken soldiers who enter to sing a music-hall style rendition of *I Don't Want to be a Soldier*, which brings the subject right back down to earth from Pankhurst's attempt at an ethical debate. Unfortunately, millions of men were never to return home to England and the next scene's treatment of the Battle of the Somme offers a damning indictment of failed leadership and suicidal decisions that led to horrific scales of death and carnage.

The Battle of the Somme

The ineptitude of Haig's leadership is emphasised throughout the 'Somme Scene' with several renditions of children's songs including *Pop Goes the Weasel* and *They Were Only Playing Leapfrog* to the tune of *John Brown's Body*. As Haig issues orders to attack, the references to playground songs suggest that he might as well be playing with toy soldiers for all the duty of care he displays towards his men. The implication is that he views the men as fodder, and worse, that he has no compunction about sending all available men to their deaths as long as he is able to secure victory by having the last man standing. Safely behind a desk at headquarters and unmoved by the news that Allied forces are facing seventy per cent casualties, he is more concerned that one of his horses dismounted the King and what this might mean for his chances of promotion. The scene suggests his distance from the action, unquestioning sense of duty, unyielding faith in his abilities and belief that he is 'the predestined instrument of providence for the achievement of victory for the British army' (p. 86) completely blinds him to the realities of war and the huge death tolls his decisions are wreaking.

Interspersed with Haig's orders and under his watchful gaze, Littlewood places short vignettes of soldiers caught up in a hopeless cause, forced to listen to the cries of the wounded stuck in no-man's-land and preparing for their imminent deaths with gallows humour. The overwhelming sense of purposelessness and defeat is enshrined in the soldiers' rendition of *If You Want the Old Battalion*, with the repeated refrain: 'We've seen them, we've seen them/hanging on the old barbed wire' (p. 89); whilst Theatre Workshop's depiction of Haig as little better than a murderer is secured by the brief appearance of a pierrot as the notorious French serial killer Landru, who stole from, murdered and burnt the bodies of ten women during the First World War. However, Haig's death toll is shockingly and starkly revealed by the newspanel that announces at the end of the scene: 'SOMME BATTLE ENDS ... TOTAL LOSS 1,332,000 MEN ... GAIN NIL' (p. 93). The implication is clear – Haig is a serial killer of unprecedented proportions.

For God and Country

Theatre Workshop stressed Haig's religiosity and the hypocrisy of institutional religion during the church scene in which the pierrot soldiers bleakly transpose traditional hymns with their own irreligious words and dark humour. The collective singing and pessimistic content of the songs places the men at sharp odds with the sentiments exhibited by the Chaplain as he singles out Haig for silent prayer and seeks God's approval and support. Once again, Haig's personal ambition and self-regard is stressed as he asks the Lord for victory, specifically 'before the Americans arrive' (p. 96) so that he can take full credit for any success. Reviewing the show in *Encore*, Marowitz commented on the fact that:

> God is seen to be the rank immediately above Field Marshall, and war, particularly in the eyes of the British, becomes a test of Christian stamina founded on the assumption that victory belongs, as if by divine right, to well-heeled, white protestants with double-barrelled names and country estates.
>
> *(Marowitz 1965: 231)*

As the soldiers depart they sing 'Whiter than the whitewash on the wall', words with multiple meanings given the context: for example, the sense that the blood of those sacrificed will be whitewashed out of history in the name of victory or that religion acts as a whitewash on the barbaric acts that are being perpetrated in its name. Whilst Haig continues to justify his actions, the on-stage soldiers are replaced by the documentary slides of real-life soldiers at war and a newspanel giving a death toll for those killed on the Western Front up to November 1916. The pierrot soldiers re-appear miming burial duty and sing a song first seen in Behan's *The Hostage* when the hostage is killed and springs back to life with *The Bells of Hell*, a defiant song of life cheated by death, which holds no victory for anybody.

The final push

As *Oh What a Lovely War* proceeds towards its climax, Littlewood chose to come back once more to the humour, compassion and resilience of the men as they dig trenches, cope with appalling physical conditions and discuss missing comrades. As the soldiers go about their everyday business, Haig delivers overly confident speeches and a nurse laments the butchery she encounters all around her. A moving sequence develops as a newspanel announces that the average life of a machine gunner is four minutes, followed by a rendition of *Keep the Home Fires Burning* and a quick-fire newspanel giving details of British losses and territory gained. Yet, rather than capitalise on this emotive atmosphere, Littlewood immediately shifts the tone to avoid any possibility of mawkishness. Encouraging the audience to join in and not look so gloomy, a female performer sings *Sister Susie's Sewing Shirts*, a light-hearted music-hall style tongue-twister, yet even this crowd-pleaser is undermined by the presence of pierrots as German, French and British generals debating when the War will end. The piece once more conveys a never-ending war game as the dates go up and up until they reach the year of production. Immediately after this a group of pierrots as French soldiers mutiny as they are ordered to advance into the trenches, proclaiming they are 'like lambs to the slaughter' they advance baaing towards the audience before a burst of gun-fire causes their collapse. When Theatre Workshop took *Oh What a Lovely War* to the Paris Festival in 1963, Goorney recalls that the show:

> ... made a tremendous impression. That the carnage and killing actually took place on French soil must have brought the horror of the First World War very close to the French audiences, and during the scene when the French soldiers are depicted as sheep going to the slaughter, the audience rose in their seat and cheered.
>
> *(1981: 157)*

As the final newspanel announces 'THE WAR TO END ALL WARS ... KILLED TEN MILLION ... WOUNDED TWENTY-ONE MILLION ... MISSING SEVEN MILLION' (p. 106), a slide sequence depicts the real-life soldiers the show represents and honours. As Paget thoughtfully informs us, 'while the play has no hero, it presents an *implied* hero who is a constant presence-in-absence. This shadow-figure, simultaneously individual and abstract, is the Unknown Soldier whose eternal flame burns in so many European capital cities' (2004: 400). It is to these heroes that transcend age, political agendas and nations that the show turns as it closes with the image of a long line of soldiers walking away from the camera toward the trench. Their final destination is open, yet what has gone before has provided a potent examination of the origins of their journey and the moving final song, *And When They Ask Us*, offers a glimpse of the memories forged in the minds of a generation of men who could never convey the extent of the horrors they witnessed.

Selling out

Owing to Theatre Workshop's lack of public subsidy, Littlewood had no option but to capitalise on the critical success of *Oh What a Lovely War*'s four-week run at the Theatre Royal with a year long run at the Wyndham's Theatre in the West End. This move was made slightly more palatable by the fact Littlewood and Raffles formed their own West End management to ensure that all the royalties would be theirs rather than in the pockets of a West End impresario. However, the transition from the East to the West End was not without difficulties and the company faced accusations of nostalgia, sentimentality and 'selling-out'. On a practical level, the larger Wyndham's stage 'produced a bigger sense of occasion' (Pryce-Jones 1963: 838), which also demanded a less subtle style of performance as events had to be underlined to ensure those at the back of the stalls could appreciate what was going on. For example, rather than the simplicity of one singer performing the songs *I'll Make a Man Out of You* and *Itchy-koo*, in the former Avis Bunnage was accompanied by a chorus of women indicating the meaning of every sentence and Fanny Carby was joined by other singers in the latter. According to Paget, the financial imperative to secure a sustained West End run also 'ensured that some accommodations to West End "taste" were made on the journey from E15 to WC2' (1990c: 244). For example, contentious elements of the war profiteers scene were edited out and several people expressed particular concern about a change to the original Stratford East ending, as Frances Cuka, who played Jo in *A Taste of Honey*, recalled:

> When I saw it at Stratford Victor Spinetti made the closing speech, which went something like 'The war game is being played all over the world, by all ages, there's a pack for

all the family. It's been going on for a long time and it's still going on. Goodnight.' This cynical speech, which followed the charge of the French soldiers, was quite frightening and you were left crying your heart out. When I saw it again in the West End, I was shocked by the change of ending. After Victor's speech the entire cast came on singing 'Oh What a Lovely War' followed by a reprise of the songs. All frightfully hearty and calculated to send the audience home happy.

(Goorney 1981: 127)

Evidence suggests that this softened ending arose because Donald Albery, the owner of Wyndham's Theatre, insisted that the show end on a light note. Murphy has spoken about the company's resentment at how economic imperatives influenced aesthetic judgements. Nonetheless, Murphy also illuminates how:

Littlewood tried to counter this weakening of the conclusion of the show by getting the cast, during the reprise of 'Oh It's a Lovely War', to 'hand back again to the men – literally, physically, pointing our hands to that screen, so that the last thing the audience saw were the actual pictures of those men'.

(Paget 1990c: 259)

Even though Littlewood capitulated to the West End audiences taste for entertainment (if with an obviously radical and critical edge), she refused to leave the focus on the actors. Instead, she provided a visual reminder that the soldiers were at the heart of the show – it was their struggle, camaraderie, resilience, humour and sacrifice that the audience should take away with them to their after-show dinners, drinks and on their journeys home. However, there were still those who saw the play as a betrayal of Theatre Workshop's original aims. In particular, MacColl offered a vociferous and typically combative assessment:

I maintain that a theatre which sets out to deal with a social and human problem like war and which leaves the audience feeling nice and comfy, in a rosy glow of nostalgia, is not doing its job, it has failed. Theatre, when it is dealing with social issues, should hurt; you should leave the theatre feeling furious.

(Goorney 1981: 128)

It is difficult to ascertain how far the 1960s audience left the theatre feeling furious, but the show certainly made a significant impact on individual audience members, critics and the development of theatre practice in the twentieth century.

Impact and influence

According to Littlewood, *Oh What a Lovely War* 'Awakened race memory in our audiences. At the end of each performance people would come on stage bringing memories and mementoes, even lines of dialogue which sometimes turned up in the show' (Littlewood 1994: 693). Melvin, a performer in the production, similarly remembered in conversation with the author how after seeing the show a family were moved to return to the Wyndham's Theatre to present him with a perfectly preserved First World War Christmas parcel. They insisted on giving this precious piece of family memorabilia to Theatre Workshop as a 'thank you' for acknowledging and honouring the men, including their father/grandfather, who served on the front line. For many, seeing *Oh*

What a Lovely War was a profoundly moving experience as a letter from the veteran philosopher and anti-war campaigner Bertrand Russell testifies:

> I have enjoyed few things as much as 'Oh What a Lovely War', which I found moving and a statement on war such as I have not experienced . . . As you know, the First War was an event which has a vital place in my thinking and in my life. All the people concerned with resistance to the war were my intimates. The great horror which affected us as the war interminably dragged on was something none of us have ever fully outlived. If there were any way in which I could make people understand how true and important your play is, I should wish to do it. I wonder it has been allowed on a London stage. After it, there was much that I should have wished to have said to you and to the performers I was fortunate enough to meet. The experience of the production had drained me, and I could only speak of ordinary things when I wanted to convey to you that I thought all that had happened to me that evening to be most extraordinary. 'Oh What a Lovely War' brings war within our grasp, which is immensely difficult.
>
> May you sweep through the world with this play, past governments and to as many people as authority permits you to reach.
>
> *(5th June 1963, TRSE Archive)*

Not only did *Oh What a Lovely War* make a personal impact, it also acquired significant critical praise and shared the best production prize at the 1963 Paris Festival with the Royal Shakespeare Company's production of *King Lear* directed by Peter Brook. In 1964, the show went to Philadelphia for three weeks followed by six months on Broadway. In Philadelphia, the critics responded in a rather bemused fashion because what publicity agents billed as a musical, turned out to be more than frivolous and diverting entertainment. As Henry T. Murdock reported in the *Philadelphia Inquirer*:

> This is not a conventional show in either material, playing or staging, but it is a potent one. It hits hard, sometimes unmercifully hard. It shouts and screams and hammers and it has no intention of letting its audience relax. But we think it will stand out in the memory and perhaps in the conscience of almost any adult audience.
>
> *(1964: 11)*

By the time the show reached New York the Vietnam War had begun. Melvin recalls how the show worked in direct opposition to the mood of 'victory fever':

> People walked out in groups during the show. I remember those marvellous Quakers who kept up a twenty-four hour vigil in Times Square against the war. They were beaten, spat upon and abused. We gave them free tickets, and they'd come back at the end to our dressing-rooms with tears in their eyes, thanking us for coming to America.
>
> *(Coren 1984: 46)*

In its substantial departure from the dominant theatre practice of the time, *Oh What a Lovely War* also 'represents a turning point in the history of English theatre' (Hayman 1979: 136). Paget has consistently referred to Theatre Workshop and *Oh What a Lovely War* as a 'Trojan Horse', a means of allowing a European, anti-naturalistic political theatre to infiltrate the British scene. In particular, the show influenced a new generation of politically motivated, socially conscious and theatrically revolutionary practitioners that emerged in the 1960s. For instance, John McGrath acknowledged that it 'had an extraordinary effect on British theatre. In the 60s it was performed and loved in almost every repertory in the country. A new generation of young actors played in it, sang the songs, and heard how Joan's actors had worked on it' (McGrath 1981: 48). The creation of the piece through collaboration inspired other theatre workers to embark on devising processes in both small and large-scale theatres, as seen with Peter Brook's US (1966) at the Royal Shakespeare Company. Equally, practitioners began employing documentary methods to create work combining dramatic scenes and factual information to interrogate social and political issues such as Peter Cheeseman's Stoke documentaries including *The Jolly Potter* (1965) and McGrath's *The Cheviot, the Stag and the Black, Black Oil* (1973). Yet, *Oh What a Lovely War*'s impact stretches beyond the theatre. In more general terms, it has also become embedded in historiography as each new generation often has their understanding of the First World War supplemented by study of the play. The historian A.J.P. Taylor was so impressed by the piece that he dedicated his *Illustrated History of the First World War* (1963) to Littlewood and when London's Imperial War Museum recently held a First World War exhibition it contained information, designs and costumes from the original production and invited Littlewood to attend the opening. The original *Oh What a Lovely War* probed the First World War in an illuminating and entertaining way through its use of documentary material and the vibrant anti-naturalistic, technologically sophisticated exchange between the stage and auditorium. Moreover, its provocative theatricality and anti-war stance continues to speak to us in the here-and-now as the 'war game' maintains potent resonance in the twenty-first century.

Further reading

Anderson, Lindsay (1958) 'A Taste of Honey', *Encore*, Vol. 5, No. 2, p. 42.
Anon (1945) 'The Flying Doctor Comes to Town', *Penrith Observer*, 4 September, p. 2.
——— (1952) 'The Travellers', *Scotsman*, 20 August, p. 6.
Ansorge, Peter (1972) 'Lots of Lovely Human Contact!', *Plays and Players*, Vol. 19, No. 10, July, pp. 18–21.
Banham, Reyner (1964) 'People's Palaces', *New Statesman*, 7 August, pp. 191–192.
Barber, John (1971) 'The Littlewood Dilemma', *Daily Telegraph*, 11 January, p. 7.
Barker, Clive (1977) *Theatre Games*, London: Methuen.
——— (2000) 'Joan Littlewood', in Alison Hodge (ed.) *Twentieth Century Actor Training*, London: Routledge.
Benedetti, Jean (1998) *Stanislavski and the Actor*, London: Methuen.
Bradbury, Ernest (1964) 'Fairy World of Dvorak Opera', *Yorkshire Post*, 21 August, p. 7.
Bradby, David and Williams, David (1988) *Directors' Theatre*, Basing-Stoke: Macmillan.
Brien, Alan (1959) 'Anyfing Goes', *The Spectator*, 27 February, p. 289.
Brown, Georgina (1993) 'Sightings of the Invisible Woman', *Independent*, 12 May, p. 12.
Coren, Michael (1984) *100 Years of Stratford East*, London: Quartet.
Croyden, Margaret (1971) 'Joan Littlewood', in Joseph McCrindle (ed.) *Behind the Scenes: Theatre and Film Interviews from the 'Transatlantic Review'*, London: Pitman, pp. 1–12.
Davies, Alistair and Saunders, Peter (1983) 'Literature, Politics and Society', in Alan Sinfield (ed.) *Society and Literature 1945–1970*, London: Methuen.
Dykes, Ivor (1998) *Oh What a Lovely War: Then and Now*, unpublished manuscript, Theatre Royal Stratford East Archive.
Eyre, Richard (2000) *Changing Stages: A View of British Theatre in the Twentieth Century*, London: Bloomsbury.
Gellert, Roger (1963) 'Tommies', *New Statesman*, Vol. 65, No. 1672, 29 March, p. 470.
Goorney, Howard (1966) 'Littlewood in Rehearsal', *Tulane Drama Review*, Vol. 11, No. 2, pp. 102–103.
——— (1981) *The Theatre Workshop Story*, London: Methuen.
Goorney, Howard and Ewan MacColl (eds.) (1986) *Agit-Prop to Theatre Workshop*, Manchester: Manchester University Press.

Hayman, Ronald (1979) *British Theatre Since 1955*, Oxford: Oxford University Press.
Hewison, Robert (1986) *Too Much: Art and Society in the Sixties 1960–1975*, London: Methuen.
Hobson, Harold (1955) 'Richard II', *The Sunday Times*, 23 January, p. 11.
—— (1958) 'Triumph at Stratford East', *The Sunday Times*, 19 October, p. 21.
Hunt, Albert (1981) 'The Changing Fortunes of People's Theatre', *New Society*, Vol. 56, No. 970, 18 June, pp. 492–493.
Laban, Rudolf (1988) *The Mastery of Movement*, 4th edition, revised by Lisa Ullmann, Plymouth: Northcote House.
Leach, Robert (1989) *Vsevolod Meyerhold*, Cambridge: Cambridge University Press.
Lewis, B. N. (1965) 'Fun Palace: Counter-Blast to Boredom', *New Society*, 15 April, pp. 8–10.
Littlewood, Joan (1959–60) 'Plays for the People', *World Theatre*, Vol. 8, No. 4, pp. 282–290.
—— (1961) 'What Miss Littlewood Demands of the Theatre', *The Times*, 12 July, p. 5.
—— (1964) 'A Laboratory of Fun', *New Scientist*, Vol. 22, No. 391, 14 May, pp. 432–433.
—— (1965) 'Goodbye Note from Joan', in Charles Marowitz, Tom Milne, Owen Hale and Richard Findlater (eds.) *The Encore Reader: A Chronicle of the New Drama*, London: Methuen.
—— (1968) 'Non-Program, a Laboratory of Fun', *Drama Review*, Vol. 12, No. 3, pp. 129–131.
—— (1994) *Joan's Book: Joan Littlewood's Peculiar History as She Tells It*, London: Methuen.
Lobsinger, Mary Louise (2000) 'Cybernetic Theory and the Architecture of Performance: Cedric Price's Fun Palace', in Sarah Williams Goldhagen and Rejean Legault (eds.) *Anxious Modernisms: Experimentation in Post-War Architectural Culture*, Cambridge, MA: MIT Press.
MacColl, Ewan (1986) 'Introduction: The Evolution of a Revolutionary Theatre Style', in Howard Goorney and Ewan MacColl (eds.) *Agit-Prop to Theatre Workshop*, Manchester: Manchester University Press, pp. ix–lvii.
—— (1990) *Journeyman*, London: Sidgwick and Jackson.
Marowitz, Charles (1965) 'Littlewood Pays a Dividend', in Charles Marowitz, Tom Milne, Owen Hale and Richard Findlater (eds.) *The Encore Reader: A Chronicle of the New Drama*, London: Methuen.
McGrath, John (1981) *A Good Night Out*, London: Methuen.
Melvin, Murray (2004) 'Memories of Laban at the Theatre Workshop', unpublished manuscript, Theatre Workshop Stratford East Archive.
Milne, Tom and Goodwin, Clive (eds.) (1967) 'Working with Joan', in Charles Marowitz and Simon Trussler (eds.) *Theatre at Work: Playwrights and Productions in Modern British Theatre*, New York: Hill and Wang, pp. 113–122.
Moussinac, Leon (1931) *The New Movement in the Theatre*, Paris: Editions Albert-Lévy.
Murdock, Henry T. (1964) '"Lovely War" Stirs the Conscience', *Philadelphia Inquirer*, 9 September, p. 11.
Newlove, Jean (1993) *Laban for Actors and Dancers*, London: Nick Hern Books.
Paget, Derek (1990a) *True Stories? Documentary Drama on Radio, Screen and Stage*, Manchester: Manchester University Press.
—— (1990b) 'Popularising Popular History: "Oh What a Lovely War" and the Sixties', *Critical Survey*, Vol. 2, No. 2, pp. 117–127.
—— (1990c) '"Oh What a Lovely War": The Texts and Their Context', *New Theatre Quarterly*, Vol. 6, No. 23, pp. 244–260.
—— (1996) 'Remembrance Play: *Oh What a Lovely War* and History', in Tony Howard and John Stokes (eds.) *Acts of War: The Representation of Military Conflict on the British Stage and Television Since 1945*, Aldershot: Scolar.
—— (2003) 'The War Game Is Continuous: Productions and Receptions of Theatre Workshop's "Oh What a Lovely War"', *Studies in Theatre and Performance*, Vol. 23, No. 2, pp. 70–85.
—— (2004) 'Case Study: Theatre Workshop's *Oh What a Lovely War*, 1963', in Baz Kershaw (ed.) *The Cambridge History of British Theatre*, Volume 3, Cambridge: Cambridge University Press, pp. 397–411.
Pryce-Jones, David (1963) 'Shot in the Arm', *The Spectator*, 28 June, p. 838.
Roberts, Peter (1961) 'We're Just Not Practical', *Plays and Players*, Vol. 8, No. 6, March, pp. 11–13.
Schechter, Joel (1985) 'Pierrot in the Great War: Theatre Workshop's "Oh What a Lovely War!"', in *Durov's Pig: Clowns, Politics and Theatre*, New York, NY: Theatre Communications Group, pp. 127–133.
Sinfield, Alan (ed.) (1983) *Society and Literature 1945–1970*, London: Methuen.
Sked, Alan and Cook, Chris (1984) *Post-War Britain: A Political History*, 2nd edition, Harmondsworth: Penguin.
Theatre Workshop (1965) *Oh What a Lovely War*, London: Methuen.
Tynan, Kenneth (1989) *Profiles*, London: Nick Hern Books.

Wells, John (1948) 'The Other Animals', *Manchester Guardian*, 6 July, p. 3.
Wells, John (1992) 'Heroes and Villians: Joan Littlewood by John Wells', *Independent Magazine*, 29 February, p. 46.

Video and audio material

Omnibus (1994) 'Joan Littlewood', BBC1, 19 April.
Talking about Theatre (1964) 'Joan Littlewood in Conversation with Carl Wildman', BBC Radio, 28 June.

INDEX

Abramović, Marina xii, xiii, xv, xvi, xvii
Adler, Stella xiv, 246, 335
Albane, Blanche 324
Allen, Maud 216
Appia, Adolphe 86, 91, 95–96, 97, 102, 108, 116, 121, 125, 176, 178, 208, 325, 332, 416
Arp, Hans/Jean 138, 185
Artaud, Antonin xiii, xvii, 245, 328, 330, 357, 397
Ausdruckstanz 151, 163, 164, 173, 175, 181–182, 185, 186, 187, 189, 190, 191, 192, 196, 197, 203, 204, 207, 214, 224–225

Barba, Eugenio xiv, xv, xvi, 106, 339, 341–342, 351
Barrault, Jean-Louis 104, 324, 327–328, 329–330, 331, 332, 334, 346, 356
Baty, Gaston 103, 104, 253, 327, 328
Bausch, Pina xiii, xvi, 173, 376, 396
Bely, Andrei 52, 238
Berkoff, Steven 124, 259, 260
Bing, Suzanne xiii, 91, 95, 98, 100–102, 105, 106, 111, 116, 118, 126, 324, 326, 327, 341
Blok, Aleksandr 51–53, 54, 57, 59
Boal, Augusto xiii, xiv, xv, xvi
Brecht, Bertolt xiii, xiv, xv, xvi, 44, 163, 255–256, 273–321, 410, 412, 434
Brook, Peter xiii, xvi, 124, 449
butoh 371–405

Chekhov, Anton 5–7, 24–25, 27, 29, 31, 33–34, 35, 38–40, 45, 47, 110, 230, 419
Chekhov, Michael xii, xiii, xv, xvi, xvii, 11, 86, 153, 230–272
commedia dell'arte xvi, 53–54, 100, 111, 114, 115, 322, 324, 325, 331, 418, 419, 436
Copeau, Jacques xiii, xiv, xvi, xvii, 86–131, 324–327, 328, 332, 333, 336, 339, 341

Craig, Edward Gordon xvi, 86, 91, 93–95, 97, 102, 116, 125, 234–235, 241, 325, 332, 334
Cunningham, Merce 169, 207, 376

dada 140, 175, 176, 184–186, 212, 214
Dalcroze, Emile-Jaques 86, 95–96, 97, 121, 137, 138, 139, 156, 160, 176, 178, 179, 182, 183, 188–189, 208, 224, 325, 326, 375
Decroux, Etienne xiv, 104, 322–370
Dullin, Charles 92, 103, 104, 105, 244, 324, 327, 328, 330
Duncan, Isadora 23, 90, 156, 176, 178, 194, 214, 376, 384

ensemble xii–xiii, xv, xvi, xvii, 3, 4, 5, 7, 14, 24, 29, 31, 34, 36, 51, 78, 79, 81, 82, 86, 90, 91, 93, 106, 127, 128, 142, 143, 161, 163, 206, 214–215, 216, 230, 242, 249, 252, 257–258, 262, 264, 284, 293, 294, 295, 297, 299, 300, 301, 305, 306, 307, 308–311, 318–319, 409, 410, 416, 422, 425, 436
Ensor, James 185
expressionism 135, 151, 159, 162, 164, 169, 174, 175, 176, 180–182, 185, 186, 187, 195, 198, 202, 203, 217, 253, 277, 279, 280, 371, 375–377, 379, 388, 392, 412, 414, 415, 420, 434, 445

Goethe, Johann Wolfgang von 199, 216, 217, 294
Graham, Martha xiv, 161, 178, 194, 195, 197, 202, 204, 207, 208, 209, 390
grotesque 53, 56, 57, 69, 72, 73, 82–83, 127, 136, 145–146, 160, 164, 166–170, 187, 190, 214, 221, 230, 236, 254, 259, 260–261, 262, 263, 276, 282, 379, 393
Grotowski, Jerzy xiii, xiv, xv, xvi, 106, 341, 342–344, 346–347, 348

Index

Hauptmann, Elisabeth 282–283, 285, 290
Hauptmann, Georg 47, 48
Hijikata, Tatsumi xiii, xv, xvi, xvii, 371–408
Holm, Hanya 178, 188–189, 192, 195, 196, 201, 202, 205, 223, 224
Humphrey, Doris 178, 194, 195, 197, 202, 209
Hurok, Sol 194–199

Ibsen, Henrik 11, 47, 48, 50, 90
improvisation 10, 18, 19, 21, 22, 57, 76, 86, 91, 95, 100, 101, 102, 106, 107, 110, 124, 132, 135, 138, 141, 143, 150, 166, 169, 170, 171, 175, 191, 235, 236, 237, 248, 249, 253–254, 325, 326, 327, 338, 348, 349, 350, 356, 376, 378, 384, 388, 396, 409, 422, 423–424, 434, 435, 436

Jooss, Kurt 133, 141, 142, 143, 144, 147, 151–153, 169–170, 191–192, 193, 248
Jouvet, Louis 92, 93, 94, 103, 104, 105, 110, 117–118, 119, 324, 326, 327, 328

kabuki 341, 374, 375, 376, 390, 391, 392–393, 398
Kandinsky, Wassily 137, 169, 186, 181, 186–187, 238
Komissarzhevskaya, Vera 49–51, 54, 55, 56
Komissarzhevsky, Fedor 2, 49
Kreutzberg, Harald 142, 159, 188, 195, 202, 375

Laban, Rudolf xiii, xiv, xv, xvi, 132–172, 175, 176, 179, 180, 181, 183–186, 187, 188, 189, 191–192, 193, 202, 209, 212, 214, 216, 217, 224, 248, 376, 377, 399, 412, 415, 419
Labanotation 142, 154, 159, 183
Lecoq, Jacques xii, xiii, xiv, xv, xvi, xvii, 87, 101, 104, 335, 338, 348, 358
Littlewood, Joan xvi, xvii, 409–452
Loeser, Ruth 143

MacColl, Ewan 410–452
Maeterlinck, Maurice 9, 10, 47, 48, 49, 51, 52, 57, 90, 234, 241
Marceau, Marcel 104, 168, 330–331, 335, 339, 346, 351
Marx, Karl/Marxism 136, 273, 275, 282–284, 285, 286, 288, 289, 295, 297, 298–299, 307, 309, 310, 318, 415–416
Meyerhold, Vsevolod xii, xiii, xiv, xv, xvi, 7, 10, 18, 43–85, 92, 121, 230, 234, 236, 240, 241, 242, 256, 290, 339, 356, 412, 434, 439
modernism 54, 173, 174, 175, 178, 191, 195, 392
Molière 91, 93, 97, 109–127, 328, 413, 418, 422
Monroe, Marilyn 250

naturalism 1, 6, 20, 33, 35, 40, 47, 48, 50, 53, 63, 88, 94, 232, 234, 237, 240, 241, 280, 410, 414, 445

Nemirovich-Danchenko, Vladimir 3, 4, 6, 7–8, 10, 15, 18, 23–24, 34, 45–46, 102, 233
noh 100, 101, 108, 212, 324, 327, 336, 341, 347, 348, 374, 375, 376, 379, 390, 391, 392, 395

Ohno, Kazuo xiii, xv, xvi, xvii, 371–408
orientalism 162, 166, 376
Ouspenskaya, Maria 235, 236, 246

Palucca, Grete 187, 188, 201, 202, 207, 215
Pilates, Joseph 196
Piscator, Erwin 284–285, 290, 412, 414, 434, 437

realism xvii, 9, 20, 26, 27, 30, 33, 36, 38, 39, 40, 63, 67, 71, 75, 97, 98, 102, 120, 124–125, 167, 186, 233, 234, 236, 240, 242, 245, 255–256, 259, 261, 262, 289, 293–294, 296, 304, 316, 318, 325, 319, 357, 361, 412, 414, 433
Reinhardt, Max 189, 230, 243, 250, 251, 279, 281

Saint-Denis, Michel 86, 102, 103, 105, 107, 108, 111, 116, 122, 326
Shakespeare, William 8, 47, 57, 86, 89, 90, 91, 93, 98, 109, 111, 115, 118, 126, 241, 243, 244, 249, 264, 273, 314, 328, 331, 411, 413, 420, 422
Shankar, Ravi 153
Shankar, Uday 248
Snell, Gertrud 143
Stanislavsky, Konstantin xi, xiii, xiv, xv, xvi, 1–42, 43, 44, 45–48, 49, 54, 55, 57, 64, 66, 73–74, 86, 91, 93, 97, 99, 102–103, 110, 118, 121, 124, 230, 231–237, 239, 240–241, 243, 244, 246, 247, 248, 251, 257, 258, 262, 280, 291, 296–297, 339, 357, 410, 412, 414, 419
St. Denis, Ruth 162, 194, 208, 209, 216
Strindberg, August 48, 240, 279, 328
Sulerzhitsky, Leopold 11, 13, 235–236, 247
symbolism 1, 9, 33, 40, 47, 48, 52–53, 56, 125, 175, 217, 234, 424

Tagore, Rabindranath 153
Tauber, Sophie 138, 175, 185

Ullman, Lisa 153

Vakhtangov, Evgeny 11, 230, 235–236, 240, 241, 244, 251, 252, 259, 264

Weigel, Helene 283, 287, 290, 293
Wigman, Mary xiv, xv, xvi, 132, 137, 138–139, 140, 141, 142, 147, 148, 156, 159, 162, 165, 166, 168, 173–229, 373, 375, 376, 377, 378, 379
Wilson, Robert xiii, xvi, 93

Zeami, Motokiyo 341, 347, 348
Zola, Emile 6, 47, 88, 414

Printed in Great Britain
by Amazon